MUNICIPAL ADMINISTRATION

BY THE SAME AUTHOR

THE GOVERNMENTS OF EUROPE
THE GOVERNMENT OF THE UNITED STATES
THE GOVERNMENT OF EUROPEAN CITIES
THE GOVERNMENT OF AMERICAN CITIES
PERSONALITY IN POLITICS
THE MAKERS OF THE UNWRITTEN CONSTITUTION
THE INVISIBLE GOVERNMENT

MUNICIPAL ADMINISTRATION

BY

WILLIAM BENNETT MUNRO

PROFESSOR OF HISTORY AND GOVERNMENT AT THE
CALIFORNIA INSTITUTE OF TECHNOLOGY

NEW YORK
THE MACMILLAN COMPANY
1934

COPYRIGHT, 1934,
BY THE MACMILLAN COMPANY

ALL RIGHTS RESERVED—NO PART OF THIS BOOK MAY BE REPRODUCED IN ANY FORM WITHOUT PERMISSION IN WRITING FROM THE PUBLISHER, EXCEPT BY A REVIEWER WHO WISHES TO QUOTE BRIEF PASSAGES IN CONNECTION WITH A REVIEW WRITTEN FOR INCLUSION IN MAGAZINE OR NEWSPAPER

Published May, 1934.

SET UP AND ELECTROTYPED BY T. MOREY & SON
PRINTED IN THE UNITED STATES OF AMERICA

PREFACE

This book deals with present-day methods and problems of administration in the cities of the United States. It reviews the existing procedure in the various branches of municipal business and indicates what possibilities of improvement seem to be suggested by the experience of the past twenty or thirty years. Obviously the subject is an extensive one and includes within its range a large number of diversified activities, for the modern city is a very complex affair; but throughout the volume an attempt has been made to keep the discussion free from details in the hope that the general picture might be somewhat clarified.

Various matters included in this book have been discussed by the author in two previous volumes, one of them published in 1915 and the other in 1923, but changes in the technique of municipal administration during the past ten years have been so frequent, and of such far-reaching importance, that relatively little of this earlier discussion has proved usable in the present instance.

To all intents, therefore, this is a new book,—in its scope, arrangement, materials, and to some extent in its point of view as well. In this connection it will be noted that chapters have been included on traffic regulation, special assessments, the abatement of nuisances, the inspection of weights and measures, the law department, hospitals, public libraries, municipal airports, and various other topics which are not ordinarily given much attention in books on municipal administration. The growing importance of these matters, however, would seem to justify the consideration that has been devoted to them here.

A number of colleagues and friends have been good enough to read portions of the manuscript and to give me the benefit of their suggestions. To them I am sincerely grateful. Likewise I am indebted to Mrs. Ethel H. Rogers for painstaking assistance in preparing the material for the press, checking the bibliographical references, and making the index.

WILLIAM BENNETT MUNRO.

PASADENA, CALIFORNIA,
April, 1934.

TABLE OF CONTENTS

I. ADMINISTRATIVE ORGANIZATION AND PERSONNEL

CHAPTER | PAGE
I. ADMINISTRATION AND PRACTICAL POLITICS 1
II. ADMINISTRATIVE PRINCIPLES AND PROBLEMS . . . 15
III. MUNICIPAL EMPLOYEES AND THE MERIT SYSTEM . . 35

II. THE STAFF DEPARTMENTS AND THEIR WORK

IV. REGISTRATION OF VOTERS 52
V. NOMINATIONS AND ELECTIONS 62
VI. THE LAW DEPARTMENT 76
VII. THE CITY CLERK 89
VIII. ENGINEERING AND CONTRACTS 96
IX. CENTRALIZED PURCHASING 107

III. MUNICIPAL FINANCE

X. THE ASSESSMENT OF PROPERTY FOR TAXATION . . . 116
XI. MUNICIPAL REVENUES 126
XII. SPECIAL ASSESSMENTS 141
XIII. BUDGET MAKING AND APPROPRIATIONS 155
XIV. MUNICIPAL DEBTS 168
XV. AUDITS, ACCOUNTING, STATISTICS, AND REPORTS . . 185

IV. CITY PLANNING AND PUBLIC IMPROVEMENTS

XVI. PRINCIPLES OF CITY GROWTH 201
XVII. CITY PLANNING 219
XVIII. ZONING 237
XIX. LAND TAKINGS AND EXCESS CONDEMNATION . . . 249
XX. STREETS 260
XXI. PAVEMENTS AND SIDEWALKS 272
XXII. WASTE DISPOSAL 285
XXIII. SEWERAGE 298

V. PUBLIC SAFETY

XXIV. POLICE ADMINISTRATION 313
XXV. THE REGULATION OF TRAFFIC 335

TABLE OF CONTENTS

CHAPTER		PAGE
XXVI.	The City Courts	354
XXVII.	Crime and Correction	368
XXVIII.	The Regulation of Buildings	385
XXIX.	The Inspection of Weights and Measures	400
XXX.	Fire Prevention	411
XXXI.	Fire Protection	427

VI. PUBLIC WELFARE

XXXII.	School Administration	440
XXXIII.	Public Libraries	461
XXXIV.	Health Administration	474
XXXV.	The Abatement of Nuisances	495
XXXVI.	Hospitals	508
XXXVII.	Public Welfare and Social Insurance	518
XXXVIII.	Housing	532
XXXIX.	Public Markets	546
XL.	Parks and Public Recreation	556

VII. PUBLIC UTILITIES

XLI.	Water Supply	569
XLII.	Public Lighting	588
XLIII.	Municipal Airports	604
XLIV.	Urban Transportation	619
XLV.	The Control of Public Utilities	635
XLVI.	Municipal Ownership	653
	Index	671

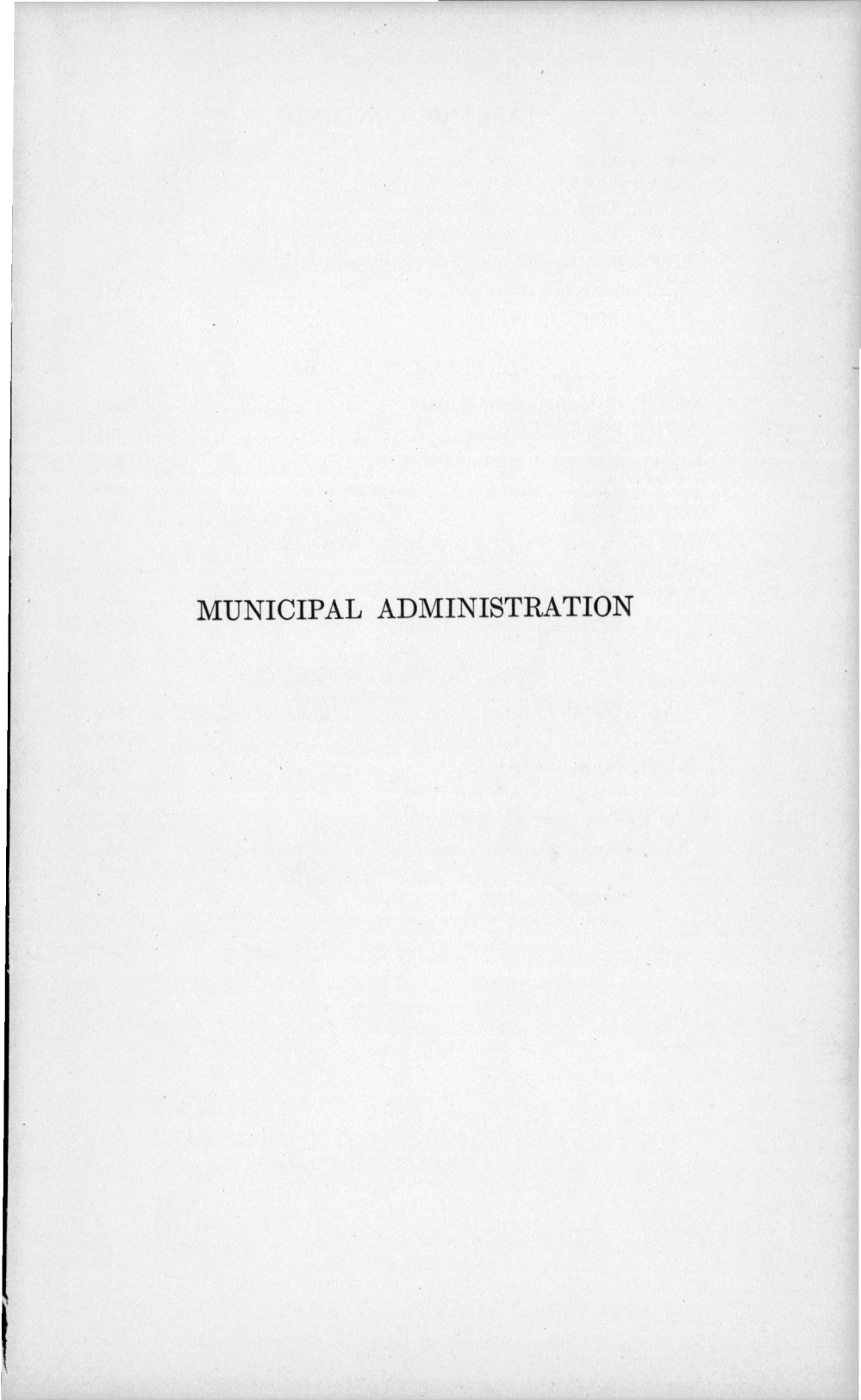

MUNICIPAL ADMINISTRATION

MUNICIPAL ADMINISTRATION

CHAPTER I

ADMINISTRATION AND PRACTICAL POLITICS

Popular government rests on the principle that it is every citizen's business to see that the community is well governed.—Lord Bryce.

In the government of the modern city there are two general tasks to be performed. First there is the determination of public policy. Decisions must be reached as to what work is to be done and how. Arrangements must be made to finance it. Authority must be given to go ahead with it and provision made for seeing that it is done properly. All this is the function of the city's legislative organ,—the city council, board of aldermen, city commission, or whatever it may be called. This body exercises the functions of decision, appropriation, authorization, and general direction which together constitute the basis of all administrative work. {The two general tasks of government.}

Declarations of municipal policy are usually made by passing ordinances, but such enactments are subject always to the superior authority of state constitutions and statutes, including the city charter which has the force of a statute. Within these limitations, municipal ordinances have the force of law and are binding not only upon the administrative officers of the city but upon all persons who come within its jurisdiction. By ordinance the municipal legislative body decides how much money shall be raised by taxation, how the proceeds shall be spent, who shall do the spending, what the functions of each administrative officer shall be, what limitations shall be placed upon their discretion, and to what regulations the citizen shall conform. {The ordinance power as the basis of administration.}

Every city, for example, has a building ordinance or code which lays down various rules which all private construction must obey. In addition it usually has a zoning ordinance which regulates the use to which private buildings may be put. Most cities likewise have a traffic ordinance, a fire prevention ordinance, and an ordinance containing all sorts of regulations in the interest of the {Policy-determining ordinances.}

public health. "And thou shalt teach them ordinances and laws," says the Pentateuch, "and shalt shew them the way wherein they must walk and the work that they must do." [1] Our city councils are obeying this decree of the law and the prophets. Whatever else may be lacking in our municipal system, there is no shortage of ordinances showing the people the way in which they must walk or pointing out to the city officials the work which they must do. Even the municipal budget is passed in the form of an appropriation ordinance. The funds which it provides do not become available until this ordinance goes into effect.

Policy-determining by resolution and by vote.

The city council also makes decisions and grants authority in ways other than by the enactment of ordinances. Much of this work it does by resolutions or by simple votes.[2] Appropriations are made by ordinance, for example, but transfers from one appropriation to another can thereafter be made, as a rule, by vote of the council or sometimes even by the mayor under authority granted by it. So with permits which the council grants, or claims which it authorizes to be paid, or contracts which it approves,—these things can also be done by resolution or vote and do not require the enactment of an ordinance. The city charter always sets forth in a general way, and sometimes in elaborate detail, the powers which the policy-determining organ or organs shall exercise and the procedure which it must follow.

The separation of legislative and administrative functions.

Most American city charters are framed on the principle that the power to determine public policy should be vested in one body of men, while the function of carrying this policy into effect should be given to another. The former should always be elective; the latter mainly appointive. Representation of the people is what is wanted in one case; administrative skill and efficiency in the other. The city council, therefore, does not (except under the commission form of government) carry its own decisions into effect. It has no machinery for doing so. It appropriates money; but no city treasurer would pay out a penny on the council's order. He insists on a warrant from the mayor, city manager, department

---

[1] Exodus xviii. 20.

[2] "An ordinance must usually have an enacting clause, a resolution need not; an ordinance must receive more than one reading on different days, a resolution need not; an ordinance usually must be published, a resolution need not. As a general rule, ordinances are used to enact a more or less permanent rule of conduct while resolutions are used in the transaction of administrative business."—Harvey Walker, *Federal Limitations upon Municipal Ordinance Making Power* (Columbus, Ohio, 1929), p. 12.

head, or other administrative official to whom the appropriation has been granted.

Spending money after it has been voted is an executive or administrative function. Executive and administrative work do not differ greatly. The executive represents the government as a whole and its functions are to a degree political in character because they permit some exercise of judgment as to the way in which the program set up by the policy-making body shall be carried out. The administrative function, by way of contrast, is generally restricted to the observance of instructions, without discretionary leeway; furthermore it is concerned with assigned portions of the general program rather than with the whole of it. Hence the higher ranks among those who execute public policy are commonly known as executive officers, while those in the lower ranks are said to occupy administrative posts. The mayor or the city manager is called the city's chief executive, while the superintendent of streets or the manager of the lighting plant is designated as a member of the administrative staff. By most people, however, the terms executive and administrative are used interchangeably. Not much confusion arises from their being used in that way, for those who execute are executives and those who administer are administrators; and in practice it is usually unimportant to draw a clear line of demarcation between the two functions.

Executive and administrative work.

One of the first things that every student of municipal administration ought to realize is the constant divergence of fact from theory in government, and of practice from principles. The actualities of government rarely follow the design. According to the principle of checks and balances the mayor of a city is an independent executive, without responsibility to the council, and free to do his work in his own way. But no mayor ever finds himself in any such position of agreeable detachment. No matter what the philosophy of the city charter may be, he finds that he must hold conferences with the councilmen, compromise with them, appoint their friends to office, and meet them halfway on all sorts of issues. Otherwise the council will manage to make his executive work more difficult by setting up all the hurdles that its ingenuity can suggest.

The divergence of theory and fact in municipal administration.

And so it is with the principle of checks and balances when you turn it the other way around. The city council's complete freedom from executive pressure is merely one of the agreeable fictions of the American municipal system. The mayor is not a member of the council (except in rare instances), nevertheless he is almost always the most important figure in its deliberations. His phantom hovers behind the presiding officer's chair at every session—encouraging or threatening as need may be. His power and his patronage are never out of the councilmen's minds. Some are his friends and some are his foes. The mayor may be balked and bullied by the council or he may be supported by it, but in no event can he be ignored.

The city council's interference with administrative officers.

The same hiatus between fact and fiction runs right down the line into all branches of the city's administrative service. The heads of departments, such as the chief of police or the superintendent of streets, are assumed to be the subordinates of the chief executive and responsible to him alone. When the city council has approved any project and voted the necessary funds it is supposed to stop there, leaving the administrative officials to do the rest without interference. But that is not what usually happens. Neither individually nor as a body do the councilmen hold themselves strictly aloof from the routine of administration. They suggest, importune, and threaten if need be. They can call the head of a department before them, heckle him, intimate that his appropriation will be cut down next year, appoint a committee to investigate his work, or pass a resolution asking the mayor to remove him. In the face of these realities the theory of administrative independence largely disappears.

The doorway through which politics comes in.

This is the doorway through which practical politics is able to influence administration. It has been generally taken for granted that by electing a high-grade non-partisan chief executive a city can eliminate the taint of partisan politics from its administrative departments. This assumption is rarely a sound one, as experience has repeatedly shown. The heads of departments are not merely the ministers of the mayor. He does not define their duties or fix their compensation. He cannot protect them against councilmanic pressure dictated by self-interest. Members of the council, on their part, do not usually inject themselves into administrative routine because they like to do it. They do it because they are beset by their constituents, by voters in their own wards or districts, who want favors which only the administrators can give. This must inevitably be so, for the councilmen are regarded as the tribunes of the people who have chosen them. They are

elected to reflect the public attitude towards the conduct of municipal business, and even the most rigid prohibitions of the city charter will not keep them from doing it in their own way. Some cities have made it a penal offense for any councilman to interfere in such administrative matters as the hiring of labor, the purchase of supplies, or the awarding of contracts; but this has merely driven the pressure into roundabout channels.

When the city manager form of government was first established there was a hope that this plan would ensure the divorce of partisan politics from administration. It was, in fact, the very kernel of the new form of government that the city manager, when once installed in office, would be given full control over all branches of community administration and permitted to run the affairs of the city as a business enterprise, making no concessions to spoilsmen or other favor-seeking politicians. Preferably he was to be an outsider, brought into the city from somewhere else, and hence having no local affiliations or political contacts such as might tempt him to favor any individual or group. By the provisions of city manager charters the councilmen are strictly forbidden to interfere with the manager in the performance of his administrative duties or to have dealings with any of the city departments except through him. In some charters any attempt at such interference is made a misdemeanor, punishable by the removal of the offending councilman from office. *The city manager plan and non-partisan administration.*

The city manager plan of government has undoubtedly diminished improper political interference in the administrative departments of those cities which have adopted it. Managers, for the most part, have been permitted a good deal of latitude in making appointments, awarding contracts, hiring employees, and planning their work. But nowhere, in these cities, has unfair pressure upon the administration been altogether eliminated or even reduced to negligible proportions. Nor is it ever likely to be so. A city administration under the control of the people, but with politics wholly eradicated, is a contradiction in terms. Where the people rule they must have representatives, and those who represent the voters as policy-determining officials will insist upon bending the administration into line with what they believe to be the popular desire. If they cannot accomplish it directly they will secure the result in some indirect way. *What it has accomplished.*

Not long ago a new city manager was appointed in a western

city. On taking office he called in the newspaper reporters and after shaking his finger wisely at them said: "Now I'm going to give this city a business administration with no politics or personal favors in it. No politicians, big or little, are going to tell me what to do." "Forget it," said one of the reporters, "it can't be done." "Why can't it be done?" queried the new city manager. "Because the city council doesn't want a business administration and most of the voters don't want it, and they won't let you stay in office if you try to give the city anything of the sort." The reporter was more nearly right than municipal reformers commonly realize.

Why city administration cannot be conducted on a strictly business basis:

There are several reasons why the administration of a city cannot be conducted on a purely business basis, with "no politics in it." For one thing the policy-determining organ of a business concern, the board of directors, is a homogeneous body, composed of men who think alike. Their decisions, on at least nine questions out of every ten, are unanimous. But the policy-framing organ of the municipality, the city council, is made up of members who represent a diversity of interests; they are rarely unanimous on anything and sometimes find themselves unable to act at all because of the wide-open division in their ranks. In many cases, therefore, the city's administrative officers are set to the task of carrying out a program which is not clearly defined but is the product of compromise and may even be considerably altered before the work is half done.

1. The diversity of interests represented.

2. The handicap of legal restrictions.

In the second place it must be borne in mind that municipal administration is hedged about by all sorts of legal restrictions which greatly circumscribe the freedom of those who are trying to carry it on efficiently. Restrictions of various kinds have been placed in the city charter; sometimes the exact salaries which heads of departments are to receive are fixed in that way. State laws set up further restraints,—for example, the frequent provision that only citizens of the United States can be employed on any form of public work, or the stipulation that every public employee must have Saturdays off duty without deduction of pay. Civil service regulations in many cities fetter the administration's discretion in selecting municipal employees and often compel the retention of those who would be promptly dismissed from the service of any business concern. These last-named restraints hark back to the long battle which cities had to wage in order to free themselves from the spoilsman's clutches. They cannot safely be relaxed—at any rate not until some equally effective way of keeping the utterly incompetent off the public payroll has been found.

Business, by way of contrast, is largely immune from these shackles. Within the general limits established by law it can pay whatever salaries it pleases. It can hire any kind of labor, citizen or alien, and pay for it by the day or hour as may be bargained for at any point above the minimum. It can select, promote, or dismiss its employees at will. Business can award contracts without competitive bidding, or purchase supplies without prior advertisement, or vary its services overnight—all of which things a municipal administration is debarred from doing even when they would be clearly to the city's financial advantage. Business administration can cut through the established routine at any time but municipal administration cannot. One enjoys a flexibility which the other does not possess. *Compared with private business.*

Then there is the possibility of testing results objectively, an advantage which business has and civic administration has not. The manufacturer knows that his business is being conducted efficiently if his output increases and his profits rise. His competitors spur him to his best efforts. But there is no equal competition between municipalities. There is no yardstick whereby we can accurately measure the relative efficiency of municipal administration in any two communities. The city makes no profits, pays no dividends, accumulates no surplus. No matter how much more one city may be paying than another for any form of service (police costs per capita, or public lighting per mile of streets, or water per million gallons) there will always be a plausible explanation to account for the discrepancy. *3. The absence of objective criteria wherewith to test results.*

Reducing unit costs in any branch of city administration does not usually bring a letter of commendation from the mayor to the head of the department concerned. What it much more often produces is a chorus of protests from those whose personal interests have been adversely affected by the reduction. A municipal administration's security in office does not depend on efficiency but on popularity. Business can sometimes be managed without obeisance to the principle that "the customer is always right," but in public administration the prejudices, caprice, and traditions of the electorate have to be taken into account at every turn. If not, there is likely to be a change at the next election no matter how great the business efficiency of the mayor or the city manager may have been.

4. The need for never-ending compromises. A successful city administration, under a democratic system of government, must inevitably be a compromise between what the people want and what their public officials think they ought to have. It is a problem of striking a fair balance between expert judgment and the public desire. The sensible administrator will never forget that the public pays the bills and consequently has some right to decide, after being given adequate information, what is the best thing to be done. Accordingly he will strive to secure the highest efficiency under conditions as they are rather than in defiance or disregard of these conditions. He will try to improve them, to gain the confidence of the voters so that they will eventually be ready to accept his judgment in place of their own. Above all, he will be patient about it and not try to regenerate human nature overnight. For this he will be called a trimmer by the idealists; but if he holds valiantly to his own realism he will eventually get results and his days will be long in the office that he holds.

The relation of good administration to the general frame of city government. It is sometimes said that good city administration can be achieved with any kind of policy-determining machinery;—that it is merely a matter of the right departmental set-up, with capable men as department heads, and the use of sound methods. That proposition, however, is not supported by municipal experience. Since administrative work must be preceded by the adoption of a program by the legislative organ of the municipality, there is a necessary relation between the two branches of the city government. To achieve satisfactory results the administrative officers must necessarily have behind them a city council which is able to do its own work promptly, intelligently, consistently, and without evasion of responsibility. Policies cannot be carried into operation until they have been clearly defined. Yet too often the city council delays in doing its part, or evades the problem, or takes ambiguous action when the time comes. It may be true that the principles of public administration are much the same no matter what kind of municipal legislature is functioning; but the results are not the same. Efficiency and economy in the conduct of the city's business are related in considerable measure to the general frame of government which the city charter provides.

So the general plan of a government is not merely a matter

ADMINISTRATION AND POLITICS

for fools to wrangle over, as the poet Pope once assured us. The general form and the results are usually related. It is easy enough to say that all will be right "if you only put good men into public office" but this merely begs the question as to how you are going to get and keep them there. Men of good sense and judgment will not put their energy behind a virtually unworkable machine, which is what some city charters provide. Improving the form of government increases the chances of getting such men. That is why the form becomes important. *Relative importance of forms and methods.*

There are four types of municipal government now existing in the United States and they facilitate good administration in varying degrees.[1] Among these the oldest, and one that still exists in many cities, is the "federal analogy" or strong-council plan of mayor-and-council government. This scheme of city government is so called because it was originally modelled on the national constitution, and its corner stone is the principle of divided powers. Chicago, Philadelphia, and Los Angeles afford the best examples of it at the present day. The essential features of their government are a mayor who possesses veto power over the actions of the municipal legislature and the right to initiate certain appointments, but whose hands are tied by a strong city council which has the right to confirm or reject such appointments and virtually controls the finances of the municipality. In some instances, as in Chicago, the city council actually prepares the annual budget through one of its committees and the mayor has nothing to do with the appropriations until after the council is through. Under this system of government the members of the city council are usually elected by wards or by districts and regard themselves as representatives of their own particular neighborhoods rather than of the city as a whole. *Four types of general framework:*

1. The strong-council plan.

The most serious defect of the strong-council plan, from the standpoint of municipal administration, is the division of responsibility which it establishes. The mayor is assumed to be the head of the city administration but he is not allowed a free hand in the selection of his own subordinates. He can only nominate the heads of the various departments, and these nominations must be confirmed by the city council before they become effective. Thus the appointing power is bifurcated, and when poor selections are made *Defects of this plan.*

---

[1] For a full account of these four types see the author's *Government of American Cities* (4th edition, New York, 1926), pp. 255–342.

there is no way of bringing home the blame. In the case of dismissals, likewise, the mayor requires the council's concurrence. So it is with the city's financial operations. The mayor, as chief executive, is expected to get results in the way of efficient administration at a low tax rate; but he is not permitted to plan the year's expenditures or to decide where the available funds may best be spent. The city council does this and usually does it on the principle of giving each ward its proportionate share of the available money irrespective of its needs. Such a scheme of government does not promote efficiency in municipal administration. In most cases it is a serious barrier to all efforts in that direction.

2. The strong-mayor plan. In the closing years of the nineteenth century many cities came to a realization of this fact and made substantial changes in their governmental framework. In New York, Boston, and Detroit, for example, the old arrangement was replaced by a new strong-executive type of mayor-and-council government. Under this plan the mayor directly controls the whole field of city administration. He appoints the heads of departments without confirmation by the city council and does not need the council's permission to remove them from office. Thus his position is even stronger than that of the President in relation to the national departments. If anything goes wrong in municipal administration under this type of government the mayor has the authority to set it right. Moreover, he prepares the annual budget (or has it prepared for him), and submits it to the council to be finally approved. The latter body is not free to change the budget at will; as a rule it is forbidden by the city charter to increase the appropriations under any circumstances. Its discretion is limited to the uncongenial work of making reductions and even when it does this the council's actions are subject to the mayor's veto.

Its merits. Where the strong-executive type of city government has been established the city council is usually reduced in size and its members are elected by the city as a whole, rather than by wards or districts. This plan of government has proved more favorable to the development of good administrative traditions than the older one; but the large powers given to the mayor, and the extensive patronage which he is able to distribute, are an incentive to the building up of a personal machine, thus helping the mayor to perpetuate himself in office. In some cities, therefore, the charter makes him ineligible to succeed himself.

ADMINISTRATION AND POLITICS

The third general type of city government now existing in the United States is known as the commission form. It originated about thirty years ago, and at one time had a considerable vogue, but has now lost most of its earlier popularity. As a scheme of local government it differs from the others in that it abolishes the office of mayor, or, more accurately, it divides the duties of that office among a small group of commissioners, usually five in number.[1] These commissioners are elected by the people of the city to serve as mayor, heads of city departments and council combined. As a body they enact the city ordinances, make the appropriations, fix the tax rate, appoint officials, and settle all questions of municipal policy. As individual commissioners they take immediate charge of the several administrative departments. One of the five, for example, assumes supervision over the department of public safety (police and fire protection), another over municipal finance, a third over public works, a fourth over public utilities, and a fifth over health and civic welfare.

3. The commission plan.

The entire administrative work of the city is thus parcelled out into five general divisions, each with a commissioner in charge of it, but with the whole commission controlling him. It was hoped that this concentration of power and responsibility would enable the administration of the city's affairs to be carried on in businesslike fashion; but on the whole this hope has not been realized. A five-headed executive does not usually function well, even when it has plenty of power. Disagreements among the commissioners, on a three-to-two basis, are likely to arise and clog the wheels. Each commissioner, being possessed of human ambitions, sets out to make a record for himself with his own department, forgetting that city administration is more than the sum of five activities struggling for success by rivalry. The commission form of government does not facilitate, in any considerable measure, the elimination of politics from administration or the development of administrative efficiency.

Its failure to fulfill expectations.

Finally, there is the city manager plan, the newest of the four types of government, having originated about twenty years ago. Under the city manager charter the people, as the stockholders of the municipality, elect a small council, or commission, or board

4. The city manager plan.

---

[1] In some commission-governed cities the title of mayor is retained for the commission's presiding officer; but the customary mayoral powers do not go with the title.

of directors—whatever it may be called. This body, in turn, appoints a city manager who directly controls all departments of administration. Having appointed the manager, the council is supposed to give him a free hand within the limits of the general program which it formulates. The city manager then appoints his subordinate officials, prepares the budget for the council's consideration, attends its meetings (but does not vote), and advises it on all technical matters. The council makes the appropriations, which are then turned over to the city manager to be spent.

Its tendency to encourage sound administrative methods.

It is the essence of this plan that the manager shall be a professional officer chosen because of his special training and experience in administrative work. This form of government now operates in more than three hundred cities of all sizes, including such large ones as Cincinnati, Rochester, Kansas City, Oakland, and Akron. It embodies a sound philosophy of municipal government by concentrating control and responsibility while keeping functions separate. There is a division of labor but no division of power. The manager controls the administrative departments and is responsible for their work; but the council controls the manager and is responsible to the people for him. In practice, as well as in principle, the city manager plan has been found to encourage, even if it does not always ensure, the use of good administrative technique.

The importance of the city council with respect to administration has not been sufficiently stressed.

In general, then, the form of a city's government is by no means a negligible consideration. On the contrary, it is fundamental to the whole quality of municipal administration. Unless programs of administrative work are wisely framed and judiciously financed, it is difficult for good administrative results to be achieved, no matter how competent the administrative staff may be. Planning and financing are the city council's business. It will be good, bad, or indifferent business depending on the size of the council, the manner of choosing its members, and the quality of the men who get themselves elected. An unwieldy council of thirty or forty members chosen by wards will rarely attract men of competence or do its work with conspicuous good sense. That proposition has been proved by the experience of American cities over and over again. Unhappily there exists in the American mentality a fixed idea that the more numerous the elective officials, the more truly democratic a government is bound to be. The contrary is nearer the truth. The people really control their government, and assure themselves capable administration, in inverse ratio to the number of names on the ballot.

So it is a serious error to assume, as is so often done, that since the city council is a legislative body its size or quality has no bearing upon the work of actual administration. Under all four types of government it is the prime source of administrative activity. It determines how much money each department shall have for its year's work and often prescribes in detail just how this money shall be spent, whether for contracts, salaries, supplies, equipment, materials, or something else. It has power to investigate the work of any department in order to assure itself that the money has been properly spent. All this gives the council an opportunity to dictate many details of administration when it feels minded to do so, as too often it does. And even when it cannot legally compel the mayor or the city manager or the head of a department to conform with its wishes, it can by resolution send him a "request" which will often meet with compliance for the sake of harmony even when the administrative officers realize that it is incompatible with the best interests of the municipality.

Councilmen are not themselves responsible for this propensity to meddle in matters which ought to be outside their province. They are merely reflecting the wishes of the voters whom they represent. The average American citizen feels that the councilman or alderman from his own ward or district is the one to whom he should turn when he has a grievance to air or a favor to ask. Nine out of every ten Americans are politicians by instinct. Their first thought, when they want something from the public authorities, is to enlist the influence of someone for whom they have voted. So when anyone wants a street light placed in front of his home he rarely goes to the lighting department and asks for it. He gets his councilman to do the asking for him. This habit of circumlocution is responsible for injecting a good deal of politics into the daily routine of city administration. *A word of defense for councilmen.*

While it is too much to hope that politics can be wholly or even largely eliminated from the conduct of municipal business, a good deal can be accomplished in this direction by care in the framing of the city charter, whatever its type may be. Particular attention should be given to those charter provisions which deal with budget-making, the transfer of appropriations, contracts, the purchase of supplies, auditing and accounting, inventories, collections, abate- *Importance of the administrative provisions in city charters.*

ments, promotions, claims, pensions, and so on. When the procedure in such matters is definitely prescribed in the city charter, the politician does not find it easy to switch things from their regular course. If it is stipulated, for example, that no property shall be purchased by the city at a figure above its assessed valuation otherwise than by regular condemnation proceedings, it becomes virtually impossible for any political interest to unload real estate on the public at fancy prices. Such a charter provision will at least eliminate this particular variety of "honest graft," as it has been termed.

The ultimate responsibility of the voter. Charters can help, but no amount of diligence and sagacity will avail to make them proof against evasion. The only ultimate and dependable safeguard against the dilution of efficiency by politics is the growth of a public sentiment which will not tolerate any such situation. Over most of the country the public schools have been cut free from political control and influence—not by the enactment of inhibitory legislation but merely because the American voter would not stand for the practice of having his children taught by some politician's daughter, regardless of her other qualifications. We will get politics out of the police and fire departments when the same voter makes up his mind that the protection of his own life and property should be regarded from the same point of view.

REFERENCES

Further discussions of the relation between administration and politics may be found in Frank J. Goodnow, *Politics and Administration* (New York, 1900), James (Viscount) Bryce, *Modern Democracies* (2 vols., New York, 1921), Leonard D. White, *Introduction to the Study of Public Administration* (New York, 1926), and *Trends in Public Administration* (New York, 1933), G. A. Weber, *Organized Efforts for the Improvement of Methods of Administration in the United States* (New York, 1919), R. M. Dawson, *The Principle of Official Independence* (London, 1922), Peter Odegarde, *Pressure Politics* (New York, 1928), Charles E. Merriam, *New Aspects of Politics* (new edition, Chicago, 1931), and W. F. Willoughby, *Principles of Public Administration* (Baltimore, 1927).

A full list of useful treatises on public administration may be found in Sarah Greer, *A Bibliography of Public Administration* (2nd edition, Part I, New York, 1933).

CHAPTER II

ADMINISTRATIVE PRINCIPLES AND PROBLEMS

The proper duty of a representative body in regard to administrative matters is not to decide them by its own vote, but to take care that the persons who have to decide them shall be the proper persons.—*John Stuart Mill.*

The administrative functions to be performed in a modern city cover a wide range and are of great variety. Moreover they are constantly increasing. A recent survey in one of the largest American communities disclosed more than three hundred such functions, ranging all the way from the regulation of traffic to the purchase of supplies, and from the assessment of taxes to the care of municipal cemeteries. Many of these administrative responsibilities are so closely related that they can be grouped within the jurisdiction of a single department, and they usually are so grouped in all large cities, but the extent to which this consolidation can profitably be accomplished is not so great as is sometimes supposed. *The scope and variety of the city's administrative work.*

The citizen who watches his city's administrative machinery piling up, and growing more complicated every year, does not always sense the primary cause of this development. The principal reason for it is to be found in the progress of applied science, the rise in the general standard of living, and the accumulation of wealth. Science has transformed the day's routine in cities during the past half-century. It has brought in the skyscraper and the automobile,—two innovations which are at the root of street congestion and have necessitated the widening of streets and the elaboration of traffic rules as well as the imposition of height limits in buildings in the downtown districts. Higher standards of living have inspired the people to demand more and better service from their local governments, while the accumulation of wealth has enabled them to pay for it. Hence the expansion of the city's administrative mechanism has been the inevitable result of civic progress, and it will continue so long as urban civilization keeps moving forward. The problem is to make sure that each new activity is carefully articulated to all the rest. *Why it is increasing.*

The first question that arises with reference to the proper organization of a city's administrative work is this: Should the number of departments and their jurisdiction be prescribed by the city charter and thus placed beyond the power of the regular municipal authorities to change, or should this matter be left to the city council for flexible determination as it may deem best? The more common practice is to embody in the city charter various provisions relating to the organization and functions of at least the more important departments. The objection to this is that it tends to stereotype the city's administrative organization, making it difficult to change even though altered conditions may render changes highly desirable. If, on the other hand, the whole administrative organization is left to the judgment of the council there is danger that stability will be lacking. For if the councilmen are permitted to change the number, organization, or functions of the city departments at any time and for any reason, they are likely to make changes after every election and in making them they are more than likely to be actuated by partisan or personal motives.

In practice it has generally been found that when new departments can be created by majority vote of the councilmen, there is a considerable temptation to increase their number in order to provide jobs for political supporters. And when a new council desires to oust department heads from office it finds an all-too-easy method of doing this by abolishing or consolidating the positions which it controls. Then it proceeds to create new positions which carry on the old functions but with new officials in charge under a different name. It is for this reason that the framers of city charters, having been warned by experience, are disinclined to entrust city councils with much discretion in the matter of departmental organization. Sometimes a compromise arrangement is devised by setting up the departments in the city charter and providing that this set-up may be changed by ordinances of the city council but that such ordinances must be passed by a two-thirds vote. Where not more than half the council's membership can be changed at any one election this two-thirds rule provides a reasonably adequate safeguard against any periodical scrabbling of the city's administrative staff in obedience to the principle that the spoils of office belong to the victors at the polls.

Assuming that a city charter undertakes to fix the number

and jurisdiction of the city departments, how far should it go in prescribing the methods which these departments must use in doing their work? For example, should the charter undertake to specify the procedure which department heads must follow in appointing their subordinate officials, hiring labor, awarding contracts, purchasing supplies, keeping accounts, and making reports? Or should the methods be left for the city council to prescribe by ordinance? Or should each department be given freedom to determine them for itself? The two first-named alternatives tend to discourage departmental initiative and to encourage the complacent following of whatever routine methods are prescribed. The third alternative almost always results in the use of inefficient or loose procedure by some departments. It is the experience of all cities that some heads of departments, when left to themselves, will continue to use wasteful and out-of-date methods for the simple reason that they do not know any better.

<small>2. To what extent should departmental methods be prescribed?</small>

On the whole it is probably the wisest plan to make compulsory, by charter provision or by ordinance, the use of those general methods which experience has shown to be advantageous in all departments,—for example, in the matter of awarding contracts, purchasing supplies, standardizing salaries, giving vacations to employees, making promotions, using official cars when not on duty, and taking an active part in factional politics. On these and some other questions it is impracticable to let each department make its own rules. Such an arrangement would produce no end of irritation and misunderstandings. Standards in each department would tend to gravitate to the level set by the lowest. In matters such as those above mentioned, therefore, the practice should be made uniform. On the other hand there are many other things which may best be left to each department for local self-determination. Within this category comes the whole field of departmental routine. Problems and tasks which are peculiar to one department should be left free to be handled by it in its own way.

<small>The need for a prescription of general procedures.</small>

One frequently hears it said that good city administration depends on the caliber of the man whom you put at the head of a department, rather than on the methods which he uses. That assertion is half true, half false. But like most half-truths it finds many believers. Successful public administration is equally a matter of men and of methods. The best results come from a com-

<small>Men *versus* methods in city administration.</small>

bination of many factors, including not only the personal capacity of the department head but the concentration of adequate power and full responsibility in his hands, the proper distribution of work among his subordinates, the skillful adjustment of prescribed and discretionary methods in doing their work, and the establishment of a system of promotion and of pay increases such as will uphold the morale of the whole department.

Good routine is not to be despised. There are right ways of doing most things, and wrong ways too. There are good ways, better ways, best ways. Many well-meaning administrators have persisted in the use of wasteful, ineffective, antiquated methods without knowing it. Often they are abetted in this by older subordinates in their department, men who have got into a rut and cannot get out of it. When a new man comes in at the top he may be full of new ideas but he rarely finds it is easy to convince the departmental staff that these ideas are worth putting into practice. They will usually conspire to confront him with all manner of difficulties and objections.

The number of city departments. How many administrative departments does a city need? That is one of the many questions relating to municipal organization which cannot be answered in a dogmatic way. To say that a city should have five, seven, nine, or eleven administrative departments would be like saying that a house ought to have five, seven, or eleven windows irrespective of its location, size, use, or number of occupants. For a city has a varying number of administrative functions to perform. The number depends upon its size, character, resources, civic standards, and traditions. Some cities have branched out into many fields of service and are engaged in many tasks of a public welfare sort. Others have gone but a short distance into such activities. Some municipalities own and operate their lighting plants and street railways, while others do not. An inland city does not need a harbor board or port director. If poor relief is wholly under the jurisdiction of the county, as is the case in many parts of the United States, the city does not require a department of charities. No two cities are alike in their needs and problems. To determine how much administrative machinery a city requires, one must first know the amount and nature of the load that is going to be placed upon it.

The number of departments should therefore be adjusted to the scope and variety of the services which the city is undertaking to perform for its people. That ought to be a self-evident proposition, if anything is, but municipal reformers have not always regarded it so. Otherwise we would hardly have "model" plans of departmental organization put forth from time to time for the guidance of all cities irrespective of their size or requirements. The commission plan of city government, for example, usually provides five departments, no more and no less, into which all administrative work must be concentrated no matter how large or how small the community may be.

It should be related to the amount of work.

Convenience of administration ought to be the controlling principle, but with two basic considerations kept prominently in mind. The first is that the number of departments should never be increased beyond what is clearly essential to the efficient conduct of the city's business. The burden of proof should be on those who want the number expanded. The second rule is that functions of a wholly dissimilar nature, or which are not somehow related, should never be crowded into the same department but should be placed in different ones. So far as practicable the number of departments should be kept down because experience has everywhere shown that the distribution of administrative work among city departments on a too elaborate scale leads to friction, duplication of effort, and unnecessary expense. The multiplication of overhead machinery always pushes up the overhead cost, and beyond a certain point it does not facilitate but rather impedes the conduct of public business. Boston, for example, has about forty municipal departments, which is a much larger number than the city needs. Some of them were created to provide jobs for friends of the mayor and are continued because each new city administration desires to retain the patronage which their existence provides. Detroit, a considerably larger city, has only twenty municipal departments; while Philadelphia, which is larger still, is able to get along with eleven.

The considerations which should determine the number.

A small number of departments, however, is not necessarily an indication of administrative efficiency. The process of grouping functions can easily be carried to a point where it hinders rather than helps the taxpayer in getting his money's worth. The evil of having too many departments has been replaced in some cities by the evil of having too few. Efficiency experts have sometimes appeared to take it for granted that the combining of two departments into one is a certain virtue in itself; but such consolidations

There is no inherent virtue in a small number of departments.

do not represent a real gain if they result in loading the merged department with functions of a diverse and unrelated character. For when a department head is given greatly diversified responsibilities, some of them are likely to be neglected, or at least given deficient attention. He will put his mind on those in which he is primarily interested. The head of the city's health department, for example, should be a man who is primarily interested in public health. Unless he be an individual of uncommon versatility he will not be interested in the inspection of weights and measures, the regulation of billboards, the supervision of the city's employment bureau, the licensing of pawn-shops, censorship of motion picture houses, or any one of a dozen other functions which ought to have careful attention from somebody whose personal interest they can command.

The dangers involved in too much consolidation. If any of these matters, therefore, are thrown into the health department for the mere reason that there are only so many departments and there seems to be nowhere else for them to go, they are not likely to get a cordial welcome or much solicitude. On the other hand it is obvious that a city cannot maintain a separate department for every municipal function. It must deal with these functions in related groups. The problem, therefore, is to work out the relationships, place kindred functions together and keep dissimilar ones apart, letting the number of departments depend on the result. In case of doubt the benefit should be given to the aspects of similarity. On this basis a city of any considerable size is likely to find that it needs at least nine or ten departments, while a large city will require perhaps twice that number.

The general grouping of administrative functions. Broadly speaking, there are at least fifteen fields of work in which the administrative authorities of any large city find themselves engaged, and these may be listed as follows:

1. *Law.* The duties of some city officials must include the interpretation of the city charter, the drafting and revising of municipal ordinances, the approval of legal documents, the giving of legal advice to the various departments, the adjustment of claims for damages brought against the city, and the representation of the municipal corporation before the courts. Every city, therefore, has a law department, headed by an officer who is known as the city attorney, city solicitor, city counsel, or by some such title.

ADMINISTRATIVE PRINCIPLES AND PROBLEMS 21

2. *Records.* Then there are records to be kept, including the minutes of the city council and of its committees. Closely related duties include the certifying and publication of municipal ordinances, the giving of all public notices which are required by law, and the handling of official correspondence both with the state authorities and with the officials of adjoining municipalities. This work is customarily entrusted to the office of the city clerk.

3. *Registration and elections.* Within this general field comes the registration of voters, the publication of the voters' lists, and all matters incidental to the holding of elections, whether for national, state, or municipal offices. The national and state governments do not conduct and pay the cost of their own elections; they pass this responsibility to the local authorities. The state laws usually provide that the latter shall select the polling places, appoint the polling officers, print the ballots, make the necessary returns after the polls are closed, and conduct a recount if one is demanded. As a rule there is a board of registrars or a board of elections in charge of the work.

4. *Personnel.* This includes the making of rules with reference to appointments, promotions, and discipline in the municipal service, and sometimes the control of demotions and dismissals as well. In most of the larger cities there is a civil service commission which receives applications, conducts the competitive examinations, and makes up an eligible list of successful candidates from which the appointees are then chosen. A few cities have personnel departments instead of civil service boards. In many smaller municipalities, however, nothing in the way of a merit system has yet been established.

5. *Finance.* The general field of municipal financing comprises the assessment of property for taxation, the collection of taxes and the custody of public funds, together with the work of approving bills for payment, paying them, auditing the accounts, compiling financial reports, selling municipal bonds, investing sinking funds, together with various other financial duties. This whole field of work may be concentrated in a single department of finance, under a commissioner of finance, or it may be divided among several officers such as the city assessor (or assessors), city treasurer, city comptroller, and the sinking fund commissioners.

6. *Public safety.* Under the general head of public safety there are various important functions such as police administration,

fire prevention and fire protection, the regulation of traffic, the inspection of weights and measures, the enforcement of the sanitary ordinances, and the inspection of buildings to see that they conform with the building code. Except in cities which have the commission form of government, these duties are usually divided among two or more departments.

7. *Justice.* This includes the organization and maintenance of the municipal courts, the upkeep of city jails and other correctional institutions, and the handling of juvenile offenders, together with the supervision of the parole and probation systems.

8. *Education.* Within this comprehensive field comes the management of the public school system, with its array of elementary schools, junior high schools, high schools, junior colleges (occasionally a municipal university), night schools, continuation classes, summer schools, extension classes, Americanization work, and a good deal more. This work is very frequently turned over to the officials of a school district, the boundaries of which are not always identical with those of the municipality. A school board, with a superintendent of schools as its chief administrative officer, is invariably placed in charge of this department. Within the field of education one might logically place the management of public libraries also, but this function is usually vested in a separate department.

9. *Parks and public recreation.* Various classes of parks and parkways have to be maintained in large cities, including downtown and suburban parks, public gardens, historic places, cemeteries, and so on. The work of maintenance usually requires the establishment of a park department. In addition to its regular duties, moreover, this department may be given charge of the city's program of public recreation including the supervision of swimming pools and bathing beaches, the management of public athletic fields, the provision of band concerts in the parks during the summer months, and the conduct of public celebrations.

10. *Public health.* The enforcement of rules relating to public health in a large city is an extensive and important responsibility. The work includes the abatement of nuisances, the inspection of food and milk, the establishment of quarantines, the prevention of epidemics, the compilation of vital statistics, and the maintenance of various hospitals—emergency hospitals, isolation hospi-

ADMINISTRATIVE PRINCIPLES AND PROBLEMS 23

tals, and general hospitals. In the largest cities these hospitals are usually administered by a separate department.

11. *Public welfare.* This generic term includes the work of administering the system of public charity in cities where poor relief is a municipal function. But in many sections of the United States poor relief is not a municipal function; it is entrusted to the county authorities. Public welfare work also includes such matters as the care of defectives and delinquents, the censorship of amusements, the maintenance of an employment bureau, and sometimes the supervision of public playgrounds, although this is a function which seems to come more logically within the purview of the school department.[1] Sometimes there is a regular department of public welfare to manage these various things, but more often the various welfare activities are distributed among the park department, the recreation department, and even the police department.

12. *City planning and zoning.* Under this head comes the preparation of a comprehensive city plan, the control of new subdivisions, the approval of new street layouts, the framing of zoning ordinances, and the hearing of requests for individual exemptions from the zoning rules. Usually there is a city planning board to pass upon all such matters.

13. *Public works.* Here is one of the most comprehensive divisions of municipal administration. It includes the construction, maintenance, and upkeep of streets, the collection and disposal of municipal wastes, along with sewerage and sewage disposal, the provision of a public water supply, and the care of all public buildings which are not under the jurisdiction of a particular department. Its problems are mainly of an engineering character. Sometimes the whole field is concentrated within a single department of public works, but more commonly the city has a street department, a sanitary department, a water department, and sometimes a department of public structures as well.

14. *Public utilities.* An important municipal function concerns the general relations between the city and the various private utilities which operate within its bounds,—railroad, telephone, gas, electric lighting, street railway, motor-bus and taxicab companies. To a large extent these utilities are now subject to regulation by the state authorities and the cities have relatively little control over them except when the time comes to review their franchises.

---

[1] See the discussion of this matter, *below*, p. 24.

On the other hand many cities own and operate their electric lighting plants as a municipal enterprise, and some have taken over the gas and street railway services as well. In such cases it becomes necessary to establish a department of public utilities or something of the kind. The water supply service is sometimes included under its supervision as a publicly owned utility, but more often it is either placed in a separate department or included with streets and sewers as a branch of the public works department.

15. *Miscellaneous.* Finally, there are many assorted functions which do not come within any of the foregoing fields. For example, a city may have a municipal printing plant (as Boston has), or a municipal university (as Cincinnati has), or a harbor to be administered, or a ferry system. It may have one or more public markets, municipal airports, municipal docks, and even municipal warehouses. It may have a municipal art gallery, a museum, a theater, a stadium, an auditorium, a recreation pier, and a number of neighborhood civic centers.

Some problems of appropriate grouping:

The foregoing list of general administrative fields will indicate an approach to the minimum number of departments which a large city will find it necessary to provide. Most municipal functions can be grouped under one of these general headings without placing extraneous things together; but there are some activities which do not seem to belong in any of the regular functional groups and yet are of insufficient importance to have separate departments for themselves. Centralized purchasing, for example, has an intimate relation to all the departments. Customarily it is placed within the department of finance. Some administrative activities seem to have an equal affiliation with two departments —for example, the work of establishing, equipping, and supervising children's playgrounds. Does this function belong to the park department or to the school board? On the one hand it is argued that the work of acquiring land for recreation purposes, improving it, and caring for it is park department business. But the playground is more than a piece of land with some apparatus on it. The school authorities look upon it as an educational institution which plays an important part in the out-of-school program of public education. Supervision and the organization of play are what count. The playground director is a more important factor than the playground itself, and his natural link-up is with the school authorities.

1. Playground administration.

ADMINISTRATIVE PRINCIPLES AND PROBLEMS 25

So although it is easy enough to lay down the generalization that in organizing municipal departments related functions should be kept together and unrelated functions apart, it is by no means easy to apply this rule in specific cases. Does the collection and disposal of garbage, for example, belong properly to the department of health or to the department of public works? In other words, is it a matter of health or merely of public convenience? Should parkways (the boulevards which connect the city's park system) be under the jurisdiction of the park department or treated as streets for administrative purposes? *2. Garbage collection.*

And what of the public library? In some cities it has been placed under the jurisdiction of the school board on the ground that it is an agency of adult education. Is that a wise arrangement? If not, where should the public library be placed as respects its administrative supervision? If the city is to have only ten or twelve departments, the public library cannot have one of these to itself. *3. Public libraries.*

Finally, should the licensing of public amusements, the regulation of commercial dance halls, and the censorship of motion pictures be entrusted to the police, or to the department of public welfare, or to some other authority? These, it will be noted, are practical questions which cannot be answered by applying any general formula. *4. The licensing of public amusements.*

Whatever the number of administrative departments, it is important that they shall be regarded as a single integrated set of administrative agencies. Instead of being viewed as isolated and independent units, they should be treated as working parts of a single organization. This is essential in order that each of them, while having its own distinct sphere of jurisdiction, shall be constrained to work in harmony with all the others towards the attainment of a common end. The task of administering a city is a unit; a rather complex unit, it is true, but nevertheless a single enterprise. No part of it should be aloof from the rest. *Municipal administration as an integrated whole.*

In keeping with this principle every municipal department should be linked to a common center with all the lines of control and responsibility converging inward and upward. Outline the whole administrative scheme on a blueprint or chart. If the resulting diagram takes the general form of a pyramid with the mayor, city manager, or commissioners at the apex, the city employees at the base, and the entire hierarchy of administrative officers coming in between—if it takes that shape the mechanism is all *The converging lines of responsibility.*

right. But if all the lines of control and responsibility do not converge toward the top; if some of them run off in tangents to the side; then the administrative set-up has not been properly designed. It means that the door is open for conflicting jurisdictions, overlapping functions, and duplication of activities—all of which spell economic waste and misdirection of energy. It is only by a complete unification of control that the danger of such conflicts and duplications can be avoided. Furthermore, unless the officials are organized and held accountable in this way, there can be no unity in the city's program of work and no solid foundation for a properly organized budget system.

The headship of a department. Every administrative department should have a recognized head. This headship may take the form of a board, or it may be vested in a single commissioner. Fifty years ago the board system of departmental management was very popular in American cities. This was due in part to a widespread feeling that city administration ought to be bi-partisan rather than non-partisan, which means that the minority political party ought always to be accorded its proper share of participation in it. Minority representation in administrative work necessitates a plural headship. A board of three or five members can provide for representatives of at least two political parties, whereas a department with a single commissioner at its head can offer no such dual representation.

The earlier practice.

Its disadvantages. But the bi-partisan plan of municipal administration often worked out badly, more especially when it was applied to such departments as police, fire protection, and public health, where there is frequent need for prompt and decisive action. Disagreements and bickerings in these bi-partisan boards were more often related to political allegiance and the desire to control patronage than to the merits of the problem under consideration. Hence the bi-partisan requirement has been gradually abolished in most American cities. Boards are still used in municipal work to a considerable extent, but with the bi-partisan requirement eliminated. And in certain departments there is a good deal to be said for using them.

Certain departments should have single-headed direction. Whether a department should have a board or a single commissioner at its head has been the subject of much controversy, but the decision in most cases is simple enough to make. Where the work is of such nature as to call for prompt and direct action rather than for prolonged deliberation the single commissioner

ADMINISTRATIVE PRINCIPLES AND PROBLEMS 27

type of organization is clearly preferable. Both in private industry and in public administration it has been demonstrated by experience that where emergencies are likely to arise at frequent intervals, where strict discipline has to be maintained, and where there can be no efficiency without promptness—that in such fields of work there must be a definite location of authority in the hands of a single individual. Accordingly, in such municipal departments as police, fire protection, public health, public lighting, water supply or sanitation, the advisability of a unified command is clearly apparent, or ought to be.

Not all departments, however, are of this character. In some of them the work does not require efficiency of the army-and-navy type. It is work which involves the exercise of discretion. It should not be done under pressure but after careful deliberation. Where the work of a department, for example, includes the drafting of rules and regulations which have the force of law and protect private rights, as in the case of city planning, or where the department deals with varied interests which need to be amicably reconciled (as in the case of schools, public libraries, and public welfare), there are sound reasons for the use of the board type of departmental organization. *Others are better suited to the board system.*

For in such branches of administration the collective judgment of several persons is likely to be wiser than the quick decision of any one individual. Hence the board system is rather generally and quite properly used in the administration of the public schools, charities, city planning, public libraries, public recreation, sinking funds, and the regulation of public utilities. It is the customary arrangement, moreover, in the case of the department which has charge of registering voters and conducting elections,—at any rate in cities where elections are conducted on a partisan basis. And even those cities which elect their own officials on a non-partisan ballot often have the responsibility for locally conducting state and national elections in which party feelings run strong.

In recent years the tendency has been to replace boards by single commissioners in city administration. The movement in that direction has possibly gone too far. The board system is in greater disfavor than it deserves to be. Its advantages have been too frequently overlooked. The board system encourages continuity of policy because only one member retires at a time. When a single commissioner goes out of office his policy goes with him. *Some neglected merits of board administration.*

Moreover, in small cities the board plan has the merit of economy because citizens are willing to serve on a board without pay, giving part-time service (and often very useful service), whereas a single commissioner at the head of a department must usually be paid a regular salary. Of course it is often argued, and it sounds plausible to say, that a single commissioner, with expert qualifications, giving all his time to the work of a department can save the city a great deal more than his salary; but as a matter of municipal reality the replacement of an unpaid board by a single paid commissioner has usually added to the city payroll someone whose expert qualifications are purely political and whose endeavor has been to spend more money rather than less of it.

The selection of department heads:

How should the heads of departments, whether boards or single commissioners, be selected? Various cities have tried at least a half-dozen methods during the past fifty years—election by the people, election by the city council, appointment by the mayor with aldermanic confirmation, appointment by the mayor without confirmation, appointment by a city commission, appointment by the city manager, and (in a few cases) appointment by the governor of the state or by the higher state courts.

1. By popular election.

The selection of administrative officials by direct vote of the people has rarely proved satisfactory. Where administrative skill and experience are desired, there is no more unlikely way of getting them than by the action of the voters at the polls. The people elect good fellows to office; but not good administrators except by accident. Election by the city council is a plan which has proved itself equally bad, or worse. Many city councilmen look upon department headships as jobs to be distributed among their friends. They should not be given the opportunity to fill posts of high responsibility with men of low qualifications. An exception should be made in the case of the city clerk who is the council's own clerical officer and hence may properly be chosen by it in spite of the likelihood that some valiant party worker will get the place.

2. By council election.

3. Appointment by the mayor.

Appointment by the mayor with confirmation by the city council has been a popular plan in a great many cities, but it is open to the objection that it divides the appointing power between two organs of government who may be hostile to each other and hence it frequently results in compromise appointments which are a credit to neither. The plan of having appointments made by the

ADMINISTRATIVE PRINCIPLES AND PROBLEMS 29

mayor without council confirmation centers responsibility for the selection and hence is distinctly a better one—provided the mayor is really desirous of giving the city an efficient administration and does not merely utilize his appointing power to build up a personal machine with the idea of perpetuating himself in office. Appointment by the commission in commission-governed cities has shown itself open to the same general objection as election by the city council, although to a smaller degree. The plan of having municipal officers chosen by the state governor or by the state courts has been tried in a few cities, but nowhere has it proved popular. It offends the spirit of municipal home rule.

The best results, in general, have been obtained through the system of appointment by the city manager if the council selects a well-qualified manager and gives him a free hand to choose all the heads of departments whether from residents of the city or from outside. They then hold him responsible for his selections. For these heads of departments are the manager's subordinates and his own tenure of office depends on whether they produce results. Unfortunately, in some municipalities which have the city manager form of government, the maximum salaries for department heads are fixed so low that good men cannot be had for the posts, even when the manager does his utmost to secure them. And in others the pressure on the manager to make appointments for partisan, factional, or personal reasons is an obstacle to the selection of the best men who would be available at the salaries prescribed.

4. Appointment by the city manager.

Civil service reformers have proposed from time to time that members of administrative boards and heads of city departments should be chosen under the merit system by a plan of competitive examination. They have urged that applications be received and referred to a committee of recognized experts in the field. Such a committee would then examine the various applicants and recommend the best one. But this proposal has not commended itself to cities for the reason that many qualities other than technical competence are required in a successful head of a department. Integrity, tact, organizing power, and good sense are needed, for example, and these qualities cannot be tested by any form of examination. An even more weighty objection arises from the fact that such an arrangement would relieve the mayor and the city manager from a responsibility which is the essence of responsible government. Compel them to work with subordinates whom they

Should heads of departments be selected by civil service tests?

have not chosen and in whom they may have no confidence—do this and you can hardly hold the chief executive to any strict accountability.

Appointments and politics.
Everywhere, even in most of the city manager municipalities, the appointment of the higher administrative officials is still bedeviled by the taint of party politics. The manager is supposed to be non-partisan and beyond the reach of political pressure; but the politicians usually get to him through roundabout channels. Where there are city bosses and ward bosses, they will not be fenced off by any mere charter provision. Hence there is hardly a single large city in the United States of which it can be said that political considerations have been altogether eliminated from the making of higher appointments or have even been reduced to a secondary place in determining the choice.

Partisan or personal influence is still the controlling factor in the majority of American municipalities whatever their location, size, or type of charter. In far too many instances the men who are at the head of such important departments as streets, sanitation, parks, water supply, and public buildings are individuals who would not be trusted with such large responsibilities in any field of private business. If any comment upon their technical skill is needed, it will be found in the fact that when they lose their positions through a change of city government, they almost invariably have a hard time finding other jobs anywhere outside the public service at half their former official salaries.

The qualities of an ideal department head.
What are the qualities of an ideal department head in the municipal service? The successful head of a city department must be honest, intelligent, fair-minded, and willing to work. He should be prompt in making decisions, ready to assert his authority, and willing to assume responsibility for it. He should give results, not excuses. He should maintain harmony within his department, enforce discipline without becoming unpopular, and deal tactfully with both the press and the public. He ought to be a reliable judge of what the people want, and hence be able to tell before he does a thing whether it will prove unpopular or not.

The capable department head need not have a greater amount of knowledge and skill than his subordinates possess. But where this is the case he must know how to use these subordinates to the utmost of their capacity. To be able to do this is a rare gift. It consists in sensing the strong qualities of other men and getting them to give the maximum service. Likewise it consists in holding subordinates back when they incline to go too far, as will often be the case. The successful department head must be able to apply the brakes at times without dulling the initiative of those under him. To be a good speaker is also a considerable help because he will be called upon at times to defend his work before the city council or at public gatherings. And if he has personal qualities which make him a good mixer among men, they will redound to his advantage. In a word, the successful head of a city department ought to be a good administrator, a good leader, a good organizer, a good technician, and a good fellow.

Of course one rarely finds all these qualities combined in any individual, and few individuals so richly endowed can be hired at the rate which cities usually pay their heads of departments. The good organizer-leader-technician can make much more profitable use of his rare abilities in private business than in the public service. So the city takes what it can get for the price that it is willing to pay. One applicant will have a fine record of technical training and experience, but may combine with this a reputation for being untactful in the handling of subordinates. Another will be a resourceful and diplomatic fellow whom everybody likes but whose technical competence is open to question. Of the two he is the more likely to get the place, because an applicant's personal qualities, including his political sophistication, are generally given more weight than they deserve in the selection of department heads. Indeed, it is an axiom, confirmed by prolonged observation, that the amount of political pressure exerted on behalf of any municipal office-seeker is usually in inverse ratio to his qualifications for the job. *Men with these qualities are hard to find.*

Getting the right men to head the various city departments is difficult. Keeping them in office, after they are appointed, is equally difficult. The public is a fastidious employer. It is more ready to find fault than to express satisfaction. The capable department head sometimes gets a chance to move over into the employ of a private concern (such as a construction company or a real estate corporation), and he takes it. More often he is let out when a new mayor or city manager comes in. City charters sometimes provide that heads of departments shall be chosen for a fixed term so that they hold over into a new administration and cannot be dismissed when it comes in; but this provision does not *And when found they are hard to keep.*

32   MUNICIPAL ADMINISTRATION

avail much. When a mayor or city manager wants to get rid of any department head he can usually accomplish it by indirection —going over his head in giving instructions to subordinates, withholding approval of plans, and so on. What we need is not more legal safeguards but better traditions. When the public insists on competence in the higher municipal posts we will get it and be able to keep it.

The internal organization of a city department. A city department, when it gets large enough, must subdivide itself into bureaus, divisions, and sections. The department of public works, for example, will divide itself into various bureaus— streets, water supply, sanitation, lighting, parks, bridges, and public buildings. Each bureau may then be further segregated into two or more divisions—for example, the bureau of water supply will be split into divisions of construction, maintenance, and finance. Finally, a division may be, and often is, subdivided into sections. Thus the finance division of the water bureau in the department of public works may have an accounting section, a collection section, and a records section. Each bureau in a department has at its head a deputy commissioner, superintendent, director or whatever he may be called; while each division or section will have its chief or foreman. In many cities the heads of bureaus, divisions, and sections are chosen under the merit system, as will be explained in the next chapter.

Two methods of organization. This internal organization of a department may be determined on a functional basis, that is, each bureau or section may be assigned a different class of work. Or it may be arranged on some other basis, such as the results which are sought to be obtained. For example, in the department of public works there may be a single bureau which prepares all the plans for the construction of streets, sewers, water mains, public buildings, and bridges. Its sole function is to prepare plans. But there will also be bureaus which have charge of construction and maintenance in each of the above-mentioned branches of the department's work. Such bureaus have many functions, all directed to the production of certain results. Thus both principles of division may be applied within the same department. The details of internal organization cannot be settled in any department by enunciating a general rule. The important thing is that all the lines of control and responsibility within the department shall center in the department head. Every bureau chief, divisional director, or section foreman should

ADMINISTRATIVE PRINCIPLES AND PROBLEMS 33

be ultimately responsible to the department head and through him to the city's chief administrative officer. This chart will illustrate the idea:

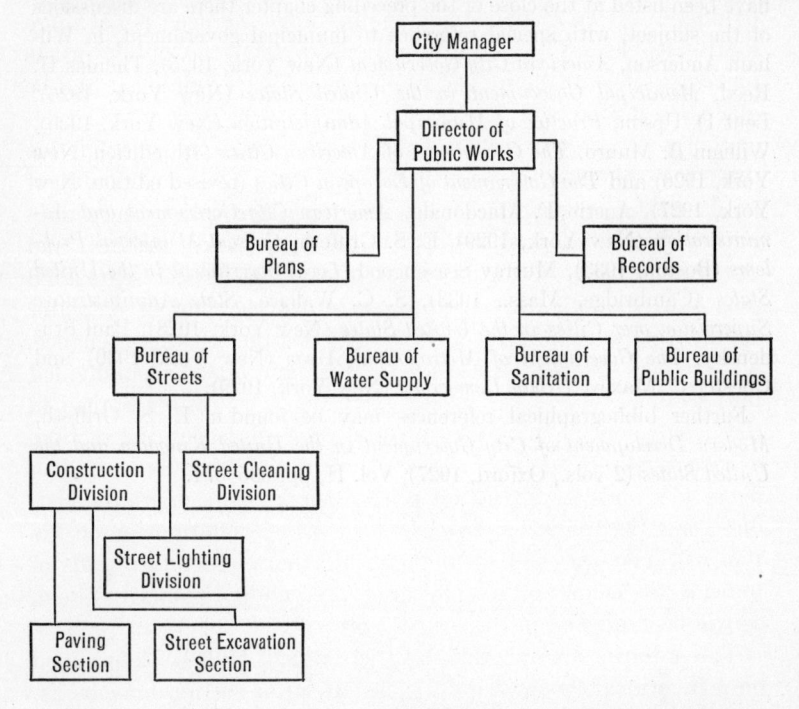

```
                         City Manager
                              |
                         Director of
                         Public Works
          _____|_____
         |                                |
   Bureau of                         Bureau of
     Plans                            Records
         |_____|
         |           |           |            |
   Bureau of    Bureau of    Bureau of    Bureau of
    Streets   Water Supply   Sanitation  Public Buildings
      |
   ___|_____
  |                |
Construction   Street Cleaning
  Division       Division
  |                |
  |         Street Lighting
  |            Division
  |_____|
  |                |
Paving       Street Excavation
Section          Section
```

There is always a danger of administrative over-organization. The segregation of duties among sections and subsections of a department can be carried too far. In some cities it has been. When this takes place, the lines of control between the bottom and the top of the department become too long and too attenuated. Responsibility is lost on the way. The city payroll becomes studded with the names of too many majors, captains, and lieutenants in proportion to the number of corporals and privates who do the real work. The amount of examining, approving, initialing, checking up, referring higher up, making reports, filling requisitions, sending communications, tabulating and conferring—it keeps piling up until it passes the point of desirability or profit. There is a law of diminishing returns in administrative disintegration although it is not always recognized by city officials.

The danger of too much mechanism.

REFERENCES

In addition to the general books on administrative organization which have been listed at the close of the preceding chapter there are discussions of the subject, with special reference to municipal government, in William Anderson, *American City Government* (New York, 1925), Thomas H. Reed, *Municipal Government in the United States* (New York, 1926), Lent D. Upson, *Practice of Municipal Administration* (New York, 1926), William B. Munro, *The Government of American Cities* (4th edition, New York, 1926) and *The Government of European Cities* (revised edition, New York, 1927), Austin F. Macdonald, *American City Government and Administration* (New York, 1929), E. S. Griffeth, *Current Municipal Problems* (Boston, 1933), Murray Seasongood, *Local Government in the United States* (Cambridge, Mass., 1933), S. C. Wallace, *State Administrative Supervision over Cities in the United States* (New York, 1928), Paul Studensky, *The Government of Metropolitan Areas* (New York, 1930), and Chester C. Maxey, *Urban Democracy* (New York, 1929).

Further bibliographical references may be found in E. S. Griffeth, *Modern Development of City Government in the United Kingdom and the United States* (2 vols., Oxford, 1927), Vol. II, pp. 635–674.

CHAPTER III

MUNICIPAL EMPLOYEES AND THE MERIT SYSTEM

Let me tell you that patriotism has been dying out fast for the last twenty years. Before then, when a party won, its workers got everything in sight. That was something to make a man patriotic. But how are you goin' to interest our young men in their country if you have no offices to give them when they work for their party?—*Plunkitt of Tammany Hall.*

Thirty years ago George Washington Plunkitt was Tammany leader of the fifteenth assembly district in New York City. Incidentally he was a political philosopher. From his favorite rostrum, a bootblack stand in the county courthouse, he expounded his theories of politics and patriotism. Plunkitt believed that all true patriotism had payroll implications and hence that no one could be a real lover of his country unless he was able to effect a short circuit between his own pocket and the public treasury.

"Let me tell you of one case," said he. "After the battle of San Juan Hill, the Americans found a dead man with a light complexion, red hair, and blue eyes. They could see he wasn't a Spaniard, although he had on a Spanish uniform. Several officers looked him over, and then a private of the Seventy-First Regiment saw him and yelled, 'Good Lord, that's Flaherty.' That man grew up in my district, and he was once the most patriotic American boy on the West Side. He couldn't see a flag without yellin' himself hoarse.

"Now, how did he come to be lying dead with a Spanish uniform on? I found out all about it, and I'll vouch for the story. Well, in the municipal campaign of 1897, that young man, chockfull of patriotism, worked day and night for the Tammany ticket. Tammany won, and the young man determined to devote his life to the service of the city. He picked out a place that would suit him, and sent in his application to the head of the department. He got a reply that he must take a civil service examination to get the place. He didn't know what these examinations were, so he went, all light-hearted, to the civil service board. He read the questions about the mummies, the bird on the iron, and

The Plunkitt philosophy.

Patriotism as the handmaid of patronage.

all the other fool questions—and he left that office an enemy of the country that he loved so well. The mummies and the bird blasted his patriotism. He went to Cuba, enlisted in the Spanish army at the breakin' out of the war, and died fightin' his country.

"That is but one victim of the infamous civil service. If that young man had not run up against this examination, but had been allowed to serve his country as he wished, he would be in a municipal office today, drawin' a good salary. Ah, how many young men have had their patriotism blasted in the same way!"[1]

The beginnings of civil service reform.

When Grover Cleveland declared that "public office is a public trust" he disgusted the politicians everywhere. For generations it had been regarded as a brand of gravy for professional patriots. But the merit system of appointment gained the favor of the national government, worked its way into the states, and filtered down into the cities. It is well that this has been the case, for the continuance of the spoils system on its old-time scale might have bankrupted some of our cities long ago.

Importance of the merit system in relation to municipal expenditures.

The municipalities of the United States are now spending, for all purposes, more than three billion dollars per year, of which more than half goes in salaries and wages to about 800,000 officials and employees. Even with the merit system operating in practically all the large cities it is a common complaint that the taxpayers do not obtain anything like full value for this payroll expenditure. This is chiefly because municipal employees give a smaller return for their wages than do those who work for private corporations. The only question is how much less. A competent city manager once gave me his opinion that city labor, in comparison with that of private concerns, is on the average about eighty per cent efficient. Many would call this estimate too high. It is hard to figure an average because the efficiency of public employees is not the same in all departments. As a rule it is highest in the schools and public libraries, while it runs lowest in those departments where unskilled labor is largely employed,—in the street cleaning and snow removal services, for example. Something also depends on the head of the department. If he doesn't insist on high standards nobody else will be much concerned about them.

Its scope and purposes.

Nearly all American cities of over 100,000 population have now adopted the merit system in whole or in part. Heads of city departments are still outside the scope of the civil service regu-

[1] William L. Riordon, *Plunkitt of Tammany Hall* (New York, 1905), pp. 26–28.

lations but most of the subordinate officials and employees are selected by competitive tests. The purpose of the merit system is twofold. It aims to prevent the appointment of persons who are clearly unfit and whose selection represents the payment of political debts. But a merely negative purpose would not be a firm foundation upon which to build a better public service. Hence the second aim of the merit system is to provide a means whereby qualified applicants may be recruited and certified to the appointing authority.

How does the merit system operate? In some features it varies from city to city, but its essentials are as follows: First there is a civil service commission or personnel board, ordinarily of three or five members, usually appointed by the mayor or the city manager, but occasionally elected by the city council. Then, whenever a subordinate position in one of the city departments is to be filled, the mayor or other appointing officer calls upon the commission to send him an "eligible list," or list of persons who have qualified for appointment. If the position is a common one, for which competitions are frequently held, there will be an eligible list on hand. For example, if the request is for a policeman, fireman, clerk, or stenographer, there is usually no delay in sending an eligible list, because examinations for these posts are held every year or oftener. But if some unusual position is to be filled, such as that of bacteriologist in the water department or chief cataloguer in the public library, it is necessary to hold a special competition. Public announcement is made; applications are received; special examiners are appointed when necessary; examination papers are made out; the tests are taken by the various applicants; and the results are figured. Candidates who have made the best showing are then certified, and the appointment must be made from among them. Ordinarily the appointing officer may select at his own discretion anyone on the eligible list, but sometimes he is required to make his choice from among the three highest.

How the system operates:
1. The civil service board.

2. Examinations and eligible lists.

It should not be assumed from this brief description, however, that civil service competitions take the form of written examinations such as are given in school or college. The tests are closely related to the work which the applicants will have to do in case of appointment. Candidates for appointment as stenographers are required to receive dictation and transcribe it. Civil service

The nature of the tests.

tests for policemen assume the form of physical examinations, an intelligence test, questions on elementary law, on criminal court procedure, on local geography (streets, public buildings, etc.), and on the duties of a policeman. These questions are usually supplied by officials connected with the police department or the city attorney's office. In the case of technical positions it is usual to enlist the aid of outside experts in framing the questions and in grading the answers. The civil service commission does not make the appointments; it merely certifies the names of those who have been found eligible.

The weight given to personal qualities. There is a great deal of difference in the nature of the various competitions. In most cases a considerable amount of weight is given to general training and experience, as well as to his character and integrity as indicated by the recommendations from former employers which each applicant is expected to file. Intelligence and capacity are tested by written and oral examinations. Where good physique is important (as in the police and fire departments) there is a rigid physical examination. Personality is rated on a basis of an interview with the examiners. These several qualities are weighed according to some agreed-upon scale which varies for different departments. It is desirable that the system of rating shall not be inflexible but the trouble is that discretion on the part of the examiners is too often a synonym for political or personal favoritism.

Non-competitive tests. In the case of some positions it is customary to give a non-competitive test if the appointing authority asks for it. This merely involves the scrutiny of some one person's qualifications to see whether he measures up to the requirements. The justification for this is that sometimes a well-qualified man will accept a position on that basis, but is not willing to compete in a general scramble for the place. Non-assembled competitions are also held in some cases, particularly for special or technical positions. In such instances the candidates do not come together for examination but send in their records, samples of their work, testimonials, etc., and the examiners give them a rating on this evidence.

Veterans' preference. In many of the states there is a legal requirement that veterans shall be given a preference by civil service examiners when they enter the competitions. In some cases the preference is an absolute one, that is, all veterans who pass the examination must be put at the top of the list and certified for appointment before non-veterans get a chance, no matter how much higher they may have rated in the competition. In other cases a veteran is given a qualified preference by adding five or ten per cent to his rating for experience. This giving of preferences has been very detrimental to the workings of the merit system. It is true that a country is under obligation to those who have served it in times of emergency, but there are less costly ways of paying such a debt than by a partial breakdown in the morale and efficiency of the public service.

Ordinarily, when an appointment is made from the civil service list it is probationary for a period of three or six months. At any time during this interval the appointing authority is usually permitted to discharge the probationer and ask for another name from the eligible list. But when the probationary period has expired the appointee goes on the permanent force and may not thereafter be dismissed except in accordance with the civil service regulations. This system of probationary service is intended to supplement the merit system by what is the only conclusive test in the final analysis, namely, whether the appointee can actually do the job. *Probationary appointments.*

It will be noted from the foregoing discussion that a civil service commission has legislative, administrative, and judicial functions all combined. It makes the rules and regulations under which the competitions are held. It administers the examinations. (The commission's secretary and his associates, of course, do the detailed work.) It hears appeals from applicants who are dissatisfied with the ratings given them at the examinations and frequently its approval is necessary before employees can be dismissed. In addition the civil service commission is often given some special administrative functions, such as the certification of payrolls, the classification of work and the standardization of pay in the municipal service, the keeping of efficiency records and the recommending of promotions. To get all this work done properly necessitates a commission of competent men, immune from political pressure, impartial, and in sympathy with the principles of the merit system which they are administering. Great difficulty has been found in securing civil service commissioners of that type. *The varied responsibilities of the civil service board.*

In Massachusetts and in New Jersey there is one civil service commission for the entire state; its members being appointed by the governor. When any post within the classified municipal service is to be filled, the city authorities call upon the state com- *How such boards are appointed: 1. By the state.*

mission to certify the necessary names. The objection to this plan is that it infringes the principle of municipal home rule; but in effect it is nothing more than the extension of a practice which has been commonly followed by many of the states in connection with their public school systems. Examinations for teachers' credentials are frequently conducted by the state department of education and only those who are certified as eligible can be appointed to any teaching position in a city school. If the examination and certification of school teachers can properly be regarded as a state function, it can hardly be deemed a gross absurdity to provide that playground supervisors, probation officers, assistants in the public library, health inspectors, assistant engineers, and so forth, in other branches of the public service, shall be similarly certified. The question is one of expediency rather than one of principle. State control of the examinations has the advantage of removing them from the influence of local politicians. It likewise secures uniformity in the administration of the civil service laws.

2. By the city.

But central control is not popular. In most of the states which make provision for the use of the merit system in their cities, a strictly local plan of administrative control is established. The mayor of each city, or the commission, or the city manager, appoints a civil service board, usually of three members. In Philadelphia, Denver, and a few other cities this board is chosen by the city council. Sometimes it is provided that both political parties shall be represented on this board; in other cities it is stipulated that the appointees shall not be active members of any political party. These municipal commissions function within their respective cities; they make the rules and conduct the examinations without being subject to the supervision of any state authority.

Weak features in the latter arrangement.

This method is more considerate of home rule sensibilities, but it has not been altogether satisfactory in practice. The civil service commission is assumed to act as a check upon the chief executive, and on the heads of departments who are his subordinates. But how can the board fulfill this function effectively when it is appointed by the authority whom it is expected to hold in restraint? It is human nature for a mayor or city manager to appoint civil service commissioners whose attitude towards patronage is akin to his own, and it is human nature for men who are thus appointed to be reasonably complaisant towards the appointing authority.

A mayor who wants to use his appointing power as a means of building up a political machine will not knowingly appoint any civil service commission which may be counted upon to stand firmly in the way of his doing so. The merit system can be riddled with loopholes whenever a civil service commission is ready to wink at evasions of its spirit and letter. The various ways in which this can be done will be explained a little later.

Then why not have the civil service commission chosen by the city council, as some cities have arranged it? This removes them from any obligation to the executive authority. Unfortunately our municipal experience does not warrant the expectation that civil service commissioners chosen by a city council will reflect a high standard of integrity or non-partisanship. The average councilman, especially if he be a ward or district representative, is not interested in civil service reform, or in reform of any other variety. He is far more concerned, as a rule, about getting jobs for his own clamorous supporters. "I try to keep up the fire of patriotism by gettin' a lot of jobs for my constituents," said Plunkitt, and there are hundreds of aldermen and councilmen in the United States who strive to keep the home-fires burning in the same way. The civil service commission which insists upon a strict adherence to merit, paying no heed to the hints, suggestions, recommendations, and protests of councilmen is likely to find itself replaced by one whose members are more amenable. *Is appointment by the city council a solution?*

As a compromise between state and local control of the merit system, New York and Ohio have provided for city-appointed commissions whose work shall be subject to the general supervision of the state civil service authorities. The local boards conduct the competitions and prepare the eligible lists; but the rules and regulations are made by the state authorities and apply uniformly to all the cities. The state civil service commission may also investigate the administration of these rules in any city, may hear appeals from the decisions of the local commissioners, and may even remove the latter from office. The value of this plan depends, of course, on the thoroughness and impartiality with which the state authorities do their supervisory work. *A compromise between state and local control.*

The problem of selecting, and maintaining in office, a civil service commission which will do its work capably, impartially, and without fear or favor, is one that has not yet been solved. The suggestion has been made that instead of a civil service com- *Public personnel bureaus.*

mission each city should have a public personnel bureau corresponding to the personnel departments which are maintained by large business enterprises. The head of this bureau would be himself selected on a merit basis. His functions would include all those now performed by civil service commissions. Such a plan would have many advantages but there has been a natural reluctance to place such large powers in the hands of anyone who is not chosen at the discretion of the people's representatives.

<small>Justification of the merit system.</small>

The merit system of selecting city employees has demonstrated itself to be a vast improvement over the older method of distributing paid offices among party workers. It has substituted fitness for favoritism and open competition for political manipulation. The spoils system rested on the proposition that all men are endowed by their Creator with an equal capacity to perform the technical duties which arise in connection with the city's engineering, accounting, sanitary, health, and recreational work—which is an absurdity. So the problem is simply this: Since special qualifications are needed in order to perform municipal business properly, how can we prevent men who are utterly deficient in these qualifications from getting into positions where they will waste the public money by giving poor service? The system of selection by competitive tests may have its defects, it is true, but its results are unquestionably far better than those of the spoils system which it replaced. If it has not always brought superior men into the municipal service, it has at least kept a great many inferior ones out.

<small>Obstacles which have been placed in its way.</small>

The merit system would have accomplished more in the way of results were it not for the serious practical difficulties that it has had to surmount. First of all the system was promoted in the United States under an ill-chosen name—civil service reform. People in general do not like any proposal that has the word "reform" tagged to it. Nowadays its friends prefer to call it the merit system, which is a better term. Second, the new plan had to be imposed upon unwilling mayors and heads of departments. Almost every public official believes, and believes honestly, that he can choose better subordinates by using his own discretion than can be found for him by any commission of examiners or any kind of competitive examinations. The merit system was accepted by mayors and city councilmen, in many instances, because the state laws imposed it on them against their own wishes. Naturally

EMPLOYEES AND THE MERIT SYSTEM 43

they have not given the plan, in its actual operations, any wholehearted support.

Failing to prevent the merit system from being established by law, mayors and heads of departments have often tried to control the boards which administer it. They have endeavored to secure the selection of civil service commissioners who would interpret the laws liberally and thus provide a reasonable number of loopholes through which patronage might be dispensed to deserving members of the party in power. For that reason the actual administration of the merit system has often been placed in the hands of persons unsympathetic with its principles.

Finding loopholes in the system.

There are various ways of providing loopholes in a civil service law when its administrators set out to do this for the benefit of politicians. One is by the frequent use of non-competitive tests. Such tests are supposed to be held in very special cases only, where a position requiring quite unusual qualifications is to be filled. But they have often been approved by civil service commissioners in cases where the only real reason is the desire of a mayor or department head to appoint someone who could not get near the top of the eligible list in any open competition. An even more common practice is the authorizing of temporary appointments. The civil service laws usually provide that when emergencies arise, and the city requires some new employees in a hurry, the civil service commission may approve temporary appointments for a short period (say three months) until a regular competition can be arranged and an eligible list prepared. This is a reasonable provision but the privilege which it confers has often been grossly abused. Examinations are frequently postponed and temporary reappointments approved. Sometimes these "permanent temporaries," as they are called, stay in the municipal service for years. They often manage to stay, at any rate, until they have learned enough about the practical work of their positions to give them an edge over outside competitors in the rating for experience and knowledge of the special duties. In a word, the game is to slip men in as temporaries and leave them in that category until they are likely to stand high in a competition where "actual experience in the work of the office" is so heavily weighted in the ratings as to give them a marked advantage over all other applicants.

The abuse of non-competitive tests and temporary appointments.

Even when a civil service commission is honestly endeavoring to

Inherent defects of the examination plan. administer the merit system in the right spirit, moreover, it is handicapped by the tools with which it has to work. Examinations and tests, no matter what their character, cannot always be relied upon to sift the best from the second-best. There is no formal procedure by which one can determine with certainty from among a whole roomful of candidates, the two or three who ought to be ranked highest in honesty, initiative, industry, tact, leadership, common sense, resourcefulness, personality, or even in general intelligence. Nevertheless these are the qualities which count for most in the administrative service. Anyone who possesses them can learn the actual duties of his post in a short time. And without them his service will not be successful no matter how much he knows about the special work that he is appointed to do. Examinations have their own defense in the fact that the world has thus far devised nothing better as a means of separating the sheep from the goats. There is a widespread popular impression that the questions asked at civil service examinations are technical and often absurd. Thirty years ago this impression had some basis but there is little or no justification for it today. Civil service tests have been greatly improved.

A common but unfounded criticism. In the circles of organized labor the merit system is often branded as "undemocratic" because it inevitably gives an advantage to applicants who have had a high school or college education. Such young men and women have learned to write legibly and correctly, to make the most of what they know, and to keep their wits about them at the examination. This objection to the merit system on the ground that it gives educated persons an advantage is hardly a valid one in a country which makes education free and compulsory; but it is widely held and accounts in part for the unpopularity of civil service reform among great masses of the voters, especially in the larger cities. The spoils system has been considerably rooted out, but the spoils spirit remains.

Recruiting the candidates. It was a fair criticism of civil service commissions in earlier days that they concentrated all their attention upon the work of making regulations and examining candidates. They gave little heed to the importance of recruiting suitable applicants. They overlooked the fact that when all the candidates are inferior, no form of examination will pick good ones from the lot. Here, again, there has been a marked improvement. Announcements of vacant positions and of forthcoming competitions are inserted in the newspapers and sent to all institutions from which applications might be expected to come. In the larger cities there are various night schools and extension classes which prepare recruits for the examinations.

The greatest obstacle to the successful working of the merit system is the existing method of making promotions in the municipal service. No plan of appointment will secure good entrants so long as it is well known that later promotions will depend on political influence. In spite of the merit system the public service is still a blind alley for the man without a pull. Increases in pay and advancement in rank are not, for the most part, determined by merit but by outside pressure. So long as this remains the case it is not likely that municipal employment will attract young men or women of unusual capacity or ambition. But there are indications of a change in this situation. Most civil service commissions now keep efficiency records which take into account the quality of work performed by every municipal employee, his punctuality, general conduct, errors and omissions, together with the confidential rating given by his foreman or bureau chief. Such records ought to be used in determining promotions, but heads of departments often prefer to use their own judgment without reference to them. *The problem of merit promotions.*

The merit system is concerned not only with appointments and promotions but with transfers, suspensions, and dismissals. The usual requirement is that no official or employee who has been appointed under civil service rules may be transferred from one department to another without the commission's approval. Nor may he be suspended or discharged except on specific written charges filed with the commission. As a rule he is entitled to a hearing on these charges. In some cities this hearing takes place before the mayor or the head of the department; in others it is the civil service commission that conducts the hearing and decides whether the charges have been sustained. An appeal may always be carried to the courts when a dismissed official or employee feels that his legal rights have been infringed. In the case of veterans there is usually a special provision for such appeals. The courts frequently order the reinstatement of dismissed officials, with compensation for the time lost. *Dismissals and hearings.*

While the mere requirement that charges shall be filed and publicly heard may not seem to afford much protection against un-

The hearing as a protection.

just dismissal, it does in fact provide a considerable measure of security. Mayors and heads of departments will put up with a good deal rather than have internal discords laid bare to the public. Public hearings on dismissals usually produce a fracas. The newspapers play up these proceedings, for anything in the shape of a fight makes good reading. The dismissed official is sure to hit back by making countercharges and setting off some fireworks. Every city official who keeps his eyes open is bound to see some things that are not supposed to be known outside his own department. There are skeletons in every city hall closet. No mayor wants to have them trotted out every few days for the benefit of his political adversaries at the next election. Hence it is sometimes said that many drones are kept on the payroll for what they know, not for what they do.

Inequities in the pay of public employees.

It is essential to the success of the merit system that public employees shall be adequately paid. They should be compensated according to the duties which they perform, not according to the amount of political influence which they can muster. Unfortunately, in many cities, there has been no classification of positions or standardization of pay. One employee may be rated as a clerk at thirty dollars a week while another, who does exactly the same work, is rated as a bookkeeper at fifty. Women employees are often put down as stenographers, typists, secretaries, confidential clerks, or assistants—not according to the kind of work which they do but merely as a way of justifying differences in pay. Ordinary laborers in all departments get a fixed rate of four or five dollars per day; but so far as the higher-ups are concerned their compensation depends upon a number of things,—political influence, personal favoritism, legislative action, length of service, individual competence, and good luck.

The classification of employees and standardization of their pay.

Various plans of employment classification and salary standardization have been worked out. Some cities have put them into operation. The first step is to send every city employee a request for a detailed statement of the duties which he is actually performing. This data is then classified into groups and grades. A standard definition of duties in each grade (accountant, draftsman, inspector, messenger, etc.) is then framed and for each of these a minimum-maximum rate of compensation is fixed. Every new employee must then be given the initial pay of the grade to which he is appointed and thereafter he gets increases depending on length of service until the maximum is reached.

But it is not enough to adopt a scheme of employment classification and salary standardization, leaving the whole thing thereafter to take care of itself. Heads of departments will find ways of handling the grades. Clerks who perform the most routine duties (copying tax bills, for example) will be put down as expert accountants in order that they may obtain the pay which goes with this higher rank. An ordinary janitor, if he has influential friends higher up, will presently appear on the list as property custodian, or heating engineer, or assistant superintendent of buildings,—anything that will serve as an excuse for higher pay without any change in duties. To protect the city against such evasions it is essential that the civil service authorities be empowered to make frequent investigations to determine just what work every city official and employee is doing. This costs money but it will prove an economy in the end. *The follow-up on these reforms.*

It is sometimes said that the pay of public employees should not be standardized but should be determined by the law of supply and demand. The trouble with this proposition arises from the fact that city employees are voters. Thus, in a sense, they are their own employers. Politically they are well organized in most American cities. In the larger municipalities the majority of these employees are virtually unionized, although their organizations are not always called unions. Some of them, however, are affiliated with the American Federation of Labor. The unionization and affiliation now includes in some large cities not only the laborers and foremen in the street, water and sewer departments, but the public library employees and the clerical staff. But it does not usually include the policemen and firemen. The members of these protective services are permitted to have their own welfare or benefit associations but are usually forbidden to affiliate with any outside labor body. *The unionization of public employees.*

The successful operation of a merit system requires, as has been said, not only fair competition in the case of original appointments but the vigorous recruiting of good applicants, a plan of promotion based on merit, securities against unjust dismissal, together with a proper standardizatior of work and pay. A final essential is a scheme of pensions for public employees. Employees grow old in the service or become incapacitated. The easiest, and at the same *The pension problem.*

time the most expensive, way of caring for such employees is to keep them on the payroll after they have ceased to give value for their wages. That has been the practice in many cities. Some of them have partial pension systems which cover certain classes of officials and employees, especially the school teachers, policemen, and firemen. But very few have comprehensive plans of retirement covering the whole range of the municipal service. The advantages of such a plan are its economy in the long run, its good effect on the morale of the service, and its helpfulness in drawing better employees into the city's employ.

Types of pension systems.

Comprehensive pension systems covering all classes of city employees, and resting upon a basis which is equitable both to the employee and the taxpayer, have been worked out for the use of cities. They are of three kinds—altogether contributory, partly contributory, and non-contributory. In the first case the employee pays for his pension by regular contributions while he is at work, the city contributing nothing. In the second place the employee and the city both contribute. In the third case the city contributes it all. There has been much controversy over the relative fairness of these three systems. The taxpayer favors the first plan while the employee argues for the last. On the whole the intermediate scheme, with both sides contributing, seems to be the fairest and the most satisfactory in its distribution of the burden. In any event the pension funds, as they accumulate, must be carefully built up on an actuarial basis, properly conserved and safely invested; otherwise the deficiency will have to be made up from current revenues.

Some questions to be settled.

Many practical questions arise with respect to the details of a retirement system. What should be the retiring age? Some city employees are outworn at sixty, while others are still capable of doing a good day's work. Should pensions be given only to those who have served for at least twenty or thirty years; if so, what about the men who entered the service late in life? Under the contributory or partly contributory system shall an employee lose all that he has contributed if he leaves the service before he reaches the retiring age? What provision should be made for the widows and children of employees who die in service or are injured in the performance of their duties?

Workers outside the public service do not always take kindly to public pension schemes. They cannot see why pensions should be given to men who have held steady jobs at good rates of pay, without any spells of unemployment, while workers in private employment are left to their own devices. Hence, municipal retirement schemes, when submitted to the people at the polls, have often been defeated. With the progress of the general movement for old age pensions, however, this popular aversion is steadily subsiding. The pension plan seems likely to spread both in public and in private employment. With proper safeguards it is a reasonable and economical measure of social insurance. *The public attitude towards pensions for city employees.*

Should men be trained for the municipal service in America, as they are in some European countries? In the United States we have schools for military and naval training, but no publicly supported schools for the training of city managers, police chiefs, paving inspectors, probation officers, park foremen, assessors, and the rest. Members of the staff in the technical bureaus (such as water analysis, engineering, and accounting) are trained in the regular institutions of education, but they form a relatively small group. In the larger cities there are short training courses for probationary policemen and firemen. But the great majority of those who serve the city have no regular opportunity to obtain instruction in the work which they are expected to do. *Training for the public service.*

It has been urged that colleges and scientific schools ought to provide courses of study leading to the municipal service and a few of them have taken cautious steps in that direction. But there are some practical difficulties in the way. First is the fact that capable young men and women do not yet look upon city employment as a worthy career in America as it is in Europe. Second, there is no assurance that graduates in municipal science could procure positions because cities are averse to appointing applicants from outside their own boundaries, however well qualified they may be. Finally, it is doubtful whether any special course of academic study can be made to serve as a real preparation for a civic post. The first two difficulties are the more important ones. Until cities make their service more attractive, with security of tenure and promotion by merit, there is scant hope of steering capable young men or women into it. *Should the colleges provide it?*

A more immediate need is for training after appointments are made. Teachers in the public schools get an opportunity to take summer instruction and university extension courses, thus keeping abreast of new developments in their fields. Their promotions *In-service training.*

often depend on taking this professional instruction. But there are no regular summer schools or extension courses for detectives, traffic officers, fire prevention officers, assessors, city clerks, paving inspectors, playground supervisors, and all the rest. In the ranks of city officials and employees there are literally thousands who would welcome the opportunity to become more expert by special study if their advancement were made to depend on it. Lacking such incentive they allow their ambitions to become atrophied. Hence the listlessness of city employees has become proverbial. The city hall reporters make it the butt of their wisecracks. But it is not hard to explain nor are the employees largely to blame for it.

REFERENCES

General discussions of the subject may be found in William Anderson, *American City Government* (New York, 1925), pp. 454–500; L. D. Upson, *The Practice of Municipal Administration* (New York, 1926), chap. iii; A. F. Macdonald, *American City Government and Administration* (New York, 1929), chap. xvii; C. C. Maxey, *Urban Democracy* (New York, 1929), chap. xvi; and Joseph Wright, *Selected Readings in Municipal Problems* (Boston, 1925), pp. 454–499.

The best and most comprehensive treatise on the subject is A. W. Procter, *Principles of Public Personnel Administration* (New York, 1922); but quite extensive discussions may also be found in W. F. Willoughby, *Principles of Public Administration* (Baltimore, 1927), pp. 211–380; and in two books by L. D. White, namely, *Introduction to the Study of Public Administration* (New York, 1926), pp. 286–398, and *Civil Service in the Modern State* (Chicago, 1930).

The history of the civil service reform movement in the United States is given in C. R. Fish, *The Civil Service and the Patronage* (New York, 1905), and W. D. Foulke, *Fighting the Spoilsmen* (New York, 1919). Mention should also be made of *Civil Service: A Sketch of the Merit System* by Edward C. Marsh (New York, 1922), and of *Civil Service Administration* by L. F. Fuld (New York, 1922).

The present workings of the merit system in American cities are fully discussed in the report on *The Character and Functioning of Municipal Civil Service Commissions in the United States*, issued by the Governmental Research Conference (1922), the *Report of the Civil Service Committee*, issued by the National Municipal League (1923), the report on *The Personnel Problem in the Public Service*, issued by the Conference Committee of the National Assembly of Civil Service Commissions (1926), and the study of *Public Personnel Problems and the Depression*, by Raymond M.

Gallagher, printed as a Supplement to the *National Municipal Review*, Vol. XXII, pp. 199–215 (April, 1933).

A monthly journal entitled *Good Government* is the organ of the National Civil Service Reform League (521 Fifth Ave., New York) and contains much current material. Reference may also be made to *Public Personnel Studies*, a monthly publication (923 East 60th St., Chicago), and to the annual *Proceedings* of the National Assembly of Civil Service Commissions.

On pensions for public employees the best volume is Lewis Meriam, *Principles Governing the Retirement of Public Employees* (New York, 1918), to which an elaborate bibliography is appended. Mention should also be made of the National Municipal League's report on *Pensions in Public Employment* (New York, 1922).

The classification of employment, the standardization of pay, the making of promotions, and many related problems are fully discussed in the books by Procter, Willoughby, and White already cited. Mention should also be made of the *Report on Classification of Positions and Schedules of Compensation* published by the City of Minneapolis in 1922.

CHAPTER IV

REGISTRATION OF VOTERS

*The freeman casting with unpurchased hand
The vote that shakes the turrets of the land.*
—*Oliver Wendell Holmes.*

The voters' list. Before a freeman can cast his vote he must first get himself registered, hence elections are preceded by the preparation of a voters' list or register of voters. The purpose of this enrollment is to make sure that no one will vote at the election unless he is legally qualified. Incidentally, the list serves as a basis for canvassing on behalf of the candidates and for the mailing of campaign circulars. In many cities it is also used in connection with the drawing of talesmen to serve on juries. The register of voters is made up on a precinct basis and the names on it are usually set down in alphabetical order but sometimes they are arranged by streets. After the list has been finally revised it is printed, and copies may then be obtained at the city hall, usually on payment of a nominal sum.

In the early stages of American municipal history there were no voters' lists. People came to the polls, gave their names, and were permitted to vote unless challenged. This plan was workable so long as communities remained small. The election officers knew almost everybody who came to the polls and strangers were sure to be questioned. But with the growth of the cities and the influx of foreigners the situation changed. The practice of allowing anyone to come forward on election day and demand a ballot led to numerous frauds. In due course it had to be abandoned in the cities, but in many rural districts of the United States there is still no register of voters.[1]

The older method of compiling it. Provision for a register of voters is now made in practically all cities of any considerable size. Originally the responsibility for compiling this register was placed upon the tax collector or on some other city official as an addition to his regular duties. To save time, these officials merely copied off names from the tax

[1] Arkansas and Texas, for example, have still no registration of voters for either cities or rural areas. In these states, however, every rural voter must produce a poll tax receipt.

rolls or from other records at the city hall. But when compiled in this way the lists were incomplete and full of errors. Moreover, it was easy for partisan officials to place on the register names that had no right to be there or even fictitious names which could be used on election day by organized squads of personators and repeaters. In the larger cities, during the seventies and eighties of the nineteenth century, it was notorious that many thousands of ballots were fraudulently cast at every election.

To provide a safeguard against these electoral frauds the practice of requiring a city-wide personal registration was adopted. New York was the first to take the step. Every person desiring to be enrolled as a voter was required to come forward and get himself listed by a board of registration officials. This did not put an end to all the evils, but it eliminated some of them and the system of personal registration gradually spread over the greater part of the country.

Personal registration.

The machinery used in securing registration of voters is by no means uniform throughout the United States, but in general each city has a board of registrars or election board, the members of which are appointed in various ways.[1] These boards have from three to five members and it is a common requirement that both political parties shall be given representation on them. Days for registration are fixed, either by statute or by the election boards, and on such days the voters must come in person to the place of registration. There the officials make a record of each person's name, legal residence, place of birth, length of residence in the state and in the city, and sometimes his occupation as well. In a few cities there is provision for absentee registration by sending a written request. If the applicant is of foreign birth, he may be required to produce his naturalization papers or otherwise prove that he is a citizen. If a literacy test is required by law, it is usually given by the registrars. The registrars may refuse to enroll anyone who does not satisfy the legal requirements, but in case of refusal their action is subject to review by the courts. The common procedure is for the applicant to secure a writ of mandate (man-

The registration procedure.

---

[1] In New York City the board of aldermen elects them; in Boston and San Francisco they are appointed by the mayor; in Philadelphia and St. Louis they are named by the governor, in Chicago by the county judge, and in Cleveland by the secretary of state. See the table printed in the *Report of the Committee on Election Administration* published by the National Municipal League (revised edition, New York, 1931), p. 14.

damus) requiring the registrars to show good reason for their refusal.

Procedure in other countries:

1. England.

It is interesting to note how voters are registered in other countries. In English cities the work of compiling the roll of electors is entrusted to the town clerk. No provision for personal registration is made as in American cities. People are not required to come and be enrolled. Instead the town clerk appoints a corps of canvassers who go about the city, from house to house, like the takers of a census. At each place of abode these canvassers put down the names of persons who seem to be qualified as voters. The names are then made up into a list and posted for public inspection. Anyone whose name has been overlooked is entitled to come forward and have it put on. Or any name that has been improperly put on the list will be stricken off in the process of revision if someone protests it. When the applications and protests have all been heard, the list is closed. The outstanding feature of the English registration system is that it requires no initiative on the voter's part unless there is some error to be remedied and this does not often happen.

2. France.

In French cities the procedure is quite different. No canvassers are sent out. The lists are made up from the records at the city hall. It should be explained in this connection that French cities maintain a perpetual census—every birth, death, disqualification, or removal from the city as well as every incoming of a new citizen is put on record in this *état civil*, as it is called. The compilation of the voters' list from these records is performed by a board consisting of the mayor (or someone named by him), a second member selected by the city council, and a third member appointed by the prefect of the department in which the city is located. This board hears and determines all appeals and protests concerning the inclusion or omission of names. When a city is divided into wards, there is a registration board for each ward. In France, therefore, as in England, the great majority of voters are listed and stay listed, without any action on their part.

The individual initiative in registration.

The American procedure is to place the initiative on the voter. It is his duty to appear at a designated place, stand in line, answer questions, take oath as to his citizenship, age, and residence, pass a literacy test if required, and be enrolled if the registrars can find no good reason for keeping him off the list. We speak of the "right to vote" as an inalienable right, but an American citizen may live his whole lifetime without having his name placed on the register of voters unless he goes and gets it done. That, of course, is not the spirit in which we compile the tax rolls or census returns. The assessors and census enumerators go from house to house and make sure that there are no omissions. But as respects the voters' lists it is estimated that fully one-third of those who are qualified to vote never register at all. Non-registration, therefore, is an important factor in non-voting.

The situation is made worse by the fact that in a good many American cities (including New York, Philadelphia, and Buffalo) a new list is made annually, which means that all voters must go through the same process of registration every year or be left off the list. The citizen is expected to keep his eye on the newspapers for information as to the dates set for enrolling voters. Too often he procrastinates until the last day and then forgets about it. Or on the last day he finds a long line of other procrastinators ahead of him and decides that it is not worth while to wait his turn. In any event a great deal of wasted time and personal inconvenience are involved in the system of annual registration. In no other country would it be tolerated. The argument for annual registration is that it automatically keeps the lists purged of names which should be deleted, that is, names of voters who have died or moved away. *Annual registrations.*

Most of the larger cities have now established systems of permanent or semi-permanent registration. These include Chicago, Boston, Cleveland, Detroit, Seattle, San Francisco, and Los Angeles. Under this arrangement, when a voter once gets his name on the register, it remains there as long as he continues to live in the city. This, of course, is a great convenience to the voter, but it means that the list will often carry names of persons who have moved away. In all of the cities a check-up is made to verify changes in address, but this is a difficult and expensive thing to do. The various ways of doing it will be explained a little later. Frauds are possible under almost any system of registration. Names that have no right to be on the list will get there and be kept there, even when great precautions are taken. It is merely a matter of trying to keep them down to a minimum. *Permanent or semi-permanent registration.*

The officials in charge of registration, even when they are thoroughly honest and competent, have difficulty in determining whether applicants are qualified or not. There is the matter of citizenship, for example. In virtually all the states it is now re- *Qualifications for becoming a registered voter:*

1. Citizenship. quired that one shall be an American citizen by birth or by naturalization in order to become enrolled as a voter. This might seem an easy requirement to apply, but in actual practice it is not. When an applicant declares himself to be a citizen by birth the registration officials usually take his word for it. Rarely is there any check-up on this statement. But if he claims to be a naturalized citizen he is usually required to produce proof of it.

With respect to married women the problem of determining citizenship has become more difficult since the enactment of the Cable Act which permits husband and wife to be of different allegiance. Until 1923 it was the rule that the citizenship of a wife followed that of her husband. When an American woman married a foreigner, she thereby lost her American citizenship; and when an alien woman married an American, she thereby acquired it. But Congress in that year saw fit to change this time-honored rule and it is now the law of the land that a woman neither loses nor gains American citizenship by the mere fact of marriage. The Cable Act, of course, is not retroactive in effect.

2. Legal residence. The determination of legal residence also gives the registrars some trouble at times. In general the requirement is that the voter, in order to be enrolled, must have been a "legal resident" of the city or the precinct for a given period of time—usually from one to six months. But legal residence and actual residence are by no means the same thing. One may be a legal resident without actually living in the city or in the state, or indeed, in the United States. Woodrow Wilson lived for eight years in the White House. During all that time he remained a legal resident of Princeton, New Jersey, although he never went there except to vote on election day. In general, a person's legal residence is where he intends it to be; but there must also be some color of connection, some address from which he can claim to be registered. Every person is entitled to have one legal residence, and one only. To have it he does not need to own or to rent property. On the other hand his claim to residence needs some reasonable foundation in fact. The matter is not determinable by applying any rigid rule; it depends on the circumstances in each particular case and the decision in the first instance rests with the registration officials. If the applicant does not like their ruling he can appeal to the courts.

This American habit of differentiating between legal residence and actual residence opens the door to a good deal of fraudulent registration. One can check up a man's real habitation, but it is not so easy to verify his intent. From time to time it is found, upon investigation, that more voters are registered from some address than could possibly be accommodated there—from some small hotel or boarding house. The voting lists in the tenement wards of the large cities often include large numbers of these "mattress voters," as they are called. During an investigation in Chicago a few years ago it was found, within a single precinct, that 100 voters were registered from addresses which did not exist; 42 were enrolled from torn-down houses; 22 from vacant lots; 21 from schoolhouses, and 18 from addresses which were outside the precinct altogether.[1]

Evasions of the residence requirement.

There are various ways of checking such fraudulent registrations. In some cities a house-to-house canvass is made prior to important elections. This is done by election clerks or by the police who are given lists of registered voters to verify. Frequently, however, the canvass is made in a perfunctory way and does not succeed in purging the lists. Even when the canvassing officers are conscientious they are often given false information by landlords who have been coached by party henchmen. Other cities take an annual census of all adult residents and check the registration lists against this census. This is a better plan because the census-takers do not know what persons are registered from each address and must therefore try to be accurate. Moreover the census is sometimes used as a basis for the assessment of poll taxes. A third method of preventing fraudulent registration is to require that all hotels, rooming houses, and lodging houses shall file with the election officers the names of their bona fide residents. This requirement, however, is often honored in the breach although it would serve as a useful check if rigidly administered.

The prevention of fraudulent registrations.

Some cities make use of the daily death reports as a means of eliminating from the lists, as a routine operation, the names of all deceased voters. Others automatically drop from the register all persons who have not voted within a two-year period. In San Francisco an official election pamphlet is mailed to every registered voter. By an arrangement with the post office all pamphlets which cannot be delivered to the addressee at the designated address are returned to the election officials. In a few cities the registration

---

[1] National Municipal League, *A Model Registration System: Report of the Committee on Election Administration* (revised edition, New York, 1931), p. 20.

lists are checked with the city directory, the telephone book, the motor car registry, and other compilations.[1] The only sure method of verification is to send every enrolled voter a registered post card with return receipt demanded, but this costs a good deal of money. Great advantage, however, can be had from the practice of requiring every voter to sign his name when he registers and sign it again when he votes. This provides a safeguard against the personation of voters who are absent from the city on election day or who are too ill to vote, or who have died since the lists were compiled. The signature requirement is now coming into general use.

3. Literacy. In many cities the registration officials are now required to administer a literacy test before enrolling an applicant. In some cities no one may be registered unless he can read, in the English language, a passage taken at random from the state constitution. Others require that the applicant shall be able to read and write, but make various exemptions from this requirement. In southern cities it is often provided that ability to give a "reasonable interpretation" of a paragraph from the constitution may be accepted in lieu of reading it, or in addition to reading it. This, of course, is a provision designed to prevent the registration of colored voters. In the cities of New York state every new applicant for registration as a voter is now required by law to present a diploma showing that he has completed a certain grade at school, or that he has passed a literacy test administered by the school authorities, that is, by the school superintendent or his assistants. This takes the test out of the hands of the registration officials altogether.

Registration and bipartisan boards. The work of registering voters, like all other work of a semi-judicial nature, demands that the officials who perform it shall be careful and unbiased. Unhappily, they do not always fulfill either of these specifications. Too often the registrars are appointed as a reward for partisan service and are expected by the party machine to look out for its interests. Their business, as they see it, is to help the party in every possible way, even if this involves placing some strain upon the letter of the law. The requirement that both political parties shall be represented in the membership of an election board does not avail to secure fair play, be-

---

[1] A full discussion of the methods used to prevent fraudulent registration may be found in Joseph P. Harris, *Registration of Voters in the United States* (Washington, 1929), pp. 214–239.

cause the representation accorded to the minority party is often a purely technical one. The mayor or governor who finds the law requires him to appoint at least one member of the registration board from each political party will usually see to it that the Republican who gets this appointment in a Democratic city is a Republican for revenue purposes only. And a Republican mayor will find the same kind of a Democrat. There are some alert politicians in every city who register themselves as members of the other party so that they will be eligible for appointment as minority representatives. The system of bi-partisan boards has not proved satisfactory and some better plan ought to be found.

There would seem to be no good reason why registrars of voters should not be chosen under civil service rules. Their work is merely to apply the rules of law, intelligently and fairly. They have nothing to do with the determination of policy. But public opinion is very reluctant to have registration boards or election commissioners chosen in this way, although the office force in the department is sometimes included within the scope of the merit system. Members of these boards are usually chosen for terms of two or four years. They work, as a rule, on a part-time basis and are paid for their services—sometimes very well paid for the amount of work that they have to do. *The selection of registrars by the merit system.*

In most cities a voter cannot be registered except on certain days which are designated for this purpose. These registration days, perhaps eight or ten of them in all, are set two or three weeks prior to the primary or election date. During the last few days of this period there is a great deal of crowding and standing in line at the registration counters in the various precincts. To avoid this difficulty the state laws provide that voters in some cities may register at any time during the year by going to the city hall or county building. The books are closed, however, a few days immediately preceding the election. This plan is a convenience to many voters of systematic habits, but to the majority of others it avails nothing. They will leave this duty till the last day or two. *Registration days.*

Getting voters registered is a more expensive business than most people realize. A recent study of this matter disclosed the fact that the cost per voter is sometimes a dollar or more.[1] On the other hand some cities get the work done for a good deal less *The cost of registering voters.*

[1] National Municipal League, *A Model Registration System: Report of the Committee on Election Administration* (revised edition, New York, 1931), pp. 20–21.

than this figure. The difference depends largely upon the relative cost of the overhead organization, including the expense incurred for "extra employees." Often the registration offices are made the dumping ground for those relatives and friends of politicians who are so poorly qualified for clerical positions that they cannot be placed in any other department.[1] There would seem to be no good reason why any city should spend large sums of money in order to have names and addresses written in a book. The compilers of a city directory can get this done for a few cents per name and their lists are often more accurate than those compiled by the city. By every objective test it seems to be demonstrated that a city which spends fifty, eighty, or a hundred cents per voter for this work is paying several times too much. A few municipalities which have set out to cut the cost find that they can effect a reduction to about fifteen cents per name.[2]

The tests of a good registration system.   There are three criteria by which the efficiency of a registration system may be tested: first, its convenience to the voter; second, the cost of operating it; and, third, its effectiveness as a safeguard against fraudulent voting.[3] The plan of annual registration may satisfy the last of these requirements (although even this is not certain), but it does so at the expense of the other two. A system which requires every voter to come and get himself reënrolled each year is obviously inconvenient. It is bound to put expense on the public treasury besides taking the voter's time, which is the equivalent of money to him. Hence there is much to be said for some form of permanent or semi-permanent registration. But this must be supplemented by an effective arrangement for checking and revising the lists, otherwise the opportunities for fraud will be almost unlimited. The work of trimming the deadwood ought to go on throughout the year and should not be left until a few weeks before the election. Whether the check-up should be undertaken by the police, or by a corps of assistant registrars, or by the assessors, or by a signature system, or by sending out registered post cards—the answer to that question must depend upon local conditions. There are a few cities which have found

---

[1] Joseph P. Harris, *Registration of Voters in the United States* (Washington, 1929), p. 242.

[2] Milwaukee and Portland, Oregon, are examples of cities in which the expense is below this figure.

[3] These criteria are set forth in the *Model Registration System*, sponsored by the National Municipal League and issued as a Supplement to the *National Municipal Review* (January, 1927; a revised edition was printed in 1931).

the police check-up a reasonably efficient way of keeping the list from being padded with ineligible names at the behest of the ward bosses, but there are other communities in which the police could not be depended upon to do this work with even a small degree of reliability because they are themselves under political control. The first essential of satisfactory work in the registration of voters is its complete divorce from the influence of partisan politics.

Because such a separation has rarely been effected there are few things less efficiently or more wastefully done in most cities than the registration of voters. The extent of the leakage is usually concealed by combining the cost of registration with that of conducting the elections. But people are beginning to appreciate the need for reform in this branch of city administration, and there is a growing demand for radical changes in the existing methods. More especially is there an increasing belief that registration should be made more convenient to the voter, for the inconvenience which is put upon him by the existing system, in some cities, is a deterrent to his getting registered at all. A situation in which one-third of the eligible voters remain unregistered, as is frequently the case, would seem to demand remedy.

REFERENCES

Brief discussions of this subject may be found in various books on elections and the party system, including P. O. Ray, *Introduction to Political Parties and Practical Politics* (3rd edition, New York, 1924), R. C. Brooks, *Political Parties and Electoral Problems* (New York, 1923), and E. M. Sait, *American Parties and Elections* (New York, 1927).

A much more detailed study is included in the excellent monograph by Joseph P. Harris entitled *Registration of Voters in the United States* (with a bibliography), published by the Brookings Institution (Washington, 1929). Attention should also be called to the pamphlet on *Registration Laws* by Helen M. Rocca issued by the National League of Women Voters (Washington, 1925), and to the *Proposed System of Registering and Canvassing the Registration Lists in Chicago*, published by the Chicago Bureau of Public Efficiency in 1923. The report on a *Model Registration System*, issued by the National Municipal League (revised edition, New York, 1931), is of great value. The *National Municipal Review* has published a number of interesting articles on the general subject of registration during recent years.

CHAPTER V

NOMINATIONS AND ELECTIONS

"In this election," said the candidate, "I propose to live up to the letter as well as the spirit of the law." "All right," replied the boss, picking up his hat, "live up to the law and be licked."—*Frank R. Kent.*

By way of introduction.   A history of elections would be a long chronicle, but not a dull one. People voted in Greece, and occasionally in Rome. In mediaeval England they chose burghers to represent them in parliament and aldermen of the town. But it was the French Revolution, with its emphasis on the doctrine of popular sovereignty, that gave balloting its first great impetus all over the world. Then, in due course, came manhood suffrage, secret ballots, party campaigns, rotation in office, short terms and frequent elections, and various devices of electoral corruption. Hardly any of these things, however, originated in the United States. Europe invented most of them long before America became politically adolescent.

Early self-determination in election procedure.   In the beginning every American town or city controlled its own election procedure. It held its elections when and as it pleased. This freedom, however, was often abused by those in control. They used their power to perpetuate themselves or their friends in office. Moreover it was deemed desirable to have local and state elections conducted simultaneously, as a means of saving expense, and this brought with it the control of the joint elections by the state authorities.

State control of municipal elections.   Today all municipal elections (even when no state officers are chosen) must be conducted in accordance with general election laws which have been passed by the state legislature. These laws usually determine the procedure in detail. But the state does not actually hold the elections. It devolves this work upon the municipal authorities, making the latter responsible for preparing the voters' lists, securing the polling places, appointing the polling officials, printing the ballots, and making the necessary returns. In all these matters, however, the local authorities must follow the procedure laid down by the state laws; they have little or no discretion of their own. Occasionally there is a state election

NOMINATIONS AND ELECTIONS

board which exercises a general supervision over all elections within the state but more often this duty is entrusted to the secretary of state or to some other regular state officer.

Subject to this general supervision, and in strict conformance with the state laws, each city holds its own elections. The machinery which it uses for this purpose is variable. In a few states there are county boards of elections appointed by the governor upon the nomination of the major political parties, and these boards conduct all local elections, including municipal elections.[1] More commonly, however, each city has a board of elections or an election commissioner appointed by the mayor. The board system is thought to be preferable because it permits the representation of both political parties, but the practice of having a single election commissioner has worked well in a number of cities and it has the advantage of concentrating responsibility.

The election board.

In any event it is the duty of the local election board, or the election commissioner, to see that due public notice of all primary and final elections is given, that ballots are prepared and polling places secured, that the polling officials are appointed and instructed, that polling places are equipped with the essential furnishings, and that the results of the election are properly certified. In most cases the local authorities are also given the duty of conducting recounts, when these are demanded, and of adjudicating disputes which arise in connection with the election results. From their rulings there is usually a right of appeal to the courts.

Its functions.

The date of the municipal election is fixed by state law or by the city charter. Almost always this election is held in the autumn or the spring. As a rule it is not held on the same day as the state election, but sometimes it comes on the same November date in off-years, that is, in years when no national or state election is being held. A separate date is thought desirable as a means of divorcing local elections from state politics. Moreover, when state and local elections are held on the same day the joint ballot becomes too long. Voters then pay too much attention to the aspirants for state office and give too little of their attention to the names of municipal candidates at the bottom of the ballot. The date of the municipal election should come before the beginning

The election date.

[1] Usually the election includes two stages, a primary and a final election. The procedure is substantially alike at both. For a discussion of the various types of primary election, reference may be made to any of the books on political parties listed at the close of this chapter.

of the city's fiscal year. This is essential in order that the newly elected mayor and council may be inaugurated and given an opportunity to study the budget before the old appropriations expire. Thus, if the city's fiscal year begins on July 1, the elections should be held in the preceding March or April.

<small>Sunday elections in Europe.</small> In the cities of continental Europe it is the universal practice to hold municipal elections on a Sunday or a legal holiday. It is believed that a larger vote is likely to be polled on such days. Moreover it is possible by this method to reduce the expense of conducting the election—by using schoolhouses as polling places and by getting volunteers to serve as clerks or watchers at the polls. Public opinion in the United States has not been friendly to the idea of Sunday elections despite the considerable economic gain that would result from such an arrangement. Assuming that it takes each voter, on the average, one hour to reach the polls, mark his ballot, and get back to work, one can easily reckon how considerable is the loss from production in the case of a week-day election.

<small>The polling precinct.</small> For convenience in balloting every large city is usually divided into wards, and these again are divided into precincts or election districts. There is at least one polling place for every precinct, and often several of them. Sometimes the city council is permitted to determine the ward boundaries and to subdivide the wards into precincts, but more commonly this is done by the state or local election authorities in accordance with regulations laid down by the state laws. These regulations usually fix the maximum size of a precinct, and require that all territory within a ward or a precinct shall be contiguous. In general a precinct should not contain more than five hundred registered voters unless there is more than one polling place available.

<small>Polling places.</small> Care should be taken to select convenient polling places. Public buildings, such as schoolhouses, fire stations, and branch libraries should be used whenever practicable. This is not only because of the economy in expense, but also because such places are likely to be easily found and easy of access. When public buildings are not available, it becomes necessary to rent voting booths in private homes, or stores, or garages. It is advisable to secure places which can be hired year after year so that the voters may become familiar with them and not have to inquire each year where their polling booths are. Buildings that are regularly used

NOMINATIONS AND ELECTIONS 65

for partisan purposes, or which have become connected in the public imagination with some form of controversial propaganda, should be avoided. Some cities have found it economical and convenient to use portable polling booths which are stored in the city yards between elections and then placed on some convenient public square or on a vacant lot when they are needed.

Polling booths require some equipment. Tables and chairs are required for the officials in charge of the poll and for the various checkers. It is desirable to have a barrier or passageway so that voters can be admitted one by one. Several copies of the voters' list should be at hand, and provision should be made for a double check on every ballot given and received. As each voter comes to the barrier he should be asked for his name and address. Two checkers should then look him up on the voters' list and having found his name, should repeat it aloud as they enter a check mark against it. Thereupon the voter is given a ballot. Along the wall of the booth there should be small compartments, each provided with a shelf large enough to hold the ballot when laid flat. These compartments should be so constructed that a voter in one of them cannot see what his next-door neighbor is doing. A pencil should be provided in each compartment and it should be securely tied or it will disappear within the first half hour. The pencils should be of soft black lead with a blunt point, for when sharp pencils are used the marking will show through the ballot, even when folded. In some cities a rubber stamp and inking pad are provided, thus doing away with the need for a pencil. After the voter has marked his ballot, and folded it properly, he should be requested to deposit it in the ballot box personally. It should not be handed to the official in charge of the poll. The most convenient type of ballot box is one which takes each ballot flat and presses it down in a pile without crumpling. This greatly expedites the count.

Interior arrangements.

One of the most difficult problems connected with municipal elections is that of securing poll officials who are competent, honest, and non-partisan. Each polling place has a chief official known as chairman, warden, or inspector. With two or more others he is sometimes a co-equal member of the precinct polling board. In addition there are usually two or more checkers and sometimes a clerk of the poll. Thus the precinct staff may include only three or four persons or it may run to a dozen. New York City, on an elec-

The polling officials.

tion day, requires twenty thousand precinct officers. All election officials are paid from the municipal treasury, the usual remuneration being from five to ten dollars for the day. As a general rule these polling officials are appointed by the local election authorities, that is, by the city clerk, or the election commissioner, or the board of elections. Sometimes the laws require that in making the appointments due representation shall be given to each of the political parties, and in any event this is the custom whether the laws require it or not. And too often, as a result, these jobs are passed out as petty patronage to half-illiterates who happen to be out of employment. The result is that gross inaccuracies are frequently found in the count of the ballots or in the returns,—not because of willful malfeasance but as the outcome of all-round incompetence. It has been suggested that polling officials should be selected under the merit system and there is a good deal to be said for this proposal.

Challengers and watchers. In addition to the regular polling officials the party organizations or the candidates are permitted to be represented by challengers or watchers and outside checkers. The services of these supernumeraries are paid for from the campaign funds; in some cases they are volunteers. The outside checkers keep tally of the voters as they come to the polls so that instructions may be given to those party workers who are engaged in bringing out the vote. The challengers may question the identity of any voter and require him to swear that he is a legal voter. If this oath is taken, the voter receives a ballot, but it is kept separate from the other ballots in order that it may be scrutinized in any subsequent legal proceeding or recount. If any other controversy arises within the polling place, the officials make their ruling and this is final so far as the immediate question is concerned. It may usually be appealed, however, to the higher election authorities or to the courts.

The unofficial workers. When it is said that a city election requires from three to a dozen officials per precinct, this does not tell the whole story of the labor required on election day. Add to the regular officials a couple of challengers per precinct, two or more outside checkers, a policeman stationed at the poll, and several messengers (either afoot or with automobiles) engaged in bringing voters to the polls. The total number of workers may run to a score per precinct and large cities have several hundred precincts. In San Francisco, for example, there are nearly nine hundred, and in Cleveland about eight hundred. Hence the actual cost of conducting a municipal election (no matter who pays it) is much larger than the official records disclose.

In the early stages of American municipal history there were no printed ballots. The voter came to the polling place, announced his choice orally, and had it recorded in the poll book. This procedure eliminated all secrecy from voting and hence lent itself to intimidation. Written and printed ballots were therefore brought into use. At the outset the printed ballots were not absolutely secret for they were merely "tickets" printed by the party organizations. They did not require the voter to mark a cross. When he came to the poll, he was met outside by agents of the opposing candidates, each of whom proffered him the party ticket. After taking whichever one he preferred, the voter then went to the ballot box and dropped it in, or he might go into one of the compartments and "scratch" the ticket; that is, draw his pencil through one name and write in another. The party tickets were printed on paper of different sizes, and sometimes of different colors, so that it was usually possible to tell what each voter was doing. The accompanying "ticket" (from the author's collection of old ballots) is one of those on which Abraham Lincoln was elected President in 1860.

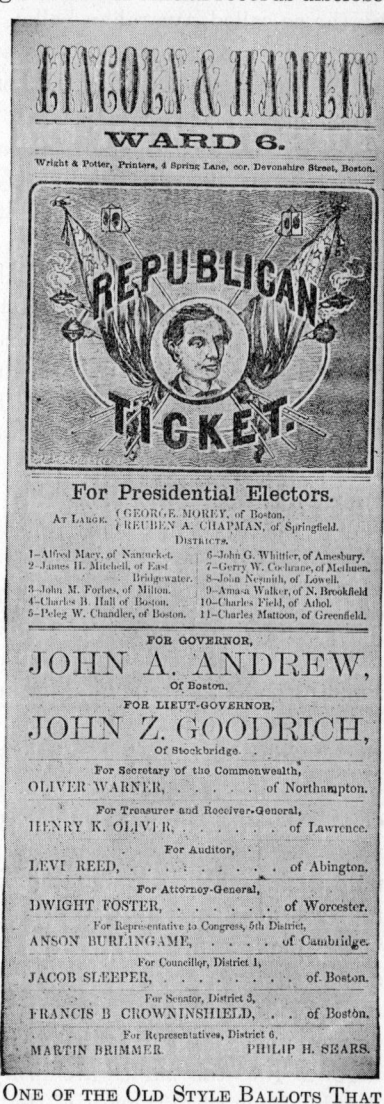

The ballot: Its early history.

ONE OF THE OLD STYLE BALLOTS THAT ELECTED ABRAHAM LINCOLN IN 1860

Ballots of this type remained in use until about the final quarter of the nineteenth century, when party tickets began to be replaced by the so-called Australian ballot. The latter is now used in virtually all American cities. It is an official ballot, printed at the public expense under official supervision,—not furnished by the party organizations. These ballots are now sealed in packages and delivered to the polling officials, with seals unbroken, in the early morning hours of election day. On the reverse of each ballot there is usually printed a facsimile of the chief election officer's signature. This is done to make sure that every voter deposits in the ballot box the identical ballot which was given to him,—and not two or three counterfeit ballots folded up. Occasionally the ballots are printed with a coupon or counterfoil attached. This counterfoil bears a serial number which serves to identify the ballot but which is torn off before the ballot goes into the box. The Australian ballot is absolutely secret. It also provides security against corruption and dishonesty in that every ballot must be accounted for at the close of the polls. When the election is over the total must check up as marked ballots, spoiled ballots, and unused ballots.

The form of the ballot is determined by the general election laws. In cities where the elections are conducted on a party basis, the names of candidates are often printed in columns with the party symbol at the head of the column and a large circle immediately below this emblem. By marking a cross in this circle one can vote the entire party ticket, or as an alternative he may split his ticket by marking crosses after the names of certain candidates in each of the columns. This column-and-circle ballot is virtually essential when there is no literacy test for voting. Some cities, however, use a ballot on which the names of candidates are listed, each with its party designation, under the head of the respective offices which they are seeking. This does away with the party column and circle; but no one can vote this ballot intelligently unless he is able to read. In still other cities the names of candidates are printed under the various offices without any party designation.

As a rule the names are printed in alphabetical order. The disadvantage of this plan is that it gives undue prominence to candidates whose names happen to begin with letters high up in the alphabet. When a considerable number of candidates are in the running, this alphabetical priority is worth a good many votes.

NOMINATIONS AND ELECTIONS

Some years ago in a certain eastern city every one of the thirteen members of the board of aldermen had names beginning with the letters A or B. Sometimes it is provided that the order of names shall be determined by lot. This merely transfers the advantage to the candidate who happens to be having his lucky day. A few cities have tried the plan of printing the names in the order determined by priority in filing nomination papers; but this merely brings a line-up in front of the election board's door for hours, or even for days, before the time set for filing the papers.

The best method, and the fairest to all concerned, is the plan of rotating the names in such way that every candidate comes at the top of the ballot an equal number of times. To accomplish this the printer first sets up the names in alphabetical order. Then, after a certain number of ballots have been printed, the presses are stopped and the top name is transferred to the bottom, whereupon another quota of ballots is printed and the same procedure is repeated. Before being sent out, all the ballots are mixed together so that each polling place gets an approximately equal proportion of ballots with a given order of names. The merit of this method is its absolute fairness, but politicians dislike it because of the difficulty in coaching the semi-illiterate voter when there is no way of knowing how the names will be arranged on the ballot which he receives. *The plan of rotation.*

Most municipal ballots are too long. They contain too many names. To make matters worse, they often have referendum questions printed on them. Ballots with fifty names and a dozen questions are by no means uncommon. This is because minor officials are often made elective and trivial issues are put on the ballot because the city council dislikes the responsibility of deciding them. Long ballots encourage random voting. The voter loses interest before he gets halfway down the list. The ballot ought to be kept short. This can be done by having all except the outstanding positions filled by appointment, not by election. *The need for shorter ballots.*

The voter marks his ballot by placing a cross after the names of candidates. This might seem to be a simple task; but the number of spoiled ballots cast at every election proves that for many voters it is not. Some of them mark for more candidates than there are places to be filled; others place the cross midway between the names of two candidates so that it cannot be counted for either; while still others merely draw lines through the names of those *Spoiled ballots.*

to whom they are opposed. Ballots are not thrown out on mere technicalities. A check mark will do instead of a cross if the voter's intention is clear. But even with this leniency a fair sprinkling of spoiled ballots is likely to turn up in every count.

Counting the ballots. The ballots are counted at the polling booths except in cities which use the system of proportional representation. In that case they are sent to central headquarters to be tabulated. In counting the ballots one official calls off the names while two others keep tally. Two crews of three persons may work simultaneously, thus expediting the count. After the count has been finished the ballots are arranged in packages and replaced in the ballot box, which is then locked and sealed up. *The official returns.* The chief official of the polling place is responsible for seeing that it goes safely back to election headquarters accompanied by an accurate tabulation on the tally sheets which have been provided. These sheets indicate the number of ballots cast for each candidate, the number of spoiled ballots, and the number of ballots which are returned unused. In some cities the responsibility for returning the sealed ballot box to election headquarters is placed upon the police officer who has been stationed at the polling place during the day.

Recounts. In case the election has proved to be a close one, it is usually possible to obtain a recount. This recount may cover only a single precinct, or a number of precincts, or it may cover the whole city. The usual procedure is for one of the candidates to present a formal petition requesting a recount of the votes. The election authorities decide whether this petition shall be granted. In some cities it is very difficult to obtain a recount; in others it is relatively easy. Where it is too difficult, this serves as an encouragement to fraudulent practices at the polls. On the other hand, some safeguards ought to be provided against needless requests for recounts, which involve considerable expense to the city authorities.

They rarely change the result. Recounts do not often change the results of an election, although they may shift a good many votes from one column to another. Almost every recount discloses an amazing amount of carelessness and inaccuracy in the original count and tabulations. It has sometimes happened that in a city with over a hundred precincts the original returns prove to have been inaccurate in every instance without exception. As a rule, however, the inaccuracies work both ways; a candidate gains in some precincts and loses in the others, with the gains offsetting the losses, and the result left unchanged.

NOMINATIONS AND ELECTIONS

Mention has been made of counting votes in accordance with the principles of proportional representation. This system (now used in several large cities) is rather complicated but may be concisely described as follows: First, the names of all candidates are printed alphabetically on the ballot and the voter indicates his choices by marking the figure 1 after the name of his first choice, the figure 2 after the name of his second choice, and so on. Then, when the polls are closed, the election officers compute the number of votes needed to elect a candidate and this is called "the quota." The quota is figured by dividing the total number of votes cast by the number of places to be filled, plus one, and then adding one to the quotient. For example, let us suppose that 10,000 votes have been cast and that there are seven candidates to be elected. Ten thousand divided by eight (seven plus one) is 1,250, and any candidate who receives 1,251 first choice votes is declared elected. If such candidate, however, has more such votes than enough to fill his quota, the surplus votes are distributed in accordance with the indicated second choices among candidates whose quotas have not been filled. If enough candidates are not elected by this process, the candidate with the smallest number of first choices is then dropped and his votes are distributed in the same way. This process of elimination and distribution goes on until enough candidates have filled their quotas or until the successive eliminations have left no more than enough to fill the vacant positions. The plan is not a model of simplicity, of course, but it is not so difficult to understand as one might at first imagine; nor in its actual workings does it present any serious complications.[1] What the voter has to do is simple enough. Insofar as there are any difficulties, they arise in connection with counting the ballots, not in marking them.

Counting ballots under the proportional representation system.

Many cities are now using voting machines instead of printed ballots. The voting machine is constructed on the principle of a cash register. The names of the candidates are displayed on banks of keys under the names of offices to be filled, or under the names of the respective political parties. The voter steps behind a curtain and presses one key after another, thus recording his choice. Every time he presses a key it locks the mechanism against additional choices for the same office unless there are two or more

Voting machines.

---

[1] For a full explanation, see C. G. Hoag and G. H. Hallett, *Proportional Representation* (New York, 1926).

candidates to be voted for. The mechanism is also arranged so that the voter cannot change his choice without having the mechanism readjusted to its original position. Voting machines have merit in that they save the trouble and expense of printing ballots; they eliminate spoiled ballots; they prevent any tampering with votes, and they make known the returns immediately when the poll is closed. Polling booths equipped with a sufficient number of voting machines, moreover, can serve a much larger number of voters during the polling hours than can be handled by the process of marking printed ballots. Fewer election officials are needed and there is never any need for a recount. On the other hand, the machines are expensive to install and to maintain. Like all other complicated mechanisms, they get out of order, and unfortunately they seem to do this at the most inconvenient time, namely, during the busiest part of an election day. Furthermore, slow-minded voters have difficulty in using the machine intelligently and are under temptation to cast a straight ballot, which sometimes can be done by pressing a single key.

Their merits.

And their defects.

Absent voting.

It frequently happens, in the nature of things, that many voters cannot conveniently be in their home districts on election day. Soldiers and sailors, commercial travellers, railway conductors, engineers and trainmen, students in universities, and various other persons are obvious examples. It has been estimated that the number of voters who are necessarily absent from their homes on election day averages about five to ten per cent of the total registration. Many others, in order to cast their ballots, are put to considerable expense and inconvenience. Accordingly, in most cities it is provided that voters who have to be absent on election day may mark their ballots before they go, or may send their votes by mail. The usual procedure is for a voter who expects to be absent to apply, sometime before the election date, to a designated official for a ballot. The ballot is then given to him. After being marked, it is returned in a sealed envelope to be counted with the other ballots. Absent voting is now permitted in the cities of forty-four states.

Compulsory voting.

Compulsory voting has often been advocated but does not yet exist anywhere in the United States. In several foreign countries where it does exist the usual procedure is to impose a fine upon every voter who, without valid excuse, stays away from the polls on election day, or, for repeated absences, to strike his name off the voters' list altogether. This compulsion rests upon the proposition that the right to vote imposes a duty to vote. A citizen must serve on juries in time of peace, and in the army during war, whether he likes it or not. Why, then, should he be allowed to shirk his duty as a voter, a duty which must be performed if democratic government is to survive? If one voter has the right to stay away from the polls, it is argued that every other voter has the same right. And if all followed this policy, no country could maintain a "representative" form of government.

All this sounds plausible enough but there are serious practical objections to any plan of compulsory voting. The voter who goes to the polls because he will be fined if he stays away is not likely to mark his ballot with much intelligence, discrimination, or patriotism. Are the votes of such men really worth counting? Moreover, it has been demonstrated by foreign experience that although you can compel a voter to go to the polls you cannot compel him to mark his ballot. In some cases it has been found that the chief result of compulsory voting is to induce many reluctant voters to avoid a fine by dropping blank ballots in the box. Voting is a duty, to be sure, but it is a duty which ought to be performed from motives of civic responsibility, not from fear of the penalties. Most citizens do not have to be forced to the polls, and it is questionable whether forcing others there would serve any useful purpose. The objections to it.

Municipal elections afford a good deal of opportunity for corrupt practices because of the shifting which takes place in city populations year by year. There is an anonymity in the crowded urban areas which one does not find in the rural sections. Electoral corruption takes various forms and some of them are hard to prevent. Personation is a common one, but not so common as it used to be. It is the offense of voting under a name which is not your own. Voters who have died since the lists were compiled, or who are absent, are sometimes impersonated by men who have no right to vote at all. Vigilance on the part of the election officers helps to prevent personation although the officials can hardly be expected to know everyone who comes to the polls. The practice of requiring every voter to sign his name, for comparison with the signature in the registration book, is of great assistance to these election officers. Corrupt practices at elections.

Then there is repeating, *i.e.*, the offense of voting twice at the

Divers fraudulent practices at the polls. same election. To do this a voter must first, by fraudulent means, become enrolled as a voter in two or more precincts or districts. Ballot-box stuffing is the practice of putting in the box forged ballots which have no right to be there. With the Australian ballot in use this practice is infrequent and when voting machines are used it is eliminated altogether. Ballot-switching is the placing of marks on the ballots, surreptitiously, while the ballots are being counted. A dishonest official, with a small piece of lead under his fingernail, has often been able to spoil or to "switch" ballots by marking additional crosses on them during the process of counting. This form of crookedness can be prevented by using rubber stamps instead of pencils in the voting compartments. Intimidation is the offense of influencing a voter's action by threats of wrongful pressure. Bribery, of course, is self-explanatory. All these practices involve turpitude and are forbidden under severe penalties. Nevertheless, they have not been entirely eliminated. Municipal elections are still won, at times, by crookedness. " I shall win," said a candidate on one occasion, "because I am willing to risk the penitentiary to do it—and the other fellow isn't!"

Practices which are illegal but not corrupt. Various electoral practices, not in themselves wrong, have been made illegal by statute because they are regarded as contrary to good public policy in that they tend to render an election undignified, or unfair, or unnecessarily expensive. Canvassing or distributing campaign literature is forbidden within a certain radius of every polling place on election day. In some cities it is required that all campaign advertisements shall bear the name and address of a qualified voter. Candidates are almost everywhere required to file with the proper authorities a statement of their campaign expenses and it is usually made illegal to spend more than a prescribed sum even for purely legitimate purposes, such as the hiring of halls and the printing of posters. The purpose of these provisions is not only to render the election a dignified affair but to give every candidate, rich or poor, as nearly equal a chance as the laws can ensure. These regulations are often evaded, it is true, but conditions would be much worse if there were no such restrictions.

REFERENCES

Materials relating to municipal elections and election procedure may be found in P. O. Ray, *Introduction to Political Parties and Practical Politics* (3rd edition, New York, 1924) with an excellent bibliography, C. E.

Merriam and H. F. Gosnell, *The American Party System* (revised edition, New York, 1929), C. G. Haines and B. M. Haines, *Principles and Problems of Government* (New York, 1926), R. C. Brooks, *Political Parties and Electoral Problems* (New York, 1923), E. M. Sait, *American Parties and Elections* (New York, 1927), H. F. Gosnell, *Why Europe Votes* (Chicago, 1930), and H. A. Bernhard, *Das parliamentarische Wahlrecht* (Berlin, 1926).

The various books on state government, such as W. F. Dodd, *State Government* (2nd edition, New York, 1928), especially chaps. xviii–xix; A. N. Holcombe, *State Government in the United States* (3rd edition, New York, 1931), especially chaps. viii–ix; and F. G. Bates and O. P. Field, *State Government* (New York, 1928), chap. v, likewise contain discussions of electoral machinery.

Mention should also be made of Edward B. Logan, *The Supervision of the Conduct of Elections and Returns with Special Reference to Pennsylvania* (Philadelphia, 1927), T. D. Zukerman, *The Voting Machine* (New York, 1925), and the handbook on *How to Conduct City Elections* published by the League of Kansas Municipalities. The *Model Election Administration System: Report of the Committee on Election Administration*, published as a Supplement to the *National Municipal Review*, Vol. XIX, pp. 629–671 (September, 1930), is of especial interest. A recent volume by Joseph P. Harris on *Election Administration in the United States*, published by the Brookings Institution (Washington, 1934), covers the subject in full detail. References to books on the short ballot, voting machines, election procedure, and proportional representation may be found in the first edition of Sarah Greer's *Bibliography of Public Administration* (New York, 1926).

CHAPTER VI

THE LAW DEPARTMENT

*Who to himself is law no law doth need,
Offends no law, and is a king indeed.*
—*George Chapman.*

<small>The law department and its head.</small>

Every American city has a law department.[1] At its head is an official known as the city attorney, city solicitor, or city counsellor. The provisions of the city charter invariably require that the person appointed or elected to this office shall be a lawyer, and sometimes the requirement is that he shall be a lawyer of so many years' standing. In the larger cities the city attorney is usually (although not always) a full-time official, receives a substantial salary, and is forbidden to carry on private practice during his term of office; but in the smaller communities a part-time arrangement is frequently made as a means of keeping down the expense.

<small>How he is chosen.</small>

In many of the larger cities the head of the law department is appointed by the mayor, but in most of the smaller ones he is chosen by the city council or elected by the people. Where the city manager form of government is in operation, the manager sometimes makes the appointment. Not as a rule, however, for this is one position which the framers of city manager charters have generally deemed advisable to place beyond the range of managerial control in order to ensure its independence. The term of the city attorney varies from one to four years, but in some cities the appointment is made without definite limit of time. As a general rule no capable occupant can be induced to hold the position very long. The responsibility is large and the pay is a good deal less than a successful lawyer can make in private practice.

<small>What is the best method of selection?</small>

Some difficult questions arise with respect to the proper method of selecting the head of the city's law department. Obviously the best method is one which will not only ensure the choice of a competent man but will place him in such position of independence

---

[1] English cities, on the other hand, do not maintain separate law departments. There the town clerk serves as legal adviser on all ordinary matters. When important questions arise, which he and his associates are unable to handle, he is usually authorized to consult outside legal specialists.

THE LAW DEPARTMENT

that he can perform the duties of his office without fear or favor. The city attorney has a variety of functions, as will be seen presently, but the most important among them is that of giving legal advice to the higher municipal authorities. Almost daily this advice is sought by the mayor, city manager, council, or heads of departments on questions relating to their respective powers, rights, duties, and liabilities. Frequently the law department becomes the arbiter of controversies among these officials, each of whom desires to apply his own interpretation of the laws. More particularly the city attorney has to act as umpire between the mayor and the city council when the two get into disagreements concerning their respective jurisdictions as fixed by the city charter.

Being placed in this quasi-judicial situation, it is of course desirable that the head of the law department shall be kept free of entanglements. His position should guarantee his independence and neutrality. In other words, he ought not to be directly under the thumb of mayor, council, or manager. For in that case he will be regarded as a partisan no matter how impartial he may try to be. Legal advice is not worth much when colored by official pressure. If the mayor appoints the city attorney, and has power to remove him at will, it is not reasonable to expect that the law department will stand in the way of what the mayor wants to do if it can find any loophole for him. City councils likewise want the law department to take their point of view and when they have the appointing power this end is usually achieved. Lawyers are human. They desire to please their clients when they can. But the real clients of the city's law department are the citizens—not the mayor or the councilmen. This department's function is to protect the public against illegalities on the part of the city officials.

The need for independence.

Hence it is suggested that the head of the law department ought to be elected by popular vote, thus placing him in a position where he can act and advise without reference to the wishes of the various officials who are immediately concerned. In many cities this plan is followed, but it has some disadvantages. One of these is the fact that popular election too often puts a good politician rather than a good lawyer into the office. The city attorney ought to be not only a lawyer but a very good lawyer, one who not only stands well in his profession but is recognized as a specialist in municipal jurisprudence. Popular election is clearly not the best

Objections to the popular election of this official:

1. It does not assure competence.

MUNICIPAL ADMINISTRATION

2. It submerges the post in politics.

way to secure such a man; on the contrary it is a reasonably sure way of excluding him. The best lawyers in the city are usually the worst vote-getters, and one might almost say that the converse is true. Popular election is never a dependable method for securing skill or expertness in public office.

There is another objection to the practice of having the head of the law department chosen by popular vote. It arises from the nature of his work. The city attorney not only serves as legal adviser but he has to do with various matters which afford him an opportunity to play politics if he is so inclined. The approving of contracts and the settlement of claims against the city, for example, afford opportunity to do political favors. An elective city attorney is thus in a position to build up a personal machine (at the city's expense) and thereby to entrench himself in office. Or, as sometimes happens, he can proceed to use the powers and patronage of his office as a means of promoting his own candidacy for a judgeship. Making the office elective is sure to draw the city attorney into politics.

Merits of mayoral appointment with confirmation.

On the whole, therefore, it seems best that the head of the law department be appointed by the mayor for a definite term, with confirmation by the city council, and that he should not be subject to removal without the council's consent. This arrangement gives him a status in which he is not entirely beholden to either the legislative or executive branches of the city government. It is quite true that the selection of the city attorney under such a plan may become a matter of trading and compromise between the mayor and council. But in such matters we are restricted to a choice among practical alternatives, no one of which is altogether free from potential dangers. The head of the city's law department is expected to work harmoniously but impartially with two branches of government which frequently disagree. It stands to reason that he should be chosen in some way which will help him gain the confidence of both.

The department's staff.

Small cities manage to get along with a part-time legal adviser, but places of 30,000 population or more usually require full-time service. Larger municipalities find work for one or more assistant city attorneys as well. And in the biggest American cities the law department becomes a formidable affair, with dozens of lawyers on its payroll and occupying a whole floor of offices. The subordinates of the city attorney are usually (but not always)

THE LAW DEPARTMENT

appointed by him. In some cities they are chosen under civil service regulations. Legal duties are apportioned among these assistants as the city attorney determines. One of them approves municipal contracts as to form, another defends suits brought against the city, another looks after all legal matters connected with the maintenance of municipal property, another has charge of claims-adjustments, and so on. In the course of time these assistant city attorneys often become very proficient in their work, but the salaries paid are not usually adequate and the best of them rarely stay in the city's law department very long. Other lawyers discover their ability and take them into partnership, or they get an opportunity to earn more in private practice for themselves. In this way the most capable assistant attorneys are often drawn out of the service while the less competent ones remain. That is one reason why the lower ranks in the law department of a large city are frequently occupied by attorneys who become so immersed in the windy side of legal technicalities that the city councilmen are tempted to echo Shakespeare's sentiment, "the first thing we do, let's kill all the lawyers."

The work of the city attorney's office requires versatility, for it covers a wide range. Most of its functions, however, can be grouped under a dozen heads as follows; but it should be emphasized that the order in which these are here stated is not necessarily their order of importance: (1) preparing bills, on behalf of the city, for introduction into the state legislature; (2) giving advice and opinions on legal matters to the mayor, city manager, city council, the various municipal boards, and to the heads of administrative departments (especially to the head of the police department) when asked to do so; (3) framing amendments to the city charter for submission to the people (or to the legislature in cities which do not have the home rule charter system); (4) drafting ordinances or resolutions to be enacted or adopted by the city council; (5) drawing or approving contracts for public work, preparing deeds or leases of city property, and drafting all other legal documents; (6) legal work in connection with the issue of bonds and other municipal obligations; (7) determining the validity of surety bonds submitted by contractors who do work for the city, and giving approval to any other papers that may need scrutiny as to their legal form; (8) serving as counsel for the city in suits at law, whether brought by the municipality or against it; (9) ad-

The law department's functions:

justing claims for damages so as to avoid litigation; (10) assisting in negotiations with public utility companies and handling petitions or protests brought on behalf of the city to the state public utilities commission; (11) attending conferences of all sorts in connection with the city's business; and (12) dealing with a host of miscellaneous functions which defy classification but which include the frequent untangling of snarls into which the city authorities get themselves by failing to consult the law department until after they have acted.

<small>1. Business with the state legislature.</small> The law department of a large city must keep in constant touch with the state legislature while the latter is in session. This is essential because a city has no inherent legal powers of its own. All its powers are derived from the constitution and laws of the state. The city charter is merely a statute. So, when the city wants any new or special powers it must go to the state legislature for them. In that case a bill is prepared by the city's law department and introduced by some friendly senator or assemblyman. Then it is supported at the committee hearing by the city attorney or by one of his assistants. A few of the largest cities employ special legislative counsel, attached to the law department, for this purpose. Any citizen or group of citizens may also have bills introduced and frequently such bills are deemed by the city authorities to be worthy of official opposition. In such cases the law department takes the responsibility of trying to get the bills defeated.

<small>The flood of bills affecting cities.</small> Bills affecting the interests of the larger cities are numerous at sessions of nearly all the state legislatures. This is true even in states where the constitution makes provision for municipal home rule. The reason is that a constitutional provision for municipal home rule restricts cities to the control of their strictly local affairs, and the major problems of city administration are no longer of merely local consequence. They are deemed to be of state-wide concern, in which case the state legislature takes them in hand. At the 1930 session of the Massachusetts legislature more than one hundred bills relating to municipal affairs were introduced. These included bills for widening streets, curtailing the powers of certain city officials, fixing tax rates, granting exemptions from the city debt limit, authorizing pensions, raising the pay of city employees, and so on. Some were supported by the municipal authorities; others were opposed by them. In either case they provided work for the municipal law departments.

THE LAW DEPARTMENT

A second function of the law department, that of giving legal advice to city officials, is perhaps the most onerous of them all. Every question upon which there is difference of opinion as to legality is referred to the law department for its interpretation and opinion. The mechanism of city administration has become so complicated by reason of numerous charter amendments, special statutes, ordinances, judicial decisions, and regulations that no one can be absolutely sure of his duties or jurisdiction in certain contingencies. So, when doubt arises on any point, the law department is asked to examine the matter and submit a ruling. If the question is of major importance the city attorney studies it himself; but minor issues are referred to one of his assistants. In either case a written opinion is finally prepared and submitted. Such opinions have virtually the effect of judicial decisions because they are usually accepted by all the parties concerned, although the issue can be carried to the courts if anyone wishes to do so. In well-organized municipal law departments these opinions are bound up and properly indexed so that they can be readily referred to when questions arise.

2. Giving legal advice to city officials.

This function of ruling on points of law enables the city attorney to exercise more influence upon the course of municipal administration than most people realize. Nearly all problems of general policy, and many routine problems as well, involve legal questions. Strictly speaking, the law department has nothing to do with the expediency of any proposed action but only with the legal issues involved; nevertheless the two are often so closely intermingled that they cannot be considered apart. The legality of a proposal sometimes depends, in part at least, upon its merits and urgency from the standpoint of public policy. A city ordinance, for example, will not be enforced by the courts if its provisions are unreasonable. But unreasonability is a question of fact; it depends on the situation to which the ordinance is applicable; hence the provisions of an ordinance may be reasonable under one set of circumstances and unreasonable under another. To exclude heavy trucking from certain residential streets may be reasonable, but to prohibit them from using the streets of the warehouse and shipping districts would certainly not be so. To require that all persons who handle food in stores shall secure health certificates may be a reasonable measure of public sanitation, but the application of the same rule to those who work in machine shops and

Importance of this function.

furniture factories would scarcely have the same measure of rationality. In any event the head of the law department can accentuate the legal difficulties of any problem or help to clear them away.

3. Drafting charter amendments. When amendments to a city charter are desired by the municipal authorities, the law department is usually asked to prepare them for submission to the state legislature or to the people, as the case may be. It is necessary to make sure that these amendments are properly worded, are consistent with the provisions of the state constitution, and fit properly with the other provisions of the charter. In states which have the home rule charter system the initiative in charter drafting is given to an elective board of freeholders. But individual amendments do not customarily require this procedure.

4. Framing the ordinances. Then there is the work of framing new ordinances and amendments to the existing ordinances. When the city council desires to enact an ordinance on some designated matter, the law department is requested to prepare it in proper form. This is the wise procedure but occasionally it is not followed. Sometimes a councilman prepares the ordinance himself and gets it passed by the council without consulting the law department at all. In such cases there is a good chance that the ordinance will be found defective and declared invalid by the courts. Laymen do not always realize that the proper drafting of an ordinance is no task for an amateur. It requires both skill and experience. This is especially true of ordinances relating to taxation, expenditures, and bond issues. Even a slight mishap in this field may prove costly.

The profusion and confusion of city ordinances. Ordinances are laws of local application.[1] They differ from statutes in that they are passed by the city council and apply, for the most part, only within the municipal boundaries.[2] Speaking generally, they deal with sanitation, the erection of buildings, obstructions in the streets, traffic regulation, markets, and such matters; but ordinances are enforced in the courts just as statutes are. In every large city they are numerous, and they are constantly being amended or repealed. So continuous is this process of change

---

[1] See the chapter on "The Place of Municipal Ordinances in Our Legal System" in Harvey Walker, *Federal Limitations upon Municipal Ordinance Making Power* (Columbus, Ohio, 1929), pp. 1–19.

[2] In special cases, however, municipal ordinances may have an extra-territorial effect, for example, in the case of watersheds, mountain parks, or airports belonging to the city but situated outside the municipal boundaries.

THE LAW DEPARTMENT

that a great deal of confusion often results. There are said to be about sixteen thousand ordinances on the records in New York City and it has been estimated that the municipal ordinances of Philadelphia (including those that are obsolete but unrepealed) would fill four volumes of nine hundred pages each. Such excessive numbers are due to the multiplication of repealing and amending ordinances. From time to time the city ordinances are revised and consolidated, with a view to lessening the bulk and confusion. This task is usually performed by the city's law department, a special appropriation being made by the city council to cover the expense.[1]

5. Preparing deeds, leases, and other legal papers. A good deal of the law department's time is devoted to the work of preparing deeds and leases, examining titles, and filing papers in connection with the taking of private property for public use. The city is constantly acquiring land for public buildings, parks, playgrounds, street widenings, and so forth. Before paying for such acquisitions, it must make certain that the seller has a good title, that the deeds or other papers are in proper form, and that they are duly recorded in the registry of deeds. The procedure in taking private property for public use is explained in a later chapter of this book.[2] City property is also sold when no longer needed, or it is leased to a tenant, or rights of way may be given over it. All such transactions involve the making of legal papers. So with contracts for public works, which are usually prepared by the engineering department, but come to the law department for approval as to legal form before they are signed on behalf of the city.

6. Legal work in connection with municipal bond issues. Whenever a city undertakes to borrow money by the issue of bonds there is a good deal of preliminary legal work to be done. The proper resolutions have to be prepared and various published notices given. Where bond issues require approval by popular vote the numerous matters connected with the calling and holding of a bond election have to be arranged with meticulous attention to the legal requirements, otherwise the bonds may not be valid. All this work falls upon the city's law department. In order to make assurance doubly sure, it is the usual practice to have the

[1] Revisions and codifications have often been crudely done—partly because of inadequate appropriations for the work. Ordinances relating to the organization of the city departments have been jumbled with those relating to individual conduct. There is need for some such orderly arrangement as is suggested in E. D. Greenman's article on "The Codification of Municipal Ordinances," in *The Municipal Index* (New York, 1925), pp. 39–43.

[2] See Chapter XIX.

validity of the bonds, including the entire preliminary procedure, approved in a formal written opinion by some nationally-known firm of bond attorneys. This is done to facilitate the sale of the bonds to brokers and investment concerns.

7. Determining the validity of contractors' bonds, etc.

Contractors are usually required to give bonds of a different character, namely, surety bonds, for the proper performance of their work. Certain city officials, especially those who handle money, must also give surety bonds. Surety bonds are likewise required in connection with permits for the occupancy of a portion of the street during private building construction and in various other connections. A surety bond is a guarantee from a responsible individual or from a bonding company, filed to protect the city against loss. The law department is usually required to pass on the validity of all such bonds and to make certain that the protection is complete.

8. Prosecuting and defending suits.

As a municipal corporation the city may sue and be sued in the courts. It brings suits against individuals and corporations from time to time and has an even larger number of actions brought against it. Cities bring suit, for example, to collect monies due, or to recover sums which have been illegally paid, or to obtain damages arising out of somebody's failure to fulfill the provisions of a contract. Actions against the municipal corporation are brought in connection with personal injuries arising from defective street pavements or other public property, or for the collection of disputed and unpaid accounts, or for the reinstatement of a dismissed official in his post, or on any one of a dozen other grounds. It is a rare week in any large city when the law department does not have to deal with a suit for damages, a petition for an injunction, an application for a writ of mandate, or a citation to appear in court on some other matter. The city attorney, or someone connected with his staff, prosecutes or defends all such actions. This involves getting the evidence ready, presenting it, making the argument in court, and preparing the appeal if there is one.

Police court work.

In addition, the law department is often enjoined by the city charter to see that "all ordinances are properly enforced." This does not mean, however, that someone from the city attorney's office must be at the police court every morning to prosecute all traffic cases and other misdemeanors. Sometimes there is a city prosecutor to do this. Most minor offenses are prosecuted in the municipal court by the police officer who has filed the com-

THE LAW DEPARTMENT

plaint or made the arrest. But the city attorney's office may be called upon to coöperate, or even to take charge when a case of major interest or importance comes up. Moreover, when the issue involved in some legal action is likely to set a precedent and is appealed to the higher courts, the law department always comes into the case and follows it through. Cases arising in the police court may concern a relatively trivial incident but may nevertheless raise an issue that goes all the way to the Supreme Court of the United States.

The relations between the city and the public utility companies (telephone, electric lighting, gas, street railway, and motorbus companies) give rise to much negotiation, controversy, and litigation. These utilities operate under franchises, and a public utility franchise is often a very complicated document.[1] Franchises expire from time to time and negotiations for their renewal have to be undertaken. Even while a franchise is in operation, many disagreements are bound to arise between the city authorities and the companies as to rates and quality of service. In all such matters the law department has the duty of representing and protecting the interests of the city and its citizens. Most of these questions are settled by conference and negotiation, but some of them have to be carried to the state public utilities commission for a ruling. If this ruling is not satisfactory to either side it may be appealed to the courts. Hence the litigation between the city and the public service companies is often long drawn out, highly complicated, and very expensive to all concerned.

9. Negotiations and handling of controversies with public utility companies.

In such contestations the municipal law department is usually at a disadvantage. The public utility corporations are quite ready to pay for the best legal and technical skill that money can buy; they are willing to spend large sums in the collection of data and evidence bearing on the issue; they do not hesitate to retain advisers who have formerly been members of the public utilities commission and know its methods thoroughly. The city, on the other hand, usually expects its side of the case to be worked up within the bounds of the law department's modest appropriation for routine matters. When the city attorney's office asks authority to engage an outside law firm with special qualifications for handling the case the city council does not always see much point in spending the extra money. What is a law depart-

The city's disadvantage in such negotiations.

[1] See Chapter XLV.

ment for if outside lawyers have to be hired whenever big cases come up?

Law and politics.

Controversies with public utility companies, moreover, are sometimes started by mayors or city councils for political effect and not because there is any expectation of winning them. From time to time it is accounted good politics to make a drive against the "interests" as represented by the gas company or the street railway corporation. Such forays enable the mayor and councilmen to pose as vigilant friends of those who have to pay the rates and fares. In such cases the law department is expected to make an uphill fight for something which it knows to be unreasonable. Then when the controversy is decided against the city there is a protest from the councilmen that the city attorney and his assistants are incompetent. Contestations into which the city enters for political effect are likely to prove unsuccessful no matter how capable the law department may be.

10. Adjusting claims.

Claims for damages are presented to the city in considerable number. Somebody trips on the pavement and is injured, or a water main bursts and floods his basement, or a truck owned by the city's lighting department runs into his car and wrecks it— all manner of injuries to person or property may provide the basis for claims. These claims, when they come in, are referred to the law department for disposition. If this department, on investigation, believes the claim to be a just one, it tries to negotiate an amicable settlement. In most cases it is successful. Relatively few claims are carried into court. It should be borne in mind, however, that cities are not liable for all the damage that their officials and employees may do. There is no legal liability in the case of those departments which perform strictly governmental functions—the police, fire, and health departments, for example. But where the functions are quasi-commercial, as in the case of the water or electric lighting departments, there is a legal liability if negligence on the part of a city official or employee can be proved.[1] A very large portion of the law department's time is absorbed in adjusting these claims and it is here that political pressure from outside is often a serious obstacle to fair action. Councilmen come in and press for the payment of money to voters whose claims would probably be rejected in court.

[1] For a further discussion of this matter see the author's volume on *The Government of American Cities* (4th edition, New York, 1926), pp. 112–132.

When conferences are held at the city hall on any matter of municipal business, a representative of the law department is usually requested to attend. In some cities such conferences by groups of city officials are held frequently. Very often, moreover, a delegation from the chamber of commerce or from some other civic organization comes seeking a conference with the mayor, the city manager, the head of a municipal department, or a committee of the city council. At such conferences it is usually deemed advisable to have someone from the law department present in case any legal questions arise. In some cities this attending of conferences takes a considerable amount of time. Nor should one overlook the demands which are often made upon the head of the law department in the way of addresses at public gatherings, especially in large cities when questions relating to franchises or the regulation of utilities are under discussion. The occupant of this post is sometimes the only one who thoroughly understands all the issues involved in a franchise controversy. 11. Attending conferences on various matters of city business.

The foregoing list does not exhaust the category of matters with which the law officers of the municipality have to deal. There are miscellaneous duties which vary from place to place and from day to day. In no two cities are they alike. The nature and number of these varied functions depend upon whether the city's legal work is all concentrated in one central law department, or whether it is somewhat decentralized by giving a separate legal adviser to each of the major departments such as police, public works, and public health. When this is done the department's own counsel can relieve the city's law department of a great many small chores. Too much decentralization is not advisable, however, because there must be uniformity in the city's legal administration, otherwise confusion will result. 12. Miscellaneous functions.

All in all, the city attorney has a large amount of responsibility and ought to be a lawyer of high competence. Sometimes he complies with that specification and sometimes he does not. In too many American cities the passport to this position has been, and still is, political or personal influence. This is invariably true where the office has been made elective, and unhappily it is also too often the case where the mayor makes the appointment. In selecting the head of the law department a mayor is under temptation to find someone whom he can trust as a political as well as a legal adviser, a lawyer who has been with him in his campaign and with Conclusion.

whom he is on terms of close personal friendship. But mixing politics with law does not usually give good results and it is to be hoped that the two will some day be divorced in city administration. Progress in that direction has already been made and seems likely to continue. There are a good many cities in which the selection of men in this important department is now made on a non-partisan basis with the incumbents remaining in office through successive administrations. And the number of such cities is likely to increase when people come to a full realization of the large influence which the legal officers of the city exert upon the direction of its affairs.

REFERENCES

The best-known work on the legal aspects of city administration is J. F. Dillon, *Commentaries on the Law of Municipal Corporations* (5th edition, 5 vols., Boston, 1911), a comprehensive, thorough, and accurate compilation. Eugene McQuillin, *The Law of Municipal Corporations* (2nd edition, 7 vols., Chicago, 1928) and *Supplement* (Chicago, 1932), is a later treatise which many law departments prefer. Shorter works are H. S. Abbott, *Treatise on the Law of Municipal Corporations* (3 vols., St. Paul, 1905), C. B. Elliott, *Principles of the Law of Municipal Corporations* (3rd edition, revised by Stewart Chaplin, Chicago, 1925), R. W. Cooley, *Handbook of the Law of Municipal Corporations* (St. Paul, 1914), and Allen B. Flouton, *Outline of the Law of Municipal Corporations* (Brooklyn, N. Y., 1926).

Mention may also be made of case-books, including J. H. Beale, *Selection of Cases on Municipal Corporations* (Cambridge, 1911), John E. Macy, *Selection of Cases on Municipal or Public Corporations* (Boston, 1911), R. W. Cooley, *Illustrative Cases on Municipal Corporations* (St. Paul, 1913), and C. H. Tooke, *Selection of Cases on the Law of Municipal Corporations* (Chicago, 1926).

Special volumes which will be found useful in their respective fields are T. M. Cooley, *Treatise on Constitutional Limitations* (8th edition, Boston, 1927), Edward F. White, *The Negligence of Municipal Corporations* (Indianapolis, 1923), H. L. McBain, *American City Progress and the Law* (New York, 1918), and Harvey Walker, *Federal Limitations upon Municipal Ordinance Making Power* (Columbus, Ohio, 1929).

Further bibliographical references may be found in the *Encyclopedia of the Social Sciences*, Vol. XI, pp. 93-94.

CHAPTER VII

THE CITY CLERK

> That low man seeks a little thing to do,
> Sees it and does it.
> —*Robert Browning.*

The office of clerk is one of the oldest in city administration. It goes back to early mediaeval days, to a time when so few laymen could read or write that a cleric had to be requisitioned to perform the duty of keeping the borough records. But despite its great age and good traditions the office is not one that gives its occupant much opportunity to impress himself on the public mind. Its duties are of a varied but mostly routine sort. They call for punctuality and painstaking, but not for much exercise of judgment or imagination. The ideal city clerk is one who possesses a good memory, who has developed habits of orderliness and accuracy, and who realizes that there is virtue in doing little things right. The city clerk's functions are unpicturesque, hence he is sometimes regarded by the public as a "low man" in the hierarchy of municipal officers; but his work has a fundamental importance which no one familiar with the inner operations of city administration can fail to appreciate. The value of this department to the whole administrative mechanism is not to be judged by the size of its staff or the amount of its annual appropriation. *A routine post of high importance.*

In England the city clerk is a lawyer and hence is able to serve as legal adviser to the municipal council. He is the officer who represents the municipality in its dealings with the central government; he supervises the registration of voters, conducts the elections, keeps the official records, and is the "key man" of the municipal service. His remuneration, as a rule, is higher than that of any other city official. Elected by the city council, he has a permanent tenure and is entitled to a pension on retirement. In a word, the clerk's office is the pivot on which the whole system of British municipal administration revolves.

Every American city, of whatever size, and whatsoever its form of government, has a city clerk, or city recorder as he is sometimes *How the city clerk is chosen.*

called. Almost invariably he is chosen by the city council. This is because he was regarded in earlier days as the council's recording secretary with no duties other than to keep the minutes of each regular meeting. Gradually, however, additional functions were assigned to the city clerk because he seemed the logical one to take them. His office, in fact, became the place for everything that did not have anywhere else to go—registering births, issuing marriage licenses, publishing official notices, arranging the details of elections, and so on. Keeping the council's records eventually became a small part of his work. Nevertheless the traditional method of filling the office has been continued. The city clerk remains, in theory, the council's scribe and mentor, appointed by it and responsible to the council alone. Even in cities which have adopted the manager form of government, and in which all the other heads of administrative departments are appointed by the city manager, the city council continues to name the clerk.[1]

Term and qualifications.
The term of office is usually two or four years, but in a few cases it is merely made dependent on the pleasure of the council. American city clerks are not chosen from the legal profession, as a rule, but anyone who holds the office must familiarize himself with the provisions of the city charter and with the general laws relating to the municipality. The selection of a city clerk is often influenced by political pressure, yet the position has acquired a fair degree of permanence. City clerks stay in office a good deal longer, on the average, than city managers, police superintendents, or city attorneys.

The need for continuity.
This is natural enough, because there must be some custodian of city hall methods and procedure, someone who knows how things have been done in the past, and to whom the councilmen can turn when they want to know the correct procedure. The business of the council would often get into a snarl if there were no experienced clerk to guide the proceedings along and to make sure that all the essential formalities are complied with. The city clerk sees to it that meetings of the council are legally called, that a quorum is recorded as being present, that resolutions and ordinances are properly introduced and given the requisite number of readings, that they are duly signed and authenticated, and that the necessary publications are made. All this is of great importance

[1] In a few cities, especially smaller cities in the South and West, the city clerk is elected by popular vote.

THE CITY CLERK

because any serious omission may invalidate all that is being done. No one knows better than the councilmen how essential is the careful and intelligent performance of this work; so when a city clerk gives efficient service, and keeps out of politics, he always stands an excellent chance of being reëlected term after term. It is not uncommon to find city clerks who have remained in office for twenty years or more. This office, in fact, has developed a stronger tradition of permanence than any other in the American municipal service. When a vacancy occurs in it, moreover, the assistant city clerk is frequently promoted to the higher post. This means that the office of city clerk is occasionally filled by a woman, and there is no good reason why it cannot be efficiently filled in that way.

Among the varied functions of a city clerk the oldest is that of keeping the council's records. The clerk attends all meetings of the council and in the smaller cities all meetings of council committees as well. He sits alongside the presiding officer and advises him on points of procedure. All papers to be considered are presented to him before or at the meeting. When they are ordered read to the council, he reads them. When a formal vote is taken, he calls the roll, records the yeas and nays, and announces the result. He keeps the official record of the proceedings and often drafts the committee reports for presentation to the council. He receives all petitions and presents them. He files all documents that are ordered to be placed on file. When the meeting is over he puts the record into proper form and sees to the publication of any matters that require such action. Virtually every item of council business clears through his hands.

Duties of the office:

1. Keeping the records.

In the larger municipalities the city clerk is not able to do all this work and perform his other administrative duties as well. Hence, there is usually an assistant city clerk who attends committee meetings and is sometimes known as the clerk of committees. Sometimes there are two or even three assistant city clerks among whom the work of the office is divided. Under them is a staff of stenographers and copyists. But no matter how large the municipality may be, the city clerk usually attends the regular council meetings in person, accompanied by an assistant to do the clerical work. He is there to answer the endless questions that will be asked of him—as to what has been done in the past, or what is the next step, or what notices must be given, or how a resolution ought to be worded. In some cities it is the practice to have the city attorney present at council meetings as an additional safeguard in the observance of legal formalities.

Importance of accurate records.

The importance of having the council's records kept with some judgment on the part of the recording officer is obvious. In the heat of debate the councilmen will sometimes say and do things which are not for the official records to disclose. Discrimination must be used in determining what needs to be set down in the book of minutes. From the tangle of motions and amendments, and amendments to amendments, the city clerk is supposed to straighten things so that they will all appear to have been done in a dignified, regular, and orderly way. This is essential, for it is to the official records that the courts will refer in case any legal controversy arises concerning the validity of council proceedings. They will not go behind the records. If these records show that an ordinance was properly introduced, read three times, voted upon, and adopted by at least a majority with a quorum present, the courts will not concern themselves with the snarls and squabbles that may have marked the journey of the ordinance through the council chamber. City councils have a good deal to do at some of their meetings and occasionally they cut the corners in getting it done. Then they leave it to the city clerk to fill the omissions.

2. Giving notices and preparing reports.

Closely associated with this work of keeping the journal is a second function—that of preparing the various notices which are required by law to be given publicly—notices of hearings, or of intention to borrow money on the city's credit, or to close a street, or what not. In some cities the clerk's office is required to notify voters of the time for registration, the date of an approaching election, the location of the polling places, and the hours during which the polls will be open. Another duty is that of putting the city's annual report in shape to be printed, and keeping a supply of city documents available for those who want them. People go to the city clerk's office for a copy of the charter or for the revised ordinances. It is a general rule that municipal ordinances, especially those of a penal character, may not be enacted by the council (except in cases of emergency) until after public advertisement. From time to time the existing ordinances are printed in book form. They are put in shape for publication by the law department; but the work of getting them printed and distributed is often turned over to the office of the city clerk.

This matter of distributing official publications has not been

THE CITY CLERK

given adequate attention in most cities. Reports are sometimes printed in large quantities and then left to pile up undistributed. In the basement or attic of the city hall you will often find a whole room full of them. Occasionally the surplus publications are turned over to the public library which mails them out to the public libraries in other cities where they clutter up the shelves. A careful advance calculation of the city's actual needs in the way of published reports would save a considerable expenditure.

Another function of the city clerk in some parts of the country is concerned with the management of elections. The procedure with respect to the filing of nomination papers, the printing of ballots, the appointment of polling officers, and the counting of the ballots is usually laid down in the election laws, but the actual work is usually devolved upon an election board or in some cases upon the city council. When the latter is given the responsibility it invariably passes all the routine work to the city clerk. In cities which have no election board he prepares the nomination blanks, gets them printed, gives them out to be signed, checks them over when they come back, arranges for a supply of ballots, voters' lists, polling books, and other paraphernalia at the primaries and elections, and takes charge of the ballot boxes when the polling is over. He does not divide the municipality into precincts, or fix the location of the polling places, or appoint the precinct officials. This is done by the city council. But the city clerk's office gets the data ready for the council to act upon.

3. The management of elections.

In cities which have provision for the use of the initiative and referendum, or in which a popular vote on bond issues is required, an additional task is thrown on the city clerk as election officer. His office then receives the initiative petitions, checks up the signatures, and (if they are found sufficient) frames the question for printing on the ballot. Sometimes it is provided that information concerning these questions shall be published and distributed for the information of the voters and the city clerk's office is often given this additional responsibility. The Model City Charter of the National Municipal League, for example, contains this provision:

Referendum elections.

"The city clerk, at least fifteen days before any election at which any measure or charter amendment is to be submitted, shall print and mail to each elector qualified to vote thereon an official publicity pamphlet containing the full text of every measure or charter amendment submitted, with their respective ballot titles, together with arguments for or against such measures or charter amendments which may have been filed with the city clerk not less than twenty days before such election. Such arguments shall be signed by the person, persons, or officers of organizations authorized to submit and sign the same, who shall deposit with the city clerk at the time of filing a sum of money sufficient to cover the proportionate cost of the printing and paper for the space taken, but no more. The text of every measure or charter amendment shall also be displayed at the polling booths in such election."

4. Preparing the jury lists. With respect to many other matters it is the function of the city clerk to find out what the councilmen have to do and then get it into such shape that they can do it speedily. By so doing he saves a great deal of their time. For example, the laws sometimes provide that the jury panels, that is, the list of citizens who are to be summoned for jury service, shall be made up by the city council. The making of these panels is quite a complicated task, but the council is relieved from all except a minor part in it. The city clerk's office takes the voters' list and eliminates all those who are legally exempt from jury service—lawyers, physicians, teachers, public officials, and so forth. A further elimination is made of all who have already been called for service within a stipulated time, for the laws usually provide that no one may be drafted on a panel oftener than once a year. In states where women are exempt from jury service their names are also taken off. The remaining names are then typewritten on individual slips of paper, folded up one by one, and brought in a box to the council meeting. There the box is passed around among the councilmen, each of whom draws out a slip and reads the name aloud. These are written down by the city clerk and sent to the clerk of the court or to the sheriff as the case may be. So far as the council is concerned, the whole proceeding takes only a few minutes, but the city clerk's office may have to spend many hours in getting everything ready. It should be explained, however, that throughout the greater part of the United States the preparation of the jury lists is a county function, in which case neither city councils nor city clerks have anything to do with it.

5. Miscellaneous functions. Finally, there are a lot of miscellaneous duties which have been imposed by law upon the city clerk. These differ greatly from place to place. Very often the clerk's office is made responsible for the vital statistics of the municipality, that is for the registra-

tion of births, marriages, and deaths. The city clerk's office issues various permits, some of which are required by the state laws and others by the municipal ordinances. In the smaller cities the clerk's office is the chief center for the issue of licenses, but in the larger municipalities a special licensing bureau is frequently maintained. Or, as an alternative, the work may be divided among several departments—such as the street, police, and health departments. State legislatures, moreover, have a habit of picking out the city clerk's office as the one on which to place responsibility for making various returns and reports to the state authorities on the city's behalf. This is not because the city clerk is necessarily the official best fitted to do the work but sometimes because the clerk is the one officer that every municipality is certain to have.

In the smaller cities the office of the city clerk serves as a general bureau for giving information and receiving complaints. Most of the larger municipalities maintain a regular information office at the city hall—usually in the main lobby on the ground floor—and this is a great convenience to the public. But some expense is necessarily involved and many cities avoid it by leaving the information service to be rendered by an office which is already overloaded. It is questionable economy. 6. Information and complaints.

No other office in the municipal service has so many contacts. It serves the mayor, the city council, the city manager (when there is one), and all the administrative departments without exception. All of them call upon it, almost daily, for some service or information. Its work is not spectacular but it demands versatility, alertness, accuracy, and no end of patience. The public does not realize how many loose ends of city administration this office pulls together. Conclusion.

REFERENCES

Printed material relating to the organization and functions of the city clerk's office is almost entirely lacking, for books on municipal administration devote chapters to virtually every city department except this one.

CHAPTER VIII

ENGINEERING AND CONTRACTS

To make the city is what we are here for. He who makes the city makes the world. For though men may make cities, it is just as true that cities make men.—*Henry Drummond.*

The range of municipal properties.

A growing municipality has a continuous need for the construction of new physical services and for the extension of older ones. These public properties include streets and bridges, water supply plants, sewers and sewage disposal works, parks, and a variety of public buildings such as police and fire stations, hospitals, branch libraries, and schoolhouses. All such structures have to be planned, with blueprints and detailed specifications; and while they are being constructed by contract or by the city's own force the work has to be inspected. Taken together, these responsibilities are usually vested in the city engineer's department.

The city engineer's office.

Every municipality of any considerable size has an engineering staff. It is headed by a city engineer who is usually appointed by the mayor or by the city manager. In the larger cities the engineering department is divided into bureaus and the work is apportioned among them. Although the duties of the department call for a high degree of technical competence, and necessitate freedom from political pressure in order to secure the best results, it frequently happens that political considerations influence the appointments in this branch of city administration. The city engineer's term of office is not more than four years, as a rule, and the pay is rarely sufficient to attract high-grade men from the emoluments of private practice.

The pressure of politics upon it.

Moreover the head of the engineering department comes into almost daily contact with the politician-contractors who do business with the city, and is expected to keep them reasonably satisfied, which he cannot always do without being in some degree unfaithful to his own professional responsibilities. The consequence is that high-grade engineers are inclined to avoid the post, while men who have failed to make headway in private practice take it as a means of livelihood. Much of the waste that has

ENGINEERING AND CONTRACTS

accompanied municipal construction is the outcome of poor designing, faulty specifications, loosely-drawn contracts, and slipshod inspection, all of which is in turn attributable to a lack of skill, diligence, or integrity in the engineering department. Here is a branch of their work in which American cities have too often practiced false economy. Poor engineering service is dear at any price. The cost of a single error may exceed a large salary many times over.

The work of the engineering department is largely staff work, in other words it is performed at the request and for the benefit of the various line-departments such as streets, public buildings, water, lighting, sewerage, parks, bridges, and public utilities. Not infrequently the engineers are working on a score of different projects at the same time, all of them undertaken on the initial responsibility of the other departments. Municipal engineering may be grouped in a general way under seven heads, namely, surveying new locations, preparing plans, making specifications, estimating costs, drafting contracts, advising on the award of these contracts, and inspecting the work when it gets going.

Work of the engineering department:

When a street is to be widened, or a new park established, or a public building erected, the first step is to make a ground survey. This is essential in order to determine the exact amount of land needed. Then the city's law department takes the necessary steps to acquire it. In the case of locations for such structures as reservoirs or sewage disposal plants, the engineering department also makes a study of the subsurface to determine its suitability.

1. Surveys.

The location having been surveyed and the land duly acquired, the next step is the preparation of sketch plans. Often this precedes the acquisition of the site and as a matter of good practice it ought to do so. When the sketch plans have been approved by the department for which they were prepared, the engineers proceed to make the working plans. If the project is one of great importance, or if it presents some special problems (as in the case of a new pumping plant or an airport), an outside specialist may be called in as consultant. Money expended in this way is usually well spent because no city engineer, however competent, can be expected to make wise decisions on all the technical problems that arise in the course of his work. He should have opportunity to check up his plans with outside experts whenever vital decisions are involved.

2. Sketch plans and working plans.

MUNICIPAL ADMINISTRATION

Outside competition in the case of public buildings.

In the largest cities some departments (such as water and sewerage) have their own engineering bureaus and do the work for themselves. This plan has the advantage of permitting specialization but it involves increased expense and sometimes results in overlapping. Likewise it stands in the way of full coördination as respects the city's engineering work as a whole. In the case of public buildings, such as fire stations, hospitals, public libraries, and schoolhouses, the plans are sometimes prepared by an architectural bureau in the engineering department; but more often the job is given to some local architect. This may be done by competition, that is, by asking architects to submit sketches and then awarding the work to the one whose sketch is preferred, or the city authorities may simply select the architect without competition. The latter method usually leads to political and personal wirepulling, with an unsatisfactory outcome. When an outside architect is employed he is customarily compensated by a fixed commission on the cost of the building.

Importance of the working plans.

In any event the careful and intelligent preparation of working plans is vital to success in any public enterprise. Many contingencies have to be foreseen and provided for. Even a small miscalculation or error may involve much delay, inconvenience, and ultimate expense. For the contractor, when the time comes, will follow the working plans precisely and let the city bear the brunt of correcting its own mistakes. It is not his business to check up and see that the measurements and materials are exactly what the city wants or needs.

The high cost of "extras."

Plans can be corrected, of course, after the work is begun, but such changes always involve a relatively heavy increase in cost. The contractor, having agreed to do the work at a certain figure, feels himself free to present claims for "extras" at his own price whenever the plans are altered. Sometimes these extras amount to a considerable percentage of the original estimated cost—thirty or forty per cent on occasions. It has been found in some instances that plans and specifications have purposely been drawn in ways that would give a favored contractor the opportunity to make a handsome profit out of changes and extras. There is only one way to prevent excess cost in public construction, which is by insisting on adequate competence, care, and honesty in the engineering department.

Along with the working plans, and supplementing them, are

ENGINEERING AND CONTRACTS 99

specifications which the city's engineering staff or outside consultants also prepare. Specifications are written or printed; they explain the drawings by indicating the precise materials and methods to be used, the time allowed for construction, and the arrangements for periodical inspection when the work is in progress. In the case of an extensive public improvement they may cover a hundred typewritten or printed pages.

3. The specifications.

The specifications, of course, are quite as important as the plans. If they omit anything, or contain ambiguities, or if there is a lack of coincidence between what the plans show and what the specifications call for, the city is almost sure to incur a penalty in the form of delays, disputes, and sometimes prolonged litigation. All that has been said concerning competence and care in the making of plans applies with equal force to the drafting of specifications. Inadequate or loosely-drawn specifications, prepared by some fledgling engineer whose appointment was inspired by political favoritism, have put American cities to trouble and expense on numberless occasions.

Their importance.

Estimates of cost, based upon the plans and specifications, are likewise prepared by the engineering department. These estimates are for the information of the mayor, city manager, city council, or commission as the case may be, and enable these officials to decide whether the project can be handled within the city's financial resources. It sometimes happens that the estimates of cost prove higher than was expected, and the enterprise is then postponed or abandoned altogether. The engineering department's estimates, in case the work is authorized, ought to be of service in checking the bids submitted by contractors, but too often they prove to be of little service to anybody because they have not been worked out with sufficient care. Preliminary figures submitted to mayors and city councils are proverbially wide of the mark, and unhappily they almost always err on the side of optimism. The contractors' bids, when they come in, are regularly in excess of the estimates, often far above them, and the ultimate cost of the improvement proves to be higher still,—sometimes twice as high as the initial figures.

4. The estimates of cost.

When it is the city's purpose to have the work done by a contractor, as is usually the case, the municipal authorities prepare a form of contract, have it approved by the law department, attach it to the plans and specifications, and advertise for bids or pro-

5. Preparation and awarding of contracts.

posals. This is done, as a rule, by inserting in the local newspapers or in the technical periodicals an announcement stating that sealed proposals will be received by the city engineer, the commissioner of public works, or by some other official on or before a certain date. The usual practice is to stipulate that each bidder shall submit, along with his figures, a bond or certified check as an assurance that he will accept the contract in case it is awarded to him. If the proceedings are in good faith, the announcement will be placed where contractors are likely to see it, and pains will be taken to send marked copies of the advertisement to all who are likely to be interested. Ample time will also be allowed for an inspection of the plans and specifications, as well as for careful figuring upon all items before the date on which the sealed proposals are to be opened. But frankness and good faith do not always feature the advertising or award of city contracts. There are at least a dozen ways whereby a competition can be so manipulated as to make sure that no one but a hand-picked favorite will have much chance of securing the award.

Manipulating these awards. Some of these manipulations may be briefly described, for not only are they common but they demonstrate how easily the spirit of the laws and ordinances can be set at naught when public officials lay themselves out to do it for the benefit of their political friends. City charters and ordinances commonly require that contracts shall be duly advertised and awarded to the lowest bidder. But they also, in most cases, permit exceptions to be made under special circumstances. These exceptions are proper, their intent being to allow the summary award of contracts without advertising or competition in cases where there is good reason, in the public interest, for such action. It is a waste of time and money, for example, to require advertising and competitive bids in the case of small jobs, amounting in each case to only a few hundreds of dollars. Some work, moreover, such as the replacement of a demolished bridge or the rebuilding of a fire station may have to be done in the shortest possible time.

The splitting of contracts. It is usually provided, therefore, that contracts involving relatively small outlays, or contracts relating to work of great urgency, may be awarded without advertising or competition. But these loopholes can be stretched inordinately, and the city authorities sometimes have no scruples in that direction. For example, they can divide one large contract into a host of small ones

ENGINEERING AND CONTRACTS

so as to bring the whole thing within the permitted exceptions. So, instead of having to earn a fifty thousand dollar contract by open competition, the contractors who are in favor at the city hall accumulate a score of small non-competitive contracts, all for different parts of the same job,—for the excavation, the foundation, the frame, the roof, the floors, the plastering, and the painting of the same building. This is commonly known as the "split contract" device and it has been widely utilized. There is no way of preventing it so long as city officials, while keeping within the letter of the law, are ready to violate its plain intent.

Another method, a rather crude one, is to give some favored contractor a copy of the plans and specifications in advance of their being made public, thus "letting him in on the ground floor." Bids are then required to be submitted in so short a space of time that no one else has a fair opportunity to figure on the work. Or, again, it is possible to slip into the specifications a provision for the use of certain patented materials which a favored contractor happens to control. It is not that these materials have any superior merit; the idea is to eliminate the other fellows. The specifications for street-paving contracts may require, for example, that a certain brand of asphaltic binder be used (there may be half a dozen other brands equally good), or may stipulate that the work be done in accordance with some patented process. Such requirements are rarely dictated by a desire to get the maximum value for the least expenditure; their almost invariable purpose is to deflect the award of the contract into friendly hands.

"Ground floor" awards.

Unbalanced bidding, so termed, illustrates still another method of awarding contracts on a basis of partisan or personal favoritism. Proposals are invited for two or more incidents of the same job. For example, a ditch is to be dug for a trunk sewer. Bidders are asked to submit piece-work figures—so much per cubic yard for excavating rock, so much for gravel, so much for clay, etc. The contractor who is in collusion with the officials will bid high on one item and low on another, being assured that he will only be called upon to do the high-priced excavation. But being low bidder on the other items he gets the entire contract.

Unbalanced bidding.

Let us suppose, however, that the newspapers and civic organizations are keeping too close a watch on the awards for any of the foregoing subterfuges to succeed. The politician-contractor will then submit a bid which is in fact the lowest among those

Paying for "extras."

that come in. But this does not mean that he expects to do the work at the price stated. He has had underground assurances that many "extras" will be needed. These have been intentionally left out of the specifications so that the contractor will supply them at his own figures, thus recouping himself on the extras for his lack of profit on the original contract.

Evading the specifications. But the most common way of putting an unearned increment into the pockets of a contractor is by letting him disregard the specifications. Bids are submitted on the understanding that the work will be carefully and regularly inspected as it proceeds; penalties are provided in the contract for any defects in the materials or for any departure from the methods of construction specified, or for not having the job finished on time. The outside bidder knows that he will be hazed and held to a strict accountability at every point, and that the penalties will be exacted if occasion arises; but the inside bidder, with influential friends among city officials, can reckon differently. He knows that he can substitute inferior materials and no one will be any the wiser. This is because officials and inspectors often owe their positions on the public payroll to the influence of the contractor and his friends. Occasionally they have been found by subsequent investigations to have been secretly on the contractor's private payroll as well as openly on that of the city. There is enough profit in this type of collusion between the contractors, the officials, and the inspectors to split the surplus three ways.

Collusive bidding. Another type of collusion which is often practiced at the expense of the city takes the form of a gentlemen's agreement among contractors to avoid all genuine competition. There are enough contracts to go around; so why not let each contractor have his share at figures which will yield him a good profit? Accordingly the word is passed along that A is to have one job and B another. Each in his turn is given a set price. The others will submit bids also, but will take care that their figures are higher than the contractor whose turn it is. Such conspiracies in restraint of competition are illegal, and punishable by the courts; but their existence is hard to prove. Nothing is put down on paper; it is merely a matter of a few words passed by a "fixer" to the right people.

The importance of inspection. Regular, honest, and strict inspection is the city's most dependable protection against inferior work on the part of those who obtain municipal contracts. Nevertheless few city employees are chosen with less discrimination than are the inspectors in the public works department. Where there are no civil service regulations these inspectors are almost invariably appointed for personal or partisan reasons, often at the behest of a ward boss who is in league with the contractors. Even civil service competitions do not succeed in supplying the city with men whose attainments are above mediocrity, or afford a guarantee that the inspectors will be men of skill and integrity. No one would assert, of course, that regular, strict, and honest inspection is never applied to contract work in American cities; but it is the exception rather than the rule. More inspectors, better pay, civil service appointments, security of tenure, and prompt dismissal for negligence or collusion are the remedies.

As a means of protecting the city against ultimate loss through the crookedness of contractors and the infidelity of inspectors it has become the practice, in many communities, to provide that all public work performed by contract must be guaranteed for a definite number of years. The contractor who paves a street, for example, must in such cases give an approved bond to ensure that any defects which may appear in the pavement during five, ten, or even fifteen years after its completion will be properly repaired at the contractor's expense. If the contractor fails to make matters right, the city does the work and collects on the bond. Occasionally a part of the contract price is held back for a term of years as an alternative to the bond. *Bonded contracts and maintenance guarantees.*

These provisions, on their face, might seem to afford the city an ample measure of protection, but in practice they rarely do so. Bonds and bondsmen often prove to be worthless; and when a portion of the contractor's pay is to be withheld for five years or more it naturally increases his original contract price. Holding back payments has a tendency to discourage competition from reputable contractors whose business methods are not adapted to the practice of waiting several years for their money. Bonds and maintenance guarantees are a poor substitute for capable, honest inspection when the job is being done. *Their unreliability.*

In view of the opportunities for favoritism and corruption which seem to be inherent in the contract plan of public construction, some cities have tried the policy of having the work done by their own employees, thus eliminating the contractor altogether. This *Day-labor work as a substitute for the contract system.*

is commonly known as the direct day-labor or "force account" plan. It ought to be the cheaper method because no private profit is loaded on the work; but in practice it rarely turns out so. This is because city labor is, on the whole, less efficient and more highly paid than is the labor employed by private contractors. The boss in politics, moreover, is more lenient than the boss who has charge of the contractor's gang. At any rate, work that is done on "force account" often exceeds the estimated cost by a good margin.

Competition between contractors and the city departments. In some cities it is the custom to let both the public works department and private contractors put in their bids on the same basis. Then the award is made to whichever is lowest. The trouble with this plan is, however, that there is no way of holding the city's own officials within their figures. If the work costs more than was originally figured, there is nothing to do but pay the excess from the municipal treasury. The officials at fault may be discharged; but that does not help the taxpayer who has to stand the extra cost. When a contractor, on the other hand, overruns his bid he or his bondsmen have to pocket the loss. The chief value of the direct-labor plan is the possibility of using it when contractors are suspected of collusive bidding. For this reason a city should always retain the alternative of doing the work with its own force if need be.

Some disadvantages of the force account plan. In point of time-saving the contract system has a distinct advantage, and this is important in cases where delay involves public inconvenience as in the case of street widenings. The contractor has everything to gain by speeding his work. Hence he expands his force and often works his men in double shifts day and night. The city's staff of workers can also be enlarged, it is true, but when the job is finished there remains the difficult problem of prying this surplus labor off the payroll. From all quarters will come political pressure to prevent any lay-off,—for example, by absorbing the men into other city departments where they are not really needed. Where a great deal of work has to be performed in a single season it is therefore inadvisable, as a practical matter, to take hundreds of men into the municipal service with the expectation that they can be summarily discharged, as a contractor would discharge them, the moment the job is done. Labor inflation is very easy in municipal administration; but cutting down again is one of the hardest things in the world.

ENGINEERING AND CONTRACTS

Students of the unemployment problem have suggested that municipal public works should be so planned that little or no construction will be undertaken when private industry is prosperous and labor is scarce. Then, in times of depression, public employment should take up the slack. In other words the idea is that large public improvements should be delayed, whenever practicable, until times of industrial depression and should then use labor which would otherwise be idle. Within certain limits this proposal has merit; but there are many public improvements (such as the erection of schools and the repair of streets) which cannot be delayed year after year until the business cycle has got around to the right point. It should be borne in mind, moreover, that the majority of those who are temporarily thrown out of employment by reason of a business depression (for example, women workers, professional men, clerks, and the whole array of "white-collar" employees) can hope for little or no relief from the speeding-up of public construction. Such work creates a demand for mechanics and plain laborers only. Furthermore, there is always a danger that needless projects will be undertaken, and large sums wasted, under color of providing work for those who need it. The experience of many American cities in this regard during the past few years has been very illuminating.

Public improvements as a means of alleviating unemployment.

Anyone who tries to figure the relative cost of a municipal construction or of any kind of public service in different cities will be impressed by the surprising discrepancies. For what is ostensibly the same thing, two cities of nearly the same size, in the same part of the country, seem to be paying widely different rates. The cost of paving streets, laying water mains, building sand filters, equipping schoolhouses, or modernizing fire apparatus often shows a measure of variation which would excite prompt suspicion in the mind of anyone uninitiated. The explanation, in nine cases out of ten, is that each city has its own way of reckoning the cost and each way is different. Until a few years ago it was only in rare cases that cities attempted to work out unit-costs at all. Even yet one may search for hours through the vast panorama of figures in a municipal report without being able to discover how much the city is paying for anything per capita, per mile, per square yard, per ton, or per anything else. But cost-accounting has made great progress in the larger cities during the

The unit-cost of municipal work.

past decade; it is one of the things which they have borrowed from private business.[1]

First costs and final costs. The initial cost, moreover, is not the only thing to be considered in determining the ultimate expensiveness of a public improvement. A small outlay at the start may involve disproportionate annual charges for maintenance; a far larger investment at the outset may prove cheaper in the end. This is true in public as in private business. A great deal of false economy has been practiced in American cities by reason of the emphasis placed on initial cost. Things are called expensive when the first cost is high, and cheap when this is low. The reverse would often be nearer the truth. The real cost of a street pavement, for example, is not the figure that happens to be paid for laying it. Durability, suitability to traffic, appearance, cost of repairs, and cost of cleaning must all be taken into account in estimating the ultimate financial burden. But city officials are elected or appointed for short terms; they want to get things done quickly so that they may point with pride to their achievements before they go out of office. As for the grief that may come later, they are content to bequeath this to their successors.

REFERENCES

A. P. Folwell, *Municipal Engineering Practice* (New York, 1916) was a useful book in its day but is now somewhat out of date. Unfortunately there is no later work on the general subject of municipal engineering and contracting. There are numerous books, however, on the special phases of municipal engineering such as Streets, Pavements and Sidewalks, Waste Disposal, Sewerage, Water Supply, and Public Lighting. References to such materials are given at the close of the several chapters which deal with these subjects.

[1] See Chapter XV.

CHAPTER IX

CENTRALIZED PURCHASING

All that is human must retrograde if it does not advance.—Edward Gibbon.

A considerable part of the city's total expenditure goes every year for the purchase of equipment, materials, and supplies. As a rule this amounts to nearly a third of the entire operating budget. Every city has to obtain commodities in almost infinite variety,—fire-fighting equipment, police uniforms and accoutrements, street-cleaning machinery, trucks, motor cars and gasoline, coal and oil as fuel for public buildings, typewriters, paper and ink, office supplies, technical equipment for the health department and the hospitals, books for the public library:—there is almost no end to the number of things which a large city buys in the course of the year. In some of them the total outlay runs into the millions, and even in small communities it is larger than most people realize. {What a city buys.}

Until about twenty years ago the purchasing of all this equipment, materials, and supplies was left to each department. The head of a department, or someone authorized by him, merely sent out and bought what was needed. Each department used its own specifications and paid whatever price it saw fit to pay. This practice, of course, resulted in a great deal of overlapping and waste. The wonder is that it was tolerated so long. Sometimes a dozen city departments (police, fire protection, public buildings, schools, hospitals, public library, etc.) were found to be buying coal from a dozen dealers at different prices and with wide variations in quality. The same was true of office supplies and stationery. Such materials as mucilage, copying paper, lead pencils, and typewriter ribbons were found on investigation to vary as much as three hundred per cent in cost to the city, with no appreciable difference in quality. {Older methods of purchasing.}

Every department, moreover, had its own friends, its own favorite dealers from whom it bought at their own prices. Seldom did any city get wholesale rates or cash discounts. The purchase of supplies, in a word, was looked upon as a form of minor patronage {Purchasing and patronage.}

to be doled out among small shopkeepers who had the favor of someone in the city administration. Sometimes the purchases were made from people who carried on no business at all,—from politicians who merely bought at retail and then added their own profit. The waste involved in this arrangement was very large. It meant that cities paid from thirty to fifty per cent more than was necessary.

How centralized buying began.

It should be pointed out, however, that the practice of piecemeal purchasing at varying prices from favorite contractors was not confined to the city's business twenty years ago. A similar condition of affairs existed in many large business concerns and in public utility companies. Gradually, however, the stress of competition forced these private establishments to recognize the advantage of centralized buying. One after another they set up regular purchasing departments with expert buyers in charge. The savings proved to be so great that chambers of commerce and similar organizations began to press the public authorities to adopt the same plan. Most of the larger cities have now done so, but many small municipalities still follow the old practice of departmental buying. Progress in the direction of improved purchasing methods has been most notable in municipalities which have the city manager form of government.

The purchasing department or bureau.

Centralized purchasing involves the setting up of a separate administrative department, or a special purchasing bureau within one of the regular departments. Large cities usually pursue the former plan, while smaller municipalities content themselves with a purchasing bureau attached to the office of the city manager, city comptroller, or city clerk. Only in rare cases is the head of this bureau chosen under the merit system, although there is every reason why he should be. The work of a purchasing agent is of a strictly business nature. His sole function is to see that all municipal purchases are made to the city's advantage. He should be chosen on the basis of his professional competence, and should be rigidly protected against political pressure.

The purchasing agent.

The office of purchasing agent is not an easy one to fill acceptably. The appointee, according to one authority, should be a man endowed with "good judgment, shrewdness, tact, a sense of real values, foresight, initiative, and, above all, common sense. Supplementing his natural equipment he should have business training and experience, a thorough familiarity with market conditions, and an intimate acquaintance with the commodity requirements of the governmental units which he serves." [1] These are specifications which a city does not often find itself able to fill at the salary that it is willing to pay.

In a small municipality the head of the purchasing bureau does not need a considerable staff; but in the larger cities he requires various accountants, inspectors, voucher clerks, warehouse checkers, and other helpers. In Detroit, for example, the commissioner of purchases and supplies has a staff of more than thirty subordinates in his department. Members of the purchasing department staff ought also to be chosen under the merit system and should have reasonable security of tenure. It has been figured that the entire cost of maintaining this department can be kept within one per cent of the total volume of purchases made by it. *His staff.*

When a centralized purchasing system has been established, the procedure in securing equipment, materials, and supplies for use by the city is in general as follows: Each municipal department, when it needs anything, is required to prepare a requisition stating the quantity and quality of the goods desired. These requisitions are made in duplicate on standard blank forms. One copy is sent to the purchasing office; the other is held on file. On receiving a requisition the purchasing agent proceeds to get what it calls for. He may do this by advertising and open competition, or by informal competition without advertising, or in some cases without competition at all. When the amount involved is large, and where time permits doing so, the usual practice is to advertise for bids. But if only a small quantity of something is needed, or if there is great urgency, the purchasing agent may ask for informal bids by telephone from dealers who are known to have the material on hand. Purchases without any form of competition are usually restricted to materials and supplies which are sold at fixed prices, including patented articles which can be obtained from one source only. *Purchasing procedure.*

Some cities have provisions in their charters or ordinances to the effect that all purchases exceeding a designated figure (usually $1,000 or $2,000) must be made on the basis of competitive bids. Such provisions can be evaded, however, by splitting one requisition into two or three. The competitive system, moreover, assumes that departments will submit their requisitions some time in *Competitive bids.*

[1] Russell Forbes, *Governmental Purchasing* (New York, 1929), p. 67.

advance of the time when the materials will be needed. This, unfortunately, they often neglect to do. They delay until something essential runs out; then they make haste to file a requisition marked *urgent* or *immediate* in red ink. This is followed by a telephone message to the purchasing agent that they simply must have the requisition filled within twenty-four hours or some important job will be held up. One of the sorriest tributes to the laxity of American municipal administration is the number of avoidable "emergencies" which arise in the various operating departments. They point to a lack of planning and are the outcome of hand-to-mouth procedure.

Purchasing days.

To provide departments with a periodical reminder of their prospective needs it has become the practice, in some cities, to designate certain days of the month as purchase days for certain groups of supplies. Dealers are invited on these days to gather at the purchasing agent's office, submit their samples, and name their prices. Representatives from the departments are requested to be on hand and look them over. If they feel that one type of merchandise is better than the others, this is the time to prove it—with rival dealers present. In the case of supplies which are needed in relatively large quantities and of a uniform kind, the best practice is to make a contract running for several months, or for a year, with the proviso that delivery will be made from time to time in such quantities as may be called for. In such cases when a requisition comes in, the order is sent directly to the firm having the continuing contract. In many instances, however, there is nothing to be gained by buying in bulk; on the contrary there is a danger of over-buying in such cases and there is the further chance that prices may go down during the term of a continuing contract.

Checking with the appropriations.

Before the purchasing agent issues an order based upon a departmental requisition he must make sure that the department has available funds from which the purchase can be paid for. This he does by sending a copy of it to the city auditor or comptroller, who certifies that there is enough money left in the department's appropriation. This, of course, takes time, for the routine at the city hall moves rather slowly. Several days may elapse between the making of the requisition and the delivery of the materials unless the procedure can be shortcircuited by the city manager or the mayor or somebody else higher up. Frequently this is done. The requisition, order, and approval may all come along after the materials have been delivered in response to telephone calls. Such procedure, although frequent, is irregular and often leads to serious abuses.

When the dealer receives his order he supplies the goods and sends an invoice of the same to the city auditor or comptroller. The latter checks the invoice with the order and with the receipt for the goods. Then he approves it for payment and forwards it to the city treasurer who issues a warrant or check for the amount. This may seem to be a rather elaborate routine, especially in the case of purchases which amount to only a few dollars; but there is no other way of plugging the loopholes through which the taxpayers' money will dribble away if it gets a chance. *Invoices and warrants.*

One of the advantages which come from centralized purchasing is the saving of time and effort in the various departments. When each department buys for itself, there are likely to be several officials spending their energies on the same job at the same time— looking up prices, examining samples, and negotiating for the purchase of exactly the same merchandise, such as typewriters, janitor's supplies, ink, paper, and other supplies. The time which they spend in doing this is taken from their regular work and the city pays for it. A considerable saving can be made by having the work concentrated in a single office. *Advantages of the centralized purchasing system:* *1. The saving of time.*

Another advantage arises from the possibility of standardizing all materials and supplies which are in general use. Under the system of decentralized purchasing each department follows its own particular whims. In one city it was found that nine different kinds of carbon paper were in use, varying in price by more than a hundred per cent, with no noticeable superiority of one brand over the others. One of the first things that a centralized purchasing office has to do is to draw up sets of standardized specifications covering all routine materials and supplies which are used by several departments. These specifications are prepared in consultation with all the departments concerned. They are asked, for example, to agree upon some brand of carbon paper which all the city offices will hereafter use. This can then be bought in large quantities, at a favorable price and of a quality that is guaranteed to be up to specifications. In some cities an arrangement has been made whereby a standing committee on specifications, representing the various city departments, is appointed to decide all such matters. Before final adoption of any specifications this committee gives a *2. The standardizing of supplies and the consequent saving of money.*

hearing to dealers and others who may be interested. Assistance is also had by studying the specifications which large industrial concerns and public utilities have prepared and put into use. Specifications covering many classes of goods have also been compiled by the United States Bureau of Standards.[1] When standard specifications have been finally adopted, and approved by the purchasing agent, all future bids are made on this basis. Materials will be rejected if they do not conform to the specifications.

3. Other advantages. This practice of standardization has various advantages in addition to that of promoting economy. Standardized equipment and materials can be easily interchanged between departments—between the street and park departments for example. One can use the surplus of the other. Standardization makes inspection a much simpler task. The question is not whether the supplies are satisfactory but whether they conform to the specifications. Likewise it gives every bidder a square deal and removes all temptation to favoritism in making the awards.

Practical difficulties in the framing of specifications. Some controversies are likely to arise when specifications are being prepared. Heads of departments do not like to be told that they must use this or that standardized commodity. They argue that their own particular needs are quite different from those of other departments, although in most cases their preference is nothing more than an idiosyncrasy. By actual test it is usually practicable to determine what is best value for the price and this ought to be specified in the taxpayers' interest, without reference to the personal preferences of city officials. Patented supplies or equipment, and goods protected by trade-marks ought to be avoided in standard specifications whenever this is possible for the reason that they are not subject to competitive bidding. This is especially true of materials used in street construction.

Buying on sealed bids. From time to time the purchasing agent calls for "sealed proposals," or bids, based on the specifications that have been adopted. His call may be advertised in the newspapers or sent to a list of known dealers. It should give definite information as to the amounts required, the time and place of delivery, and everything else that a bidder needs to know. Bids should be asked on groups of commodities, such as stationery of all kinds, rather than on separate articles such as paper, ink, pencils, and so forth. In some

---

[1] See the *National Directory of Commodities' Specifications* (Washington, 1925).

cities there is an understanding that local bidders shall have preference, even if their figures are above those submitted by outsiders. "The city should patronize its own merchants, who pay the taxes." It is a plausible contention but one that is certain to increase the cost.

When bids are called for, the customary provision is that the contract for purchase must be awarded to the lowest bidder provided he can qualify by giving adequate security in the way of a bond or a deposit. Each bidder is usually required to post a certified check or a cash deposit as a guarantee that he will accept the contract if it is awarded to him. Bids unaccompanied by this security are rejected. Then, when signing the contract, the successful bidder must put up a bond (usually furnished by a bonding company) to guarantee that he will deliver materials which comply with the specifications at the price agreed upon and promptly on the designated time. The requirement that contracts shall go to the lowest responsible bidder is a justifiable one in order to prevent political and personal favoritism; but there is one difficulty of a practical nature connected with it. The lowest bidder, for example, may be financially responsible, but he may also be someone with whom the city has had unsatisfactory dealings in the past. Naturally the departments do not wish to have anything more to do with him. Bonds put up by the contractors, moreover, do not always give the city adequate protection. Suit may be brought against the bonding company when the contractor fails to live up to the letter of his agreement; but such litigation is costly, tedious, and does not prevent much inconvenience meanwhile. City officials prefer to deal with those who have given full satisfaction in the past—even if this does cost a little more.

Awarding contracts for supplies.

In many cases the city charter provides that no one who is connected in any way with the city government may enter into a contract with the city for work or supplies. Sometimes the rule is so rigid that no corporation in which any city official is a stockholder may become a qualified bidder. Such a provision works injustice in the case of business men who are members of unpaid commissions, such as the city planning board, hospital board, or public library commission, and who happen to be small stockholders in concerns which would otherwise be eligible to submit bids.

The exclusion of city officials from contracting with the city.

It is not enough to adopt standardized specifications, ask for

The inspection of supplies. bids thereon, and require that contractors shall submit their proposals accordingly. Care must be taken to see that the city gets exactly what it has bought and paid for. This necessitates a system of rigid inspection covering both the quantity and quality of the goods supplied. Otherwise inferior materials may be substituted (as in the case of oil, gasoline, coal, lumber, cement, and fertilizer) or shortages may occur in delivery. To guard against this the purchasing agent should have a staff of qualified inspectors whose business it is to make a careful and continuous check-up and no bills should be paid until they have been certified both as to quantity and quality. In some cases the inspectors are employed by the comptroller or auditor and are responsible to him—not to the purchasing agent. In any event great care has to be taken lest there be collusion between contractors and inspectors. Many cities have been heavily mulcted in that way.

Central receiving depots. Rigid and honest inspection is greatly facilitated when the city maintains a central storehouse and yard to which all materials and supplies are delivered. Some materials, of course, must be delivered on the job, wherever it is; but for most supplies a central depot is a great protection, as well as a convenience in that it enables a reserve stock to be kept on hand. In connection with the storehouse some of the larger cities maintain a testing laboratory for such supplies as cement, coal, gasoline, and oil. The central receiving depot plan also facilitates the taking of regular inventories and lessens the temptation to pile up supplies in departmental offices. Finally it encourages the sale of surplus materials and discarded equipment whenever this becomes desirable. No such sales should be permitted at the discretion of the departments themselves but should be authorized by the chief municipal executive on recommendations approved by the purchasing agent.

Summary. The more significant advantages of centralized purchasing may therefore be summarized as follows: It permits the city to buy in larger quantities at better prices, saves the time of department officials, permits the standardization of materials and supplies which are in common use, provides a check-up on deliveries, helps to prevent over-buying, facilitates the taking of inventories, and brings the city's procedure into line with the best practice in large business concerns. Reputable vendors greatly prefer this plan to the older method of soliciting piecemeal orders from individual departments. There are some objections to the system of central-

CENTRALIZED PURCHASING

ized purchasing but they are mainly connected with the workings of the plan rather than with the principle itself. Purchasing officials have sometimes been unduly rigid in their methods and have built up a needless amount of red tape in their offices. In some cases, moreover, they have persuaded the departments to take unsuitable supplies because these happened to be available at bargain prices. A purchasing department is no better than the man at the head of it.

REFERENCES

The best book on this subject is *Governmental Purchasing* by Russell Forbes (New York, 1929). It contains an elaborate bibliography. A forty-four page booklet on *The Organization and Administration of a Governmental Purchasing Office* by the same author was published in 1932 by the National Association of Purchasing Agents (11 Park Place, New York), and a compilation of *Purchasing Laws for State, County, and City Governments* (1931) is obtainable from the same organization. A booklet on *Purchasing for Small Cities* by Russell Forbes is included in the Public Administration Service series (1932).

Mention should also be made of A. G. Thomas, *Principles of Government Purchasing* (Baltimore, 1919), John C. Dinsmore, *Purchasing Principles and Practices* (New York, 1922), H. D. Murphy, *The Fundamental Principle of Purchasing* (New York, 1923), N. F. Harriman, *Principles of Scientific Purchasing* (New York, 1928), and the excellent chapter on "Purchasing" in A. E. Buck, *Municipal Finance* (New York, 1926).

CHAPTER X

THE ASSESSMENT OF PROPERTY FOR TAXATION

Property has its duties as well as its rights.—Benjamin Disraeli.

Why assessments precede taxation. With most cities, as with most individuals, the hardest problem is to make both ends meet. If governments had an unlimited income, most of their problems would disappear. But their revenues are not unlimited. They can be increased, for the most part, in one way only—which is by putting more taxes, or higher taxes, on the people. Of itself a government earns no money. Every dollar that it gets must come from someone who has done the earning. Before it can tax property, moreover, a government must first assess it. This is a fundamental principle of public administration, for it assures that taxes shall be levied with due notice as to their character and amount. Taxation without assessment would be unsystematic, uncertain, and arbitrary.

An assessment defined. An assessment is a formal valuation of property or income as the basis for levying a tax which has been authorized by law. The laws determine what may be assessed and by what procedure. In most parts of the country the function of assessing property for taxes, whether state, county, or municipal, is entrusted to the municipal assessors; but in some states there are two separate assessments of the same property, one by the county and the other by the city.

The assessors. In any event the work of assessing property for taxation is performed by public officials who are known as assessors. Fifty years ago these officials were almost everywhere elected by popular vote, and in many rural communities they are still chosen in that way; but in the cities it has now become the more common practice to have the assessors appointed by the mayor or by the city manager. Sometimes there is a single chief assessor, with one or more assistants or deputy assessors; more often the work is done by a board of assessors all of whom have the same rank. The centralized plan, with a single head, is now regarded as the better one. Assessors have little or nothing to do with questions of policy. Their duty is to do as the law directs.

Once a year, or once in every two or three years, as the laws may require, the assessors make a formal valuation of all the taxable property within the city, including land, buildings, and personal property. They are expected to appraise this property at its true value or at such fraction of its true value as the laws prescribe.[1] The assessors go around the city from place to place and set down on their rolls a provisional valuation. Sometimes they divide the city into districts, each assessor or deputy assessor taking one of these areas. As a rule they make a distinction between land and buildings, setting a separate valuation on each. It is desirable that this separation be made, even though it is not always a simple thing to do. When personal property, such as merchandise, machinery, and household effects, is subject to taxation, it is assessed at the same time. Determining the true market value of personal property, such as furnishings in a hotel or merchandise in a second-hand store, is also not a very simple task. Procedure in making assessments.

How is the true value of a parcel of land determined? The principal factors in the value of a city lot are its location, utility, shape, and size. Land has value in proportion to its accessibility. But it must also be of sufficient area to permit the erection of a suitable building and be so shaped that it can be fully utilized. Ordinarily a triangular plot of land would not be of the same value as a square plot having the same area and in the same location. Corner lots, likewise, have additional value. On the other hand the value of any parcel of land, either downtown or uptown, may be impaired by the proximity of some objectionable feature, such as an elevated railroad. All these things have to be considered in determining the true value of land for taxation. Figuring the value of urban land.

In other words, the assessment of urban land can be approximated to a science and in the larger municipalities this is now being done. But in smaller communities the work of assessing land is still, for the most part, on a guesswork basis. Ten years ago I happened to ask an assessor what scientific rules he employed for the determination of downtown land values in his city of 100,000 population. "I don't use any scientific rules," he replied, "I use How it is usually done in small cities.

---

[1] In various states the laws use the words "fair value," "full value," "market value," or "cash value." The fractions designated run from twenty per cent to eighty per cent.

my horse sense." But his equine sagacity, as I happened to know, was well tinctured with political favoritism. In some states the assessors require the owners to file sworn lists of their property with a statement of its true value, but these lists and statements are not dependable.

Data which can profitably be used. A much better method, in the case of real estate, is to keep track of all sales made during the year. Such figures can usually be obtained from the registry of deeds or from the real estate exchange. Helpful information can also be obtained from the probate records and from official valuations filed by trustees or guardians. As respects newly erected buildings the assessors can usually secure reliable data from the office of the building inspector where plans have to be filed before a permit is granted. What has been paid for property is common knowledge among realtors. Real values cannot be properly determined, however, by the prices paid at forced sales, such as sales resulting from the foreclosure of mortgages. Prices realized at voluntary sales, moreover, often indicate the price trend rather than the true value.

Capitalizing the rental value as a basis. Another method commonly used by assessors is to find out what property rents for and then capitalize this rental. In some states the laws require that all leases for more than six months must be registered with the recorder of deeds. A rule-of-thumb procedure is to assess real estate at ten times the annual rent; but in capitalizing rentals a different multiplier ought to be used for different kinds of real property. Residential properties are sometimes worth a good deal more than ten times their rental, while some types of business property are worth less than that. None of the foregoing are trustworthy methods of approaching the true market value, but they are useful as check-ups after values have been provisionally determined in some other way.

The unit-foot method of land valuation. Scientific methods of assessing land in cities start with the unit foot. The unit foot, for appraisal purposes, is one foot of frontage by 100 feet in depth, or whatever the normal depth of city lots may happen to be. This unit foot is located in the center of each block, midway between the two nearest cross-streets. After a careful study of all the available information, a tentative value is assigned by the assessors to this unit foot; then the next step is to determine the allowance to be made for lots which have more or less than the standard depth. Various tables have been devised for this purpose, but all are based on the principle that the major portion of the value is in the front half of the lot. In other words, if a lot which is 100 feet in depth is assessed at $1,000 per front foot, then a lot alongside which is 75 feet in depth would not be assessed at $750 per front foot but only at $600 per front foot or less.

Having determined the value of land per front foot at the center of the block, and having made due allowance for any irregularities of shape or depth, the assessors also estimate the enhancement of value which results from proximity to the street corners. A corner lot almost invariably has a higher value; but of course the increased value which accrues from a double frontage is not the same in all parts of the city. Nor is there any agreement among real estate experts as to how far the corner influence extends to inner lots near the corner. On the principle, however, that it gradually diminishes as the distance from the corner increases until it disappears altogether at the middle of a block—on this principle various schemes for computing the enhancement of values due to corner proximity have been devised. A corner lot at the intersection of two heavily congested streets may have very high value for retail business purposes; while a corner location in the financial district or wholesale section often has no advantages over an inside location except those of better light and ventilation. In residential sections of the city a corner situation is sometimes regarded as a disadvantage because of the noise due to intersecting traffic.[1] Other factors must also be taken into account, such as the presence of an alleyway in the rear of business property. In other words the basic values are computed in such way that the assessment on each parcel of land shades into the one alongside.

Corner values.

But these various calculations and formulas are not intended to be applied mechanically. They are not designed to replace brains and intelligence in the assessing department, but are for the use of skilled appraisers who understand how to apply them and when to make variations. Their service is to keep the minds of the assessors focussed upon things which fundamentally determine true land values, without paying undue attention to other factors which may be only of transient consequence. Land, as land, does not necessarily acquire an increased value because it happens to

All valuation formulas should be flexibly applied.

---

[1] The table showing rules for determining the enhancement of value due to corner influence may be found in John A. Zangerle, *Principles of Real Estate Appraising and Unit Value Land Maps* (Cleveland, 1924), p. 96.

have a fine building on it. Or because the post office is located next door, for the post office may move.

How assessments are recorded.
When any parcel of real property is assessed it must be designated on the assessment roll with such definiteness and accuracy of description that it cannot be confused with any other property. Hence, it is not customary to assess land in the name of the owner, but merely by its legal designation—for example, "the west exact half of Lot No. 32-A, in Block 7-B of the Smith and Jones Tract, as recorded in Book 17 of the Records of the County of Bristol, etc." Some difficulties arise, however, in connection with the recording of assessments in this fashion. It involves an unduly large amount of clerical labor in making up the assessment roll and nevertheless affords no assurance against overlooking small remnants of land. City lots are periodically divided and subdivided, then consolidated again in whole or in part, until the legal descriptions become long and technical. In this shuffling of boundaries some small pieces of land are likely to escape the eyes of the assessors and remain untaxed, sometimes for several years, until a new survey is made. The method of recording assessments by legal description, moreover, puts owners to much inconvenience whenever they have to look up matters relating to their taxes. This is because very few owners can remember, offhand, the exact legal description of their properties. They have to copy it from the deeds whenever the occasion to make inquiry arises.

Block and lot maps.
To meet these objections many cities have now provided themselves with a "block and lot map" for assessment purposes. This is a detailed topographical plan of the city showing every block and lot in it, each with its own number. Every parcel of land within the city limits is described simply as Lot ——, Block ——. On each lot is indicated, moreover, its area and street number. This greatly simplifies the work of compiling the assessment rolls and places very little strain on the owner's memory. No parcel of land, moreover, can possibly be overlooked by the assessors under this system, because the total area of the lots must check with the area of the block.

Airplane surveys.
Block and lot maps are made by means of a careful survey on the ground, and are checked by using airplane photographs. It is by such surveys that the cities have discovered various small parcels of extremely valuable land (little strips and wedges in the downtown districts) which have been overlooked by the assessors

ASSESSMENT OF PROPERTY

and hence not taxed at all. Preparing these maps in the case of a large city is a rather expensive undertaking at the outset. Moreover they have to be kept up to date by making the necessary changes whenever the dimensions of lots are changed by the transactions of their owners. Because of this expense most cities still leave their assessors unprovided with any map equipment except the atlas which title insurance companies prepare for their own use and sell to anyone who wants a copy of it.

Another useful instrument for aiding the assessors and for keeping the property owners satisfied is a land value map. This differs from a block and lot map in that it shows tax values rather than designations or dimensions. By means of figures printed on the four sides of every block these maps indicate the value per front foot, or, in the case of unsubdivided property, the value per acre. In this way the relation of tax values on neighboring streets, or on opposite sides of the same street, or in adjacent blocks, is made clear at a glance. Every property owner can then determine whether he seems to have been fairly assessed with reference to adjacent property. Points showing high values will grade off towards others showing low values and everywhere the scale of appraisal from one street should interlock with those on the next in a way that can be seen, understood, and compared. The foregoing maps, it should be explained, do not show buildings on the land and have nothing to do with the value of buildings. They are concerned only with the designations, dimensions, and values of urban land. *Land value maps.*

The assessment of buildings is a separate problem. Most cities list separate tax valuations on land and buildings but the differentiation is for the most part made by a rule-of-thumb method, as follows: first, the assessor estimates the total value of the property; then he subtracts his estimated value of the land, and the remainder is set down as the value of the buildings. This method is sometimes justified by pointing out that the value of a building cannot be completely dissociated from its site, and that even a poorly built structure may have a high market value if it is well adapted to its location. On the other hand the value of a first class building may be almost negligible if it is unsuited to the best use of the land upon which it is placed. *The problem of assessing buildings.*

As a matter of fact many considerations have to be regarded in determining the true value of a warehouse, factory, office building, store, or apartment house. These factors include location, type of construction, utility, age, obsolescence, state of repair, as well as the facility with which the building could be remodelled to serve some other use. Tables and formulas can be used to some extent in evaluating these various factors, but individual judgment must obviously be allowed a good deal of leeway. For example, the cost of construction per cubic foot in the case of new buildings can readily be obtained from contractors and architects. General tables showing the normal deductions for depreciation and obsolescence are also available. But the rapidity with which a building becomes obsolescent depends upon the rapidity and direction of city growth. Its suitability for existing use depends upon the drift of business in the section where it is located. Its value is also determined, in part, by the question whether the exterior architecture of the building is in style or out of style. These elements of value are not easy to figure by using any kind of formula or tabulation, hence much dependence must be placed upon the sagacity and good judgment of the assessors. If these officials are competent they will keep close watch on sales, mortgage loans, foreclosures, leases, court appraisals, and all other items of information which are relevant to their work. Having nothing to do but figure property values the assessors might reasonably be expected to develop a high degree of expertness in this line of work.

But unfortunately there are so few things less expertly done in the average American city than is the work of assessing real estate for taxation. The chief reason for this is the failure of the municipal authorities, and of the citizenship in general, to recognize the fact that the task of appraising and reappraising property is one that requires an uncommon amount of skill, shrewdness, integrity, and experience. It is not a job for which the average man, much less the average politician, can qualify. The real estate market, in some cities, undergoes fluctuations almost as erratic as the stock market. Fortunes are quickly made and quickly lost in it by realtors and land speculators. And unless the assessed valuations are kept measurably in line with these changes in market value a good deal of injustice is done—either to the city by letting the assessment remain too low or to the owner by keeping it too high. Cheap assessing is false economy. The idea that any successful vote-getter can qualify as an assessor is one that ought to be discarded. Assessors should be as carefully chosen and as well paid as city engineers, health officers, or city attorneys. Their work calls for at least an equal standard of competence. Moreover, they should be kept in office long enough to let them profit by experience. Hence the practice of electing assessors by popular vote is the very negation of what the office requires. In a number of states the attempt is being made to improve the work of assessing property by providing supervision at the hands of a state tax commission or tax commissioner with power to revise local assessments. In a few cases this central authority may even remove the local assessors for incompetence, neglect of duties, or favoritism.

Lack of integrity on the part of assessors has been an even more widespread shortcoming than lack of intelligence. It is easy for assessors to show favoritism when no tax value maps are available for inspection by individual property owners. Land and buildings can be assessed at figures far below their true value, with nobody knowing about it except the assessor and the property owner concerned. In this way assessors often manage to build up a powerful political machine which ensures their perpetuation in office. Chicago afforded a conspicuous example of this manipulation during the years 1920-1930. The shameless underassessment of large areas in the loop district continued year after year until the loss of taxes brought the city into serious financial difficulties. Not only that, but an inflated net-earning-power accrued to this property by reason of the low tax burden, and when a general upward-revision of assessments took place there was a severe shrinkage in downtown property values. This, in turn, brought heavy losses to the banks and mortgage companies which had loaned money on the inflated values. Chicago's experience proves that a city gains nothing in the long run by allowing the control of assessments to pass into the hands of politicians who use it for the advantage of their friends. *The vice of political and personal favoritism in assessments.*

Finally, there is the matter of assessing personal property, which is of two kinds: (1) tangible personal property which includes merchandise, equipment, furniture, etc., and (2) intangible personal property which includes stocks, bonds, notes, bank deposits, and other securities. The first of these classes presents no very serious problem because it is in plain sight for the assessor to see and appraise. In the case of industrial corporations and other *The assessment of personal property.*

1. Tangibles.

business concerns, moreover, the personal property and equipment is carried on the books of the company at a stated valuation. Nevertheless the assessment of personal property imposes a good deal of labor upon the assessors and they often try to do it by short-cut methods. One device is to apportion the city into several zones, one containing the poorest tenements and residences, another the somewhat better homes, another the still better ones, and so on. Then a uniform assessment for household furniture and personal effects is placed on the occupant of every home within a zone. The better the zone the higher is this assessment. This method works out fairly well on the whole. It is supplemented by going over the list of automobile registrations and tacking on additional assessments for cars.

2. Intangibles.

The assessment of intangible personal property (such as stocks and bonds) is much more difficult because these securities are not in plain sight for the assessors to see. They are stowed away in safe deposit boxes. Hence there is virtually no way in which the assessor can estimate the value of an owner's intangible property unless the latter discloses it. In some states the laws require that every owner of stocks, bonds, mortgages, notes, etc., shall make a detailed return to the assessors before a certain date. Anyone failing to make such return is liable to a penalty in case his ownership of unreported stocks and bonds is subsequently discovered. A check-up for such discoveries is then made by requiring banks, brokerage houses, and other financial institutions to provide the assessor's office with transcripts of customers' accounts, showing what securities they have bought or sold during the year. If the assessors find that a resident of the city has made no return, they may impose an arbitrary assessment on him, even though they have made no discovery of intangibles actually owned. In that case, however, the person so assessed may secure an abatement by entering a protest and proving that he has no intangibles subject to taxation. Opportunities for evasion are numerous, nevertheless, and a large amount of intangible property escapes assessment altogether.

Appeals from assessments.

When the assessment lists have been completed they are made available for public inspection. Anyone who believes himself to have been over-assessed may then appeal to some higher authority. Commonly this is a board of review which is set up for the purpose but occasionally the appeals are heard and decided by the county commissioners or by the city council. A further appeal may be carried to the courts. As a rule, however, the courts do not reexamine the facts on which the assessment is based but pass only upon questions of law.

REFERENCES

Good books in this field are Charles Knox, *Principles of Real Estate Appraising* (Youngstown, Ohio, 1924), John A. Zangerle, *Principles of Real Estate Appraising* (Cleveland, 1924), Frederick M. Babcock, *The Appraisal of Real Estate* (New York, 1924), and *The Valuation of Urban Real Estate* (New York, 1932), R. M. Hurd, *Principles of City Land Values* (4th edition, New York, 1924), Stanley L. McMichael and Robert F. Bingham, *City Growth and Values* (Cleveland, 1923), Stanley L. McMichael, *McMichael's Appraising Manual* (New York, 1931), W. W. Pollock and K. W. H. Scholz, *The Science and Practice of Urban Land Valuation* (Philadelphia, 1926), Ernest M. Fisher, *Advanced Principles of Real Estate Practice* (Ann Arbor, Michigan, 1930), John P. Kennedy, *The Basis of Real Estate Values* (Los Angeles, 1925), Roger D. Washburn, *Principles of Real Estate Practice* (New York, 1930), H. D. Simpson and J. E. Burton, *The Valuation of Vacant Land in Suburban Areas* (Chicago, 1931), Cuthbert E. Reeves, *The Appraisal of Urban Land and Buildings*, Public Administration Service Publications, No. 11 (New York, 1928), and J. B. Stoner, *Systems of Equalizing, Assessing and Collecting Taxes* (Austin, Texas, 1924).

Attention should also be called to the pamphlet by Lawson Purdy on "The Assessment of Real Estate" published by the National Municipal League (4th edition, New York, 1929), and to the manuals for the guidance of their assessors which have been published by some of the large cities such as Detroit and Washington.

CHAPTER XI

MUNICIPAL REVENUES

> The essence of a tax, as distinguished from other charges by government, is the absence of a direct quid pro quo between the taxpayer and the public authority.—*F. W. Taussig.*

The city's greatest problem. Revenue is the first essential of government. No administration can be carried on without it. Hence the control of municipal administration by the city council arises from its authority to grant or withhold appropriations. Raising money, in fact, is the most important and at the same time the most difficult thing that city governments have to do. Not only that but it is getting to be more difficult as time goes on. This is because more revenue is needed year by year, while the sources from which this revenue can be secured are not proportionately increasing.

The expanding need for revenue. More revenue is needed because city governments are continually taking on new functions and expanding old ones. Many things can be better and more economically done by the public authorities than by each citizen for himself. Hence the people are insisting that their local governments shall take over one new responsibility after another. They want the city to trim the trees in front of their houses, cut the weeds on vacant lots, provide band concerts in the parks, maintain a public golf course, organize community dances, and do a hundred other things which the people of a generation ago were supposed to do for themselves. Each additional function is urged upon the city with the plea that the cost will be very little. But the total cost proves to be very large. At any rate the public keeps pressing for more service and better service, all of which means a bigger budget and the necessity of raising more revenue. That is why the tax rate keeps going up.

Limitations on the municipal power to tax. In all cities the bulk of the public revenue is raised by taxation. This does not mean, however, that a city is permitted to tax what it pleases. It is limited by the general laws as to what may be taxed and how. Taxation is never a matter of local discretion. The power to tax is of such far-reaching scope and potency that no

126

branch of American government is permitted to exercise it without constitutional restraint. The taxing power of the federal government is limited by the national constitution; the taxing power of the states is limited both by the national and the state constitutions; while the taxing power of the municipalities is limited by the state laws as well. Hence the city must raise its taxes from within a field which has been limited by defining what may be taxed and (in some cases) what the maximum rate of taxation may be.

In addition there are limitations of a practical sort which often put the city government on the horns of a dilemma. The voters call for services which cost money that can only be had by raising the tax rate. Simultaneously they demand economy and insist that taxes be kept down. This inconsistency of attitude is exemplified at the city hall every week in the year. One deputation of citizens will arrive to urge new playgrounds or increased pay for policemen or an extra half-holiday for city employees. Its arguments are convincing. But this group is quickly followed by another from the chamber of commerce or the real estate exchange or the taxpayers' association. Its members argue in an equally convincing way against higher taxes of any kind. The city council listens to both pleas and devoutly wishes that governments were so constituted that councilmen could please everybody. In the end they usually do whatever seems to be good politics, and the voters who want money spent appear to be more numerous than those who want it saved. *The issue of political expediency in taxation.*

How much money do the cities of the United States raise in taxes every year? The exact amount cannot be figured because the methods of tax-accounting are not uniform. But the total, in all probability, is not less than two billion dollars annually— which is about four per cent of the entire estimated earnings of the national population. Federal, state, county, township, and district taxes take six or seven billions more. At least twenty per cent of the national income goes to pay taxes. This is a heavy burden upon the earning-power of the people, although by no means so onerous as in some European countries. It amounts to about $75 per head of population or something like $300 per family on the average. And all of it comes from the same source, from the earnings of the people. The money which American cities raise each year is virtually all contributed from *Tax burdens in their totality.*

rents, profits, salaries, wages, and the other channels of private income.

The general sources of municipal revenue.

In their order of normal importance the sources of municipal revenue may be classified as follows:

1. Taxes:
   a. General property taxes and taxes on real estate.
   b. Classified property taxes, including taxes on personal property, whether tangible or intangible, and income taxes.
   c. Business taxes, which are sometimes levied on the volume of business done, or at a flat rate upon certain types of business (such as pawn-shops, transient traders, etc.).
   d. Poll taxes.
2. Licenses and permits, especially building permits.
3. Special assessments.
4. Fines and forfeits.
5. Grants-in-aid from the state or county.
6. Interest on municipal funds.
7. Profits from public service enterprises, owned and operated by the city, such as water, gas, and electricity.
8. Franchise payments from public service enterprises when privately owned.
9. Rental from properties owned by the city.
10. Pension assessments upon policemen, firemen, etc.
11. Miscellaneous, including sale of surplus supplies, copies of documents and of records, etc.

Taxes are not proportioned to benefit.

Taxation is the principal source of municipal revenue and taxes are assumed to be levied on the basis of ability to pay. Therein they differ from most other payments. Virtually all other payments that people make are in proportion to the benefits which they receive. The one notable exception is the payment of taxes, which have no direct relation to individual benefit. People who pay very little in taxes, either directly or indirectly, sometimes receive a large return in the form of public services. For example, a man may be a large municipal taxpayer and yet not live in the city at all. As a non-resident owner of vacant lots, for example, he pays taxes to maintain the public welfare departments of the city. He sends no children to the public schools, but that fact does not relieve him from the obligation to pay his share of what public education costs. Taxes are compulsory payments, which become due and payable without any bargaining.

MUNICIPAL REVENUES

Taxation cannot be proportioned to individual benefit because there is no way of ascertaining how much benefit any individual receives from the work of public administration. Who benefits the more from good street lighting, for example,—the property owners along the street, or the people who use it for traffic? And even if it were practicable to determine the relative benefit obtained by each individual citizen, this would not be a workable basis of taxation. Those who get the most advantages from public administration are in some cases the least able to pay for it, and the general welfare requires that everyone should have police protection, public health service, free education, and recreation facilities whether he is able to pay for them or not. *The reason for this.*

A tax may therefore be defined as "a compulsory contribution from the people to their government for use in the public service without reference to individual benefits conferred." It is assessed upon property or persons in accordance with their assumed ability to contribute. Property which has a high market value is required to contribute more to the public treasury than property which has a low market value. This is because the owner of the more valuable property is assumed to be able to bear the increased burden. Earners of large incomes pay more than small income-earners, on the same principle. The government, by its taxing power, takes from those who have, in proportion to what they have. To state the matter more bluntly, it confiscates each year a portion of everyone's property and income for the public use, and the justification of this procedure is that government could not be carried on without doing it. *Taxes and the ability to pay.*

The principal source of municipal revenue in the United States is the taxation of real estate. During the nineteenth century general property taxes were almost universally levied. A general property tax is a levy made at a uniform rate on all property— land, buildings, machinery, merchandise, furnishings, stocks and bonds. With the increased diversification of wealth, however, the general property tax became inequitable. It placed so heavy a burden on intangibles as virtually to compel evasion. A three per cent tax on the value of real estate is not necessarily excessive because the owner usually receives a gross income of ten or twelve per cent from such property; but a three per cent tax on the market value of bonds and stocks would take from the owner half his income from these securities, and often more than *Forms of municipal taxation:*

1. *The general property tax.*

half. Hence the tendency today is in the direction of a classified property tax, or a series of graded taxes on different kinds of property, with an income tax in some cases as a substitute for the older levy on the value of intangible property.

2. The classified property tax.

Under a classified property tax system the rate of taxation varies with each class of property. Intangible property, such as stocks, bonds, and notes, are taxed at a much lower rate than that fixed for real estate. In some cases a different rate of taxation is fixed for land and buildings. The idea underlying the classified property tax system is that the burden should be equitably adjusted so as to remove any strong temptation to evasion. The objection usually urged against the plan is that it places too much discretion in the hands of the public authorities who are likely to be guided by political motives. Where politicians do the classifying they will think more of politics than of equities. They will temper the wind to those property owners who possess the votes. The power to classify property, and to tax each class at a different rate, inevitably conveys power to discriminate in favor of one class of owners and against another. People are naturally reluctant to place this authority in the hands of political officeholders.

3. Income taxes.

In a few cities the attempt to tax intangible property has been given up altogether. A tax on the income from these securities has been substituted. This income tax is assessed and collected by the state authorities and the proceeds are then turned back to the municipalities on some equitable basis. Every resident is required to make a sworn return of his income for the year, provided this income exceeds a designated minimum. Then an income tax is assessed on the basis of this return. Certain property and incomes, however, are exempt from state or local taxation. These exemptions include all property owned by any government (federal, state, or municipal), the salaries of all federal officers, together with the income derived from United States bonds and certain other bonds which have been designated by Congress as tax exempt. State and municipal bonds are also, as a rule, free from state and local income taxes within the state. The property, and usually the income, of various semi-public institutions such as colleges, hospitals, and museums, are also exempt from taxation in most cities.

Everywhere throughout the cities of the United States one hears the protest that real estate is too heavily taxed. Sometimes half the net income derived from an office building, apartment house, or store building is taken in taxes. Such a situation discourages investment in these forms of property and forces a high scale of rentals. It is true, of course, that the owner of rented real estate does not himself bear the burden of taxes laid upon his property under normal conditions. He passes it to his tenants if he can. They, in turn, try to pass it along to their customers or employees. Thus the taxes on occupied property are shifted from shoulder to shoulder until the burden finally reaches somebody who cannot unload it on anyone else. Real estate taxes thus percolate into rents, prices, salaries, and wages, in other words into the cost of living. *Is real estate too heavily taxed?*

This is not to imply, however, that all real estate taxes are so shifted, or that the entire tax bill can be passed along. Taxes on vacant land cannot be immediately shifted, for there is no one to whom they can be passed. In the case of occupied property the rent is sometimes insufficient to pay the taxes and yet leave the owner a fair return on his investment. This happens when the amount of such property, available for rental, exceeds the demand—as occasionally happens in the case of stores, office buildings, apartment houses, or single dwellings. But in general, and over considerable periods of time, taxes become a factor in the general cost of living and everyone gets part of the burden saddled on him, whether he realizes it or not. *Limits on the shifting of property taxes.*

Too often the average voter does not realize this shifting of the incidence of taxation. Not being himself directly assessed for taxes, and not receiving a tax bill each year, he gets the idea that the taxes are being paid by the landlord. This is one of the great American delusions. Its existence is responsible for the readiness with which people approve wasteful and extravagant public expenditures. The man who pays fifty dollars per month for his house or apartment would be amazed to find that ten dollars of this is really taxes, not rent. Yet the tax proportion is usually that, or more. More service and better service from the city inevitably means higher rents and higher prices. The voters would display a greater personal interest in the tax rate if they realized this elementary fact. *The myth of the non-taxpayer.*

How is the rate of municipal taxation fixed for any given year? Fixing the tax rate is merely a problem in simple arithmetic. The assessors, having made up their assessment rolls and revised them, *How tax rates are fixed.*

turn in the totals of assessed valuation for the whole city. Meanwhile the city manager or mayor or a committee of the city council is at work on the municipal budget. This, as will be explained in the next chapter, is a tabulated forecast of estimated revenues and expenditures for the ensuing fiscal year. By totalling the anticipated expenditures and deducting the amount of revenue to be obtained from sources other than property-taxation (*e.g.*, from licenses, fees, etc.), the balance represents the total tax levy. Divide this last-named sum into the total property valuation as reported by the assessors and you have the tax rate. It is expressed in so many dollars per thousand, or so many cents per hundred dollars, or so many mills per dollar. Thus one city announces its tax rate as twenty-seven dollars, another as twenty-seven cents and still another as 2.7 mills,—it is all the same thing.

Theory and practice in tax-rate fixing.

But as a practical matter the procedure above outlined is not usually followed. Instead, the city officials make a number of tentative calculations of the tax rate when they are considering items of estimated expenditures in the compilation of their budget. They do this because they are concerned to make up a budget which will not entail an increase in the preceding year's tax rate. Hence the process of figuring a tax rate is sometimes just the reverse of that described in the preceding paragraph. Mayors and city councilmen do not make up the budget and then inquire what rate of taxation will be needed to balance it. They first ask how much money they will be able to spend if the existing tax rate is maintained. Then they proceed to budget the expenditures up to that limit, or, if they think the people will tolerate an increase in the tax rate they enlarge the appropriations accordingly. In other words the tax rate is first agreed upon in a tentative way and then the expenditures are adjusted to whatever revenue this rate is estimated to produce.

Municipal tax limits.

It is sometimes provided by the general state laws or by the city charter, however, that the municipal tax rate must not exceed a certain figure—say twenty dollars per thousand of assessed valuation. But money raised to pay interest on the municipal debt, or repayments of the principal, is not usually included within this limit. An alternative form of limitation is the provision that the amount of taxes levied in any year shall not be more than a certain percentage above that of the preceding year. In a few cases the limit is fixed at so many dollars per head of population. Whenever any of these limitations are imposed, the municipal authorities must keep within them, in form at least.

But tax limits can be evaded. When the limit is fixed in terms of assessed valuation, the city authorities can get more revenue by the simple device of raising the assessments. If the tax limit is twenty dollars per thousand, for example, a horizontal increase of five per cent in the assessed valuations will give you the same total revenue that would be obtained from a tax rate of twenty-one dollars on the earlier valuations. This method of circumventing a statutory tax limit has been commonly used by cities. Another method is to keep within the limit and leave a deficit at the end of the year. Then the same procedure is repeated until so large a floating indebtedness is piled up that it has to be funded by the issue of bonds. Per capita limits are evaded by juggling the estimates of population between the census dates. Some cities get considerable amounts of revenue, to defray what are really current expenses, by levying special assessments.[1] Finally, there is a method of evasion by creating special taxing districts such as sanitary, lighting, or library districts. Such districts take over the cost of certain services, thus relieving the municipal budget and enabling the city tax rate to be kept within the statutory limit. But the combined municipal and district rate is above this limit and the property owner loses the protection which it was the intention of the statute to provide. *How they are sometimes evaded.*

Statutory tax limits are of doubtful advantage. They seldom place an effective check on city expenditures. On the other hand they incite the city authorities to divert money from special funds for general purposes, or encourage the inadequate upkeep of public property, or lead to all manner of subterfuges or evasions. Most taxpayers believe in tax limits and vote for them when they get the opportunity; but this is only because the average property owner does not realize their ineffectiveness. Better than any rigid limitation of the tax rate is the requirement that the municipal tax rate shall be approved by some designated state authority before it goes into effect. In Indiana, for example, the state laws provide that after a municipal tax rate has been provisionally fixed, any ten taxpayers may petition the state board of tax commissioners for an investigation and review of the rate. This commission, if it sees fit, may order the budget revised downward and *Administrative control is better than a statutory limitation.*

[1] See Chapter XII.

the tax rate correspondingly lowered. A few other states have adopted somewhat less drastic plans of administrative control over the expenditures and tax rates of their cities. Such action is criticized on the ground that it involves an interference with the principle of local self-government, but it seems to operate successfully and it has a degree of flexibility that is not possessed by any method of statutory control.

The need for additional sources of municipal revenue.
In the last analysis, however, the only effective safeguard against excessive tax rates is the development of an interest in the city's financial affairs on the part of all the citizens. To this end a broadening of the tax base is desirable. The city's revenue should not be derived wholly, perhaps not even largely, from taxes on real and personal property. Resort should be had, wherever practicable, to other forms of taxation so that the largest possible number of voters shall be brought within the category of conscious taxpayers. This has been accomplished to some extent by means of a sales tax on certain commodities. For example, it has become a nation-wide practice to levy taxes on gasoline, and although these are usually collected by the state authorities, the proceeds from such taxes are often distributed, in part at least, to the municipalities. Or, as an alternative, main highways are built and maintained by the state, even those stretches which are within the city limits. This relieves the cities from considerable highway expenditures which would otherwise fall on them.[1]

Business and sales taxes.
In some states the cities are allowed to impose business taxes, or "licenses for revenue" as they are occasionally called. Such taxes are levied upon the various professions and trades in proportion to the volume of business done, or the number of employees, or on some other basis. Objection is frequently raised to these impositions on the ground that they tend to slacken trade and retard the expansion of industry. A similar objection is urged against the imposition of taxes on retail sales, but such taxes are now being levied in a number of the states. In some cases the state keeps the entire proceeds, while in others a portion is distributed to the cities. Poll taxes are not a large source of revenue anywhere. The possibility of requiring every resident to file an income tax return and pay a minimum of two or three dollars has

---

[1] F. G. Crawford, *The Administration of the Gasoline Tax in the United States*, Public Administration Service Publication No. 38 (3rd edition, New York, 1932).

MUNICIPAL REVENUES 135

been suggested as a substitute for the poll tax and deserves consideration. In general the tendency is to provide that new taxes shall be levied by the state, not by the individual municipalities, but with a provision that at least a portion of the proceeds shall be turned over to the local governments.

Some municipal revenue is obtained from regulatory licenses. These licenses are not established for the purpose of securing revenue but serve as a means of keeping certain forms of business under supervision and control. Incidentally, however, they bring in a good deal of money. If you look over the schedule of regulatory licenses in any large city you will find that they make a rather formidable list. They are used to regulate pawn-shops, second-hand stores, pool and billiard rooms, bowling alleys, dance halls, auctioneers, transient traders, peddlers, massage and beauty parlors, stores which sell firearms or explosives, truckmen, taxicabs, milk vendors, soft-drink establishments, and so on. The number of activities thus made subject to the city's police power through the requirement of licenses is steadily increasing, and the extension is usually defended on grounds of public safety or sanitation. The courts have upheld the city's right to insist on licenses wherever the nature of the business is such as to make public regulation desirable, provided, of course, that the amount of the license fee is not excessive. {Income from licenses.}

A certain amount of revenue also comes in from fees and fines. Fees are usually exacted for building permits, for the placing of temporary obstructions in the streets, for making cuts in the pavement in connection with sewer or water connections, as well as for the inspection of boilers, elevators, weights and measures, dairies, and markets. Such fees are usually collected by the department which grants the permit or makes the inspection. Then they are turned over to the municipal treasury. Fines levied in the municipal police courts, together with forfeited bail, are also turned into the city's exchequer. The imposition of fines by the courts should never be regarded primarily as a source of public revenue, but unhappily the work of the police court is sometimes looked upon by the municipal authorities as an income-producing enterprise. {Fees and fines.}

It is taken for granted that public utility companies which obtain privileges in the city streets shall contribute to the municipal revenues, but the methods of making them do so have varied {Franchise taxes.}

greatly from city to city. Many cities impose franchise taxes based upon the capital, gross income, or net earnings of each company. Sometimes, however, the company's property is taxed as ordinary real estate. This plan is rarely satisfactory because a public service corporation often does business in several adjoining cities and owns property in all of them. Portions of the property cannot be readily segregated for assessment, because all of it forms part of a single-going concern and each parcel is related in value to the others. Other methods of getting adequate revenue from public utility corporations are available, as will be pointed out in a later chapter.[1]

Profits from the municipal utilities.
Then there are the net profits which the city obtains from its own public enterprises. Almost invariably it owns the water-supply service. Sometimes it also operates a municipal lighting plant and occasionally a street railway system. The water department contributes to the general revenues and sometimes the other publicly owned utilities are also profitable. More often, however, the net profits of these municipal enterprises are padded on the books by exempting them from taxation, or by failing to load them with overhead expenses which they ought to bear. Most municipally owned utilities show a balance of net profit on the books, but the number of those which contribute substantially to the general revenue is relatively small.

What should be done with them?
This raises the question whether such utilities, when they make a profit, should turn it over to the general funds of the city or keep it for themselves. In some cities the laws provide that this net profit must not be paid into the general funds but must be kept separate to provide for extensions of the plant, to meet interest and debt retirement charges in connection with the enterprise, or to provide a surplus. The argument is that since the patrons of the public enterprise (that is, the users of light, power, or transportation) are not identical with the general body of the taxpayers, the latter should not have the benefit of any profit accruing. On the other hand it ought to be remembered that a municipal enterprise is acquired or constructed out of funds provided by the whole municipality which pledges its credit for the payment of the bonds and which assumes responsibility for liquidating any deficit that may arise. It seems hardly fair that the general taxpayer should be responsible for the deficit, while only the patrons of the utility

[1] See Chapter XLV.

should get the benefit of the surplus. A municipal lighting plant, for example, belongs to the whole city and not merely to the customers of the plant; it should be taxed like any private enterprise, and should be saddled with its proper share of overhead cost. If there is a profit, the city as a whole should have a share in it.

Looking over the items of revenue received by any large city one will find a few which need explanation. One of these is the item entitled "loans in anticipation of taxes." This is not revenue at all, although it temporarily serves the purpose of revenue. Temporary loans of this kind are essential because municipal taxes are usually assessed in the spring and collected in the autumn. Meanwhile the city has to pay its bills. In order to do this it borrows money from the banks for a few months on short-term notes. Then, when the taxes come in, the loans are paid off. Sometimes, unfortunately, the loans turn out to be larger than the receipts, in which case a floating debt is carried over to the next fiscal year. In the municipal accounts these loans are carried in the revenue column while the repayments appear in the list of expenditures. One thus offsets the other but the totals of revenue and expenditure are inflated above the actualities. *Loans in anticipation of taxes.*

Another item in the list of revenues is represented by the money received from uncollected taxes of previous years. Taxes become due on a designated date, but they are not always paid at that time. The usual provision is that when taxes become overdue a penalty of five or ten per cent is imposed. After the lapse of a certain further period the property is put up for sale and somebody buys it in for the amount of unpaid taxes. Tax arrearages and tax sales greatly increase during a period of depression. When property is sold for taxes this does not mean that it is irretrievably lost to its owner. He has the right to redeem it within a certain time by paying the overdue taxes plus the penalty and various other costs. When tax arrearages are paid, either by the owner or by the buyer at a tax sale, the money goes into a new year's budget because the books for the previous year have been closed. Sometimes the total amount received in back taxes is a very large sum. It is one of the items in a municipal budget that cannot be accurately estimated because of its close dependence upon general business conditions. *Tax arrearages.*

Many cities have found it extremely difficult to make both ends meet during the past few years. For this they are themselves a good deal to blame. During the era of economic expansion most of them piled up large debts, inflated their payrolls, raised property valuations and assumed all manner of new obligations. Then, in 1930, they suddenly found themselves confronted by the necessity of reducing assessments, cutting tax rates, and trimming expenditures. The task did not prove to be a simple one nor was it always performed with good judgment or discrimination. In many cases severe reductions of expenditure were ordered at points where the retrenchment could not be made without impairing the public service.

Tax exemptions. In their endeavor to secure a balanced budget many cities have carefully investigated the possibility of increasing their revenues without raising tax rates or levying new taxes. Such studies have focussed attention on the large amount of property which is entitled to tax exemption or to tax abatement. It has been the common practice in cities to exempt from taxation altogether, or to make an abatement of the taxes levied upon the properties of such institutions as homes for the aged or for orphans, day nurseries, settlement houses, churches, colleges, and sometimes even private schools if they are not operated for profit. One such exemption or abatement leads to another until a large amount of property is relieved from its share of the public burden. In some cities it has been estimated that the total amount which is lost in this way amounts to one-fourth of the entire municipal assessment, or, to put it in another way, that the tax rate could be reduced twenty-five per cent if there were no exemptions or abatements at all. It has been suggested that this property ought to be taxed at the regular rates and that the city council should then have power to give them appropriations in lieu of the tax exemption if it saw fit. Were this done it can be taken for a certainty that cities would be far less generous to eleemosynary institutions than they now are.

Larger license fees. Another proposal is that the licensing power of the city should be extended, and much larger amounts collected from this source. It is now customary, for example, to exact a fee of only $50 or $100 a year from motion picture theaters. Even a one per cent tax on the gross income of these establishments would yield a large revenue to the municipality. The same is true of boxing arenas, football games, professional baseball games, public dance halls, and all other forms of public amusement. In any event the schedule of licenses and fees in most of our cities needs overhauling. But the practical difficulty is that whenever a city council proposes to secure additional revenue in this way the interests which happen to be affected are promptly mobilized in opposition while the taxpayers who would get the benefit are rarely heard from at all. Meanwhile the need for more municipal revenue has become imperative. The annual expenditures of cities are more likely to grow than to dwindle. Existing sources of revenue are not adequate to provide the public services which the people demand. The theory of the general property tax is that new income resulting from increased property valuations will normally take care of a city's new requirements, but this theory breaks down when property values undergo a year-after-year decline. A broadening of the income-base is essential if cities are to drive home to the mind of every citizen the fact that what all the people demand must be paid for by all the people, not by a small portion of them. Taken by itself, the injustice of any tax is easy enough to prove. It is inequitable to make real property, or personal property, or incomes, or retail sales bear too large a part of the public burden. Justice in taxation requires the framing of a tax system which will include taxes of several kinds, so that those who escape too lightly from one form will be required to contribute their share by another. Too much discussion has usually been centered upon individual taxes and not enough on a tax system.

REFERENCES

A useful bibliography of books on public finance and taxation is included in Harold E. Batson, *A Select Bibliography of Modern Economic Theory, 1870–1929* (New York, 1930), pp. 101–112.

Discussions of municipal revenue may be found in the various books on public finance such as C. C. Plehn, *Introduction to Public Finance* (5th edition, New York, 1926), H. L. Lutz, *Public Finance* (2nd edition, New York, 1929), J. P. Jensen, *Problems of Public Finance* (New York, 1924), M. H. Hunter, *Outlines of Public Finance* (revised edition, New York, 1926), H. Dalton, *Principles of Public Finance* (London, 1923), C. J. Bullock, *Selected Readings in Public Finance* (3rd edition, Boston, 1924), M. C. Mills and G. W. Starr, *Readings in Public Finance and Taxation* (New York, 1932), W. J. Shultz, *American Public Finance and Taxation* (New York, 1931), A. C. Pigou, *A Study in Public Finance* (London, 1928), and G. Findlay Shirras, *The Science of Public Finance* (London, 1924).

There are also many special treatises on taxation, such as E. R. A. Seligman, *Essays in Taxation* (10th edition, New York, 1925) and *The*

Shifting and Incidence of Taxation (5th edition, New York, 1927), A. P. Comstock, *Taxation in the Modern State* (New York, 1929), H. W. Peck, *Taxation and Welfare* (New York, 1925), H. A. Silverman, *Taxation: Its Incidence and Effects* (New York, 1931), G. Armitage-Smith, *Principles and Methods of Taxation* (London, 1924), J. P. Jensen, *Property Taxation in the United States* (Chicago, 1931), S. E. Leland, *The Classified Property Tax in the United States* (New York, 1928), R. G. Hutchinson, *State-administered Locally-shared Taxes* (New York, 1931), Herbert D. Simpson, *Tax Racket and Tax Reform in Chicago* (Chicago, 1930), and H. G. Brown, *The Economics of Taxation* (New York, 1924).

Reference should also be made to the annual *Proceedings* of the National Tax Association, the quarterly *Bulletin* of the same organization, the *Tax Magazine* published monthly by the Commerce Clearing House of Chicago, the *Tax Digest* issued monthly by the California Taxpayers Association, the publications of the Municipal Finance Officers' Association (850 East 58th St., Chicago), and various studies of the tax burden issued by the National Industrial Conference Board during the past few years.

Current discussions of tax problems may be found in the *American Economic Review*, the *Quarterly Journal of Economics*, the *Journal of Political Economy*, and the other economic periodicals. A tabulation of the comparative tax rates of cities is published annually in the *National Municipal Review*.

CHAPTER XII

SPECIAL ASSESSMENTS

I never knew any man who could not bear another's misfortunes like a Christian.—*Alexander Pope.*

There are three ways of financing large public improvements such as the widening of streets, the establishment of parks, or the installation of sewers. The first method is to pay the cost out of the city's current income from taxation, but this is rarely found practicable on any extensive scale, except in the case of street pavements. Here the proceeds from the gasoline tax are sometimes available, in part at least, for the improvement of the city's main thoroughfares. The second plan is to pay for them by the issue of bonds on the general credit of the city, these bonds running for a considerable term of years with provision for a gradual amortization or for a sinking fund which will liquidate them at maturity.[1] Cities in the eastern portions of the United States have used this plan extensively. {Three ways of financing public improvements: 1. From taxes. 2. From loans.}

The third method is to defray the cost, in whole or in part, through the levy of special assessments upon such private property as is assumed to have been directly benefited by the public improvement. This special assessment plan of financing has been more widely used by cities in the western part of the country. It is not always essential to the validity of a special assessment, however, that the benefit to the property shall be an actual and demonstrable one. In some cases it is legally permissible to apportion the cost of a public improvement among all the property owners in the neighborhood on the general assumption of benefit without reference to the specific advantages accruing in each case. {From special assessments.}

The term special assessment is not an easy one to define. It is used with various meanings by writers on taxation and is employed in several different ways in various parts of the country. In general, however, it is "a compulsory charge on real estate imposed by the public authorities, usually in some proportion to {Special assessments defined.}

---

[1] For an explanation of the difference between serial bonds and sinking fund bonds see *below*, pp. 177–180.

the special benefits conferred upon such property by an improvement of a public character." In some respects, therefore, a special assessment is analogous to a tax, but it is not a tax in the strict sense of the term. Ordinary taxes and special assessments are alike in that they both have the element of public purpose; both represent an exercise of the government's taxing power and both are compulsory upon the individuals affected. On the other hand the primary element in a tax is that it imposes a general burden on the theory of a common benefit to all, while the primary test of a special assessment is its implication of a special advantage and the adjustment of its burdens accordingly. Hence a special assessment is imposed without regard to the rules of uniformity and equality which the constitutions of various states require to be observed in the imposition of taxes. Special assessments are like fees in that they rest on the doctrine of equivalent return.

The philosophy of the general tax system is that taxes shall be levied in accordance with ability to pay and without respect to individual benefit, while the theory of the special assessment plan is that the levy shall be made with regard to individual benefit irrespective of ability to pay. On this basis the courts have generally held that a special assessment is not a tax within the meaning of this term as it is used in constitutions and statutes. Accordingly, when the charter of a city imposes a tax limit, this limit does not apply to special assessments. On the other hand, where property has been given exemption by law from general taxes (as in the case of schools and colleges), such property is not exempt from special assessments.

Taxes, again, may be progressive, that is, they may have lower and higher brackets, as income taxes often do; but in the nature of things a special assessment cannot be progressive. It must be proportional, that is, levied at a uniform rate on all frontage, acreage, or assessed values which come within the same category. It may also be noted, as another practical difference between the two, that whereas all general taxes are collected by the public authorities, this is by no means invariably the case with respect to the special levies. In many instances these special assessments are not collected along with the regular taxes but by a special procedure which will be explained a little later on.

Special assessments represent an old financial device, apparently known to the Romans, for one of the imperial edicts contained the provision: *Construat vias publicas unusquisque secundum propriam domum.* The special assessment has long been used in England where it is known as a "betterment tax." As far back as 1662 a provision was made in London for the assessment of house owners in proportion "to their several interests" in a public improvement. Likewise it was utilized to some extent in colonial America but gradually dropped out of favor and was not revived on any extensive scale until the closing years of the nineteenth century. Of late, however, it has come to be widely employed as a means of paying for the large volume of public improvements (street pavements, sewers, and sidewalks) which have been needed by rapidly growing communities, especially in the western part of the United States. In many of these cities it seemed impracticable to finance all these neighborhood improvements by the issue of municipal bonds. Municipal debt limits, set up by state constitutions and laws, interposed a legal barrier to any such policy. Moreover the issue of municipal bonds, on the general credit of the city, often requires an affirmative vote of the people and it is rarely practicable to obtain this popular endorsement for projects which inure to the special benefit of a single locality. The chief reasons for the spread of the special assessment system, therefore, have been the rapid growth of cities in the western portion of the country, the insistent demand of the people for costly public improvements especially in the new suburban districts, and the impracticability of financing these projects by any other method.

Origin of special assessments and reasons for their use.

Moreover, the special assessment plan has some weighty arguments in its own favor, apart from the difficulties involved in the use of any other method. Most people are inclined to look upon it as an entirely equitable method of financing such improvements as street widenings, street paving, the building of sewers, curbs, and gutters, the establishment of neighborhood playgrounds, and the installation of ornamental street-lighting systems, for the reason that such improvements almost always increase the market value of the neighboring property. No one can have failed to observe, for example, the way in which real estate promoters play up the advantages which their building lots possess in the way of well-paved streets, water, light and sanitary facilities, proximity to schools and playgrounds, and so on. If the owners of this property expect financial benefit from such public improvements, why should they not be required to bear the cost, in whole or in part?

Their justification.

144   MUNICIPAL ADMINISTRATION

The special assessment provides a way of compelling them to take the burden as well as the benefit.

Objections to the system. This general principle is sound and it is being widely accepted. To a steadily increasing extent the cities are demanding that those whose property is likely to be enhanced in value by reason of a public improvement shall bear a larger share of the burden than those whose property is not so beneficially affected. But in the application of this idea many practical difficulties are encountered. A rule which is easy to state sometimes proves by no means so easy to apply. "The burden should be in accordance with benefit." Yes, but the exact degrees of benefit are often very hard to determine. For example, when a main thoroughfare is widened will the enhancement of property values confine itself to this one street, or will it accrue in some measure to properties which are on adjacent streets, half a block away? In some cases the relief of traffic congestion, by reason of a street widening, has increased the value of property on other streets which run into the widened thoroughfare. One should also bear in mind that a street does not belong to those whose property fronts on it. It is for the use of the entire citizenship and the whole community gets some benefit when it is improved by widening, straightening, or repaving. Hence it is argued that at least a portion of the cost should be paid out of the general taxes. But how can the proper apportionment in cases of this kind be determined? It is usually a matter of compromise and adjustment.

How far does a zone of benefit extend? Or, to take another example,—the case of neighborhood playgrounds. Should their cost be covered by the levy of special assessments, and if so how far does the zone of benefit extend? The outlays involved in the building of a school are almost never financed by a special levy, for schools are regarded as instrumentalities of the entire educational system, even though the location of a school may be of direct and demonstrable benefit to property values within walking distance. Should the same principle be applied to playgrounds? So with many other types of public improvements. The practical difficulties involved in the equitable spreading of the levies become very considerable when the project concerns the erection of a new bridge, or the turning of the waterfront into a parkway, or the erection of a new civic center.

Generally speaking, there are two kinds of special assessments, namely, those levied for special services of a recurring sort, and those which are imposed, once for all, in connection with permanent improvements. Under the former head are included such special assessments as are imposed to meet current expenses for the cleaning, sprinkling, or oiling of streets, the flushing of sewers, the cutting of weeds on vacant lots, the care of shade trees along the curb, the lighting of streets, and the removal of snow from the public thoroughfares. The theory in these cases is that such current services confer localized benefits in excess of those accruing to the city as a whole.

Two kinds of special assessments:

But here again a not-altogether-logical practice has been forced upon the municipal authorities by purely practical considerations. Cities which have had a limit imposed by the state legislatures upon the size of their annual tax rates frequently find it impossible to provide out of their general revenues all the special services which the property owners demand. They cannot trim trees, cut the grass on parkings, provide a semi-weekly removal of rubbish from stores and homes, maintain expensive street lighting systems in residential sections and remove the overhead wires into subsurface conduits—they usually cannot do all such things and stay within a tax limit of twenty dollars per thousand of assessed property valuations, or whatever the maximum figure may be. Resort has therefore been made to the use of special assessments as a means of providing these services without putting the burden upon the general tax rate. Officials try to justify it on the ground that the benefits resulting from such services are special rather than general, but the distinction in some cases does not seem to be either logical or clear. Not all cities, of course, have been driven to this method of financing a portion of their administrative costs. The majority of them continue to pay the current cost of street maintenance and cleaning, the flushing of sewers, the removal of snow, and the care of street trees, out of their general funds.

1. For special public services.

The other form of special assessment, namely, for covering the whole or a portion of the cost of a permanent improvement, is much more widely employed. In almost all cases, however, a legal restriction is placed upon the extent to which such special assessments may be imposed. In some states this limit is set in terms of the total cost of the project; in other words, it makes provision that not more than fifty per cent or some other percentage of the entire outlay may be apportioned upon adjacent property in the form of a special assessment. In other states the limit is set in

2. For permanent public improvements.

terms of the value of the property affected. For example, in New York City the statutes provide that in no case shall any improved or unimproved property be levied upon by special assessment for more than one-half its fair value. This has been construed to mean the value at which the property is assessed for taxation on the city tax roll. In some other cities it is stipulated that no special assessment shall be imposed upon any property until a certain period of time has elapsed since the last levy, or unless it immediately adjoins the improvement. And as a general rule (although there are exceptions) the amount of the special assessment must not exceed the actual enhancement in value. This last-named restriction, of course, is hard to apply because the extent of the increased value is a matter on which expert opinions may differ widely.

<small>What kinds of property may be assessed?</small>
With reference to the kinds of property which may be subjected to special assessment there are some variations in practice throughout the country. In some cities the levy is made upon real estate, which includes not only land but the buildings. In other cities the assessment is levied upon the land alone without reference to the buildings which may be erected upon it. Where the assessment is levied in terms of so much per foot frontage, this distinction is of no account; but in cases where the assessment is apportioned over an entire district on a basis of the assumed enhancement of the property in value, the distinction becomes a highly important one. Personal property, such as stocks in trade, machinery, and household furniture, are not subjected to special assessment, nor is intangible property in the form of stocks, bonds, mortgages, and notes. On the other hand, real estate which is ordinarily exempted from the general tax levy (such as small homes owned by war veterans) are compelled to pay their quota in the case of special assessments. This principle has been carried so far, indeed, that property of a county, when located within the borders of a city, is frequently required to pay along with the rest.

<small>The maximum amount of the levy.</small>
The cost of a public improvement, for the purpose of determining how much may be charged to assessed property, is reckoned as including not only the actual expense of construction but all incidental expenses such as legal costs and fees for preliminary engineering. Occasionally, however, the city assumes the cost of paving street intersections on the theory that these intersections do not actually abut on any private property. In other

SPECIAL ASSESSMENTS 147

cases these costs are prorated over all the property along the street to the next intersection. The intersections, of course, are integral parts of a highway and there seems to be no reason for treating them as different from other portions of the highway surface.

There are several methods of apportioning special assessments on a basis of the benefit which different parcels of land are assumed to have received from a public improvement. The first and simplest plan is the front-foot rule. Under this arrangement the cost is spread over all property directly abutting upon the improvement, the apportioning being made at so much per front foot for each parcel or lot. This method has been rather generally followed with respect to assessments for street paving, the installation of curbs, gutters, sewers, wire conduits, and ornamental lighting standards. It rests on the assumption that no property other than that which is immediately adjacent to the improvement receives any benefit at all, and that the contiguous property benefits in proportion to its frontage. In its actual workings, however, this plan sometimes turns out to be inequitable as between deep and shallow lots. It is also unsatisfactory as applied to lots of irregular shape. A fifty-foot frontage, with a hundred feet of depth, pays no more under the front-foot rule than a similar frontage of only half that depth, although its area is twice as large. Likewise a lot may be triangular, with its short or long sides abutting on the street. Then the owner will find himself in luck or out of it as the case may be. In paying the cost of street widenings the front-foot rule is often productive of serious injustice; nevertheless it has been considerably used. The area of benefit, in the case of such work, almost invariably extends beyond the frontages immediately concerned.

<small>How the apportionment may be distributed:</small>

<small>1. On a front-foot basis.</small>

The second method of levying assessments is to apportion the cost upon the property immediately adjacent to the improvement but on a basis of superficial area rather than of frontage. This plan has been considerably used in the case of storm sewers and some other improvements, including at times the paving of streets. It has defects similar to that of the frontage levy but in the opposite direction. In other words it frequently proves inequitable in its application to property which has a large superficial area but a relatively small frontage. These lots, as has been shown elsewhere, carry most of their market value in the front portion of the area.

<small>2. On the basis of superficial area.</small>

Moreover, in the case of parks, playgrounds, bridges, waterfront improvements, and civic centers, it is obviously unjust to confine the levy to properties immediately fronting on the improvement. When the costs of such improvements are being apportioned it is desirable to use some plan which will distribute the burden at varying rates over an entire district.

3. On the basis of proximity.

This has led to the devising of a third method of levying special assessments which is nowadays being widely used. This plan involves the creation of a special district which is mapped out to include all the property within the assumed zone of betterment. Such a district takes in everything within a certain radius of the work. The assessments are then spread over this entire district according to the relative value of each piece of property at the time the project was begun. Sometimes no distinction is made between properties which are located in close proximity to the improvement and those which are located some distance away. More often, however, a combination of proximity and area or value is used as the basis of apportionment. In such cases the nearer properties pay the bulk of the cost while those farther away pay a small portion of it.

Inner and outer zones.

The usual procedure under this zone-and-area or zone-and-value rule is to map out the improvement district in a series of zones, the inmost zone being given the highest rate. For example, the zone immediately adjacent to the improvement may be required to bear, say forty per cent of the entire levy, while the second zone, a little further out, pays twenty per cent, the next zone ten, and so on, with descending percentages imposed upon the zones still further outlying. This (see map on p. 149) is better than levying upon the whole district uniformly, but even the concentric zone does not go far enough to provide an adequate safeguard against injustice in individual cases. Hence some cities have gone farther and devised a complicated set of rules by the application of which each individual piece of property is given an assessment based upon all the factors involved, namely, its proximity to the improvement, its value, its frontage, its area, its configuration, and its topography. The use of this method involves, of course, the preparation of a district map showing every parcel of property in the district with the amount of the levy calculated on each. As a method of ensuring even-handed justice to all property owners, this plan has everything in its favor except that it puts the public authorities to a good deal of trouble preparing the maps and making the individual calculations.

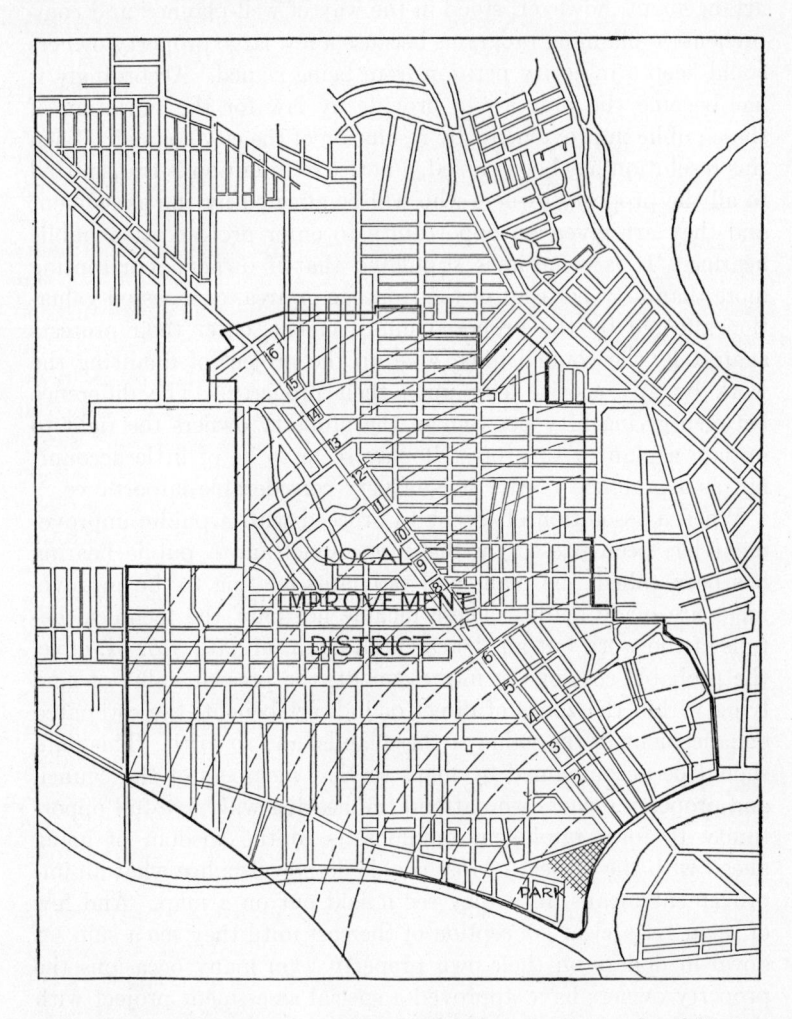

Until recent years the right to initiate a project of public improvement, the cost of which would be met by special assessments, was usually vested in the abutting property owners. Proceedings were begun by the filing of a petition signed by a majority of the property owners concerned, or, to be more accurate, by owners representing a majority of the frontage concerned. Without such

The procedure in financing by special assessment:

1. The petition and resolution of intent.

petition the undertaking of a public improvement, to be financed by a system of special assessments, was not usually possible. This arrangement, however, stood in the way of well-planned and comprehensive planning programs because a few large property owners could keep a majority petition from being signed. Accordingly it has become the practice to provide by law for the initiation of these public improvements by resolution of the city council. When this resolution has been passed, a notice of intention is transmitted to all the property owners who will be affected by the assessment and they are given an opportunity to enter protests at a public hearing. It is sometimes stipulated that if owners representing more than fifty per cent of the frontage or area, or assessed valuation affected by the proposed improvement, enter their protests against it, the council must give up the project of financing the work by any special levy upon their property. The difference between giving fifty per cent of the property owners the right to initiate a plan or to protest it may seem to be of little account, but as a practical matter it is of very considerable importance.

2. The hearing.

When a resolution of intent to proceed with a public improvement has been passed by the city council and a public hearing has been called, the plans and estimates relating to the improvement are made ready. These include not only the technical details of the work but all the essential financial data—for example, the probable cost of the improvement, the present value of land lying within the zones of direct or indirect benefit, the estimated enhancement in the value of these lands, and so forth. This data should be accompanied by maps so that members of the council and property owners who attend the hearing will have full opportunity to form intelligent opinions as to the wisdom of going ahead with the project. Most people do not visualize what an improvement means until they see it laid out on a map. And few of them get a clear conception of the cost until they see a sum set down in dollars on their own property. On many occasions the property owners have approved a special assessment project with the idea that the cost would be far less than it ultimately proved to be. Then they have come to the council chamber in high dudgeon with a demand that they be relieved from the excess burden.

3. The levy: (a) By prior payment.

In some cities the practice is to levy the special assessments and collect them or convert them into liens against the property before the improvement is actually undertaken. The ostensible advantage of this arrangement is that it permits the city to pay the contractors in cash, while the property owners get the advantages of an installment plan.

But the plan of having the city pay at once and the property owners pay later is open to some serious objections. It complicates the bookkeeping over a term of years. It pledges the general credit of the municipality for what is usually a neighborhood project. Thus it gives the city an appearance of being more heavily in debt than is actually the case. Moreover, such special assessments are levied on the basis of what the work is estimated to cost, and, as everyone knows, public improvements often entail a much greater expenditure than the original estimates forecast. In the event of such an excess the practice has been to levy a supplementary assessment upon the property, and this procedure always stirs up a great deal of resentment on the part of those who have to pay the bills. The plan of prior payment has the additional disadvantage of making it difficult for the city to change the plans after the hearing has been held and the assessments levied. The property owners feel that they ought to be consulted with respect to such changes, but it is hard to get them together and even harder to get them to agree.

Objections to this plan.

On the whole it is better to levy the special assessments after the work has been completed and the entire cost accurately determined. Prior to the completion it is good financing, if the laws permit, to have the city pay the contractor out of the proceeds of temporary loans made for the purpose. These loans can then be paid off, with interest, out of the lump-sum assessment levies. But in cases where the special assessments are made payable over a term of years, the problem of financing the contractor out of money temporarily borrowed by the city becomes a more complicated one and the use of this procedure opens the door to serious abuses. The city authorities, yielding to the political pressure of the property owners, sometimes fail to insist upon the full collection of the special assessment over the entire term of years, in which case there are insufficient funds to pay off the loan and the taxpayers as a whole make good the deficiency. Meanwhile the work has been paid for, which means that the contractors have ceased to worry; the property owners aggressively look out for their own interests, and the unorganized taxpayer finds that this arrangement is advantageous to everyone but himself. Arrearages

(b) By payment after completion.

and defaults on special assessments have been common in cities where this plan is used. The theory is that the city will enforce the payment of these levies in the same way that it compels the payment of its general taxes, namely, by selling the property if need be; but political pressure often intervenes to prevent such action.

(c) By the issue of local improvement bonds.
Some cities, therefore, have tried the plan of paying the contractors, during the progress of the work or at its completion, by giving them local improvement bonds which do not pledge the city's credit but are merely a lien on the private property concerned. They are, in effect, a first mortgage on the individual properties which have been benefited. The contractors then sell these bonds to banks or bond brokers who generally resell them to private investors. Since the credit of the city is not behind these obligations they bear a higher rate of interest than is paid on regular municipal bonds and are rated as a somewhat speculative investment. In some cases the holders of the local improvement bonds are left to do their own collecting from the property owners, but more often the city's tax collecting department performs this function as the agent of the bondholders. This is an economy and a convenience to all concerned, but it should be reiterated that in most instances the cities have given no guarantee, express or implied, that either the interest or the principal of these local improvement bonds will be paid when they become due.

Abuses connected with the system.
Various abuses have arisen in connection with the special assessment system, especially in boom-town communities. Real estate promoters manage to get streets paved, sewers laid, and ornamental lighting standards installed in their new suburban areas. Then they sell the building lots with a whole series of special assessments to be liquidated by the purchasers. The burden often proves heavier than the new owner anticipated and presently he finds himself unable to make the periodical payments, with a resulting loss of his property. When a man buys property in one of these real estate subdivisions he often buys on the installment plan a street pavement, a sidewalk, sewers, water mains, and street lights as well as a piece of land, although he does not realize it. Whole tracts have sometimes reverted to the holders of local improvement bonds under this arrangement. In such cases the financial credit of the city is weakened in the minds of investors despite the absence of any guarantees on its part.

SPECIAL ASSESSMENTS

Some states have now made it a requirement that these local improvement bonds, instead of being a lien on individual pieces of property, shall be a charge on all the property within the assessment district or even on the city as a whole. In other words they require that the credit of the entire district or of the whole city be pledged for the payment of interest and principal in the case of special assessment bonds. This plan places a damper on a too-lavish expansion of local improvements based on the optimism of real estate promoters and land speculators. Incidentally it reduces the interest rates for such bonds to the normal rate for other municipal obligations, with a consequent saving to the assessed property owners. *A method of restricting them.*

Special assessment bonds are usually issued in the form of straight serials, that is, the amount of amortization is equal each year. If the amount assessed against a given piece of property is $2,000 and the term is ten years, then ten bonds of the face value of $200 each would be issued. Under this arrangement, however, the burden on the property owner is not uniform. Assuming interest at the rate of six per cent he would pay $320 the first year, $308 the second year, and so on down. In certain cases that is as it ought to be, for some public improvements, such as street paving, giving him the highest value in the earliest years. But there are other improvements, such as parks, in which the highest value comes with the lapse of time. Hence the distribution of the total burden on the property owners ought to be adjusted not only to the benefit which each is supposed to obtain but to the degree of benefit as related to the term over which the assessment is spread. In other words, the principles that apply to municipal bonds in general should be applied here also. *Serializing the local improvement bonds.*

The likelihood is that special assessments, as a method of financing municipal improvements, will be even more widely used in the future than in the past. The procedure and methods are being gradually improved. The abuses are being remedied. The equity of the plan appeals to most people, the property owners included. When local improvements are financed from general taxes, or by regular municipal loans, the work goes to those localities which can exert the heaviest political pressure. The benefit thus accrues to the politically influential without their having to pay for it. The special assessment plan has its shortcomings but it is better, on the whole, than the usual alternative. *Conclusion.*

REFERENCES

The best brief discussion of special assessments is the chapter by Philip H. Cornick in A. E. Buck, *Municipal Finance* (New York, 1926), pp. 384-439. Attention should also be called to the twenty-one page pamphlet on *Special Assessments* issued by the National Municipal League's Committee on Sources of Revenue (3rd edition, New York, 1929). A good discussion of the subject may be found in E. R. A. Seligman, *Essays in Taxation* (10th edition, New York, 1925), pp. 413-420, and pp. 433-451. Most of the treatises on public finance likewise devote attention to the problem of levying special assessments. For a list of these books see the references at the close of Chapter XI.

A volume on *Special Assessments* by Victor Rosewater (New York, 1898) was the pioneer in this field and is still of value on the historical aspects of the subject. For the cities of New York State a valuable compilation by Arthur R. Burnstan on *Special Assessment Procedure* is issued by the State Tax Commission (Albany, 1929). Mention should also be made of J. I. Tucker, *Special Assessments in California* (Los Angeles, 1930), and G. A. Graham, *Special Assessments in Detroit* (Urbana, Illinois, 1932).

Useful information with respect to the levy of these assessments for particular types of public work may be found in many of the books relating to city planning and municipal engineering. In Thomas R. Agg and John E. Brindley, *Highway Administration and Finance* (New York, 1927), for example, the subject is discussed in its relation to street pavements (pp. 195-221) with interesting maps and tables. Legal phases of the subject are discussed in Harold F. Kumm, *The Law of Special Assessments* (Minneapolis, 1927).

CHAPTER XIII

BUDGET MAKING AND APPROPRIATIONS

"I see," said Alice, trying to look as if she did. "And what are budgets?"
"You know midgets?" said the man.
"Yes," said Alice, "I have seen pictures of them."
"Well, budgets are just the opposite," said the man. "And they're getting bigger every year——." —*Alice in Wonderland (American Version)*.

All the revenue that a city raises is spent. It is only on rare occasions that a municipality has a surplus at the end of the year, although the city officials often try to make the people believe there is one. There are various ways of misleading the taxpayers on this point. The most common method is to announce the considerable amount of cash that the city treasurer has on hand and say nothing about the larger total of unpaid bills still outstanding. Or, if need be, the bills which should have come in during the closing month of one fiscal year can be held off until the opening month of the next, thus permitting the officials to show a fictitious balance on the city books. When a mayor goes out of office he congratulates his successor on the heritage of a fine surplus in the treasury but the new administration is rarely able to find it with a microscope. In nine cases out of ten the municipal surplus is a myth.

Revenues are entirely spent.

There are now about a thousand cities of all sizes in the United States. These municipalities are spending at least a billion and a half dollars per annum and probably as much as two billion.[1] This total is more than double what it was twenty years ago. Most of the increase took place during the years 1917-1929, an interlude during which the aggregate municipal expenditures grew more rapidly than the growth of population or property values. While this expansion was going on, the city authorities explained that a considerable part of it was due to the higher level of prices and wages which resulted from the war and the post-war boom. The higher cost of materials, equipment, and labor, they explained, had to be met by raising the appropriations. But when the general

Municipal expenditures and the price level.

---

[1] The exact amount cannot be figured because the financial statistics gathered by the United States Census Bureau cover only cities of over 30,000 population.

level of prices started downward in 1929, the expenditures of the cities did not diminish at the same pace. On the contrary they were reduced, on the whole, by a relatively small fraction. In some departments they were considerably retrenched while in others they underwent a large increase. In public welfare departments, for example, the problem of caring for the unemployed necessitated a much larger outlay, as it always does in an era of economic depression. The most impressive financial lesson to be drawn from American municipal experience during the past twenty years is this: that public expenditures readily follow the price level upwards but display no such readiness to follow it down.

The law of increasing costs in municipal administration. Wholly apart from the price level, however, the tendency of municipal expenditures is irresistibly upward. This is because cities have been growing, and expenditures are related to growth at a greater than proportionate rate. In other words the larger the city's population, the higher is the usual cost of public administration per capita, per thousand of assessed valuation, per square mile, or per anything else you care to use as a basis of reckoning. It might be thought that in municipal administration, as in many industries, the possibility of doing things on a large scale would mean a smaller cost per unit, but this is almost never the case.

This law illustrated. The per capita cost of government varies directly with density of population. To illustrate this proposition, let us assume that the cost of administration in a city of 50,000 population is two million dollars per year, or about forty dollars per person. One might suppose that if the population were to double, and become 100,000, the expenditures would increase in the same proportion or even less, and hence that the cost per capita in the enlarged community would be no greater than it was before. This, however, is not what happens. When the population of a city doubles, the expenses are usually more than doubled. Sometimes they are tripled or even quadrupled. That is why we say that municipal administration is conducted under the law of increasing costs per capita. The existence of this law is sometimes overlooked by financial planners, but it is fundamental in municipal finance.

Why it operates. Why does the cost of municipal administration move upwards at a more rapid rate than the growth of the city? It is because standards of administrative service rise with the growth of urban population. A large city requires not merely more service than a smaller one, but better service as well. In a small city, for example,

BUDGET MAKING AND APPROPRIATIONS

a few policemen at low rates of pay perform the work of maintaining law and order. But let the city grow in size and the police officers expect higher rates of pay; a detective bureau is added; the traffic problem becomes more acute and demands special officers; members of the police force have to be detailed for work at railway terminals and in the theater district. A municipality of 20,000 population can get along with one policeman for every 2000 people. A city of a million requires one policeman per thousand. New York City has one for every 500. Growth in population and in property valuation makes the work of the police department more diversified and requires more specialization. The same principle holds in the other city departments such as public health and education. The bigger the scale, the larger is the cost per capita.

The average business man does not usually appreciate all this. Otherwise he would not be so ready to believe that if more industries could be brought to the city, more people would come to occupy more houses, hence there would be more property to assess for taxation and the tax rate would be proportionally reduced. More industries, more buildings, and more people provide more resources from which to draw the city's revenue, to be sure, but they also bring demands for more police, better fire protection, more parks and playgrounds, a vocational high school, branch libraries, street widenings, a new city hall—for more and better service all along the line.[1] A city in this respect is like an organism; in its lower and simpler forms it has few and simple needs, but in its more complex stages its needs become more diversified and its administration more expensive. To expect a declining tax rate in a growing city is to coddle a futility. *Why municipal expenditures keep rising.*

The city's revenue, when it comes in, is turned over to the city treasurer who is under bonds to keep it in safe custody and not to pay it out except on proper authorization. He deposits the money in approved local banks, usually distributing it among several of them. Some of the revenue goes into designated funds which the city charter requires to be kept separately; for example, into the sinking funds for the ultimate repayment of bonded indebtedness. Occasionally, moreover, certain revenues are allocated directly to the support of the public library, or for social welfare work. The *The city treasurer.*

---

[1] See L. D. Upson, *The Growth of a City Government*, published by the Detroit Bureau of Governmental Research (1931).

city charter or the state laws may also require that income accruing to the water department or to the municipal lighting plant shall be kept separate from the general funds and not merged with the latter. All revenue that is not specifically allocated goes into the general fund and from this fund it is expended in accordance with such appropriations as the city council may see fit to make in the annual budget or otherwise.

How the city treasurer is chosen. Originally it was the general practice to have the city treasurer elected by the people at the polls. This practice is still continued in many cities because of a desire to keep the treasurer free from control by any other city official so that he will not be under pressure to pay out money without full authority. It is also a widespread popular belief that if the office of treasurer is kept elective, the incumbent will be changed from time to time, and that in connection with each change a thorough audit of the treasurer's accounts will be made. But if the treasurer is an appointive official, he may be kept in office year after year without any such rigid accounting. Hence the elective plan is believed to afford a sort of automatic safeguard against large defalcations.

Independence and integrity in this office. These arguments in favor of keeping the office elective are hardly entitled to be given much weight under present day conditions. The city treasurer can be placed in a position of independence even when his office is appointive. This can be done by having the city charter or the ordinance specify his responsibilities in such a way that he cannot yield to sinister pressure without violating the law and becoming himself liable. And the best way to secure the city against defalcations in the treasurer's office is to have frequent and thorough audits by someone outside the treasurer's control.

Appropriations. When revenue goes into the city's general fund, it does not get out again except by an appropriation duly made according to the established procedure. The making of an appropriation is the first step in the spending of public funds. The initiative in recommending an appropriation sometimes belongs to the mayor, but the concurrence of the city council, or other legislative body, is always necessary before an appropriation can become effective. In cities which have the commission form of government, the appropriations are initiated, adopted, and even expended by the commission itself. This is an arrangement which has been criticized because it concentrates the appropriating and the spending

BUDGET MAKING AND APPROPRIATIONS 159

power in the same hands, with a consequent removal of the usual checks on expenditure. Under the city manager form of government the appropriations are recommended by the manager and are then voted by the council. Some cities do not entrust the function of recommending appropriations either to the mayor or to the city manager, but vest it in the hands of a special committee of the city council. This plan is an unsatisfactory one in that it permits an evasion of responsibility when wasteful appropriations are made.

Most of the appropriations for the fiscal year are embodied in a formidable document known as the municipal budget. The consideration of this budget is perhaps the most important task that the city council finds itself called upon to perform. The city's whole program, in fact, is determined each year by the budget because there is very little that can be done without an appropriation on the one hand, while on the other hand the amount of the appropriation determines what can be done. A municipal budget may therefore be defined as a plan of city financing for the incoming fiscal year. It is a program which involves an estimate of revenues on the one hand and of expenditures on the other. These estimates are made in detail and sometimes in very great detail. A properly drawn budget should show an anticipated excess of revenue over expenditure and most city budgets do this when they are prepared, but the surplus frequently fades into a deficit before the fiscal year comes to a close. This is because the probable income is so often over-estimated while various emergencies arise unexpectedly during the year and cause the appropriations to be exceeded. *The city budget.*

How is a municipal budget prepared? The first step is to call upon the heads of the various city departments for their estimates. Fire protection, streets, public works, police, parks, and all the rest,—each department prepares an itemized estimate of what it would like to spend. To facilitate the making of these estimates the comptroller or auditor sends to each department head a standard form upon which he has set down the actual expenditures of the department during the fiscal year preceding, or sometimes for two or three years preceding. The heads of departments go over these forms in consultation with their chief subordinates, put in the new figures, and then return the sheets to the mayor or the city manager or whoever has the responsibility of presenting the *How it is prepared.*

budget to the city council. Meanwhile the city auditor, or comptroller, or other financial officer makes up his figures of probable revenue from all sources other than taxation. In conference with the assessors he also figures out informally just how much revenue would be received from taxes if the tax rate of the preceding year is applied to the current year's assessed valuation.

Reviewing the estimates. When all of these estimates have been received, they are recopied, arranged in orderly fashion, and consolidated into a single bulky document. Then the figures are ready for review by the mayor, city manager, board of estimate, or by a committee of the city council, as the city charter may provide. Almost invariably the total estimates prove to be too high. In other words they exceed by a considerable margin the probable revenue of the city unless the tax rate is increased. Accordingly the revising authority proceeds to pare them down. Sometimes this is done by ordering a horizontal cut, say a ten per cent reduction in the estimates of every department except those in which the expenditures are uncontrollable. It should be explained in this connection that some municipal expenditures are not amenable to any cutting-down,— for example, interest on the municipal debt, the payment of maturing bonds, funds for the maintenance of the courts, and for the payment of pensions, the cost of holding elections, and so forth. In some cases the salaries of department heads, municipal judges, or even policemen and firemen, are fixed by the city charter or by state laws and must be covered in full by the appropriations. At times as much as forty per cent of the whole budget is represented by these uncontrollable items. Accordingly the remaining estimates are the ones which have to stand all the pruning.

Making the budget balance. Reviewing the estimates and making both sides balance is a difficult and by no means an agreeable job for whoever has to do it. No mayor or city manager or council committee in a large municipality can perform it unaided except in a perfunctory way. Sometimes there are budget examiners whose function it is to go through the estimates with a fine-tooth comb and pick out the places where savings can be made. Heads of departments are called into conference and asked about the proposed reductions. They protest, of course, that they have already cut things to the bone; but often they are overruled. After a fortnight, perhaps a whole month of conferring, discussing, dickering, and refiguring, the budget is ready for consideration by the council. Its two ends

BUDGET MAKING AND APPROPRIATIONS   161

have been made to balance, either at the existing tax rate or by means of a proposed increase.

Anyone who is acquainted with the sinuosities of municipal politics will tell you that the foregoing process is often accompanied by a good deal of shadow-boxing to impress the public. For example, when the estimate-sheets are sent out to the various departments, the mayor sometimes passes out a tip that he wants the opportunity to make some drastic cuts when the time arrives. The heads of departments take the hint and pad their estimates accordingly. The totals then prove to be sky-high, whereupon the mayor calls in the newspaper reporters and with a great show of indignation assures them that he is not going to stand for any such extravagance as these heads of departments propose. On the contrary he is going to insist on drastic reductions all along the line, thus performing his full duty to the taxpayers. So the newspapers proclaim in flaming headlines: "Mayor Promises to Cut a Million Dollars from the Budget," and half the people believe it. *The politics of budget making.*

But it is all a publicity gesture and involves no saving at all. The mayor merely takes out of the estimates what should never have been put in. And after he has finished doing this it usually turns out that the totals are still considerably in excess of what was appropriated for the preceding year. The tax rate goes up, and when people complain about it the mayor assures them that nothing but his stern economizing prevented the taxes from being raised a good deal more. This sort of thing has been worked off on the taxpayers of some American cities year after year. It is a marvel that they do not get tired of it. *The alibi for increases.*

But to continue the story of how a municipal budget is made. After the estimates have been duly revised and reduced, they are transmitted in the form of a general appropriation-ordinance to the city council for approval. This should be done at least a month before the beginning of the new fiscal year. The council then refers the whole document to its committee on finance, or on ways and means, or whatever it may be called. If the council is a small body of only seven or nine members the usual practice is to consider the estimates directly, as a committee of the whole, without referring them to a smaller group. *The budget before the city council.*

In virtually all cities there is a provision for public hearings before the budget is finally adopted by the council. Representatives of various civic organizations appear at these hearings and *Public hearings.*

speak their minds on proposed appropriations. The heads of departments are also summoned to explain their figures and are questioned by the councilmen. These questions as a rule are not motivated by a desire to have the department head reduce his figures, but rather to have him increase them for the benefit of the councilman's district or constituents. Hearings may consume several days or even weeks. In large measure they represent a waste of time. Councilmen stretch their legs and yawn while reformers and others come in and dilate on the extravagance of city governments in general. Someone from the taxpayers' league argues for a reduction of estimates all along the line. Then he is followed by someone from the civic improvement association who urges the council to push the totals up.

Limitations on the council's powers. At any rate, when everybody has been heard, the council votes to make such changes as it thinks desirable and the budget is then accepted by it as a whole. In some cities there is a charter provision that the council may make changes by way of reduction but not by way of increase. Anyone who knows a city council will realize that this circumscription of its power means that the council will usually make no changes at all. Councilmen are not interested in taking away some patronage that is already in sight. Cuts in the budget nearly always create political resentment. They mean that somebody loses his job or has his pay reduced, or that some section of the city must go without a public improvement for which it has been clamoring. In scanning a budget the councilmen follow the injunction to "look up, not down."

The final step. Then comes the last step. The budget as finally approved by the council in the form of an appropriation ordinance is given its three formal readings, and sent to the mayor for his signature. The mayor may veto the budget ordinance, as in the case of other ordinances, subject to repassage over his veto. Where the city manager form of government is in operation, the city council is the final authority as respects the appropriation ordinance. The city manager has no veto power in relation to it. When the appropriation ordinance has been finally adopted and has become effective, the head of each department is notified that a designated amount of money has been appropriated for him to spend. He then proceeds to authorize expenditures out of this appropriation. But before any bills are paid they go to the city comptroller or auditor to make sure that his appropriation covers them.

BUDGET MAKING AND APPROPRIATIONS 163

This work of getting the estimates ready, reviewing them, and having them adopted may consume two or three months and this delay may carry the matter into the new fiscal year. Meanwhile the various city departments need money to carry on their work, and in order to provide this the custom is to make temporary appropriations. For the first month of the new fiscal year a sum equal to one-twelfth of the money spent by each department during the preceding year is usually allocated. Then, if the new budget is not passed within another month, another one-twelfth is granted, and so on until the new funds become available. These temporary appropriations are then deducted from the amounts voted in the regular budget when the latter goes into effect. *Provisional appropriations.*

There are three types of municipal budget, commonly known as lump-sum, segregated, and allotment budgets. Under the lump-sum plan the estimates are submitted in some detail but the appropriations are voted to each department in totals—so much for materials, so much for labor, and so on. The park department, for example, may be given a million dollars for "personal services" and may apportion this amount for salaries of higher officials, clerical help, manual labor, and so forth as it thinks best, subject, however, to the provisions of the civil service laws when such are in operation. It may spend a large amount one month and a smaller amount the next if such action seems desirable. So long as the head of the department does not spend more than the total amount appropriated to him, he may use his discretion as to the manner and time of the expenditure. *Types of municipal budget: 1. The lump-sum budget.*

This method has the merit of flexibility; but unless the head of the department is a very careful planner, he usually finds that the last dollar of his lump-sum appropriation is gone before the year is out. Then the city council must choose between giving him a supplementary appropriation or letting the city go without some essential service until the new fiscal year begins. The former alternative provides the city with a deficit; the latter brings a storm of protest from the employees who have been laid off. The head of a department who gets himself into this fix ought to be dismissed, but he can usually find plausible excuses as well as political influence to back them up. Because of its various shortcomings the lump-sum budget system has now been abandoned in most of the larger cities and is losing ground in the smaller ones as well. *Its advantages and defects.*

Under the segregated budget plan the appropriations are voted

2. The segregated budget.

in detail, a definite sum being allocated for every item of proposed expenditure. The segregation may be carried to any degree desired. In some cases there is an itemization of the salary appropriated for every official on the city payroll. Specific sums are put down for each piece of equipment that the city expects to buy and for each type of material. As a rule, however, the segregation does not go so far. Most cities prepare their estimates in detail but in voting the appropriations there is a lumping together of those items which are closely associated (stationery supplies, for example) and these are then voted by subheads.

Its value.

But even with this grouping the appropriation ordinance becomes a somewhat formidable document in any large city. The outstanding merit of segregation is that it compels a careful planning of all city expenditures and thus helps to avoid needless outlays. It places each department in a situation where it must justify every dollar that it asks for. On the other hand it is obviously impossible for any department head, however far-sighted, to calculate in advance all the detailed expenditures which will be necessary in his field of work during the course of the fiscal year. Emergencies will arise and accidents will happen. Moreover, through some change in conditions it may become very desirable to spend a little more money on one group of items and less on another—more on street-cleaning equipment and less on labor, for example. When a budget is too minutely segregated, the freedom of a department is hampered in such cases. A certain amount of leeway can be given, of course, by allowing each department a reasonable sum for use in emergencies, or by leaving a larger sum in the budget as a general reserve from which appropriations may subsequently be made to the various departments which happen to need it.

Transfers from one appropriation to another.

Transfers from the general reserve fund usually require action by the city council. But transfers of money from one appropriation to another, within the same department, may be made in some cities with the approval of the mayor or the city manager or the comptroller. Such transfers are numerous. To some extent they are inevitable, but to a larger extent they are the outcome of insufficient care in making the original estimates. It is astonishing how many "unforeseen" needs arise in city departments. They are unforeseen because of deficient foresight. Sometimes, before the fiscal year is finished, there are no unused balances in the departmental appropriations and nothing left in the general reserve fund. Then the city council is called upon to make supplementary appropriations and it often does so with no additional revenue in sight. Such action starts the next fiscal year with a deficit.

Realizing that both the lump-sum and segregated budget systems have their shortcomings, some cities have attempted to work out a combination of the two systems. This is commonly known as the allotment budget plan, under which lump sums are appropriated to the various departments but on a monthly or quarterly basis. Under this system the estimates are submitted in detail, but this is for the information of the appropriating authorities only. The appropriations themselves are made in lump sums to each department, but with a provision that the mayor or city manager or comptroller shall make each month or each quarter a definite allotment to each department from its lump-sum appropriation in accordance with its demonstrated needs. This plan has some advantages, especially when it is accompanied by a definite work program. It serves as a safeguard against too free spending in the early part of the fiscal year, with shortages at the other end. It does away with the need for transfers. It enables the needs of each department to be periodically reëxamined so that new opportunities for economy may be found. It keeps the departments constantly figuring, and not merely figuring their needs once a year. On the other hand it gives them a greater amount of latitude, when they really have special requirements, than the usual type of segregated budget affords. *3. The allotment budget.*

Not all the city's income and expenditures are budgeted. Certain departments and agencies are sometimes authorized to spend, without central supervision, such special revenues as they receive in the way of fees, gifts, or income from trust funds. This is not a desirable arrangement but because of constitutional or legal restrictions there is occasionally no way of avoiding it. It is an undesirable arrangement because considerable amounts of money come from the pockets of the public and are expended without any action on the part of the appropriating authorities. No public revenues of any sort should ever be paid out of a public treasury except in pursuance of a formal vote taken by the representatives of the people. *Expenditures outside the budget.*

This objection applies, although in somewhat smaller degree, to the practice of making permanent or continuing appropriations. Quite often the state laws or the city charter provide that certain *Permanent or continuing appropriations.*

minimum appropriations must be placed in the budget, year after year, for certain departments such as schools, health, or public libraries. This is done to protect such departments against undernourishment. Since they yield relatively little patronage for the benefit of the politicians, these departments might be mulcted for the benefit of others, such as public works, in which there are more favors to be passed around. Occasionally this protection is worth while, but for the most part it fails of its purpose. The departments in question soon find that they need a good deal more money than the minimum prescribed for them and they have to get it by asking the budget-makers to supplement this amount. Minimum and continuing appropriations should be avoided. The financial requirements of any municipal department depend on its program of activities for the year, and this program should be made the subject of an annual scrutiny.

Loan budgets

Ordinarily the municipal budget does not include either the revenue obtained from the sale of bonds or the expenditures to be made from this revenue. Public improvements, if financed by borrowing, are regarded as special projects and the regular budget is looked upon as a plan which covers ordinary operations only. In most communities these special projects come up at irregular intervals and have no connection with one another. A few cities, however, are adopting the practice of preparing from time to time a bond budget, or loan budget, with the idea that all borrowing projects shall be considered in connection with a comprehensive program of public improvements.

Every year the United States Bureau of the Census is required by law to publish a volume giving statistics of expenditure in all American cities of over 30,000 population. On a basis of these figures it will be found that our cities are now spending, from their regular revenues, about $40.00 per head of population. Some cities, of course, spend a great deal more than this, while others disburse considerably less. In the main it depends on the size of the city but in part it also hinges on the relations between the city and the county in which it is situated. In some states the relief of the poor is a county function and so is the hospitalization of the sick. In other commonwealths these functions are assumed and paid for by the city. So with the school expenses. Sometimes these are included in the regular city budget, but more often there is a separate school district with its own budget. Offhand one might

BUDGET MAKING AND APPROPRIATIONS

think it a very simple matter to figure out and compare the per capita expenditures of different cities. Just divide their budget totals by their populations. The result would be sadly misleading. To obtain a fair comparison one must first reduce their expenditures to a comparable basis, which is a difficult thing to do.

REFERENCES

The theory and practice of municipal expenditures are discussed in M. L. Walker, *Municipal Expenditures* (Baltimore, 1930), a volume to which an extensive bibliography of the subject is appended. The *Financial Statistics of Cities Having a Population of over 30,000*, issued annually by the United States Bureau of the Census, gives data on all phases of municipal expenditure.

Good discussions of the municipal budget problem may be found in A. E. Buck, *Public Budgeting* (New York, 1929), *Municipal Budgets and Budget Making* (New York, 1925), and *Municipal Finance* (New York, 1926), pp. 31–142; L. D. Upson, *Practice of Municipal Administration* (New York, 1926), chap. iv; and Robert Emmett Taylor, *Municipal Budget Making* (Chicago, 1925). This last-named book contains an elaborate bibliography.

Mention should also be made of several volumes which deal with the broader phases of budget making, for example, F. A. Cleveland and A. E. Buck, *The Budget and Responsible Government* (New York, 1920), E. A. Fitzpatrick, *Budget Making in a Democracy* (New York, 1918), W. F. Willoughby, *The National Budget System with Suggestions for Its Improvement* (Baltimore, 1927), and the various chapters on the budget in his *Principles of Public Administration* (Baltimore, 1927), pp. 435–504. Some excellent bibliographical references will be found in this volume (pp. 701–705).

The National Municipal League published in 1928 *A Model Budget Law*, and in 1931 the Public Administration Service issued a useful pamphlet by A. E. Buck, entitled *Budgeting for Small Cities*. Other pamphlets which deserve special mention are C. E. Ridley and O. F. Nolting, *How Cities Can Cut Costs* (Chicago, 1933), F. W. Herring and others, *Municipal Costs and Finance* (Chicago, 1933), and D. L. Judd, *Budget Making and Administration with Special Reference to Cities* (Washington, 1933).

See also the books on public finance listed at the close of Chapter XI.

CHAPTER XIV

MUNICIPAL DEBTS

> Desires extend themselves with the means of satisfaction; the horizon is enlarged in proportion as one advances, and each new want equally accompanied by its pleasure and its pain becomes a new principle of action.—*Jeremy Bentham.*

Why cities borrow. Not all municipal expenditures can be defrayed out of revenue. Such enterprises as the construction of a new city hall, or the acquisition of a new park, cannot usually be financed from the funds which the taxes provide. All cities, therefore, have the right to borrow money under regulations prescribed by their charter or by the general state laws. And virtually all American cities have availed themselves of this privilege. They have borrowed money frequently and in large amounts. The bonded indebtedness of all the cities in the United States now totals more than ten billion dollars.

The philosophy of municipal borrowing. Within reasonable limits a municipal debt calls for no apology. It is the earmark of a go-ahead city. It indicates that the authorities are following a sound philosophy of municipal finance. No progressive city can do justice to its taxpayers without borrowing money. Current expenses, of course, should be paid out of current revenues, but the entire cost of permanent improvements ought not to be saddled on those who receive only a small part of the benefit. A new city hall will serve the municipality for perhaps thirty or forty years. Hence it is only fair that the taxpayers of each year during this period should bear their equitable share of what the structure costs. In the case of a new city park the usefulness is greater after twenty or thirty years than at the outset. Burden should be spread according to benefit. Scrupulous care should be taken, however, to make sure that future generations of taxpayers are not loaded with an undue share of the cost, for they will have enough new commitments of their own when the time comes.

Municipal debt comparisons. Much humbug is passed out to the people concerning municipal indebtedness. When the elective officials of any city desire to

MUNICIPAL DEBTS

prove to the voters that the place is being economically governed they prepare figures showing that its per capita indebtedness is lower than that of other nearby cities. Such tabloid statistics prove nothing and are usually misleading. They take no account of the purposes for which municipal debts have been incurred, or the value of the assets (such as waterworks or lighting plants) which have been built up from borrowed money, or the amount of the sinking funds which have been accumulated to pay off the debts at maturity.

Neither do they usually include the indebtedness which has been incurred by "local improvement districts" within the city, or of the city's share in the indebtedness of some larger governmental subdivision, such as a county or a metropolitan district. Indebtedness incurred by the school authorities, for example, may be reckoned as part of the regular city debt, or it may be regarded as the obligation of a separate district, even though the city and the school district cover exactly the same territory. Money borrowed for a sewage disposal system may be included (as in New York), or it may be left out of the city's debt total (as in Chicago) and set down as the separate obligation of a sanitary district. To figure out the per capita net indebtedness of several cities on a comparable basis is by no means a simple problem. *Why they are often misleading.*

And in any event these per capita figures do not mean much, even when they are accurately compiled. A city does not borrow money on the security of so many heads of population. It sells bonds on the basis of its total property valuation. Bankers do not lend money to a city because there are so many people in it, but because there is so much property to secure the loan. The indebtedness of the city constitutes a lien or mortgage upon all real estate within its boundaries; in other words it is an encumbrance upon the property of the citizens. For the money that is needed to pay interest on the debt, and to liquidate it at maturity, must be obtained by raising the taxes on this property if it cannot be had in some other way. *Public debts as a lien on private property.*

Before discussing the methods of borrowing and the limitations on municipal indebtedness it may be well to explain a few technical terms. A city's *funded* or *bonded* debt is that part of its total indebtedness which has been taken care of by the issue of bonds. These bonds come due for payment at designated future dates. *Varieties of indebtedness:* 1. Funded and floating debt.

The *floating* debt, on the other hand, is that part of the city's indebtedness (usually a small part) which has not been covered by the issue of bonds but is merely carried on the books. It includes such liabilities as unpaid judgments in suits against the city, short-term notes given to banks for loans in anticipation of next year's taxes, overdrafts at the banks, unpaid bills, and so on. The existence of a large floating debt is usually the result of bad financial planning. Frequently it results from the carrying of one year's deficit over to the next, and then adding some more to it. When a floating debt gets too large it becomes embarrassing to the municipal authorities. Accordingly they try to clear the decks by funding it through the issue of bonds—and they usually succeed. In this way the future generation is saddled with what ought to be a current burden.

Anticipatory borrowing and floating debts.

Anticipatory borrowing is the practice of getting money from the banks in order to defray municipal expenses until the taxes or other revenues come in. This is because the date upon which taxes are due, or license fees payable, does not synchronize with the beginning of the city's fiscal year. The fiscal year may begin in January, while the taxes become payable in May or even in September. Having little or no cash on hand from the preceding year the city must meet its payrolls and defray its other expenses during the interval by getting temporary loans. This procedure is not objectionable if the taxes, when they come in, are used to pay off the temporary loans and not diverted to some other purpose.

Mention should also be made of anticipatory borrowing in connection with public improvements. When a city authorizes the issue of bonds to pay for the construction of a new building, bridge, or park it does not need all the money at once. It pays as the work proceeds. To do this it often secures temporary loans. Then, when the work is finished, it sells the bonds and uses the proceeds to pay off these loans. In this way there may be a considerable saving in interest charges. The procedure is financially sound when it is properly controlled. Unhappily the work sometimes costs more than was anticipated; the temporary loans pile up; the proceeds of the bonds do not suffice to liquidate them; and there is a hangover which passes into the floating debt.

2. Gross and net debt.

A clear distinction should also be made between *gross* debt and *net* debt. The city's gross debt is the sum of its funded and floating debts without reference to any offset. It represents total liabilities. The net debt, on the other hand, is the gross debt less the total amount of sinking funds which are already in hand for the redemption of the funded debt when it matures. In some municipalities these sinking funds represent a large fraction of the gross indebtedness, so that the net debt is relatively small. In others there are no sinking funds; the bonds are issued with serial maturities and are paid off, one by one, as they fall due. In such cases the gross and net indebtedness are the same. Debt comparisons, when made, should be on a net basis.

Then there is the distinction between *general* and *special* indebtedness. A city's general indebtedness includes all obligations which have been incurred for city-wide benefit, and for the repayment of which the full faith and credit of the municipality is pledged. Special indebtedness represents the debt which has been incurred on the security of a certain portion of the city (a local improvement district, for example), or a designated public utility owned by the city, or under some other arrangement which does not pledge the credit of the municipality as a whole. When a city buys out the lighting plant of a private company, for instance, it may pay for the same, and sometimes has done so, by issuing bonds which are a mortgage on the plant itself, and not a general obligation of the city. Such mortgage bonds are not often issued because investors will not buy them unless the bonds bear a higher rate of interest than those protected by the city's general credit.

3. General and special debts.

Much more common, particularly in western cities, is the special indebtedness which has been incurred under the local improvement system. As has been explained in a previous chapter, the general laws usually provide that whenever a street is to be widened, or some similar local betterment made, the city authorities may create an improvement district or special assessment district. The cost of the work is then defrayed by the issue of bonds or warrants on the security of the private property within the district, each parcel of property having a share of the obligation definitely allocated to it. These local improvement bonds or warrants are spread over a term of years and the money to liquidate them is usually collected as an addition to the regular taxes on the property within the district.

Special assessment debts.

A city, as a municipal corporation, has no inherent power to in-

Limitations on municipal indebtedness.

cur indebtedness. To possess such power it must be given borrowing powers by its municipal charter or by the general laws of the state. This power is in fact always granted but under various limitations. These limitations usually control not only the procedure by which borrowing may be authorized, but the total amount of debt which may be incurred, the purposes for which bonds may be issued, the term for which they may run, the maximum amount of interest that may be paid, and the provisions which must be made for repayment of the debt at maturity. Few things in municipal administration are now more strictly regulated by law than the issue of municipal bonds.

How debt limits are fixed.

As for the limit on total indebtedness, the usual plan is to fix this in terms of a percentage of the assessed valuation of all taxable property within the municipality. The usual figure is five per cent, although some cities are given a leeway of twice this percentage. In any event the city may issue bonds up to the percentage limit and must stop there. For example, if the total assessed valuation is sixty million dollars, a city can have a maximum net funded debt of three million if the limit is fixed on a five per cent basis. Each year, however, as the valuation of property increases, the borrowing power automatically expands and this gives a spread for additional bond issues. While debt limits are usually fixed in terms of assessed valuations, a few cities have their debt limits related to municipal revenue. The usual provision in such cases is that the city may not incur a funded net indebtedness in excess of the amount represented by one year's municipal income. As the taxes increase, the borrowing power expands.

Debts which are exempt from the general limitation.

In the case of all debt limits, however, whether related to valuation or to revenue, it is customary to exclude from the computation such debts as have been incurred in connection with self-supporting utilities, such as the municipal water supply system or the lighting plant. This is done on the ground that such indebtedness imposes no burden on the general taxpayer and hence does not need to be rigidly controlled. Nor does the municipal debt limit apply to the indebtedness of incorporated school districts or sanitary districts within the city limits. Local improvement bonds are also excluded from the reckoning, but are sometimes controlled by a special limit of their own. In general, therefore, the municipal debt limit applies to only a portion of the city's total obligations.

Every student of public finance realizes that some form of limitation on municipal indebtedness is essential, for otherwise the politicians who so often control the city's financial affairs would muddle them into virtual bankruptcy. They have managed to do this in some cities despite the limitations. On the other hand it is not easy to devise a plan of debt limitation which will prove effective and yet be sufficiently flexible. The practice of fixing the limit in terms of assessed valuation has not proved to be an altogether satisfactory arrangement because a city's needs in the way of borrowing do not have a direct and close relation to the wealth of its citizens. One community with very large property valuations may have smaller requirements in the way of parks and playgrounds, for example, than another in which the property valuations are lower. High property valuations also make it practicable to pay for some public improvements out of current revenues. *Evils of inflexible debt limits.*

But the most serious objection to the practice of fixing the debt limit in terms of property valuation is the fact that city authorities can increase the borrowing power by jacking up the assessments. This subterfuge keeps within the letter of the law but violates its intent. Unfortunately, moreover, this horizontal boosting of assessed valuations produces no general resentment on the part of property owners if the tax rate is reduced proportionately. In other words, if assessments throughout the city are raised ten per cent and the tax rate lowered ten per cent, the tax bills stand unchanged and the taxpayer has no cause to complain. But this juggling of figures will enable the city authorities to get more borrowing power, which is what some of them are always looking for. In some cities the assessed valuations have been pushed well above the actual values of property so that the municipal indebtedness, while standing at only five per cent of the total assessment, is much above that figure in terms of current market values. *Evading the debt limit by raising the assessments.*

Another weakness in the fixed debt limit plan may be found in the fact that it permits the municipal authorities to borrow freely until the limit is reached; then they must either find a method of evading it or stop borrowing altogether. What cities often do, when they find it no longer possible to move the assessed valuations any higher, is to plead with the state legislature for special favors. They petition for special laws which will permit them to *Borrowing outside the debt limit.*

borrow outside the debt limit for some assertedly urgent purpose. The need being obvious, it is hard for the legislature to refuse. Moreover the city usually mobilizes its own state senators and assemblymen to logroll the proposition through. Then this action becomes a precedent for some other city to use. In several eastern commonwealths these petitions for borrowing beyond the debt limit come before the state legislature in considerable profusion at every legislative session. Occasionally the matter has been taken out of the legislature's hands by embalming the debt limit in the state constitution, but this arrangement makes it virtually impossible to give a city additional borrowing powers in an emergency. It is too rigid.

Legislative versus administrative control of municipal borrowing.

The American plan of limiting municipal indebtedness is different from that pursued in the various countries of Europe. Across the Atlantic the practice has been to place no fixed limit upon what a municipality may borrow. In England, for example, every proposal to incur municipal indebtedness must be approved by the national authorities before it can go forward. With such approval, which is given or refused in each instance on its merits, a city can borrow and keep on borrowing; without such approval it cannot borrow a single shilling. In other words the American practice is to place a constitutional or legislative limit on municipal borrowing; while the European practice is to make the limit a matter of administrative discretion. The latter, of course, is a much more sensible and flexible arrangement. One may express the hope that some plan of administrative control over municipal borrowing may ultimately be worked out in the United States.

The Indiana-Iowa plan.

A beginning has been made in Indiana and Iowa where the laws provide that any proposed municipal bond issue must be submitted for approval to the state board of tax commissioners if objection is raised by any ten taxpayers in the municipality. After a hearing on the protest of the taxpayers the board may approve the bond issue or may withhold its approval.[1]

Municipal bonds:

1. Their forms.

What is a municipal bond? It is a promise, made by the municipality on its faith and credit, to pay a designated sum on a certain date with a stipulated rate of interest meanwhile. Municipal bonds may be issued either in registered or coupon form. A registered bond is recorded on the books of the city treasurer in the

---

[1] See the discussion in Schuyler C. Wallace, *State Administrative Supervision over Cities in the United States* (New York, 1928), especially p. 100.

MUNICIPAL DEBTS

name of its owner, and the interest is sent to him by check twice a year without any action on his part. A registered bond is transferable from one owner to another by written endorsement, and this endorsement must be registered on the city treasurer's books. A coupon bond, on the other hand, is payable to bearer. It is transferable by mere delivery, over the counter; hence the name of the owner is not recorded in the office of the city treasurer, and interest is obtained by periodically clipping the coupons which are attached to the bond. As a rule the purchaser of a coupon bond can have it converted into a registered bond on application to the proper authorities. Registered bonds are safer against loss by theft or fire, hence investors often prefer them. Coupon bonds are more readily negotiable, which is the reason why banks and brokers usually choose this type.

Municipal bonds run for varying terms, all the way from one year to fifty years. The term is prescribed by the city council or other borrowing authority, but its discretion in this matter is limited by the city charter or the state laws which usually require that the maximum term of a bond shall be related to the purpose for which the indebtedness is incurred. For example, bonds issued to fund the floating debt are customarily restricted to a term of three years or less; while bonds for the purchase of departmental equipment (such as fire engines) are ordinarily limited to five years. Street paving bonds generally have a ten-to-fifteen-year term; while bonds issued for the construction of public buildings are permitted to run from twenty to forty years. Bonds running for a longer term than this are not common, although some cities are permitted to give them a longevity of fifty years or even more in the case of bonds issued for the purchase of park land, water power sites, and similar property which inures to the city's benefit forever. *2. Their terms.*

The principle involved is this: that the term of the bonds should in no case exceed the estimated life of the equipment or the improvement for which the debt has been incurred. If a particular type of street paving has a reasonable life-expectation of ten years, then the paving bonds should be dated to mature within this period. Otherwise a new pavement may have to be put down before the old one is all paid for. That is what has happened in many cities through undue optimism concerning the probable life of a public improvement. It is highly important that such estimates be made conservatively. *The principle involved.*

176 MUNICIPAL ADMINISTRATION

Procedure in municipal bond issues. What is the procedure when a city desires to borrow money by issuing bonds? The first step is taken by the city council, usually on the recommendation of the mayor or the city manager. The council passes a loan order or resolution which authorizes the loan. Sometimes a two-thirds vote of the council is required to pass such resolutions. This order or resolution sets forth the purpose of the borrowing, the term for which the bonds are to run, the rate of interest, the place where the interest shall be payable (usually the city treasurer's office), and the provisions which are to be made for liquidating the bonds as they mature. If a ratifying vote of the people is necessary under the provisions of the city charter or the state laws, the question of authorizing the bond issue is placed on the ballot at a special or regular election. Meanwhile a detailed statement of the proposal is published for the information of the voters. In some states a three-fifths or a two-thirds vote at the polls is necessary to validate a proposed municipal bond issue.

Selling the bonds. If these various requirements are fulfilled the bonds are then put up for sale. The laws usually provide that they must be sold publicly and likewise require that this public sale shall be preceded by advertising for a stated period. The practice is to advertise for bids, to be opened at a given time and place in the presence of the appropriate municipal authorities. Unless there are strong reasons to the contrary, the bonds are sold to the highest bidder. Bids come from bond brokers and investment bankers. They are usually submitted in the form of an offer to take the entire issue at a certain premium on the face value of the bonds. For example, a brokerage concern or a bank may offer to take a million dollar issue of four and one-half per cent bonds at 102,—in other words it offers a premium of $20,000 for the issue. This method of receiving and accepting bids is not altogether satisfactory because it gives the city more money than it has been authorized to borrow. A better method is to ask for the bid in terms of the amount of bonds required to produce a certain sum,—for example, what amount of bonds will the bidder require in order to furnish the city with a million dollars? The bidder in the preceding illustration would answer $980,400. The advantage of this plan is that the city gets the exact amount of money which it has been authorized to borrow.

The final steps. At any rate, when the highest bid has been figured out and accepted, the bonds are printed under the supervision of the city

MUNICIPAL DEBTS

treasurer; they are then signed by him and turned over to the successful bidder in return for his check. Before this last step is taken, however, a legal opinion to the effect that the bonds are in all respects a valid obligation is obtained from some firm of lawyers who specialize in this line of work. If the city is borrowing for an enterprise which will take a year or two for completion, it does not usually sell the entire issue of bonds at a single stroke, thus having a large unused sum of money on hand before it is needed. It may borrow on short-term notes from a bank and sell the bonds to liquidate these temporary loans when the work is finished, or it may sell the whole issue of bonds in several installments. As a third alternative it may sell the whole issue to one bidder but require him to take and pay for them in designated installments over a stated period.

Sometimes the limitations which the laws place upon the sale of municipal bonds prove too rigid and tie the city's hands unreasonably. For example it is often stipulated that bonds shall be issued at a certain rate of interest and shall not be sold below their par value. This provision is all right when money is plentiful and interest rates are low, but in an era of tight money it may mean that cities are unable to borrow at all. Under ordinary circumstances good municipal bonds are popular with banks, bond houses, and private investors. Such cities as Philadelphia, Baltimore, St. Louis, and San Francisco can usually sell at a premium bonds bearing four and one-half per cent or four per cent interest. During the World War period, however, interest rates on municipal bonds went above five per cent and even at this rate cities found it difficult to sell them at par. Banks and bond houses sometimes buy municipal bonds as a permanent investment, but more often they take large blocks for resale to their own customers. Municipal bonds are usually issued in denominations of $500 or $1,000. From time to time it has been suggested that denominations of $50 or $100 should also be used, as in the case of some national government bond issues; but this proposal has not found general favor. *Fixing the maximum rate of interest.*

When a city issues bonds it may provide for their ultimate liquidation in either one of two ways. The earlier method was to provide for the creation of a sinking fund into which the city treasurer would be instructed to pay a certain amount every year. These annual payments into the sinking fund, together with the accretion of interest, would suffice to retire the whole issue at its *Paying off municipal debts: The sinking fund and serial bond plans.*

date of maturity. The other plan, now more commonly used, is to issue the bonds in a series, making one or more of them mature in each successive year of the loan period. One may illustrate the difference as follows: A city desiring to borrow a million dollars for a twenty-year period in 1933 might make all of these bonds mature in 1953, meanwhile accumulating a million dollars for their repayment at that date by means of the sinking fund process; or it might make $50,000 of the bonds payable each year during the twenty-year interval, thus avoiding the need of a sinking fund altogether. In the latter case the city must raise enough money in its annual tax revenue to pay off the bonds which mature year by year.

Advantages of the serial plan. Under ideal conditions there is no reason why either of these methods should be better than the other; but there are various practical difficulties connected with the sinking fund plan which the serial arrangement does not encounter. For example, the sinking fund plan involves the special custody and safe investment of the funds which are accumulated each year. For this purpose most cities have boards of trustees known as sinking fund commissioners who are supposed to keep the money earning interest all the time. On the whole these trustees have handled sinking funds wisely, but there is always a danger that any group of men, however competent, will make unwise investments and lose some of the money that is entrusted to their care.

The political manipulation of sinking funds. Nor is this the only danger. Sometimes men who represent various banking interests have manoeuvered to get themselves or their friends appointed to the sinking fund commission in order that public funds may be kept on deposit in their own banks or trust companies. Then, if such institutions become insolvent, the funds are short when the time comes to pay off the bonds. Again, when a city finds trouble in selling newly issued bonds on the open market its officials have sometimes put pressure on the sinking fund trustees to buy these bonds with money on hand, hoping that they can be unloaded upon the investment market later on. Such hopes are not always realized.

Using the sinking funds for current expenses. A more common and even more objectionable practice is that of lending money out of the sinking funds for current municipal expenses on the promise of the city officials that such temporary loans will be repaid with interest when the taxes come in. Then the city finds itself with a deficit and the temporary loan is extended until it becomes virtually a permanent one. A kindred practice, equally objectionable, is that of omitting the stipulated payment into the sinking fund whenever the city treasury gets into a tight place. Assurance is always given that the deficiency caused by such omissions will be made up later, when times are better; but experience demonstrates that such promises are not always to be depended upon. Miscalculations, moreover, are frequently made in estimating what the sinking funds will earn. Then at the maturity of the bonds the trustees have more money than is needed to pay them off, or they have less money,—usually the latter. In a word, the sinking fund plan involves the piling up of large sums under conditions which afford a temptation to use some of it injudiciously.

The serial plan does away with all these difficulties and mishaps. No trustees, no accumulations, and no reinvestments are necessary; there are no financial favors to be bestowed upon "pet banks"; the city cannot omit its contribution for any year, nor can it use the cash, even temporarily, for any purpose other than debt-repayment. A serial bond issue, as its name implies, falls due in installments and payment of these installments must be made on time. The serial plan also lends itself to flexibility in the distribution of the tax burden by enabling the peak of the load to be placed in the early, middle, or later years of the loan, as may be desired. In the case of some public improvements (such as street pavements, bridges, or public buildings) the maximum usefulness comes in the earlier years. The service rendered to the community by an improvement of this kind gradually diminishes as the years go by. Accordingly the heaviest burden connected with the cost of such improvements should be borne by the taxpayers in the years immediately following the construction, and the load should gradually diminish year after year thereafter.

Flexibility of the serial plan.

But there are other improvements, such as parks and recreation grounds, where the maximum value to the community is not usually reached for ten years or more, that is, until the trees have grown up and the recreation spaces have become used to their full capacity. In such cases the process of repaying the cost should not be expedited at the outset, but should be so arranged that the peak of the load will have to be borne by the taxpayers some years in the future. This is particularly true of money which is borrowed for the purchase of land. This flexibility is made practicable by arranging that more of the serial bonds shall fall due in the earlier or later portions of the loan period as the case may be.

But this flexibility may be abused. But some dangers lurk in this discretion. Municipal authorities are under temptation to issue the bonds in such way that the initial installments will not begin to be payable for several years. This is known as the "deferred serial plan" and can hardly ever be justified. State laws and city charters frequently prohibit it altogether. The amortization of every bond issue should be so arranged as to place an equitable amount of the burden on the taxpayers of each year throughout the entire loan-period. If there is any doubt as to the equities it is good policy to make all the installments equal. Under that arrangement the burden automatically lessens each year through the decreasing interest charges upon the amount of bonds outstanding.

Relative cost of the two systems. As between the relative cost of the sinking fund and serial plans there is no appreciable difference provided the conditions are identical in both cases. If one makes the same assumptions as to rates of interest paid and earned, the aggregate cost of a municipal loan will be the same under either plan. This assumes, however, that money will be paid into the sinking fund promptly, and invested immediately, at a rate of interest equal to that which is paid on the bonds outstanding. It also assumes that there will be no poor investments and no losses. Such assumptions, when made in connection with the average city government, take far too much for granted. The sinking fund plan gives too many hostages to fortune and it is now being abandoned by most cities.

How municipal debts have grown. Viewing the situation as a whole, the net indebtedness of American cities has been increasing too rapidly. Taking all the municipalities with populations exceeding 30,000, and reckoning not only the debts of the cities proper but of overlapping incorporated areas, the total was about two and one-half billion dollars in 1920. During the next ten years, that is, between 1920 and 1930, this figure rose to over four billion dollars. The national government of the United States during these ten years reduced its indebtedness from twenty-six to sixteen billion by careful financial planning and the exercise of rigid economy. But neither the states nor the municipalities followed the national government's example during this decade; on the contrary they increased their borrowings for all sorts of public enterprises and when the depression arrived in 1930 many of the cities found their credit so seriously impaired that they were unable to secure further loans except by borrowing from the national government.

Four or five causes account for this tendency to over-borrow on the part of American municipalities. In the first place it has been partly due to the lack of effective state regulation. The practice of fixing rigid debt limits by state constitutions or state laws has not encouraged careful financial planning but has rather discouraged it. City authorities have been tempted to borrow freely until the debt limit has been reached; then they have found themselves prevented from borrowing at all. In this exigency they have naturally sought ways of evading the debt limit or they have manoeuvered to obtain special exemption from it. The traditional American method of restricting municipal indebtedness by general laws has everywhere been a failure, partial or complete. Far better is the European plan of administrative supervision over municipal borrowing. In every state of the Union there should be a board of control to which all proposals for municipal borrowing would go. Without the approval of this central authority no loans should be authorized.

Reasons for this rapid increase:

1. The ineffectiveness of debt limits.

A second and widespread cause of excessive municipal indebtedness has been the custom of borrowing money for recurrent expenses, that is, expenses which do not have to be met every year, but which do recur every few years. The cost of fire-fighting apparatus, motor trucks in the street department, and playground equipment are examples of such expenses. Even police and fire stations might be put in the same category. Many large cities find that they must build a new police precinct station or new fire house every two or three years. Usually they raise the money by means of bond issues instead of taking it out of current revenues. But this way of doing it merely postpones the day of reckoning, with interest added on. And presently the city finds itself raising more taxes to pay interest and maturing bonds than would be required to finance the new construction.

2. Borrowing for recurrent expenses.

Our heavy municipal indebtedness is also due in part to loose methods of accounting which serve to conceal the true situation from the public eye. Whenever a new proposal to borrow money is brought forward, the people of the city are fed with propaganda in the form of catch-word statistics showing that the annual cost of the new loan will be almost negligible, only a few cents per thousand dollars of valuation. They are always assured, moreover, that the city's debt is exceedingly small when compared with the

3. Loose accounting methods.

indebtedness of other communities. Anyone can prepare a tabulation of this sort, in any city at any time, if he is sufficiently adept in the art of juggling figures. Most voters do not realize that the city debt is much concern of theirs anyhow. A proposal to build a new city hall and pay for it by a forty-year bond issue does not look like a cause for real worry on the part of this year's taxpayer or next's.

4. Popular delusions as to the debt burden.

In many of the states there is a belief that an adequate check on excessive municipal borrowing can be provided by requiring that no bonds shall be issued until after the voters have approved the issue at a bond election. This, however, has not proved to be a dependable restraint. Thousands of voters are always ready to vote for every bond issue in the belief that it will put money into circulation, give employment, and help business generally. When you ask a voter whether he wants the city to undertake some public improvement for his own benefit, and let his grandchildren pay for it, there is not much doubt what his answer will be. Not one property owner in a hundred realizes that every dollar of the city's indebtedness is a mortgage on his shop or home, and that it sometimes constitutes a pretty heavy mortgage.

5. The bond issue ballyhoo.

Finally, our cities have been too optimistic. They have listened to the high-pressure salesmanship of real estate promoters about the impending growth of population and the inevitable inflation in property values. Too often, unhappily, the chamber of commerce and the service clubs have joined in this civic ballyhoo. Over and over again such organizations have combined in campaigns to build an elaborate civic center or to widen some main thoroughfare at a far higher cost than the city could properly afford. Under the pressure of this realtor enthusiasm many cities have discounted the future too heavily. The country runs into a depression and the expected inflation in values does not materialize, but the debts are there to be liquidated out of decreased revenues. Some American cities have now reached the point where as much as a third of their annual revenue goes to pay interest on bonds and the repayment of serial issues.

Pay-as-you-go proposals.

Having regard to this heavy burden and to the desirability of preventing a further increase in it, the advocates of the pay-as-you-go plan have been renewing their advocacy of that arrangement. They urge that virtually all public improvements be financed out of current taxes. They would include the construction of

MUNICIPAL DEBTS

schoolhouses, police stations, and fire houses, as well as the paving of streets and the establishment of new parks. Those who argue in favor of the pay-as-you-go plan lay stress on the fact that every public improvement must ultimately be paid for by the taxpayers. The average voter does not realize how heavy this exaction is. When he authorizes borrowing for a new schoolhouse, let us say, at a cost of $100,000 and spreads the bonds over a period of thirty years, it does not occur to him that this schoolhouse is going to cost more than $200,000 before he is through with it. To say that the city owns its city hall, schoolhouses, police stations, and playgrounds is in many cases to speak after the manner of an individual who "owns his home" subject to a mortgage for more than it is worth. What most cities really do is to pay rent for such buildings, an annual rental in the form of interest and serial repayments which extends throughout the entire life of the structures.

Of course the pay-as-you-go plan is not popular with the individual citizen. He makes his own purchases on the installment plan. Perhaps he has an automobile, a radio, a vacuum cleaner, or even a suit of clothes that are being paid for in this way. He sees no good reason why the city should not follow the plan of "pay while you use." And in any event the transition from the borrowing system to the pay-as-you-go plan inevitably means a radical increase in the tax rate at the time when the shift is made. No city administration likes to take the responsibility for such action. *Unpopularity of the idea.*

Is it possible for a city to default on its debts and go bankrupt? Of course it is possible, although some milder term is customarily used when a city becomes insolvent. It is said to be in financial difficulties and to have "deferred the payment of its obligations." On a good many occasions a city has found itself in this situation. City officials and employees have had to go for a time without their pay checks and holders of municipal bonds have had their coupons sent back with the notation "no funds." But cities cannot stay insolvent. Taxes must be increased to provide for the servicing of the debt. If this does not suffice, a petition for assistance goes before the state legislature with a request for the loan of state funds. Even the national government may be importuned to extend financial aid. As a last resort the state may place the city in a virtual receivership by placing an appointive commission in charge of its financial affairs as has been done in some cases during recent years. *Municipal defaults and bankruptcy.*

REFERENCES

Chapters on municipal indebtedness are included in A. E. Buck, *Municipal Finance* (New York, 1926), pp. 470-509, and in L. D. Upson, *Practice of Municipal Administration* (New York, 1926), pp. 105-125. A more general discussion of public credit and its use may be found in H. L. Lutz, *Public Finance* (2nd edition, New York, 1929), and in the other books on public finance listed at the close of Chapter XI. Mention should also be made of Lane Lancaster, *State Supervision of Municipal Indebtedness* (Middletown, Conn., 1923), Ward L. Bishop, *An Economic Analysis of the Constitutional Restrictions upon Municipal Indebtedness in Illinois* (Urbana, 1928), Paul Studensky, *Public Borrowing* (New York, 1930), Schuyler C. Wallace, *State Administrative Supervision over Cities in the United States* (New York, 1928), Fraser Brown, *Municipal Bonds* (New York, 1922), W. L. Raymond, *State and Municipal Bonds* (2nd edition, Boston, 1932), Lawrence Chamberlain and G. W. Edwards, *The Principles of Bond Investment* (revised and enlarged edition, New York, 1927), and J. G. Fowlkes, *School Bonds* (Milwaukee, 1924).

The Financial Statistics of Cities . . . *over 30,000* issued by the United States Bureau of the Census contains data on municipal debts. An informing study of *Municipal Debt Defaults: Their Prevention and Adjustment* was published in 1933 by the Public Administration Service (850 East 58th St., Chicago). A tabulation of comparative city indebtedness is printed annually in the *National Municipal Review*. *A Model Municipal Bond Law*, prepared by a committee of the National Municipal League (309 East 34th St., New York), was published by that organization in 1927.

CHAPTER XV

AUDITS, ACCOUNTING, STATISTICS, AND REPORTS

The waste, extravagance and misappropriation of funds in our cities have been largely due to the fact that the financial administration has not been sufficiently concentrated.—Charles A. Beard.

In private business concerns it is customary to have the books audited periodically, at least once a year. This is done to provide a safeguard against defalcations as well as to obtain from an independent source a statement of financial conditions. But an audit also furnishes a means of determining the exact amount of profit or loss which has been realized on the year's operations. Now a modern city is in effect a large business concern, operating vast properties, carrying on extensive operations, employing a numerous force of workers, raising money, spending it, borrowing it—all of this professedly done in an efficient and economical way. One might suppose that great care would be exercised in protecting the city's business operations against financial malfeasance, leakage, diversion of funds, and other such mishaps—as much care, in any event, as is taken by private business corporations for the protection of their stockholders. Such, however, has not always been the case. In the matter of auditing many American cities are still in the primitive stage. This is possibly because the spending officials are usually the ones who prescribe the type of audit service.

<small>The auditing of municipal accounts.</small>

Small cities have no municipal auditors or comptrollers. Books of account are kept by the city treasurer and city clerk, but as a rule these books cover only the cash receipts and expenditures. Once a year a firm of outside auditors or accountants is hired to go over them. This firm makes a report certifying that all receipts have been properly accounted for, and that the expenditures appear to have been properly authorized. Such audits are not often thorough or wide enough in scope; they do not check transactions back to their source. Indeed, the whole procedure in many cases amounts to little more than checking book-entries against the vouchers and adding up the columns of figures. No attempt is usually made to list the unpaid bills, nor is there any inventorying

<small>Checking receipts and expenditures.</small>

of city equipment, materials, and supplies to make sure that all of it is actually on hand. An audit of cash transactions is useful so far as it goes, but something more than this is needed to afford full protection.

Why this alone is not enough.

Such a restricted audit may show, for example, that all the cash coming into the municipal treasury has been accounted for, but this leaves open the question whether the city has received all the cash that was coming to it. Licenses, for example, or rentals from city-owned property may have been left uncollected, or may have been collected by officials who did not turn in the money. Equipment may have been bought and paid for, but never received. Surplus materials may have been sold and the proceeds pocketed. Merely checking up vouchers and cash items affords no adequate protection against such malfeasance. Shortages, defalcations, and divers other varieties of crookedness have been so common in smaller municipalities because of restricted audits that the state authorities are now in many cases insisting upon a more thorough examination of their books and more rigid supervision of their accounting methods.

State control of local audits.

During recent years a varying degree of control over the auditing of accounts in smaller municipalities has been established in a number of states, notably in Ohio, Indiana, Iowa, New York, and Massachusetts. In Indiana the audit is ordered whenever a designated number of municipal taxpayers petition for it; in New York it is made whenever the state authorities decide. In Ohio the requirement is that an examination of all local government accounts shall be made at stated intervals by the state auditor's office, the expense being borne in each case by the municipality concerned. State control of auditing has not yet been applied to the larger cities nor does it seem to be necessary in their case, because most of these larger cities have made provision for a continuing audit, in other words for a day-by-day check-up of transactions throughout the year. This work is done in the office of the comptroller or city auditor.

Inside and outside audits.

In addition to the continuing audit some of these cities provide for periodic audits by outside accountants. This represents to some extent a duplication of effort, but it provides an extra safeguard. It is a way of making sure that the city's own financial and auditing officers are not in collusion. Yet notwithstanding all such checks and double-checks the opportunities for peculation seem to continue. Defalcations of city treasurers still figure in the headlines all too frequently. It is difficult to close every loophole because of the mass of detail which is costly to check. When one is barred, another opens. Public accounts can be juggled with an ingenuity which seems to defy the sleuthing of auditors, no matter how proficient they may be. There is no substitute for personal integrity in city treasurers.

What are the functions of a city auditor? It is his duty to examine every bill which has been presented to the city for payment, to determine whether it comes within the scope of a properly authorized appropriation, whether the goods or services have actually been received, whether all revenues have been properly accounted for, and whether the balance on the city treasurer's books is accurate. In a word it is the auditor's business to trace every transaction through the books from start to finish. An outside auditor, when called in to do this once a year, finds himself confronted with a long job. Sometimes it takes him several weeks or even months to get it done. Consequently his findings are greatly delayed and the city's annual report is not published until long after the fiscal year has closed. *The city auditor: His functions.*

In the case of large cities the practice of maintaining a regular auditing department has been found more satisfactory. One advantage is that a continuing inside audit permits all questionable bills to be stalled before payment is made. When bills against the city come in, they are first sent for approval to the head of the department which has incurred the obligation. Then they go to the office of the city auditor or comptroller; who makes sure of three things: first, that the expenditure comes within the authority of the department; second, that there is an appropriation available from which to pay the bill; and third, that the payment would be a legal one. If he is in any doubt on the score of legality he consults the city's law department. When the auditor is satisfied on all three counts, he approves the bill and a warrant for payment is issued to the city treasurer. The treasurer then issues his check on one of the banks in which the city keeps its funds. A city treasurer assumes no responsibility with respect to these payments other than to see that they are made on properly certified warrants. *The procedure in auditing.*

From the nature of the city auditor's duties it is essential that he be given a position of independence, free from control by those who might have an interest in forcing his hands. For that reason *Should the auditor be an elective official?*

the city charter sometimes provides that the auditor shall be elected by popular vote. Popular election gives him a position of independence, but too often it results in the choice of an auditor who is altogether unqualified to do the work. Many large shortages in city accounts have been permitted by slovenly auditing at the hands of elective officials. The post demands not only independence but skill and integrity. Neither of these qualities is guaranteed by the process of popular election.

Or by whom should he be appointed?

On the other hand, if the auditor is appointed by the mayor or by the city manager, and if he is subject to dismissal by these higher officials at any time, he must inevitably be under temptation to approve payments which he would not certify if he were free to use his own judgment. To meet this objection it is sometimes provided that the auditor shall be chosen by the city council. In practice, however, this plan has not proved satisfactory. The councilmen are disposed to treat the position, like all others on the public payroll, as a form of patronage to bestow upon some politically influential friend, irrespective of his special qualifications. It has been urged that city auditors ought to be appointed under civil service rules, by open competition on a merit basis; but public opinion has not yet been educated to the point where it is ready to approve this step. On the whole it would seem best to have the auditor appointed by the mayor or other executive head of the city, but with a provision that he may not be removed from office except by a two-thirds vote of the city council. Such a system permits the appointment of a qualified man and yet gives reasonable protection to his independence.

Accounting

Municipal accounting:
1. Its scope and purpose.

Municipal accounting involves a good deal more than mere auditing. Accounting is the science which undertakes to gather and explain the data of business. It is an elaborate bookkeeping procedure devised for the purpose of obtaining prompt and accurate information concerning revenues, expenditures, indebtedness, assets and liabilities, profit and loss. This information is for the use of those who determine business policy and are in charge of the executive operations. It is utilized by them as a basis for the exercise of judgment. Hence the purpose of a municipal accounting system is to inform the city council, the administrative staff, and the public to such an extent concerning the financial operations of

AUDITS, ACCOUNTING, STATISTICS, REPORTS

the municipality that they will be able to form intelligent opinions and reach wise conclusions.

No large business tries to get along without a system of accounts. If it did it would pass into bankruptcy. Some cities, however, attempt to do it, at any rate they endeavor to get along without a system of accounting which achieves the ends described in the preceding paragraph. All cities keep a record of their revenues and expenditures, to be sure, but in many small cities these transactions are never reduced to statements of final account which reflect administrative results in any intelligible way. The result is that both the city officials and the public remain in the dark. *2. Its inadequacy in many small cities.*

With the enormous growth in scope and complexity of the city's business activities during the past thirty years, however, the system of municipal accounting has been steadily improved and extended. Today, in all the larger cities it is closely modelled upon the general plan of accounting which is used in large business corporations but with such additional agencies of control as are made essential by the special nature of municipal business. In private business the purpose of an accounting system is to tell the operating executives what they need to know in order to be wise executives. In public business the objective ought to be exactly the same. A satisfactory accounting system should enable the city authorities to visualize clearly the results of all municipal activities so far as their financial implications are concerned. It should simplify the problem of making up their minds, hence the quick usefulness of the data is all-important. *3. Its steady improvement in the larger ones.*

Auditing and accounting are so closely related that both functions are usually consolidated under the supervision of a single officer. He is frequently given the title of city comptroller. It is a measure of economy to combine the two kinds of work in the same office, but the double duty carries a dual responsibility. As auditor the official should have a position which makes him independent of those who spend the money. On the other hand, as the city's chief accounting officer he should have a close relation to the various spending departments. This close relation is made desirable by the fact that the comptroller is the one who translates the detailed financial operations of the departments into intelligible generalizations. The problem is to give him a position which will make independence possible, but not isolation. Unusual qualities of firmness and tact are required in the occupant of such an office. *The functions of auditor and comptroller distinguished.*

Cash accounting.

Every city, of course, keeps a record of cash received and cash expended, but some of the smaller municipalities do little more than this. One New England town, some years ago, had a treasurer who kept his official accounts in a vest pocket notebook tied with a piece of string. In this book he set down with a lead pencil a record of whatever money came in and went out. The annual audit consisted of totalling up his figures to make sure that he had added them correctly. This is an extreme case, no doubt, but there are numerous small communities in which the official bookkeeping is of the most fragmentary sort. In others the records are more elaborate but sometimes they are about as orderly as a squirrel's nest. In any event a mere record of cash transactions is of little or no value in helping a city council to determine policy or in assisting the administrative officers to test the results of their work. As a matter of fact such a record is likely to be misleading. It may show a surplus when none really exists, for revenues which belong to one fiscal year may be credited to another when they happen to come in a little early or a little late. It is not difficult to show a surplus on the cash books by deferring the payment of current bills until after the accounts have been closed for the fiscal year.

Accounting on an accrual basis.

A proper accounting system should, therefore, take cognizance of all revenue which is due but not yet paid in; also of liabilities which the city has incurred but not yet liquidated. Accrued income should be credited to its proper fiscal year whether it is actually collected within that period or not. Municipal accounts should show, for example, not only the amount of taxes due and collected in a given year but also the amount due and uncollected. They should likewise disclose the amount of uncollected license fees, rentals from city-owned property, and other payments which will be received in due course but do not figure in the current cash balancing. Incidentally such figures enable one to form judgment concerning the efficiency of the city's collection department.

Its value in enabling departments to keep within their appropriations.

So with liabilities incurred but not yet paid off. They should be charged against the revenues of the year in which the expenditures were authorized and not pushed over into the next. A proper accounting system makes record of all liabilities as soon as they are incurred and debits the departmental appropriations at that time. Under such an arrangement no contracts can be awarded and no orders given for supplies or materials until after the approval of the chief accounting officer has been obtained. This

AUDITS, ACCOUNTING, STATISTICS, REPORTS

ensures that any balance in the department's appropriation at the end of the fiscal year will be a real one. It also enables the head of each department to ascertain, at any time, how much money he still has to spend. Department heads, for the most part, want to keep within their appropriations, and the city's accounting system should be set up so as to help them do it.

Most cities own a great deal of property including land, public buildings, repair shops, storage yards, equipment, supplies, materials, and so on. A proper accounting system provides for the accurate listing of all this property. Everything sold or discarded is stricken off the list and everything acquired by the city is put on it, thus giving a perpetual inventory under central control. This should be checked by taking a hand inventory, that is, by comparing the list with the property, item by item, once a year or oftener. A good deal of minor corruption has resulted from the failure of cities to maintain such a control system. City employees have been found giving away or selling off old equipment on their own responsibility with no proper accounting for it. No municipal property of any kind should be sold until after it has been appraised by a representative of the accounting office. Finally, the accounts should make a clear distinction between expenditures for the upkeep and maintenance of city existing property and those for new purchases. The former outlays should come out of current revenues. The latter, in some cases, may properly be paid from the proceeds of bond issues—for example, a new pumping plant or a fireboat or a garbage incinerator. Too often, unfortunately, a defective accounting system has permitted the payment of current expenses out of borrowed funds.

<small>Inventory accounting.</small>

Then there is the matter of funded obligations. It is self-evident that the accounting office ought to have a complete and accurate record of all bond issues, all payments of interest on these bonds, all maturities, and all monies in the sinking fund to liquidate these bonds on maturity. It should be possible to find out, on any date, the actual gross debt of the municipality, the net debt, and the amount which the city still has power to borrow within its constitutional or statutory debt-limit. Periodic statements should reflect, to the city authorities and to the public, the true condition of affairs in this domain of municipal finance.

<small>Debt accounting.</small>

The accounting system should also make provision for the checking of all payroll payments. It should ensure the city against any-

<small>Payroll accounting.</small>

one drawing pay at higher than the authorized rate or for work that has not actually been performed. Payroll padding has been one of the traditional forms of petty grafting in American cities. Time and again municipal investigations have shown that political idlers, dead men, and persons who never existed at all were regularly drawing pay—at any rate somebody was drawing pay for them. In the case of day labor the foreman who has charge of the job usually makes up the rolls and certifies them under oath. But he can put his friends on the list, even those who have never turned a hand, unless it is somebody's task to check him by an actual count at unexpected times. Nor is it sufficient to take a foreman's certificate that so many men have been at work even though the number be accurate. How much work have these men accomplished? The answer to this question involves the use of job records which show the number of cubic feet excavated per man per day, or the square yardage of street surface repaired, or the number of water meters daily inspected per employee, or whatever it may be. A payroll clerk in the accounting office, by comparing these records, can usually determine whether the city is getting value for its wage outlays.

The test of a good accounting system.
The whole purpose of accounting is to supply knowledge,—and knowledge is power. It is power in the realm of city finance as in every other field of human activity. Without it there can be no consistent making of wise decisions in the complex business of the modern city. Hence the criterion of a good accounting system is not its conformance to the principles of commercial bookkeeping. The true test is whether it does in fact provide with promptness and accuracy the information that the higher city officials need to have in order to judge past results and determine future policy. The problem is one of setting up the accounts in a form that will meet this requirement. How to do it is a highly technical matter which requires the advice of experts in the science of public accounting. The task is made more difficult by the fact that cities, by state laws or by the provisions of their municipal charters, are often directed to set up all sorts of special funds for special purposes, such as pensions, the care of certain parks, or the maintenance of the public library. Other statutory provisions also make it impossible, in some cases, to follow the simple procedure which good accounting would otherwise dictate.

Most of the deficits in city administration result from the overspending of departmental appropriations. Yet it has been said, and it is probably true that nine out of every ten department heads want to keep within their appropriations and make an honest endeavor to do so. The trouble is that honest intent does not of itself guarantee success in this direction. At any rate many department heads fail to achieve it. It is partly because most of them are men of no experience in business planning, and little appreciation of the vigilance that is needed to make accounts come out square at the end of the year. But it is also because some accounting systems make it virtually impossible for department heads to find out just where they stand, month by month. Statements are given to them several weeks overdue. Loose record-keeping causes various items to be overlooked. So guesses occasionally take the place of figures and in the absence of exact information a department head will stretch the laws of probability in his own favor.

Good accounting and the prevention of deficits.

The results, unfortunately, do not often justify his optimism. That is why so many city departments end the year with a deficit and a bumper crop of excuses. Some emergencies, moreover, are likely to arise even in the best-managed departments and too often the reserve set aside for such contingencies proves inadequate. All in all, there is no way of preventing departmental deficits except by the exercise of rigid accounting control. City officials often chafe under this supervision, grumble about it, and call it red tape; but the idea that the average department head can get the best results by doing everything in his own way is one of the myths of municipal administration which post-mortem financial investigations have exploded long ago. He gets the best results when he is held to a strict accountability.

STATISTICS

A system of accounting is not in itself a system of statistics; it merely provides the records and data from which informative statistics may be compiled. In order to inform the city officials and the general public concerning the financial operations of the municipality, it is desirable that accurate statistics, based on the accounting data, should be compiled and made public from time to time. Expenses should be reduced to terms of unit cost,—for example, the cost of cleaning streets per square yard, or of collecting refuse per ton, or of providing water per million gallons. It is

Relation of accounting to statistics.

only by reducing expenditures to such basis that the head of a department can tell whether his work is becoming more efficient. It is only on such a basis that public work can be compared with private work, or work in one city can be compared with work in another. When unit-cost data is at hand, the mayor or the city manager can press for a reduction in the figures, and each successive department head can be set to the task of bettering his predecessor's record. To prepare such data, accurately and without overlooking anything, is not always a simple problem. It involves keeping track of each individual job as respects all payments for supplies and material, for labor involved, equipment used, the exact proportion of overhead expense, and every other item that ought properly be reckoned in. Differences of opinion often arise as to some of these apportionments.

The value of unit-cost statistics. When compiled on a uniform basis these unit-cost statistics perform a most valuable service in providing objective tests of inter-municipal efficiency. A comparison of total expenditures in the same department of any two cities does not tell one anything worth while. There may be good reasons why one city of 200,000 population should spend more for street paving or for water supply than is spent for the same services in another city of the same size; but there is no good reason why it should spend more per square yard for laying a certain type of street pavement, or more per million gallons for chlorinating water, or should use more gasoline per thousand miles in its municipal motor trucks. When such things are reduced to a common denominator in neighboring cities the figures often become enlightening. They call for an explanation of discrepancies. Many savings have been made in civic expenses during recent years by the simple process of asking officials to tell why their unit-costs are so high. The most common answer is that they can be reduced, and will be.

Making them accurately comparable. Great care should always be taken, however, to make sure that these tabulated figures of unit-costs in different cities are truly comparable. Many of the tabulations which are published from time to time by interested parties serve no purpose but to mislead. This is particularly true of the per capita tabloids, which are so popular with rule-of-thumb statisticians. To obtain these figures one merely divides cost by population. Then comes the announcement that fire protection or police or some other municipal service costs so much per capita in one city and a good deal less in another,

AUDITS, ACCOUNTING, STATISTICS, REPORTS 195

the implication being that the former is spending its funds wastefully. This is unfair, because the cost of fire protection in any city depends upon the nature, construction, and use of its buildings rather than upon the number of people included within its boundaries. One community may be largely residential with most of its people living in detached single dwellings and with no serious fire hazards anywhere, while the other may be heavily industrialized, with most of its people living in tenements or frame apartment houses. So with the per capita cost of maintaining the police, or the health service, or street lighting, or the public library. A high per capita cost does not necessarily imply wastefulness. Nor does a low cost per head argue for efficiency. A fair comparison requires something more elaborate than the mental arithmetic of simple division. It necessitates the making of careful allowance for all the factors involved.

The average citizen dislikes statistics. He resents having to read them or to hear them read. And when the figures are crudely presented in dreary columns of digits he can hardly be blamed for this aversion. It is not essential, however, that the presentation of statistics should take the form of long and complicated tabulations. Statistical data can be presented in graphic form, that is, by using the visual devices which every expert statistician knows how to employ. This enables the information to be set forth in compact and vivid fashion so that any citizen can readily grasp its significance. *The art of making statistics interesting.*

Municipal income and expenditures for different years, or by the various departments, can be made quickly comparable by the use of bar charts; while the financial operations month by month lend themselves to graphic illustration by means of the so-called curve chart. This latter device is also useful in portraying comparisons of unit-costs. For operations covering a long period of time it is customary to use line charts with a logarithmic scale. This gives a ratio chart with vertical intervals representing ratios of increase. Diagrams portraying differences in area or in volume are also helpful devices for setting forth statistical information. The cost of government in one city, for example, can be compared with that of another city by circles or squares of proportionate area or by cubes of relative dimension. Circle charts, with sectors representing the relative expenditures of the various departments, are frequently used in municipal publications. They are *Illustrative graphs and charts.*

easy to understand and within certain limits serve a useful purpose.[1]

REPORTS

The city's annual report. At the close of each fiscal year, or more commonly after a delay of some months following that date, every city issues an annual report. In the larger municipalities the common practice is to issue a series of reports, one for each administrative department. Then these are consolidated into a single large volume. How elaborate these reports may become in a large city may be judged from the fact that the annual report of the police department in New York City for 1929 by Commissioner Grover Whalen made a volume of 337 pages. Printed on book paper with vermilion binding it weighed three and a half pounds. If every department in New York City had been as prolific in printed matter as this one, the complete résumé of administrative activities in the metropolis would have run to more than 5,000 pages, thus rivalling the city directory in its bulk.

Departmental reports. The annual reports of the various departments are submitted to the mayor or the city manager, who is supposed to read and study them, which of course he rarely does except in a perfunctory way. Most of what the reports contain is already known to him in a general way and he is usually not interested in bygone details. Since there are all varieties of department heads, so there are great variations in the quality of their reports. Some go to great pains in preparing the statements, while others look upon the work as a tedious chore and turn it over to a subordinate. Some departmental reports turn out to be interesting human documents, while others are nothing more than a transcript of figures culled from the comptroller's records. In some cities the department reports are merely bundled together without revision or editing and sent to the printer with a preface or introductory survey by the mayor or the city manager; in other municipalities they are condensed, arranged into orderly form, provided with graphic illustrations, and issued as an attractive booklet. The best municipal reports are very good, while the worst of them serve no purpose but to provide a printing contract. Instead of encouraging the citizen to take an interest in his government some of these reports provide him with a powerful temptation not to do so.

[1] For illustrations of these various charts see A. E. Buck, *Municipal Finance* (New York, 1926), chap. vii.

AUDITS, ACCOUNTING, STATISTICS, REPORTS

In any event few citizens ever read a municipal report and still fewer ever understand one. This is not surprising, for much that goes into these publications is unintelligible except to persons who are versed in the work of individual departments. Too often they are cluttered with needless details and fail to record the major facts of departmental administration. Only in rare cases does anyone find in these reports any clear-cut statement of what a department has been trying to do, what it has actually done, what the exact cost has turned out to be, and what program the department has in mind for the future. Instead these documents frequently contain long enumerations of salary increases, lists of delinquent taxpayers, tabulations of sinking funds, rosters of licensed undertakers and pawnbrokers, tributes to deceased aldermen, and laudatory paragraphs concerning public officials still in service.

Defects in municipal reports.

Anyone who has occasion to study the departmental reports of a number of cities will be tempted to wonder whether the average department head ever visualizes the audience which he is supposed to be addressing. If a municipal report is not going to be read, it is surely not worth printing. A magazine or a newspaper which showed so little sense of what the public is willing to read would soon find itself in the hands of a receiver. Yet the all-too-frequent aridity of these departmental reports is about what one ought to expect under the circumstances, for the head of a department is not chosen because of his ability as a ghost writer or rewrite man. He possesses no editorial expertness. Rarely is he a man of much imagination and even less often has he any capacity to use his pen in an effective way. Not only that, but the preparation of municipal reports has been regarded as a mere incident, not as an essential operation in the process of government. As documents they have had no definite purpose. No one has been sure whether the reports were intended to inform the mayor, or to impress other city officials, or to provide data for municipal researchers, or to enlighten an unconcerned public, or merely to inflate the city's printing bill.

The need for better publicity work.

Public reporting will not become vital until it is accepted as an integral and important municipal activity, worthy of entrustment to skilled hands. An editorial bureau, through which all the departmental reports were compelled to pass on their way to the printer, would be a real economy in most of the larger cities. It would

A concrete suggestion.

reduce the printer's bill considerably and at the same time make the reports much more appealing to the public. Such a bureau of information, editing, and publicity might profitably be established even in cities of 100,000 population or less. The cost would not be large because a single competent individual could probably do the work. A pound of facts is worth a ton of public indignation. Combine the two and you are likely to get an evil remedied. Nor should one overlook the opportunities which are afforded to city officials in the way of making known their work through public addresses and radio broadcasts. There are thousands of citizens who prefer listening to reading. An annual municipal exhibit showing the work of the various departments, such as is held in some cities, is also a useful agency of public education if it is properly advertised so as to bring large numbers of people to see it.

Newspaper reports on municipal affairs. In addition to the information which the city provides in its official reports, a good deal is given to the citizen by the local newspapers. This, however, is often colored by the newspaper's own attitude towards the existing city administration. In any event the press is mainly interested in the unusual, the picturesque, and the controversial happenings at the city hall, not in the routine business which makes up ninety per cent of the city administration. Some newspapers are interested, most of all, in municipal scandals, in charges and countercharges of malfeasance and corruption. Such things usually get a cross-page headline with the biggest type in the plant. That kind of reporting is apt to give the average citizen a wholly distorted opinion of his city officials, their competence, skill, and honesty. On the other hand there are cities served by newspapers which report to their readers with fidelity, fairness, and illumination most of the things that they ought to know.

Reporting by citizen agencies. Citizen agencies of various kinds also help to inform the people concerning the work of their municipal authorities. Civic leagues, good government associations, and chambers of commerce serve the public in this way through their published bulletins and membership meetings. Bureaus of municipal research now exist in more than thirty cities, and they are contributing effectively to the enlightenment of local public opinion by their studies and publications.

Federal and state reporting. Finally, a great deal of useful reporting is done by agencies of the federal and state governments. These agencies undertake the most difficult of all financial reporting, the presentation of comparative data. Each year the United States Bureau of the Census publishes a volume containing the comparative financial statistics of all American cities having populations of over 30,000. These figures are for the most part collected by the bureau's own agents. They are comprehensive, accurate, and to students of comparative administration they are invaluable. Many of the states, moreover, require that every city shall make uniform reports of its financial operations to some central state authority. In most cases these are tabulated and published. They serve a useful purpose to public officials but the information which they contain does not percolate down into the ranks of the citizenship. Despite all these channels of public information it is to be feared that the average citizen does not know—does not know that it is worth while to know—how his city is being managed. Nor, when all is said and done, would he find it easy to get the information if he set out in quest of it.

REFERENCES

A. E. Buck, *Municipal Finance* (New York, 1926), contains good chapters on general accounting and reporting, cost accounting, and graphic statistics. An informing discussion of municipal accounting may also be found in L. D. Upson, *Practice of Municipal Administration* (New York, 1926).

Other sources of information are Francis Oakey, *Principles of Governmental Accounting and Reporting* (New York, 1921), W. B. Lawrence, *Cost Accounting* (New York, 1925), R. H. Montgomery, *Auditing Theory and Practice* (4th edition, New York, 1927), W. D. Gordon and J. Lockwood, *Modern Accounting Systems* (revised edition, New York, 1926), Lloyd Morey, *Introduction to Governmental Accounting* (New York, 1927), the same author's *Manual of Municipal Accounting* (New York, 1927), Walter R. Darby, *Outline of Uniform System of Accounts for Municipalities* (revised edition, New York, 1927), J. H. McCall, *Municipal Audits and Finance* (London, 1925), S. Whitehead, *Municipal Accounting Systems* (London, 1924), H. R. Hatfield, *Accounting: Its Principles and Problems* (New York, 1927), DeWitt C. Eggleston, *Municipal Accounting* (New York, 1914), and E. F. McDonald, *Municipal Accounting* (Philadelphia, 1924).

The art of statistical presentation is explained in Edmund E. Day, *Statistical Analysis* (New York, 1925), with bibliography, pp. 453–454, Harry Jerome, *Statistical Method* (New York, 1924) and Horace Secrist, *Introduction to Statistical Methods* (New York, 1921).

On the subject of municipal reports there is some excellent material in the booklet by Wylie Kirkpatrick entitled *Reporting Municipal Government*, issued by the Municipal Administration Service in 1928, and in the more extensive study of *Public Reporting*, prepared by the National Committee on Municipal Reporting and published by the same service in 1931. Mention should also be made of H. C. Beyle, *Governmental Reporting in Chicago* (Chicago, 1928).

CHAPTER XVI

PRINCIPLES OF CITY GROWTH

I never learned to tune a harp, or to play upon a lute; but I know how to raise a small and inconsequential city to glory and greatness.—*Themistocles.*

However primitive their life may be, men feel the need of a rendezvous. They desire a haven of common refuge, a shrine for the observance of religious rites, a market-place, a place for coming together. The Etruscan oppidum, the Teutonic burg, the Slavic gerod, the Kaffir kraal, and the Indian pueblo all testify to the social nature of barbaric man. Probably the earliest consideration was protection against an enemy, for warfare is as old as humanity and the problem of defense is as old as war. At any rate, the original location of almost every ancient and mediaeval city was determined by defensive facilities. Athens at the Acropolis, Rome on her Seven Hills, Paris on an island in the Seine, and mediaeval London surrounded by almost impenetrable swamps are conspicuous examples. Other ancient and mediaeval towns grew up at centers of religious observance or around the shrines and monasteries which were built at the graves of early martyrs. These formed places of assemblage the sanctity of which was deemed to afford some protection against wanton attack. Other mediaeval villages developed around the fortresses or castles of feudal lords. As these small communities developed they surrounded themselves with walls within which the people could be huddled with their flocks and herds when danger threatened. But their work lay outside the enclosure and in normal times they did not live within the circumference of the walls.[1] In the pastoral and purely agricultural stages of economic progress this was not possible.

Then in due course came the beginnings of industry and of trade. Merchants and artisans took up their abode within the walls. Moreover trade pushed out along trade routes. These paths of commerce, which lay along the lines of least resistance

The beginnings of cities.

Places of refuge and assembly.

The early industrial town.

---

[1] For an interesting discussion see the chapter on "City Origins" in Henri Pirenne, *Mediaeval Cities* (Princeton, 1925).

between the source of certain products and their place of exchange for other goods, greatly stimulated the growth of old towns and led to the founding of new ones. The consideration of chief importance in the location of towns shifted from a military to an economic basis. Facilities for trade became of greater consequence than the hills and marshes which had given protection. Urban locations were now chosen at points where a break in transportation took place. Such strategic locations were found at a natural harbor, or at the head of navigable waters, at the fords of rivers, at the junction of mountains and level country, or at any other place where topography required a change of carriers.

Trade and town building.
Whenever a trade route, for example, traversed an ocean or lake it was natural that a town would have its beginnings at the point of landing, and this point of landing would be chosen for its easy topographical approach to the region served by the trade. The mere transfer of goods in early days required a large amount of human effort and where it was accompanied by a change of ownership the transfer brought with it a need for storage as well as for some plan of financing and credit. During the period from the tenth to the eighteenth centuries, therefore, most new cities owed their locations to the energy and genius of the trader. Most older cities owed their growth to the same inspiration. Nevertheless there were some cities which owed their expansion to other causes, to political reasons, for example, as in the case of national capitals such as Berlin and Madrid.

Navigable waters and urban locations.
But the commercial town, located at a break in transportation, would have remained little more than a market-place if commerce had not succeeded in attracting industry. The two factors go together. Industry furnishes the materials of trade, and trade provides an outlet for the industry. With the industrial revolution, therefore, the heyday of rapid city growth began. Then came the railroads and these new traffic arteries largely superseded all other land trade routes, although they did not succeed in pulling the cities away from locations on navigable water. Apart from the political capitals virtually all the great cities of Europe are located on the seacoast or upon navigable waters. In the United States there are only two or three cities of over 300,000 population located elsewhere than on the two oceans, the Great Lakes, the Gulf of Mexico, or major navigable streams such as the Ohio and the Mississippi.

PRINCIPLES OF CITY GROWTH

Applying these various considerations to cities of the United States it will be noted that New York, situated at the junction of a navigable river with the sea, owes its extraordinary growth to the fact that there is only one topographically easy route from the middle Atlantic coast through the Appalachian range to the West. The Erie Canal followed this sea-level route in early days and so did the railroads when they came. Boston chose its location because of an excellent harbor, while Philadelphia is at a point where ocean and river navigation join. The same is true of New Orleans. Albany owes its site to the fact that the navigation of the Hudson stops at that point. St. Louis is at a river confluence. Harrisburg had its nucleus at a ferry across the Susquehanna River, while Memphis came into existence because of the deep water in the river frontage. *Some American illustrations.*

Proximity to raw materials has also been a factor, although by no means the only factor in the location of various American cities. Lumber in the case of Saginaw, Grand Rapids, and Seattle; wheat in Minneapolis; iron and coal in Pittsburgh; gold and silver in Denver; salt wells in Syracuse; oil wells in Cleveland; salmon canneries in Portland; citrus fruits in Los Angeles; meat packing in Chicago, Kansas City, and Omaha;—the list might be considerably prolonged. On the other hand an equal number of cities have successfully specialized in industries the raw materials of which are brought from a long distance. In the cities of Massachusetts and Rhode Island a great textile industry has developed although these communities are far away from the sources of raw cotton and wool. Detroit's supremacy in the automobile industry has not resulted from easy access to steel or rubber. Schenectady and Lynn have no claim of proximity to the raw materials which enter into the manufacture of electrical appliances. The great collar-and-shirt industries of Troy are far removed from the cotton fields. Proximity to a large market for its finished products is more important to an industry than is nearness to the source of raw materials. Water power was also influential in determining the location of industrial towns a century ago, as in the case of Minneapolis, Spokane, and Lowell; but with the easy transmission of hydro-electric power it has ceased to be of consequence. *Proximity to raw materials.* *Proximity to markets.*

Climate likewise has had its part in the location and upbuilding of some cities. A summer or winter resort on the seacoast or in the mountains gradually develops into a year-round community. *Other factors in city growth.*

Ostend and Nice in Europe; Atlantic City, Saratoga, Newport, and Long Beach in America will serve as examples. Historic associations also count for something in giving a place prestige, attracting tourists, and creating business. This factor is of greater importance in Europe than in America because there are more such places. Athens, Rome, Jerusalem, Weimar, and Stratford come quickly to mind in this connection. Educational institutions have become the nucleus of important communities on both sides of the Atlantic. Oxford and Cambridge, Heidelberg and Göttingen, New Haven and Princeton, Urbana and Berkeley—they are no longer exclusively college towns but higher education has been the mainspring of their prominence. The forces which create cities in modern times are more varied than they were in earlier days.[1]

How topography affects the direction of city growth:

Once a city is located, the main direction of its growth is usually controlled by topography. Cities on one side of a harbor or a wide river naturally expand on that side since any broad expanse of water prevents easy development in any other direction. The increasing pressure for more building land, however, will project a city's growth across a narrow stream and sometimes will carry it across a wide one as well. The ability of a river to hold expansion on the side where the city has originated depends not only on its width but upon the area and relative advantages of the sites on the two banks, modified to some extent by the persistence of land speculators. Thus in the case of St. Louis and Kansas City, where the river is wide and the land on the other side of it not particularly suitable for urban development, the Mississippi has formed a serious barrier to the growth of large communities on the further shore, although the handicap has been to some extent overcome. On the other hand, in the case of Cincinnati and Pittsburgh, the interposition of a relatively broad stream has not proved a very serious obstacle at all.

1. Rivers.

2. Marshes and hills.

Tracts of marsh or swampy ground also stand in the way of urban expansion until a certain point is reached. Then, when the demand for accessible land becomes strong enough, it will usually cause a draining or filling of the low land, as in the case of Boston's Back Bay and certain portions of San Francisco. Steep hills like-

---

[1] For a discussion of this subject, see the chapter on "The Location of Cities" in Herbert B. Dorau and Albert G. Hinman, *Urban Land Economics* (New York, 1928), pp. 44–60.

PRINCIPLES OF CITY GROWTH   205

wise are obstacles in the path of city growth, but a growing community will ultimately climb right over them as San Francisco, Seattle, and Providence have done. Wide valleys and deep ravines similarly check expansion temporarily, but even these impediments are forced by the handiwork of man to give way before the onward march of an expanding community. Nor does Nature provide the only obstacles to the projection of new streets and the sale of building lots. To some extent artificial barriers are interposed across the paths in which expansion would naturally proceed,—for example, there are such artificial blockades as large public parks, railroad yards, and great industrial plants. Streets cannot be pushed through these tracts of land, and the necessity of skirting around them is often a deterrent to normal city growth in the regions where they are located.

3. Artificial barriers.

When a town takes its original location on a harbor or river bank, its early development runs tangent to the harbor or parallel to the shore of a waterway. The same is true of communities which start in a small way at some point on the railway or on a well-travelled motor thoroughfare. The beginnings are casual and undirected. The pioneer residents of the place have no thought of town-building as their ultimate goal. But the hamlet grows on their hands until presently the place decides to become incorporated. Then it becomes community-conscious, organizes a chamber of commerce, nurtures grandiose hopes, and proceeds to stimulate its own development. Residences on the main highway or river bank soon give way to business blocks and seek new locations for themselves on new streets intersecting or paralleling the original locations. If the people of the community are wise and far-sighted at this stage, they zone the vacant land and plan for future growth in an orderly way, with due provision for such public services as are likely to be needed; but unhappily most new communities in the United States do not display any such prevision. The expansion is generally left to follow its own caprice.

The usual process of expansion.

When left to itself the process of growth will normally proceed along highways leading to the community's next neighbor, particularly if there is a larger city not far away. When it has moved some distance from the point of origin it then spreads laterally, in which case the influence of topography becomes important. In a general way the influence of topographical factors may be summarized by saying that level land usually attracts retail

Factors affecting it.

business, while land at a moderate elevation tends to become a residential district. On the other hand land situated slightly below the normal level will provide the natural route for transportation lines, while filled-in land is commonly used for warehouses, manufacturing, and cheap tenements. But not all communities have sufficient land of these four varieties, hence one will sometimes find industries and residences locating themselves outside their natural locations. The direction of the prevailing winds is a consideration which occasionally determines the question as to where the best residential sections will establish themselves in an industrial community. They will not go to the leeward side of the smoke-belching factories.

The evolution from simple to complex. In the process of city growth there is always a gradual development from simple to complex, and from the general to the specialized. The small village can satisfy its primary needs with a general store, a post office, a public garage, a school, and a church. A place of a hundred homes can get along with these simple facilities. But as the community increases in size, a diversification must take place both in the facilities which are provided and in the locations at which the service is performed. The former usually precedes the latter. More places of business come in and cluster around the original location. When this region becomes well developed, there is a tendency for newcomers to seek other points of vantage.

The sequence of events in the evolution of a new American community is about as follows: first comes a small general store carrying not only groceries but a few of the more staple dry goods. It is often combined with the post office. A school and one or more churches are usually in the immediate neighborhood. Then a gasoline station arrives and a small public garage, followed by a café or other eating place, sometimes with a pool room in connection. Other small business places presently filter in—a news stand, a real estate man's office, and perhaps an auto camp. These are followed in due course by the regular specialty establishments, a drug store (with soda fountain and tobacco counter), a regular grocery, a small hotel, and possibly a chain store. Along with these a barber shop trails in and before long a motion picture house. All these establishments stay close to the original location; but a point is ultimately reached at which the pressure for space compels them to move outside these bounds. And from that point onward the drift and direction of community growth, as well as its rapidity, will depend upon a great variety of factors which cannot be generalized upon. For as a community grows there is not merely a multiplication of shops and houses but a process of differentiation as well.

Because business establishments tend to concentrate in and around the original community location, this naturally becomes the area of highest land values. An increase in rents is the result and this has the effect of driving the residences out of the high-value zone. They, with the non-business establishments and smaller shops seek refuge in the outer, less expensive regions. The direction which they take will be determined by the interaction of proximity and costs, in other words they always look for less costly sites while keeping as close to the area of highest values as they can. This spread from the center outward, modified by topographical factors, goes hand in hand with increased population. Step by step, as it proceeds, the value of land in and around the original location becomes higher. Buildings are torn down and structures of greater height are erected in order to make the investment yield a fair return in view of the expanded land values. Some lines of business find that they cannot afford to occupy these new premises and are forced off into the less accessible, lower-priced areas. Thus there is a constant overflow from the center along the lines of radius.

<small>Locations and land values.</small>

By the time the community has reached a population of 100,000 or more, its whole area may be divided into three general categories of land, namely, that used for business, for residences, and for public or semi-public buildings. The business sites will presently become subdivided into four further classes, those used for retail business, for wholesale business, for banks and offices, and for industry. Residence areas will likewise be subdivided into several sections ranging from streets of high-class, expensively built homes through those which are lined with less costly ones down to the region of flats and tenements. The land used for public or semi-public buildings includes the parks and playgrounds, the sites occupied by the schools, city hall, post office, public library, fire stations, churches and hospitals, as well as the railroad right-of-way, the freight yards, and the public markets. But these categories of urban land cannot be rigidly marked off with a pencil and ruler for they are usually interspersed with one another.

<small>General categories of urban land.</small>

The lines of gravitation:

1. Retail stores.

The locations regarded as most desirable by the various subdivisions of occupancy are about as follows: Retail stores and small shops tend to group themselves around the original site of the community in the earlier stages of its growth. Then as the land becomes more valuable they move to parallel or intersecting streets. Exceptions are found in cases where a small business grows with the growth of the community and manages to hold its location in spite of increased land values. All forms of retail business prefer to be where there is a good deal of pedestrian traffic. They endeavor to stay close in, on level, well-kept, well-lighted streets, preferably on those which are served by the street cars. The display of goods in windows is regarded as very important in most branches of retail trade, and shade is necessary for good display without damage to the merchandise. Hence the side of a street which is well shaded during the shopping hours is greatly preferred by many retailers, especially by those whose business is largely with women. Property on the shaded side usually acquires an added value.

2. Wholesale concerns.

Wholesale establishments, from the standpoint of their site-preferences, are of two kinds. First there are those which handle merchandise of great weight or bulk but of relatively small value. Such wholesale houses naturally seek locations near the transportation lines for economy in the handling of goods. The development of transportation by motor truck has somewhat reduced the importance of this contiguity to freight terminals and harbor warehouses, but many wholesale concerns still desire to be where a spur track can be run alongside their premises. Those dealing in merchandise which occupies a relatively large amount of storage space (such as agricultural machinery, furniture, coal, building materials, etc.) also find it desirable to secure locations with transportation facilities but in a region of moderate rentals and values. In the second place there are wholesale establishments which deal in merchandise of small bulk with high value. These usually desire to be located in proximity to the retail stores with which they do their business. Such concerns can afford to pay at higher rates for the relatively small space which they occupy.

3. Factories.

Industry, in a general way, follows the same course. Those engaged in light manufacturing (such as tailors, silversmiths, cigar-makers, etc.) tend to keep company with the retail district, while the heavy industries move off to points where land is less expensive. In their case, moreover, convenient access to the waterfront or railroad lines is very important. The movement of both mercantile business and industry, moreover, is nowadays kept under control by the zoning regulations which most cities have put into effect. These regulations set bounds to the areas which different types of industries may invade.[1]

4. Banks and offices.

Banks, trust companies, insurance companies, theaters, newspapers, and some professional offices stay in the retail business district or very close to it. They desire to be on the main currents of travel and also to have locations which possess advertising value. What some of these concerns acquire, when they buy or lease a corner lot at the intersection of two busy retail streets is not merely land but a franchise, in other words the exclusive right to do business at a choice spot. The cost of this location may be charged up as rent or interest but much of it is in reality a payment for prestige and advertising.

The segregation of kindred establishments.

When a city grows beyond a certain size, say 500,000 population, the tendency is for those engaged in similar lines of business, or in similar professions, to group themselves somewhat closely together,—for example, the newspaper offices, the theaters, and even professional men such as lawyers, physicians, and architects. This is because customers and patrons seem to find such groupings convenient. In a word the distributions and the segregations rest on a purely economic basis. It is not a matter of sentiment at all. The better a location from the standpoint of its suitability for various types of business, or of professional work, the more bidders there will be for it, and the higher value it will soon attain. When the location becomes too high-priced for some of the bidders, they drop out, leaving the field to other concerns which can afford to do business on costly land—for example, the department stores, the jewelry stores, or the fashionable shops for women's clothing, footwear, and millinery. The others distribute themselves out of the way as best they can.

5. Residences.

By way of contrast to all this, the chief determining factor in the case of residence values is not economic but social. Well-to-do people choose their home environment for a variety of reasons—attractive topography, a good view, reasonable proximity to the business center yet not too close, a suitable street layout, the

[1] See Chapter XVIII.

absence of nuisances—but above all else they desire to be among congenial neighbors. The personnel of a neighborhood is the basis of its residential values. Thus it often happens that a few families of social prominence build their homes in a certain section; then some of their friends migrate to the same vicinity and the area takes on a social distinction. Living in this neighborhood gives prestige. Presently one finds people of moderate means and somewhat lower social status moving to the outskirts of this high-class residential district, getting as near to it as they can without spending too much for the privilege. And so on down the scale of wealth and social gradation. The ambition of all city folk is to improve their own social standing, or at least the appearance of it. Hence, there is a constant pressure towards the best residential district. It is sometimes said that business property is selected by the man from an economic standpoint, while residence property is chosen by the woman from a social standpoint. The city as a place of residence is an aggregation of neighborhoods. People will do business willingly with those who are not of their own social categories, but they want to live among those who are like themselves.

6. The tenements.

As for the poorest families, they take whatever residence areas remain available. Usually such areas are on the immediate flanks of the land occupied by railroad terminals, by industrial establishments, wharves, railroads, warehouses, and the like. Here one finds a zone of workers' homes and tenements, cut through by rooming-house districts which utilize old residences from which the former occupants have moved to more desirable sections. Where the transportation facilities are good, however, many workers take up their homes in suburban or commuters' zones which are situated some distance from the downtown districts of the city, but these commuting suburbs often utilize land which is not marketable for any higher-grade residential use.

7. Hotels and apartment houses.

In the case of high-class apartment houses and family hotels the social factor likewise comes into play; but as respects the cheaper range of apartments and flats the basis of value is economic and conforms closely to the principles governing business properties. Commercial hotels naturally seek locations on or adjacent to the retail business streets, while the so-termed apartment hotels prefer sites on streets which run through or near the best residential areas. It is a significant fact that when the best residential district of the city becomes fixed, the main growth of retail business is likely to move in that direction. The reason is that shops and stores, when they are patronized by customers from the high-class residential district gain prestige thereby and are then sought by people from other parts of the community. This consideration was more important, of course, a generation ago than it is today when motor transportation has relaxed the emphasis on proximity; but in most cities the invasion of the best residential districts by high-priced specialty shops had gained momentum before motor vehicles came into use. One may note in this connection the gradual ousting of fine residences by retail business establishments on Fifth Avenue in New York City, on Boylston Street in Boston, on Michigan Avenue in Chicago, and on Euclid Avenue in Cleveland.

In the case of large department stores, which draw their customers from all classes and sections, the most desirable location usually coincides with the point of highest land value in the community. This will invariably be at or near the center of access, which is not necessarily the center of population. The center of access is the point which can be most conveniently reached (whether in street cars, subway trains, motor cars, or on foot) by the largest number of people within the shopping radius. Its location is therefore determined by the railroad terminals, subway stations, street railway routes, traffic thoroughfares, and to some extent by the amount of traffic congestion. Towards this center of access the department stores will gravitate and by following them one can usually find the points of highest land value in the city. A few exceptions to this general rule will be found in the largest cities where the banking and office building districts average higher in land values than the area around the center of access. 8. Department stores.

Up to a certain point the growth of a city is centripetal. The pressure of business is towards the downtown areas. The residential districts, during these earlier stages, also keep close in. But there comes a point at which the axial outflow of the residential areas will give rise to a demand for neighborhood shopping centers. Then the growth of the city becomes in some degree centrifugal. Business no longer crowds toward the downtown section; on the contrary there are certain forms of it which tend to scatter here and there at vantage points through the residential suburbs. The result is seen in the numerous small business communities of varying size which spring up at considerable distances The point at which business begins to decentralize.

from the general center of access and seek their patronage among residents of their respective neighborhoods.

Neighborhood shopping centers. Neighborhood shopping centers they are usually called. Everyone who lives in a large city is familiar with them. Invariably they begin at the intersection of two important traffic thoroughfares or residential streets and spread from the four corners outwards. It might be thought that the greatly increased use of motor transportation would give these outlying stores and shops a serious problem because people would prefer to go in town where they can obtain a wider range of choice and usually lower prices as well. But things have not worked out that way. The expansion of automobile traffic has helped rather than hindered the growth of neighborhood shopping centers. This is because the heavy traffic congestion in the downtown retail areas has made shopping a tedious and somewhat inconvenient process there. Consequently the female head of the suburban home (who usually handles the household shopping problem) prefers to do the ordinary day-by-day purchasing at convenient places near by, reserving a trip to the downtown business district for supplies which are not of a routine character. Under this procedure the neighborhood shopping centers become the resort of customers for meats, vegetables, fruits, drugs, and the like, but not ordinarily for clothing, shoes, furniture, or house furnishings.

What they usually include. Contributing to the growth of these localized shopping centers has been the chain store, a development of the twentieth century which has gone forward with great rapidity. Another influence is the motion picture theater which always selects its suburban site in close proximity to a neighborhood shopping center. In fact, the typical center is made up of a chain store or two, a filling-station, a motion picture house, a meat and vegetable market, a fruit stand, a drug store, a clothes-cleaning-and-pressing establishment, a restaurant, a barber shop, and a few other small concerns of varying kinds. Cheap structures and low rents are characteristic of them all. One-story buildings, designed as economically as the ordinances will permit, testify to the feverish haste of land owners to convert their property into profitable use with the least possible outlay. Very seldom is the neighborhood shopping center a place of architectural artistry. Bizarre little buildings, and residences partly converted to business use, usually alternate with vacant lots that are used as parking places or covered with flaming

PRINCIPLES OF CITY GROWTH

billboards. Too many outlying street intersections have been zoned for business at the behest of ambitious property owners and real estate speculators. Fewer and better-built neighborhood shopping centers would be an advantage to all concerned.[1]

The foregoing are some principles of city growth, if it is allowable to call them principles. More accurately they might be termed tendencies, for all of them are open to numerous exceptions. In general, however, they represent the chief forces which influence the direction of growth in a growing city. But what determines the measure of a city's expansion? Why is it that one city develops with great rapidity while another, despite the high ambitions of its people, fails to grow at all? The answer is that the growth of a city depends *on the breadth of its economic base.* And from this point of view it is possible to group all cities into five or six classes—such as the agricultural service city, the one-industry city, the diversified industrial city, the satellite city, the industro-commercial city, and the metropolitan city.

The grouping of cities according to the breadth of their economic base:

First of all we have in the United States a very large number of what may be called agricultural service communities. These places, like Emporia, Kansas, Sioux City, Iowa, or Fresno, California (their name is legion) depend for their growth and sustenance upon the rich agricultural areas which they serve. They are the local centers to which farmers bring their products and through which they procure their supplies. Such communities obviously have a slender economic base and unless they are able to broaden it by the attraction of industries, or in some other way, they have little prospect of growing into cities of any considerable size. Even the primary services which they perform have been considerably narrowed during the past generation by various factors. For example, the coming of motor transport and the building of good roads have encouraged the farmer to do some of his marketing in larger communities farther away. Likewise the development of mail-order business by large mercantile concerns in the metropolitan centers has seriously cut into the business of merchants in these agricultural service communities. For these and other reasons most of them have failed to grow appreciably in business or population while some have actually lost ground.

1. The agricultural service community.

---

[1] See the article by J. C. Nichols on "The Planning and Control of Outlying Shopping Centers" in the *Journal of Land and Public Utility Economics*, Vol. II, pp. 17–22 (January, 1926).

2. The one-industry city.

Then there is the city which largely depends upon a single resource other than agriculture—for example, on oil production, mining, lumbering, fisheries, a single large industrial plant or group of such establishments, an educational institution, or on the fact that it is a political capital. We have many such cities in the United States and examples will readily come to hand. Tulsa rests on oil, Scranton on coal, Butte and Douglas on minerals, and Gloucester on fisheries. Dayton is associated in the public imagination with cash registers, Akron with automobile tires, Grand Rapids with furniture, Troy with collars, Bridgeport with machine tools, Rochester with kodaks, Manchester (N. H.) with textiles, Hollywood with motion pictures, Schenectady with electrical products, Pittsburgh, Gary, and Youngstown with steel, Minneapolis with flour, and Detroit with automobiles—the list could be almost indefinitely extended.

Institutional forces which give impetus to city building.

Educational activities have built some other communities. Ann Arbor, Lawrence, Palo Alto, Eugene, Ithaca, Chapel Hill, and other seats of universities throughout the country owe their growth, such as it has been, to the impetus of higher education. Harrisburg, Sacramento, Topeka, Austin—and above all, Washington, depend heavily upon their status as political capitals. Miami, Colorado Springs, San Diego, and other happily situated communities have capitalized the tourist trade, while Battle Creek has thriven on the industry of health restoration. All this is not to imply, however, that the cities above named, or others like them, are wholly dependent upon a single resource, either industrial or institutional. In many cases they have a supplementary diversification of resources; but the mainspring of their progress has been, and still is, the industry or institution which they prefigure in the public imagination. Hence, the economic base is a relatively narrow one and under ordinary conditions this stands in the way of anything beyond a moderate measure of urban growth. A one-industry city ties its future to that industry. Sometimes that is sufficient unto greatness—as in the case of Detroit—but not often.

3. The diversified industrial city.

More fortunate, on the whole, is the city of diversified industries. Its economic base has been broadened to a point where the community does not depend upon a single resource but on several. New York, Chicago, Philadelphia, Baltimore, Boston, Los Angeles, and Buffalo are good examples; but most American cities with populations of over 500,000 fall into this class, with Cleveland, Pittsburgh, and Detroit as conspicuous exceptions. Many cities with less than half a million population have likewise developed a high degree of industrial diversification.[1] Take Providence for example. It began as a marketing and distributing point for Rhode Island, and as such alone the city would not have amounted to much. But it is also the state capital and the seat of an important university. Likewise, it has attracted a considerable diversification of industries and has the advantage of transportation facilities by sea. This combination explains why the smallest state in the Union has built up the second largest city in New England.

Diversification of its urban resources gives a city strength and stability. A recession in any single field does not, in such cases, involve a serious setback. Entire dependence upon one industry, such as oil production or mining, means that a breakdown in this particular branch of economic activity spells disaster for the whole community. In many portions of western America one can find blighted mining towns which were on their way to prosperous cityhood until the veins of ore receded. The ambitious city, if its people are wise, will spare no effort to promote industrial diversification and thus to extend the economic foundation upon which the community rests. The promoters of urban growth, such as chambers of commerce and realty associations, are active in this direction, being fully alive to its importance. And there is need for their vigilance, because the natural tendency is towards industrial concentration. When an industry establishes itself in any city and makes good headway, other concerns of the same type are likely to come because a supply of skilled labor is already at hand. Then, in due course, some closely affiliated establishments will cluster around the main industries. Shoe factories, for example, will attract concerns which make laces, buckles, thread, paper boxes, and shoe polish. This natural tendency towards integration needs to be offset by active efforts on the part of a city's industrial planners. *The value of diversification.*

Industry and commerce go together. One cannot develop far without the other. Every large industrial city, therefore, becomes of necessity a center of commerce. Indeed, it cannot become a *4. The industro-commercial city.*

[1] See the article by Glenn E. McLaughlin on "Industrial Diversification in American Cities" in the *Quarterly Journal of Economics*, Vol. XIV, pp. 131–149 (November, 1930).

great industrial community if facilities for the development of commerce are lacking. Nor does one often find a great port of commerce with no large industrial development to support it. Mention has already been made of the significant fact that virtually all the world's great cities except a few political capitals are situated on navigable waters. All of them, without exception, are well served by railroads. Every American city of a half million population or more is an industro-commercial city. It could not grow to such proportions otherwise. And when it reaches this stage, or even earlier, it begins to develop its ring of encircling satellites.

5. Satellite cities. The term satellite cities has come into use as a means of designating those communities, chiefly industrial, which cluster outside a larger center but within its orbit. Factories move to the outer ring under the impulse of cheap land, low taxes, and elbow room, taking their workers with them. A town springs up and in due course becomes a satellite city, politically independent of the mother community but within its marketing area. Every very large industrial city has its girdle of satellites, big and little,—its Ivorydale, Flint, or Sugar Creek, its Homestead or Bessemer, its Hammond or Gary. Once established they spread inward not outward. Gradually the areas intervening between the large community and its satellites is built up and annexation sometimes follows. Thus a metropolitan city arises.[1]

6. The metropolitan city. The metropolitan city is largely a product of the last hundred years. It is the economic capital of a designated large area. Boston serves New England in this capacity, Chicago the Middle West, Minneapolis the Northwest, and Los Angeles the Southwest. Size alone does not make a metropolitan city, but size plus the radiation of economic influence. The metropolis of an area is the axis at which the accumulation of merchandise takes place, the center from which the large-scale distribution is made, and hence from which the banking and credit facilities are supplied. Such cities develop like a spider's web. The axial lines are thrown out from the center and then the concentric fasteners are put in. Everything points inward, all roads lead to Rome. Thus Greater New York began as a town on the tip of Manhattan Island, spread northward, then gave birth to Brooklyn and other satellites which she subsequently annexed, overflowed to Long Island and above

[1] C. B. Purdom, *The Building of Satellite Towns* (London, 1925).

the Bronx, and finally poured her surplus population across to the Jersey shore. But the development of each and every point on the periphery of this great community has been conditioned by its accessibility to Lower Manhattan where the process of growth began.

It should be mentioned, of course, that the entire area of a metropolitan city is not usually within the purview of one municipal government. Metropolitan Boston is an aggregation of more than thirty municipalities, all within a radius of fifteen miles from the center. This unity of economic interest within a metropolitan area, combined with political decentralization, gives rise to various problems.[1] Unity of planning becomes difficult and sometimes virtually impossible. Each municipality has its own restricted plan which does not articulate with those of its neighbors. The development of a regional plan for the New York metropolitan area is intended to overcome this difficulty. The political decentralization in a metropolitan community also operates as a hindrance to efficient police and health administration. Neither malefactors nor epidemics pay any heed to municipal boundaries. The metropolitan city, as such, has no charter, no officials, and indeed no definite boundaries.

Municipal and metropolitan boundaries.

Nevertheless it is a reality, recognized by the statisticians of industry and even to some extent by the census bureau. The simplest method of solving the problem is by outright annexation but this is rarely practicable. Communities which have enjoyed municipal independence are reluctant to give it up. The alternative is some plan of municipal federation which will enable the individual cities to preserve their political integrity while providing for centralized management of certain administrative functions in the interest of the whole. This has been successfully accomplished in London and Berlin. To work out such a plan for any metropolitan area in the United States, however, is difficult and to secure its adoption is even more so.

REFERENCES

Herbert B. Dorau and Albert G. Hinman, *Urban Land Economics* (New York, 1928) and Richard M. Hurd, *Principles of City Land Values* (4th edition, New York, 1924) are excellent books in this field. Stanley L.

[1] See Paul Studensky, *The Government of Metropolitan Areas* (New York, 1930), and C. E. Merriam, S. D. Parratt, and A. Lepawsky, *The Government of the Metropolitan Region of Chicago* (Chicago, 1933).

McMichael and Robert B. Bingham, *City Growth Essentials* (Cleveland, 1928), is a work along similar lines with some new material. Mention should also be made of Harland Bartholomew, *Urban Land Uses* (Cambridge, 1932), E. M. Fisher and R. F. Smith, *Land Subdividing and the Rate of Utilization* (Ann Arbor, Michigan, 1932), J. M. Gries and James Ford, *Planning for Residential Districts* (Washington, 1932), and F. Longstreth Thompson, *Site Planning in Practice* (New York, 1923).

More general discussions may be found in Ernest W. Burgess, *The Urban Community* (Chicago, 1926), Nels Anderson and E. C. Lindeman, *Urban Sociology* (New York, 1928), J. G. Thompson, *Urbanization* (New York, 1927), H. Paul Douglass, *The Suburban Trend* (New York, 1925), Scott E. W. Bedford, *Readings in Urban Sociology* (New York, 1927), Maurice R. Davie, *Problems of City Life* (New York, 1932), Niles Carpenter, *The Sociology of City Life* (New York, 1931), and Graham R. Taylor, *Satellite Cities* (New York, 1915).

Much excellent material is embodied in the publications connected with the Regional Plan of New York and Its Environs, especially Vol. I on *Major Economic Factors in Metropolitan Growth and Arrangement* (New York, 1928), and in the monograph by R. D. MacKenzie on *The Metropolitan Community* issued under the auspices of the President's Research Committee on Recent Social Trends (New York, 1932).

See also the references at the close of Chapter XVII.

CHAPTER XVII

CITY PLANNING

Architecture has its political uses. Public buildings being an ornament of a country, it establishes a nation, draws people and commerce, and makes the people love their native land.—*Sir Christopher Wren.*

City planning is the science of designing cities or parts of cities so that they may be more convenient and more attractive places of human abode. It aims to control and guide the development of cities and towns in such way as to make them serve their purpose in the highest degree. Hence in its wider aspects it comprises the planning of local transportation facilities, including subways and airports, the general street layout, the arrangement of new suburbs and subdivisions, the development of the waterfront, the provision of motor traffic thoroughfares, the location of public buildings, parks, and playgrounds, the securing of an adequate and safe water supply, the effective disposal of the city's sewage and other wastes, the control of private property by zoning, the encouragement of better housing, the devising of an adequate and equitable system of municipal revenues, the promotion of sound political traditions, and the developing of a rational civic pride in the minds of the people. In fact there is no department of municipal administration which city planning, in its more comprehensive sense, does not call into coöperation. {What city planning includes.}

Two popular misconceptions with respect to city planning have arisen in the public mind. One is the notion that such planning is entirely concerned with physical improvements,—with street widenings, public buildings, new boulevards, and such things only. The average American thinks of city planning in terms of better public architecture. But the chief objective of all city planning is convenience and utility rather than beautification, although the latter is by no means to be despised. Hence the primary aim of city planning is social, not physical. Widened streets and new traffic arteries are not designed and built for the mere purpose of giving the city a better appearance but because they conduce to the greater convenience and comfort of the whole citizenship. {Two popular misconceptions relating to it: 1. That it is a physical enterprise only.}

Attractiveness is thrown in for good measure, as it ought to be. Landscape architects have been in the forefront of the city planning movement during the past thirty years and they have naturally laid stress upon those aspects of the work which come closest to their own interest. But comprehensive planning goes far beyond the confines of aesthetic interest. It is an enterprise that serves to forecast and to provide for the city's future needs in all directions,—physical, social, legal, financial, and administrative. Laws and tax systems need straightening as well as streets.

<small>2. That it involves a heavy spending of public money.</small>

The second popular error is embodied in the idea that city planning involves a great deal of drastic tearing down and reconstruction at the public expense, with big bond issues and large additions to the city debt. Sometimes, it is true, considerable money must be spent in order to correct past mistakes, but the principal aim of city planning is to make sure that such mistakes will not occur again. To this end the city planners try to figure out the growth and needs of the community for a generation ahead. Then they persuade the municipal authorities to direct this growth into orderly channels and to make provision for oncoming requirements before the days of urgency arrive. How often, in our municipal yesterdays, have we heard public officials predict that a city would double its population within a decade or two, yet lift not a finger to meet the problems which so rapid a growth would inevitably bring! City planning seeks to eliminate from municipal administration the haphazard, makeshift, hand-to-mouth, snap-judgment methods which have so freely characterized it in the past, replacing these by carefully thought-out plans and prevision.

<small>Early examples of city planning.</small>

The idea that cities should be planned is, of course, by no means a new one. It goes back to ancient Greece and beyond.[1] Excavations have disclosed that the streets of Athens in certain sections of the city were constructed according to a regular plan. Rome, after the great fire of Nero's reign, was in part rebuilt according to a definite scheme of street reconstruction. The first notable writer on the art of city planning was a Roman of the imperial age, Vitruvius, whose *Ten Books of Architecture* are not without interest even at the present day.[2] Many of the provincial cities of the Roman Empire grew out of military camps, and their street lay-

---

[1] A general sketch of city planning in Egypt and Babylon may be found in Karl B. Lohmann, *Principles of City Planning* (New York, 1931). A more extensive discussion may be found in F. Haverfield, *Ancient Town Planning* (Oxford, 1913).

[2] A translation by Morris H. Morgan (Cambridge, Mass., 1914) is available.

CITY PLANNING 221

outs were merely elaborations of the Roman castra with avenues and streets intersecting one another at right angles. Here may be found the genesis of the so-termed gridiron scheme of street layout which is characteristic of so many modern cities.

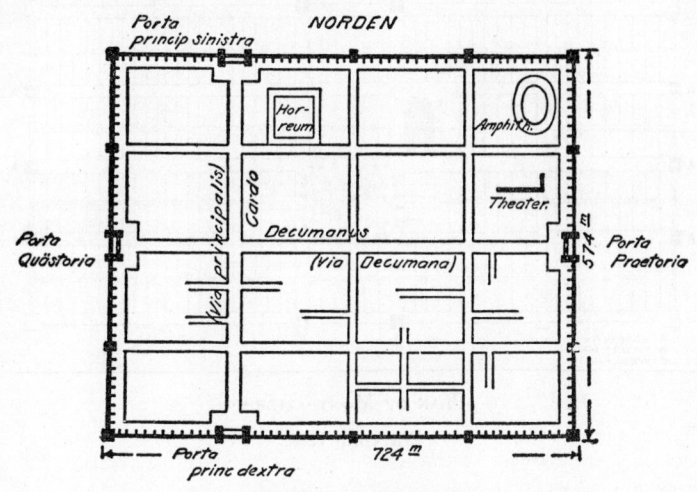

THE ROMAN CASTRA [1]

The fortress towns or bastides of the mediaeval period usually followed this general plan, although the sites reserved in the Roman layout for amphitheater and forum now became the locations of church and market-place. The plan of Montpazier, in southern France (see next page), will indicate the indebtedness of the mediaeval fortress town to the Roman castra in its fundamental features.

But with the fall of the Roman Empire city planning became a lost art. The cities of mediaeval Europe grew up in rare disorder, their populations huddled into alleyways of squalid hovels behind circular walls of defense. Often the genesis of a mediaeval city was the lord's castle, from which a few narrow and crooked streets wandered outward to the city gates. Within the walls were safety and protection. In time, however, conditions of life became less precarious; the walls were no longer needed; they were torn down and the cities went sprawling out beyond these ancient limits. Little or nothing in the way of orderly planning was attempted in

Mediaeval town planning.

[1] Reproduced from Raymond Unwin, *Town Planning in Practice* (2nd edition, London, 1911), p. 51.

222   MUNICIPAL ADMINISTRATION

any European city for more than a thousand years after the fall of Rome.

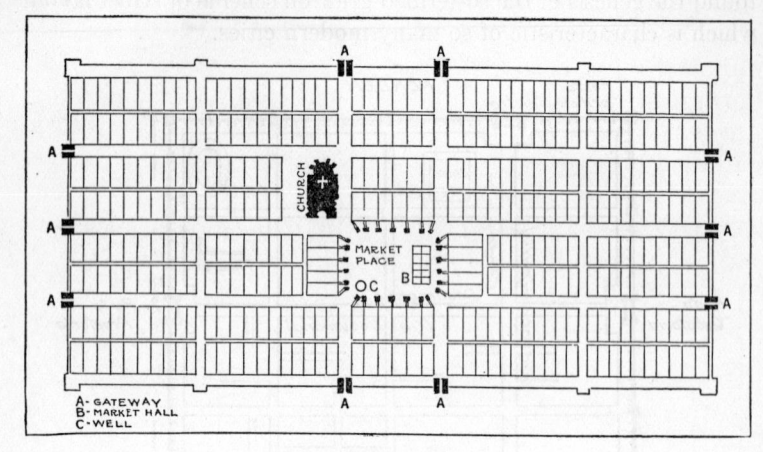

PLAN OF MONTPAZIER [1]
FOUNDED 1284

Sir Christopher Wren.   The earliest among modern city plans was the one prepared by Sir Christopher Wren after the great London fire of 1666. London

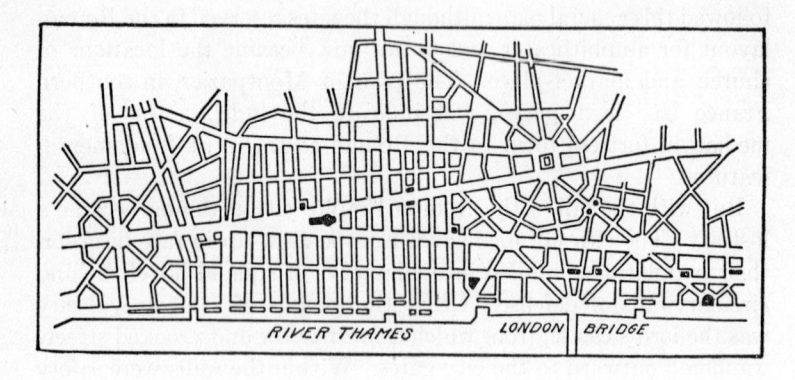

before this great fire was a typical product of mediaeval negligence—congested, unsanitary, wallowing in filth, and scarcely ever free from plague. Wren, the foremost architect of his day, was

[1] From T. H. Hughes and E. A. G. Lamborn, *Towns and Town Planning: Ancient and Modern* (Oxford, 1923).

CITY PLANNING 223

commissioned by the authorities to make a new plan upon which the city could be rebuilt. He executed his commission with great skill. Briefly, he provided for three principal avenues, ninety feet in width, straight through the city but not running exactly parallel, with intersecting cross-streets sixty feet wide at regular intervals. Provision was also made for some public squares with radiating streets. Two of the main avenues converged at St. Paul's Cathedral and two at the Royal Exchange. The area in the region of London Bridge was planned with great ingenuity. But unhappily very little came of the whole scheme. Influential land

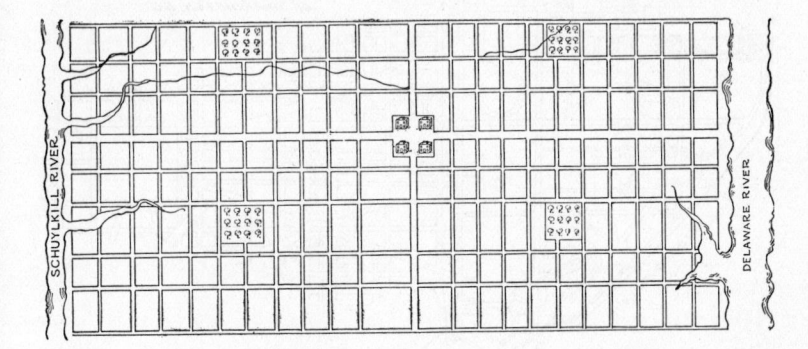

owners opposed the adoption of the plan and although some features of it were carried into effect, the city on the Thames was rebuilt upon substantially the old lines. Thus the finest opportunity for city planning ever given to a great metropolis was lost and the misfortune has cost London, during the years since 1666, a sum that is beyond calculation.

A few years later an opportunity came to America when William Penn in 1682 laid out his new city of Philadelphia covering about two square miles. Penn's plan was simple; in the center of the new community he provided an open space upon which it was his intention that the public buildings should be erected. The rest of his tract was laid out in checkerboard fashion with arterial thoroughfares and cross-streets intersecting at regular intervals. Four large square spaces were reserved for parks. *William Penn's Philadelphia plan.*

A little more than a century later Major L'Enfant was brought over from Paris to make a plan for the new national capital on the banks of the Potomac. L'Enfant's plan, when it was finally completed, extended over an area of about forty square miles. His *The planning of Washington by L'Enfant.*

ideas were admirable but were conceived on rather too elaborate a scale. For his street layout L'Enfant used a combination of the gridiron and radial plans with provision for the diagonal avenues which are important features of the Washington scheme of traffic circulation today. To use his own quaint language he "first made the distribution regular, with streets at right angles, north south and east west." Then he "opened others in various directions as avenues to and from every principal place, wishing by this not

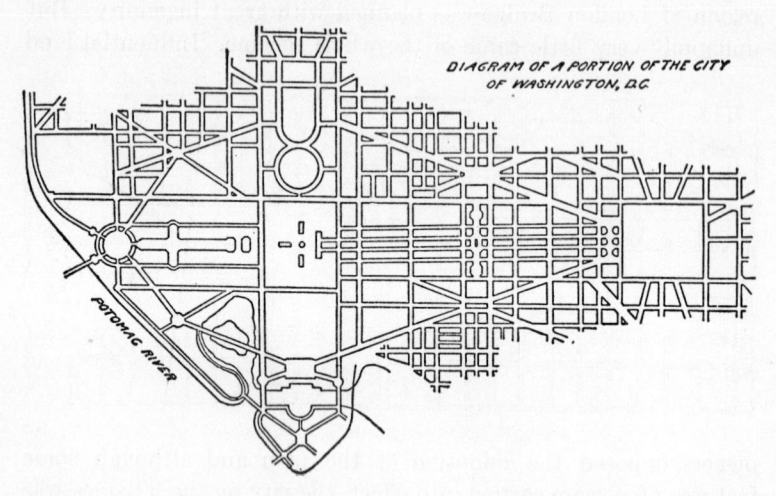

DIAGRAM OF A PORTION OF THE CITY OF WASHINGTON, D.C.

merely to contrast with the general regularity but principally to connect each part of the city with more efficacy by making the real distance less from place to place."[1] Considerable modifications in the original plans were made from time to time during the nineteenth century, and there have more recently been large extensions; but despite these changes the present ground plan of Washington is substantially as the great French engineer prepared it.

The planning of Manhattan Island.

But neither Philadelphia nor Washington form the model which other large American cities have generally followed. New York is the community that set them their example. The metropolis, of course, made a bad start because its oldest section was not planned at all. It grew out of a primitive Dutch settlement which squatted on the lower end of Manhattan Island. But as the com-

[1] An account of L'Enfant's work may be found in W. B. Bryan, *History of the National Capital* (New York, 1914), chaps. vi–vii.

munity grew and spread northward some regulation of this growth became imperative. In 1807, therefore, a commission was appointed to make a street plan for the upper portion of the island, and this group turned out to be an unimaginative body. With a pencil and ruler it merely laid off the whole area from river to river in straight gridiron fashion with avenues running lengthwise and numbered streets sprinting across them at uniform intervals. In this way the commission cut the whole tract into two thousand city blocks, each two hundred feet wide, no more and no less. The only deviation from regularity was that involved in leaving Broadway to continue its diagonal course northward across the face of the plan.

The whole arrangement was just what the real estate promoters liked, and they pushed their sales of the land with great rapidity. New York grew fast during the next six or seven decades and became the envy of other communities. It was quite natural, therefore, that such cities as Chicago, Cleveland, St. Louis, and San Francisco should have followed the New York example, as they did. The checkerboard layout spread everywhere and became orthodox, paying little or no account to differences in topographical conditions. Streets went straight uphill and down again. Anyone who could draw a straight line qualified as a city planner.

Towards the close of the nineteenth century, however, the inevitable reaction came. Americans who went to Europe came home impressed with the beauty of Edinburgh, Paris, and Vienna. The versatility and variety of almost every European community contrasted strongly with the drab, dull symmetry of the typical American town. Meanwhile the movement for more extensive recreational facilities was crystallizing into the acquisition of extensive outlying parks and reservations, thus giving an organized exemplification of conscious city planning. And the World's Fair at Chicago in 1893 gave the whole country an inkling of the possibilities. The much-admired White City, which was created for this exposition, promoted a renaissance in civic good taste. In the minds of those who came and went, its orderliness and beauty left a deep impression. People returned to their own communities with a feeling that utility and dignity in city building could be combined by proper planning. *Later stages in planning.* *Chicago's example in 1893.*

Automobile traffic, moreover, began to make new demands upon American city streets. New arterial thoroughfares were needed and how should they be planned? Likewise the aesthetic *The effect of the automobile.*

standards of the New World moved higher as the frontier era receded into the distance. As a result of these various influences, public attention began to be drawn toward comprehensive planning and during the past thirty or forty years the progress in this direction has been remarkable. But Chicago still holds her place as the outstanding American pioneer in the new movement. The mid-western metropolis has planned comprehensively and has adhered to her plans more faithfully than has any other large American community. But every large city in the United States, and most of the small ones, have set up city planning boards whose function it is to guide the growth of the community, and projects of urban replanning have been placed under way all over the country.

Regional planning. Finally, the planning of cities has matured into the planning of metropolitan counties and regions. When several urban communities are located in the same area it has been found that each cannot satisfactorily plan its traffic thoroughfares, or its transportation system, or even its housing restrictions without reference to the others. Hence planning, in such cases, must be a coöperative enterprise. The largest enterprise of this sort during recent years has been the development of a regional plan for the New York metropolitan region, an area that reaches into three states and includes a very large number of incorporated urban communities. Surveys and studies of an elaborate sort have preceded the framing of such regional plans.

Procedure in city planning. City planning begins with the establishment of a planning board which is usually composed of from five to fifteen persons. As a rule they serve without compensation. They are commonly appointed *The planning boards.* by the mayor in cities which have the mayor-and-council form of government, or by the city council in city manager cities. In some cases various city officials are ex-officio members of the commission. Usually the city planning commission has its headquarters at the city hall and is provided with a permanent paid staff, which in the larger cities consists of a secretary, various engineers, landscape *Their present powers.* architects, and draftsmen. The powers of city planning boards, however, have been for the most part advisory. They are entrusted with the function of preparing general plans for consideration by the city council, making recommendations with respect to zoning ordinances, and advising the city authorities with respect to applications for changes in the zoning rules. In a few cases it is provided that city planning boards, in addition to rendering general advice, must be given the opportunity to report upon certain matters before final action can be taken by the city council, and in any case it is the custom in all large communities to refer projects of public improvement to the city planning board before adoption. The next step in the development of city planning will be to endow these planning boards with some mandatory powers. In time they will doubtless be given authority to veto projects which they deem incompatible with the well-ordered growth of the community. This is a power which the planning authorities of European cities already possess. *The next step.*

All city planning should be based upon a preliminary survey, in other words upon a careful compilation of the facts relating to the physical character and future requirements of the city. Every community, and indeed every section of it, has its own problems, needs, and individualities. Good planning should adapt itself to these peculiarities. Moreover, the planning authorities never have a clean slate to start with; there are always a good many established situations to which they must conform whether they like it or not, and of course it is essential, first of all, to determine what these situations are. A city planning survey results in the preparation of accurate topographical maps showing the existing layout of streets, the location of all water, sewer, and gas mains and electric conduits—in a word every physical feature which may be affected by replanning operations. *City planning surveys.*

It also results in the compilation of accurate data concerning the present distribution of population, its probable increase over a period of years, the nature and characteristics of the city's industrial resources, the character and use of transportation facilities, the distribution of parks, recreation grounds, and other public spaces, the community's present resources and probable future needs as respects public buildings, along with much other data of the same general sort. The city planning survey also involves the study of the city's legal powers, its charter, its financial resources, whether from taxation or by borrowing, and its general administrative organization. All this is important because city planning is not merely a matter of engineering and architecture. It must look out for legal powers, ways and means, and even the political difficulties. Many excellent projects have come to grief because the city planners have not sufficiently taken into ac- *Its extensive scope.*

count the legal and political obstacles that lay scattered along the path.

Interpreting the survey and making the plans. After the planning survey has been completed, the next step is to interpret the data. Interpreting data is more difficult than gathering it. Hence it is at this point that expert consultation becomes imperative. From a study of all the data a general plan can then be evolved, with various recommendations for the prevention of undesirable developments in the future. A good city plan constitutes a program extending over a long period of years, but it should never be a cut-and-dried affair. It should always remain tentative and flexible, subject to modification when need arises. The right sort of city plan is a living organism, an ever-changing compilation of ideas and projects. Emphasis goes on one feature today and on another tomorrow. Some parts of the plan may never be realized; others may have to be carried through little by little over a considerable period of years.

City plans should be flexible. Fashions change in city building as in the construction of homes. Civic needs undergo great alterations within a single decade. Hence nothing could be more detrimental to well-ordered urban growth than a stereotyped plan with no provision for changing it. For this reason it is the function of a city planning board not merely to prepare a plan and to stand guard over it, but to keep constantly recommending changes in it, adapting it to new civic requirements and varying some of its features day by day. In this way city planning becomes not only elastic but educative. The public discussion of proposed changes helps to make the citizens more familiar with the growth, problems, needs, and resources of their own neighborhoods. It provides a vigorous stimulant to civic interest and pride.

What does a city plan include? What matters are included within the scope of a comprehensive city plan? There are at least five general subjects and often more. The first concerns the means of circulation, that is, the facilities for getting goods and people from place to place within the city, whether by water, by railroad, by the street railways (including surface, elevated, and subway lines), by freight trucks, by motor-bus, and by private cars using the streets, or on foot. Nearly all large cities have a good deal of water-borne traffic, requiring harbor and dock facilities, space for warehouses, and connection with railroads. These need skilled planning to avoid acute congestion. Steam railroads rush great quantities of freight into the city and out of it, and this requires a careful coördination between the freight terminals, the trucking services, and the heavy-traffic street layout. Likewise the railroads pour their loads of commuters into the city every morning and take them back in the late afternoon hours. Good planning for the handling of this throng involves the provision of convenient terminals with quick access to the subways or surface lines. Likewise good planning involves the problem of bringing the railroads into the city in such way that the regular traffic streets will not be blocked by the trains. It is a hard problem in most large cities because the railroads arrived and took their rights of way long before the city planners came on the scene.

Then there is the street railway. It has been one of the chief factors in promoting the growth of suburban areas and also in contributing to congestion on the downtown streets. As this congestion grows more acute in the larger cities, it becomes necessary to re-route the cars, or even to take the surface trolleys off the street altogether, placing them either overhead or underground. Forty years ago it was thought that elevated structures would provide a solution for the problem of rapid transit, but they have not proved altogether satisfactory because of their noise and unsightliness. No more elevated lines are being built in downtown sections. Subways are expensive to construct, but are far more satisfactory in the long run.[1] Linking together the various forms of steam and electric transportation so that they will serve the public convenience in the highest degree and at the lowest practicable cost—that is one of the most difficult problems that confront the makers of city plans.

Urban transportation in the city plan.

An increasing amount of surface transportation is now being handled by trucks, motor-busses, and taxicabs. The motor-truck is already a formidable competitor of the railroad while the motor bus has entered into vigorous competition with railroads and street railways alike. These vehicles have cut down the traffic of these older utilities and have eaten into their net earnings. Motor-busses have an advantage over both railroads and street railways in that the amount of capital needed per unit of transportation is very small. They do not have to maintain trackage and rights of way. They pay very little in taxes. Only to a slight extent are they subjected to rigid regulation by the public authorities. Hence they

Planning for motor traffic.

[1] See Chapter XLIV.

are enabled to carry passengers at low rates of fare. Likewise the taxicab has become an important factor in urban transportation and a very serious one in traffic congestion, especially at rush hours of the day. As for private cars they occupy more space on the streets than all other traffic carriers put together. Street cars, busses, trucks, taxicabs, and cars—when they all crowd upon the street surface they leave room for nothing else. Eventually the congestion proves intolerable, despite the efforts of the traffic authorities. Then the city planning experts are given the problem of finding a solution.

Street layouts:

1. The gridiron plan.

The ease or difficulty of circulation in a city is closely related to its primary street layout. Street plans are traditionally of two general types, regular and radial. The regular or checkerboard plan is the one which American cities have most extensively utilized. The widespread adoption of this arrangement has been due not alone to the early example set by New York, but to the fact that it coincides with the interests of the real estate promoter. For it is economical in the amount of land which must be dedicated to public use, and leaves the maximum amount of ground for private sale. With a straight gridiron layout nearly seventy-five per cent of a subdivision remains available for sale in the form of building lots to private buyers. The lots, moreover, are of standard size and shape.

Its merits and defects.

Much criticism has been showered upon the checkerboard plan, not all of which has been deserved. Its aesthetic shortcomings are considerable, but it has some advantages. Certainly it facilitates the task of finding one's way about. No one need ever get lost in New York City above Fourteenth Street; it is not so in London or Paris,—or even in Boston. The gridiron plan, moreover, lends itself excellently to automatic traffic regulations, as recent experience in many American cities has shown. People call the checkerboard arrangement monotonous, but only because it looks so to them on the map. It is not so in reality. Versatility in architecture can be exemplified on straight streets and square corners, as anyone who wanders along Fifth Avenue will soon discover. It is in accordance with the American spirit to cut straight across things, which is what these early street planners did.

2. The radial plan.

The other general type of street plan, commonly known as the radial type, has been very popular in Europe. It somewhat faintly resembles a spider's web. Centers are established here and there

CITY PLANNING 231

throughout the city and from these centers main avenues radiate. In this way right-angled intersections are for the most part avoided and the building lots assume a variety of shapes and sizes. Baron Haussmann, in his reconstruction of Paris during the Second Empire, used this arrangement extensively. Broad avenues and boulevards, converging in open plots called *Places*, which could be used for the erection of monuments, were run through the central sections of the city with no thought of formal regularity. In this reconstruction many of the old, crooked passageways were widened and brought more directly into the new avenues. Haussmann's

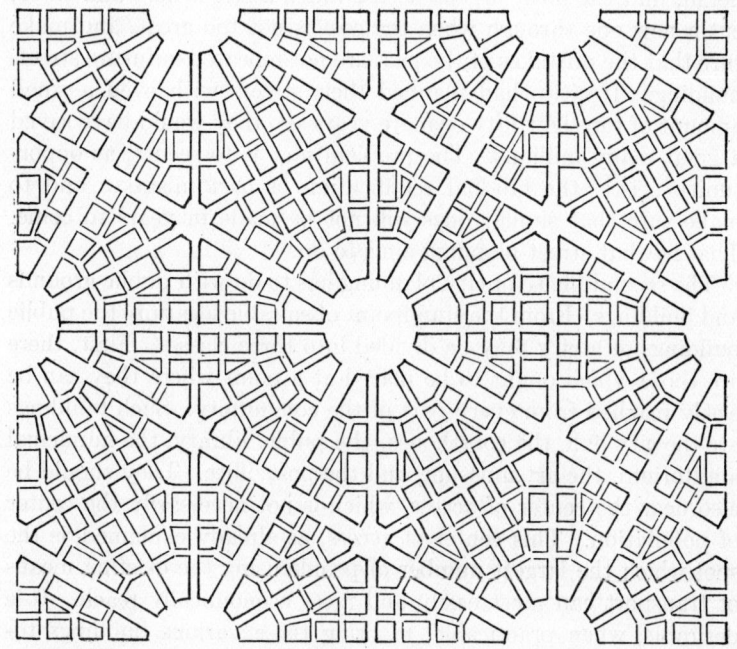

A Section of the "Governor and Judges" Plan for Detroit (1807)

idea was that the streets of the new Paris should be artistic, capacious, and, what was not of less importance, available for the rapid mobilization of troops.

In the United States the so-called Governor and Judges Plan for Detroit, prepared in 1807, affords an even better example of the radial arrangement. Happily it was never fully carried out, for it would have made the city an extremely inconvenient place

232 MUNICIPAL ADMINISTRATION

under modern conditions of traffic. L'Enfant, as has been pointed out, made use of both types, superimposing one upon the other. The gridiron layout forms his basis, with diagonal thoroughfares cut across it at various points. And in the newer suburban areas of many large American cities the same idea has been utilized. In various combinations the two plans can be made to work out very well together.

Street planning and the rectification of mistakes.

Of course it is impossible to replan and rebuild all the streets of a city. Such an enterprise would be too costly. The best that can be done is to take the existing layout, study its shortcomings in full detail, find the most urgent needs, widen a street here and there, cut a new one through when the cost is not too great, and make sure that the mistakes of the past are not repeated in future street-building. If cities had planned their streets with even a small amount of foresight fifty or more years ago they would have saved a great many millions. The problem now is to secure, as opportunity arises, the gradual rectification of past mistakes and to make sure that similar ones will not be made in years to come. That is what street planning aims to do.

Planning locations for public buildings:

The second phase of city planning has to do with public grounds and buildings. From the standpoint of suitable location, the public buildings of a city may be divided into three classes. First, there are those which ought to be placed at a point where they can be easily reached from every part of the community. Such buildings are the city hall, the courthouse, the public library, the municipal auditorium, the art museum, and the post office. They should be also near the center of access, which is not necessarily the center of population. This center of access, as already explained, is the spot which the largest number of people using the existing means of transport can most easily and most economically reach. It is desirable, when practicable, to bring these various buildings together in a civic center, but this, of course, cannot always be done. Too many different authorities are connected with the work. The federal government determines the location of the post office, the county authorities control the placing of the courthouse, and the city council determines the location of the public library. Only by something akin to a miracle can all three groups be brought into coöperation. Nevertheless civic centers have been constructed in a number of American cities, including such large communities as Cleveland and San Francisco.

1. Those which require a central location.

CITY PLANNING

On the other hand, there are various public buildings which must be located in different parts of the city. These include the fire and police stations, the elementary schools, the branch libraries, the health centers, and the public recreation buildings. From the nature of their use these must be scattered, but this does not mean that they have to be located at haphazard. Too often, unfortunately, that is what happens. For if the placing of these buildings is not made a matter of careful study by the city planning authorities, the sites will inevitably be determined by political pressure. Influential politicians will buy up cheap parcels of land, or get options on them, with the idea of making a good sale to the city. Howsoever unsuitable a location may be for the purpose in hand, these political fixers will try to manipulate enough votes in the city council to have it purchased, and they will usually succeed unless the planning authorities are prepared for them with proof that a better site can be had for less money.

2. Those which must be scattered.

Some other public buildings require specialized locations. Public bathhouses, for example, must go to the water's edge wherever it is. The municipal market must be accessible to the freight terminals. The city hospital should be situated outside the zone of heavy traffic, but sometimes it is not so located. And there are various other public structures, including the prison, the house of refuge, the garbage disposal plant, the incinerator, and even the airport— no residential neighborhood wants them in its vicinity. Some of them are unwelcome in any section of the community, yet they must be placed somewhere. Timely planning helps to solve this problem by securing convenient sites before the city grows too large. Everyone knows that various services will become necessary when a city reaches a certain size, but rarely is much thought given to the problem of searching suitable locations for them in advance. As a rule the municipal authorities wait until the growth of suburbs has made the problem a very difficult one. It is the function of the city planning board to supply the prevision which the other officials of the city so frequently lack.

3. Those which require specialized locations.

There is still another phase of city planning, and thus far it has received too little attention. For want of a better name it may be called social planning. This phase of the work is non-physical in character. It does not deal with streets, buildings, parks, or sewers, but with human relations. It includes the planning of the city's educational system, its recreation facilities, and the many other

Social planning.

things which conduce to the social strength of a community. It includes the promotion of good will between all classes of the city's population. And last, but by no means least, it comprises the endeavor to develop an active interest in civic affairs among the people, for without this all the other phases of city planning will avail but little. For a vigorous and well-sustained public interest is the foundation of good city government. Only on such a basis can a satisfactory city charter be obtained and made workable. Only under such circumstances can properly equipped men be brought out and elected to public office. City planning, therefore, has to do with charters and public opinion and sound politics as well as with schools, playgrounds, and art museums.

Financial planning.

Of great importance, finally, are the financial aspects of city planning. These are of high importance because no project of physical or social reconstruction can be carried through without spending money,—sometimes a great deal of it. The chief problem, very often, is not one of plans and specifications but of ways and means. There are a hundred men who can show you how to build a new parkway, as an engineering proposition, for every one man who can tell you how to get the money for it. Tax limits and debt limits often stand in the way. How much of the cost should be paid out of current taxes, how much out of funds borrowed on the city's credit, and how much of it should be defrayed by levying special assessments on adjacent private property? The decision of this question is not always a matter of laws or logic but of what the political exigencies will permit. City planning, therefore, involves the finding of money by the raising of tax limits and debt limits if need be, as well as by devising methods whereby special assessments can be more equitably levied. Inadequate attention has been given to this phase of city planning, and many well-framed projects have come to grief as a result. It avails nothing to make plans for something that a city cannot afford, and the time to determine what it can afford is before the plans are made.

Planning in relation to private property.

City planning does not confine itself to the regulation of public property alone; it deals also with the regulation of private property in the public interest. And this is important, for no matter how much the city itself may do in the way of improving its thoroughfares and erecting fine public buildings, much of this effort will be wasted so far as civic attractiveness is concerned unless the owners of private property are thereby influenced to raise their standards.

CITY PLANNING

Good planning therefore involves the coöperation of the citizens. To the extent that such coöperation is fundamentally essential for the orderly growth of the community it is usually enforced by the enactment of a zoning ordinance which divides the city into zones or districts, and in each of these districts regulates the height, bulk, arrangement, and construction of the buildings as well as the use to which such buildings may be put. But zoning is too important a matter to be covered in a few paragraphs, and the next chapter will be devoted to it.

REFERENCES

The literature of city planning is quite voluminous. References to virtually all of it that is worth while have been included in Theodora Kimball, *Manual of Information on City Planning and Zoning* (Cambridge, Mass., 1923), supplemented by Theodora Kimball Hubbard and Katherine McNamara, *Planning Information Up to Date* (Cambridge, 1928), and *Manual of Planning Information and Supplement* (Cambridge, 1929).

Books that may be singled out as likely to be of special value to the student of municipal administration are John Nolen, *New Towns for Old* (New York, 1927), *Twenty Years of City Planning Progress* (Cambridge, Mass., 1927) and *City Planning* (2nd edition, New York, 1929), Nelson P. Lewis, *The Planning of the Modern City* (2nd edition, New York, 1923), Frank B. Williams, *The Law of City Planning and Zoning* (New York, 1922), Karl B. Lohmann, *Principles of City Planning* (New York, 1931), Harlean James, *Land Planning in the United States for the City, State and Nation* (New York, 1926), Theodora K. Hubbard and Henry V. Hubbard, *Our Cities—Today and Tomorrow* (Cambridge, 1929), George B. Ford, *Building Height, Bulk and Form* (Cambridge, 1931), H. Paul Douglass, *The Suburban Trend* (New York, 1925), C. M. Robinson, *Modern Civic Art* (4th edition, New York, 1918), R. L. Duffus, *Mastering a Metropolis* (New York, 1930), Russell Van Nest Black, *Planning for the Small American City* (Chicago, 1933), Thomas Adams and others, *Recent Advances in Town Planning* (New York, 1932), and A. E. Wood, *Community Problems* (New York, 1928).

Books dealing with city planning in Great Britain are S. D. Adshead, *Town Planning and Town Development* (London, 1923), T. H. Hughes and E. A. G. Lamborn, *Towns and Town Planning: Ancient and Modern* (Oxford, 1923), and H. V. Lanchester, *The Art of Town Planning* (London, 1925).

The publications of the Committee on a Regional Plan of New York and Its Environs (10 vols., New York, 1927–1931) constitute a monumental work of the highest value to all students of city planning. Special attention should be called to the final volume on *The Building of the City* by T. Adams, H. M. Lewis, and L. M. Orton (New York, 1931). Current discussions may be found in the *Proceedings of the National Conference on City Planning* (130 East 22nd St., New York), issued annually since 1910, and in *City Planning*, a quarterly review (9 Park St., Boston).

See also the references at the close of Chapters XVI and XVIII.

CHAPTER XVIII

ZONING

*The city is built
To music, therefore never built at all,
And therefore built for ever.*
—*Tennyson.*

Zoning may be defined as a method of procedure whereby the city authorities endeavor to control the use or occupancy of land within the city limits by restricting such land to certain designated uses or to certain types of structures. The idea came from European cities, more particularly from Frankfort-on-the-Main, where the general principle of controlling the use of private property was put into operation during the early years of the twentieth century. It aimed to prevent the haphazard development of cities with resulting difficulties in public administration. {Definition.}

The chief argument in favor of zoning at the outset was the desirability of simplifying some tasks of the city administration. Proponents of the plan contended that the invasion of an industrial section by residences, or of a residential section by industries or business, inevitably complicated the problems of the various municipal departments. Assessors, for example, find difficulty in making fair tax-valuations when an area is in process of being transformed from residential to mercantile use. Land values in a transition area are unstable and speculative. Likewise the school authorities encounter difficulties when rapid changes are taking place in the character of a district through the invasion of industry. Within a few years nearly half the enrollment of an elementary school may disappear through the exodus of families from a section of the city that is ceasing to be residential. The cost per pupil in these half-emptied schools is naturally excessive. On the other hand the schoolrooms in other sections have to absorb this migration and become overcrowded. {The value of zoning.}

So with other branches of public administration. Police costs are increased by the intermingling of diverse activities within a single area. A strictly residential section is easy enough to patrol, {Police and fire protection.}

but with the encroachment of factories and shops the problem becomes more difficult. Pool-rooms, all-night lunch rooms, speak-easies and hang-outs edge their way in. Dwellings and apartment houses are transformed into cheap lodging houses or worse. So it is with fire prevention and fire protection. One does not need to argue the point that every invasion of a home area by factories and shops is certain to bring greater fire hazards and hence to accentuate the difficulty of providing adequate fire protection except at increased cost.

The safeguarding of a community's long-range interests.

The prime purpose of zoning, therefore, is to promote the growth of a city along orderly lines so that the problems of public administration may be made easier of solution. Haphazard and unplanned growth results in lower land values, higher taxes, public inconvenience, and impaired governmental service. Left without regulation, the development of a growing community will follow whatever seem to be the lines of least resistance at the moment. Promoters will push their business into any region that seems to offer profit, without any regard for the long-range interests of the city as a whole. Then the whole body of taxpayers is penalized by the resulting increase in the cost of police, fire protection, schools, health service, and public recreation.

By stabilizing real estate values.

But zoning is designed to benefit the individual as well as the community. It aims to protect every property owner against an unjust shrinkage in values. It seeks to ensure that the street on which a man buys a home shall not be open to the sort of industrial intrusion which makes the place no longer suitable for a home. It is based on the proposition that home owning can be encouraged by giving reasonable stability to residential values, and this stability cannot be achieved if anybody who wants to start a public garage or a meat market is permitted to place it wherever he chooses, irrespective of the wishes and interests of the immediate neighborhood.

Summary.

Comprehensive zoning, in a word, seeks to map off the city in such way that the use of every parcel of land will be restricted to its appropriate purpose from the standpoint of the public interest. It provides every form of business with a suitable and adequate area set apart for its exclusive use. It reserves designated sections for strictly residential use. Each area is then protected against encroachment by anything that does not appropriately belong to the zone. Such action accomplishes the threefold purpose of ensuring orderly civic development, lowering the expensiveness of public administration, and giving property values a reasonable measure of stability.

The first large American municipality to undertake a zoning project was New York City in 1916. This initial action created a threefold division of the city into industrial, mercantile, and residential areas. It did not, however, differentiate as between various classes of residential property such as apartment houses, duplex dwellings, single dwellings, and so on. New York's example was quickly followed by some other large cities and soon the zoning movement spread rapidly throughout the country. Within a dozen years zoning ordinances had been passed by the city authorities in the great majority of American municipalities. As the movement made headway the procedure was improved, particularly in the way of increasing and refining the classifications of districts. Today there are few American cities, large or small, which do not have zoning regulations of one sort or another.

History of the zoning movement.

It should not be assumed, however, that the provisions of a zoning ordinance relate only to the general type of building which may be erected in a designated area or to the occupational use which may be made of such buildings. As a rule the ordinance places limits on the height of structures, irrespective of their type or use. This limit is usually, but not always, related to the width of the street on which the building fronts. Likewise it is customary to restrict the percentage of area which may be built upon. Ordinarily from one-fourth to one-third of each city lot must be kept free for the admission of light and air. The zoning ordinance also deals with setbacks, that is, in residential districts it may prohibit the construction of any building within so many feet of the front property line, thus enhancing the appearance of the street. It has been suggested that restrictions should also be placed upon the type of architecture which may be used by property owners when erecting buildings, but zoning ordinances have not yet gone that far.

General scope of zoning provisions.

Ordinarily the first step in the process of zoning a municipality is taken by the city planning commission or by a special zoning commission appointed for the purpose. City planning commissions, as has already been explained, are usually authorized by the city charter or by state law; they consist of five or more members who are usually appointed by the mayor, city manager, or city council.

The city planning commission and the zoning survey.

The city planning commission or special zoning commission proceeds to examine the municipal maps and to make a study of the local situation. This usually involves the hiring of experts and the preparation of new maps showing the purposes for which all buildings in the city are already being used, the height of all structures, the density of population, the setbacks, and the range of property values. Along with these special maps a great deal of statistical data has to be gathered, all of which involves the spending of considerable time and money. Because of this some of the smaller cities have gone ahead and drafted their zoning ordinances offhand, without adequate preliminary data, and guided largely by the personal judgment of the city councilmen. Such action has usually proved to be false economy in the end. It has often resulted in faulty ordinances and costly litigation. Poor zoning is in some respects worse than no zoning at all.[1]

Drafting a zoning ordinance. Following the completion of the survey, the next step is the drafting of the zoning ordinance, which is submitted to the city council with a map of the districts. The proposals are then discussed at public hearings in order that full opportunity may be given for protests and objections. In many states the laws provide that public hearings with adequate notice must be held before a zoning ordinance can be legally adopted or amended. In addition the ordinance is usually presented for discussion to the various civic and neighborhood organizations so that the rank and file of citizens may become properly acquainted with the purpose and scope of the new regulations. Such discussions are highly useful, not only because they help to dissipate misunderstandings but because they uncover defects in the draft-ordinance and often point the way to an improvement in the various provisions.

The final stages. After the public hearings have been concluded, the planning commission or special zoning commission takes time to go over all the objections and suggestions which have been made. This done, its recommendations are transmitted to the city council which alters the provisions in accordance with these recommendations if it sees fit. Then the zoning ordinance, having been given its final form, is put through its regular stages by the city council and passed to enactment. The provisions of such ordinances are not

---

[1] For further details see the article on "Zoning Survey and Procedure" by Earl O. Mills in the *Annals of the American Academy of Political and Social Science*, Vol. CLV, Part II, pp. 69–73 (May, 1931).

usually retroactive. They do not require that already established industries shall move out of areas which have been zoned for residential purposes, but merely provide that no more industries shall move in.

Some zoning ordinances make classifications which are quite elaborate. For example, some have designated at least five zones, namely, (a) single residence, (b) apartment and income residential, (c) mercantile, (d) light industrial, and (e) heavy industrial. The rules relating to maximum height, bulk, type of construction, and setbacks from the street are usually different in these various zones. Such an arrangement obviously simplifies the problems of street construction and street lighting as well as those of policing and protecting property from fire. *The number and character of the zones.*

The enactment of a zoning ordinance is a legislative function, but the enforcement of its provisions is an administrative responsibility. The official who is commonly charged with the administration of these provisions is the building supervisor, or chief building inspector, or whatever he may be called. Before any building can be erected, or radically altered, an application must be made to his office for a building permit. This he will not issue unless the proposed structure and its proposed use are in accordance with the provisions of the zoning ordinance. It is the function of the buildings department to see that the provisions of the ordinance are strictly followed in the matter of setbacks, the type of construction, the height, the fire hazards, the sanitary requirements, and all other legal stipulations. To this end the application must be accompanied by preliminary plans of the building and a careful scrutiny of these plans is made by one of the building inspectors before the permit is granted. After the building is finished, a certificate of occupancy must usually be obtained before the place can be occupied. This is to make sure that all the conditions of the permit have been fulfilled. While building inspectors are supposed to be strict in their administration of the rules, there is sometimes a good deal of laxity in their work. Political and personal considerations often intervene on behalf of favored contractors and buildings which are out of conformance with the zoning regulations sometimes get through. *Enforcement of the zoning regulations.*

Zoning ordinances should not be made of cast-iron. They should have some flexibility. This means that provision must be made for the granting of exceptions to the general rules wher- *Making exceptions to the rules.*

ever good reasons for such action arise. Otherwise the terms of the ordinance may work much hardship in individual cases and thereby engender unpopularity. So a safety valve is usually provided by setting up a board of adjustment with power to grant special permits or to transfer a parcel of land from one classification to another. In some municipalities the city council retains this function for itself.[1] In any event it is often difficult to protect the integrity of the zoning ordinance because of the political pressure which inevitably comes to the aid of property owners who desire special favors. Real estate dealers find that they can sell certain plots of residential land at high prices if they can get permission to build apartment houses thereon. Forthwith they mobilize their influence to secure the exemption of this land from the general provisions of the zoning ordinance. Consequently there has developed a great deal of "spot zoning," that is, the making of exceptions in favor of particular parcels of land, thus eliminating them from the classification in which they were originally placed and putting them in another.

"Spot zoning."

Objections to it.

Applications for spot zoning usually develop into a battle royal between two sets of private interests, namely, those who own the property in question and expect to profit by the change, and those owners of neighboring property who fear that the change will result in loss to themselves. All other considerations, for the most part, are lost to view. Very rarely does a board of adjustment or a city council explore the question whether the change, if made, will increase or simplify the difficulties of municipal administration, or whether it is in line with the process of orderly plan and regulated growth which the municipality has laid out for itself. The issue is usually determined by the respective amounts of political and personal influence that each of the opposing interests can bring to bear.[2]

The public attitude.

This does not mean, however, that spot zoning is always inadvisable. There are times when it is warranted by considerations of general well-being, even though it may be detrimental to private property in the immediate neighborhood. Unfortunately the neighbors rarely see the matter in that light. Many owners of residen-

[1] See the chapter on "Zoning" in T. K. Hubbard and H. V. Hubbard's *Our Cities Today and Tomorrow* (Cambridge, Mass., 1929), pp. 162–191.
[2] "A Danger Spot in the Zoning Movement" by William B. Munro, in the *Annals of the American Academy of Political and Social Science*, Vol. CLV, pp. 202–206 (May, 1931).

tial property, because of assurances given them by enthusiastic real estate dealers at the time of purchase, have come to feel that they have a vested right in the provisions of the zoning ordinance and hence that any change in it, if made to their detriment, is a breach of faith on the part of the public authorities.

Such a point of view, although natural enough on the part of the private owner, betrays a false philosophy of law and public administration. The purchase of property in a zoned area carries no guarantee, express or implied, that its environment will never be suffered to undergo a change. Zoning is not intended to serve as an impregnable shield to private property against the vicissitudes of time and circumstance. No one can acquire a vested interest in public policy, or in the laws of the land, or in the city ordinances. It stands to reason that so long as we have a system of government by all the people, there must be reasonable discretion on the part of the public authorities to modify the ordinances in such way as to serve the greatest good of the greatest number. Hence no one has either a moral or legal right to insist that any general rule (whether it relates to zoning, or traffic, or the salaries of public officials, or any other administrative matter) shall be maintained intact because a change in the rule would be detrimental to his own private interest or advantage. To concede any such right would be to clog the wheels of civic progress and make zoning a barrier rather than an incentive to orderly municipal growth. *It is often unreasonable.*

In this, therefore, as in many other fields of municipal administration one finds a head-on collision of two philosophies, both of them false. One assumes that land ought to be re-zoned whenever there is a pecuniary profit in doing it; the other holds that it should never be done if somebody nearby is to suffer pecuniary loss. Both lose sight of the major considerations. Unhappily the promoters of a change are usually the more influential and emerge as the victors. Accordingly many small parcels of land, sometimes single lots, are lifted bodily out of one zone and placed in another while all the surrounding land remains classified as before. Somebody with sufficient political or personal influence wants the place as a location for a gasoline station or a block of stores. He and his friends set to work, pull all the strings, until by dint of plausibility and persistence they get what they are after. They argue that the re-zoning will enable a new building to be erected, thus increasing *A conflict of philosophies.*

property values for taxation, and, best of all,—providing work for the unemployed. Any large construction, no matter how inappropriate to the neighborhood, can be advocated as providing work. Indeed the more inappropriate the structure to the environment of a residential district, the more work for the unemployed it is likely to provide.

Regulating the height of buildings. Zoning, as has been said, restricts not only the character and use of property, but regulates the height of buildings as well. The chief reason for regulating the height of buildings in cities is the desire to ensure adequate light and air to smaller adjoining structures; but there is also the motive of protecting the adjacent streets from overload on their surface capacity. It has been demonstrated by various surveys that the number of persons concentrated in certain areas of New York and Chicago is greater than the adjacent streets can accommodate. The day-population of some metropolitan skyscrapers runs as high as three thousand. These throngs of people are poured out into the streets at the lunch hour and at closing time with acute congestion as a result. Hence it has become the practice to limit the height of buildings in accordance with the width of the street on which they front. The New York zoning ordinance of 1916 recognized this relation between building height and street width by devising the step-up-and-step-back or decreasing volumetric arrangement which has worked such a picturesque modification in the architecture of tall buildings in the metropolis during the last fifteen years. The higher the building, the farther it recedes from the street at successive stages and the less its additional volume becomes. In smaller cities the usual plan is to restrict the height to one and one-half times the width of the street in front.

The constitutionality of zoning. Zoning has been upheld as constitutional under the police power of the municipality. That is, the power to zone the city is included within its general right to make reasonable regulations for protecting the "public health, safety, morals, and general welfare." This was established in an interesting decision some years ago. In 1922 the city council of Euclid, Ohio, passed a comprehensive zoning ordinance which excluded industries from the entire municipality. Euclid lies just outside Cleveland and seemed to be in the line of industrial growth and development, but its citizens wished to preserve the place as a residential community and sought to do this by erecting the zone barrier. Thereupon a certain real estate company brought action to annul the ordinance on the ground that it was a deprivation of property without due process of law and hence unconstitutional.

The case found its way to the United States Supreme Court and was decided by this tribunal in 1926. The decision upheld the authority of the city to pass the ordinance in question and laid down certain general principles in relation to zoning which are now recognized as the law of the land. More particularly the court established the point that the provisions of a zoning or city planning ordinance are to be construed, as to their reasonability, with reference to particular circumstances and localities and not by abstract considerations. *A significant decision.*

"Whether the power exists to forbid the erection of a building of a particular kind, or for a particular use, is to be determined not by an abstract consideration of the building or of the thing considered apart, but by considering it in connection with the circumstances and the locality. . . . The exclusion from residential districts by zoning ordinances of business and trade of every sort, including hotels and apartment houses, cannot be said to be so clearly arbitrary and unreasonable and to have no such substantial relation to the public health, safety, morals and general welfare as not to be within the police power. . . . The exclusion of places of business from residential districts is not a declaration that such places are nuisances or that they are to be suppressed as such, but it is a part of the general plan by which the city's territory is allotted to different uses in order to prevent or at least to reduce the congestion, disorder and dangers which often inhere in unregulated municipal development." [1]

Zoning is sometimes criticized as undemocratic. Its opponents contend that it tends to segregate the well-to-do in one part of the city and the industrial workers in another. By setting apart a certain district for industries it encourages the herding of the workers into tenement houses near by, while the restriction of other sections to single-family dwellings is an incentive to the concentration of the well-to-do in these parts of the city. This is doubtless true but it is not necessarily an argument against zoning. Most people prefer to live in homogeneous neighborhoods with others like themselves. Nothing is gained from the mere juxtaposition of diversified tenants in adjacent houses. Such contiguity gives no assurance that they will understand each other better. Zoning *Is zoning undemocratic?*

[1] Euclid vs. Ambler Realty Company, 272 *U. S.* 365.

merely promotes and conserves what is and ought to be the natural order of urban life.

Zoning and monopoly locations. A more serious objection to zoning, and one that cannot well be remedied, is the fact that it often operates to establish monopoly locations. When a zoning ordinance is passed, there may be one or two retail stores already located in a residential district. As the ordinance is not retroactive these stores are permitted to remain, but no more may come in. This means that they are shielded from competition and hence have no incentive to keep prices low. Moreover those properties become valuable through the legal advantages which they enjoy. To some extent the objectionableness of this situation can be mollified by spot zoning other locations for retail business right alongside when conditions warrant such intervention.

Regional zoning. When several municipalities are located close to one another, it is desirable to have the zoning planned on a regional basis, that is, the zones should be mapped out for the whole area and not for each municipality by itself. In that way it is made possible for each community to acquire and keep its own distinctiveness. Regional zoning, moreover, prevents competition among neighboring cities, with each trying to attract industries or apartment houses by lowering the restrictions. It is desirable, if practicable, that heavy industries should be concentrated in one part of the region rather than decentralized into one section of each municipality within the region. This is because the freight terminal, trucking roads, and other facilities can be organized to do better service in that case. So with mercantile and residential areas. Zoning here is more efficient when established on a regional basis.

Zoning against billboards. Closely related to zoning is the question of protecting the attractiveness of a community against eyesores of various sorts. One of the most persistent offenders against good taste in this respect is the flaming billboard which thrusts itself before one's gaze at every turn. From every vacant lot, from the roofs of buildings, as well as from walls and fences these monstrosities of wood and paper shout their commercial messages to the passerby. They mar the hillsides and inject their raucous presence into every agreeable vista. Numerous cities, finding their parks, boulevards, and residential streets defaced by billboards, have endeavored to find a way of abating the nuisance. There are, however, some serious legal obstacles in the way because billboards cannot be suppressed for the mere reason that they happen to be unsightly. Mere unsightliness does not constitute a sound reason for depriving any man of his property—at least the courts have thus far held that it does not.

Billboards may be subjected to restriction in the interest of public safety or public morals; they may be forbidden in residential districts unless certain conditions are met; and they may be subjected to reasonable taxation. Regulatory ordinances and laws may therefore require that billboards be made of strong construction so that they will not be blown over by the wind, that they be built in such way as to constitute no fire hazard, that they be limited in size, and set a certain distance back from the public highways. By one regulation or another short of actual prohibition some communities have been able to make the billboard business unprofitable. A proposal has been made to prohibit all billboards on highways as an interference with safety in driving, since the driver of a motor car cannot read billboards and watch the road at the same time; but it is questionable whether the courts would uphold this extension of the police power. Some day it is not improbable that the courts will concede the point that billboards may be treated as structures and zoned out of certain districts altogether, just as lumber yards and gas tanks now are. It would be a logical and desirable step to take.

Can the billboard nuisance be eradicated?

REFERENCES

Short discussions of zoning may be found in H. B. Dorau and A. G. Hinman, *Urban Land Economics* (New York, 1928), pp. 298–321; S. E. W. Bedford, *Readings in Urban Sociology* (New York, 1927), pp. 125–132; Austin F. Macdonald, *American City Government and Administration* (New York, 1929), pp. 480–504; John Nolen, *City Planning* (revised edition, New York, 1929); Stanley L. McMichael and R. F. Bingham, *City Growth Essentials* (Cleveland, 1928), pp. 359–377; and in the *Proceedings* of the American Society of Civil Engineers, Vol. LI, pp. 153–217 (February, 1925) and pp. 434–446 (March, 1925).

The entire issue of the *Annals of the American Academy of Political and Social Science*, Vol. CLV, pp. 1–230 (May, 1931), is devoted to the subject of "Zoning in the United States" under the editorship of W. L. Pollard. An excellent classified bibliography, compiled by Katherine McNamara, is appended (pp. 213–227) and covers every phase of the question.

Useful books on the legal aspects of the subject are James Metzenbaum, *The Law of Zoning* (New York, 1930), Newman F. Baker, *Legal Aspects of Zoning* (Chicago, 1927), Helen M. Werner, *The Constitutionality of Zoning Regulations* (Urbana, 1926), and H. S. Swan, *The Law of Zoning,* issued as a Supplement to the *National Municipal Review,* Vol. X, pp. 517–536 (October, 1921).

A summary of recent legal decisions relating to zoning, by Frank B. Williams, appears in each annual issue of *The Municipal Index, e.g.,* 1930, pp. 132–150; 1931, pp. 154–162; 1932, pp. 134–143. A *Standard State Zoning Enabling Act* (revised edition, Washington, 1926) is the work of the Advisory Committee on Zoning in the United States Department of Commerce.

See also the references at the close of Chapters XVI and XVII.

CHAPTER XIX

LAND TAKINGS AND EXCESS CONDEMNATION

Interest reipublicae ut quisque re sua bene utatur.—Latin Proverb.

In connection with nearly all public improvements the city finds it necessary to acquire land from private owners. It needs this land when new streets are being laid out, or old thoroughfares widened, or when parks and playgrounds are established, or new public buildings erected. One of the serious problems connected with public works administration in all cities is that of getting land without having to pay too much for it. The procedure which the municipal authorities are required to follow in this matter should be fully explained, for it is by no means simple and it has frequently opened the door to a considerable amount of waste and corruption. {Acquiring land for public use.}

When privately owned land is needed by a city for a public improvement, how is it obtained? It may be acquired in one of three ways. In the first place, the land may be donated or dedicated to the city by its owners in connection with schemes of real estate promotion. This is the usual method when streets are being laid out in newly opened suburban areas. What happens is about as follows: A realty concern or syndicate obtains a tract of outlying land, purchasing it at so much per acre. A surveyor or planner is then called in and instructed to subdivide the tract into suitable building lots, with due reservations for streets. When the plan is finished it is submitted to the city authorities with an offer to donate the land indicated on the plan as street area in return for permission to go ahead and sell the building lots. If the city accepts the offer the streets become municipal property and are thereafter maintained as such. They become "dedicated" to public use. {The methods: 1. By dedication.}

Some cities make it a rule to accept no donation of street land, in connection with a new real estate subdivision, unless a specified minimum of the whole tract is included within the street area so dedicated. This is intended to serve as a deterrent to avaricious promoters who otherwise would put as little area as possible into {Acceptance of dedicated street areas.}

street reservations in order to have as much as possible for sale in lots. Many cities go even farther and require that promoters of real estate subdivisions shall not only dedicate a sufficient amount of street space for public use but shall lay the water and sewer mains, besides grading and paving the streets before they are accepted by the city. In any event the usual practice is to refer all new subdivision plans to the city's planning department for study and recommendation as to the adequacy and suitability of the proposed street layout. This is a wise precaution because the subdivision owner is primarily interested in a street plan that will give him the largest return from the sale of his lots, and such a layout may not be to the best interest of the whole neighborhood. In rapidly growing communities a great many subdivision plans are submitted every year and large numbers of new streets are acquired in this way without any cost to the municipality.

2. By purchase.

The second method of acquiring land for public use is by purchase. In the older, thickly settled parts of the city, very little street area is ever obtained by dedication. When land is needed in the downtown sections for a street widening or for the location of a public building it can be purchased in the open market, if the city authorities so desire, by making an offer to the private owners of the land and inducing them to accept it voluntarily. But this method is not usually practicable. The city is at a disadvantage as a buyer in the open market because the private owners, who know that the city must have the land, are likely to hold out for high prices. At times, it is true, the two sides manage to get together amicably on a project of public improvement, with the city agreeing to go ahead with the work on condition that the private owners turn over their property at a stated figure, but such occasions do not arise with great frequency.

Advance bargaining in connection with special assessments.

More often, perhaps, the city finds it possible to make an agreement whereby it obtains land for the widening of a street with the stipulation that the price shall be offset, in whole or in part, by a designated levy upon the remaining property of the private owners because of its increased value due to the widening. In this connection it should be explained that municipalities usually have the right to recoup themselves, in part at least, for the outlay involved in connection with a street widening by laying special assessments on adjacent private property which may have been enhanced in

LAND TAKINGS AND EXCESS CONDEMNATION

value by reason of the improvement. The procedure in levying these special assessments has already been explained.[1]

The third method of acquiring land is by condemnation. This system is widely used because much of the land which a city requires in connection with the expansion of its public activities cannot be obtained by gift nor will the owners agree to part with it in what the municipal authorities believe to be a fair bargain. The only alternative, in such cases, is to condemn the land, in other words to take it regardless of the owner's consent.

3. By condemnation.

The method of taking land in this way is a somewhat complicated one, and to understand it some familiarity with the principle of eminent domain is necessary. This principle starts from the postulate that the needs of the community should take priority over the wishes or interests of the individual citizen. Hence it is a rule of law that the *domain* (or ultimate ownership) of the state is *eminent* or paramount over private property. The national or state governments may take private property at any time for a public purpose, provided always (and this proviso is very important) that the private owner shall be given "just compensation." Such a requirement as to just compensation is stipulated in both the national and the state constitutions. The state government, moreover, may delegate its right of eminent domain to a city, county, school district, or even to a public utility corporation such as a street railway company. When this is done, the city or the public utility corporation is privileged to take whatever private property it may need for a public or semi-public use on condition that the owners are duly compensated.

The legal basis of land takings.

By virtue of this privilege the municipal authorities do not have to pay whatever price the private owners of property may demand. If an exorbitant figure is demanded they can proceed to take the land by formal condemnation and settle the price later. The procedure in doing this differs from city to city but in general it is as follows: Whenever a public improvement is under consideration the city engineer's office prepares a plan and exact description of the privately owned land that will be needed in connection with the project. If the project is then approved by the municipal authorities the city council passes an ordinance setting forth its intention to proceed, and the next step is to make sure that the land is acquired by "due legal process" as the constitutions in

Condemnation procedure.

[1] See Chapter XII.

most of the states require. To this end the procedure is turned over to the city's law department which prepares such public notices and arranges for such hearings as are required by law. At these hearings a protest against the improvement from the owners of a majority of the frontage affected may be filed and in such cases it is sometimes stipulated that a protest of this kind puts an end to the project. Occasionally it is provided that any owner may intervene to raise the question whether the taking of the land is necessary for a public use and may have this issue decided by a jury.

Final steps. When the various formalities have been concluded (and they sometimes take considerable time), the final step is either to file a condemnation in the registry of deeds or other office provided by law (whereupon the title passes to the city) or, in some states, to have the issue submitted to an eminent domain commission or other statutory authority. From its decision as to the necessity of the taking and the amount of compensation to be awarded an appeal may be carried to the regular courts. In some other states the issue goes directly to these courts without being first heard by a commission of any kind. In some cases the city does not take the land but only a right-of-way over the property, leaving the title with the private owner. Such action follows the same procedure as when the property itself is condemned. Taking only a right of way or easement in the case of streets has not been found to be wise policy, on the whole, because difficult questions often arise as to whether pipes and conduits can then be placed under the surface without calling for further compensation.

Defects of the condemnation procedure. There are few matters on which the procedure differs so greatly from place to place as in this field of land takings under the law of eminent domain. Almost everywhere, however, the proceedings are tedious and technical. Notices have to be given, hearings held, and resolutions passed. A city is fortunate if it gets possession of condemned land within six months or a year. Rarely, moreover, is it practicable to satisfy the owner whose land has been taken from him. He has his recourse at law, it is true. He can prosecute a suit against the city for the full amount that he claims. The constitution gives him that privilege. If he avails himself of it, his suit is duly entered, placed on the court calendar, and heard after a delay of several months as a rule. At the trial he produces testimony as to the value of the land, but real estate experts and valuators

LAND TAKINGS AND EXCESS CONDEMNATION 253

will also appear on behalf of the city. Each side will present widely varying estimates of true value, and the court will sometimes appoint its own impartial experts to assist it in reaching a fair conclusion. When the testimony is completed the lawyers make their arguments, the issue goes to the jury, and in the end a judgment is given.[1] It may be for all that the owner asks, or for what the city has offered, or for some amount between the two. Usually it is for an in-between figure. If either party is dissatisfied with the award an appeal may be taken, in which case the matter goes for review to a higher court.

All this means that litigation in land-taking cases is slow and costly. Both sides are wise to avoid it when they can. Nevertheless a great many such cases go to trial every year. This is partly because the value of urban land is a matter which lends itself to wide and honest differences of opinion. Real estate appraisers will sometimes vary, in good faith, as much as fifty per cent or more. Juries are in the habit of splitting the difference, which is hardly a fair way of dealing with either side. Few reforms would be of greater aid to efficient city planning than a reform and simplification of the procedure now used in connection with the compulsory acquisition of land for street widenings and other such purposes. *The need for reforms in it.*

Mention has been made of the fact that the taking of land for public improvements has often opened the door to corruption. It provides opportunity for what is known as "honest graft." For naturally it is the politicians who get the earliest information concerning the city's plans. When the city proposes to widen a street or to build a police station or to establish a new playground they are the first to know about it. Immediately some of them, through intermediaries, go out and purchase or get options upon the land that will be needed in connection with such plans. Options are more common than outright purchases because they do not take so much money. *Land acquisitions and honest graft.*

At any rate, when the plans are publicly announced and the city proceeds to acquire the land it is with politically influential personages that the authorities have to negotiate. Strong pressure is brought upon them to pay the price that is asked. Repeatedly it has been shown, in the course of investigations, that cities have paid exorbitant prices to officeholders and their political allies for *Buying from politicians at fancy prices.*

---

[1] In some states the suit may be heard without a jury.

land that had been purchased by them with the sole purpose of unloading it on the municipality. Such deals are always cloaked from public view by having the title or the option recorded in the name of someone other than the politician himself, a "straw man" as he is called, who merely serves as a go-between and gets a small commission for his services. The only adequate safeguard against this mulcting of the city is a provision in some cities that unless the owner is willing to accept say fifty per cent above the assessed value of the land the award must be left to the court for decision.

A few questions raised but not answered.

Can land be taken for one public purpose and then used for another? Can land belonging to one municipality be taken for use by another? For example, can a county condemn land already owned by a city if it needs such property as a site for the county courthouse? Is the compensation for land based upon its value when the proceedings are started or its value when they are ended? There may be a considerable rise or fall in the period of a year or two which often intervenes. This is hardly the place to discuss such intricate legal questions.[1] They are raised to show that the whole subject is by no means a simple one and that the present discussion has covered only its very general aspects.

Excess condemnation.

One more of these general phases remains to be mentioned, namely, the taking of excess land. As a rule it is not allowable to condemn any greater area of land than is actually required for the public purpose in hand. But the courts have been liberal in their construction of the term public purpose. They have held that to condemn land for streets, parks, police stations, schoolhouses, hospitals, and so on is clearly to take it for public use; likewise they have permitted the compulsory acquisition of land for street railway terminals, subway stations, garbage reduction plants, airports, or power-houses. But they have usually insisted that the city must not take more land than it actually needs. Unless it has been specifically empowered to do so, a municipality is not allowed to take excess area with the idea of reselling it at an enhanced price after the improvement has been completed and thereby getting back part of the outlay. For example, the city authorities are not permitted, under ordinary circumstances, to condemn a strip on either side of a new street with the design of resurveying this area into building lots which may be sold at a profit.

Its limitations.

[1] They are fully discussed in the books listed at the end of the chapter.

LAND TAKINGS AND EXCESS CONDEMNATION 255

Nor has it usually been possible to control the immediate surroundings of a new city hall, public library, or art museum by acquiring the land around about and then reselling it under restrictions which would ensure its appropriate use. Hence it frequently happens that the value of a street widening from the standpoint of traffic facilitation is considerably offset from an aesthetic point of view by the rows of cut-in-half and patched-up buildings which line the enlarged thoroughfare. Or the new public library finds itself fronted on a row of dilapidated tenements.

Why excess takings are at times desirable.

Moreover the principle that a city must not condemn surplus land for resale has often proved a barrier to the successful financing of public improvements, especially in the case of downtown street widenings where the original building lots are badly cut into, leaving only land remnants which, by reason of their inadequate size or odd shape, are not suitable for anything but small buildings of awkward construction. In such cases the city loses financially because it cannot recoup itself through adequate special assessments on the abutting property. The remnants of land are not of sufficient value to be heavily assessed. Their value is reduced by their unsuitability for building sites.

The avoidance of remnants.

Here is a problem of law, finance, construction, and aesthetics combined. The city, let us say, has a crowded fifty-foot street which it desires to widen into an eighty-foot one. The lots on each side are fifty to sixty feet deep. To take a fifteen-foot strip on both sides for the widening project would reduce the depth of the lots in some cases to thirty-five feet—too shallow for profitable use. Moreover, if the street is a crooked one and needs to be straightened in the widening, there will be various remnants which are smaller still. To consolidate these shallow lots with lands in the rear or alongside is rarely practicable by any process of voluntary agreement among the different owners. Hence it often happens that a newly widened street remains for years with unbuilt shreds of land on both sides of it, most of them serving as sites for billboards. That is not what the city spent money to create. If, however, the city were permitted to take a broad zone of land, say one hundred feet in depth, on each side of the improved street, it could then lay out suitable lots of sufficient depth and sell these to private purchasers for the erection of office-buildings, stores, hotels, theaters and so forth under proper regulations as to construction and appearance. In this way the city treasury might

An illustration.

not only recover a substantial part of the original outlay, but would greatly facilitate the work of rebuilding upon the abutting property.

<small>Constitutional provision to facilitate excess condemnation.</small>

Cities, however, are not permitted to do this unless they have been specifically given the power of excess condemnation by constitutional amendment. For the constitutions of virtually all the states contain a stipulation that private property shall not be taken by the authorities *except for a public use*. To take property for resale to private purchasers is to stretch the term "public use" beyond what the courts have usually been willing to permit. During the past thirty years, however, a number of American states have amended their constitutions to confer a restricted authority on their municipalities to take land in excess of actual public needs. In such cases the city authorities are permitted to condemn not only the land that is directly required for a public improvement, but also as much additional property in the immediate vicinity as may be needed to resurvey the excess land or to protect the improvement from being surrounded by ill-assorted and unsightly private structures. Compensation to the private owners is given in the usual way. When the improvement has been completed, the re-surveyed excess land is sold to the highest bidders. In this way, if the project is skillfully handled, the city may get back a substantial portion of what the improvement cost.

<small>Financial dangers in the plan.</small>

Unfortunately the handling of such projects is not always skillful. Too often there is political jugglery in the sale of the land. Hence, as a practical matter, too much stress should not be laid upon the financial advantages of the excess condemnation procedure. Experience has shown that American cities more often lose than save money when they undertake public improvements on this expansive basis. And there are reasons why this is likely to be the case. Municipal authorities in the United States have rarely proved themselves to be good bargainers. They usually pay too much for land. They are slow in getting improvements completed; hence the excess land is held too long with interest charges piling up. Then it is often sold at snap-auctions to favored purchasers at prices below what might have been obtained for it if the proceedings were open and above-board. There are exceptions to all this, of course, but they are none too common.

LAND TAKINGS AND EXCESS CONDEMNATION 257

Excess condemnation should not be used unless there are considerations other than purely financial ones at issue. It should be regarded as an instrumentality of good taste rather than of good business. In other words its justification ought to be primarily in the importance of the aesthetic considerations involved. Nor should one overlook the dangers which lurk in any free use of the power to condemn land in excess of purely public needs. If our cities develop the habit of projecting street-widening schemes on the theory that they can traffic in real estate and emerge with a profit, the taxpayers are apt to be sadly disillusioned. Syndicates of municipal politicians will hardly permit such opportunities of self-enrichment to pass unutilized. They will manage to load the city with land that nobody will buy back at what it cost. There are few ways in which large sums may be more quickly dissipated than in land speculation. Cities should keep out of this maelstrom. They are not well equipped to deal with sharp realtors. Excess condemnation should be an exceptional, not a regular procedure.

The power to take excess land should be used sparingly.

In European cities the conditions are somewhat different. There the practice of excess condemnation has long been followed because no constitutional barriers have intervened. The first use of the procedure on a large scale was in connection with Baron Haussmann's construction of the great Paris boulevards during the middle years of the nineteenth century. In this case the authorities condemned wide swaths of territory through which the new avenues were laid out. Then the surplus land, after having been suitably re-surveyed, was put up for sale. It sold readily and brought good prices; but the proceeds were below expectations, and the net cost of the whole enterprise was very large. Whatever its results may have been in the way of urban beautification, the experiment was not regarded as a financial success and the procedure has not since been much used in Paris.

European experience:
1. Paris.

London, however, has undertaken many public improvements during the past fifty years under this general plan. One of the most extensive was the fine thoroughfare known as the Kingsway, which runs from Holborn to the Strand. Financially the results in this instance proved to be somewhat disappointing as the gross cost of the highway turned out to be a good deal more than the authorities had counted upon. Other European cities have had varying experiences with excess condemnation, but on the whole

2. London.

their figures of profit and loss do not warrant the expectation that American municipalities can hope to utilize this plan on any extensive scale with financial success. It should be reiterated, however, that the financial aspects of the matter are not the only ones involved. Even though the use of the excess-condemnation procedure may prove to be more costly than the other alternatives, it may nevertheless be the wiser one under certain conditions. For only by using it can the city, in some instances, get what it wants, namely, a guarantee that a fine highway which has been built or widened at heavy cost will not be fringed on both sides by vacant remnants of land or by odd-shaped and tawdry structures.

Relatively small use of excess condemnation in the United States. Twenty-five years ago there was more interest in excess condemnation than there is today. Much effort was put forth at that time to secure the removal of constitutional barriers, and when this had been accomplished a number of cities began to use the plan. But only in rare cases were the results altogether satisfactory. Under ordinary circumstances it has been found that more net advantage to the city can be gained by carrying through public improvements under a plan of special assessments levied upon the private property which has been benefited.

REFERENCES

The most comprehensive studies of this subject are John Lewis, *A Treatise on the Law of Eminent Domain in the United States* (3rd edition, 2 vols., Chicago, 1909) and Philip Nichols, *The Law of Eminent Domain* (2nd edition, 2 vols., Albany, 1917). A good brief survey may be found in the chapter entitled "The Acquisition of Land" which is included in Flavel Shurtleff and F. L. Olmsted, *Carrying Out the City Plan* (New York, 1914), pp. 22–51.

On the condemning of surplus land a useful volume is R. E. Cushman, *Excess Condemnation* (New York, 1917). There is also a good discussion in F. B. Williams, *The Law of City Planning and Zoning* (New York, 1922), pp. 59–160. Mention may likewise be made of the Massachusetts Constitutional Convention Bulletin on *Excess Condemnation* (Boston, 1918), and the Illinois Constitutional Convention Bulletin on *Eminent Domain and Excess Condemnation* (Springfield, 1920). See also the symposium on "Excess Condemnation in City Planning" in the *Proceedings* of the American Society of Civil Engineers, Vol. LI, pp. 1416–1452, 1861–1872 (September–November, 1925).

The methods used by British cities are explained in R. A. Gordon, *Handbook on Compulsory Acquisition of Land and Compensation* (London,

1929). Information concerning the practice of cities in the countries of continental Europe can be found in the various standard manuals of administrative law such as Hue de Grais, *Handbuch der Verfassung und Verwaltung in Preussen und im deutschen Reich* (25th edition, Berlin, 1929), and Gaston Jèze, *Principes généraux du droit adminstratif* (3 vols., Paris, 1925–1930).

CHAPTER XX

STREETS

> That living flood, pouring through these streets, knowest thou whence it is coming, whither it is going? A thousand carriages, and wains, and cars come tumbling in with food, with young rusticity, and other raw produce, inanimate or animate, and go tumbling out again with produce manufactured. Friend, thou seest here a living link in that Tissue of History which inweaves all Being: watch well, or it will be past thee and seen no more.—*Thomas Carlyle.*

Arteries of traffic.

There is something about the city streets that has always stirred the imagination of man. The streets have been called the city's arteries, the sluiceways through which its life-blood of traffic flows. They have also been likened to the bones of the human body in that they determine the general frame and contour of the urban community. And they have been called the nerves of the metropolis because it is through them that the myriad civic activities are made to respond. There are flaws in all such analogies, no doubt, but they testify to the vitally important part which is played in the life of every city by its network of thoroughfares.

Services which the streets perform.

Nor does all the service which a street performs for the community make itself visible to the naked eye. Everyone realizes, of course, that the city streets bear on their surface an enormous amount of traffic in the form of street cars, motor busses, taxicabs, trucks, delivery wagons, private motor cars, and throngs of pedestrians. It is also apparent that the streets afford locations for lamp-posts, trees, hydrants, signs, patrol boxes, telephone poles, and various other public installations. Overhead they sometimes carry elevated railway structures and they are usually strung with wires of all varieties. But the average citizen does not always stop to remember that below the ground they provide for subways, water mains, sewers, gas pipes, wire conduits, and almost every type of public utility. Nor does he realize that the streets are the main channels through which light and air come to the shops and dwellings, or that they are the carriers of surplus rainfall, or that they are sometimes the only playgrounds the children have. Most men, if you asked them to define a city street, would tell you that it is a strip of ground set aside for people to ride, drive, or walk upon; but it is in fact a great deal more than that. A street is of three dimensions, surface, subsurface, and overhead. In all three it renders service of the highest importance.

The planning, construction, and maintenance of city highways (but not including the regulation of traffic) is usually entrusted to a separate department, with a superintendent or commissioner at its head. In some cities, however, there is a department of public works which includes highway administration along with sewerage, water supply, and sometimes public buildings. The advantage of the latter plan is that it brings street administration into close relation with other physical activities which are closely allied to it. The head of the street department is usually an engineer,[1] appointed by the mayor or the city manager, and there is need for an engineer's imagination in connection with the work; but politicians with neither technical skill nor experience have sometimes found their way into this post, with expensive results to the taxpayers in the way of waste and incompetence. *Organization of the city street department.*

The street department, or the street division of the public works department, is a favorite objective of the spoilsmen who wish to get control of patronage. It is a large purchaser of land, materials, equipment, and supplies. In addition it is a large employer of labor. The political bosses naturally look upon its opportunities with an avaricious eye. To protect its best interests against them at all times is no easy task. The most dependable way of accomplishing it is to provide the department with a well-qualified head, appointed for a fixed term and safeguarded against removal except for proper cause. *The department head.*

Should this head of the department be a qualified engineer or a layman? This question has been much discussed in administrative circles. The engineer inclines to become absorbed in the technical aspects of the work and to overlook considerations of public policy which are equally important. The layman is likely to disclose these shortcomings in the reverse order. He tends to over-stress political expediency. The engineer functions best so far as planning and directing the operations of a street department are concerned, but the layman is often more successful in maintaining harmonious contact with the heads of other departments, with the mayor or *Engineer or layman?*

---

[1] In smaller cities the position of street superintendent is usually combined with that of city engineer.

city manager, with the press, and with the public. So the question whether a skilled engineer or a skilled executive should be placed at the head of the department depends on which of the two functions, technical or administrative, seems to be the more important in any given case. And this usually depends on the size of the city. The importance of political judgment and administrative resourcefulness in this department may be said to vary directly with the population of the community. The appended chart, prepared by Clarence E. Ridley, is intended to illustrate the point.

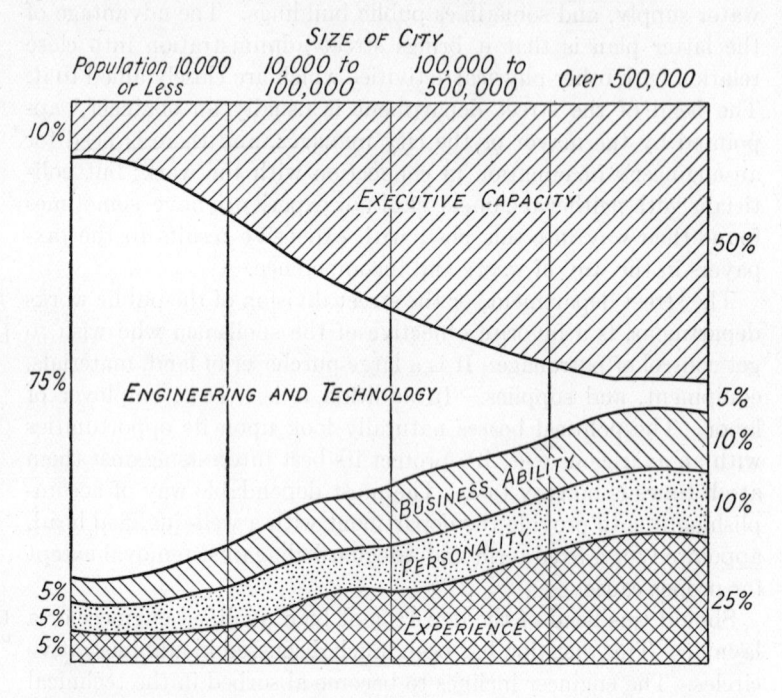

SIZE OF CITY

| Population 10,000 or Less | 10,000 to 100,000 | 100,000 to 500,000 | Over 500,000 |

- 10% — EXECUTIVE CAPACITY — 50%
- 75% — ENGINEERING AND TECHNOLOGY — 5%
- BUSINESS ABILITY — 10%
- PERSONALITY — 10%
- 5% / 5% / 5% — EXPERIENCE — 25%

Importance of personal qualities. Diagrammatic illustrations like the foregoing should not, however, be taken too literally. Allowance must be made for local conditions which often vary considerably as between cities of the same size. Nor can the personal equation be disregarded. Good engineers are far more plentiful than good administrators. There are ten capable men who can tell you how to widen a street for every one man who can wisely advise you how the cost can best be defrayed. It is sometimes said that the place for the technical expert is "on tap, not on top"—in other words, that he ought to be the second or third man in the department rather than at the head of it. Such a formula ought not to be generally applied. Engineers are sometimes good administrators. One should not take it for granted that a trained mind has no resiliency. The most successful city managers have been engineers. Finally, it need hardly be reiterated that personal honesty, a high sense of obligation to the public welfare, and at least a normal endowment of common sense are essential to the successful administration of this or any other department, no matter which type of official, engineer or layman, is placed at its head.

What functions are included within the work of a street department? This department, or division, has three fields of work to cover in any city of considerable size. *First*, there is the duty of laying out new streets. This includes the task of determining their location, width, and grades, taking into account the topography of the neighborhood and the problem of acquiring the necessary land. *Second*, there is the work of constructing these new streets or widening old ones, paving them, and keeping the pavements in repair. *Finally*, there is the function of protecting them from obstruction, preventing their breakdown by too heavy trucking loads, safeguarding them against needless tearing-up for repairs to water pipes, sewers, gas mains, and conduits, granting permits for temporary locations on the street surface when buildings are under construction, providing them with street signs and other aids to traffic, designating some of them as one-way streets, and a miscellaneous list of other such work. All these duties are ordinarily imposed upon the street department; but there are various others, somewhat closely related, which frequently seem more advantageously placed elsewhere. The work of cleaning the streets, for example, is often handed over to the sanitary department; the regulation of traffic on the city's thoroughfares is almost always entrusted to the police; while street lighting in some of the larger cities is placed under the control of a separate department of public lighting.

General functions of the department.

By its streets is a city known. Visitors form their general impressions of a place from its main thoroughfares. Americans think of Paris in terms of the Grand Boulevards and the Champs d'Élysée. They associate London with Regent Street and Piccadilly, Berlin with Unter den Linden and the Friedrichstrasse, and Vienna with her famous Ring. New York, to the American imagination, is

The diversity of thoroughfares.

Fifth Avenue, Wall Street, and Broadway. And what would Boston be without Commonwealth Avenue, or Cleveland without Euclid Avenue, or Chicago bereft of her Michigan Boulevard? Yet every city has a great variety of thoroughfares, famous and infamous, broad and narrow, straight and crooked, showy and sordid, good and bad. Some urban highways are industrial, some mercantile, some residential, while some are a combination of all three; some, again, are main streets, some are side streets, and some are in the twilight zone between. Streets can be classified to almost no end: there are about as many types as there are streets themselves. No two are exactly alike in their character of functions, and the differences have a direct relation to the proper determination of widths, paving, lighting, cleaning, traffic regulation, and general maintenance. Hence no rules-of-thumb can be applied to all kinds of city highways.

Classification of streets. There are several ways of grouping streets into classes. They can be arranged, for example, according to the amount and nature of the traffic which they convey, or according to the character of the abutting buildings (whether industrial, mercantile, or residential), or with respect to the position which they occupy in the general street plan of the city. But whatever the basis of classification, the grouping ought to be flexible, for many streets will fall on the border line between two groups and some streets will be found to be in process of passing from one category into another—from the residential to the mercantile group, for example. Everyone has seen this transformation under way. It begins at an intersection with the incoming of a neighborhood grocery, a drug store, or a news stand. Then other small shops edge their way in, one after another, putting shop windows in the fronts of residences. Presently a business block goes up on the corner and before long a considerable area running out from the intersection is found to have changed its character. It will be recalled that one of the objects of zoning is to control and regulate this development.

A suggested functional grouping. As a tentative general classification of streets the following may be suggested, although it is by no means exhaustive, for each general group of streets may be further divided and subdivided:

 (1) *Arterial streets*, or through-traffic highways. In this class come the streets which are direct routes of through-the-city and across-the-city traffic, particularly for trucks, motor-busses, and motor cars. They link up with the state or county roads. From the standpoint

of the abutting property they may be business or residential streets, but when the traffic becomes busy, especially at night, they soon cease to be desirable for residential purposes. Their prime characteristic is their use as trunk thoroughfares to accommodate a stream of rapidly moving traffic, little or none of which is of local origin or destination. Owned and maintained by the city, they are largely used by people who live outside its bounds. Every city has a few such streets; the smallest community has at least one of them. In some cases the county or the state has taken over the responsibility for the upkeep and maintenance of these streets, defraying the expense from the proceeds of the gasoline tax.

(2) *Retail business streets.* Every urban community, be it ever so humble, has at least one street of this type, one "main street," as it is colloquially called. A large city will have many of them. Such streets are the ones most heavily congested by pedestrian, vehicular, and street-car traffic. They bear also the largest number of impediments in the way of poles, tracks, wires, signs, and so on. All too often these streets are too narrow for the purposes which they are called upon to serve, especially when lines of parked cars are set next the curb on either side, as is usually the case. The majority of busy retail streets in large American cities were never meant to be such. They have been converted from the residential use for which they were originally designed.

(3) *Streets of the industrial, wholesale, shipping, and market districts.* Here the pedestrian traffic is not large, nor is the street car usually a factor in congestion; but slow-moving vehicles are numerous and the streets must be adapted to their use. Even the most durable pavements have difficulty in standing up under the heavy traffic of these areas.

(4) *Streets in the financial and office districts.* Such streets are heavily used by both foot and vehicle traffic during the day hours from nine till five. Thereafter they resemble a deserted village.

(5) *Main streets of residential districts.* In these street areas the traffic of all kinds is relatively light, but much of it is quick-moving, and some of it is cross-city or through-traffic. The chief problem is to keep these streets clean, attractively planted, well lighted, and free from too much noise.

(6) *Minor streets of residential districts.* Streets in this category bear only local traffic but what they carry is highly diversified. They form by all means the most numerous class of streets in any city and also the simplest from the standpoint of the administrative problems which they present.

(7) *Boulevards, esplanades, and parkways.* Roadways of this type are used almost wholly for pleasure driving; heavy traffic is usually

excluded; light paving can be used and there is no problem of congestion.

(8) *Alleys, lanes, courts, and passageways.* This group includes the narrow public ways which are used almost altogether by delivery wagons, refuse and garbage collectors, peddlers, and what not. Sometimes they are "private ways," owned and maintained by the owners of properties which they serve.

<small>Streets which cannot be classified.</small>

Now a little reflection will serve to show that these various classes of public ways have altogether different requirements as regards layout, width, pavements, sidewalks, cleaning, tree-planting, and lighting. Hence each type of public thoroughfare presents its own set of problems for the street department. To place each street in an accurate classification it becomes essential not only to make a property survey but to undertake a traffic census as well, that is, an actual count and tabulation of the pedestrians and vehicles using each thoroughfare on typical days. Such surveys will almost always indicate, however, that there are many streets which do not fall in any one of the usual groups. A long street, for example, may pass through several districts (industrial, mercantile, and residential) in the course of its mileage. Nevertheless the great majority of streets in any city run true to type and are of such a character that their classification can be easily determined.

<small>Street widths.</small>

How wide should each class of city streets be? In the mind of the average citizen there is some confusion as to what is meant by the "width of a street." And this is not surprising for the term may be used in any one of three senses. It may mean (and in popular parlance usually does mean) the actual driving surface from curb to curb. Or it may mean the roadway and sidewalk combined (the city officials use the term in this sense), that is, the space from property line to property line. Finally, it may be taken to include the entire stretch from the buildings on one side to those on the other, thus including land which belongs to private owners but is subject to a setback, in other words cannot be built upon. So there are three lines to be considered in laying out a street, namely, the curb lines, the property lines, and the building lines. In a strict sense the width of a street extends from property line to property line, that is, it includes only the area which the city owns. In some cases, however, the city expects the owners to build and maintain sidewalks, outside their property lines, and even to care for the grass parkings and trees which lie beyond the sidewalks.

Assuming that a street is reasonably level, its width is the most important factor in its usefulness. During the nineteenth century it was the common practice to lay out streets in widths of exactly forty, sixty, or eighty feet from property line to property line. Minor streets in residential districts were usually plotted either forty or sixty feet in width, while business streets and avenues were given a width of sixty or eighty feet. In any event the distance was fixed in round numbers, in multiples of ten. No one thought of laying out streets in multiples of eight or nine. This way of doing things was, of course, without scientific basis whatever; it used arbitrary figures which bore no relation to the work that a street would be called upon to do. The result is that in all the older American communities there are many streets which now turn out to be a few feet too narrow or a few feet too wide for the purpose that they are expected to serve. When a street is even a few feet too narrow it becomes congested, with a resulting irritation and loss of time to all who use it. When it is a few feet too wide there is a waste of public money in lighting, cleaning, and maintaining space that is not needed. Every square foot of unnecessary street space is an imposition on the taxpayers, for it has to be kept cleaned and lighted year after year. If a city could take from some streets the surplus area which is never used, and give this to other streets in which a few feet of extra width are badly needed, many difficult problems of street administration would be quickly solved. The taxpayers of today are being mulcted for the unscientific street planning of a generation ago.

Anyone who watches traffic moving along a city's streets will notice that it passes in streams, deviating from its direct course only when obstacles come in the way. Two lines of vehicle traffic, and sometimes four lines, keep moving in opposite directions, each keeping to the right in its own lane and requiring a certain sluiceway or zone to move in. This zone of traffic, or strip of street surface which is needed to allow a stream of traffic to pass conveniently, is the unit nowadays used in the determination of street widths. An adequate zone for motor vehicles is ten feet. A line of cars parked alongside the curb takes about eight feet. In order to provide space for parked cars on both sides, and two zones of moving traffic between them, a street should be thirty-six feet in width from curb to curb. This leaves only four feet for sidewalks in the case of a forty-foot street, which is too little. The minimum for a minor residential street should be at least fifty-two feet and if planted with trees it should be sixty-six feet from property line to property line. If four lanes for moving traffic are desired the entire width should be eighty-six feet. Ten feet should then be added for each additional traffic zone. The calculations may be made clearer, perhaps, by a glance at the accompanying diagram.

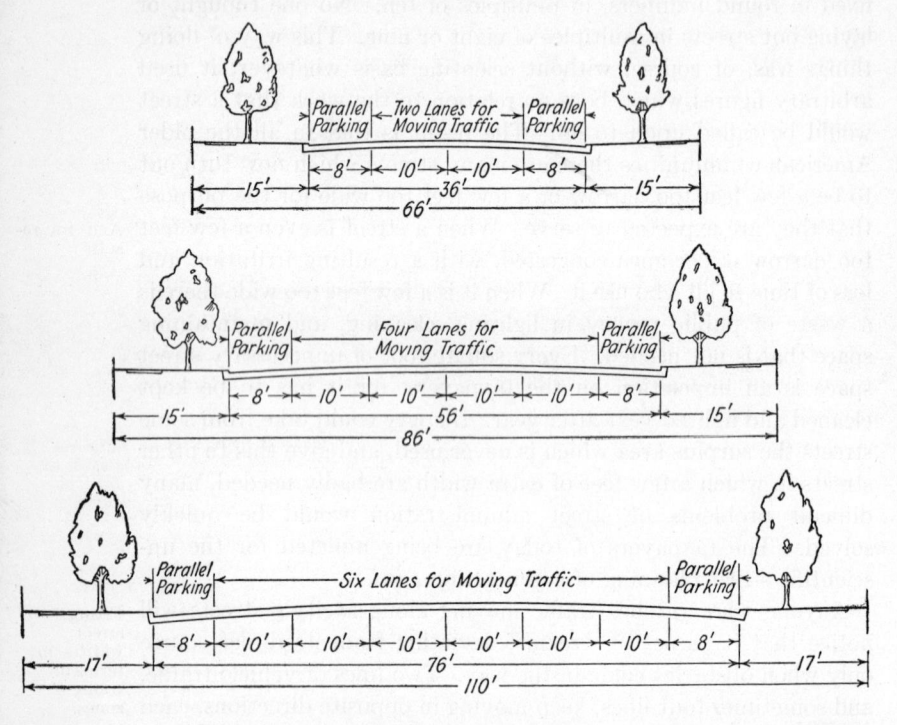

Car tracks in relation to street widths.

In the case of a business thoroughfare which is used by street cars, a double-track car line, with due clearance space, requires eighteen feet. In highways which were laid out before the advent of the trolley there is no way of avoiding the use of the street car's zone by ordinary vehicles as well, but in a properly designed new street it should not be necessary for motor vehicles to encroach upon a trolley right-of-way. As a minimum there should be at least eighteen feet of roadway on each side of the area used for street-car movement, one zone of ten feet for motor traffic and one of eight feet for parked vehicles. This would make a total width of fifty-four feet from curb to curb. Add eight feet for sidewalks on each side and the minimum convenient street width is seventy feet.

The obvious way to increase the usefulness of a too narrow street is to widen it. But this cannot always be done because of the expensive buildings which have to be condemned and torn down at heavy cost. Occasionally, however, much relief can be had by eliminating the bottle-necks which sometimes exist on older streets, that is, the places where a street narrows for a block or two and then resumes its usual width. In some cases it has been found practicable to widen the roadway by narrowing the sidewalks but unhappily the streets which need widened roadways are usually the ones which require wide sidewalks also. Occasionally relief can be had by arcading the sidewalks, that is, moving them within the property lines. This plan is less expensive than condemning the buildings and it has been considerably used abroad— for example, on the Rue de Rivoli in Paris. The idea of double-decker streets has been broached and much discussed in the United States. Wacker Drive in Chicago is regarded as a successful example of such a two-story street, but such projects are highly expensive and they would greatly mar the attractiveness of most downtown thoroughfares.

<small>Relieving congestion on too narrow streets.</small>

Apart from widening a street, or arcading or double-decking it, there are various ways in which its traffic capacity can be increased and the congestion ameliorated. One of them is by putting improved paving on parallel streets so as to encourage a diversion of traffic. Another is to keep obstructions at a minimum. The free flow of traffic is often seriously impaired by street excavations (for the repair of pipes and conduits), by fencing off a portion of the street when new buildings are being erected, by placing cumbersome traffic signals in the middle of the street, by allowing all-day parking, and by permitting stands for the sale of newspapers to occupy locations on the sidewalks at congested corners, thus diverting pedestrians to the pavements. The removal of railroad grade crossings from city streets is also a means of increasing traffic capacity although often an expensive one.

<small>The removal of obstructions.</small>

It has been suggested, however, that a street is something more than a mere channel for traffic to squeeze through, and hence that its width should have some relation to the size of the buildings

<small>Social significance of the street.</small>

which are likely to be erected on both sides of it. The nature of such building development, however, is difficult to forecast. Nevertheless, in laying out a new street, it should always be borne in mind that those who are likely to work or dwell upon its borders will have as much interest in its width and arrangement as those who pass along its surface. In other words the city authorities should give more attention to the sociological significance of the street, its proportions and design, its outward attractiveness, its importance as an area of sunlight and ventilation, or of recreation and play. People are known by the streets they live on. Environment has a large influence upon our ways of life.

Undue width is a detriment. In all this, however, there is a danger of going too far, and some cities have done it. Finding their older streets too narrow, they have determined that no such shortcoming will ever be found with streets in the newer parts of the city. These, accordingly, have often been given a width of one hundred and twenty feet or more, in some cases two hundred feet. Streets in the suburban areas that are never likely to become traffic thoroughfares have been given boulevard proportions. This not only involves a waste of valuable building-land but entails a continuing excess of cost for repaving, lighting, and cleaning, the care of trees and of grass-plots, all of which must be paid by the abutting owners or by the the general taxpayer. Grandiose street planning may be found as much a burden by the next generation as niggardliness of street space has imposed upon the present one.

Good and bad street planning. The streets of a city ordinarily absorb from twenty-five to thirty-five per cent of its entire area. The older cities approach the lower percentage, especially in their downtown sections; but modern city planning follows the policy of insisting upon at least thirty-five per cent of the land for streets in new subdivisions. Washington has proportionately a larger street ratio than any other city in America. L'Enfant, who drew the original plan for this city, was prodigal in his allowances, devoting over fifty per cent of the city's area to highways, squares, and circles. But his successors in other American cities did not follow this example. They tried to save land for private owners. Not only that but they permitted the streets to be laid out with offsets, blind alleys, and bottle-necks. Even within recent years, indeed, there has been too much planning of streets in subdivisions without reference to the probable needs of new suburban communities as a whole.

Utility is not the only test of a well-planned street. Attractiveness in appearance is also a desideratum, and trees are an important factor in making the city streets attractive, especially in the residential districts. But trees cannot perform the function of beautifying a street unless they are intelligently selected and properly placed.[1] This choice and arrangement must depend upon the width and character of the street, the climatic conditions, and the relative ease with which the trees can be cared for. The important thing is to avoid a monotonous and standardized installation, so that the foliage may accentuate the individuality of each thoroughfare. Other factors in attractiveness are the right proportioning of the street area between roadway, sidewalks, and tree space, the enforcement of proper setbacks, the use of simple but well-designed lighting standards and the safeguarding of the street from the installation of unsightly poles and wires. The streets represent the largest amount of public property that a city owns. They deserve even more official interest and attention than has been spent upon them.

Making the streets attractive.

REFERENCES

Most books on city planning (see references at the end of Chapter XVII) contain chapters on the arrangement and design of streets. C. M. Robinson, *City Planning with Special Reference to the Planning of Streets and Lots* (New York, 1916) is an older work which retains considerable value because of its clear statement of principles and the excellence of its style. There are good discussions of street design in F. S. Besson, *City Pavements* (New York, 1923), pp. 97–136, and in Thomas R. Agg, *The Construction of Roads and Pavements* (4th edition, New York, 1929), pp. 111–157. Material on the design and maintenance of streets may also be found in W. W. Crosby and George E. Crosby, *Highway Location and Surveying* (New York, 1928), and in J. H. Bateman, *Highway Engineering* (New York, 1928). There is some useful street data in the publications of the Regional Plan of New York and Its Environs, especially Vol. III on *Highway Traffic* (New York, 1927).

See also the references to books and periodicals at the close of Chapter XXI.

[1] See the chapter on "Trees for City Planting" in F. S. Besson, *City Pavements* (New York, 1923), pp. 404–413.

CHAPTER XXI

PAVEMENTS AND SIDEWALKS

> We hold the money of the people in our hands, to be used for their purposes and to further their interests as members of the municipality, and it is quite apparent that, when any part of the funds which the taxpayers have thus intrusted to us are diverted to other purposes, or when, by design or neglect, we allow a greater sum to be applied to any municipal purpose than is necessary, we have, to that extent, violated our duty.—*From a Veto Message of Grover Cleveland, Mayor of Buffalo (1882).*

Streets and local topography. The efficiency of a street depends upon several factors—its layout, width, grade, and paving. The gradient should come close to level and in any event should not exceed four per cent, but this, of course, is not always practicable. In many places the topography is such that the streets have to run up and down steep hills, so that there is no alternative to a high gradient except to excavate or tunnel at high expense. Lowering a hill street, moreover, leaves the building lots on both sides high above the street surface, thus making them inconvenient of access and reducing their value. Steep grades are a serious detriment, especially in heavy-traffic areas. Such cities as San Francisco, Seattle, and Providence are considerably handicapped by topographical considerations in this respect. Sometimes the handicap can be partly overcome, as in Los Angeles, by cutting traffic tunnels through the highest elevations.

Relation of pavements to local needs. The nature and condition of a street pavement are also matters of great importance, as city authorities have everywhere come to realize. The ideal pavement is easy to define but hard to obtain. It should be inexpensive, durable, smooth, non-skidding, dustless, easy to keep clean, and economical to keep in repair. Of course no type of pavement satisfies all these requirements. Granite blocks, which have been so much used in the shipping and warehouse districts of eastern cities, make a pavement of great durability and one that is easy to keep in repair—but it is rough on the surface, unattractive in appearance, difficult to keep clean in wet weather, and expensive to install. A pavement of oil-bound crushed stone, on the other hand, usually costs a good deal less to con-

PAVEMENTS AND SIDEWALKS 273

struct; in addition it has a smoother surface and a better appearance; but it is apt to break down under heavy traffic, hence the cost of maintenance may be large. Pavements of concrete, brick, wood blocks, and sheet asphalt all have their merits and their shortcomings, depending upon where and how they are used.

So there is no such thing as an ideal pavement for all streets irrespective of their character. On the other hand, every type of pavement has some talking points in its favor, and if sufficient emphasis be laid on these its claims become strong. The market, moreover, is full of patented pavements which are urged upon the city authorities by the methods of high-pressure salesmanship. Most of these do not represent any new form of pavement but are merely different processes of combining crushed stone with bituminous or asphaltic binders.

There is no ideal pavement.

If you go about any large city and pay careful attention to the street surfaces, you will see many examples of poor judgment in the selection of paving materials. On one street will be found a light asphalt surface which has been broken down under heavy trucking; on another you will find a six-inch bed of concrete with little or no traffic of any kind passing over it. Here you will see a suburban side-street, its modest homes separated by a fifty-foot strip of costly, patented materials, while just around the corner is a broad avenue along which the motorists jolt their way over the broken macadam. Why do we not have a better exercise of judgment in the selection of pavements with reference to the particular requirements of each individual street, avenue, or boulevard?

Why unsuitable pavements are so often laid:

The answer to that question is not a simple one. First of all it should be borne in mind that the selection of a pavement is sometimes made by the city authorities and sometimes not. When the cost of the paving is paid from the general funds of the city the selection is virtually always made by its officials, that is, by the superintendent of streets or the city engineer. But even when he is given the responsibility of making the choice he is not always permitted to use his own expert judgment. The mayor or the city council, in authorizing the work and voting the money for it, sometimes specify the type of pavement that must be used. And their action, now and then, is influenced by the wire-pulling of those who have some special brand of paving to sell.

1. Expert judgment does not always control the selection.

2. Political influence of paving contractors. Paving contractors, in many cities, are men of political influence. Not infrequently they are generous contributors to the campaign funds of mayors, aldermen, or city councillors. This gives them an influence which often counts for more at the city hall than the advice of the municipality's engineering experts. In other instances the officials of the street department and engineering offices are themselves in league with the paving contractors. When these officials are political appointees, as is often the case, they let their judgment be swayed by considerations of political expediency. On many occasions it has been disclosed, in the investigation of street-paving scandals, that city officials have knowingly and shamelessly sacrificed the public interests to the avarice of their own political friends in the selection of materials and the awarding of contracts. That is one of the reasons why unsuitable pavements are sometimes found on city streets.

3. The caprice of property owners. But there is another reason that operates more often, namely, the caprice of the property owners along the street. When the cost of a new pavement is borne by the owners of the abutting property under the plan of special assessments it has been the practice to let these owners have a voice in deciding what type of surface the street shall have. The argument is that since they are paying for the work their wishes in the matter ought to be consulted. What happens in such cases is that the paving-salesman takes advantage of his opportunity. Going to the property owners one by one he endeavors to convince them that his particular brand of pavement is the one they ought to have. And before he gets through with them they are frequently induced to sign a petition asking for it. Many a street surface in American cities owes its decrepit existence to the activities of some smooth-tongued fellow working on commission.

The best remedy for these difficulties. The wasteful results of this arrangement have led many cities to provide that the entire discretion in selecting pavements shall rest with the public officials, no matter how the work is to be paid for. This is a step in the right direction, although it has not provided an altogether adequate remedy in cases where the work is financed by the levy of special assessments. For even though it is stipulated that the selection of materials shall not be made by the property owners, they continue to feel that their wishes ought to be taken into account and they frequently enter a protest against the decisions made by the city's engineering officers. Such protests can be disregarded, of course, but it is not good political tactics to do this too often. Accordingly it becomes the duty of the city officials to convince the property owners that good reasons have dictated the choice and that the selection of just any other type of pavement would be unwise. This is not always easy to do.

Such difficulties are lessened when the city has adopted a comprehensive paving program. A program of this nature, prepared by its engineering department, will indicate what type of resurfacing is to be placed on each street when the time comes. It should be prepared after a careful study of each thoroughfare, with a counting and classification of the traffic on all busy streets in order to make an accurate determination of the needs. A good paving program should likewise endeavor to forecast the approximate dates at which the repaving will become desirable in each case and should include plans for financing the work. Ordinarily it should cover a period of at least five years and preferably ten. *Street-paving programs.*

The selection of suitable and economical pavements for the city streets may seem to be a relatively simple phase of municipal engineering; at any rate the average citizen very often assumes it to be so. But a few moments' reflection should convince one that this is not the case. On the contrary it is a very complicated and technical problem. Take the matter of what a pavement really costs, for example. Figures must be compiled showing not only the initial cost but the probable expense for maintenance during the estimated life of the pavement. The cost of keeping the surface clean is also an item that has to be reckoned. There is a considerable difference in this respect as between different types of street surfacing. Moreover there is the matter of facility in drainage, the nature of the subgrade underlying the street, and the suitability of the pavement not only for present traffic but for what may be expected in the future. Every street presents its own problems which have to be considered in relation to the general street program. Emphasis should be laid on this articulation to the city-wide program, for a street does not belong to those who live on it. It belongs to the whole city and the whole city has an interest in it. All questions relating to it should therefore be left to the judgment of those who represent the municipality as a unit *Determining the place of each street in the general program.*

and these officials should be safeguarded against political pressure in reaching their decisions.

Structure of the pavement:
1. The subgrade.
A street pavement, in its broader sense, consists of three layers, known as the subgrade, the base, and the surfacing. The subgrade is the soil or gravel below the base. It is laid bare by excavating where the natural grade is too high or by filling-in when it is too low. In laying a pavement the subgrade is first prepared, levelled, rolled, and provided with proper drainage. Where any portion of it has been made by filling a depression with earth there should be a thorough puddling and rolling down before the base is laid. It frequently happens, of course, that a dirt or gravelled roadway has been in use for some years before the city proceeds to make it a paved street. In such cases there is already at hand a well-compacted subgrade on which to build.

2. The base.
On top of this subgrade goes the base or foundation. It may be of coarse stone, bituminous concrete, or hydraulic cement concrete. Usually it is the latter. The thickness and quality of the base depend on various considerations such as the nature of the subgrade soil, the weight of the surfacing that is to be laid, and the character of the traffic which the pavement is expected to bear. Ordinarily it runs from six to ten inches. In the case of a cement concrete base much depends upon the proportions of the mix (cement, sand, and crushed stone or gravel), and these should be specified with the utmost care. There should also be rigid inspection and tests to make sure that both the materials and the methods of mixing are up to the specified standard, for a surface is no stronger than the base on which it stands. More pavements have suffered from poor base work than from poor surfacing. Inferior workmanship in the base, moreover, can be slipped through and covered up. Of course no surfacing should be permitted until the base has had time to set. This takes several days under the most favorable conditions.

Reasons for poor pavement foundations.
Unsatisfactory results in street paving are frequently due to the pressure for speed. Merchants and householders dislike to have the street closed in front of their stores and homes for even a few days. Hence they press for a quick job and sometimes get an inferior one. It has become a common practice nowadays to do half the street at a time, finishing from the center to one curb before starting on the other side. This permits the street to be used (although with some inconvenience) while the work is in

progress and has lessened the pressure for speeding it up. Poor work has sometimes resulted, moreover, from laying the base in very cold weather. All pavement work should be suspended when the thermometer gets considerably below the freezing point.

Laying the surface is the final step, and here the range of choice in the matter of materials is large. Granite blocks, set on a concrete base and with a concrete grouting between them, have been very popular in the heavy-trucking areas of the larger cities. By having the blocks trimmed to a smooth surface this type of pavement has been greatly improved. Cement concrete is now being very widely used for surfacing as well as for the base, especially on state and county highways. But concrete, when laid in this monolithic way, is affected by changes in temperature and tends to become cracked, even when expansion joints are installed. Repairs can easily and cheaply be made, however, by filling the cracks with bituminous filler. Cities have experimented widely with creosoted wood blocks and with vitrified brick. Wood blocks were favored in the days of horse-drawn vehicles because they provided a pavement that was relatively noiseless, but with the motorization of traffic this advantage has become negligible. Brick paving has been much used in some eastern cities, especially on hilly streets; but it is now losing ground. Sheet asphalt has also had a widespread and well-deserved popularity as a surfacing in residential districts and on other light-traffic thoroughfares. It is smooth, easy to keep clean, and looks well; but has the disadvantage of being rather slippery for traffic in wet weather. Taking the country as a whole, the most widely-used surface today is one of bituminous or asphaltic concrete. This is a mixture of sand or finely crushed stone with heavy oil asphalt laid to a depth of a couple of inches upon a base of broken stone or cement concrete. Oil asphalt is a by-product in the refining of petroleum. Various types of bituminous mixtures have been patented and are sold under trade names. They all use the same materials—sand, crushed stone, and asphalt or bitumens—but in different proportions or by a variety of mixing processes.

<small>3. The surface.</small>

One might summarize the problem of selecting a pavement surface in some such tabulation as is given below, but bearing in mind that any order of rating will vary in different parts of the country. Costs vary from place to place, depending on the relative proximity of materials. Climatic conditions affect the durability

<small>A tabulation of surface qualities.</small>

of pavements and the difficulty of keeping them clean. Individual opinions will vary, moreover, as to the relative attractiveness of the different surfaces in point of general appearance. Hence this table is presented as a basis for discussion and argument, not as embodying a series of conclusions:

Economy in Construction	Economy in Upkeep	Durability	Cleanliness	Appearance
1. Water-bound macadam 2. Bituminous or asphaltic concrete 3. Sheet asphalt 4. Cement concrete 5. Brick 6. Wood blocks 7. Granite blocks	1. Granite blocks 2. Cement concrete 3. Wood blocks 4. Brick 5. Sheet asphalt 6. Bituminous or asphaltic concrete 7. Water-bound macadam	1. Granite blocks 2. Cement concrete 3. Wood blocks 4. Brick 5. Bituminous or asphaltic concrete 6. Sheet asphalt 7. Water-bound macadam	1. Sheet asphalt 2. Cement concrete 3. Bituminous or asphaltic concrete 4. Wood blocks 5. Brick 6. Granite blocks 7. Water-bound macadam	1. Sheet asphalt 2. Bituminous or asphaltic concrete 3. Cement concrete 4. Wood blocks 5. Brick 6. Granite blocks 7. Water-bound macadam

Paying the cost of pavements. The differences of opinion which may be provoked by any discussion of the foregoing tabulation will at least serve to reinforce the proposition that there is no ideal pavement for all streets under all conditions. The emphasis to be placed upon the factors of cost, durability, and appearance will differ from time to time and from place to place. It will depend upon the grade of the street, the amount and nature of the traffic, the general character of the neighborhood which the street serves, and the amount of money that is available for the work. As elsewhere discussed, there are three methods by which the cost of paving a street, or of constructing any other public improvement, may be defrayed. It may be paid out of current taxes, but this plan is rarely used. It may be covered by an issue of street bonds on the general credit of the city, with the interest and repayment of charges borne from the general tax funds over a period of ten or twenty years. Difficulties have frequently arisen through the issue of these bonds for a longer term than the life of the pavement, hence the laws in many of the states now impose limits upon the maximum term for which street bonds may run. Finally, the cost of the pavement may be levied upon the owners of abutting property by means of special assessments, as already explained.[1] The cost of maintaining and repairing a pavement, after it has been laid, is paid from the city's annual income.

The work of constructing a street and paving it is sometimes done by using the city's own men and materials, but for the most part the work is entrusted to those contractors who put in the lowest bid based upon the street department's plans and specifications. Regular inspection of the work by city officials is depended upon to enforce a strict compliance with these specifications, but this trust is sometimes found to have been misplaced. The paving inspectors employed by the city have frequently been put on the payroll by politicians who are in collusion with the contractors. The result is that inferior materials and workmanship often get palmed off on the city in lieu of what the specifications require. There is no place in the entire municipal service where rigid integrity and strict vigilance are more important than in the inspection branch of the public works department. The men engaged in this field, however, are all too often selected for personal or partisan reasons with little regard for their technical qualifications. They are not well paid by the city, as a rule, and consequently find it hard to resist the temptations which contractors throw in their way. It has been argued that the way to be sure of a good paving job is to have the city do it with its own force, but as has been pointed out elsewhere in this book there are defects in that arrangement also.[2]

Checking up on the paving contractors.

The repairing of pavements, however, is almost always handled by the city's own employees. In the case of sheet asphalt or bituminous concrete the "cold patch" method is successfully used. It consists in mixing crushed stone or sand with bituminous binders which can be used without heating them. For more extensive repair jobs the surface of the street is scarred and then treated to a top dressing of oil and finely crushed stone. An asphaltic or bituminous concrete surfacing is sometimes laid over a worn granite-block, brick, or water-bound macadam surface. This, however, is not a desirable procedure unless the base is sound, which is not usually the case with old pavements. The cost of keeping pavements in repair forms a considerable item in city budgets; it usually averages from two to three cents per square

Keeping pavements in repair.

[1] See Chapter XII.   [2] See Chapter VIII.

yard of street surface annually. In a city with several hundred miles of streets this makes a substantial yearly bill.

Car tracks and the breakdown of pavements.

Streets which have to accommodate car tracks present a special problem in the matter of pavement. The vibration caused by the heavy cars is likely to injure both the paving surface and the base unless precautions are taken. Water then gets into the cracks at the track-joints and causes a further deterioration. Engineers have now devised methods of overcoming this difficulty by using a more rigid form of track construction and by strengthening the track substructure. It is a common practice of cities, in granting or renewing franchises, to require that the street railway company shall pave and keep in repair that part of the street which it occupies as a right-of-way, or, in some cases, that the cost shall be divided between the city and the company, with the latter bearing the main share. Much friction has marked the relations of the two authorities in this matter because the traction companies do not want to spend on this work any money that can be saved. It is better, in the long run, to relieve the street railways from this obligation and have them pay into the city treasury enough taxes to have the work properly done by the public authorities. The burden in any event falls on the car-riders, not on the company, which means that it comes chiefly on the workers and their families.

"Corporation cuts."

Another problem is connected with street openings or "corporation cuts" as they are sometimes called. Nothing has been a source of greater injury to the paved streets of American cities than the practice of allowing gas and electric lighting companies a relatively free hand in tearing up pavements to install or repair mains, pipes, and conduits. The city's own water and sewer departments have also been at fault in this regard. The spectacle of a new pavement torn up within a few months after it is laid has become so common that people have almost ceased to give it passing notice. Sometimes it has seemed as though there were an organized conspiracy to prevent any newly paved street from remaining intact for more than a few months at a time. Much of the trouble arises from a failure of the city departments and the public service companies to work together. Too often each has made its own plans without consulting the others.

Fortunately, however, this situation has undergone a marked improvement during recent years and there is now more coöper-

PAVEMENTS AND SIDEWALKS 281

ation than there used to be. When a new pavement is to be laid, the practice of street departments nowadays is to notify the public service companies and the other city departments some time in advance, so that all connections and repairs may be made before the street work is begun. Care is also taken to make sure that when pavements are opened they shall be replaced with proper attention to the subgrade and base as well as to the surfacing. To this end it is often provided that the city shall do the replacing itself, with the cost charged to the company or the property owner, as the case may be. *The problem of keeping them to a minimum.*

Even at the best, however, pavements will have to be torn up from time to time, for no one can foresee all the eventualities. House connections with street mains will get out of order, pipes and mains will break, freeze, or give out unexpectedly, and to make the necessary repairs in such cases the pavement must be excavated. It has sometimes been said that in planning and constructing their trunk sewers the larger American cities should have followed the example of Paris where these subsurface tunnels were made large enough to carry the various utilities, such as water mains and wire conduits. This solves the problem of excavations in the pavement, for it permits the repairs to be made from below and not from above. The cost of providing trunk sewers of sufficient size to do this, however, is very large as Paris has discovered. *A European solution.*

Most people have very little idea of the extent to which the streets of a large city are dug up here and there each year. In Boston, with a total street length of approximately five hundred miles, there are about fifteen thousand openings per year, aggregating in combined length about one hundred and fifty miles. The ratio in other cities would probably not be different. The inconvenience to traffic is serious but even worse is the permanent injury done to the pavements themselves. Rarely is it practicable to restore the street surface to its original condition. Especially in the winter months it is extremely difficult to replace the frozen earth and the concrete base in such a way that it will have the same bearing strength as before. After a time the subsurface is likely to give way; then the top dressing drops below the surrounding street level or breaks through under the strain of heavy traffic. *Extent of the damage that is now being done.*

The street pavement ordinarily includes gutters and curbs.

Gutters and curbs.

The same contract covers all three. The gutters are usually of cement concrete, no matter what the pavement itself may be. The curb is also of cement concrete as a rule, but sometimes blocks of granite or sandstone are used. When both the curb and gutter are of concrete they are usually built integral, the junction of the two being rounded to facilitate cleaning. The height of the curb is determined by considerations of appearance and economy, but six inches is generally considered to be the maximum height desirable and five-inch curbs are the most common. Expansion is provided for by building the curb, or the curb and gutter, in six-foot sections with a very narrow space between each section. Where sidewalks terminate at the curb, as in the case of street intersections, a wider expansion space is necessary because sidewalks tend to increase in length with age.

Sidewalks, width and design.

The design and construction of sidewalks for pedestrian traffic is rather simple and fairly well standardized. But the proper apportionment of width between roadway and sidewalk is something that cannot be fixed by any general rule. It should vary with local conditions. On outlying residential streets a five-foot walk is usually adequate, while well-built residential streets require sidewalks from six to eight feet in width. Streets in the wholesale and shipping districts require maximum teaming space but are well served with a minimum of sidewalk width. A wide sidewalk in such districts is an actual nuisance, because so much heavy merchandise has to be carried across it from the warehouses to be loaded on trucks and wagons standing at the curb. In retail business sections the volume of pedestrian traffic is so heavy, especially at certain periods of the day, that sidewalks twenty feet in width are sometimes none too large.

Materials and construction.

Sidewalks are nearly always built of cement concrete, although brick walks are not uncommon in the older residential districts of many cities. In building concrete sidewalks the ground is first tamped down solidly; then a four- to six-inch layer of lean concrete is set and finished off with a half-inch wearing surface of stronger mixture. Sidewalks are finished smooth except on steep grades. They are grooved off into sections, usually four feet square, to create lines of weakness along which cracks due to expansion may run rather than spreading irregularly through the whole surface. Expansion joints, which are merely open joints about an inch in width, ought to be provided at points where two sidewalks intersect or where a walk terminates at the curb. When the edge of a sidewalk is adjacent to the curb, a longitudinal expansion joint filled with bitumen or other resilient substance should also be installed.

In some cities the entire cost of building the sidewalk, whatever its width and material, is borne by the owner of the adjoining property. In such cases owners are usually allowed a free choice as to the material and methods used. In the case of new subdivisions they naturally choose what is cheapest. Hence the quality of these walks is usually poor and they often have to be relaid a few years after the lots are sold. More supervision should be given by the city authorities to those pavements, gutters, curbs, and sidewalks which are built in connection with real estate promotions. Indeed it is a question whether the city would not be better off, in the long run, if it put sidewalks on the same basis as curbs and gutters, thus taking full responsibility for their design and quality. For although the practice of leaving to private owners the entire initiative and discretion in providing what is really a public passageway has lightened the direct burden upon the public treasury, it has certainly not saved any money to the citizenship as a whole. *Who should pay for sidewalks?*

The usefulness of a street is furthered, to a greater extent than most cities realize, by the proper installation of street name signs. The absence of such signs at intersections is a cause of congestion, delays, confusion, and inconvenience. Name signs should be of at least four-inch letters and printed so as to be easily read by anyone approaching in a motor vehicle on the right-hand side of the road. Preferably they should be within range of the street lights. In some cities they are placed on the lamp standards. Wooden printed signs have been found preferable to those made of enameled metal. Tests have shown that non-tarnishing gold leaf on a background of sanded dull black makes the most legible sign. The signs should project over the roadway, semaphore fashion, about fifteen feet above the street surface.[1] House numbers, painted on the curb, are also a great public convenience. Some cities do this work and make a nominal charge to each property owner for it. *Street name signs.*

---

[1] For a full discussion see A. J. Post and G. A. McCaffrey, *Street Name Signs*, Municipal Administration Service (National Municipal League), Publication No. 8.

REFERENCES

There are several good sources of information on the design, construction, maintenance, and financing of city pavements and sidewalks. Among these are F. S. Besson, *City Pavements* (New York, 1923), A. H. Blanchard and R. L. Morrison, *Elements of Highway Engineering* (2nd edition, New York, 1928), Thomas Radford Agg, *The Construction of Roads and Pavements* (4th edition, New York, 1929), Thomas R. Agg and J. E. Brindley, *Highway Administration and Finance* (New York, 1927), E. W. James, *Highway Construction, Administration and Finance* (Washington, 1929), W. G. Harger and E. A. Bonney, *Handbook for Highway Engineers* (4th edition, New York, 1927), V. J. Brown and C. N. Conner, *Low-Cost Roads and Bridges* (Chicago, 1933), A. H. Blanchard, *The American Highway Engineer's Handbook* (New York, 1919), W. H. Barton and Louis H. Doane, *The Sampling and Testing of Highway Materials* (New York, 1925), and Wilson G. Harger, *Rural Highway Pavements—Maintenance and Reconstruction* (New York, 1924).

Mention should also be made of the various bulletins on road building and paving issued by the Bureau of Public Roads in the United States Department of Agriculture. Current discussions may be found in the *Proceedings* of the American Road Builders' Association (National Press Building, Washington) as well as in those of the American Society of Municipal Engineers (4359 Lindell Building, St. Louis) and in the various publications of the American Automobile Association (Pennsylvania Ave. and 17th St., Washington), the Highway Education Board (1723 N St., Washington), the American Society of Civil Engineers (33 West 39th St., New York), the Highway Research Board (Corner B and 21st Sts., Washington), and the Asphalt Institute (801 Second Ave., New York). Many articles in this field appear in *Good Roads*, a monthly which is published at 53 West Jackson Boulevard, Chicago, the *Engineering News-Record*, a weekly published at 330 West 42nd St., New York, the monthly issues of *The American City*, and lists of current discussions are printed in the annual volumes of *The Municipal Index*.

See also the references appended to Chapters XVI–XVII, XX, and XXV.

CHAPTER XXII

WASTE DISPOSAL

Ye swear that ye shall well and diligently observe that the pavements in every ward be rightfully kept in order, and that the ways, streets and lanes be kept clean from dung and other filth, for the honesty of the city, and that if ye know of any violation ye shall report it to the alderman that he may make due redress therefor.—*The Scavenger's Oath* (*Twelfth Century*).

Sanitation is one of the oldest and at the same time one of the youngest among municipal enterprises. Scavenging in some crude form is as old as the oldest community; but scientific scavenging is mainly the product of the past two or three generations. It is the science of removing objectionable wastes on a large scale in a safe and economical way. For many centuries preceding the nineteenth there were thoughtful men who suspected a connection between filth and disease, between human wastes and human ailments, but they knew nothing about the transmission of infection by the living organisms that thrive in all varieties of uncleanliness. Not until the epoch-marking discoveries of Pasteur and others did the world gain a clear inkling of the extent to which the physical well-being of the people is menaced by the waste materials which urban life causes to accumulate. This knowledge of the major routes of infection now forms the foundation of modern sanitary science, and its applications are steadily extending. Public cleanliness is the basis of public health. *Sanitation as a science.*

But public sanitation is not merely a health enterprise. If that were the case we might save the effort now put forth by cities to secure the prompt removal of some wastes (such as ashes, for example) which are in no way a menace to health. Public sanitation is an enterprise not only for the protection of health but in the interest of public convenience and orderliness. In fact there is no limit to what the citizen desires from his community along these last-named lines. He wants not only the safe disposal of sewage, but the frequent collection of garbage and rubbish from his place of business or his home, the abatement of smoke nuisances, the removal of snow from the streets, and the flushing of *Its steady extension.*

the pavements. Hence the field of public sanitation is constantly broadening its scope so as to suit the aesthetic tastes of the people and serve their convenience, as well as to safeguard their health. Few people realize how greatly every large community depends upon the sanitary work of the public authorities. A modern city could get along for a while without street lights or parks or even without pavements; but a breakdown in the service of public sanitation would subject its population to no end of discomfort and inconvenience within a very few days. In a week of warm weather it would make most cities unlivable.

The volume of urban wastes. The volume of waste which a thickly populated community throws off each day in the year is almost unbelievably large. First of all there is the output of ashes from industrial establishments, shops, and homes. This daily output is now much smaller than it used to be because oil has been replacing coal as fuel for furnaces. Rubbish is a second large item in the total volume of daily waste material. Business establishments and places of residence alike contribute a vast amount of it. Garbage is also contributed in large quantities every day by hotels, restaurants, markets, factories, and homes. Add to this the city's daily volume of sewage, which includes most of the water that comes from the taps and goes back to the sewers. Reckon also the refuse that is swept from the streets, all the waste materials that building-contractors accumulate, and, finally, most of the rain and snow that falls on the pavements—put all these things together and you will gain some idea of what has to be collected and safely put out of the way by the sanitary departments of a modern municipality. Taking it as a whole,—ashes, rubbish, street refuse, garbage, and sewage,—the amount probably exceeds a ton a day for every head of the population. In Chicago, with well over three million inhabitants, it reaches the stupendous total of nearly a billion and a half tons per annum. Of course a large portion of this goes of its own accord into the sewers, but, even so, this does not solve the problem of ultimate disposal. On the other hand, a great deal of the waste material cannot be put into the sewers but must be gathered up and carried away in rubbish trucks and garbage wagons.

How it may be classified: The first general division of municipal wastes, therefore, is a differentiation between sewage and all other forms. The collection and disposal of sewage presents so many special problems

WASTE DISPOSAL

that the discussion of that subject is reserved for the next chapter of this book. All other forms of municipal waste can be classified into public and private categories, the former comprising street refuse and snow, while the latter includes ashes, rubbish, and garbage.

The amount of public waste now handled in cities is less than it used to be. This is because of the virtual disappearance of horse-drawn traffic from the streets. Thirty years ago the daily tonnage of animal manure that had to be removed from the streets of a large city ran into the tens of thousands. The motor vehicle has solved this problem. Moreover, the modern pavement has greatly lowered the volume of refuse which is nowadays swept from the highways as compared with the earlier era of cobblestones, rough granite blocks, and old-style macadam. But there remains a considerable daily accumulation of dead leaves, soot, and dust, sweepings from sidewalks and buildings (for it is a frequent practice in the tenement districts to sweep from the buildings into the gutters); likewise there is a voluminous grist of paper, fruit skins, cigar butts, matches, and other litter dropped by pedestrians and by passing vehicles, together with what the wind blows into the streets from back yards and rubbish barrels. Some of this refuse is washed by the rains into the sewers where it is collected in the catch-basins which have been put there for the purpose and are cleaned out by hand at intervals. A much larger amount of the waste material remains on the pavements, to be gathered up by machine sweepers or by hand labor and carted away.

1. Street sweepings.

How large is the quantity of street refuse that has to be collected in this manner? It varies with the season of the year to some extent. Ordinary street sweepings increase during the summer months. It also depends upon the section of the city. A street which is lined with tenement houses, especially when these are inhabited by workers of foreign birth, will always provide more litter than a high-grade residential avenue. Down in New York's east side, until the authorities intervened, it was the custom of many tenement dwellers to wrap their daily garbage in an old newspaper and hurl it out into the gutter—the bundle being locally known as "a pigeon." Likewise those sections of the city in which the public markets and the heavy industries are located will contribute more than their share. Something also depends upon the kind of street surfacing used. A pavement of sheet

Their extensive amount.

asphalt is easy to flush off and thus keep refuse from accumulating. The same is almost equally true of bituminous concrete pavement. A street surface of bituminous macadam is not so easy to keep clean and the same holds true of both wood and brick pavements because of their surface irregularities. The older types of granite block pavement are even harder to maintain in sanitary condition.

Street-cleaning methods. Until fifteen or twenty years ago the work of collecting this street refuse was mainly done by hand. Men with pushcarts ambled along from street to street, sweeping up the litter with a broom and trundling it away. In New York City these employees of the street-cleaning department were colloquially known as "white wings," because they wore uniforms which had originally been of that color. To some extent hand methods are still in use, especially in smaller cities; but most of the work is now done by motor-driven machinery. A much-used device is a rotary-broom sweeper equipped with a sprinkling mechanism. This machine, in one operation, wets down the pavement and sweeps everything to the curb where it is then collected by a pick-up gang with removal trucks. Other types of street-sweeping machinery use the vacuum process. For the most part the work of machine sweeping is done during the night hours. This arrangement is designed to minimize the amount of interference with traffic, but it is also made essential by the fact that rows of parked vehicles occupy so much of the street surface during the day hours. The refuse, after being collected, is usually taken to the city dumps or used for filling low land. In the old days it was sometimes sold as fertilizer but with the passing of the horse from the city streets it no longer has any commercial value.

2. *Snow removal.* In northern cities, especially during winters when the precipitation is heavy, the removal of snow from the streets is a difficult and costly enterprise. A heavy snowfall sometimes ties up the whole traffic in a few hours. Emergency crews, with trucks and shovels, then have to work night and day to make the highways passable. In such cases the first attention is devoted to the business thoroughfares and to the vicinity of fire hydrants. Apart from waiting for a change in temperature there is only one way of getting snow removed from the streets, which is by carting it away. A certain amount of it can be scraped or dumped into the sewer manholes; but most of the snow has to be trucked to the nearest

WASTE DISPOSAL

waterway or to vacant land which has proper drainage facilities. The chief desideratum is to get the snow off the streets as quickly as possible, and to do this with the least possible blocking of traffic by those who are doing the work. It is a high-pressure problem, with full crews working all night.

The work of removing snow from the streets is expensive because it requires a large addition to the regular street-cleaning force during the emergency. These workers are obtained by hiring men from the ranks of the unemployed or by letting contractors do it. Under such conditions it is hardly to be expected that a high degree of labor efficiency will be shown. Some progress has been made in the development of mechanical truck-loaders and it is probable that costs will eventually be reduced by using them. Meanwhile the budget of the street-cleaning department in many cities is a difficult thing to prepare, because no one can foresee just how much expense may be incurred under the head of snow removal. In some years it is very small, while in others it amounts to a very large sum. *Why it is expensive.*

Sometimes the responsibility for keeping the streets clean is devolved upon the street department, although this work has almost no kinship with construction and paving. More often, however, it is turned over to a department of sanitation, or sanitary service, along with the work of removing rubbish and garbage from shops and homes. But every city of considerable size ought to organize the work of street cleaning into a regular division or department with a single superintendent or director in charge of it. Preferably he should be a man of engineering education and a general knowledge of sanitary science besides being one who can efficiently organize a group of workers and get work out of them. The daily routine should be carefully planned in order to secure the maximum results without undue cost and there is especial need for vigilant inspection to make sure that portions of the street surface are not being overlooked. The street-cleaning service, unfortunately, does not have the most capable portion of the city's labor force assigned to it. Men who have grown too old or too infirm for work in the other outdoor departments are often transferred to the street-cleaning division as a way of making it easier for them. But this practice does not make it any easier for the official who has charge of the work. The problem of keeping the streets clean can be reduced in difficulty, however, by a sustained *The street-cleaning department.*

campaign of education, beginning in the schools and continued by the newspapers and civic organizations, for a very considerable portion of the litter that goes upon the city streets is the outcome of public carelessness or indifference.

Public cooperation in keeping the streets clean.

People do not seem to realize that every bit of waste material thrown on the street increases the tax rate. Somebody has to be paid for picking it up and his pay comes out of the municipal treasury. Some years ago a resident in one of the larger eastern cities told of seeing a young man, evidently of foreign birth, amusing himself by tearing a newspaper into small shreds and letting the wind blow it scurrying along the street surface. Stepping up to the thoughtless one, he said, "Don't you know that what you're doing is poor citizenship? Somebody's got to pay for picking up all those scraps of paper that you're scattering on the street." "Oh, no," was the reply, "nobody pays for that. The city does it for nothing." It is a common delusion—that when the city renders free service to its citizens, nobody pays for it.

Private wastes:

1. Ashes.

Then there is the problem of removing private wastes. These include large quantities of ashes, the most innocuous and most uniform of all urban waste materials. Ashes present a relatively simple problem of collection and disposal, both because of their relative cleanliness and because the total amount does not vary much in quantity for several months at a time. In northern cities the output of ashes has been reckoned at about one hundred and fifty pounds per year for every head of population, but the amount is steadily becoming smaller with the use of oil fuel in industries and of gas for cooking in homes. If ashes are kept free from rubbish and garbage, they make excellent filling for low or swampy lands, and in most cities they are disposed of in that way. Serious difficulties are involved, however, in persuading or compelling householders to keep their ashes separate from other forms of waste.

2. Rubbish.

Rubbish is the generic term applied to an assortment of waste which defies exact definition, for it includes almost everything in the nature of castaways—wood, paper, leather, tin, glass, rubber, and what not. In southern cities they call it "trash." The problem of getting this material out of the way is one of no great technical difficulty, but it sometimes involves considerable expense. Most of the smaller cities collect ashes and rubbish together, carting both to the same "dump" or tract of low land where the rubbish is burned and the ashes spread out. In larger cities the same plan is sometimes followed, but it becomes steadily more expensive as a city grows larger. This is because the length of haul to suitable dumping places is increased as the close-in lands become filled.

In such cases it is often found cheaper to incinerate the rubbish, either separately or along with garbage, at some central spot. Occasionally, before incineration, it is picked over by city employees at reclamation stations, or by junkmen who pay an annual sum for the privilege. Everything that can be further utilized is taken out during this sorting process. Some years ago it was commonly believed that rubbish incinerators could be used to generate steam and develop electric power, but experiments in this direction have not been generally successful. The fuel efficiency of rubbish is low, and a large amount of extra handling is required because the rubbish cannot easily be dumped from above but must be fed uniformly to the incinerator in order to keep up a steady fire. Incineration is still frequently used to produce steam, but only for the forced draft of the incinerator itself. In some seacoast cities it has been the practice to load the rubbish on scows for dumping at a distance from land. This plan has been found objectionable, however, in that much of the lighter material floats back to litter the beaches. It has been abandoned in Europe and is now being discarded in America. *Disposal of rubbish by incineration.*

Some cities collect rubbish from business establishments and from private residences free of charge. Some give free service to homes but collect a fee from places of business. And some merely give licenses to private rubbish collectors who require both shops and homes to pay for the removal. In some cases, moreover, the city does the work with its own employees and rubbish trucks; while in other instances it pays contractors for doing the job. There has been a great variety of practice in this field. Experience seems to indicate, however, that the most satisfactory results are obtained when the city assumes the function of collecting rubbish free of charge except in the case of industrial establishments. It can do the work much more cheaply than it can be done by each householder for himself. *Fees for collecting rubbish.*

Finally, there is the type of waste known as garbage. It is made up of waste matter from the kitchens of hotels, restaurants, and dwellings, together with offal from markets, decayed fruits and vegetables from shops, along with various other putrescible wastage. In amount and character it varies in different parts of the *3. Garbage.*

city and at different seasons of the year. The summer volume of garbage is often double that of the winter and the annual average is about one hundred and fifty pounds per inhabitant.[1] Many smaller cities make no provision for the collection and disposal of garbage, but merely leave it to be burned by the householders and thus to become a public nuisance, or to be collected by licensed scavengers who dispose of it by feeding to hogs. In some larger communities the garbage is gathered by city employees and sold to hog farms outside the municipal limits. This plan has the merit of affording a cheap solution of the disposal problem but it is offensive in thickly settled areas and can hardly be called a sanitary method anywhere, although with good management the objections to it can be greatly reduced. It also makes essential the separation of garbage from all other household waste, which is not an easy thing to secure because householders in the crowded sections of large cities find it more convenient to dump garbage, rubbish, and ashes into the same barrels or bins.

Its use as hog fodder.

Some cities do not insist on this separation but use the garbage, mixed with other wastes, for filling low land and natural ravines. When the material is buried in thin layers, treated with a deodorant, and well covered with soil, this plan is not objectionable. It has been found that land so filled is not usable, however, for several years. Dumping or burying garbage in shallow trenches has nowhere been found satisfactory as a method of disposal, for such dumps soon become infested with rats and develop into public nuisances. Some cities send their garbage (as well as their rubbish) out to sea, which is a harmless plan if the scows are towed far enough from shore. Other cities incinerate their garbage along with rubbish. The incineration of garbage is more extensively practiced in Europe, however, than in America.

Disposal by interment.

The utilization of garbage in a reduction plant has been found practicable in a number of large cities. Ordinary urban garbage yields about three per cent grease. This is sixty pounds per ton, and quite sufficient to cover the cost of its recovery when the scale of operation is large enough. Rarely is garbage reduction profitable in a city of less than 200,000 population, however, and in no event are the profits sufficient to cover the cost of collection. In the reduction process the garbage is conveyed into tanks or digesters

Disposal by reduction.

---

[1] H. R. Crohurst, *Municipal Wastes: Their Character, Collection, and Disposal*, United States Public Health Service Bulletin No. 107 (Washington, 1920).

holding from eight to ten tons each. The lids of the digesters are then screwed down and steam is injected at high pressure. In this way the garbage is "cooked" for several hours, at the end of which time it has the consistency and appearance of apple butter. Then it is run through a press which forces out the moisture and grease, leaving dry "tankage" to be sold as fertilizer base. The moisture and grease are separated, the grease being used for making soap or other marketable products.

Another process, known as the dry-heat method, is also in use. The raw garbage is crushed and dried with heat. Then the dry solids are placed in sealed, jacketed tanks into which a grease solvent (usually of distillate) is pumped. The solvent releases the grease, which is then run off and utilized, while the solvent is distilled off, to be used again. After the extraction of the grease the garbage is sold as tankage. This process has the advantage of low operating costs, but the drying results in a large volume of odorous gases which become a nuisance to the neighborhood unless they are successfully treated.[1]

Garbage disposal by any form of reduction, however, is open to serious objections. Even under the most favorable conditions no one wants one of these plants in his part of the city. Hence the reduction plant has to be located away off by itself, which greatly increases the cost of hauling the garbage to it. The reduction method of disposal also necessitates strict enforcement of a rule that garbage shall be kept by householders and others in separate receptacles, unmixed with ashes and rubbish. It is almost impossible to enforce compliance with this requirement in cities which have a large foreign-born population. Moreover the profits from reduction plants have proved smaller than was anticipated when they were established. This is because the prices obtained for the recovered greases have not been up to expectations and the tankage has not proved easy to sell at a profit either as poultry feed or as a base for fertilizing material. Some reduction plants have shut down because of their failure to make both ends meet. The incineration of garbage is now regarded by many sanitary experts as a better method of disposal under ordinary conditions.[2]

General objections to the reduction method of disposal.

---

[1] Victor M. Ehlers and Ernest W. Steel, *Municipal and Rural Sanitation* (New York, 1927), p. 137.

[2] Some experiments are being made with the Beccari method which has been developed in Italy. The raw garbage, under this system, is placed in brick pits where it is allowed to ferment for a month or more. The liquid drains out at the

Disposal of garbage by incineration.

Many of the earlier garbage incinerators were not satisfactory because they operated at relatively low temperatures. The result was an incomplete combustion of the gases and vigorous complaints of foul odors. This defect has now been remedied by the use of garbage destructors which operate under forced draft at a temperature of twelve to fifteen hundred degrees Fahrenheit, thus ensuring complete decomposition of the gases so that they can be released through the smokestack without danger of creating a nuisance in the vicinity. Garbage contains from eighty to ninety per cent moisture, hence rubbish is often burned with it to provide sufficient combustible matter. If this combination is not made, some other fuel is necessary.

Methods of garbage collection:

Much difficulty has been encountered in the matter of getting garbage promptly collected. There are two methods, namely, to have the work done directly by the city's own trucks and employees, or to have some contractor do it for an agreed-upon figure.

1. By contractors.

The contract plan of collection is often cheaper, but not so satisfactory as the work done by the city's own employees. The man who seeks and obtains a garbage-collection contract is not customarily an idealist. He is not acutated by considerations of sentiment or aesthetics. His aim is to make an unpleasant job yield a profit. To do this he often employs the cheapest form of labor and as his contract is usually for a short term of years, with no certainty of renewal, he uses inexpensive equipment and cuts the corners wherever he can. The labor unions protest because his men are underpaid and the citizens complain because the service is slovenly.

2. By city employees.

So the contract method of garbage collection has been replaced in nearly all the larger cities by a system of collection in which the city's own employees do the work. Sanitary experts are inclined to believe that the best results can be obtained when the city provides its own teams or trucks and operates them by its own labor on a flexible schedule under the supervision of inspectors. In most cases the cost will be greater than under the contract system, but the merits of direct collection are believed to be worth the difference. Horse-drawn wagons are much used for the house-to-house

---

bottom but the top of each pit is sealed to prevent the escape of odors, while provision is made for the entry of enough air to expedite the process of fermentation. The gases arising from the pits are converted into sulphate of ammonia. The fermented tankage, when it becomes dry enough, is removed and sold (or given away) as fertilizer.

collections because the frequent stops make the cost of collection by motor truck unduly expensive. Moreover two men are required when a truck is used for collecting wastes, one to drive it and the other to load, whereas a team of horses can be trained to move along periodically while the driver does the loading. For long hauls from district transfer stations to the place of ultimate disposal the truck is much more economical.

The number of garbage collections per week depends on various factors—the density of the population, the section of the city (whether residential or business), the climate, and the season of the year. It should never be less frequent at any season than once a week, and there ought to be a daily service during summer months in congested or downtown sections. In the operation of an efficient collection system, moreover, there are certain rules which must be made and enforced. Receptacles should be specified in a general way with a view to reasonable uniformity—for example, their maximum size should be limited. Uncovered garbage containers should be forbidden. Some cities require householders to set the containers out at the curb. This is an economy in the labor of the collectors, but the line of garbage cans and rubbish barrels along a residential street is not a sight that moves anyone to aesthetic enthusiasm. Other cities permit the material to be placed at any convenient spot in rear of the private premises. *Frequency of collection.*

The collection of garbage should be made in water-tight wagons, easy to dump and to clean, with provision for top coverage. Tarpaulins, heavily waterproofed, are commonly used as covers. Rubbish vans do not require these precautions. All waste collections should be made during the daylight hours in spite of the fact that this procedure results in a parade of unsightly garbage and rubbish vehicles through the streets. Night collections are noisy and evoke loud protests from the sleeping populace. Since the employees in the collecting service do not like night work, they can usually be counted upon to make their operations audible. New York City, many years ago, tried the night collection plan but was quickly forced by a ruthlessly awakened citizenship to abandon it. Much can be done through proper planning to put most of the work into the early morning and evening hours—say from five to nine at both ends, which gives the workers their eight-hour day. *Garbage collection equipment.*

The collection service, in any event, should be flexible. Peak

296   MUNICIPAL ADMINISTRATION

Keeping the public satisfied. loads, in the case of garbage, come in the summer, at the very time when collections have to be made with the greatest frequency. Few branches of municipal administration, moreover, elicit so many complaints from householders. There should be well-organized facilities for receiving such complaints, checking up on them, and using them as a spur to improved service. Many complaints relate to sins of omission and some cities have found it advisable to have a light truck available to make special calls whenever such complaints are telephoned in. Because of variations in the seasonal load it is necessary to rearrange the routes and redistribute the equipment from time to time.

The cost of waste collection and disposal. In discussing the problem of waste disposal it is usual to give some data concerning the relative cost of the various methods. Such figures, however, are apt to perform the disservice of misleading the reader. Every city, of course, should keep accurate records of cost on a unit basis. The cost of street cleaning is usually reckoned in terms "per curb mile," in other words the cleaning of half the street parallel to each curb, including intersections, for a distance of one mile. This is because the cost of cleaning the streets is in large measure the cost of cleaning the gutters next the curb. The expense of snow removal is figured per cubic yard, while the collection of rubbish and garbage is figured so much per ton.[1] But considerable variations in cost must be expected from one community to another. There can be no "standard" unit-costs because no two cities are alike in such matters as the frequency of collection, length of haul, the proximity of low land for filling, the kind of equipment used, the availability of suitable sites for incinerators or reduction plants, and the ease or difficulty with which the separation of the various wastes can be enforced. This last-named factor depends upon the texture and traditions of the city's population.

The setting-up and maintenance of an efficient and economical system of waste collection and disposal is a problem in sanitary engineering which requires careful study and elaborate figuring by competent experts who will take into account all the local factors involved. There is no best method for all communities. Nor is the question one of economy alone. A city owes something to the

---

[1] See the report on *The Measurement and Control of Municipal Sanitation* published by the International Association of Street Sanitation Officials (Chicago, 1930).

development of aesthetic standards among its people, even in the regions of the unadorned tenements. It should set an example of orderly housekeeping.

REFERENCES

General works dealing with the collection and disposal of municipal waste include Rudolph Hering and S. A. Greeley, *The Collection and Disposal of Municipal Refuse* (New York, 1921), Victor M. Ehlers and Ernest W. Steel, *Municipal and Rural Sanitation* (New York, 1927), C. H. Kibbey, *The Principles of Sanitation* (Philadelphia, 1927), W. L. D'Olier, *The Sanitation of Cities* (New York, 1921), Victor M. Ehlers, E. G. Eggert and E. G. White, *Applied Municipal Sanitation* (Austin, Texas, 1926), and H. B. Wood, *Sanitation Practically Applied* (New York, 1917). In 1920 the United States Public Health Service issued a useful ninety-eight page bulletin (No. 107) dealing with *Municipal Wastes: Their Character, Collection, and Disposal* (Washington, 1920). This bulletin contains an extensive bibliography. Mention should also be made of the pamphlet on *The Measurement and Control of Municipal Sanitation* prepared in 1930 by a committee of the International Association of Street Sanitation Officials (923 East 60th St., Chicago).

References to the reports which are prepared by various American cities from time to time on rubbish collection, snow removal, street cleaning, incineration, garbage reduction, and other topics within this general field can be found in the annual volumes of *The Municipal Index*.

CHAPTER XXIII

SEWERAGE

In my youth people talked about Ruskin; now they talk about drains.—
Mrs. Humphry Ward.

The most dangerous of all urban wastes. Sewage is the community's liquid waste, consisting mainly of the water supply which has been used in habitations and industrial establishments together with part of the rainfall which descends upon the paved streets. To the casual eye it is not an offensive-looking product, being ninety-nine and nine-tenths per cent water, and hardly differs in appearance from the ordinary flow of an industrial river such as the Merrimack or the Monongahela. The Chicago drainage canal is not a thing of beauty, to be sure; but its waters are not visibly dirtier than those which flow through the famed canals of Venice on which the gondolas ride. The death-dealing powers of a great body of sewage are of course enormous. This effluvia is the most dangerous of all the wastes of civilization. In the course of history it has cost more lives than gunpowder has done. Sewage has been a bigger factor than warfare in keeping populations down.

Early methods of sewage disposal. From earliest times the menace of sewage to health has been recognized, although vaguely at first, and its safe disposition has been regarded as a public function. There were great public sewers in ancient Rome, and one of them (the Cloaca Maxima) is still in use. After the decline of Rome public sanitation passed into an eclipse, and it was more than a thousand years before any city again reached the point where Rome had left off. During these ten centuries all great communities emptied their wastes into the nearest body of water and often drew their water supplies from the same lake or river. It is small wonder that they were plagued with fever and dysentery year in and year out. They would have been scourged to extinction had it not been for the beneficence of Nature which so often protects man against his own ignorance and folly. The amount of sewage in those early centuries was relatively small, and the water courses were usually large. Dilution saved the race. The oxidizing power of the Tiber, Thames, and Seine

SEWERAGE

helped to keep Rome, London, and Paris from being wiped out by mediaeval pestilences. It was not until the beginning of the nineteenth century that the world's great cities roused themselves to a full appreciation of the close relation between disease and polluted water. Then began an era of rapid progress in public sanitation which has continued to the present day.

This has been a fortunate circumstance, for the volume of sewage has enormously increased during the past hundred years. In the modern city it runs from a hundred gallons to two hundred gallons per capita daily,—sometimes even more. The load on the sewerage system varies, of course, with the seasons, and with the amount of rainfall. Something also depends on the character of a city's industries and on the habits of its people; but under ordinary conditions an American city of half a million people will have a hundred million tons of sewage to get out of the way during the course of a single year. This is a stupendous volume of liquid waste. What becomes of it?

The daily volume of sewage.

First of all it has to be collected—from homes, factories, shops, street surfaces, and the roofs of buildings. There are two systems of sewage collection, known as the separate and the combined systems. American cities, for the most part, use the latter plan. In the separate system the surface water and the trade wastes are collected by one large set of mains, while the domestic sewage is carried away by an independent network of smaller pipes. The surface water and industrial wastes are given a rough treatment and run into some neighboring body of water, while the domestic sewage is put through a sewage disposal plant. In the combined system the same mains take care of the entire volume, surface water and domestic wastes alike.

Separate and combined sewerage systems.

Both plans have their merits and both have their shortcomings; the choice between the two depends upon a variety of conditions such as the density of population, the amount of rainfall per annum, the concentration of this rainfall, the topography of the place, and the facilities for ultimate sewage disposal without undue cost. The last-named factor is probably the most important, for if the sewage is merely poured into a lake or ocean, the advantages of the separate system are far less than when all of it has to be put through some form of treatment or disinfection. The question is one for decision by experts after a thorough study of all the factors involved.

Their merits and defects.

A thorough study by sanitary experts, in fact, is the basis of all

Sewerage planning. good sewerage planning. Whatever system is used, it ought to be designed to carry off the maximum amount of sewage that may be forthcoming at any season of the year, and should also take into account the inevitable need for expansion as the load increases with growth of population. For not only will population continue to grow in most cities, but the volume of sewage per capita is likely to increase as well. A great deal of money has been wasted by American cities during the past hundred years through lack of efficient sewerage planning. Countless miles of sewers have had to be torn up and replaced within a few years because of their inadequacy to meet increased demands.

Sewer construction. All the earliest sewers were built of wood or masonry, but nowadays there is a considerable range of choice among materials. In the case of street mains of ordinary size (up to forty inches in diameter) vitrified clay tile or concrete is generally utilized. House connections, being only four or six inches in diameter, are usually of cast iron. The large trunk mains, sometimes six or eight feet in diameter, are almost always of concrete or of hard-burned brick. The determination of sizes and materials is a matter of fundamental importance, requiring careful figuring and expert judgment. Industrial sewage, containing a high proportion of acid matter, has a deteriorating effect upon concrete mains. In a word, the sewerage system of a city must be regarded as a whole, but with special problems in various localities. Planning involves first of all the determination of lines and gradient. This again depends upon the topography and general layout of the city, or of the new suburban section for which the system is being planned.

Subsurface maps. Hence it becomes essential to have accurate topographical and subsurface maps, showing not only the nature of the soil and rock but the existing location of all water-pipes, gas mains, wire conduits, and other potential obstructions to the direct passage of the sewers. Much of this information can be obtained from the files at the city hall, but to dig it out takes time and money. Consequently the officials have often practiced false economy by proceeding with plans of sewerage construction in the absence of complete data. One of the great sources of waste in American cities has been the construction of inadequate and defective sewer mains.

Laterals, house connections, and fixtures. Equal in importance with a well-devised system of trunk mains, laterals, and house connections is the efficiency of the plumbing in homes, factories, and shops. Although this is installed by the private owners and not by the public authorities, it is properly made subject to regulation by the latter. To this end most cities have enacted comprehensive plumbing codes or plumbing ordinances.[1] These codes cover such matters as the size of house pipes, the character and location of traps and vents, the protection of dead ends, and the minimum quality of plumbing fixtures. It is usually provided that plumbers shall obtain permits before proceeding to install fixtures and that the work shall be inspected by officials of the city buildings department before it is completed. Usually there are two inspections, one after the "roughing in" is finished and a final look-over when all the fixtures have been placed. A certificate of occupancy is not granted until this final inspection has been satisfactorily passed. Unfortunately, however, much of the inspection has been lax, especially in smaller cities. This laxity is too often abetted by contractors and property owners who desire to cut the corners in the way of cheapness.[2]

When surface water from the pavement is allowed to run into the sewers it becomes necessary to provide inlets or gratings at frequent intervals. Unless the grade of the sewer is sufficient to ensure it a self-cleaning velocity, moreover, catch-basins must also be installed to prevent clogging by the bulky refuse which flows in with the surface water. A velocity of about two or three feet per second is regarded as essential in order to give a sewer main this self-cleaning capacity; where the flow is less than this it sometimes becomes necessary to clean the mains by flushing. This makes desirable the installation of automatic flush tanks which release water at intervals, usually once a day. Manholes, or surface entrances, are also placed where clogging is likely to take place for any reason, particularly where a sewer changes direction, and a non-automatic flushing apparatus is frequently installed in such manholes as are likely to require periodic clearing by this method. *Keeping the sewers clear.*

There are certain wastes which should not be allowed to pass into the sewers. These include the effluvium from glue factories and cement works, likewise all such strongly acid wastes as are likely to damage concrete or cast-iron mains. Large quantities of *The exclusion of certain wastes from the sewers.*

[1] The Bureau of Standards, United States Department of Commerce, has issued a publication entitled "Recommended Minimum Requirements for Plumbing in Dwellings and Similar Buildings" which may well be studied by those who are charged with the drafting of plumbing ordinances. A full discussion of the subject may be found in chap. xvii of Victor M. Ehlers and Ernest W. Steel, *Municipal and Rural Sanitation* (New York, 1927).
[2] For a further discussion see Chapter XXVIII.

exhaust steam or hot water should not be discharged into the sewers, for they may dissolve the bituminous joints in mains or in extreme cases may even crack the pipes. With the greatly increased use of automobiles the discharge of waste gasoline and oil from garages has become a danger and hence most cities now have ordinances which forbid the discharge of gasoline waste and other volatile oils into the sewers lest they become ignited after vaporization. Incidentally there is no such thing as "sewer gas," although public officials sometimes use that term. What we call sewer gas is not a gas of definite chemical composition but merely air which has come into contact with decomposing organic matter. It may, however, contain some gases which result from decomposition (*e.g.*, carbon dioxide) and its entry into homes ought to be prevented.

The noteworthy sewers of Paris.

In the matter of providing efficient systems of sewage collection, the larger cities of Europe have been ahead of American municipalities, although the gap between them has been narrowed since the World War. The sewerage system of Paris is perhaps the most elaborate and the best known among these European installations. During the Second Empire, and particularly in the decade 1860–1870, a comprehensive scheme of sewerage construction was carried to completion by Napoleon III and his reconstructors of Paris,— Belgrand, Deschamps, and Haussmann. This has been considerably extended during the past sixty years and now consists of three great trunk sewers, one following each bank of the Seine and the third traversing the Montmartre district of the city. These trunk sewers are of arched masonry and fifteen to twenty feet in diameter. Lateral mains connect with the main tunnels at each street corner.

Sewers and the public utilities.

Near the top of the tunnels are galleries which carry the city's water mains, the conduits for the electric lighting, telegraph and telephone wires, the pneumatic postal tubes, and pipes containing compressed air for power. The plan of using the trunk sewers for these various utilities was a Haussmann idea which has not yet found adoption in other cities because it involves such heavy expense at the outset; but it has great advantages in the way of making pipes and wires accessible for repair without the necessity of tearing up the street surface. Gas mains are not carried in the sewer galleries because of the possible danger from explosion; they are laid under the sidewalks. Trips of inspection through the trunk sewers are made by the officials in an electric motor boat, and visitors to Paris who obtain permission to accompany the inspectors find the experience instructive without being in any way unpleasant.

One of the most extensive among American sewerage projects is the Chicago Sanitary District, which includes the city and some adjacent territory, an area of nearly four hundred square miles. Over thirty years ago the flow of the Chicago River, which at that time carried the city's sewage into Lake Michigan, was reversed and turned southward. It now passes through a great drainage canal for a distance of about thirty miles to Joliet, where it reaches the Des Plaines River and flows thence to the Illinois, by which it ultimately makes its way to the Mississippi and the sea. This project involved the deepening of the river beds and the digging of a great canal, as well as the construction of locks, dams, and power plants. Some difficulties have arisen, however, in connection with the large amount of water which has to be diverted from the lake, thus affecting the levels to the detriment of navigation. Originally a continuous diversion of 4,167 cubic feet per second was authorized, but in the course of time more than twice that amount was being actually diverted. The federal government has now ordered Chicago to install sewage treatment plants as a means of preventing a further drain on the lake. *The Chicago sewerage system.*

This Chicago enterprise, when it was originally put through, attracted nation-wide attention because of the litigation which resulted. St. Louis and other cities on the Mississippi objected to the plan of using the Father of Waters as a sewage outlet and carried their opposition to the Supreme Court of the United States. This tribunal accumulated a great mass of testimony concerning the pollution of waterways and the conditions under which sewage may be rendered innocuous by dilution. In the end it decided that no contamination of a serious nature had been shown after a flow of more than three hundred and fifty miles, which is the water distance between the two cities in question.[1] *The litigation connected with it.*

Collecting a city's sewage is only half, and sometimes less than half, the whole problem. Getting rid of it, after it has been collected, is sometimes a far more difficult undertaking. The specific problem is to find and follow a method of disposal which will be *The disposal problem.*

---

[1] Missouri *vs.* Illinois, 180 *U. S.* 208 and 202 *U. S.* 598. A digest of the evidence in this remarkable case may be found in *Water Supply and Irrigation Paper No. 190*, edited by M. O. Leighton and issued by the United States Geological Survey.

safe, convenient, and at the same time economical. Here, again, topography plays an essential part in determining the ease or difficulty of solution. In some cities, especially those located on high ground with the ocean at their doors, there is no problem of disposal at all, or almost none. But inland communities, built upon low ground, with a water supply drawn from small rivers or lakes, often find great difficulty in handling large daily volumes of sewage during summer and winter alike. Great as are the purifying capabilities of streams and lakes, an intolerable burden can easily be placed upon them by growing communities. Hence the construction of sewage-disposal plants is in such cases the only alternative to a serious health menace.

Its relation to geography.

The problem is not one of purification but of disposal. This should be given emphasis because a good deal of nonsense has been written about the "purification of sewage." No city attempts to filter its sewage and make the effluent available as a water supply. That could be done, of course, but at prohibitive cost and public sentiment would rebel against the idea. Sewage disposal and water supply are interrelated problems, but the two physical plants are quite independent. The problem of water supply is to provide a commodity which is pathogenically pure; that of sewage disposal is to get rid of waste material in such way that the former problem is not made unduly difficult.

Its relation to water supply.

It happens, not by accident of course, that most of the world's largest cities are located at tidewater. In such cases the easiest plan of sewage disposal is to turn it into the sea. This is done by running an outfall sewer a considerable distance, often several miles from the shore. Sometimes the sewage is held in storage while the tide is coming in, and is then released while the tide is going out. Disposal into the ocean through an outfall sewer is an economical and on the whole a safe method provided the sewage is carried to a point where it will not be brought back by tides or currents. Failure to do this has sometimes caused the pollution of oyster beds and bathing beaches.

Disposal by outfall sewers.

Other large cities are located on the shores of the Great Lakes or of rivers, such as the Mississippi and the Ohio. The temptation to empty untreated sewage into these lakes and rivers is strong because of the small expense involved, but the practice is a dangerous one whenever the amount of outflow is large. It is true, of course, that large bodies of fresh water can digest an enormous

Dangers of sewage disposal into bodies of fresh water.

daily diet of sewage, and by the process of dilution render it reasonably harmless. It converts the putrescible matter into nitrates or other mineral substances, a process in which the noxious bacteria are destroyed.

Anyone who has an elementary knowledge of chemistry is aware of the fact that organic matter, in the absence of sufficient oxygen, will decompose or putrefy. If, however, it is placed in contact with sufficient oxygen, it will oxidize or nitrify. When there is enough water, accordingly, and therefore enough oxygen, the sewage will oxidize the organic matter which it contains. The question whether there is enough water, in proportion to the amount of pollution, is something that cannot be determined by any general rule; it depends on a number of factors such as the velocity of the flow, the hardness of the water, its temperature, the strength of the sewage in bacteria, and the duration of the diluting process, all of which vary widely in different cases. It is sometimes said that satisfactory oxidation or nitrification can be accomplished whenever the body of water has at least fifty times the volume of the sewage turned into it, but sanitary experts usually put the proportion somewhat larger. *The safeguard in oxidization by dilution.*

In any event it is amazing how large a body of sewage can be treated in this way. It has been estimated that the Mississippi receives nearly three billion gallons of sewage a day. Many cities on the Great Lakes, including Detroit, Cleveland,[1] and Buffalo empty their sewage without any preliminary treatment other than screening, yet the lower St. Lawrence is as free from pollution as is any ordinary surface stream which flows through well-settled areas. On the other hand the waterways adjacent to Philadelphia, Washington, Milwaukee, and various other large cities have not been deemed large enough to carry the sewage of these communities without some form of preliminary treatment.

When no large body of water is at hand, or where the process of dilution cannot be depended upon safely, the raw sewage must be treated to reduce its solid content before the effluent is discharged. There are various ways of doing this and the selection of the most effective method is sometimes a problem of serious technical difficulty. It is not one which any layman ought to try his hand at solving, but requires the assistance of experienced and compe- *Modern methods of sewage treatment: 1. Screening and roughing.*

---

[1] During the past few years Cleveland has been installing two large activated sludge treatment plants.

tent sanitary engineers. The simplest form of treatment is screening. The sewage is merely passed through stationary or rotating screens to remove the larger particles floating in it. The screened material is then carted away and either buried or incinerated, while the effluent is allowed to pass into the nearest river or lake. Straining or roughing is the term commonly used to describe a somewhat more elaborate process by which the sewage is slowly passed through a grit chamber containing coke, stone, or coarse sand, to which the heavy inorganic matter adheres. So much matter is deposited in these beds, however, that they must be cleaned out at frequent intervals, hence it is usual to have at least two grit chambers at each treatment works. There is a feeling among sanitary engineers that the roughing process is expensive out of proportion to the results obtained.

2. Plain sedimentation.

A better removal of the suspended solids in sewage can be obtained by the process known as plain sedimentation, which is used by many cities both in the United States and abroad. This process consists in allowing raw sewage to flow slowly into and out of storage tanks so that the suspended particles may be deposited at the bottom. This may be done in either of two ways, by the fill-and-draw method or by permitting a continuous flow at low velocity. In either case the sludge, which accumulates at the bottom of the tank to the extent of from four to six cubic yards per million gallons of sewage, must be removed once a week or oftener. This, of course, involves having at least two sedimentation reservoirs to permit continuous operation. Plain sedimentation is usually effective in removing from fifty to seventy per cent of the suspended matter.

3. Chemical precipitation.

When the volume of sewage is large, and where there is much suspended matter, it is customary to hasten the process of coagulation and sedimentation by the use of various chemicals such as calcium oxide or lime, sulphate of aluminum or alum, ferrous sulphate or copperas, or sulphuric acid and sulphur dioxide. These chemicals, when put into the sewage, act as precipitants, but the degree of clarification depends upon the care with which the process is controlled. Under favorable conditions, however, from eighty to ninety per cent of the total suspended matter can be removed. The sewage of London, for example, is treated in this way before the effluent is run into the Thames, while the precipitated sludge is ferried out to sea on scows and dumped overboard.

During recent years a number of commercial processes have been promoted in which an electrical current is passed through sewage with the purpose of (a) expediting precipitation, or (b) oxidizing the organic matter by the nascent hydrogen and oxygen produced by electrolysis of the water, or (c) disinfecting and deodorizing the sewage by the production of hypochlorites from the salt contained in it; but "the consensus of opinion among leading engineers seems to be that there are no results of electrolytic treatment of the sewage which cannot be obtained more cheaply and more directly by other more common treatment processes."[1]

4. Electrolytic treatment.

Screening, roughing, sedimentation, and precipitation remove a varying large proportion of the suspended solids and organic matter. When a more thorough removal is desired, this can be accomplished by certain septic tank methods whereby the solid content of the sewage is partially liquified by bacterial action and the accumulation of sewage solids, or sludge, is correspondingly diminished. The general principle is the same as in sedimentation, but provision is made to hold the sludge until its character has been changed by biological action. A septic tank, as its name implies, is a covered reservoir in which the sewage is stored until it becomes digested and decomposed, leaving a much smaller amount of black, alkaline, humus-like residuum which is then discharged upon drying beds. The effluent meanwhile is passed out of the tank for treatment by disinfection or filtration before it is discharged into a waterway. The best-known and most widely used type of septic tank is the Imhoff tank which contains two compartments, one above the other. The upper compartment is V-shaped with a slot at the bottom. The solids are first deposited in this compartment but are then allowed to run down into the lower part of the tank for decomposition. This decomposition is the work of anaërobic bacteria which become active and break down the solid organic matter when oxygen is shut out. The treatment of sewage in Imhoff tanks is regarded as satisfactory for small and medium-sized installations; it is not recommended by sanitary engineers for large communities.

5. Septic tanks.

A more recent development is the activated sludge process. This consists in putting the sewage into specially constructed aëration tanks where it is mixed with activated sludge, that is,

6. The activated sludge process.

[1] Leonard Metcalf and Harrison P. Eddy, *Sewerage and Sewage Disposal* (2nd edition, New York, 1930), p. 467.

with sludge which has been agitated by using compressed air until it has assumed a frothy or flocculent appearance. The mixing of the activated sludge with the raw sewage is accomplished by forcing air into the bottom of the tanks for a stretch of three or four hours at a time. The purpose of this aëration is to supply the mixture with an ample amount of oxygen, thereby promoting the aërobic action of the bacteria. The agitation is violent enough to ensure the continuous and intimate contact of the activated sludge particles with the entire volume of sewage. Ordinarily the introduction of compressed air produces sufficient activation, but mechanical agitators are sometimes used to reduce the air requirement and thereby secure a considerable economy in power costs.

Nature of the bacterial action. The activated sludge process is thus the antithesis of the septic tank treatment. In the former it is the aërobic bacteria, encouraged by an ample supply of oxygen, which do the work of biological decomposition; while in the latter it is the anaërobic bacteria, aided by the exclusion of air. In both cases, however, the organic matter is oxidized by bacterial action. After activation for several hours the mixture passes into clarification tanks where the sludge settles and the liquid is drained off,—clean, odorless, and free from solid matter. Part of the sludge is pumped back into the first aëration tank to inoculate the fresh sewage coming in; the rest is usually dehydrated and sold as fertilizer. On the whole the results of this system have been found satisfactory, but the expense varies with the cost of power for pumping the air and the salability of the dried sludge for fertilizer purposes. The effluent is treated with a disinfectant, such as chloride of lime, before being turned into a water course.

7. Intermittent filtration systems. Various methods of treating sewage by filtration are in use throughout Europe and America. There are at least a half-dozen such methods. The simplest is the plan of intermittent filtration in contact beds, a plan which has some important advantages whenever suitable land is available at low cost and climatic conditions are favorable. Contact beds are large, water-tight basins filled with broken stone, cinders, coke, or other inert matter, with suitable drains underneath. The raw sewage is run upon the bed until it submerges the contact material; then it is slowly drained from below, whereupon the beds are allowed to rest for a few days. How long the sewage is left in the contact bed depends upon the strength of the sewage and the condition of the contact material.

SEWERAGE

During this settling period the solids and colloids are deposited in the contact bed material. In the course of time the contents of the contact bed have to be removed and cleaned. Some difficulty with the use of this plan is encountered in cold climates where the sewage freezes before it can be drained.

Various types of trickling, percolating, and sprinkling filters represent improvements on the contact-bed plan. These filters are reservoirs from five to ten feet deep, filled with broken stone. They are not filled to the brim with raw sewage at a single stroke, but after preliminary treatment to remove the heavier solids the sewage is allowed to trickle upon the stone, or is sprinkled over it in a fine spray. Sprinklers are allowed to operate for a few minutes and then given a somewhat longer rest period, so that the bed absorbs oxygen continuously. The effluent passes through drains at the bottom of the tank and is usually given a disinfection prior to its final discharge. The principal advantage of this plan is the rapidity with which a large volume of sewage can be handled.

8. Trickling and sprinkling filters.

Sewage disposal by broad irrigation is used by some of the larger European cities, such as Berlin and Paris, but has found very little favor in America. It involves the discharge of raw sewage upon land which requires water. Berlin has tracts comprising about 20,000 acres of sewer farm land. When the sewage reaches these farms it is pumped into a reservoir or standpipe, from which it is conducted to small open ditches running through the fields. The land is dosed at the rate of about 4,000 gallons per acre daily. In the colder periods of the winter, when the sewage will not run easily, it is stored in reservoir fields which are reserved for that purpose. About one-quarter of the entire sewer-farm area is tilled by city labor; the rest is rented to tenant farmers. While the plan has been regarded as successful in Berlin, it has not been widely used in the United States because a sufficient amount of irrigable land is hard to find in close proximity to most of the larger cities. There is the additional objection that in localities where the winters are severe, or where the rainfall is heavy, the broad irrigation plan must provide for extensive storage during such seasons. Likewise there is a popular prejudice against the establishment of sewage farms in the neighborhood of settled communities. Experiments have been tried with the system of broad irrigation, especially in some California cities; but in almost every instance the plan has been given up.

9. Broad irrigation.

10. Sewage disinfection.

Finally, there is the process known as the sterilization or disinfection of sewage by dosing it with various sterilizing chemicals, more particularly the chlorine compounds or derivatives, such as chlorine gas, liquid chlorine, chloride of lime, or calcium hypochlorites. This reduces the bacterial content of the sewage by a varying percentage, depending somewhat upon the amount of solid matter in the liquid to which the process of disinfection is applied. While the exact manner of accomplishing bacterial disinfection by chlorine remains uncertain, there is no question as to its disinfecting efficiency under certain conditions. But raw sewage which contains large amounts of suspended matter cannot be adequately sterilized by this means because the larger solids are not penetrated by the chlorine. Chlorination should be used, therefore, as a supplement to one of the other methods of sewage treatment, and it is widely employed to disinfect the effluent after sedimentation or after treatment by the activated sludge system. Thus it becomes an adjunct to one of the other plans rather than an independent method of sewage disposal.

The problem of sludge disposal.

Getting rid of the sludge is not so simple a problem as disinfecting the liquid. Every million gallons of raw sewage treated by the activated sludge process will produce from 3,000 to 6,000 gallons of sludge, which must be taken out of the settling tanks and dried or otherwise disposed of. The common method of drying sludge is to run it on sand beds and allow the moisture to seep away or evaporate. Mechanical driers are also used to some extent. When properly dried the sludge has a considerable nitrogen content and is of value as a commercial fertilizer; but the problem of securing a satisfactory market for it has not always proved an easy one.

Which is the best plan?

To the layman's question: "Which of these disposal systems is the best?" it is impossible to give any categorical reply. No one can say that one process is better than the others under all circumstances. The volume of sewage to be handled, the presence or absence of industrial wastes, the topography of the city, the availability of cheap and suitable land for a disposal plant, the cost of oil or coal for operating it, the size and character of the adjacent waterways, the climate, the amount of rainfall, the city's financial resources, and (not least important) the preferences or prejudices of the municipal voters—these and many other factors must be taken into account. Hence it is sometimes found desirable to treat different portions of a city's sewage by different methods

SEWERAGE

or to use a combination of two methods, or to vary some standard plan to meet local requirements.

Consequently there is one proposition which cannot have too much emphasis, namely, that the choice of a sewage-disposal plan for any city should never be left in the hands of laymen, or even of the local sanitary officers unguided by the highest type of technical advice. To copy the installation of some neighboring city, because it seems to be giving satisfaction there, is to incur the risk of a costly error. Money spent for expert study of a local sewage-disposal problem almost invariably turns out to be money well spent. So, when a city shrinks from paying what it costs to obtain the advice of high-grade sanitary engineers on problems of this kind, and prefers to throw the whole responsibility on its own officials, it is indulging in penny-wise economy.

A question which only the experts can safely answer.

REFERENCES

A standard work dealing with this problem in all its phases is Leonard Metcalf and Harrison P. Eddy, *American Sewerage Practice* (3 vols., New York, 1916). A new edition, by Harrison P. Eddy, is in process of publication, the first volume having already appeared (New York, 1928). There is also a condensed one-volume edition of the three volumes entitled *Sewerage and Sewage Disposal* (2nd edition, New York, 1930).

Other books of value are G. W. Fuller and J. R. McClintock, *Solving Sewage Problems* (New York, 1926), A. P. Folwell, *Sewerage* (10th edition, New York, 1929), L. P. Kinnicutt, C. E. A. Winslow, and R. W. Pratt, *Sewage Disposal* (2nd edition, New York, 1919), Harold E. Babbitt, *Sewerage and Sewage Treatment* (3rd edition, New York, 1929), S. H. Adams, *Modern Sewage Disposal and Hygienics* (New York, 1930), Arthur M. Buswell, *The Chemistry of Water and Sewage Treatment* (New York, 1928), G. Bertram de B. Kershaw, *Sewage Purification and Disposal* (New York, 1926), T. H. P. Veal, *The Disposal of Sewage* (New York, 1928), T. P. Francis, *Modern Sewage Treatment* (London, 1932), C. J. Nurse, *Purification and Disposal of Sewage* (London, 1931), W. E. Adeney, *Principles and Practice of the Dilution Method of Sewage Disposal* (Cambridge, England, 1928), A. J. Martin, *The Activated Sludge Process* (London, 1927), General Filtration Co., *The Activated Sludge Process of Sewage Treatment* (Rochester, N. Y., 1926), and Karl Imhoff and G. N. Fair, *The Arithmetic of Sewage Treatment Works* (New York, 1929).

Mention should also be made of the United States Public Health Bulletin No. 132 on *Sewage Treatment in the United States* (Washington, 1923) and the American Public Health Association's report on *Standard Methods for the Examination of Water and Sewage* (7th edition, New York, 1933).

Bulletin No. 12 of the Division of Municipal and Industrial Research, Massachusetts Institute of Technology, entitled *Principles of Sewage Disposal* (1931) contains a concise survey of the subject.

Articles and current references may be found in the *Engineering News-Record* (weekly), the *Proceedings* of the American Society of Civil Engineers (monthly except June and July) and the *Sewage Works Journal* (quarterly).

CHAPTER XXIV

POLICE ADMINISTRATION

Policemen are soldiers who act alone; soldiers are policemen who act in unison.—*Herbert Spencer.*

Police protection is one of the oldest among public functions. Guardians of the peace walked the streets of Nineveh and Babylon. There were centurions and a captain of the guard in Jerusalem when the Messiah came. Imperial Rome had her prefect of police (*praefectus vigilum*) with seven thousand armed men under him. These *vigiles* were distributed into districts and precincts, each with a regular police station (*excubitorium*) and fixed patrols. During the long era of the Middle Ages the cities of continental Europe were policed by armed retainers of the feudal lord, but with the breakdown of feudalism these gave way to soldiers of the king. Everywhere, except in England, the policing of towns was regarded as a military function, a safeguard against treason and insurrection. In England, where there was no standing army, the work of patrolling the city, especially during the night hours, was entrusted to civilian watchmen who often spent more of their time in the alehouses than on the streets.

Early policing.

With the rapid growth of London after the incoming of the nineteenth century this system broke down. The untrained "Charleys," as they were called, could not cope with the epidemic of crime which accompanied the expansion of the metropolis. Accordingly, in 1839, Parliament passed a statute, commonly known as Peel's Act, which established a system of full-time, uniformed police constables under centralized control for the whole London metropolitan area. This enactment marked the beginnings of urban police administration as we have it today, for the precedent set by Peel was soon followed in America. New York City, in 1844, abolished the old system of watchmen and wardens, replacing these inefficient guardians of the peace by a regular police force which in due course was closely modelled on the London plan, even to the cut and color of the uniforms which the officers wore.[1]

Advent of modern police systems.

[1] The "new police system" was momentarily unpopular both in England and in America. In facetious tribute to Sir Robert Peel, who fathered the Metropolitan

313

Other American cities quickly followed the example of New York and within a short time the "new police system" had entirely displaced the ward constables or watchmen in all the larger communities.

State control of municipal police.

With the advent of the new police came the inauguration of state control in most of the larger American municipalities. This was true of New York, Chicago, Boston, Detroit, Cleveland, Baltimore, Cincinnati, St. Louis, New Orleans, and Kansas City. In each of these cities a police board, with its members appointed by the governor or elected by the state legislature, was placed in complete control of the municipal police establishment. The ostensible reason for this change was the alleged failure of the city authorities to maintain proper standards of law and order; although the real reason in most cases was a desire on the part of the state politicians to get control of the police patronage. But the move was not popular in any of the cities and local opposition to the continuance of state control grew steadily stronger. So it was gradually abolished in most of these cities, and today the policy of state control is continued in only four of them, namely, Baltimore, St. Louis, Kansas City, and Boston. In Baltimore there is a state board of three members who are elected by the two houses of the Maryland legislature in joint session. In Missouri the state police forces for St. Louis and Kansas City are appointed by the governor, but in each case the mayor of the city is an ex-officio member. In Boston the police commissioner is chosen by the governor of Massachusetts with the confirmation of the governor's council.

Arguments in its favor

The chief argument in favor of state control is the need for removing the municipal police department from control by local politicians. When a city's government passes into the power of corrupt or self-seeking officials, the morale of the police force is usually the first to suffer. Hence it is argued that the governor or the state legislature, having no intimate connection with local politics, should be given power to select municipal police boards or commissioners who will not be subject to the pressure of sinister

Police Act, the new officers were nicknamed "peelers" and "bobbies." These nicknames persist in London today. Peel was anxious to quiet the public fear that the new policemen would become the nucleus of a military force. To this end the officers were uniformed in blue coats with copper buttons, blue helmets, and black belts, in sharp contrast to the British infantrymen who were clad at that time in red coats with buttons of shining brass, white helmets, and pipe-clayed belts. The police buttons were a very distinctive feature of the new uniforms, hence the nickname "copper," which we have abbreviated in America to "cop."

local interests. It is further pointed out that the city police are in reality state officers, the courts having repeatedly declared them to have that status. Their chief function is to enforce the state laws, not the municipal ordinances. Without the coöperation of the municipal police it is not practicable for the state authorities to maintain order, security, and law observance. For this additional reason it is contended that the state has both a legal and moral right to insist that local police administration shall maintain a reasonable standard of efficiency. If it becomes necessary to establish direct state control as the only practicable way of securing this end, then such action is justified by the logic of facts even though it be an affront to the principle of municipal home rule.

But there is another side to this issue. Those who favor state control take it for granted that the transfer of authority will remove the police from the influence of local politics. Of course there is no absolute assurance that this will be the result in all cases. Appointments made by governors have not been more free from the taint of political patronage than those made by mayors. Everything depends on the traditions of the state or city concerned. In some parts of the country a system of state control over municipal police would unquestionably be used by governors and other high officials as a means of promoting their own political interests in the cities. It should be borne in mind, moreover, that the policy of state interference in this or any other branch of municipal administration is almost always resented by the taxpayers of the city who have to pay the bills. For state control means not only control over police work but over the expenditures of the police department. And not being responsible to the local taxpayers the state authorities have no strong incentive to keep the expenditures down. It may be good legal doctrine to regard city policemen as state officers but the average citizen does not look upon them in that light. He only knows that they get their pay checks at the city hall, that they ordinarily have no jurisdiction outside the city limits, and that the insignia which they wear is that of the municipality, not the state. It is hard to convince him that state police control is not a ruthless invasion of his right to municipal home rule.

The need for state control over municipal police, as a means of ensuring the enforcement of state laws, has been considerably

Local objections to it.

Independent bodies of state police.

lessened by the practice of establishing a regular state constabulary, that is, a body of trained police officers who are maintained by the state and paid from its treasury. These state police forces are mobilized at various convenient points from which they can be sent out to patrol the rural highways, or to supplement the work of the city police when need arises, or to enforce the state laws when the local authorities prove too lax in this direction. Many of the states have established police systems of this type. They have, for the most part, maintained high standards of equipment, discipline, and integrity.[1]

The evolution of municipal police organization:

The methods of organizing a municipal police department have passed through several stages in the United States. In early days the police were supervised by a committee of the board of aldermen or the city council. That plan of supervision was borrowed from England where it still exists; but in American cities it did not prove at all satisfactory, as can well be imagined. Since there were at that time no civil service regulations to control appointments to the police force, every alderman or member of the city council looked upon each vacancy as a fair chance to put one of his own relatives or friends on the city payroll. Unseemly scrambles for the patronage were a common occurrence among the city councillors and presently the whole system got itself so hopelessly enmeshed in the worst phases of local politics that gross inefficiency, favoritism, extravagance, and corruption became the earmarks of American municipal police administration almost everywhere.

1. The committee system of control.

2. The board system.

To remedy this situation it was decided to set up separate police boards, quite independent of the city council. The members of these new boards were usually appointed by the mayor, although in some cases they were elected by popular vote. A frequent but ill-advised requirement was that both the major political parties should have representation in the police-board's membership. This nearly always resulted in a great deal of friction within the board itself, whereupon the next step was to require that members of police boards should not be affiliated with any political party, in other words that the police board should be a non-partisan body, made up of men who had not been active in partisan politics.

Objections to the board system.

Even in this non-partisan form, however, the board system of police administration has rarely given satisfaction. Unity of com-

---

[1] For a full discussion, see Bruce Smith, *The State Police* (New York, 1925).

POLICE ADMINISTRATION

mand and promptness in making decisions are absolutely essential to an effective police administration and these can rarely be supplied by a board, no matter how honest, capable, and non-partisan its members may be. For members of a board must meet, confer, and discuss, often at some length, when quick action is urgently needed. Of course it is the theory of the board system that the immediate command of the force as well as the details of administration shall be left to the chief of police, while the board concerns itself only with matters of general procedure and policy.

But in practice the system does not usually work out that way. General procedure cannot always be sharply separated from routine. For example, should there be a training school for new police officers, and if so how should it be conducted? Should officers be detailed to the bureau of criminal investigation from the regular uniformed force or should they be specialists, chosen and trained for the purpose? Should a policeman be given extra time off as a reward for a conspicuously good piece of work? Should a patrolman, while on duty, be permitted to canvass his beat, selling tickets for the policeman's ball? Are these questions of general policy or of routine? A board usually goes on the principle that any question in which its members are interested is a question worth discussing and deciding. What is worse, the individual members of the board sometimes interfere in matters of discipline, occasionally overruling the actions of the police chief. This, of course, is destructive of the morale in any department. Police boards are rarely unanimous in their decisions and the lack of unanimity reflects itself throughout the rank and file of the force. Under such conditions no chief of police can hope to make a good record or even to remain in office very long. *Its theory and practice do not conform.*

It is time to recognize that the work of maintaining law and order in any large municipality is at best a highly complicated and difficult enterprise. It cannot be successfully performed by a group of well-intentioned citizens who give only their spare time and thought to the task. A unified command is as essential in a police force as in a military organization. Both European and American municipal experience have proved the high desirability of placing at the head of the police department, in the larger cities, a single commissioner or director who possesses final authority and takes undivided responsibility. This commissioner should be appointed by the chief executive of the city, that is, by the mayor *3. The single commissioner plan.*

or the city manager, and should be removable by him at will. He ought to be a civilian, not a professional police officer. The chief of police, not the commissioner, should be the professional head of the force. The commissioner should bear the same relation to the chief that the secretary of war bears to the commanding general of the army. It goes without saying that the police commissioner should not be a man who is given the post as a reward for party services; but as a practical matter this stipulation is much easier to lay down than to enforce. So long as mayors are themselves politicians they are likely to appoint men of their own type to the headship of the police department. One of the advantages of the city manager plan of government is that it strongly encourages, even if it does not always assure, the appointment of non-political heads in this as in the other municipal departments.

Combining police and fire departments. In some cities the police and fire departments are combined under one commissioner into a department of public safety. This is done to economize the administrative machinery and is based on the idea that police and fire protection are functions of much the same nature. Superficially they are. Both policemen and firemen are engaged in protecting life and property. But there the analogy ends. The day-by-day problems of the two departments have little in common. The police deal almost wholly with human relations, while the work of the firemen is largely related to physical property. The element of wrong-doing enters almost always in the one case and only at rare intervals in the other. In cities of any considerable size the police department ought to be a separate entity under its own commissioner.

Qualifications of a police commissioner. What are the qualities of an ideal police commissioner? He should be a man of high intelligence and alertness of mind. In addition he ought to possess in large measure that quality of intestinal fortitude which is more commonly expressed in a short four-letter word. On the other hand he should be a tactful man, able to get along with the public, the newspapers, and his own subordinates. The successful police commissioner must also be a good organizer, with broad social sympathies and the capacity to grasp the relationship between the problem of crime and the other social problems of the community. The civilian headship of the police department is no place for a fanatic or hobby-rider, or indeed for anyone who lacks a sympathetic understanding of the varied elements which make up the population of a large municipality.

The ideal police commissioner is not a routineer but a man with initiative, a willingness to experiment, and a determination to keep the methods of his department in tune with ever-changing conditions. Finally, his moral fiber and his integrity must be temptation-proof, for plenty of allurements to wrong-doing will be set across his path, all of them cleverly disguised. A wise serpent rather than a harmless dove is what the duties of this position require.

Obviously it is difficult to secure for the civilian headship of the police department a commissioner who possesses all these qualities or even most of them. Cities have tried experiments of every sort in their quest for the right man. They have given the position to business men, to lawyers, journalists, army officers, experts in criminology, clergymen, social workers, and to men who have risen through the ranks of the police department itself. About the only conclusion that anyone can reach from this process of experimentation is that good police commissioners are excessively rare and that a city which finds one has reason to be congratulated. Some of the men who have been put into the office might have turned out to be good commissioners if they had been left there long enough, but public opinion in relation to police is usually impatient and insists on getting results right away. *Rarity of these qualifications.*

That is why so few heads of municipal police departments in the United States have managed to remain in office more than three or four years. At almost every municipal election the work of the police becomes a campaign issue; indeed it is probable that more mayoralty campaigns have been fought upon this than upon any other single phase of municipal administration. Yet it ought to be apparent, on brief reflection, that we can never have an efficient police administration in our larger cities until the work is completely divorced from local politics as school administration has been in many of these communities. *Police work and politics.*

The difficulties in the way of securing this divorce are formidable. Tradition is against it because the miscegenation of police and politics is one of long standing. The social fluidity, the emphasis on personal liberty, the cynical disrespect for law even on the part of many who deem themselves good citizens, the lax administration of criminal justice by the courts—these and many other considerations afford a strong incentive to keep the police department under strict control and scrutiny. This control de- *Can the two be divorced?*

volves, of course, upon the elective authorities of the city whose mental orientation is in almost all things political and who find it hard to understand why the police should be treated differently from any other department. Strange, is it not, that no such confusion exists in the minds of the national authorities as respects the army, which is to all intents a police department writ large? It is given a special status and placed almost wholly outside the reach of partisan interference.

<small>The chief or superintendent of police.</small>

Immediately under the police commissioner or police board in the larger cities is a professional administrator commonly known as the chief of police or police superintendent. In smaller cities the commissioner or board is usually eliminated and the police chief is made directly responsible to the mayor or the city manager. Almost invariably the police chief is someone who has risen through the ranks. His selection, however, is not always a matter of seniority alone. Usually it is a combination of seniority, personal qualifications, and political influence. It is the business of the police chief to carry out the general policies laid down for him by the chief executive of the city, or by the police commissioner or police board, as the case may be. He recommends appointments to the force and approves promotions within it. As a rule he also arranges for the assignment of duties to officers, recommends changes in their remuneration, approves suspensions and dismissals,—in a word he has the immediate supervision of police discipline. It is to him that all subordinate officials of the police department look for their instructions and orders. To use a military metaphor, he is the chief of staff who directs a brigade of armed men.

<small>The rank and file of the force.</small>

For the police force of a great city is a body of enlisted, sworn, drilled, and disciplined men whose first duty is to obey their superior officer's command. It is organized into battalions, companies, platoons, and squads. It is strategically dispersed in barracks which we call police stations, with men on duty and men in reserve. Its officers are captains, lieutenants, and sergeants with quasi-military rank; its patrolmen are equipped for service with automatic pistols and frequently with riot guns, submachine guns, armored cars, and tear gas bombs. In numbers, moreover, they constitute the equivalent of a regiment or a brigade. The police establishment of New York City now includes more than 12,000 men, which is a larger body, by the way, than Washington had under his command when he won the most important battles of the Revolutionary War. Under modern conditions of warfare no sensible government thinks of sending an army into action with a politician at its head, and the critical nature of the campaign against crime in American cities ought to dictate that the same disregard of political considerations be observed with respect to the police establishment.

Police departments are composed of two main divisions and sometimes three. First there is the uniformed force, which performs the regular work of patrolling the streets and other places of public resort. Second comes the division of criminal investigation, more commonly known as the detective branch of the service; and third there is the traffic division which may be a separate unit or merely a temporary assignment from the uniformed force. Regular patrolmen, of course, form by far the largest element in the police personnel. The general nature of their work is known to everyone and requires no explanation. Not everyone realizes, however, the varied nature of the duties which the ordinary patrolman is expected to perform. In every large city he has a thousand-and-one laws, ordinances, regulations, rules, and orders to enforce— the mere task of keeping track of them all is no inconsiderable task.

General scope of their work.

As for the bureau of criminal investigation it has been the general practice to select its personnel from the uniformed force by taking from the various stations those officers who appear to have displayed, in their routine patrol duties, some special aptitude for detective work. Too often, unfortunately, the selections have been colored by the taint of personal favoritism or political influence. For the most part these men have usually been given no scientific training either before or after their assignment, although the service of detection and investigation is the most highly technical of all the duties that a police department is expected to perform. Most of the serious crimes which are committed in a large city are the work of professionals who have become specialists in their own particular varieties of law-breaking and racket. In recent years the police authorities have awakened to a realization of this fact and it is now the practice in most of the largest communities to meet the criminal on his own ground by organizing and training squads of police officers who are also specialists. Hence the maintenance of a homicide squad, a narcotic squad, a pawnshop detail, a stolen-automobile squad, a vice squad, a pickpocket detail, a racketeer squad, and various other special

The detective service.

services made up of officers who are chosen and trained to match the malefactor with his own degree of skill and experience. Even greater specialization of this sort will be needed if police departments are to do efficiently what is expected of them.

Centralized and decentralized organization of the work.

In some cities the detective corps work is stationed at headquarters, in others it is distributed among the precinct stations, while a few cities use a combination of both methods. The centralized plan has the advantage of promoting uniformity in procedure and encouraging the specialization of work, but it loads upon the police headquarters a vast amount of minor investigating which might better be handled by men from the local stations who are familiar with the neighborhood. The decentralized method overcomes this objection but leads to great diversity in procedure and prevents the development of such specialization as the other alternative not only permits but encourages. Under the combination plan a few plain-clothes officers are assigned to each precinct for the handling of complaints which originate in that area; but whenever a serious crime is reported the call goes to headquarters and members of the specialized squad are sent out to deal with it.

Lack of continuity in methods and practice.

One serious difficulty with the whole system of criminal investigation in American cities arises from the practice of making transfers of officers from one assignment to another as a means of meeting some political or other exigency. Trouble also results from the habit of abolishing or reconstructing the various special squads from time to time in accordance with the crochets of newly installed police commissioners or police chiefs. Whenever a new head of the department is appointed he proceeds, as a rule, to alter the policies of his predecessor. These periodic changes do a great deal of harm to the morale of the force.

The problem of criminal identification.

Coöperating closely with the detective or investigating division is the bureau of identification and records. This bureau has become an invaluable adjunct to efficient police work. It houses the memory of the police deparment. The earliest method of identifying criminals was by means of photographs kept in what was known as the rogues' gallery at police headquarters. But this method did not prove satisfactory because the dissipated life which the average criminal leads may effect a considerable change in his countenance within a relatively short time. Photographs, moreover, are difficult to index in such way that they can be quickly and accurately found when needed—especially when there are many thousands of them to be kept on file. As a supplement to the rogues' gallery, therefore, the anthropometric or Bertillon method of identification by bodily measurements was borrowed from Paris and became generally used in American cities during the latter years of the nineteenth century. This method rests on the proposition that there are certain groups of physical measurements which in any given individual do not change throughout adult life and which are not alike in any two individuals.[1]

Bertillon's method.

A more recent development, now universally used, is the method of identifying by dactyloscopy or the use of finger prints. This plan has the merit of being very simple; it provides records which are easy to classify and it is unfailingly accurate. The papillary lines on the surface of the finger tips have never been found to vary in pattern from infancy to death or to be alike in any two individuals. Dactyloscopy came into use about the beginning of the twentieth century and has now generally supplanted the Bertillon system, although some cities use the two plans in combination. To assist cities in the identification of criminals who move about from one place to another there has now been established at Washington a national bureau of identification in connection with the Department of Justice. The effort is made to gather and keep on file at this bureau the finger prints of all persons who have criminal records in any part of the United States.

The finger print system.

Records for the identification of criminals are not the only ones which a police department requires. Efficient police work rests on the prompt and accurate compilation of data in relation to the frequency and location of the various crimes, the methods used in each case by the criminal, and the results of the police investigation. Certain crimes appear to come in epidemics. Most professional criminals have a technique of their own and do not vary it. A successful safe-blower or second-story man or pickpocket does not change his procedure from one job to another. He goes at each one in much the same way. Hence the keeping of accurate records is often a means of connecting the same sus-

Modus operandi files.

---

[1] For example, no two individuals (except identical twins) are ever found with precisely the same head length, head breadth, middle-finger length and foot length when measured with scientific instruments. The system took its name from Alphonse Bertillon, head of the Criminal Identification Department of the Police Prefecture in Paris who devised it for use in that city fifty years ago.

pect with two or more offenses. When these *modus operandi* files are kept on a uniform basis in different communities, moreover, it is possible to associate a suspected person with offenses committed outside the city in which he has been arrested. Much progress has been made in recent years as respects the keeping of uniform crime records and the compilation of reliable statistics relating to crime. Spot maps are also useful aids to effective police work. They are maps which show by varicolored pins or dots the location of different crimes. These maps soon indicate the regions which require special vigilance.

Distribution of the uniformed force.
The methods of organizing and distributing the personnel of a city police force are much the same throughout the country. First there is a central headquarters from which the operations of the whole force are directed. Here the clerical work and record keeping is usually concentrated. Then the city is divided into police precincts of varying size. These precincts include smaller areas in the downtown districts than in the outlying sections of the city. In the larger cities the precincts are sometimes combined into police districts with an inspector in charge of each. In any event each precinct has its police station, with a captain in charge of it by day, while a lieutenant ordinarily goes on duty during the night hours. Attached to each station is a group of sergeants and patrolmen. Some of the sergeants are assigned to desk work in the station, while others perform inspectorial duty on the streets of the precinct. The patrolmen, as their name implies, are for the most part assigned to "beats" or stretches of patrol which they cover on foot, on motorcycles, or in automobiles.

Patrolling.
Every police precinct is divided into patrols or beats, the length of each beat being determined by the character of the neighborhood. In the downtown and thickly populated sections of the city they are shorter than in the outlying districts. Likewise at night, when more patrolmen are on duty, the beats are shorter than by day. A patrol beat may contain a designated number of city blocks, but more frequently it extends along a single street with the inclusion of intersecting streets for half a block on each side. Most patrolling is done on foot, especially during the day hours, but for the residential or outlying sections of the city it is now becoming the practice to provide patrolmen with motorcycles or with automobiles in order that longer routes may be covered. Mounted officers have been used to some extent in the busi-

POLICE ADMINISTRATION

ness districts of cities, but they are more picturesque than effective. By the use of motor equipment the range of a policeman can be increased several times over.

Patrolling is the basis of effective police work. The patrolman is the eye, ear, and nose of the department. His duty is to cover his beat within the time designated, prevent crime, keep an eye on suspicious persons and places, make arrests when necessary, enforce the observance of countless regulatory ordinances, report accidents, furnish information when requested by strangers, and follow any special instructions that may be given him from his station. Hence his work is of a varied and exacting character, demanding intelligence, integrity, patience, and personal courage. Alertness is also required, for the patrolman should be able to communicate with his station, or be called by it, at any time. A system of patrol-boxes or post-telephones is in common use for this purpose supplemented by signal lights which flash at various points on a patrolman's beat when he is wanted at his nearest patrol-box. Some cities have also found it desirable to locate police booths at strategic points in every precinct. Two motorcycle officers are usually assigned to each booth, one remaining there to receive calls while the other does the patrolling. *The patrolman's functions.*

But signal lights and motorcycle booths are now being rapidly superseded by the radio call system. Automobile patrols containing two or more officers are equipped with radio receiving sets. Contacts can be quickly made by the central station with any designated car or a general broadcast can be sent out to reach all patrolling cars. One disadvantage of this plan, however, is its publicity. Anyone who owns a radio receiving set can hear the reports and instructions. In many cases this is a hindrance to the police in their work. Hence the radio teletype is being brought into use by police departments. Reports and calls, instead of being shouted aloud, are recorded on a printed slip at every station within the area. In due course it may be practicable to have this device used in communicating with patrol cars as well. The patrol booth at strategic points is still useful as a means of closing avenues of escape for criminals when an alarm is sounded. *The radio call system.*

There are two ways of keeping patrolmen on their beats. One is to have regular inspections made by sergeants who go out from the precinct stations. The other is to require that every patrolman shall ring in a report from designated patrol-boxes or post- *Inspections and reports.*

telephones from time to time. These methods are ordinarily employed in combination because neither provides a sufficient check-up when used alone. Pulling a box at intervals does not guarantee that a patrolman will be vigilant meanwhile; on the other hand the inspectorial check-up cannot be a continuous one.

The platoon system. Police duty is usually divided into three platoons, each of which works an eight-hour shift. These platoons are not of equal size because a larger number of patrolmen are needed on night duty than by day. And since it would be unfair to keep men continuously on the night shift, the practice is to transfer men from one platoon to another at regular intervals, so that each member of the force has approximately an equal amount of day and night work during the course of the year. Not all the available men, moreover, can be sent out on patrol duty. Some of them must be kept at the station as a reserve in case of emergencies. To this end a certain number of men are required to sleep in the police station even when they are technically off duty. In general the distribution of work is so arranged that when one platoon is on active duty, another (or a portion of it) is held at the station in reserve, while the third platoon is off duty altogether.

Policeman and public. Taking one consideration with another, a policeman's lot is not a happy one. He must perform a lot of disagreeable duties without infringing the rights of citizens or stirring up too much resentment. His word is law on many small matters, particularly in the foreign districts of the larger cities. There he prefigures not only the law but the courts and the government. A policeman, to the mind of the average citizen, is merely a sauntering symbol of law and order who holds a soft job and has influential friends somewhere among the politicians. The newspapers cartoon him as a beetle-browed fellow, over-expanded at the equator, who talks with a brogue while he indulges his appetite for beer and corned beef. Most widespread of all popular impressions concerning the policeman is the conviction that he can never be found when he is wanted. Ideas of this sort may have had some foundation a half-century ago but they possess little or none today. Yet such popular traditions die slowly and so long as they remain alive they do harm. Not until people realize the real difficulties of effective police work will they insist that capable men be chosen for the work and properly paid for it. Not until then will public

POLICE ADMINISTRATION

opinion demand that the standards of alertness and probity be kept as high in this as in the army and navy.

In most cities until quite recent years it was the practice to appoint recruits to the police force without any form of competitive selection. Politicians sent names to the police board or police chief and those who had the strongest backing usually got the jobs as vacancies occurred. Apart from satisfying a none-too-rigorous physical examination and being a resident of the city there were no formal requirements. Young men with nothing more than a grammar school education, and sometimes not even that, had only to make application and get somebody to endorse it. The principal qualification, in the case of many applicants, was that they had failed to make good at any other job. Yet if they possessed sufficient influence they were usually taken on the force, given uniforms, and turned into the streets as probationary patrolmen with virtually no training or instruction whatsoever. Under such a system it is not surprising that police departments failed to represent a high level of intelligence or integrity. Incompetence and corruption were the earmarks of American police work almost everywhere. Scandals in the department, followed by legislative and other investigations, were of common occurrence.

Gradually, however, all this has been changing. In most of the larger cities the new patrolmen are now selected by open competition under the merit system. There is a rigid physical test and a written examination supplemented by an oral test. The written examination usually covers such things as an intelligent officer might be expected to know, including the geography of the city concerned (*i.e.*, the names and locations of the principal streets, car lines, stations, public buildings, and other places of general resort). Complaint is often made that many applicants who would make good policemen are eliminated by the rigor of these requirements but there is no reason to believe that such complaints are well founded. The only practical alternative to the merit system is the spoils system, and long experience with this iniquity of American municipal politics has proved its utter inadequacy as applied to police recruiting. Tests under the merit system are not of an academic character; they are related to the work which the applicant is expected to do. Moreover, they are reinforced by a rigid investigation into the applicant's past history. Those who stand

Methods of recruiting the force:

1. The earlier plan.

2. The merit system.

highest in this series of tests are given probationary appointments for a period of three or six months during which time they are also sent for certain hours each day to the police training school or given special instruction by senior officers if no regular school has been established. If a recruit fails to make good before the end of his probationary period he may be dropped from the force.

Its defects as applied to police recruiting.

One serious defect in this method of selection is its uniformity for all applicants in spite of the fact that a police department requires different types of human ability. The qualities which make a good patrolman do not necessarily, or even probably, ensure success as a detective or criminal investigator. Yet the same procedure is used in recruiting both branches of the police service. No higher degree of intelligence is insisted upon in one case than in the other. That is why the work of criminal investigation is so often performed in a clumsy and unintelligent way. Shrewd newspaper men frequently get the right clue before the police have even thought of it. Separate tests for the two general branches of police work, patrolling and investigation, ought to be devised and applied. Investigators ought to be selected from civilian life and given special training. To secure a place on the detective staff it should not be necessary to spend some years patrolling the streets and doing routine duty.

Police training schools.

For the training of probationary patrolmen there are regular training schools in all the largest cities. These schools, which are conducted by senior officers of the department chosen for the purpose, provide formal courses of instruction in elementary law, the gathering and presentation of evidence, the methods of criminal investigation and identification, first aid, police psychiatry, local geography, police procedure, report making, and so on. Usually this indoor work is supplemented by outdoor drill and by instruction in the use of riot guns and tear-gas bombs. Pistol target practice is often included. But no amount of schooling or drill will suffice to make a competent policeman unless he has the right qualities of character and temperament. Few fields of human activity demand a higher degree of mental alertness and rigid personal integrity than does the daily routine of the police profession. A patrolman works alone; he must do his own thinking, and think fast. He must use tact or firmness as the occasion demands. In a twinkling he may be put at peril of his life. Temptations will cross his path at every turn. He will find that it is to the profit of a great many people to keep him from being one hundred per cent honest. In view of all this a city cannot be too careful in the selection of new patrolmen or too rigorous in its weeding out of the inferior material during the period of probation and training.

Promotions in the police force are sometimes made under civil service regulations on the basis of formal ratings, but more commonly they depend upon the recommendation of the higher officers. In the latter case the recommendations are likely to be influenced, in some degree, by the amount of political pressure that the various eligible aspirants can bring to bear upon the captain or the chief. Seniority is supposed to count in making promotions, but it can be set aside. Hence a great deal of wire-pulling goes on continually within the ranks of almost every police force with respect to impending promotions. Apparently the only sure method of putting an end to this situation is to have competitive tests for all promotions with a provision that the advancement goes to one of those who stand highest. Some cities pursue this plan.

Promotions.

Suspensions and dismissals are made by the chief on his own authority in some cities. In others there must be a trial before a board of police officers appointed by the chief or the commissioner who has power to approve or disapprove the board's findings. Occasionally the aggrieved policeman has a right of appeal to the courts. The problem is to secure reasonable protection and justice to the individual officer without opening the door to such frequent reversals and reinstatements as will impair the standards of discipline within the department. For when the higher authorities find themselves persistently overruled by commissions or courts they will go easy in the maintenance of discipline and presently there will be very little discipline maintained.

Suspensions and dismissals.

Much criticism is levelled at police departments because of their reliance on the "third degree"—the badgering and maltreatment of accused persons in order to obtain confessions. So grossly have the police abused this right to question their prisoners that juries now look upon all confessions with mistrust and give them little weight as evidence against the accused. Before police work can be raised to a plane of confidence in the public mind there must be a curtailment of this indefensible abuse. It has been suggested that all questionings at police headquarters or stations be recorded

Police malpractice: the "third degree."

as talking pictures, these to be subsequently shown to the jury. This might be a help if we could be sure of no tampering with the film and sound records before they are shown. If the protection of accused persons cannot be assured in any other way it may become necessary to provide by law that no questioning of any kind shall be carried on except in open court. The use of "stool pigeons" or hired informers has also served to lower the work of police departments in the public estimation. So with wire-tapping and the "planting" of evidence. Prisoners should be taken out of police custody at the earliest possible moment and placed in houses of detention. These places of detention should not be under police control but ought to be in charge of guards appointed by the courts. The police station should be a center for law enforcement, not a place of punishment for law-breakers.

The aversion to change in police methods. Police methods have undergone considerable improvement during the past generation but they are still a long way from excellence, much less from perfection. Police departments are much better equipped than they used to be, but in the methods which they use there has been amazingly little change or improvement since the turn of the century. One reason for this may be found in the fact that every high officer connected with the uniformed force comes up through the ranks. He knows only one method, which is the method that he himself used when he was a patrolman or sergeant or lieutenant. No new blood, and hence no new ideas, come in at the top save in the case of the commissioner and he is hardly in a position to improve the technique of police work. New ideas are rarely welcomed in police departments as they have been, for example, by the city school authorities.

Women police officers. Women policemen were unknown in the United States until about twenty years ago. Now they are employed in almost every city of any considerable size. The largest municipalities have regular bureaus of policewomen, sometimes with a deputy commissioner in charge. These policewomen do not perform regular patrol duties but take assignments to special lines of work for which they are assumed to be better qualified than male officers. Their work, for example, usually includes the supervision of public dance halls and other places of commercialized recreation. Doing duty in plain clothes they are often able to obtain information which could not be secured by male members of the force. Juvenile delinquencies come largely within their range, especially when

POLICE ADMINISTRATION 331

young girls are concerned. In some cities it is the practice to have all female prisoners questioned by a policewoman and not by the desk sergeant or other interviewing official.

The cost of police protection varies directly with the size of the city, being higher per thousand of population in large municipalities than in small ones. This is because police administration follows the "law of increasing costs per capita." Large cities require not only more police but a greater diversification of police work than are needed in small places. Likewise the problem of traffic congestion becomes more acute in the larger centers and this involves the diversion of a large number of men for traffic regulation. This function of traffic control, in fact, has grown to a point where it now absorbs the energies of a substantial fraction of the entire force in all the larger urban communities. There has been some question in the minds of municipal administrators as to whether traffic control ought to be a responsibility of the police department at all. With its continuing growth in extent and complexity it may be found advisable to place the whole work of traffic control in the hands of a separate department, with a personnel selected and trained for this purpose alone. The traffic problem, however, is reserved for discussion in the next chapter of this book.

The cost of police protection.

Meanwhile it may not be amiss to remark that the average American city now spends a good deal more on its police than it disburses for health protection or for public libraries and public recreation put together. Police expenditures are much higher in American cities than in European communities of comparable size. But the results of this larger outlay are not apparent. More crimes are committed in American cities; fewer arrests in proportion to the crimes are made, and fewer convictions are obtained. The American municipal taxpayer seems to get relatively less for his dollar from the expenditures of the police department than he obtains from the city's outlay for schools, fire protection, or the maintenance of public grounds.

A comparison with European cities.

Most of the larger cities, and some of the smaller ones, have made provision whereby a police officer who reaches a designated age after serving a prescribed number of years in the service may be retired on a pension. The age limit is usually sixty and the pension is customarily fixed at one-half the rate of active pay at retirement. Officers who become permanently incapacitated by injuries received in the line of duty are also entitled to benefits under these

Police pensions.

pension systems. The problem of providing pensions for municipal employees has been discussed in an earlier chapter but it should be mentioned that pension arrangements applying to the police department alone, or to the police and fire departments, exist in many cities which make no such provision for employees in other departments. This is because the work of a police officer is deemed to be hazardous and also because it is essential to the efficiency of the force that no one be continued on active duty after he has passed the point where his physical vigor is seriously diminished. It is desirable, however, that the police pension system be established on a contributory basis, with the city and the members of the department each paying their share of the cost. Great care should also be taken to provide a sound actuarial set-up so that the funds in hand shall be sufficient to pay the pensions in full when the time comes. In many cities they have proved insufficient and the deficit has had to be covered from the general taxes.

The right of the police to organize. Members of the police department are usually organized into an association which is ostensibly for benevolent purposes such as the payment of sick benefits and funeral allowances. Once a year or oftener in almost every city this association arranges a policeman's ball or a summer picnic and these functions provide the opportunity for a general levy upon the people through the sale of tickets. It is supposed to be a voluntary contribution but many citizens do not look upon this house-to-house ticket sale by uniformed officers as anything of the sort. Nor is the purpose of these police associations altogether benevolent. They have the additional purpose of promoting the interests of the police in the matter of higher pay, more liberal pensions, and other concessions which add to the taxpayer's burden.

The right to strike. Some years ago, in a number of cities, these associations became affiliated with the American Federation of Labor and asserted their right to strike if their demands were not granted. A couple of important police strikes did take place and in one of them the whole issue was put to the test. In this instance the strike led to disorders which were quelled with the aid of troops, whereupon the striking policemen were permanently dismissed and their places given to others. The outcome of this Boston police strike in 1919 made it clear that while public opinion is willing to let the police organize and promote their own interests in any reasonable way, it is not ready to countenance any right of the police to desert their posts and leave the community unprotected. The public safety is paramount.

Police administration is not one of the things to which American cities can point with pride. The fault, however, lies more with the public than with the police. There has been too little realization of the need for better-paid police officers, for a system of appointment which will assure the selection of high-grade officers, for adequate training, for the use of scientific methods in the work of criminal investigation, and for a more coöperative attitude on the part of the citizenship. The standards of personnel and the methods used in police departments cannot be appreciably improved without intelligent and continuous support from the public. Moreover there is need for better support of the police by prosecuting attorneys and local courts. For nothing is more destructive of police morale than the turning loose, on probation or suspended sentence, of persistent offenders whose detection and arrest have given no end of trouble. An improvement in the work of the police courts is an essential preliminary to the betterment of police standards.

Improving police work.

REFERENCES

Two volumes by Raymond B. Fosdick, *European Police Systems* (New York, 1915), and *American Police Systems* (New York, 1920), are of excellent workmanship and still of much value despite the lapse of time since they were written. E. D. Graper's book on *American Police Administration* (New York, 1921) deserves mention and Inspector Cornelius F. Cahalane, *The Policeman* (New York, 1923) contains a full explanation of police procedure. A volume by Arthur Woods, formerly police commissioner of New York City, entitled *The Policeman and the Public* (New Haven, 1919) is an illuminating and readable survey. The same author's book on *Crime Prevention* (Princeton, 1918) may also be mentioned, as well as a smaller book by H. R. Gallagher on *Crime Prevention as a Municipal Function* (Syracuse, 1930). The *Cleveland Crime Survey*, edited by Raymond Moley (Cleveland, 1922) contains a great deal of useful information, as does also the *Missouri Crime Survey* by the same editor (New York, 1927). The report of the Citizens' Police Committee on *Chicago Police Problems* (Chicago, 1931) is interesting and informing. Likewise there is much data of value in the volumes issued in 1931 by the National Commission on Law Observance and Enforcement, commonly known as the Wickersham Commission.

In 1929 two special numbers (May and November) of the *Annals of* the *American Academy of Political and Social Science* were devoted to *Modern Crime: Its Prevention and Punishment* and *The Police and Crime Problem* respectively. Other works that should be mentioned are Mary E. Hamilton, *The Policewoman: Her Service and Ideals* (New York, 1924), Chloe Owings, *Women Police* (New York, 1925), Bruce Smith, *The State Police* (New York, 1925), J. Collyer Adam, *Criminal Investigation* (2nd edition, Toronto, 1924), J. A. Larson, *The Single Fingerprint System* (New York, 1924), and the volume on *Uniform Crime Reporting: a Complete Manual for Police*, issued by the International Association of Police Chiefs (New York, 1929).

The Police Journal (110 West 34th St., New York) specializes on modern police practice. Bibliographical references, together with useful summaries of current progress in this department of municipal administration, are included in the annual issues of *The Municipal Index*.

CHAPTER XXV

THE REGULATION OF TRAFFIC

Method is good in all things. Order governs the world. The Devil is the author of confusion.—*Jonathan Swift.*

Street traffic congestion is not a new problem. Even in ancient Rome it gave the authorities a good deal of trouble. For the streets of the imperial city were so thronged with pedestrians that all wheeled vehicles had to be excluded during the daylight hours. Then, during the whole night, there was an incessant clatter of wagons rumbling over the rough pavements with their loads of farm produce and building materials. The streets of all ancient and mediaeval cities were so narrow and crooked that they became easily congested, and this situation persisted down into the modern centuries. Even after the chief thoroughfares had been widened, the problem persisted and in some large cities had reached an acute stage before the coming of motor vehicles. London, for example, had great difficulty in handling the enormous volume of horse-drawn traffic that passed through her streets during the later years of the nineteenth century. Large numbers of policemen were assigned to this special duty.

An age-old problem.

But advent of the motor car made the problem of regulating traffic a much more serious one everywhere. For one thing it greatly increased the number of vehicles using the streets. The growth of motor traffic can be dated from about 1895, in which year there were about 300 cars produced. Five years later the number of automobiles in the entire world was less than fifteen thousand; today there are over twenty-five million cars and trucks in the United States alone. In some American cities there is now one registered automobile for every two or three persons. If all of these were put upon the streets at once there would be no space for anything else. Moreover, the automobile has increased the speed of traffic and consequently the hazards of street use. During the year 1930 more than 30,000 persons were killed by automobiles in the United States, and of these fatalities over one thousand were in New York City. Serious injuries totalled nearly three-quarters

Its accentuation by the motor car.

of a million and the property loss has been reckoned at nearly a billion dollars.[1] Hence the motor car has converted the street into a place of continuous peril to life and limb. The citizen can avoid a fire-trap building or an unsafe bathing beach after the risk has been pointed out to him, but he cannot go anywhere and keep off the streets.[2] He must use them and take the risks.

The monetary loss due to traffic congestion. But the increased bodily hazard is not the only problem that the motor vehicle has brought to the city streets. The loss of time through over-congestion and the slowing-down of traffic at various points, especially at street intersections, is enormous. When traffic is stalled, every minute represents a monetary wastage. For motor cars and trucks keep using gasoline and oil while they wait in line; their drivers lose time and sometimes their tempers also. Attempts have been made to calculate the cost of traffic congestion in terms of this time-and-fuel wastage, but it is impossible to do this with any close degree of accuracy. Taking the United States as a whole, it is figured that the economic loss can hardly be less than a couple of billion dollars per annum. It has been estimated that motor vehicles in most large cities spend at least ten per cent of their time waiting for somebody to get out of the way. The narrowness of the downtown city streets is in part responsible for this reduction of traffic efficiency to ninety per cent or less. The parking of cars on such streets, when it is permitted, intensifies the congestion. Some of the trouble also arises from the mingling of fast- and slow-moving vehicles such as light cars and heavy trucks in the same line of traffic. And not a little of it is due to badly devised traffic rules, the work of officials who have given inadequate study to the problems involved.

The two objectives of traffic regulation. Traffic regulation has two main purposes. The first is to speed the flow and keep it from interruption. The second is to make traffic safe for both vehicles and pedestrians. These two objectives, however, are to some extent in conflict. It is easy to accelerate traffic at the expense of safety. It is likewise easy to make traffic safe by slowing it down. But to speed it up and at the same time keep the traffic hazards at a minimum is a problem which taxes all the skill and ingenuity that highly trained traffic experts can command. Too many cities have looked upon this problem as one

[1] Statistics relating to automobile production, use, and traffic are compiled and published annually by the National Automobile Chamber of Commerce, 366 Madison Ave., New York City.
[2] Miller McClintock, *Street Traffic Control* (New York, 1925), p. 7.

that any police chief or street superintendent can solve. The welter of needlessly obstructive rules, misplaced intersection stops, and badly timed signals in most of those cities is the outcome of this impression. Street traffic control is a science. Drafting the regulations and keeping them in accord with rapidly changing conditions is a task that requires a high degree of expertness. By looking upon the problem in this light some of the larger cities have found that speed and safety can be reconciled to a much greater degree than was formerly deemed possible.

The first step in any scientific approach to this problem is the making of a traffic survey. To control traffic effectively one must first know all the more important facts relating to its normal volume, speed, direction, and character. Many serious errors have been made by basing traffic rules upon casual observation. Officials take note of a serious congestion at some one point and proceed to remedy it. Frequently their action merely creates a center of congestion somewhere else. To explore the causes of the trouble to their ultimate source is a task that calls for the collection and careful analysis of reliable data, in other words for a traffic survey conducted on scientific lines. What does such a survey include? In general it involves the obtaining of full and accurate information concerning every factor which enters into the traffic problem directly or indirectly. So many of these surveys have been made during recent years that their scope and procedure is now well defined. *Traffic surveys:* *1. Their value.*

Broadly speaking a traffic survey produces data with respect to the volume of traffic, its variety, origin, and destination, the existing street plan and its effects on traffic through the creation of bottle-neck points and one-way thoroughfares, the nature of the buildings and industries at or near the points of congestion, the probable increase of population and business in the sections affected, the available parking facilities, the location and nature of special street hazards such as three-way intersections, the normal speed of traffic at various points, the centers of pedestrian congestion, and so on. *2. What they cover.*

Much of this information has to be obtained by an actual count, taken by tabulators who are stationed for the purpose at strategic points in the streets day after day until a sufficient body of figures for averaging can be secured. The technique of a traffic count has been worked out by experts to a point where no factor of any *The traffic count.*

importance is overlooked. Standard forms for recording the count are now available and the methods of analyzing the results have been worked out in full detail.[1] Information of value in a traffic survey is also obtained from the records of the police, fire, and building departments of the city. The making of such a survey takes time and costs a good deal of money. One need only glance through the published results of surveys already made in some of the larger cities to realize how much labor and expense is involved in any such project.[2] Yet they invariably prove to be worth far more than they cost. For the monetary wastage involved in traffic congestion is so great that even a slight amelioration will justify a large expenditure to bring it about.

Traffic has outgrown the streets. What do these surveys generally indicate as the principal causes of traffic congestion? The first and most fundamental among them is the inability of the existing street space to carry a sufficient number of vehicles at a reasonable rate of speed. In other words most of our large cities have outgrown their street capacity. This is not surprising, for the majority of downtown thoroughfares have exactly the same area that they had fifty years ago, while population, business, and traffic have trebled or quadrupled during the interval. Indeed, the total street area available for traffic movement is now much smaller than it was a half-century ago because of the parked cars which now occupy a zone of the street surface along the curb. And to make this situation worse, the need for parking space happens always to be most urgent along the busy retail streets where the necessity for a free flow of moving traffic happens also to be most imperative. Likewise, it is one of the ironies of this situation that the streets which most sorely need to be widened are the very ones which cannot be widened except at prohibitive cost.

The fundamental cause of street congestion. The increase of a city's population does not of itself create a traffic problem of serious dimensions. It is not the size of the population but its distribution in relation to the city plan that causes most of the trouble. Congestion is caused by the concentration of too many people in the business districts during the day-time

---

[1] "Methods for Studying Traffic Control Problems" by Dwight McCracken, in *The Municipal Index* (1931), pp. 320–337.

[2] For example, *Chicago Metropolitan Street Traffic Survey* (1926), *A Report on the Street Traffic Control Problem of San Francisco* (1927), *The Street Traffic Control Problem of the City of Boston* (1928), *A Traffic Control Plan for Kansas City* (1930), etc.

THE REGULATION OF TRAFFIC

hours, and this results from the reluctance of business to expand horizontally. Business prefers to expand vertically, that is, by going up into taller buildings. Likewise the department stores, as has been mentioned in a previous chapter, tend to group themselves in sections where the streets are already congested.

So it is with recreation facilities. There are said to be at least one hundred places of amusement with a total seating capacity of over one hundred thousand people within four blocks of the intersection of Broadway and Forty-Second Street in New York City, yet the street space available for the use of this nightly concentration is no greater than it was fifty years ago. The growth of population would not overburden the downtown streets so badly if a sufficiently extensive development of neighborhood shopping and recreation centers in the outer residential areas could be promoted. But when the people of a city insist on doing a twelve-story business on three-story streets they should not marvel at the human flood which is poured into these avenues of traffic to the great discomfort of everyone concerned.

Inadequate street space is a fundamental cause of traffic congestion but not the only one. Part of the trouble may result from a faulty layout of the streets. Sometimes they are adequate in width but have been constructed as dead-end thoroughfares and hence are avoided by their proper share of the traffic. This throws an undue burden upon parallel highways. Bottle-neck streets are also a frequent cause of traffic congestion. Such streets are sufficiently wide to accommodate the traffic except at certain points where they become narrower for a few blocks. Wherever this narrowing occurs, the traffic tends to pile up in a jam. The elimination of these bottle-necks is one of the most effective means of expediting the traffic flow. Heavy grades are likewise a cause of much difficulty, for streets with steep hills are generally avoided by motorists. And when cars avoid certain streets by reason of the heavy gradients, they overburden the more level thoroughfares in the same vicinity if there are any. This trouble can be alleviated by the building of traffic tunnels, as has been done in Los Angeles. *Its relation to the street plan.*

Finally, it is often found in the course of traffic surveys that a considerable amount of traffic congestion is the result of defective street pavements. For whenever the surface of a street is permitted to get into poor condition, the speed of traffic on that route is appreciably reduced and there is a crowding of vehicles which *Defective pavements as a cause of congestion.*

would not occur if they were able to get through at a normal rate of movement. Such conditions can often be relieved by a relatively small expenditure for paving repairs. Mention may also be made of the temporary areas of traffic congestion which are produced from time to time by street work and by the practice of granting building permits which allow private contractors to use a part of the street space for the storage of materials during the process of construction.

The diversity of speed and its results. Traffic congestion is often created or accentuated by the fact that slow-moving vehicles percolate into the zone of potentially rapid movement and slow it down. The variation in normal and safe speed between a light passenger automobile and a heavy commercial truck is several miles per hour. Street cars and motor-buses also bring upon the streets two factors which retard the normal flow by reason of their frequent stops and the safety zones which have to be marked off for them at stopping places. Formerly it was a requirement that all other vehicles should stop while street cars and buses were taking on or letting off passengers, but in most cities they are now permitted to pass by at slackened speed so long as they do not encroach upon the safety zones. In the nature of things, however, these zones create bottle-necks of their own and sometimes result in serious traffic retardations. In some of the larger cities the cruising taxicab, which moves along at a slow rate of speed in the hope of picking up passengers, has also come to be regarded as a factor of some importance in slowing down the normal flow of traffic. Such taxicabs naturally frequent the busiest thoroughfares during the busiest hours.

The pedestrian's part in traffic congestion. Finally, in discussing the causes of vehicular congestion, one must not overlook the pedestrian, especially the oblivious pedestrian commonly known as a jay-walker. When people afoot are compelled to refrain from crossing the streets except at intersections, and then only in compliance with signals, the problem of ensuring their safety is not a difficult one. But when they make a practice of disregarding the signals or scurrying across the roadway at any point, darting in and out among the wheeled vehicles, the hazards are greatly increased and the uniform flow of the traffic is interfered with.

Controlling the jay-walker. Yet jay-walking is difficult to control. The mere enactment of rules will not accomplish it. Pedestrians seem to regard themselves as having a sort of priority in the use of the streets. Many of them resent the enforcement of rules against jay-walking while on foot but highly approve of strict enforcement when they are driving. A traffic count in Chicago not long ago disclosed that several hundred pedestrians were crossing a single street intersection every hour in violation of the rules. Such practices increase the number of accidents. They also result in slowing down the vehicle traffic, thus increasing the cost of transportation. Stationing a policeman at each busy street intersection improves the situation, but jay-walking cannot be eliminated by police watchfulness alone. The pedestrians themselves must be educated to the point where they will voluntarily coöperate, and some cities have proved that this is by no means an impossible or even a very difficult task.

These, in brief, are the causes of traffic congestion. What are the remedies? The answer to that question must of necessity be neither a short nor simple one. For the remedies must relate themselves to the causes as disclosed by a careful traffic survey and these causes are sometimes such that they cannot be removed except by the interaction of several remedies. In some cases no halfway measures will avail. There are occasional situations in which no appreciable relief can be had except through an increase of the street area. Many downtown streets will never satisfactorily carry their existing volume of traffic, much less an increase in it, no matter what regulations may be made or enforced. Widening is in such cases the only remedial measure that will suffice. Where the actual widening of the street would be too costly an enterprise because of the valuable buildings which have been erected on both sides of it, there is sometimes a possibility of arcading the sidewalks and thus permitting the paved roadway to extend as far as the property lines. Even this is an expensive way of securing the increased street surface, but it costs much less than the alternative of demolishing the entire fronts of the buildings concerned.

Remedies for traffic congestion:

1. Widening the streets.

As respects those streets which are not yet lined with tall and costly structures, a good deal can be accomplished by taking thought for tomorrow. Good city planning can see to it that the future growth of traffic on retail streets is anticipated to the extent of enforcing setbacks in the case of all new buildings so that the widening can eventually be carried through without exorbitant cost. Intelligent zoning will also restrict the growth of business to those sections of the city in which streets are sufficiently spacious to serve the increased traffic that business would bring. No street

2. Planning and zoning.

now used for residential purposes should be zoned for business unless it is wide enough or can be made so at reasonable cost. And the cost, whatever it is, should be borne by the property owners concerned.

3. Restricting the height of buildings. Restrictions should also be laid upon the height of buildings in sections of the city where the traffic has already reached the capacity of the streets. It may be mentioned in passing, however, that high buildings do not necessarily add to street congestion. It depends upon the use to which the building is put.[1] An office building of ten or twelve stories will put a smaller burden upon the adjacent streets than a three-story department store. Something can also be accomplished by locating the public buildings outside the congested areas. Structures such as the post office, the public library, the courthouse, and the city hall always draw considerable throngs of people. Intelligent planning, in a word, will not only alleviate some conditions which already exist but will forestall more serious situations in the future.

4. Double-decker streets. Proposals have been made for the construction of double-deck streets in congested portions of the city. Chicago has constructed a good example (Wacker Drive) with the upper level restricted to fast-moving traffic. Two-level streets involve the erection of steel or concrete pillars carrying a structure similar to that used by an elevated railway. Provision is made for ramps running from the ground to the upper level at frequent intervals. It is contended that such construction more than doubles the street area because it makes possible the abolition of all cross-traffic interference and under favorable conditions can give the major traffic stream an over-all operating speed of better than forty miles per hour. The newer type of elevated highway or "limited way" may be defined as a roadway on which there is no cross-traffic and from which there is no direct access to abutting property. Thus it eliminates the two principal causes of congestion. New York City has already made substantial progress on this type of construction in the so-called West Side elevated highway which will shortly be completed from Canal Street to Riverside Drive. It is not improbable that all the larger metropolitan communities will ultimately have to adopt this "limited way" type of street expansion. By care-

---

[1] Those who are interested in the relation of building heights to street traffic may be referred to the discussion of this matter in the *National Municipal Review*, Vol. XVII, pp. 405–418 (July, 1928), Vol. XVIII, pp. 94–96 (February, 1929), and Vol. XVIII, pp. 171–173 (March, 1929).

THE REGULATION OF TRAFFIC 343

ful design and refinement most of the objectionable features of the old elevated railway structures can be eliminated.

Another suggestion is to construct vehicular tunnels such as have been used so largely in New York and Boston for street railway transportation. One such subway, a double tube nearly two miles in length known as the Holland Tunnel, connects New York City with the New Jersey Shore and has been for some time in successful operation. Shorter vehicular tunnels have been constructed in San Francisco and Los Angeles. Such tunnels offer great advantages over the elevated roadway, but they also present some practical difficulties. One of these is connected with the problem of adequate ventilation in view of the enormous amount of exhaust gas that pours forth from motor-driven vehicles. Financing the work from municipal bond issues is virtually out of the question in view of the heavy indebtedness already assumed by most of the larger cities, and it is doubtful whether any large portion of the heavy cost could be defrayed by the levy of special assessments. Vehicular tunnels on any large scale are probably not for the immediate future. On the other hand short subways as a means of avoiding grade crossings at railways have advantages which usually justify their cost and pedestrian tunnels for the use of foot traffic serve a good purpose when they are constructed across wide thoroughfares carrying a large amount of rapidly moving traffic.

5. Vehicular tunnels.

Less comprehensive proposals for relief take the form of by-pass highways. A generation ago it was a common belief that all traffic passing through a city ought to be brought through the main business streets in order that the merchants might get the benefit of it. But shopkeepers have now come to realize that cross-city traffic does not profit the retail business man very much. It adds to the congestion of the retail business streets without appreciably adding to the volume of sales. So the city planning authorities are now encouraged by the business interests to make provision for cross-city thoroughfares, somewhat removed from the congested areas, through which fast-moving traffic can slip across the city with the least possible delay. To provide one of these by-pass highways usually involves the connecting of two or three existing streets, widening them in whole or in part, paving them properly, articulating them to the state highway system, and setting up road signs to ensure the proper diversion of cars to the new route.

6. By-pass highways.

7. Belt-line thoroughfares.

Then there is the problem of adequately providing for what is known as intra-city traffic, in other words the traffic which moves through the congested business districts on its way from one residential section of the city to another. Sometimes a community has been laid out in such fashion that there is no convenient way of getting to the east end from the west end, or from the north side to the south side, except by passing along some of the busiest mercantile or industrial streets. This greatly adds to the congestion but relief can sometimes be obtained by providing cross-town or belt-line thoroughfares which skirt the business district instead of passing directly through it. Following such routes may mean that intra-city traffic has to cover more distance but there is a saving of time through its more rapid movement. Belt-line highways are usually planned by taking several existing streets and connecting them into a single avenue of uniform width with suitable paving. This matter of suitable paving ought to have reiterated emphasis in any discussion of traffic facilities, for it is well known that both passenger and commercial vehicles avoid badly paved streets even when such avoidance entails a longer distance to be travelled.

8. Minor physical improvements in the streets.

Finally, there are minor street improvements of various kinds that can be made without much cost but which often serve appreciably to relieve vehicular overcrowding. Streets with dead-ends can be carried through. Sometimes the necessary extension is only a few hundred feet and the cost only a few thousand dollars. Sharp curves in streets always cause a slowing of traffic but they can frequently be considerably reduced in their degree of curvature without excessive cost. Offset streets present a more difficult problem, and almost every large city has a good many of them. They are a heritage from the days of auctioneer planning when real estate promoters laid out streets in such way as to get the largest number of salable lots and without any reference to what was already in existence on either side of their subdivision. All manner of jogs and offsets were the result. Streets coming from opposite directions failed to meet by a half block or so. These offsets involve a double turn for all traffic with a resultant slowing down and increased collision dangers as well. Look at the map of any city that has grown by accretion, as many American cities have done, and you will realize the price which traffic is now paying for the avarice of suburban subdividers in days gone by.

To remedy the situation, now that the offset streets have been built upon, is costly beyond what most cities can afford.

Aside from physical changes in the highways, a good deal can be accomplished by traffic regulation. Effective traffic control requires, first of all, a traffic ordinance or traffic code which has been prepared by experts with skill and intelligence, not by the local police authorities with an eye to the simplification of their own enforcement problem. The traffic code should contain explicit provisions covering such matters as the maximum speed in various sections of the city, the limits on parking, rights of way, procedure at street intersections, driver's signals in making turns and in stopping, loading and unloading vehicles, passing street cars and other vehicles, left-hand turns, one-way streets, safety zones, boulevard stops, and all the other incidents of traffic regulation. The drafting of such a code is a technical job which ought to be performed in each city with a full appreciation of local conditions, but too often one city merely copies the rules which have been established somewhere else. Or, quite as likely, it tries to enforce some peculiar regulation of local origin which ultimately proves futile but meanwhile gives inconvenience and trouble to traffic which comes from outside. To secure reasonable uniformity some state legislatures have enacted state-wide traffic codes embodying all the principal rules and leaving to the municipal authorities only the minor regulations. The movement towards national uniformity in the basic principles of traffic regulation, moreover, has been greatly facilitated by the uniform statutes and ordinances drafted by the National Conference on Street and Highway Safety under the sponsorship of the United States Department of Commerce.

9. Systems of traffic control.

The traffic code.

But a traffic code, by whomsoever enacted, ought not to be regarded as a stereotyped affair. It should be capable of prompt and easy alteration to meet rapidly changing conditions. Traffic regulation is becoming a science but it is still in the experimental stage. When one bears in mind that virtually its entire development has taken place within the last twenty years, it will be appreciated that this field of administrative regulation has hardly achieved finality as yet. Much has been accomplished in the way of expediting traffic without increasing its hazards but a good deal more remains to be done. Consequently there ought to be, in every large city, a traffic engineering bureau under competent direction with the duty of making a continuous study of local traffic prob-

Keeping this code up to date.

lems. The officials of this bureau should recommend to the city council such changes in the traffic code as they find desirable. It is only in some such way that the rules can be kept abreast of the times.

The question of speed limits. For the times change and public sentiment changes with them. In the matter of maximum speed, for example, opinion has undergone a complete reversal during the past decade or thereabouts. A dozen years or more ago it was the almost universal belief that the maximum speed of motor vehicles should be absolutely limited within the city limits, and as a rule this maximum was fixed at fifteen miles per hour. Anyone driving at a faster rate than this was subject to arrest and punishment regardless of the fact that a greater rate of speed might be quite safe on wide streets with little traffic and an unobstructed view. But the absurdity of a rigid maximum gradually seeped through the public mind and today the practice of definitely fixing a uniform rate of maximum speed for motor vehicles on all streets within the city limits is being generally abandoned. Instead the more common provision is that vehicles must be driven at a *reasonable* rate or at a rate compatible with the public safety. Usually this is accompanied by the further provision that a rate exceeding twenty or twenty-five miles per hour will be regarded as presumptive evidence of over-speeding but not necessarily conclusive evidence. Thus the present tendency is to leave the fact of undue speed to be determined in the light of all the surrounding conditions. Even twenty miles per hour may be excessive at a busy downtown intersection, while cars can be safely driven at a much higher speed on the broad expanse of through-traffic highways. Over-speeding should, of course, be distinguished from reckless driving; it is entirely possible to drive recklessly while keeping within the established speed limits.

The parking problem. Then there is the parking problem. Every city, no matter what its size, seems to have difficulty in keeping some of its streets reasonably clear of standing vehicles. The city streets were built for travel, not for storage, yet considerable portions of them have been converted to the latter use even in those regions where the need of street area for traffic is most acute. The reason is that downtown merchants have generally believed that liberal parking rules are good for business. Today they are veering away from that belief and are inclined to favor the placing of time-restrictions on parked cars in the business districts. In some cases they have

THE REGULATION OF TRAFFIC 347

supported the entire prohibition of parking in the most congested downtown areas. Incidentally it may be mentioned that there is no question as to the city's legal right to limit parking or even to prohibit it altogether. Back in the heyday of horse-drawn vehicles a famous English decision declared that "the king's highway is not to be used as a stable-yard" and American courts have followed the same general principle in ruling that public property cannot be used as a garage except on sufferance of the public authorities. No one has a vested right to park his car anywhere on a city street. He has such privileges in that respect, and only such, as the framers of the traffic ordinances may choose to give him.

Regulations as to parking are somewhat difficult to elaborate in a way that is equitable to all concerned. This is because all standing vehicles are not alike and cannot be subjected to uniform rules. In general, however, most of the vehicles standing at the curb fall into one of three classes. First, there is the car or truck which has stopped to load or unload merchandise. Such vehicles play an essential part in the process of urban transportation and it is quite proper that they be given reasonable facilities for their work. Restrictions should nevertheless be applied to them to make sure that they do their loading or unloading without undue delay. The second class of standing vehicles includes those which are left at the curb with drivers in charge. The practice of leaving cars or trucks for varying lengths of time with someone in the driver's seat is commonly known as live parking. Such vehicles do not form dead obstructions to traffic for they can be moved out in case of need. Hence the traffic rules usually permit live parking in places where unattended cars are not allowed to stand, for example, in front of fire hydrants. *Varieties of parked vehicles.*

But the great majority of parked cars fall into the third class, namely those which are left standing at the curb with no one in charge. This use of the street surface is the most prevalent but the least defensible of the three because it involves the use of public property for private convenience, often without any limit as to time. All-day parking is extremely common wherever it is permitted. Usually it is permitted on streets outside the business districts. Within the latter areas there is almost invariably a time-limit, ranging from fifteen minutes to an hour, and this limit is made known to drivers by signs which are set up at intervals along the street. The strict enforcement of these limitations is not *Dead parking.*

an easy matter and a great deal of overstaying takes place everywhere.

Forms of parking limitations. Various other limitations have been found desirable and are more easily enforced. Dead parking is prohibited, for example, at bottle-neck points in the streets and in narrow thoroughfares as well as within a certain distance of fire hydrants. It is also forbidden in the space which intervenes between the street-car safety zones and the curb. Likewise there are certain reserved spaces, indicated by painted curbs, in which no dead parking is permitted. These spaces are usually in front of public buildings, theaters, department-store entrances, and other places where the public convenience is served by providing free access at all times. As a rule vehicles must be parked parallel to the curb, but when the street is sufficiently wide there is much to be said for the practice of angle parking. This permits a larger number of vehicles to be parked in a given street length. Parking at an angle is also a desirable safety measure in the case of streets that have steep gradients.

Future provision for parked cars. With the increasing use of motor vehicles in urban communities it is inevitable that parking privileges will have to be still further curtailed. This means that facilities elsewhere than on the streets must be greatly increased—for example, by more numerous public garages and parking lots. Places of business are beginning to realize that when they construct new premises they should make provision for basement garages or for outside parking spaces which can be used by their patrons and employees. In the absence of such facilities many banks, stores, and other concerns are now arranging with private garages and parking lots to accommodate the cars of their customers without charge. For the most part, however, the car owner who leaves his vehicle in a public garage or outside storage space must himself pay a small fee for the privilege. And this is not inequitable. All transportation systems have to pay for their terminal facilities. Motor transport should expect to do the same.

Traffic officers and traffic signals. At the outset motor traffic along the city streets was regulated by stationing police officers at busy intersections. They used their arms as semaphores and often went through gyrations which were difficult for even sophisticated drivers to understand. But with the steady increase in traffic this method became too expensive and automatic signals have been rapidly taking the place of uniformed officers, although the congestion at some intersections

THE REGULATION OF TRAFFIC

is so great as to require both signals and officers during certain hours of the day. Much progress has been made during recent years in the design and mechanical efficiency of automatic signals.

In the early stages of traffic-signal development each intersection was operated independently, that is, without any relation to signals at adjacent intersections. Thus it was only by chance that a driver might expect to be met by a "go" signal as he approached the intersection. The next step in signal timing was to coördinate a series of signals along a street so that all of the signals would show green or red to the main highway at the same time. This is called simultaneous timing. All vehicles move on the main street simultaneously, and then all are stopped for the full length of the street so that traffic on the cross-streets may have its chance. This system is still in use on Fifth Avenue in New York and on Michigan Avenue in Chicago. *The older plans.*

The next step in the refinement of traffic-signal timing was the introduction of what is known as "flexible progressive control." By this method a series of traffic signals along a main street are coördinated in such a time sequence that a driver who starts at one end of the street with a green signal and operates his car at the speed for which the system is set, will be given a green signal as he approaches each intersection. Thus he may progress along the entire length of the street without a single interruption. Of course it is true, as every driver knows, that it is not always easy to keep the exact speed which the system contemplates, and this is especially true during the hours when the traffic is congested; but the plan of flexible progressive control in signal-timing is a marked improvement upon the methods of timing which preceded it. *The newer method of timing the signals.*

Traffic-actuated signals are now being looked upon with favor for isolated intersections. Such signals are controlled by the traffic itself through electrical or mechanical contacts which are put into action by a vehicle when it approaches the intersection. Thus a traffic-actuated signal may always show a green light or a "go" signal to traffic on the main highway except when a vehicle on the cross-street needs such short interval as may be required for its crossing, after which the signal automatically reverts to a "go" signal for the main thoroughfare. In the same general category are the hand-operated signals of the customary automatic type which can be put into play at isolated intersections by pedes- *Traffic-actuated signals.*

trians who desire to cross a street where the vehicle traffic is moving rapidly.

Enforcing the traffic rules. The enforcement of the traffic regulations is everywhere entrusted to the police department. This is not the result of a planned development; it has simply happened so. When the need for traffic regulation arose in the largest cities the police undertook the work of enforcing the rules because there was no one else to do it. Men from the uniformed force were assigned to this duty, a few of them at the outset but in gradually increasing numbers until the work of traffic regulation in some cities now absorbs nearly one-quarter of the entire police personnel. Traffic control has grown to be one of the major functions of police departments everywhere. Yet in many cities the work remains poorly organized. Patrolmen with no special aptitude for traffic duty are sometimes given this assignment as a matter of discipline, especially in the winter months. Or, in pleasant weather, men are occasionally given easy traffic posts as a matter of personal favoritism. Officers are frequently stationed at points where automatic signals could do the work quite as well and at much smaller cost.

Special traffic divisions in the police department. Police administrators, however, are rapidly coming to the conclusion that the work of traffic regulation is so different from other forms of police duty, and requires such qualifications of a special nature, that it can best be performed through the organization of a separate traffic division in the police department. Such divisions have now been organized in many of the larger cities. They are under the command of special executives (usually with the rank of captain or higher) responsible directly to the chief or superintendent of police. Patrolmen are carefully selected, and after a period of special training are permanently assigned to this division. The results have become noticeable in greater efficiency and better discipline.

Proposals for a separate traffic organization. The suggestion has sometimes been made that better results at lower cost might be had by creating a special traffic department, wholly independent of the regular police administration. Such a department would be officered by men selected for this work directly from civilian life. They would be paid a lower scale of salaries than is customary in police departments and would not need to pass the rigid physical tests which are demanded of those who qualify as patrolmen. They would be sworn in as special officers with the right to make arrests for traffic violations but would not perform any other police duties. The objection to this plan is that there might be friction between the two departments, especially as the regular police would have to be called in when fatal accidents occur through reckless or negligent driving. Traffic regulation is law enforcement and there are dangers involved in any plan which contemplates dividing the responsibility for law enforcement between two city departments.

Then there is the problem of dealing with those who violate the traffic rules. Until a few years ago the customary procedure was to summon offenders into the regular police courts where they were arraigned with the usual morning grist of malefactors. But with the increased number of traffic infractions this led to serious congestion in the police courts of the larger cities. In addition it put the defendants to the great inconvenience of waiting in court, often for several hours, until their cases were reached on the calendar. Most of the largest cities have therefore established special traffic courts which handle these cases exclusively. This has been done, for example, in New York, Chicago, Philadelphia, Detroit, Cleveland, Pittsburgh, and Baltimore. In other cities the police department has established a violation bureau where drivers who have been ticketed for minor violations of the traffic regulations can appear and pay a stipulated fine, thus obviating the need for their coming into court. The duty of dealing with those who appear at the traffic bureau is given to an experienced police officer and the success of the plan depends very largely upon the good judgment with which he is chosen. Most of the smaller cities retain the old plan of handing the offender a police court summons.

Traffic courts.

Favoritism, discrimination, and petty graft have been unfortunately too prevalent in the enforcement of traffic regulations everywhere. Public officials often set a bad example by violating the rules. People of influence expect to be let off when an officer hails them for traffic infractions. Local politicians make a practice of "fixing" things for those of their friends who get into trouble by over-speeding or wrongful parking. The first thought of too many citizens, when the traffic officer hands them a ticket, is to seek out someone who can get the matter adjusted without payment of a fine. "It is an unfortunate reflection upon American justice that in almost every city a person who knows an alderman, the mayor, a high police officer, a clerk in some of the courts, or

The public attitude toward traffic violations.

even knows somebody who knows one of these individuals can have his ticket torn up." [1]

The need for more effective penalties. There are cities, moreover, in which expensive cars are given virtual immunity from the rules while drivers of more humble vehicles, especially those which seem to be approaching the junk-heap stage, are held to a rigid observance of them. Such practices encourage a disrespect for the law and for the administration of justice. Moreover the imposition of a fine means a real penalty to the man in humble circumstances, while it is no punishment at all to rich offenders. Even heavy fines, repeatedly imposed, do not always deter certain classes of well-to-do violators. For this reason the jail sentence is gaining favor as a means of law enforcement in the case of habitual reckless driving. Likewise there is much to be said for the practice of impounding the driver's license in such cases. This power to suspend or take away an operator's license is sometimes vested in the courts but more often it requires action by the state authorities.

REFERENCES

Street Traffic Control by Miller McClintock (New York, 1925) is the standard treatise in this field, and William P. Eno, *Fundamentals of Highway Traffic Regulation* (New York, 1926) is also a useful volume. Mention should be made of the publication entitled *Municipal Organization for Street Traffic Control* by Miller McClintock and Sidney J. Williams issued by the Municipal Administration Service (1930). An entire issue of the *Annals of the American Academy of Political and Social Science* (September, 1927) is devoted to *Planning for Street Traffic*. The *Traffic Officer's Training Manual* by Clarence P. Taylor (Chicago, 1930) is an excellent handbook in its field. Much data on the subject is included in the publication entitled *Highway Traffic in New York and Its Environs* by Harold M. Lewis and Ernest P. Goodrich, issued in connection with the Regional Plan of New York and Its Environs (New York, 1925).

Among important studies of the traffic problem in individual cities the following deserve mention: *The Street Traffic Control Problems of the City of Boston* (1928), *Chicago Metropolitan Street Traffic Survey* (1926), *A Traffic Control Plan for Kansas City* (1930), *The Street Traffic Control Problem of the City of New Orleans* (1928), *Traffic Survey, City of Providence* (1928), *A Report on the Street Traffic Control Problem of San Francisco*

[1] L. D. Upson, *The Practice of Municipal Administration* (New York, 1926), p. 359.

(1927), and the *Parking and Garage Problem of the Central Business District of Washington, D. C.* (1930).

The National Conference on Street and Highway Safety and Traffic Control and Facilitation (1615 H St., N. W., Washington, D. C.) has published *A Model Municipal Traffic Ordinance* (1930) as well as numerous reports and bulletins on traffic control, traffic signals, the relief of congestion, enforcement of traffic rules, the causes of accidents, etc. The Highway Research Board of the National Research Council (B and 21st Sts., Washington, D. C.) is now conducting an extensive study of "Traffic Survey Methods and Forms" which will be published at an early date.

The Municipal Index contains from time to time some excellent articles on traffic regulation problems, and an elaborate bibliography on "Traffic Control and Facilitation" may be found in Vol. VIII, pp. 340–341 (1931).

CHAPTER XXVI

THE CITY COURTS

> Justice in the minor courts—the only courts that millions of our people know—administered without favoritism by men conspicuous for wisdom and probity, is the best assurance of respect for our institutions.—*Chief Justice Charles Evans Hughes.*

The status of municipal courts.

Strictly speaking, there are no such things as municipal courts in the United States. It is true that there are courts which bear that designation, but it is not an accurate one even when the judges are elected by the voters of the city and receive their salaries from the city treasury. Notwithstanding the fact that these tribunals may be mainly concerned with the enforcement of municipal ordinances, they are a part of the state judicial machinery; their jurisdiction and procedure are determined by the state laws, and their decisions may be appealed to the higher courts of the state. The judges, justices, magistrates, recorders, or whatever they may be called in these city courts, are regular members of the state judiciary, their status is often fixed by the state constitution, and in some states they are appointed by the state authorities. If in other states they are elected by the people of the municipality, it is usually because the state legislatures have regarded this method of selecting them as the most expedient one.

Scope of their work.

Why, then, should a discussion of these courts be included in any survey of municipal administration? The answer is that although they are an integral part of the state judicial system, the local courts are so closely related to certain phases of municipal administration that they cannot be left out of the reckoning. For example, their relation to the work of the police is obvious and intimate. It is upon them, in the main, that the police department depends for the upholding of its hands. If probity of local justice gives way, the police morale goes with it. Likewise several other departments of municipal administration depend upon the local courts for the enforcement of their regulations—for example, the buildings department, the health department, the sanitary service, and the fire-prevention bureau. Hence these city tribunals have a great deal of work to do. Most people do not realize that the so-termed municipal courts deal with more cases in the course of a year than all the higher courts of the United States, both state and federal put together. In Chicago, for example, the municipal courts hear about ten thousand cases a month.

Not only is the work of these courts extensive but it is of great social consequence. Being courts of the first instance they stand in a peculiarly close relation to the people, especially to the poorer classes in the crowded sections of the city. Those who dwell in the tenements rarely come into contact with any other courts, hence it is from these police courts and other city tribunals that they obtain their conceptions of what American justice or injustice implies. Even more, the ideas of these people concerning the honesty and efficiency of the whole city government are moulded in large part by their personal contact with police justices, bail brokers, court clerks, and public prosecutors. If any of these are venal or susceptible to political influence, the entire underworld is sure to discover it. And having discovered it, they make full use of their opportunities. Apart from all other considerations, arbitrary methods, incompetent magistrates, tribunals governed by petty politics, and slovenly proceedings at the point at which the great mass of the population come in contact with law enforcement, give a bad impression of the administration of justice as a whole and most seriously impair respect for and obedience to law generally.[1]

Their high importance.

Yet it is upon these two branches of local government, the police and the judiciary, that the greatest amount of downward pressure is always brought to bear. They are the most difficult of all to keep on a high plane of honesty and good faith. For there is cohesive force among those elements of an urban population which stand to profit from the lax or crooked administration of the law. In unity these elements work to break down the integrity of the police, the impartiality of the public prosecutors, and the probity of the courts. They even reach behind the courts and try to control those by whom the municipal justices are appointed. Or, if these judges are elected, they endeavor to work the control of the nominating machinery into their own hands. It is not surprising, therefore, that the general standards of municipal administration, when

The sinister pressure that is exerted upon the city courts.

[1] National Commission on Law Observance and Enforcement (Wickersham Commission), *Report on Criminal Procedure* (Washington, 1931), p. 6.

they begin to deteriorate, give their first indications of weakness in the law enforcement mechanism. The defense of municipal institutions at this most vulnerable point is absolutely vital to the preservation of American democracy. For democracy cannot endure without justice, and the justice that is administered by local courts, at the behest of the local police, is the only kind of justice that most of the people know.[1]

Evolution of the municipal court system:

1. The colonial era.

In their development during the last three hundred years the municipal courts of America have passed through several stages. During the colonial era no attempt was made to set up local courts as separate branches of city or town government. In New York and Philadelphia during the seventeenth century, for example, the mayor and aldermen made the ordinances, executed them, and sat on the bench to punish violations. When serving as a judicial body these officials constituted the court of mayor and aldermen. There was no separation of legislative, executive, and judicial authority. It was taken for granted that the men who made the laws were the ones best able to enforce them as well as to penalize the law-breakers.

2. After the Revolution.

Then came the Revolution, followed by the adoption of the federal constitution. With this change, as everyone knows, there came into the public mind a conviction that the three functions of government (legislative, executive, and judicial) should be kept distinct and separate. And this new philosophy soon worked its way into the administration of the cities. Mayor and aldermen were gradually deprived of their judicial functions, or at any rate ceased to exercise them. The change was expedited by the fact that with the growth of towns and cities there was more judicial work to be done and the regular city officials did not have time for it. Moreover, the cases became more difficult, involving a knowledge of law and legal procedure which mayors and aldermen did not usually possess. So the responsibility for presiding in the municipal courts was given to magistrates or justices of the peace chosen for this purpose alone. In the eastern cities these judicial officers were usually appointed by the city council, or in some cases by the governor of the state.

3. The Jacksonian era.

The third stage in the evolution of the municipal court system was reached during the Jacksonian period, which roughly covered

[1] For a full discussion of this point see R. H. Smith, *Justice and the Poor* (New York, 1919).

the years between 1825 and 1840. This interlude was marked by a great wave of popular democracy which arose in the West and backwashed into the states of the Atlantic seaboard. With it came a nation-wide demand for a new deal. Andrew Jackson and his supporters believed that all judges, alike in the higher or lower courts, should be directly elected by the people and should hold office for short terms. Courts should be representative of public opinion, just as legislatures and city councils were. Hence the practice of electing municipal judges and justices of the peace began in the New West and in keeping with the agrarian philosophy spread over a large part of the country. In many of the states any plain citizen was deemed qualified to be a judge. Men without any education whatever, and sometimes unable to read or write, became justices in both rural and urban communities. The administration of local justice, accordingly, was not only inefficient in such cases but soon became perverted by the influence of partisan politics. Men who had no qualifications except as vote-getters managed to be elected and then intrenched themselves in office by doing judicial favors for their friends. Serving on a part-time basis these elective justices were usually paid by fees and hence were able to use their powers in an extortionate way.

Such a system was bound to break down with the growth of large urban communities. The iniquities of it fell most heavily upon the poor, especially upon the emigrant who was usually uninformed concerning his legal rights. In most of the larger cities, therefore, the elective justices were gradually supplanted by regular salaried magistrates who gave all their time to the work of administering local justice. Sometimes these magistrates continued to be elected by popular vote, but in many cases they were made appointive. From the larger cities the practice of having regularly organized municipal courts spread to the smaller ones, but the movement did not proceed at a uniform rate in different parts of the country. Hence there is today a considerable variation as respects municipal court organization and procedure throughout the United States. Every state has its own plan and no two of them are exactly alike.

4. Later developments.

The local courts, which now administer justice in American cities, are known by a variety of names—municipal courts, magistrates' courts, district courts, police courts, recorders' courts, and justice courts. The judges, magistrates, or recorders are sometimes

Present-day organization of city courts.

elected by the people of the city, sometimes appointed by the mayor or by the city council, and sometimes named by the governor of the state in which the city is located. Their terms range all the way from a couple of years to life tenure. As a rule, but not always, they must be men of legal training. Their jurisdiction defies any attempt at concise classification. Sometimes these courts deal only with violations of the city ordinances; in other instances they also have jurisdiction over minor offenses against the state laws. Sometimes they hold the preliminary hearings in serious criminal cases and likewise have jurisdiction in civil controversies where the amount at issue does not exceed a designated sum. Sometimes they have the right to impanel juries but more often they do not. Usually they are courts of record, that is, they are provided with a clerk and the proceedings are available for use by the higher courts in case of an appeal.

Division of their work. Following the establishment of regularly organized municipal courts with salaried judges it presently became apparent that no single tribunal could handle all the business that developed from day to day in large and growing cities. Some division of the work became essential. Hence arose the practice of dividing the municipal court into sections, or establishing branches of it in different parts of the city. As a result of this process some of the larger cities came to have six or seven municipal courts sitting in different parts of the municipality, hearing cases of the same sort, yet virtually independent of the other and under no unified supervision. Such an arrangement proved unsatisfactory because the same offense might be differently penalized in different parts of the city, and often that is what happened. Moreover since each court had to deal with cases of every variety there was no chance to develop special competence in any branch of judicial administration. When a court is required to deal with such widely varied matters as ordinary misdemeanors, traffic violations, juvenile offenses, domestic relations, and even small civil claims, it can hardly expect to become proficient in handling any of them.

The growth of specialization in court work. The latest stage in municipal court development has therefore been marked by a recognition of the need for judicial specialization. Several of the larger cities have now unified their judicial machinery by consolidating it into a single municipal court with a number of divisions, each of which deals with cases of a designated type. In other words, the division is functional, not geo-

THE CITY COURTS

graphical. In Chicago, for example, there are now more than thirty municipal court justices. From this active corps of municipal judges the chief justice makes assignments to the several divisions. These divisions deal with traffic cases, juvenile offenses, domestic relations, small claims, misdemeanors, civil controversies, violations of the liquor laws, and so on. They confine themselves to cases within their own special fields.

The Chicago plan.

One need only glance over the master calendar of the municipal court in any large city to realize how great is the variety of the cases which come up for adjudication. In some cities the plan has been to set up special juvenile courts, traffic courts, and courts of domestic relations, rather than to have this work performed by regular divisions of the municipal court. In New York City a separation between criminal and civil jurisdiction is still maintained. Many of the criminal cases are first heard in the magistrates' courts but the more serious offenses go directly to the higher tribunals. Special magistrates' courts, however, are established for traffic cases, night court cases, the trial of juvenile offenders and cases arising out of domestic relations. The magistrates are appointed by the mayor. Minor civil cases come before the justices of the municipal court who are elected by popular vote.

The New York plan.

The night court is a relatively new feature. Prior to its establishment any person arrested in the late afternoon or evening usually had to stay in jail until the court opened the following morning or else get himself bailed by a professional bondsman who charged a stiff fee for his services. Now, where such courts have been established, the hearing can be held at once. In a few cities a special court, or division of the municipal court, has been established to hear all cases in which the complainant or defendant is a woman. Most cities have now made special provision for the hearing of cases in which the offenders are under a certain age. Sometimes there is a regular juvenile court, or a juvenile division of the municipal court, but more often the regular judges deal with such cases at a special session. The hearings in a juvenile court are informal, with the judge doing most of the questioning. It has sometimes been suggested that similar arrangements ought to be made for the trial of adult offenders whose mental age has never advanced beyond the early juvenile stage as psychiatrists can testify. Obviously a sense of personal responsibility is not a matter of years alone but of mental and moral development.

Courts of special jurisdiction.

Night courts, women's courts, and juvenile courts.

Reasons for the unsatisfactory functioning of city courts:

These various improvements in the organization of American municipal courts have accomplished a good deal; yet the administration of local justice in the cities of the United States is still far from being satisfactory so far as any effective dealing with the problem of crime is concerned. Recent investigations have demonstrated this fact beyond any question.[1] The reasons for the existing situation are not altogether easy to explain, nor will they be simple to eradicate. In a general way, however, they may be summarized under some general headings, as follows:

1. The method of choosing the judges.

First, the method of selecting and removing municipal judges. No reform in municipal court organization will avail greatly if the judges are not selected in such way as to ensure the choice of capable, honest, and impartial men. There is a widespread popular belief in the United States that judges of the municipal and state courts should be elected by the people as the only sure way of keeping them in close touch with public sentiment and restraining them from becoming arbitrary in their methods of administering justice. This is a hangover from the days of pioneer democracy. In a frontier environment there was a good deal to be said for it, but under the conditions which now exist in urban communities popular election not only fails as a method of getting capable judges but it no longer serves to keep the courts responsive to public sentiment as a whole. For popular election, as a rule, means the nomination of the candidate at the behest of the party leaders. It means the waging of partisan campaigns financed by party campaign funds, with consequent obligations to the party machine. Worst of all it often involves a personal participation in bitter and undignified political controversies. Even when the election of municipal judges is ostensibly on a non-partisan basis, the candidates must build up organizations, raise campaign funds, and seek support from influential elements in the electorate. The idea that a well-qualified, appealing candidate can be elected by merely placing his claims before the people is one of the myths of practical politics which ought to have been exploded long ago. The office should seek the man, but it hardly ever does.

In populous communities the great masses of the voters know very little about the qualifications of judiciary candidates. And in

---

[1] For example, see the bibliography on "Crime Surveys," etc., in the *Report on Prosecution* issued by the National Commission on Law Observance and Law Enforcement (Washington, 1931), pp. 258–265.

any event their choice is restricted to the nominees whose names have been placed on the ballot by action of political organizations, or the bar association, or by the local party bosses. Popular election keeps the courts responsive to those elements which have been mainly instrumental in getting the judges elected, not the people as a whole. On the other hand, it is by no means certain that appointments by the mayor or by the governor would ensure better results. For these appointing officials are themselves subject to the pressure of politics, and an incompetent or partisan executive can hardly be relied upon to appoint competent and non-partisan judges. Nevertheless the system of appointment has proved more satisfactory than the method of popular election, especially when accompanied by reasonably long judicial terms. A good lawyer will not give up his private practice for a judgeship unless he can be assured of something more than two or three years on the municipal bench. Judicial salaries should also be made commensurate with the importance of the work which the judges are expected to do. *Election vs. appointment of city judges.*

Second, political interference with the regular course of municipal justice. No matter how the justices of a municipal court may be chosen, they are bound to be subjected in some degree to the pressure of political influence. For one of the first things that violators of the law usually do is to seek the aid of somebody who is influential in politics. They desire him to intercede with the prosecuting officer, or with the judge, or with some friend of the judge before the case is called. Go into the lobby of the municipal courthouse any week-day morning. You will find a dozen local politicians ranging around, in and out. One and all their errand is to see that some offender gets less than what is coming to him. In fact, it is through the doing of such favors that the political boss builds up his machine. Much of this chicanery never exposes itself to public view because it is manipulated through indirect and invisible channels. Every political machine has its little corps of fixers who will try to straighten out anything from a traffic tag to a murder case. There can be no even-handed administration of local justice until both the courts and the prosecutor's office are divorced from politics. *2. Political interference with judicial work.*

This last-named office is almost as important as the court itself. In some large communities the prosecuting function is left to the police, but in most of them there is a city prosecutor, or prosecuting *The prosecuting officer.*

attorney, who is responsible for the presentation of cases in court. Sometimes he has a considerable staff of deputy or assistant prosecutors. The public prosecutor has a large amount of discretion. He can prosecute a case relentlessly and press for the full penalty, or he can choose to be lenient and recommend that it be placed on file. He can enter a *nolle prosequi* or suggest that a plea of guilty to a lesser offense than the one charged be accepted. Even when an offender has been convicted he can recommend a suspended sentence or release on probation, and as a rule the court will follow his recommendations. The incumbent of this office, with his large discretionary powers, is everywhere filled by popular election and too often it is occupied by a prosecutor who has the ambition to go higher in politics.

Conditions in this office.

Under such conditions there is a strong temptation to use the discretion of the prosecutor's office in ways which will accumulate political strength. So much time and thought is often given to politics, moreover, that the routine work of the office is badly done. "The cases are not well prepared, witnesses are almost never interviewed before their appearance . . . the work is perfunctory and careless in the extreme . . . some of the assistants scarcely rise above the illiterate grade . . . the assistant prosecuting attorney is usually lounging against the bench engaged in casual conversation with every passer-by, careless, unimposing, undignified and indolent . . . he usually picks up the complaint and attempts to extract testimony from witnesses whom he has not seen before." [1]

This description of conditions in one large American city would hold true in many others. The office of public prosecutor should be filled by appointment. Where practicable the selection ought to be made by the courts and the incumbent should have the same term as judges. It might also be well to provide that no one who serves in the office of public prosecutor shall be eligible for election to any other office until some years after his prosecuting duties have ceased. For only in some such way can the powers of this office be safeguarded from abuse in the furtherance of political ambitions.

3. The maze of limitations and technicalities.

Third, the welter of technicalities, delays, new trials, and appeals. American judicial procedure is over-friendly to the accused. It gives the malefactor a better run for his money, if he has the money, than would be obtained in any other country of the world.

[1] From the *Illinois Crime Survey* (Chicago, 1929), p. 406.

THE CITY COURTS

Shyster lawyers do their best to clog the wheels of justice by resort to every conceivable technicality. They enter pleas in avoidance, secure postponements, file exceptions, move in arrest of judgment, ask for new trials, and resort to other devices of procrastination. When all these fail, they still have the right to appeal from the decisions of the lower courts. These numerous appeals clog the calendars of the higher tribunals and get them so far in arrears that the accused person has a marked advantage when the case comes up for final adjudication. And even if the appeal is unsuccessful, there is still an opportunity to ask for probation or for suspension of sentence or for the minimum sentence. Finally, if the offender actually goes to jail there is the possibility of getting him released on parole or pardoned by the executive authorities.

Under such circumstances there need be no surprise that most of the crimes committed in the larger cities of the United States go virtually unpunished. Let us take a typical case and follow it from start to finish, just to show how prolific are the opportunities for an offender to evade payment of the full penalties which the law imposes. A man is found seriously wounded in his home, alone, with a bullet in his chest and a revolver lying on the floor. The police are called. If they are well trained they will see that the revolver is not handled in a way to obliterate any finger prints that may be on it, and they will otherwise take care that nothing is disturbed which might serve as evidence. Such care, however, is not always exercised. The police rush into the place, search the victim's pockets, turn out the contents of the bureau drawers, ransack the attic, call in the neighbors for questioning, and assure the newspaper reporters that they are right on the trail of the guilty one. Presently they decide that someone ought to be arrested, whereupon a complaint is filed and a warrant issued. If the suspected person has not made a getaway, in view of the thinly veiled newspaper intimations, he is brought in, locked up and probably given the "third degree" in an effort to extort something incriminating from him.

Then comes the preliminary hearing at which the prisoner is arraigned, and if a prima facie case is made out he is held for action by the grand jury or for trial before a higher court on the basis of information filed by the prosecutor's office. At a preliminary hearing the accused is entitled to have counsel if he chooses to employ one himself. Or, if he is financially unable to retain an

A typical case:

1. The police investigation.

2. The preliminary hearing.

attorney, but desires the assistance of one, the court will usually designate somebody to represent him without fee or at the public expense. Some cities have a salaried official known as the public defender whose duty it is to perform this service. In very few serious cases, however, is an accused person unable to secure the services of a lawyer for himself. In every large city there are plenty of professional defenders, or "ambulance-chasers" as they are often called, who will defend anyone, against any charge, for a small fee or even for the promise of compensation after the prisoner gets loose again and is able to pay it. This lower stratum of the legal profession includes many politician-lawyers who specialize in the work of rendering aid and comfort to law-breakers and racketeers of all varieties.

3. Release on bail. At the preliminary hearing a request for release on bail will be made. If this request is granted by the court, the amount is fixed, and one or more bondsmen are called in to provide it. Often they are professionals who will go surety in any case provided they get their fee. Such bondsmen are frequently in collusion with the police or the court clerks. The prisoner is released on bail and if he does not appear when he is wanted in court his bail is forfeited. But such forfeitures are often set aside, sometime later, by the court and only a small percentage of forfeited bail bonds are ever collected. Much injustice is done through the requirement of heavy bail in cases where the accused cannot pay the bondsman's fee.

4. The trial. If the prisoner is not acquitted at the preliminary hearing his case goes forward for indictment and trial in a higher court. Such trials, when the offense is serious, are usually by jury, although in some states the prisoner may elect to be tried by a judge alone. In any event the case is put on the court calendar and is supposed to be ready for trial on the date assigned; but often it is not. The defendant frequently asks for a postponement and almost as frequently his request is granted. In fact there may be two or three successive postponements. However, when the trial does begin, the first step is to impanel a jury. The prisoner's counsel may challenge any prospective juror. As a rule he has a stated number of peremptory challenges which he can use without giving any reasons, and in addition may challenge any prospective juror for cause. His challenges for cause are usually without limit, the validity of the reasons being decided by the judge. In the matter of challenges the

THE CITY COURTS

public prosecutor has the same right as the counsel for the defendant. Whole days and even weeks may be spent in securing a jury. After this task has been finished the prosecutor outlines his case and calls his witnesses one by one. He questions them on direct examination; then the defense attorney cross-examines them, and finally the prosecutor may question them in rebuttal or redirect examination.

In the course of these proceedings there are various opportunities to delay the progress of the case. The defense may move to quash the indictment and may argue this matter at length. The defendant's attorney may object to questions which the prosecutor puts to the witnesses, and the prosecutor has the right to repay him in his own coin. Exceptions may be taken to the judge's rulings on points of law, and sometimes the jury is excluded from the room while the rival lawyers thresh out their differences in arguments of pitiless length. When the prosecution has finished the presentation of its case, the defense brings on its witnesses for examination and cross-examination. Finally, the attorneys make their closing arguments to the jury, the judge gives the jurymen their instructions on legal points, and the jury retires to find a verdict.

5. The opportunities for delay.

Unless the twelve jurors are unanimous they report a disagreement, whereupon the prosecuting attorney may put the case on the calendar for a new trial, before a new jury, with the entire proceedings gone over again. But if the verdict be one of acquittal, this ends the case. No accused person, when a verdict of not guilty has been rendered, can ever again be placed on trial for the particular offense involved. On the other hand, if the verdict be adverse to the defendant, the case is not necessarily ended. His counsel may move for a new trial on the ground that the verdict was contrary to the weight of the evidence. He may move in arrest of sentence. He may plead for the imposition of a suspended sentence, with the convicted person placed on probation instead of going to jail. If overruled on these motions he can usually appeal and go before a higher court asking for a new trial on the allegation that some of the judge's rulings were wrongly rendered or that there were other irregularities in the proceedings. Meanwhile the execution of the sentence is delayed and the convicted offender is sometimes allowed his freedom on bail. Several months may pass before the appeal is heard, and then if the higher court finds some serious flaw in the earlier proceedings a new trial is ordered. If it

6. The verdict and after.

finds no such defect, the sentence imposed by the trial court is confirmed and then there is little for the defendant's attorney to do but seek a pardon for his client from the governor of the state, or failing success in that direction to go before the parole board and seek to have the prisoner released as soon as possible.

<small>The need for reforms in judicial procedure.</small>

It is small wonder that with such procedure as this the malefactor is willing to take chances. The chances are heavily in his favor. When a crime is perpetrated with any reasonable amount of skill, the likelihood that its perpetrator will be detected, arrested, tried, convicted, and made to serve the sentence prescribed by law—the chance is small. Taking all cities, and the whole category of crime, the chances are probably not one in ten. Greater severity of punishment is not the remedy for this situation. Greater certainty of arrest and conviction would be more helpful. The lawyers who practice in the lower criminal courts are in a considerable measure to blame for the general inefficiency with which justice is now administered by these tribunals. In the eyes of the law, a lawyer becomes an "officer of the court" whenever he appears before it as counsel; but some of those who come before the bar as defenders of crooks, gangsters, racketeers, blackmailers, kidnappers, and yeggmen do not demean themselves in that capacity. Their energies and ingenuity are sometimes directed toward the doing of injustice to the community rather than the securing of justice for the accused. Any reformation of municipal court organization and procedure, if it is to be satisfactory and permanent, must be with the coöperation of the legal profession. For lawyers form a large element in legislative chambers and without their aid there is little in the way of procedural reform that can be accomplished.

REFERENCES

An elaborate bibliography of books and articles relating to the organization of the courts, judicial procedure, defects in the administration of justice, criminal prosecution, and the remedies for judicial maladministration may be found in the *Report on Prosecution* issued by the National Commission on Law Observance and Law Enforcement, commonly known as the Wickersham Commission (Washington, 1931), pp. 233–289. Mention should also be made of the *Report on Criminal Procedure* by the same investigating body.

Books on the general subject which may be consulted with profit are W. F. Willoughby, *Principles of Judicial Administration* (Washington,

1929), C. N. Callender, *American Courts: Their Organization and Procedure* (New York, 1927), Roscoe Pound, *Criminal Justice in America* (New York, 1930), A. Lepawsky, *The Judicial System of Metropolitan Chicago* (Chicago, 1932), A. A. Bruce, *The American Judge* (New York, 1924), R. H. Smith, *Justice and the Poor* (New York, 1919), James P. Kirby, *Selected Articles on Criminal Justice* (New York, 1926), Raymond Moley, *Politics and Criminal Prosecution* (New York, 1929), *The Long Day in Court* (New York, 1929), *Our Criminal Courts* (New York, 1930), and *Tribunes of the People* (New Haven, 1932), M. C. Goldman, *The Public Defender* (2nd edition, New York, 1927), and H. R. Gallagher, *Crime Prevention as a Municipal Function* (Syracuse, N. Y., 1930).

An article by Roscoe Pound entitled "The Administration of Justice in the Modern City," printed in the *Harvard Law Review*, Vol. XXVI, pp. 302–328 (1913), deserves special mention. Current discussions may be found in the bimonthly *Journal of the American Judicature Society*. See also the references at the close of Chapters XXIV and XXVII.

CHAPTER XXVII

CRIME AND CORRECTION

There was a man and he stole. I don't know what he stole or why. But I do know that the result was six months of housing and food provided for the man at the public expense and six months of starvation for his wife and children.—Victor Hugo.

Definition of a crime.

What is a crime? The legal dictionaries define it as any act or omission which is in contravention of a law. But it does not follow that the act or omission is necessarily reprehensible, much less that it involves moral turpitude. Issuing a bank check without sufficient funds is a crime in some jurisdictions, even though the maker of the check was acting in good faith. Actions which are criminal in one place are legally permissible in another. The sale of intoxicants, for example, is a crime or a legitimate form of business depending on the outcome of the last local option campaign. Violations of the state laws or municipal ordinances are not penalized because they indicate the violator to be morally deficient but because these laws and ordinances represent the endeavor of society to protect the common interest of its members and thus to promote the general welfare. A crime, in other words, is a wrong against the public, a defiance of the mechanism whereby the social order is trying to protect itself. Offenses against individuals, as distinct from offenses against the social order, are known as torts or civil wrongs. To steal a man's property is a crime, but to trespass on his land is a tort. The public prosecutes the offender in one case, while the aggrieved individual brings suit in the other.

The classification of crimes:
1. The older division.

It has been the custom to classify all crimes as treasons, felonies, and misdemeanors. Treason is an attempt to overthrow the state. Felonies are grave offenses (such as murder, manslaughter, burglary, or forgery) punishable by execution or by a term of incarceration in a state prison, while misdemeanors are less serious violations of the law such as parking a car on the wrong side of the street or selling milk without a license. This threefold division, however, is too simple for use in the complexities of urban civiliza-

CRIME AND CORRECTION

tion, and much more elaborate classifications are now being employed.

For example, crimes may be grouped to include: (a) offenses against the safety of the state, such as treason and sedition, (b) offenses against the public peace and order, such as rioting, (c) offenses against the administration of justice, such as perjury and contempt of court, (d) offenses against public morals, such as bigamy, vagrancy, and adultery, (e) offenses against the person, such as murder and assault, (f) offenses against property, such as theft and embezzlement, (g) offenses against business morals, such as forgery or receiving stolen goods, and (h) miscellaneous offenses which are forbidden by statute or ordinance, such as bringing goods into the country without paying certain duties or operating an airplane without a license or failing to file a tax return. *2. The newer grouping.*

In any event the category of crimes is being steadily expanded, for as human relations become more complex there is greater need for the regulation of individual conduct. And this control must often take the form of a commandment to do something, or to refrain from doing something, with any violation of this order rated as a crime. Thus the network of criminal laws and penal ordinances gradually spreads itself over the land like a huge spider's web, and often traps even the well-intentioned, unwary citizen, but through which the truculent malefactor seems able to break his way at will. *The expanding category of criminal acts.*

The statistics of crime in American cities do not make agreeable reading. Offenses against the laws of the land have been steadily increasing. This holds with respect to both major and minor crimes. The increase has been much more rapid than the growth of population. No matter what method of calculation may be employed, it will be found that serious offenses, especially those accompanied by violence, are more numerous in the United States than in any other country. In homicides, burglaries, and robberies America holds the world's record by a wide margin. More than half a million persons are sentenced to jail or to other penal institutions in this country every year. The result is that the correctional institutions of the United States have a larger enrollment than all the colleges and universities put together. Moreover they have a bigger percentage of post-graduates, although their alumni do not voluntarily come back for reunions. The direct and indirect cost of detecting, convicting, and punishing criminals in the United *The high criminal record of American cities.*

States is nearly as large as the entire amount expended on public education.[1]

Reasons for it. In recent years there has been a flood of discussion concerning the reasons for this unhappy situation, this persistence of a crime wave, as it is called. To some extent it is not unlikely that the rising figures are due to the fact that more accurate statistics of crime are now being kept than was formerly the case. A generation or two ago most of the less serious crimes were never reported or placed upon the police station records. There was no central compilation of crime statistics on a reliable basis. Today we are getting the whole story and it is naturally a longer one. Many things, moreover, are forbidden today which were unknown to the law books of a few decades ago. Take the entire traffic code, for example, and the whole range of industrial codes, the increased strictness of the health and fire-prevention ordinances and the rules regulating radio broadcasting. The advance of civilization is making it steadily more difficult for people to keep from technical violations of the law. But even with all due allowance for the keeping of better statistics and the listing of new offenses, it seems beyond question that the crime ratio in American cities has been rapidly rising and that it is now the highest in the world so far as violent crimes, such as murder, manslaughter, burglary, and robbery are concerned.

What the investigations disclose. The basic reasons for this high crime ratio are not easy to untangle from the skein of superficial causes, nor is their relative importance a simple matter to estimate. Extensive investigations of the crime problem have been made by many agencies during the past dozen years without reaching much in the way of definite and satisfactory conclusions. As a matter of fact we know less about the fundamental causes of crime than we do about the causes of disease. The reason, perhaps, is that sociologists have been studying the one and scientists the other. It seems to be the general consensus of opinion among the experts in criminology, however, that the uncommendable record of the American city in the matter of serious crimes is the outcome of no single factor but of many working in combination. The spirit of pioneer independence among the people, the lack of settled traditions, the unduly liberal guarantees of individual freedom, the popular

[1] Included is the loss by thievery, the cost of insurance against theft, and many other items of indirect expense.

tolerance of wrong-doing, the venality or incompetence of police and prosecutors due to the pressure of politics, the relative inefficiency of the municipal courts, the delays and technicalities which clog the administration of justice, the maudlin sympathy so often shown by the public when a convicted criminal is about to be punished, the abuse of the probation and parole systems, the too-free granting of reprieves and pardons,—all these and a dozen other factors have had a share in transforming the American city into a malefactor's elysium. No single panacea, therefore, will solve the crime problem. There must be a revamping of mechanism and ideas all along the line.

Meanwhile there is something intriguing about the criminal as a type. From Homer to Conan Doyle men have been writing books about him and his ways. The greatest of all the Shakespearean plays, the immortal tragedy of Hamlet, revolves about a crime. Some of the most interesting characters in Dickens are fellows who ought to have been in jail. Victor Hugo and Émile Zola made a specialty of criminals. Most normal readers are interested in detective stories, and their interest is not always confined to the detective in the plot. Crime and criminals bulk large in the news of the day, and the more extraordinary the crime the livelier is the public interest in it. *The public interest in crime.*

Why do we have criminals, so many of them? It is said that "some men are born criminals, some are made, and some are both born and made." This may be so, but it is not a very illuminating generalization. Heredity may have something to do with the making of criminals, but in spite of elaborate studies we do not know whether it is a small or large factor. In so far as low mentality is inherited, however, it serves as a predisposition to delinquency. Environmental influences undoubtedly have a great deal to do with the proportion of crimes. Even the weather may have something to do with it, for crimes against the person (such as murder, manslaughter, and assault) are relatively more numerous in warm climates than in cold, while crimes against property (such as larceny and fraud) are more numerous in the reverse order. The same holds true, in a general way, of the summer and winter seasons. Some races, again, are more addicted to certain types of crime than are other races living in the same community. *The making of criminals.*

There has been a prevalent impression in the rural portions of the United States that most of the crimes committed in the cities are

Relation of crime to race, age, sex, and other factors.

the work of the foreign-born population or of those who are of foreign parentage. But the criminal statistics disclose that there is no real basis for this impression. Age and sex, however, have a definite relation to criminality, in so much as the great majority of offenders brought before the courts are male persons between the ages of eighteen and thirty. The crime ratio likewise has a demonstrable relation to business conditions, for it declines when business is good and rises when an economic depression comes. This, of course, is not surprising because an economic depression throws large numbers of people out of employment. And when people are idle they find their way into mischief more readily than when they are fully employed.

Another significant thing about the crime ratio is that it tends to drop in wartime, but rises rapidly after the war comes to an end. The Napoleonic wars in Europe left a legacy of increased crime throughout the old continent. The American Civil War was followed by crime waves which continued throughout the reconstruction period in both the North and in the South. It is not strange, therefore, that the World War, as the greatest conflict in history, has been followed by a recrudescence of criminality all over the world. War unstabilizes the social organization and unsettles the routine of life. It is an era in which hate, violence, and force are preached in the name of patriotism. Neither soldiers nor civilians can discard, all at once, the idealization of violence which has been drilled into them during the course of a prolonged military struggle. Moreover, the close of a great war generally ushers in an era of reconstruction, and time is required for the people to adjust themselves to the new order. During the transition there is an impatience with the old virtues.

Its relation to density of population.

But most significant of all, for our present purposes, is the fact that crime increases in something like geometrical progression with increased density of population. There are more crimes per thousand of population in small cities than in the rural districts, and still more in large cities than in the smaller ones. Occasional exceptions may be found, but the rule seems to hold in a general way throughout the world. Consequently, as a shifting of population takes place from the rural districts to the cities, and as cities grow larger in size, the crime ratio for the whole country is bound to undergo a substantial increase. Undoubtedly this is one of the factors contributing to the increasing crime ratio of the United

CRIME AND CORRECTION

States,—the strong drift of the population into the larger cities. Today the cities of the United States contain a little more than half the total population of the country, but they contribute nearly nine-tenths of all the crimes.

This naturally raises the question why large cities should have a criminal ratio so much above the rest of the country. An offhand reply would be that the cities contain more than their share of the alien population. But this would not account for the relatively high criminality of European cities as compared with the rural districts in their respective countries. Allegiance seems to have little or nothing to do with it. Much more to the point is the greater opportunity which the city, as compared with the rural district, affords for the commission of such crimes as burglary, robbery, embezzlement, forgery, and fraud. Take bank hold-ups, as an illustration. From the nature of things these are virtually confined to the business centers of towns and cities. Then the facilities for escaping detection and arrest are also greater in the cities. Despite the highly organized police department of the urban community, every wrong-doer knows that it is easier for a criminal to slip away from the clutches of the law in the slums than on the prairies. Hence the great majority of crooks, bandits, forgers, pickpockets, stick-up men, porch-climbers, yeggmen, gunmen, gangsters, thugs, bootleggers, confidence-men, counterfeiters, racketeers, and other practitioners of the iniquities prefer to have their permanent headquarters in the more congested parts of the largest cities. They are also influenced by the fact that a big city offers safer and more convenient facilities for the disposal of stolen property, as well as liquor dens and brothels for the dissipation which usually follows. In the large city, moreover, the crook can always find company, and it is there that he can best count upon ward politicians, bail-bondsmen, and gumshoe lawyers to help him if the law finally manages to run him down.

Why cities supply most of the criminals.

Every police officer knows that a large city always contains a number of localized centers in which the criminal can find shelter. The old-time saloon was one of them; later the speakeasy and bootlegging dive usurped its place. Hide-outs where narcotic drugs are illegally sold also serve as the rendezvous of the criminal element. This traffic in drugs has gained a considerable foothold in all the large cities of the United States during the past twenty years. Then there are such places as unregulated public dance

The localized crime centers.

halls, pool rooms, all-night lunch stands, cheap lodging houses, night clubs of the rougher type, third-rate hotels, disorderly houses, and various other establishments which very often serve as centers of resort for those who are trying to escape detection for one crime while planning another. When the police throw out a dragnet, therefore, it reaches first of all into these localized centers around which so much that is sordid in the life of a great city revolves. A map of any large city indicating the locations at which certain classes of crimes have been committed, moreover, will show that the distribution is by no means even. On the contrary it often shows a concentration of criminal offenses at spots here and there, usually in convenient proximity to the hide-outs and hang-outs of crooks. An example of a spot map showing such places is appended:

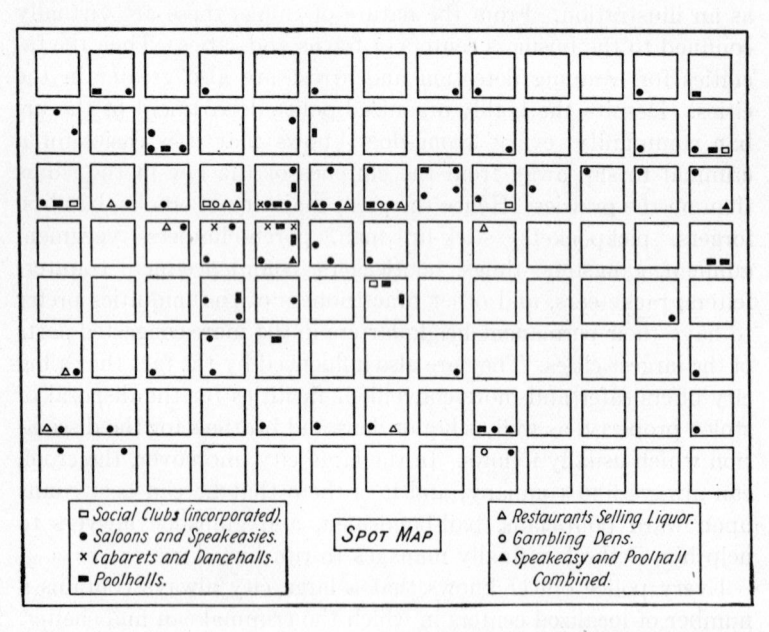

SPOT MAP

□ Social Clubs (incorporated).
● Saloons and Speakeasies.
× Cabarets and Dancehalls.
■ Poolhalls.
△ Restaurants Selling Liquor.
○ Gambling Dens.
▲ Speakeasy and Poolhall Combined.

The abbreviated biography of a typical crook.

Social and economic influences of an environmental nature have much to do with the nurture of criminals, and the city provides these influences in generous measure. Take the biography of any typical public enemy. In all probability he was born in the overcrowded section of a large city, the child of poor uneducated parents, one or both of whom were addicted to the use of alcohol or drugs. From them he inherited coarse features and a subnormal mentality. As a small child he was undernourished and often ill. The constant squabbling of his parents made him irritable and developed in his immature mind a disrespect for them and an aversion to his home. No parental interest was taken in his schooling; he played truant whenever he could, and presently joined a street gang of other youngsters who spent their energies in mischief because there was nothing else for them to do—no organization or supervision of neighborhood play and recreation. By the age of ten or twelve, he thus became proficient in telling falsehoods to his parents and teachers, in juvenile pranks of an annoying sort and perhaps in petty thievery from fruit stands and cigarette counters. *As a child.*

A few years later he left school without getting beyond the seventh grade and went out to look for a job. Unable to get one, or to hold one, he began idling his hours on the street corners and in the pool rooms where he presently made a contact with bootleggers, drug peddlers, pimps, or dice shakers. At about this stage he found a girl and needed money for her entertainment at picture shows, dance halls, and beach resorts, as well as to buy liquor for himself. To get it he climbed through the back window of a house while the occupants were away, stole some jewelry and pawned it. With a part of the proceeds he bought a gun and staged his first hold-up. Success in these initial escapades emboldened him to do more of it, especially because he now had a girl of easy virtue to use all the money that he could supply. *As a youth.*

But after a little the police got him and he made his first appearance in the municipal court. Having no previous record he was let off on probation. Within a few weeks, however, he was in trouble again and the second arraignment brought him a six-months term in a reformatory, for he was not yet regarded as beyond the pale of redemption. Emerging from this institution with no job in sight, and no well-formed habits of personal responsibility, he returned to his old haunts and before long was once more in the prisoner's dock, this time for a more serious offense which resulted in his being sentenced to a term in the city prison. With the aid of a skillful lawyer, however, he managed to have the sentence stayed pending an appeal, and when the appeal came on the calendar the prosecuting attorney consented to having the sentence suspended. *As a man.*

But now he had his lawyer's fee to pay and his training gave him no honest way of getting the money. Accordingly the career of crime was renewed with an ultimate destination in the penitentiary. A stretch of two, three, or five years at this institution merely hardened his criminal propensities and on the expiration of his term the career of bootlegging, narcotic peddling, and hold-up ventures was soon renewed. A second term in the penitentiary was followed in due course by a third and in the end he found himself classed as a habitual criminal whom society was under obligation to support and supervise for the rest of his days. This, with sundry variations, is about the way in which the life story of the average hardened criminal runs.

In its attitude toward the treatment of criminals the civilized world has passed through several stages. Primitive society looked upon punishment as a form of individual retaliation. "Whoso sheddeth man's blood, by man shall his blood be shed." Gradually, however, custom began to prescribe limits upon the amount or form of individual vengeance which might be taken. Then, in due course, it fixed a schedule of payments in lieu of physical retaliation. It was provided by the early laws of Saxon England, for example, that a slayer should atone for his offense by paying a definite wergild or fine to the family of the slain individual. If he did not have wherewithal to make this payment his relatives and friends had to make it good.[1]

Then came the next stage, the evolution of an idea that society as a whole had an interest in the discouragement of wrong-doing and that injuries which were ostensibly done to individual citizens were in effect a threat to the whole social order. So the community took upon itself the duty of imposing punishment whenever the rights of its individual members were violated. With this came a new philosophy of punishment; it was no longer a matter of retribution but of deterrence. Penalties came to be looked upon as a means of discouraging others from committing similar offenses. Hence they ought to be of great severity. So criminals were often beheaded and their heads impaled upon the city gates in order that malefactors might be duly terrified. Even the great English jurist Blackstone, in the closing decades of the

[1] There was a scale of fines for various other offenses. See William Stubbs, *Select Charters* (Oxford, 1895), pp. 63–66.

eighteenth century, accepted the principle that the purpose of punishment is to serve as a deterrent and an example.

During the past century, however, the world has gradually come to regard crime as a social ailment, due to a combination of causes for which the individual offender is not altogether responsible. Society should not, therefore, content itself with merely visiting its retribution upon him. Nor should it use his misfortune as a means of terrifying others. So the punishment of a criminal has now come to be looked upon as a means of either reforming the criminal or of protecting society against him if his reformation seems improbable. To this end punishment should be certain rather than severe, and should be corrective rather than retributive. More than one hundred years ago an eminent English reformer, Jeremy Bentham, pointed out that certainty of punishment is a more effective deterrent than severity. The whole history of punitive justice bears out the truth of this aphorism, but the world has taken a long time to recognize it. In dealing with a criminal, therefore, the first thing to determine is whether he is beyond hope of reform. If he is not, then the possibilities in the way of suspended sentence, probation, and parole are worthy to be explored. If, on the other hand, he is adjudged by competent experts to be beyond the pale of reform, he should be put and kept where he will do society no further damage; but his treatment should not be any more harsh than is necessary to secure his safe detention.

3. Punishment as a means of reformation or of social protection.

Until relatively recent years, accordingly, criminal law set up its scale of penalties in accordance with a retributive philosophy. It permitted the courts to exercise very little discretion. A convicted offender had to be sentenced to a designated institution for a prescribed minimum term of years. Today this method has been almost everywhere abandoned. The criminal code and the statutes now give the courts a wide measure of latitude in the matter of fixing sentences for convicted offenders. Only in rare cases does the law prescribe a definite penalty which must be imposed under all circumstances. As an aid to the proper exercise of the court's discretion, moreover, provision has now been made in many of the larger communities for the scientific study of each convicted person before sentence is determined. This study takes the form of an examination into the mental capacity of the individual, his physical condition, his antecedents, his life history, his

New methods in the treatment of convicted offenders.

The indeterminate sentence.

education, and his moral deficiencies. The purpose of such an examination is to place the court in a position where it can prescribe the type of treatment best calculated to reform the offender and at the same time give society the protection to which it is entitled.

Suspended sentences. First among the possibilities open to the court, on the basis of a favorable report, is the release of the prisoner on suspended sentence. This disposition is frequently made when the convicted person is shown to have no previous court record, or when the offense is merely a misdemeanor. In such cases a definite sentence is put upon the court records but with the stipulation that it is to be suspended during good behavior, and sometimes requiring that the offender shall remain within the jurisdiction of the court and report to it from time to time. If anyone who is out on suspended sentence gets into trouble, the suspension is forthwith revoked and he must serve the full term that was originally imposed.

Release on probation. In the case of serious crimes the practice of release on probation is now more commonly used. When an offender has been convicted of a serious crime, but where there are extenuating circumstances, he is usually permitted to apply for probation. Such applications are not received, as a rule, after conviction for murder, first-degree manslaughter, burglary, or the embezzlement of public funds, nor is it customary to ask for probation in the case of those who have already served a prison term. In any event the application is referred to the probation department for study and report before sentence is finally imposed. The judge, on receiving the probation officer's report and recommendation, decides what is best to do in the case. If he is convinced that more will be gained by releasing the prisoner under vigilant supervision than by confining him for a term in an institution of punishment, he grants the application. If he decides otherwise, the customary sentence is imposed and must be served.

Probation officers and their work. An offender, when placed on probation, is committed to the supervision of a probation officer, and must report to him at regular intervals. This officer is supposed to help his probationers in getting employment, to assist them in settling their personal problems, and in general to act the part of a helpful adviser. To perform these difficult functions successfully a probation officer must be an individual of quite unusual temperament and qualifications; but too often it happens that positions in this department are bestowed as political patronage upon men and women who utterly lack the capacity to win the confidence of those under them or be helpful in any real sense. The philosophy of the probation system is sound enough but in actual workings it is no better than the men and women who administer it.

If probation is denied and imprisonment decided upon, it usually becomes the duty of the judge to determine the proper length of the prison term. This is one of the most difficult things that a judge has to do, and nowhere does an incompetent jurist disclose his shortcomings more palpably than in badly adjusting the penalty to the merits of the case. For in this matter the courts are given very wide discretion, being some times empowered to punish a given offense by a sentence which may vary all the way from one to twenty years. Occasionally, however, the judge merely fixes the minimum and maximum, in which case a special prison board determines the exact term. After this is done, the actual duration of the imprisonment depends in some measure upon the prisoner's conduct and his apparent progress towards reformation. But no release can take place until the minimum term has been served, less the usual allowance for good behavior. The value of the indeterminate sentence is that it encourages the prisoner to become a coöperating agent in rehabilitation. And if he responds to this incentive he becomes eligible for release on parole any time after the completion of his minimum term. In most states there is a parole board which considers applications on behalf of prisoners for release in this way. After being given his freedom on parole, an ex-prisoner is expected to report to his parole officer at intervals and if he violates his parole by getting into trouble he can be rearrested and committed for the balance of his full term without any further court procedure.

Prison boards and paroles.

Finally, as a means of alleviating the rigor of punishment, there is the prerogation of pardon. Pardoning is not a part of the judicial process, but an executive act, which intervenes to mitigate the course of justice. Ordinarily any person confined in a state institution may apply to the governor for a pardon and anyone incarcerated in a city prison for offenses against the municipal ordinances may apply to the mayor for similar consideration. A pardon may be requested on the ground that the ends of justice have been served without further infliction of punishment, or because the original sentence was too severe, or because some ex-

Pardons.

tenuating circumstances have since come to light. Before acting on any petition for a pardon the executive authorities usually refer it to some appropriate board or official for investigation. Several of the states have placed limits upon the pardoning power of the governor by requiring the concurrence of a board of pardons, or by giving such a board the final decision upon such petitions. This is because the pardoning power, when left in the hands of a single executive officer, is likely to be abused. Governors and mayors have occasionally made use of it for political purposes.

Short term prisoners in city jails. When convicted persons are sentenced to prison for serious offenses, they usually go to institutions maintained by the county or the state, and the municipal authorities have no responsibility for their safekeeping. But every city has its own municipal jail or city prison, a house of detention which is used to incarcerate those who have been given short sentences for minor offenses as well as those who are awaiting trial. Very often those who are serving short terms are doing so because they have been unable to pay the fines that have been levied upon them. The practice of giving convicted persons a sentence of "ten dollars or ten days" is common, but archaic. The ten days often constitute nothing but a penalty for being poor. Those who cannot pay a fine should be allowed to go on suspended sentence until they can earn enough to cover it. Such an arrangement would save the city a large sum each year, for more than half the prisoners who have to be cared for and fed in municipal jails are there for the non-payment of their fines.

The segregation of prisoners. Until very recent times, moreover, the treatment of prisoners in city prisons afforded a striking illustration of man's inhumanity to man. Offenders of every type, young and old, whether convicted or awaiting trial, were thrown together without any segregation on a basis of age, color, or previous conviction of servitude. Confined in small, unsanitary, vermin-ridden, ill-ventilated and poorly lighted cells, they were often given poor food or insufficient food with little or no opportunity for exercise, bullied around by guards or keepers, and accorded every incentive to become hardened in their disrespect for the institutions of government. Even yet such conditions have not disappeared throughout the United States, although the cause of prison reform has made progress along many lines. Among other things it has succeeded to some extent in compelling the segregation of prisoners. Proper segre-

CRIME AND CORRECTION

gation means that prisoners shall be classified and kept in separate categories. Those who have not yet been convicted but are merely awaiting trial are given special consideration and not treated as incorrigibles. Young prisoners, even after conviction, are kept segregated from those of more advanced age. To accomplish this it is essential that alcoholics, drug addicts, and degenerates shall not be mingled with the general run of normal prisoners. Opportunity is also given for daily work, preferably in the open air at a prison camp.

All this means that the old-type city prison, with its rows of cell-blocks, is now obsolete in progressive communities. Instead of a single high-walled structure with iron-barred windows and dungeon cells, the up-to-date city prison is an institution that looks like an apartment house. Sometimes it occupies the upper floors of a building in which the courts hold their sessions. Facilities are available for keeping different classes of prisoners in separate sections of the building. The small cell gives way to the large ward or dormitory which a number of prisoners occupy together. Workshops are also provided in which various forms of industry are carried on. The practical difficulty in this connection is that of finding products which will not compete with private industries. In some cities it is the custom to pay prisoners a small daily wage for their work, these payments going to their dependents or being accumulated until they themselves have been released. *Gradual disappearance of the old-type prison.*

The city jail is under the supervision of an official known as the warden or superintendent. In some cities he is appointed by the mayor or the city manager, but more frequently there is a prison board, the members of which are appointed by the city's chief executive, and they in turn select the warden. The board system of management does not seem appropriate in this branch of municipal administration and it has rarely been found satisfactory. Too often the members of the prison board are selected from among local politicians and they choose one of their own kind to have immediate custody of the institution. In spite of the high importance of this post, the wardenship or superintendency of a city prison is either turned over to the chief of police ex officio or it is regarded as a choice plum of patronage to be handed over to some valiant supporter of the mayor. The average jail warden is inclined to think that he has done his whole duty if he keeps prisoners *Organization of the city jail.* *The warden or superintendent.*

from getting away. Few men in this position ever realize their opportunities for constructive work.

His staff. Under the warden or superintendent are a deputy and various guards, matrons, keepers, and other subordinate officials. They also are usually chosen by reason of their political influence, although in some cities they are now selected under civil service regulations. In the bright lexicon of human kindness the prison guard does not occupy a conspicuous place. His job is one which seems to make a special appeal to the man of domineering temperament who gets pleasure from tormenting the helpless and is callous to every variety of physical or mental suffering. Few of those who have immediate charge of prisoners in city jails are men with any real qualifications for their work or who have had any training in it. The essence of their technique is to enforce the rules by rigid discipline and to break the spirit of anyone who does not respond with a show of cheerfulness. For this situation the intermingling of jails and politics is mainly to blame.

The division of penal jurisdiction. Further administrative difficulties also result at times from the scattering of corrective authority over four areas of government in the United States—federal, state, county, and municipal. There are federal penitentiaries and other institutions of custody for those who have violated the federal laws and have been convicted in the federal courts. Likewise there are state prisons, reformatories, and reform schools maintained by funds from the state treasury and officered by persons who usually hold their appointments from the governor or from a prison board named by him. The county, again, has its house of correction, or county jail, or whatever it may be called. This is either under the jurisdiction of the county sheriff or of a warden who is appointed by the county board. Finally, there is the city jail or house of detention. Each of these institutions is independent of the others. Each has its own methods of procedure, discipline, and reformation. Each may have a different philosophy concerning the functions that it is expected to perform.

Obstacles in the way of prison reform. Penal correction has not yet advanced to the stage where it can be called either an art or a science. Its slow progress has been mainly due to the almost irreconcilable divergence at all points between prison reformers and prison officials. Prison reformers have been for the most part a well-intentioned but very sentimental group. They have had too much confidence in leniency as a way of reformation. Prison officials, on the other hand, are in general of an unbending type, averse to relaxing the rigidity of their ideas. Between the two groups it has not been easy to effect a reconciliation and the result, too often, has been a compromise that fails to satisfy either of them.

A satisfactory program should have in view, first of all, the ultimate transfer of all responsibility for penal incarceration from the city and county to the state. The city and county jails should be places of detention for those awaiting trial or held as material witnesses. No convicted person should be detained in them. It is only by following some such plan that adequate provision can be made for classifying and segregating prisoners, for ensuring them treatment that will be both scientific and humane, while keeping in mind the need of adequate protection against those who cannot or will not fit into the social scheme. Some day the work of penal correction ought to disappear from the list of municipal activities.

Some suggestions.

REFERENCES

John L. Gillin, *Criminology and Penology* (New York, 1926) is an exhaustive study covering all phases of this subject. It contains elaborate classified bibliographies. Lists of references may also be found in A. F. Kuhlman, *A Guide to Material on Crime and Criminal Justice* (New York, 1929). Mention should likewise be made of E. H. Sutherland, *Criminology* (Philadelphia, 1924), and of F. H. Wines, *Punishment and Reformation* (New York, 1919), an older book which is still of much value.

Other books that will be found of interest are Philip A. Parsons, *Crime and the Criminal* (New York, 1926), C. Phillipson, *Three Criminal Law Reformers: Beccaria, Bentham, Romilly* (New York, 1923), T. M. Osborne, *Prisons and Common Sense* (Philadelphia, 1924), L. N. Robinson, *Penology in the United States* (Philadelphia, 1921), Frank Tannenbaum, *Wall Shadows: a Study in American Prisons* (New York, 1922), K. R. O'Hare, *In Prison* (New York, 1923), William Healy and Augusta F. Bronner, *Delinquents and Criminals: Their Making and Unmaking* (New York, 1926), F. Alexander and H. Staub, *The Criminal, the Judge, and the Public* (New York, 1931), N. F. Cantor, *Crime, Criminals, and Criminal Justice* (New York, 1932), S. A. Queen and D. M. Mann, *Social Pathology* (New York, 1925), J. O. Stutzman, *Curing the Criminal* (New York, 1926), and *The Handbook of American Prisons*, issued in 1925 by the National Society of Penal Information (114 East 30th St., New York). The *Annals of the American Academy of Political and Social Science* devoted its issue of

May, 1931, to a series of articles on "Modern Crime: Its Prevention and Punishment."

Useful books on special topics are E. J. Cooley, *Probation and Delinquency* (New York, 1926), F. R. Johnson, *Probation for Juveniles and Adults* (New York, 1928), and A. A. Bruce and others, *Parole and the Indeterminate Sentence* (Springfield, Illinois, 1928).

The National Commission on Law Observance and Law Enforcement published in 1931 a *Report on Criminal Statistics*, with a check-list of official reports on the subject. In 1927 the National Crime Commission (120 Broadway, New York) issued a report on *Criminal Statistics and Identification of Criminals: on Pardons, Parole, Probation, Penal Laws, and Institutional Correction.*

Current discussions appear in the annual *Proceedings* of the American Prison Association (135 East 15th St., New York), and in the various publications of the National Committee on Prisons and Prison Labor (250 West 57th St., New York), as well as in the *Journal of the American Institute of Criminal Law and Criminology.*

See also the references at the close of Chapters XXIV and XXVI.

CHAPTER XXVIII

THE REGULATION OF BUILDINGS

> When we mean to build,
> We first survey the plot, then draw the model;
> And when we see the figure of the house,
> Then we must rate the cost of the erection.
> —Shakespeare, *King Henry IV*.

It is now more than seven hundred and fifty years ago since Henry Fitz-Elwyne, Lord Mayor of London, issued the pioneer ordinance known as the Assize of Buildings.[1] In this decree he set forth certain regulations under which all structures within the city should thereafter be built. It was stipulated, for example, that party walls must be three feet thick and made of stone. But arches one foot deep might be placed in these walls for cupboards. And no party wall could be torn down save with the consent of both owners. Roofs must be tiled and could no longer be covered with thatch. Various provisions were made regarding down spouts and gutters.

A pioneer building ordinance.

This early effort to provide for the safety of life and property in an urban community is the first in a long line of building codes leading down to the elaborate compilations of today which sometimes cover several hundred pages. It was followed, after the great London fire, by the Statute of 1667, which may be regarded as the first modern building code because it divided buildings into various classes and made definite rules as to the kind of construction permitted in each class. This code, moreover, was quite modern in that it fixed ceiling heights, established the thickness of walls, determined the minimum size of joists and girders, and provided that district surveyors should be appointed to enforce the law. Step by step, as cities have become more numerous and larger, the rules which govern the construction of buildings have grown more detailed, more technical, and more rigid.[2] Now-

Its numerous successors.

---

[1] This famous *Assize*, issued in 1189, is printed as a Supplement to the *National Municipal Review*, Vol. XVII, pp. 555–563 (September, 1928).

[2] "A Concise History of Building Codes from the Earliest Days" by Frank Burton may be found in *Engineering and Contracting*, Vol. LXVIII, pp. 82–85 (February, 1929).

adays, in every large city, the building code prescribes in great detail, from cellar to garret, the limits within which all new construction must be kept as respects both materials and methods.

<small>Objectives of a modern building code:</small>

<small>1. Structural stability.</small>

A building code has three protective purposes in view. First it aims to ensure that buildings shall stay up, and not fall down. Accordingly, some of its provisions are in the interest of structural stability. Regulations in the interest of structural safety are essential to protect the occupants of business establishments and homes from the avarice of speculative promoters and contractors who would build in the cheapest and most flimsy way if they were permitted to do it. Many buildings are put up to sell, and the speculative builder cares very little what becomes of them after the sale takes place. Regulations to ensure structural stability are especially needed in regions which may be visited by violent windstorms, heavy falls of snow on roofs, or earthquake shocks. Provisions with respect to the reinforcement of walls and the strengthening of chimneys, such as would not be essential under normal conditions, are urgently desirable in communities which lie in the vicinity of active geological faults. In all cases the requirements should be such as to provide a reasonable margin of safety but they ought not to go beyond this because every additional degree of structural strength means considerable expense and to that extent operates to retard the erection of new buildings. This, in turn, increases the scale of rents so that the occupant eventually has to pay the bills.

<small>2. Fire prevention.</small>

Second, the regulations embodied in a building code are designed to afford protection against the outbreak and rapid spread of fires. Perhaps half the provisions in a building code, or more than half, might be classed as fire-prevention rules. Such regulations are not uniform as respects all classes of buildings. Their scope and character depend upon the amount of fire hazard to which certain types of buildings are likely to be subjected by reason of their location or use.

<small>3. Sanitation and health protection.</small>

Finally, the building code contains numerous provisions which have nothing to do with either structural stability or fire prevention but are solely in the interest of sanitation and health. Its detailed provisions with respect to ventilating and plumbing come within this category. One may say, therefore, that all the regulations contained in a modern building code, no matter what their

THE REGULATION OF BUILDINGS 387

nature, have been placed there for the purpose of safeguarding either life, property, or health.

From what source do the city authorities derive their power to impose these requirements on owners of private property? Where do they get any right to dictate the maximum height to which a man may erect a building on his own land, or how thick its foundation walls must be, how wide its stairways, or how numerous its windows? By what legal authority does a city assume to tell the private builder how his heating apparatus must be installed, his plumbing put in, or his electric wires run through the walls? The answer is that every city, as a municipal corporation, is invested with a broad range of authority commonly known as its "police power." This general power, conveyed to the city by its charter or by the general laws of the state, includes the right to take all reasonable and appropriate measures for safeguarding the life, property, health, and morals of its people. The building code merely represents an exercise of this power, although a very comprehensive one. Even the rights which normally accrue to a private owner must give way before the urgent necessities of public well-being. *Salus populi est suprema lex.* Private ownership of land does not carry with it the right to create and maintain a nuisance, a menace, or an infringement upon the rights of others. *The code's legal basis.*

But in framing and enforcing a code of building regulations the city must not go beyond the purposes for which its authority was conferred. It must be prepared to convince the courts, when litigation arises, that every provision in the code can be defended as a reasonable and appropriate measure for the protection of the public safety, health, or morals within the scope of its police power as above explained. Thus a city cannot dictate the architectural design of a private building. It cannot prevent the erection of an eyesore, provided the building is safe and sanitary. The courts have not yet been willing to concede that the aesthetic sensibilities of the people need the same legal protection that is being accorded their personal safety or their health. Even within the bounds of its police power, moreover, the city's authority must not be used in an arbitrary way. For example, as between materials and methods which are equally safe for use in the construction of a building the regulations cannot prescribe that one must be used instead of the other. The private owner has a right to choose his *Limitations on the city's power to regulate buildings.*

materials and his methods so long as he keeps within the bounds which are demanded by reasonable precautions in the interest of safety and health. In general, however, if there is any doubt, the building code gets the benefit of it.

What a building code includes. A building code is a comprehensive ordinance, or, in some cases, a group of ordinances. Some cities have a building code and a separate plumbing ordinance, as well as an electrical inspection ordinance. A survey made by the United States Bureau of Standards in 1931 indicated that more than fifteen hundred American cities have codes of building regulations, many of them modelled upon the recommendations of the National Building Code Committee.[1] An effective code must of necessity cover a great variety of matters, such as the proportion of the available ground which a building may occupy, the maximum height of buildings, the range of materials which are permitted to be used, the structural strength of foundations, walls, floors and roof, the design of party walls and fire-stops, the construction of stairways and elevators, the adequacy of exits and fire escapes, the minimum provisions for light and air, the protection of furnaces, fireplaces, and chimneys, along with numberless rules relating to gas pipes and vents, plumbing fixtures, electric wiring, and water supply. Specifications with respect to signs and billboards are usually included but may be enacted in a separate ordinance. Finally, the building code establishes an agency for the enforcement of its provisions.

Who enforces its provisions? A few cities have consolidated the entire responsibility for enforcing all provisions of the building code in the hands of a single administrative department or division. This single department is given complete charge of all matters relating to structures, materials, plumbing, and electrical installation, as well as the inspection of elevators and steam boilers on the premises. A larger number of cities concentrate most of the work, but not all of it, within a single department, the buildings department, but place some of the responsibility elsewhere. For example, the inspection of plumbing is in some cities entrusted to the health department. In others the responsibility for electrical inspection has been turned over to the fire-prevention authorities. In New York City there is a separate bureau of buildings for each of the

---

[1] Publications of this Committee may be had from the Superintendent of Documents, Washington, D. C.

THE REGULATION OF BUILDINGS

five boroughs, but boiler inspection is a function of the police department and the inspection of electrical work has been devolved upon the department of water supply, gas, and electricity. A considerable number of cities, most of them not in the largest class, have entirely decentralized the responsibility for enforcing their building codes by dividing the work among a number of the regular city departments. In such cases the enforcement of the various regulations is divided around among the city engineer's office, police department, fire department, bureau of public lighting, health department, and licensing board. Occasionally the work of electrical inspection is not performed by the city authorities at all but is turned over to the fire underwriters.

There is some difference of opinion as to whether the integrated or disintegrated plan of enforcement is the more effective. On the one hand it is argued that all the provisions of a building code have a unified purpose, namely, to ensure the safety and bodily welfare of those who occupy the buildings concerned. From that point of view the consolidation of the entire responsibility under unified supervision is in accordance with the principles of sound administrative organization. Moreover, there is some danger of friction if inspectors representing different departments of the city insist on doing the work in their own time and way. *Centralized vs. decentralized enforcement.*

Likewise there are various economies which can be realized by the use of a single clerical force in connection with the inspectional work. When permits and certificates have to be obtained for each kind of construction, a great deal of inconvenience is placed upon builders and contractors through the necessity of visiting the various departments one by one to obtain these permits. It should be explained, of course, that the integrating of the responsibility does not mean that the same inspector must pass upon structural features, plumbing, electrical installation, and all other phases of the work. It is quite practicable to have different inspectors, each qualified in his own field, dividing the work among them. It is merely that under the unified system of enforcement they are all responsible to the same department head.

On the other hand there are some valid objections to this system of centralized inspectional responsibility. It can be argued, for example, that the regulations in the building code with respect to plumbing are placed there as a health measure and that their enforcement should be approached from the health point of *Objections to the centralized plan.*

view. But a plumbing inspector in the buildings department is a plumber, not a health expert. Hence he is likely to do his inspecting from the standpoint of what constitutes good workmanship rather than of what constitutes good hygiene. So with electrical inspection. The provisions in the building code with reference to wiring are placed there as a fire-prevention measure. They have nothing to do with structural stability, public health, morals, or convenience. It is contended, therefore, that the fire-prevention bureau rather than a central buildings department should be given the responsibility for enforcing such provisions.

Keeping even with the work. Every contractor knows, at any rate, that some branches of building construction must be finished before others can begin. The rough plumbing must be completed before walls are plastered or floors laid. Electrical conduits must be placed and inspected before they are covered by other work. Sometimes the interval between the finishing of one process and the beginning of another is very short and the inspection must take place during this brief interval, otherwise the work will be delayed. It is the essence of a good inspectional service that such delays shall be kept to a minimum. For when work is held up, pending the arrival of inspectors, there is both inconvenience and expense to all concerned. There are those who argue that the likelihood of these delays is smaller when a single department takes the whole responsibility than when it is shared by several of them.

Specialization in the work of enforcement. The work of building inspection obviously requires in every large city a considerable degree of specialization. This specialization assumes its most extreme form in New York City where one finds a chief inspector, assistant chief inspectors, engineer inspectors, inspectors of iron and steel, inspectors of carpentry and masonry, inspectors of plastering and fireproofing, inspectors of elevators, and inspector-specialists in every other line. Smaller cities do not carry things to such an extreme. At the same time it is obviously desirable to meet the feeling, which exists among contractors and builders, that an inspector who is perfectly competent in steel construction may know relatively little about brick work or carpentry, and may know nothing at all about plumbing or electric wiring. Unless a city is in the very largest class, however, the employment of special inspectors for each type of work means increased expense as well as the opportunity for friction and delay. The problem is one of working out a satisfactory compromise between the employment of specialists for every branch of building construction on the one hand, and the using of the same inspectors for all branches of it on the other. In this connection it should be borne in mind, however, that no building inspector is ever sent out to use his own discretion. His business is to enforce the rules. And if the rules have been framed with adequate preciseness, very little is left to the judgment of the individual inspector. Under such conditions it does not require a high degree of specialized expertness to determine whether the regulations are being observed.

This raises a question, however, concerning the advisability of making the regulations so specific and definite that they leave little or nothing to individual judgment or discretion. Materials and methods of building construction are constantly being changed and improved, so that some provisions of a code are bound to become inappropriate within a relatively short time after they have been framed. When this happens, the inspectors ought to have some leeway to approve work which meets the intent of the code even if it does not conform to the letter of the requirements. Otherwise the use of new and better materials is discouraged. All this is particularly true with respect to the plumbing and electrical trades in which changes come frequently. Rigid insistence on a literal interpretation of the rules in such cases does not result in better buildings but merely operates to increase the labor and expense through the continued use of materials, designs, or methods which have become out of date. Unfortunately this retention and enforcement of obsolete provisions in the building code is often inspired by local trade associations or labor unions in order that as much work as possible may be provided for members of these organizations. *The avoidance of too much detail in building codes.*

Provision should be made for keeping the building code in process of constant revision. It should be gone over at least once a year and minor adjustments made. Otherwise the inspectors will be placed under strong pressure to overlook small deviations and after a while they will develop the habit of overlooking more important ones. Moreover a building code should avoid the practice of requiring that certain specified materials, and no others, must be used. It should lay down the general specifications which the materials must meet, and within these limits the choice should be left to the builders. Unless this is done the city authorities *The need for frequent revisions.*

will be continually pressed to favor something which is under the control of local firms with political influence and which can only be procured through them.

The sinister pressure of private interests. This points to an ever-present danger against which cities should be placed on guard. Those who have patented materials or fixtures to sell, or who have a monopoly of certain processes, will do their best to force them on the market through the provisions of the building code. They will maintain a city hall lobby and bring political pressure to bear on the councilmen. All sorts of patented roofing materials are being sold with the assurance that they are fireproof, and every vendor feels that his product should be favored under the rules. Electrical contractors will insist that all concealed wires shall be placed in conduits, although this adds more to expense than to safety where small buildings are concerned. So with the cement manufacturers, steel jobbers, brickmakers, wired-glass vendors, plumbers, furnace men, gas-fixture merchants, and even the makers of so-termed fireproof paint—they all want provisions which might be desirable if owners did not have to consider the cost. City councils should remember that the provisions of a building code defeat their purpose if they impose requirements which, however technically desirable, result in raising the cost of construction to an excessive figure.

Uniformity and variety in the regulations. It is not possible to devise a code of building regulations which will suit all cities of varying sizes located in different parts of the country. Materials which are cheap in one section may be much more expensive in others. The methods which are used in individual localities, if they serve the ends reasonably well, ought not to be warped into conformance with provisions of a uniform building code. Some flexibility should be allowed to take care of variations in local practice. On the other hand it is desirable that there should be a reasonable amount of uniformity in the building codes of those cities which are located close together in the same region; otherwise there will be some unfair competition among them. For speculative builders will be tempted to operate in those communities which have lax building regulations and have lower construction costs on that account. The difference between the cost of construction in a city which has stringent building regulations and one in which the rules are lax may be as much as seven to ten per cent. Moreover, a strict building code will prohibit certain types of buildings which lax regulations allow.

Whole streets of jerry-built structures, such as three-decker tenements, are sometimes rushed up in those municipalities which are willing to tolerate them. In the long run a city pays the penalty for laxity in its building regulations, but for the moment it may experience a building boom and gain some advantage through the increased tax-value of the land on which these structures are erected.

A building code should classify structures according to their occupancy and use. In a city of any considerable size there will be at least a half-dozen classes of buildings. First, there are buildings of a public or semi-public nature in which the safeguarding of life is vitally important,—for example, in auditoriums, theaters, schools, and other places of large public resort. Buildings of this kind require a special margin of safety and should be subjected to stringent rules concerning the use of fire-resisting materials, the adequacy of exits, the width of stairways, and so forth. In the second place there are buildings which, from the nature of their use, have a high fire hazard; such, for example, are garages, paint factories, dry cleaning establishments, sash and door mills, lumber storage sheds, and all industries which keep large quantities of inflammable or explosive substances on hand. Buildings in this class are subjected to stringent regulations, not so much for the protection of persons but of property. The endeavor is made to keep them isolated by distance or by fire-walls from other buildings.

Third, we have buildings occupied by such industrial establishments as do not have a high fire hazard but in which there are large bodies of employees whose safety might be endangered by deficiencies of structural strength. Textile factories, makers of ready-to-wear clothing, cigar factories, and the like are in this category. In the fourth class are warehouses, wholesale establishments, retail stores, offices and similar buildings in which the rules are not usually so strict unless the buildings are of considerable height. Fifth, there are the hotels and large apartment houses, boarding houses, and other places of residence which have a dozen or more sleeping rooms. In this class it is customary to include hospitals and other institutions for the sick or indigent. Sixth come the duplex and three-family dwellings, likewise the bungalow courts, auto courts, and other groups of small structures situated very close together; and finally there is the large class of

The classification of buildings.

single-family homes. It should not be understood, however, that the foregoing classification is anything more than illustrative. Every city works out its own scheme based on local conditions.

Special provisions for each class. Each class of buildings should have a section of the code devoted to it. Provisions in this section should indicate the type of construction which must be used, the percentage of the lot which may be built upon, the distance which the building must be located from each boundary line of the lot (including the street boundary), the permissible materials to be used in the construction of foundations, walls, partitions, floors and roof, the limitations on minimum size of rooms and height of ceilings, the regulations as to stairways and elevators, the requirements as to standpipes, fire extinguishers and other fire-fighting apparatus when such are prescribed, the number and location of exits, the regulations as to plumbing installations, including traps and vents, the requirements as respects the protection of heating apparatus, the rules in relation to the materials and methods of electric wiring, and all the other incidents of construction which are deemed worthy to be subjected to regulation.

Arrangement and interpretation of the building code. When such things are specified for each class of structures, it can readily be seen that the building code of a large city is by no means a brief or simple document. On the contrary it is usually an elaborate compilation filled with intricate provisions and technical terms. As a rule the ordinary layman cannot make much out of it. Rather it serves as a textbook for architects, contractors, and building inspectors. Even they do not always understand it. To make matters worse, most building codes are poorly arranged, without a proper or logical grouping of the various provisions, and sometimes unprovided with an index. Amendments have to be made frequently, and since these amendments are not always consistent with the other provisions of the code, the outcome is sometimes a hopeless jumble of rules, provisions, qualifications, and exceptions which cannot be enforced without a great deal of misunderstanding and resentment. Careful attention should therefore be given by the city authorities not only to the contents but to the arrangement of the building code, and if the amendments are numerous the entire compilation should be thoroughly revised and reprinted every few years. The cost of this reprinting can be defrayed by making a nominal charge for copies of the code whenever architects, builders, or owners ask for them.

THE REGULATION OF BUILDINGS

Although there is little uniformity among cities as to the provisions of their building codes, there is a considerable degree of uniformity as respects the granting of permits and the methods of inspection. In the first place it is everywhere required that any owner desiring to construct a new building or remodel an old one, no matter what the character of the structure may be, must first obtain a building permit at the city hall. Such permits are required for everything in the way of structural work except minor repairs. In order to obtain the permit an application must be filed stating the nature of the work to be done and the approximate cost. In the case of a new building, or of a considerable remodelling, it is usually required that complete blueprint plans be also filed. *The machinery of enforcement:* *1. Building permits.*

These applications and plans are thereupon examined by the officials of the buildings department to make sure that they conform with the requirements of the code. Most cities require that the plans be filed in duplicate so that one may be returned when the permit is granted while the other is retained in the archives of the department. If the officials find that the plans do not entirely conform with the requirements, they delay the granting of a permit until the discrepancy has been set right. But if a careful examination proves the plans to be satisfactory, the permit is forthwith granted on payment of the calculated fee. Architects and builders who are doing construction work in any city make it their business to become thoroughly familiar with the provisions of the code and hence do not often submit plans which fail to gain approval. *2. Examination of plans.*

On receiving his building permit the owner or contractor can go ahead with the work, but at various stages in the construction he must notify the authorities that his job is ready for inspection. Thereupon the inspector whose business it is to examine the foundations or walls or framework will come around and sign his name to a certificate which is posted in some conspicuous place adjacent to the work. Again, when the plumbing is roughed-in, there is a further notification and another inspector comes around. So with the electrical work, the plastering, and the finished plumbing. A half-dozen or more inspectional visits may be made in the course of the construction. Finally, in some cities, there is a requirement that an occupancy permit must be obtained when the building is completed, this document certifying that the inspection requirements have been satisfied at every stage of the work and that the building may now be occupied. *3. Inspections.* *4. Certificates of occupancy.*

Special inspections.

Obviously it is essential that all requests for inspection shall be promptly complied with, otherwise the progress of work will be seriously delayed. To expedite this work the larger communities are usually mapped out into districts with a quota of inspectors assigned to each. These inspectors receive each day a record of all the requests that come in, and an endeavor is made to comply with them within the next twenty-four hours. The work of an inspection department, however, is not completed when the building is finished. At intervals thereafter the building code usually requires that certain features of a building shall be inspected, for example, boiler plants in industries, elevators in office buildings and other high structures, exits in theaters and auditoriums, fire escapes in school buildings, and the fire-extinguishing apparatus in various structures of a hazardous nature.

Securing compliance with the building rules.

What happens if the owner or contractor proceeds with work which has not received the inspector's approval? Sometimes the inspector posts a "Stop Work" order which is enforced by the police if necessary. And every violation of the building code is usually declared to be a misdemeanor which can be punished by fine or imprisonment. In addition some cities have provided for the licensing of all contractors including plumbing and electrical workers. In such cases if a contractor fails to observe the regulations his license can be suspended or taken away from him. As a matter of fact, however, the inspectors have little difficulty in securing compliance with the provisions of their code when they insist upon it, but these officials are not always exacting, especially when they owe their appointment to the backing of political friends. Too many inspections are of a casual sort because the officials are being hurried from one job to another and frequently lack the time that is needed to do their work carefully. Evasions of the code are not uncommon for this reason and also because inspectors sometimes tolerate minor ones rather than make trouble for owners or contractors who are politically influential.

Appeals.

As a rule the inspector's decision in any matter is not final. If the buildings department refuses to issue a permit, or if the inspector insists on a too-rigid interpretation of the rules, the owner or contractor usually has a right of appeal to a special board which is established for this purpose. Members of this board are generally paid for their services on a per diem basis. The owner or contractor also has a further appeal to the courts if he feels that the rules are

THE REGULATION OF BUILDINGS

arbitrary or unreasonable and hence constitute a deprivation of property without due process of law. Application can be made in such cases for a writ of mandate (mandamus) to compel the issuance of a permit.

The size of the inspectional force varies with the size of the city and the amount of construction that is going on. In boom times an increase in the number of inspectors is necessary and even at that they are hard pressed to get over the ground. Then, when a depression comes and building operations drop off, the force is reduced by dropping inspectors from the payroll at a time when it is difficult for them to find any other employment. This is penny-wise economy on the city's part because it gives vogue to the impression that the inspector's job is a precarious one and does not provide much assurance of permanent tenure. Experienced inspectors should not be laid off when new construction slackens but should be used to make reinspections of older buildings, in order to search out cracked walls, shaky stairways, rotted timbers, broken-down plumbing, and other things which need correction. It is not enough to make sure that buildings are safe and sanitary when erected. They ought to be inspected at intervals to make sure that they remain so. *The corps of inspectors.*

In many of the larger cities the building inspectors are chosen by civil service competition. A customary requirement for eligibility is that the applicant shall have had experience as an architect, construction engineer, builder, or foreman in charge of building operations. The written examination is usually a rigid one, covering such matters as the strength of materials, structural design, load distribution, and construction methods, besides exacting a thorough familiarity with the provisions of the code. In some types of inspection the positions are limited to engineers who have been graduated from recognized educational institutions. Unfortunately, however, the civil service regulations often provide for the making of temporary appointments, without examination, and these appointees may manage to hold their jobs on such basis for several years. A stricter enforcement of the merit system would raise the general standards in the inspectional service. *Their selection by civil service tests.*

The cost of administering the provisions of a building code, including the inspections, is defrayed from the fees for permits. It is sometimes argued that no charge should be made for permits and inspections because the building code is a public measure, in *Financing the cost of inspection.*

the interest of safety and health, and should be enforced at the public expense like any other municipal ordinance. But the generally prevailing view at the city halls of the country is that these costs should not be saddled on the public treasury because they may properly be regarded as necessary items in the expense of construction. Much controversy has been carried on with respect to this issue. Owners and contractors assert that they derive no direct benefit from the city's scrutiny of their plans or from the visits of the inspectors. They see no more reason why they should pay for such services than that the motorist on the highway should pay a fee to the policeman who stops him to inspect his brakes or his headlights. But the custom of charging for building permits has become virtually universal and most citizens believe it to be a proper one, provided the fees do not exceed the amount necessary to reimburse the city for what it spends on the work.

How fees are fixed. There are two methods of fixing these fees. The more common method is to base the charges upon the estimated cost of the building, but in a descending ratio,—for example, a fee of five dollars for the first thousand dollars of estimated cost, then two dollars per thousand up to fifty thousand, and one dollar per thousand thereafter. The other plan is to base the fee upon the cubic content or floor area of the building—for example, ten cents per thousand cubic feet or two dollars per thousand square feet of floor area. In any event the contractor usually includes an allowance for these fees in his bid and assumes them as part of the contract price. As a rule the payments are made to the buildings department and then turned in by it to the general city treasury.

The advantages of adequate and vigilant building inspection are not usually appreciated by the public until some disaster, such as the collapse of a badly built structure or a preventable fire involving loss of life, stirs the whole citizenship to indignation. Then the civic conscience becomes aroused and there is a city-wide demand for the punishment of those whose laxity has been at fault. But it is obviously better to prevent than to punish. A policy is better than a protest—it will save more lives and property.

REFERENCES

There is no book on the general subject covered in the foregoing chapter, although a treatise on building codes and their enforcement is much to be desired. The best source of information in this field is the series of publications which contain the annual *Proceedings* of the Building Officials' Conference of America (District Building, Washington, D. C.). The various publications of the National Building Code Committee, United States Department of Commerce, are also useful. These include a report on *Recommended Practice for the Arrangement of Building Codes* (revised edition, Washington, 1926).

In 1931 a *Tabulation of Building and Plumbing Codes* was issued by the United States Department of Commerce, and attention should also be called to the *Proposed Building Code for New York City* prepared by the Merchants' Association of New York in 1932. A useful pamphlet on *The Preparation and Revision of Local Building Codes*, by G. N. Thompson, was issued in 1927 by the Municipal Administration Service. The National Board of Fire Underwriters (85 John St., New York) issued the fifth edition of its *Fire Underwriters' Code* in 1931, and it has also sponsored a *Code of Suggested Ordinances for Small Municipalities*. Much serviceable information is likewise contained in the booklet on *The Administration of Regulatory Inspectional Services in American Cities*, by Edna Trull, published by the Municipal Administration Service in 1932 (pp. 81–117). The *Book of Standards* (2 vols., Philadelphia, 1927), issued by the American Society for Testing Materials (1315 Spruce St., Philadelphia), is a reference book of prime value to building inspectors.

CHAPTER XXIX

THE INSPECTION OF WEIGHTS AND MEASURES

There shall be one measure of wine throughout our whole kingdom, and one measure of ale, and one measure of grain, . . . and one width of dyed cloth . . .; and of weights, moreover, it shall be as of measures.—Magna Carta, Section 35.

<small>The fixing of uniform standards for the entire country.</small>
There is a common impression that jurisdiction over weights and measures is exercised by the national government, an impression which seems to have arisen from the mere fact that the standards are uniform throughout the United States. It is true that the national Constitution gives Congress the power "to fix the standard of weights and measures," and under this provision various units of length, mass, and capacity have been established by federal law; but there is no federal agency charged with the enforcement of these standards or with the inspection of weights and measures throughout the country. This duty of inspection has been left to the states, and by them it has frequently been devolved upon the municipal authorities.

<small>The Bureau of Standards.</small>
The Bureau of Standards at Washington is the custodian of the national standards of weights and measures. One of its primary functions is to supply the states with exact replicas of these national standards so that uniformity may be ensured, but the Bureau thereafter acts in an advisory capacity only and takes no active part in the work of inspection or enforcement. In other words, Congress has placed the problem of weights and measures' supervision squarely up to the various states, leaving them free to provide such enforcement machinery as they deem advisable. As a result of this discretion the several states have handled the problem of organizing their inspectional systems in a variety of ways, but most of them can be classified into three groups on a basis of the general methods which they use.

<small>Three plans of enforcement:</small>
In some states the entire responsibility for the work of inspection is exercised by state officials who function directly under the control and supervision of a central state supervisor of weights and measures. The inspectors under his immediate jurisdiction

go about the state from one community to another, testing all appliances, the local authorities being given no responsibility whatever. This plan promotes a high degree of uniformity in weights and measures' supervision throughout the state. It makes the rules and specifications state-wide in their operation and ensures that exactly similar methods of testing will be used by all the inspecting officers. State jurisdiction provides the simplest plan of enforcement and is in many ways the most satisfactory. But it involves the centralization of all authority at the state capitol and for that reason is sometimes regarded by the municipalities as repugnant to the principle of municipal home rule. ^{1. State inspection.}

The second plan is a dual arrangement under which state and local inspectors divide the work between them. But the division of responsibility does not proceed along the same lines in all the states which have adopted this plan. In general the customary practice is for the state inspectors to assume the task of testing commercial weights and measures in the rural sections and in the small urban communities, while resident municipal inspectors are given responsibility for the work in cities and in the larger incorporated towns. In addition the state department sometimes exercises a general supervision over these resident municipal inspectors. The dual plan of inspection is thought to have the advantage of economy in that it provides resident inspectors in the thickly populated sections where there is need for full-time officials, while supplying state service for those rural and small communities in which the inspectional work may take only a few days of an official's time each year. Left to themselves these rural communities would not appoint full-time inspectors because of the expense involved; on the other hand a part-time official, paid by the day, rarely proves to be expert at his task. Moreover, the plan of leaving these small communities to do the work for themselves would result in a lack of uniformity among them. 2. Division of responsibility between the state and local authorities.

A number of states pursue the third plan, which is to delegate the entire responsibility for inspection and testing to the local communities. Sometimes the work is made a county function, with provision, however, that the larger municipalities within the county may have inspectors of their own. This is a good arrangement in that it permits the use of full-time inspectors exclusively. Some states which follow the plan of local autonomy in this field of administration have nevertheless provided for the maintenance 3. Municipal inspection.

of a central state office with a general supervisory jurisdiction over the work of the county and city inspectors. Other states make no such provision but leave the local inspectors wholly unsupervised. And there are a few states in which no provision has been made for the regular inspection of weights and measures by anyone either in the state or municipal service. Occasionally, in these last-named states, the local authorities have been given statutory power to provide inspectional service if they desire to do so. In such cases the more populous communities generally establish something of the kind while the rest do not.

Scope of the inspector's functions. There is a popular notion that the sole duty of a weights and measures' inspector is to protect the interests of the retail purchaser, in other words to see that the local storekeepers or marketmen do not give short weight to their customers. But the inspector's duty is much more comprehensive than this. It is his function to safeguard the interests of all who are concerned in a sale, both those who buy and those who sell. His business is to protect the merchant to the same extent as the customer. And it occasionally happens that the inspector finds a piece of weighing or measuring equipment which is in error against the vendor and in favor of the customer. Nor is the inspector concerned with retail weighing and measuring appliances solely. Retail devices, it is true, receive the major portion of his attention, but this is merely because the number of weights and measures used in retail establishments is so large. Often a single small retail store will have a dozen or more scales, measures, and containers which must be tested and approved, whereas a wholesale dealer in coal, grain, or potatoes may have only one set of platform scales in his entire establishment.

His services to the public convenience. Furthermore, the retail purchaser has no practicable opportunity to safeguard his own interests. The wholesaler or jobber or commission merchant can easily check up on his bulk purchases, but the small customer at retail cannot reweigh and remeasure everything that he buys. To expect him (or her) to do this would be to impose great inconvenience on thousands of shoppers. The public must therefore be given assurance that their interests are being safeguarded by a thorough and frequent inspection of all weighing and measuring appliances. And this is not simply to protect the customer against intentional fraud on the part of those who sell to him. Most deviations from exact weight and measure are not the result of fraudulent intent. They are the outcome of carelessness, or in some cases misapprehension. The inspector's duty is to see that all deviations are corrected, no matter how they are caused.

The daily routine of a weights and measures inspector includes a number of things. First of all, he is supposed to inspect and test, by means of his own standardized equipment, all mechanical devices of whatever sort that are used in connection with the purchase and sale of merchandise. This may sound like a simple task, but the average citizen does not visualize what it implies. It means that the inspector is going to find himself confronted with railroad scales, truck and wagon scales, platform scales, counter scales, computing scales, prescription scales in drug stores, baskets and containers of a hundred varieties, liquid-measuring devices, milk jars, gasoline pumps, electric, gas, and water meters, yardsticks, tapelines, and taximeters, not to speak of avoirdupois weights, troy weights, and weights of a dozen other kinds ranging from those ponderous discs which are used to determine whether a truck is loaded above the maximum permitted on the highways to the almost invisible slivers of metal which go on the delicate balances of the apothecary's counter. The inspector is assumed to possess an expert's knowledge of all these devices and weights, to have means of accurately testing them, and to be able to make whatever adjustments are needed to ensure their accuracy. *Variety of the appliances that have to be tested.*

Nor is the work of the inspector restricted to testing and adjustment alone. For even though a tradesman's weights and measures are found to be accurate, it is still possible for him to do his customers injustice by including paper containers within the net weight, or by failing to give full measure as defined by the regulations, or by using divers other small stratagems which are known to shopkeepers of questionable integrity. Accordingly the inspector is supposed to come around unexpectedly and check weighed or measured parcels which have been wrapped for delivery. Likewise he drops in at filling stations where he is not known to the operators. With a carefully measured quantity of gasoline in his regular tank, or with an auxiliary tank, he instructs them to "fill her up" and then checks on the result. He calls a taxicab on a given street corner and then asks to be driven over a stretch that has already been measured. In some cases he or his deputies go into places of business and make purchases themselves, specifying the exact amount which they desire and then bringing the parcels *Investigating alleged violations of the law.*

to the central office for a verification test. Some of this investigating work is done in response to complaints which come from patrons of retail stores, milk dealers, gasoline stations, produce markets, and taxi stands. Such complaints, if verified by the inspector's investigation, usually result in a warning for the first offense, but if this warning is not heeded the evidence is turned over to the proper authorities for prosecution.

Inspections to determine quality.

Then there is the matter of enforcing the rules of law as to quality of merchandise. In many cities the functions of the weights and measures department are not confined to quantitative tests and investigations. Where there are laws and ordinances relating to the quality of the merchandise which may be sold, the additional duty of enforcing such standards is often imposed upon the weight and measures department. These qualitative standards apply to such commodities as milk, vinegar, gasoline, oil, and coal. The inspection of milk is customarily entrusted to the health department, as is quite proper; but qualitative tests of gasoline, oil, and fuel are made by the inspectors of weights and measures as part of their regular routine. For this purpose the chief inspector of weights and measures maintains a small testing laboratory if there is work enough to be done, but in smaller communities the samples are usually sent to state headquarters for analysis. It is not within the province of the weights and measures inspectors to enforce the regulations as respects the purity of food and drugs, but when a vigilant inspector in the course of his routine finds reason for suspecting the quality of meats, fish, fruits, vegetables, or drugs, he is supposed to impart his suspicions to the health officials.

Primary, office, and field standards for testing.

The federal government has supplied to each of the states a complete set of uniform standards. These are retained at the state capitol under special guardianship. "The primary standard of mass (or weight, as it is commonly called) is a cylinder of specially treated platinum-irridium alloy; the corresponding standard of length is a bar of similar material and of unusual cross-section, the defining lines being so finely engraved that a microscope is required for observing them. From standards of this high order there extends a long sequence of standards of lesser refinement, until finally we reach the cast-iron weight and the wooden yardstick of trade."[1] Using the set of primary standards in the custody of

---

[1] Ralph W. Smith, *Weights and Measures Administration*, Handbook Series of the National Bureau of Standards, No. 11 (Washington, 1927), p. 100.

the state, a sufficient number of "office standards" are made and these are delivered to the cities and counties. From these office standards a set of working standards or field standards is provided for each inspector. Field standards are tested with the office standards from time to time, and these again with the primary standards. For heavy testing (*e.g.*, coal and hay scales) the state authorities usually provide such special equipment as is necessary, and this is loaned to municipalities when needed.

In cities of over 100,000 population it is customary to have a department or bureau of weights and measures consisting of a chief inspector (sealer) and one or more subordinates. The chief official is usually appointed by the mayor or the city manager, but sometimes the choice is made under civil service rules. All the inspectors, including the head of the organization, ought to be chosen in that way. The work is of a specialized character and requires expertness as well as integrity. Political appointments, with consequent inefficiency in this branch of municipal administration, are sure to be costly to the public. Where the inspectional staff consists of several persons, it is sometimes the practice to divide the work on a functional basis, with certain inspectors devoting their entire attention to gasoline pumps, others to platform scales, and others again to small retail weights and measures. In the largest cities a special inspector is assigned to the testing of taxicab meters. Smaller cities frequently combine the work of inspection with various other duties such as the supervision of the public market or the inspection of buildings in process of construction. In such cases the work is apt to be ineffectively done. *Organization of the inspectional staff.*

When a new employee is taken on the staff, he is usually given a certain amount of instruction before being set to work. He is required to familiarize himself with the design, construction, and operation of the various types of scales, linear-measuring devices, and meter services. In addition he studies the laws, specifications, and tolerances relating to weights and measures. Finally, he is instructed in the technique of testing. When this is finished, an experienced inspector takes the recruit along with him on one of his regular tours of duty. The new man first observes the inspector's work, then assists him in it, and presently is fitted to go out alone. The rapidity with which a new employee learns the art is dependent upon his native intelligence and his mechanical sense. The competent official, moreover, does not quit learning when he *The training of inspectors.*

has finished his probationary period. He keeps abreast of developments by informing himself about the various new appliances, and the modifications of older devices, which are being put on the market by manufacturers of scales, measures, weights, and containers.

Number and nature of inspections. The number of inspectors required in a city depends somewhat upon its size but to an even greater extent it is dependent upon the frequency and thoroughness with which inspections are made. Some state laws and city ordinances specify annual inspection, while others require that they be made semi-annually. In addition it is usually provided that certain weights and measures shall be tested at more frequent intervals, for example, taximeters, gasoline pumps, milk bottles, and scales used for weighing ice. The requirement in such cases is for quarterly or even monthly inspection. It is also assumed that the inspectors will make surprise visits from time to time, or "try-out inspections" as they are called, and likewise will make visits to investigate complaints. Attempts have been made to work out tables showing the normal amount of inspectional work which a competent inspector may reasonably be expected to do within a given period of time, but these attempts have not proved fruitful because of the wide variation which exists in the requirements of cities. A recent survey, for example, showed that over 120,000 tests were made in Buffalo during the course of a single year, resulting in the discovery of about 1,500 incorrect weights or measures. In Seattle, a city about three-fifths as large, there were during the same year only 20,000 tests, but more than 2,000 appliances were found incorrect. Obviously the testing must have been done with a good deal more thoroughness in the latter city than in the former; but in any event the figures show how great a disparity can be found in different parts of the country.[1]

Fees for inspection. Originally it was the custom to defray the cost of weights and measures inspection by charging certain fees, and this practice still continues in some communities, although it is being generally abandoned. The argument usually advanced in favor of the fee system is that the inspector performs certain services which are not required by law or ordinance,—for example, in making slight

---

[1] See Edna Trull, *The Administration of Regulatory Inspectional Services in American Cities*, Municipal Administration Service Publication No. 27 (New York, 1932), p. 155.

INSPECTION OF WEIGHTS AND MEASURES

repairs or corrections to scales and balances which are found to be out of adjustment. But the system of charging fees is open to serious practical objections, particularly in that it inclines the owners of weighing and measuring devices to look with hostility upon the inspector's visits. They feel that he is making a profit from the discharge of his official duties and hence is under temptation to inspect more often than the occasion requires. Moreover the fee system places the inspector under pressure to make a good financial showing. It encourages him to do his work quickly so that he can cover more ground and make more collections.

Why the fee system is objectionable.

The inspection of weights and measures ought to be regarded solely as a matter of mutual protection for vendor and purchaser. It should not be looked upon as the means of raising municipal revenue. Consequently the officials of the weights and measures inspectional service should be paid regular salaries like all other municipal officials and employees, and these salaries should be fixed at a point where they suffice to draw competent men into the service. Apart from the chief inspector, the usual remuneration of officials in this branch of city administration is about $2,000 per year, which is hardly sufficient to obtain and keep the best men in the service. On the other hand it is high enough to attract the covetous eyes of young politicians who find themselves unable to hold steady jobs in private employ.

Salaried inspectors are preferable.

An inspector of weights and measures is not entitled to use his own discretion. His business is to enforce the laws and ordinances. Accordingly the provision of these laws and ordinances should be clear and specific in their requirements. They should definitely prescribe the ways in which particular kinds of commodities may be sold. For example, the law should determine whether vegetables and fruits shall be sold by weight or by measure. It should define such terms as barrel of apples, cord of wood, loaf of bread, print of butter, brick of ice cream, and so forth, because such terms mean different things in different parts of the country. Likewise all cartons, cases, cans, boxes, packages, and other containers should be required to bear a statement of their net contents.

Making the rules specific.

The inspector's task is simplified when the regulations are clear and definite, allowing no reason for controversy. Laws and ordinances relating to weights and measures should likewise provide appropriate penalties for those who are convicted of violating them. A distinction, however, should be made between offenses

Enforcing them by prosecution.

due to carelessness or negligence and those which are the outcome of a fraudulent intent. Giving short weight or deficient measure to customers day after day, even when due to carelessness, should not be regarded as a light offense, to be dismissed with a warning or placed on file, but should be penalized by the imposition of a fine. The keeper of a store or filling station who deliberately defrauds his customers should be punished with greater severity.

Allowing leeway in the form of tolerances.

It is not to be expected, of course, that weights and measures of all kinds will be found absolutely accurate at every inspection. Even with reasonable care and strict honesty some deviations from perfection will be found. Parts of scales will become outworn, screws will work loose, dust will collect on certain parts of the mechanism, and other slight misadjustments will occur. Mechanical weighing and measuring devices are not always perfectly accurate when they leave the factory. In any case they deteriorate with use. Hence, it is customary for the laws and ordinances to provide what is known as a "scale of tolerances," in other words a scale of maximum variations from the true standard of performance which the inspector is permitted to allow when he tests commercial weighing and measuring devices. A generation ago it was customary to leave the breadth of such variations to the judgment or discretion of the individual inspector, but this led to much confusion because each inspector had his own code of strictness.

The old method.

The new plan.

So today the general practice is to fix the scale of tolerances with such definiteness that there can be no possibility of misunderstanding. More particularly it has been found advisable to apply this definiteness to what are known as "commodity tolerances," in other words the limits of permissible variation in the amount of commodities which are packed and delivered with certain designations of weight or measure on the wrapper, can, box, bottle, or other container. It is obviously impossible for the net contents of these containers to be in all cases absolutely uniform. Hence, a reasonable amount of excess or shortage from the announced weight or measure must be tolerated. As a rule it is not deemed advisable to make this scale of tolerances public, because the publication of permissible variations might encourage packers and dealers to aim at the minimum quantities permitted by the tolerance table rather than the full amounts represented on the package. Some cities have endeavored to meet this problem by specifying their tolerances in average rather than in individual

INSPECTION OF WEIGHTS AND MEASURES 409

limits. In other words they require that the average variation in a given number of samples shall not be greater than the limit which the ordinance prescribes.

When a weights and measures inspector finds that scales or weights are inaccurate beyond the prescribed limits of tolerance, he prohibits their further use until necessary repairs or adjustments have been made. In many cases he is able to make the slight adjustments himself. Otherwise he condemns the appliances until they have been sent out for repairs, in which case a retesting is necessary after they come back. In extreme cases the inspector may condemn the weighing and measuring devices permanently. When either a temporary or a permanent ban is imposed, the equipment is marked with a red tag which the inspector signs. This tag is then attached to the rejected device by means of a lead seal but in such a way that the sealing does not interfere with the making of repairs. A severe penalty is provided for any unauthorized person who removes this seal, or for anyone who uses the condemned apparatus until it has been retested and approved. {Condemning appliances.}

The National Conference on Weights and Measures, which has been in existence since 1905, has done a great deal to improve the standards of weights and measures administration throughout the United States. Its membership includes state, county, and municipal inspectors, together with representatives of those concerns which manufacture weighing and measuring appliances. The objects of the conference are to promote uniformity with respect to laws, specifications, and tolerances, to standardize methods of testing, as well as to improve the technique of inspection and enforcement. The conference has worked in close coöperation with the National Bureau of Standards. Actions of the conference have no mandatory application but are merely recommendations to the public authorities, but they have carried great weight with legislatures and city councils throughout the country. {The National Conference on Weights and Measures.}

REFERENCES

The most useful manual on this subject is Ralph W. Smith, *Weights and Measures Administration*, included in the Handbook Series of the National Bureau of Standards (Washington, 1927). The *Proceedings* of the National Conference on Weights and Measures are also published annually by the Bureau of Standards. The American Institute of Weights and Measures (33 Rector St., New York) has issued a sixty-four page booklet entitled

Our American System of Weights and Measures (New York, 1924). A good chapter on the "Regulation of Weights and Measures" is included in *The Administration of Regulatory Inspectional Services in American Cities* by Edna Trull, published by the Municipal Administration Service in 1932 (pp. 135–160).

CHAPTER XXX

FIRE PREVENTION

> Never did any public misery
> Rise of itself; God's plagues still grounded are
> On common stains of our humanity;
> And to the flame that ruineth mankind,
> Man gives the matter, or at least gives wind.
> —*Fulke Greville.*

The protection of life and property against fire includes two different enterprises, namely, fire prevention and fire fighting. American cities have been maintaining highly efficient fire-fighting units for a long time, but until relatively recent years they have given very little attention to the problem of reducing the number of fires that need to be fought. So much intelligence and money have been devoted to the improvement of the extinguishing apparatus and to the better training of personnel that municipal fire-fighting services in the United States are far superior to those found in any European country. They excel in machine technique, in speed, and in their knowledge of fire-fighting tactics. {Our efficiency in fire fighting.}

But there the superiority ends. As respects the science of fire prevention, as distinguished from the art of handling fires after they start, the cities of the United States have lagged far behind. This lack of balance is somewhat surprising in view of the large amount of care that has been bestowed on preventive work in other municipal departments,—in the health department, for example. The main objective of a city health department is to prevent an epidemic of disease from breaking out. It does not content itself with elaborate preparations for the handling of such outbreaks after they occur. At any rate the placing of inadequate stress upon fire prevention has helped to defeat the purpose for which a fire department exists,—that of keeping fire losses down. These losses have not been kept down. They have been increasing more rapidly than the growth of population. The population of the United States just about doubled in the forty years intervening between 1890 and 1930, but during this period the annual fire losses more than quadrupled. {But not in fire prevention.}

412 MUNICIPAL ADMINISTRATION

Vast extent of fire losses in the United States.

Few people have any conception of the total property wastage which annually takes place through this form of destruction. For the calendar year 1930 the loss of property by fire in the United States amounted to over half a billion dollars, which is more than the total loss sustained in all the countries of Europe put together. Reckoned in terms per capita this loss amounts to more than four dollars, whereas in Great Britain it is less than one dollar and in France less than fifty cents per head of population. The discrepancy is all the more striking in view of the relatively small amounts which European cities spend on their fire-fighting equipment. In the eyes of the American tourist a European fire department with its old-fashioned apparatus and leisurely pace is a subject for witticism; but it gets the work done because there is so little of it to do. Judged by the results, the cities of the Old Continent have no reason to envy the communities on this side of the Atlantic which daily hurtle their huge motorized fire-fighting machines through the streets with shrieking sirens in a frantic endeavor to keep a half-million dollar fire from becoming a million dollar one.

Some illustrations.

Berlin and Chicago, for example, are not far apart in area or population; but Berlin loses by fire one-tenth as much as Chicago. There is some question as to whether New York is bigger than London, but there is no question as to the relative size of their annual fire losses. Every year, in the United States, we burn up more wealth than it took to create the Panama Canal. The factories, shops, and houses that are annually destroyed by fire, if grouped together, would make a city the size of San Francisco or Pittsburgh. They would line a street reaching from New York to Chicago. Nor do these figures of direct property loss tell the whole story. Fires interrupt the normal course of industry, throw workers out of employment, increase the burden of insurance premiums and, worst of all, result in a considerable loss of life. More than ten thousand persons met their death by fire in the United States during the year 1930. Twice as many were injured, a large proportion of them seriously. "A fire a minute" is not a slogan that anyone can get enthusiastic about, yet that is about the average which the United States has been maintaining for several years. One fire every minute, with a loss far exceeding a million dollars a day, is the tribute which America pays to the most destructive of all elements in her national life with the single exception of war.

What are the reasons for this great destruction of property by fire in American cities as compared with losses in the urban communities of other countries? First of all, it should be pointed out that the comparative figures are somewhat misleading unless one takes into account the difference in the scale of property values on the two sides of the Atlantic. Buildings of the same size and character have had a somewhat higher monetary value in American than in European cities. This, of course, has helped to swell the published figures of loss in the United States. Moreover there is a wide difference between European and American cities as regards the materials which are used in the construction of their buildings. The cities of Great Britain, France, and Germany are largely built of fire-resisting materials. The factories, office buildings, stores, dwellings, even farm houses and barns, are nearly always of stone, brick, concrete, or other non-combustible construction. This is partly because lumber is scarce and expensive in Europe, but it is also because most of the larger European cities have been prohibiting the erection of frame buildings for a long time as a measure of fire prevention. In Berlin, for example, no new frame buildings have been permitted to go up for more than sixty years, with the result that such structures now form an insignificant part of the whole, less than one per cent. Even in the smaller English, French, and German cities the fire-resisting buildings constitute at least seventy-five per cent of the whole, whereas in the average American city this proportion is reversed and the combustible buildings form more than seventy-five per cent. *Why fires are more common in American than in European cities.*

Lumber has been cheap and plentiful in the United States, with the result that it has been largely used. Whole areas, even in the downtown districts of large cities, have been covered with wooden buildings. This situation will doubtless change in the course of time because every large American city now has its fire-limits, within which no new frame structures can be erected. The old fire-traps are gradually being demolished and replaced by new structures of a fire-resisting type. Due to the increased price of lumber and the decreased price of steel, the difference in cost between the old and the new type of building is not now so great as it used to be. Ultimately the physical fire hazard in American cities will be no greater than it is in Europe, but this will hardly be accomplished for another half-century or so. Meanwhile fires break out in European cities almost as often as they do in the United States. *Our combustible urban areas.*

414   MUNICIPAL ADMINISTRATION

London, for example, has more than 5,000 fires a year, but they rarely get far. Apart from the interior furnishings there is little for them to burn. In the United States, on the other hand, figures of loss are heavily increased by fires which start in one building and spread to several others before being brought under control.

<small>And lax fire-prevention rules.</small> Another reason for the great destruction of property by fire in American cities may be found in the lax public control that has been exercised over the design and use of private buildings. American cities have been built, for the most part, on the principle that the design of a building is the builder's business, not that of his neighbors. Hence if an owner has desired to erect an office building with an unenclosed elevator shaft, or with no means of getting from the interior to the roof, this has too often been regarded as his own private concern. Or if he has desired to store oil in his cellar within easy range of the furnace, that likewise has been looked upon as an example of his own foolhardiness rather than as a violation of the law. Until two or three decades ago, very few American cities provided effective restrictions on the design or use of private buildings in the interest of fire prevention.

<small>These are now being stiffened up.</small> But nowadays such restrictive rules are everywhere becoming numerous and far-reaching. Likewise they are steadily becoming broader in their application and better enforced. Look through the building code of any city that has given serious study to the problem of fire prevention. You will see that this code has not been framed on the principle that owners of property have a right to build as they please. Section after section of every building code is devoted to such matters as fire-limits, structural design, basements, party walls, fire doors, stair-wells, elevator-shafts, roofs, chimneys, heating systems, electric wiring, access to attics, wiredglass for windows, exits, automatic sprinklers, standpipes, shutters, fire escapes, fire extinguishers, and spark arresters. By the rigid enforcement of such regulations the physical hazards are being steadily reduced in cities all over the country.

<small>Fire insurance and fire protection.</small> A third reason for the heavy fire losses in our cities can probably be found in the traditional American attitude toward fire insurance as a protection. Everybody, or almost everybody, has his place insured. There is a general impression that it is easier and cheaper to get adequate insurance than to incur the trouble and expense of making one's premises safe. Insurance companies have contributed to this shifting of the risk and responsibility. Energetic

agents encourage people to carry all the insurance they can. Naturally so, because more insurance means a larger premium, and a large premium means more commission for the agent. It is only in rare cases that an insurance company makes any careful inspection of the property which it insures and even more rarely does it obtain any valuation to make certain that a place is not being insured for more than it is worth. The result is that in many cases an owner stands to profit rather than to lose by a fire. That does not mean, of course, that he will try to realize the profit by setting fire to the premises. Most property owners are honest. On the other hand it is self-evident that overinsurance does not conduce to the exercise of greater vigilance on the owner's part. It tends to make him careless and neglectful of the various small precautions which he would take if the place were insured for less than its value.

There is a popular impression in the United States that when the insurance company pays, nobody loses. One frequently sees in the newspaper report of a fire the significant announcement: "There was no loss, the property being fully insured." Of course there was a loss, for all destruction of property involves a loss, and the owners of property throughout the country have to make it good in their insurance premiums. They have to make good the dishonest as well as the honest losses. A careful study of forty incendiary fires in a certain American city during the year 1932 revealed that in thirty of these cases the insured value was higher than the full value as determined by the tax assessor. In a number of cases it was fifty per cent above this figure. The sums collected from the insurance companies to repair the damage caused by these fires proved to be far in excess of the figures given in the building permits for the same repair jobs.[1]

Finally, something must be attributed to the American temperament. One phase of this temperament is its cheerful tolerance of waste. The people of the United States, especially those who live in the cities, are to an amazing degree undaunted by the prevalence of waste in all its forms. They see it going on continually, right under their eyes, without being even mildly perturbed—the waste of water, of light, of printer's ink, and of public funds. Waste through the destruction of property by fire seems to make no stronger impression upon the mind of the average citizen than does

The American leniency towards avoidable waste.

---

[1] George D. Fairtrace, "Overinsurance as a Factor in Fire Losses" in *Public Management*, Vol. XV, p. 263 (September, 1933).

any other kind of wastage. The American spirit lives in the future and does not cry over spilled milk or worry about the past. Accordingly, even before the ashes from a conflagration are cooled off, workmen are on the grounds erecting new buildings and the old ones are forgotten. People are much more interested in what the new buildings are going to cost than in how the loss of the old ones might have been prevented.

The lack of accurate data on the causes of fires.

Hence it is only on rare occasions that any rigid investigation into the cause of a fire is made, unless there has been some loss of life. Fire departments try to keep a record of causes, but too often they put down whatever simple explanation the owner happens to give them. No inquest into the cause is held as in European cities. Yet a city cannot devise effective measures for the prevention of fires unless it has accurate information as to how fires originate. It is only by eliminating or reducing the hazards that outbreaks of fire can be prevented. Unfortunately the figures relating to the principal causes of fires are neither conclusive nor altogether reliable. To some extent this is unavoidable because a fire always proceeds at once to destroy the place of its immediate origin. Rarely does anyone see the start of what proves to be a serious conflagration. If he did he would extinguish it at the outset.

Guesswork statistics.

Every fire, no matter what its finish, is the same size when it starts. The first five minutes at a fire are worth more, for putting-out purposes, than the next five hours. In the absence of direct testimony there must necessarily be resort to circumstantial evidence, or to conclusions based upon the process of elimination. Frequently there is little but guesswork to go upon. So if you look over the fire department records, you will find many instances in which the cause of a fire is put down as "defective wiring," "spontaneous combustion," or "origin unknown." What ought to be put down is that nobody has taken the trouble to find out where or how the trouble started. The firemen go back to their stations; the insurance company makes out its check to cover the loss, and the owner or tenant stands absolved of the carelessness or negligence which a rigid investigation would frequently disclose to have been the real cause.

The personal equation in fire prevention.

At any rate it is the opinion of fire-prevention experts that the personal equation is responsible for fire losses to a greater degree than all other factors combined. They believe that more than half the fires which occur in American cities are the result of somebody's carelessness, negligence, forgetfulness, or evil intent. Personal carelessness takes a multitude of forms. Householders forget to place the screen in front of the fireplace when they leave the room; ends of cigarettes are thrown into the wastebasket; chimneys are allowed to go uncleaned and unrepaired; rubbish is permitted to accumulate in the basement within a few feet of the furnace; oily rags are piled in a closet corner; leaky gas pipes are left unmended until a vagrant spark does its work; electric wires are overloaded with heaters and hot-plates till they blow the fuses, whereupon the fuses are bridged and the wires overheat (for many people do not realize that it is just as foolish to doctor a fuse with a non-fusing wire as to tie down the safety-valve of a steam boiler); children are given matches with which to start bonfires; electric irons are left unattended, grow hot, and ignite whatever is near them; naphtha is used in cleaning clothes under circumstances which cause it to be ignited—there is almost no end to the varieties of individual negligence or thoughtlessness in connection with fire hazards.

And the application of science to the household arts is steadily expanding the list of potential fire-causes. Every year some new heating, lighting, cooking, or cleaning device is brought out, and few of them are fool-proof. Moreover, all sorts of products having a nitro-cellulous base are being put upon the market, often without adequate caution concerning their liability to ignition. Combs, eye shades, knife and fork handles, boxes, trays, clocks, picture frames, even collars and candlesticks are made of substances which bear a variety of trade names but are so inflammable that they may sometimes be ignited by the heat of a steam radiator or electric light bulb. Explosions in automobile mufflers frequently result in fire losses. Motion picture films of the nitrate variety are highly combustible and when ignited give off stifling fumes. The use of house-lighting circuits for radio aërials is deemed by the fire-protection authorities to be a hazardous practice, although it is exceedingly common.[1] Some years ago a group of experts on fire prevention undertook to make a complete list of fire causes. They found nearly a hundred of them, ranging from defective chimneys to outright incendiarism and from short circuits to the ignition of gasoline vapor by castaway matches.

New devices and new dangers.

[1] *Safeguarding the Nation against Fire: a Fire Prevention Manual for High Schools*, published by the National Board of Fire Underwriters (New York, 1932), p. 63.

Incendiarism. Incendiarism is the cause of many fires; how many it is impossible to say. The offense of maliciously setting fire to property is known as arson, a severely punishable felony, but the evidence necessary for a conviction is usually difficult to obtain. The culprit makes certain that no one sees him start the fire. In fact he usually plans to be far away from the spot, and to have a perfect alibi when the fire is discovered. To this end he need only set a lighted candle where it will come into contact with some highly inflammable substance a couple of hours later, or he can rig up an alarm clock to start the blaze,—there are many ways of doing it. Most incendiary fires are the result of a desire to collect insurance. Crooked business men or house owners who get into serious financial difficulties are under a temptation to "sell out to the insurance company" at an excessive valuation. It has been found that such fires are more frequent when business is poor than in times of economic prosperity. The remedy lies chiefly with the insurance underwriters. There will be fewer fraudulent fires when overinsurance becomes less easy to obtain. Appraisals should be made in advance with the same care that mortgage and loan companies exercise. After property has been burned is a poor time to estimate its value.

Spite fires. Not all incendiary fires, however, are due to the avarice of property owners. Sometimes they are the work of pyromaniacs who set fire to buildings for the pleasure of seeing them burn. This strange and malicious malady is well recognized by authorities on mental diseases. And sometimes property is burned as a means of wreaking revenge upon its owner for a real or fancied wrong that he has done. Spite fires are part of the procedure known as racketeering. When one competitor wants to put another out of business, there are gangsters in most of the large cities who can be hired to help him do it with bomb or torch. In some of the largest centers this form of racketeering has become a well-organized underworld profession. To combat these various types of incendiarism some of the biggest cities have established arson squads in their police departments. The specialists in these squads investigate every suspicious fire and endeavor to trace its source. Arrests and convictions are relatively few, however, because convincing proofs of guilt are so hard to obtain.

Every match is potentially a conflagration. Nearly three hundred billion matches are lighted in the United States every year,

FIRE PREVENTION

and matches do not think with their heads. Nor, on all occasions, do the people who use them. Add to this the occasional sputterings of pocket lighters, the sparks from chimneys, the electrical ignitions, and all the other initial agencies of combustion; then mix them with the element of human negligence, carelessness, thoughtlessness, and avarice; keep in mind also that America is a land of wooden habitations filled with all manner of combustibles, from overstuffed furniture to wicker wastebaskets—the wonder is that we do not have an even greater loss from fire. *(The initial agencies of fire loss.)*

To recapitulate, then, there are three important factors which contribute to the occurrence and spread of fires in American cities. The first is the *physical hazard* due to the faulty design of structures and to the combustible materials which are so largely used in their construction. A large frame building with a shingle roof is a fire hazard no matter what its use, location, or design. Buildings with large undivided interior areas, or long corridors unprotected by fire-doors, or open stair-wells running from basement to roof are also hazardous even though the walls and roof be of fire-resisting construction. A wooden floor separating the basement from the street level also constitutes a fire hazard and large numbers of fires have their origin in basements. In the older tenement house districts of American cities the physical hazard is particularly high by reason of both the design and the materials. *(Recapitulation of fire loss causes: 1. The physical hazard.)*

Second, there is the *occupational hazard* which arises from the use rather than from the construction of buildings. Many buildings in cities are occupied by industries of a necessarily hazardous character. Offhand anyone can think of many such establishments,—planing mills, oil refineries, paint and lacquer factories, public garages, junk shops, shoddy mills, and what not. Theaters have a high occupational hazard by reason of the painted scenery which is stowed behind the drop curtain, hence stringent regulations are everywhere in force to reduce this danger. Occupational fire hazards are kept in bounds by zoning laws which restrict the use which may be made of buildings in different parts of the city. *(2. The occupational hazard.)*

Finally, there is the *moral hazard*, in other words the risk which arises from personal negligence, carelessness, or willful intent. This hazard depends not only on the character of the owner or occupant, but to some extent upon his financial circumstances. Property occupied by its owner is accounted by insurance companies a better moral risk than is property leased to a tenant. *(3. The moral hazard.)*

Buildings occupied by pool rooms, gambling resorts, all-night lunch rooms, and other places where loafers congregate are obviously not in the preferred class. A heavily mortgaged home constitutes a higher moral hazard than one which is clear of debt. A prosperous business is a better moral risk than one which is running behind. It is a well-known fact that fires break out less frequently in well-kept homes than in those which have no sense of order or cleanliness. Carelessness and negligence, when they become stereotyped into personal habits, constitute a moral hazard no matter how honest an owner or occupant may be.

How these hazards may be reduced.

Now the purpose of fire prevention is to lessen all three of the foregoing hazards. Fire prevention does not seek merely to compel the building of fire-resisting structures, although an increased number of such buildings in every large city is highly desirable. It is equally important that the use of buildings be controlled in such way as to lessen the occupational hazard so far as this can be accomplished without unduly restricting legitimate business. In this respect a carefully drawn zoning ordinance can accomplish a great deal. By zoning it is possible to segregate the hazardous industries in sections of the city where danger of a general conflagration can be minimized. The lessening of the moral hazard, finally, can be encouraged by various measures such as a rigid investigation of all suspicious fires, the establishment of an alert arson squad in the police department, and the encouragement of precautions against overinsurance. Many insurance companies now safeguard themselves by declining to insure property for more than a certain percentage of its appraised value, thus requiring the owner to become a co-insurer as respects the balance.

Fire zones in cities.

One effective way of reducing physical hazards throughout the city is by fixing what are known as fire zones and limiting the type of buildings which may be constructed within such zones. Fire zones have been established in European cities for a century or more; but in the municipalities of the United States they are mainly the product of the last thirty or forty years. Moreover the laws and ordinances which establish these fire zones in American cities are not retroactive, that is they do not apply to buildings already in existence. Hence it is only when new construction or extensive remodelling takes place that the restrictions can be applied.

It is true that under certain circumstances a city may, by the exercise of its police power, require the demolition of buildings which are such obvious fire hazards that they menace the surrounding region and hence can be classed as nuisances. But a frame building is not a nuisance *per se*. Fire-prevention ordinances, in order to keep within the bounds of legality, must not go beyond what is essential to the protection of the public safety. To secure this protection, however, it may be necessary to make the requirements retroactive as respects certain buildings or parts of buildings—for example, to require that frame buildings used as junk shops shall be vacated, or that additional fire escapes be attached to all buildings of a designated size or class. But it would hardly be permissible to require that all buildings of a certain type already erected within the fire limits shall be moved out of this area or torn down. *Extent of the city's police power.*

The regulations applying to the fire-zone areas differ from city to city, but as a rule they stipulate that no new buildings may be constructed within the industrial or principal business zones unless they are of fire-resisting construction in accordance with the specifications laid down in the building code. It will be noted that the term "fire-resisting," not "fireproof," construction is used. For strictly speaking there is no such thing as a fireproof building. No building, howsoever designed or constructed, is proof against destruction by fire if the fire is hot enough. And a great conflagration will develop sufficient heat to sweep any sort of structure out of its path, as was demonstrated in the San Francisco fire when even steel beams melted and cement columns disintegrated into a heap of ruins. *Types of permissible construction.*

Fire resistance is a relative term, hence the fire-prevention ordinances usually differentiate between three or four types of fire-resisting construction. As a rule they require that large industrial, mercantile office buildings within certain zones shall be of Class A construction, that is of fire-resisting materials throughout, with no wood used except for floor surfacing and interior trim. This type of construction is now also required, as a rule, in the case of theaters, schools, hotels, large apartment houses, factories, public garages, and various other buildings no matter where they may be located. *Class A construction.*

A less rigorous type of construction, sometimes known as Class B construction, is permitted in the outer zones and sometimes even within industrial or downtown business areas under certain cir- *Class B construction.*

cumstances. This type of construction permits the use of wood in floors and partitions but not in the exterior walls. Similar restrictions are usually placed upon tenement houses wherever located. A tenement house is commonly defined as any structure housing three or more families. Small shops and stores on minor retail streets are usually permitted to be built in this way. Single dwellings and two-family houses throughout the residential sections are ordinarily allowed to be of frame construction with shingle roofs. It is the function of the buildings department to see that the requirements as to fire-resisting materials are enforced.

Special regulations applying to factories, theaters, etc. The effort to lessen occupational hazards has absorbed much thought and energy on the part of fire-prevention experts during recent years. This has resulted in the framing of numerous special regulations which apply to such individual structures as factories, theaters, department stores, tenement houses, public garages, and other places where lives may be endangered by a fire even though the building itself is of slow-burning construction. It would be impossible to summarize these regulations here because each type of occupancy has its own set of requirements and some of them are very technical. However, the rules which are customarily applied to theaters and motion picture houses will serve as an illustration. Buildings occupied for such use in all the large cities must now be of fire-resisting construction. Automatic sprinklers are usually required in dressing rooms, work rooms, and under the stages. A cut-off in the form of a steel and asbestos curtain must separate the auditorium from the back-stage sections of the building. The apparatus used for projecting pictures must be housed in a room or compartment which can be quickly shut off in the event of a fire arising there. Exits from the auditorium must be adequate in number, easy of access, conspicuously lighted, and indicated on the theater program at every performance. Fire-extinguishing apparatus as specified in the regulations must be installed and kept ready for instant use. The lobbies and aisles must be of regulation width and no temporary seats may be placed in them because this would interfere with the rapid emptying of the auditorium in case of an emergency. And there are various other regulations of the same sort.

Tenement houses. As regards tenement houses, on the other hand, the fire-prevention regulations are naturally of a different character. Such buildings are usually permitted to be of less expensive construction, but various special requirements are insisted upon. One of these is the provision that there must be no inflammable connection between the basement and the rest of the building. The street-level floor must usually be of concrete, although a veneer surface of wood may be laid upon it. Open stair-wells, through which the flames can rise rapidly to the roof, are prohibited in most cities. Party walls in various portions of the building must be of fire-resisting construction. Adequate fire escapes are required with access from each apartment. Light wells must have fire-resisting walls and usually wired-glass windows. And there are other requirements of a similar type. Now and then one hears it argued that all tenement houses should be made "absolutely fire-proof." Such a requirement might be practicable but it would greatly increase the cost of construction and lead to a general rise in rents. Regulations of a too drastic character always overreach themselves and produce a reaction in the public mind.

All such regulations, moreover, are easier to make than to enforce. To pass a fire-prevention ordinance does not cost much time or money; but to enforce it is a task that requires both. Too many American communities have contented themselves with the enactment of regulations, making no special provision for seeing that the requirements are strictly observed. In general the buildings department is given the responsibility for enforcing the rules so far as physical hazards are concerned. Its officials and inspectors are supposed to make sure that the materials and design of new buildings are in strict accordance with the code. But as respects the enforcement of the rules relating to the occupational hazards it is customary to place this responsibility upon the fire department. This department is usually expected to provide such inspectional supervision as will secure the enforcement of the rules relating to the storage of inflammable substances, the keeping of adequate hand extinguishers, the prevention of overcrowding in theaters, the clearing of exits, and so forth. *The enforcement of fire-prevention rules.*

In every city of considerable size there should be a bureau of fire prevention within the fire department.[1] The firemen assigned to this bureau should make periodic visits to all places where violations of the fire-prevention rules are likely to occur. They should be on the lookout for minor as well as major infractions. *Fire-prevention bureaus.*

[1] This recommendation has been made by the National Board of Fire Underwriters in its *Suggested Fire Prevention Ordinances* (85 John St., New York, 1930).

These should be brought to the owner's attention and if not remedied at the next inspection should be reported for legal action. Intelligent and alert-minded firemen should be detailed for this task, but in many cities it is the practice to devolve the inspectional work upon old or partially disabled members of the fire-fighting force who are no longer able to do full active duty. Thus the fire-prevention bureau has tended to become a place of assignment for the superannuated or infirm rather than a vigilant branch of the city's law enforcement service. This is unfortunate because no one except the inspector is likely to be actively interested in a rigid adherence to the rules. The owner is likely to cut the corners if he can; the police will usually take the easy course by regarding these infractions as outside their jurisdiction; and the public is not particularly interested—until a catastrophe comes.

The keeping of records.

In addition to its inspectional work a fire-prevention bureau should also keep accurate records of all fires, their origin, extent, location, amount of loss, amount of insurance, names of owners or tenants, and all other relevant matters. These records will indicate the points at which greater emphasis on fire-prevention work is necessary. All these things, however, cannot be done without spending money, and the appropriations which American cities make each year for fire-prevention work are pitiably small. Municipal authorities have been slow to realize that money spent in this way is money saved in the appropriations for the maintenance of a fire-fighting force. In fact the main function of a fire-prevention bureau is to make less work for the engines and ladders.

Fire prevention as a state function.

To a large extent the prevention of fires is a local problem and the municipal authorities have adequate power to deal with it. Moreover, every city has a fire department to which the work of enforcement can appropriately be entrusted. Nevertheless a good deal may be said in favor of making fire prevention a state function. When several municipalities, for example, are located close to one another, it is difficult for one of them to make and enforce a strict code of fire-prevention rules without the coöperation of the others. The city which tries to maintain a high standard places itself at a disadvantage in rivalry with its neighbors which do not, for lenient fire prevention and lax inspection are among the allurements which draw land speculators and building promoters to a community. Accordingly it is desirable that the regulations shall show a reasonable approach to uniformity over the whole metropolitan area and shall be enforced with the same degree of strictness everywhere. In most cases there is no way of getting this done except through the intervention of the state. Several of the states now have state-wide fire-prevention laws and are maintaining fire marshals or fire-prevention commissioners to enforce them.

State control of fire-prevention work, in its broader aspects, is also justified by the self-evident fact that no city is safe from conflagration if serious fire hazards (unsupervised forests, for example) are permitted on any of its flanks, outside its own borders. Fires pay no heed to municipal boundaries. Whatever endangers one city is a matter of concern to its immediate neighbors, especially in communities which crowd so closely upon one another that one begins across the street from where the other ends. There is no good reason, moreover, why rules relating to fire prevention in factories should differ from city to city; an unprotected elevator-shaft is just as much of a fire hazard in Cleveland as in Cincinnati. A three-decker frame tenement does not become any less of a fire trap because it is located in Buffalo rather than in Rochester. To prohibit such things in one city while permitting them in another leads only to misunderstandings, resentment, and confusion. Municipal self-determination, in this field, merely encourages inter-municipal rivalry to operate in the direction of lower standards. *Its justification.*

In fire prevention, as in other civic activities, entire reliance cannot be placed on laws, ordinances, and inspectors alone. Individual carelessness, which is the most prolific cause of fires, cannot be eliminated by the action of lawmakers or the promptings of public functionaries. Much can be accomplished in this direction, however, by educating the public to the use of greater caution in all that concerns fire hazards and much has been done along this line in recent years. The best place for beginning this educational work is in the schools. More than a million copies of a small text on fire prevention, prepared with the coöperation of the United States Office of Education, have been printed and distributed to public schools for their use.[1] Newspaper articles, circulars, and addresses on fire prevention likewise have their value and the same is true of public exhibits showing the methods whereby hazards can be reduced. There are few fields of elementary knowledge in which the people stand in more urgent need of enlighten- *Public education in this field.*

[1] *A Fire Prevention Manual for the School Children of America* (New York, 1931).

ment than in this one. In many American cities it is the practice to designate one day in the year as fire-prevention day with appropriate instruction in the schools concerning the methods of protecting life and property against fire.

REFERENCES

The *Handbook of Fire Protection* by Everett U. Crosby, Henry A. Fiske, and H. Walter Forster (7th edition, New York, 1925) contains a great deal of detailed information on the methods of fire prevention. Gorham Dana and William D. Milne, *Industrial Fire Hazards and an Encyclopedia of Hazardous Materials* (Framingham, Mass., 1928) is an exhaustive study of the subject. Joseph K. Freitag, *Fire Prevention and Fire Protection as Applied to Building Construction* (2nd edition, New York, 1921), and T. F. Dougherty and P. W. Kearney, *Fire* (New York, 1931) are also useful.

Harold A. Stone and Gilbert E. Stecher, *Organization and Operation of a Municipal Bureau of Fire Prevention* (Syracuse, N. Y., 1927) is serviceable on the special phase of the subject which it covers. Mention should likewise be made of Charles C. Dominge and Walter O. Lincoln, *Fire Insurance Inspection and Underwriting* (4th edition, New York, 1929), G. E. Keay, *Fire Waste* (London, 1927), and the volume by Miller McClintock and H. L. Bond on *The Problem of Fire Waste and Insurance Rates in the City of Boston* (Boston, 1930). A valuable booklet by Kenneth F. Akers on *Fire Protection Engineering as Applied to Municipalities* was issued a few years ago by the Boston Society of Civil Engineers (715 Tremont Temple, Boston). The best book on incendiarism and its prevention is L. Benoist, *Manuel de la prévention de l'incendie* (Paris, 1923).

Various helpful publications have been issued by the National Fire Protection Association (60 Batterymarch St., Boston), by the National Board of Fire Underwriters (85 John St., New York), the National Fire Waste Council (1615 H St., N. W., Washington, D. C.) and the Underwriters' Laboratories (207 East Ohio St., Chicago). The National Fire Protection Association publishes a quarterly journal which contains current discussions of new fire-prevention methods. A bibliography of books and articles on Fire Fighting and Fire Prevention is printed in *The Municipal Index*, Vol. VI, pp. 647–648 (1929).

CHAPTER XXXI

FIRE PROTECTION

Behold how much wood is kindled by how small a fire!—*James iii, 5 (Revised Version)*.

In the matter of reducing fire losses there is much that can be accomplished by laying emphasis on the work of fire prevention, but no matter how much progress may be made in this direction, it is inevitable that fires will break out in cities and that some of them will spread to serious proportions. Every city must therefore make adequate provision for dealing with such outbreaks of fire, in other words it must supplement fire prevention by a system of fire protection. This involves the maintenance of a fire-fighting force, thoroughly organized, properly distributed, and equipped with suitable extinguishing apparatus. Developments in the apparatus available for fighting fires have been extensive during the last thirty years. There are few fields of public activity in which the technical progress has been greater than in this. Fire-fighting has become a highly developed science in American cities, and one in which they lead the rest of the world. *The science of fire fighting.*

How is a municipal fire department organized? A generation ago this department was usually placed under the direction of a civilian board. Frequently there was a requirement that the membership of this body should be representative of both the major political parties, and this provision inevitably drew the department into politics. The board system continues in some cities at the present time but it is being almost everywhere abandoned. In its place most fire departments now have a single head, known as the fire commissioner, fire marshal, or fire chief. As a rule this official is appointed by the mayor or the city manager. In some cities, especially in those which have the commission form of government, the police and fire-fighting forces have been combined into a single department of public safety, and such a combination may superficially appear to be a logical one. But the differences between the work of policemen and firemen are far-reaching and fundamental. Policemen work for the most part *How a municipal fire department is organized.*

individually, while firemen act in groups. The patrolman's place during his duty hours is on the streets, while the fireman spends most of his time within the walls of his station. Police duty continually involves the exercise of tact and patience, for the policeman is continually dealing with people of all varieties; while the fireman's contact is mainly with physical things, with fire apparatus and flaming structures, not with the individual citizens and human relations. Hence the qualities demanded from the personnel of the two departments are wholly unlike, and it is doubtful whether the practice of combining them under a single head has much in its favor save the argument that it permits some economy of overhead expense in smaller cities.

<small>Fire commissioner and fire chief.</small>
A single commissioner or chief, appointed by the mayor or other principal executive of the city, properly secured against the pressure of political interference,—this has been found to be, on the whole, the most satisfactory method of securing administrative competence at the head of the city's fire-fighting forces. In large cities the fire commissioner should be chosen from the citizenship at large and ought not to be someone who has come up through the ranks of the department. A fire chief, immediately subordinate to the commissioner, should provide whatever technical advice may be needed. The commissioner's responsibility is to handle the finances of the department, direct its general policy, serve as its connecting link with the other high municipal authorities, keep the department in a progressive frame of mind, and strengthen it in the confidence of the public. The duties of the fire chief under this arrangement include the immediate command of the force, the recommendation of appointments and promotions, the assignment of firemen to the different stations, and the general maintenance of technical efficiency. In moderate-sized and small communities, on the other hand, the functions of commissioner and chief may be combined, in which case it is usually preferable to select someone who has had experience in the work of fighting fires. It has usually been found, however, that a chief who has come up through the ranks of the department is case-hardened in his ways of doing things and reluctant to make any departure from traditional methods.

<small>Qualifications of this official.</small>
Finding a capable civilian head for the fire department of a large city is not a simple problem. He ought to have the qualities of a commanding general, which means that he must needs be

FIRE PROTECTION

alert-minded, an organizer of unusual capacity, a disciplinarian, and a strategist. Fighting fires is like fighting any other enemy; it requires careful attention to both strategy and tactics. By strategy is meant the careful planning which enables all possible emergencies to be foreseen and provided for. Tactics, on the other hand, comprises the maneuvering of apparatus and men in the immediate presence of the fire. One supplements the other. No amount of strategy will avail to prevent heavy losses by fire if the technique of quenching the flames is amateurish and crude. Nor will the finest of fire-fighting tactics accomplish much if the apparatus and personnel has been badly distributed among the stations and hence cannot be quickly mobilized at points where it is needed in emergencies. A capable fire commissioner, assisted by a competent fire chief, will see that high standards are set in both directions.

But the standards of fire-department efficiency in many cities have suffered much from the injection of politics into the choice of both commissioners and chiefs. One of the mayor's right-hand men during his political campaign is frequently given the commissionership as a reward. He, in turn, tries to transform the personnel of the department into a body of workers for the mayor's reëlection when the time comes. Men who become fire chiefs through promotion from the ranks do not always, or even usually, owe their preferment to reasons of professional capacity alone. Captains or battalion chiefs with a flair for politics, and a high degree of usefulness to politicians, are frequently moved ahead of those who would have far better claims to promotion if personal capacity were the only consideration. Municipal fire departments often seethe with local politics. Some of them are veritable hotbeds of wire-pulling. Firemen have so much time to sit around the stations, waiting for a call, that they are under a strong temptation to think politics, talk politics, and play politics,—especially when they see their higher officers doing it. *Politics in the department.*

The organization of a fire department is much the same in all cities, irrespective of size. First there is a department headquarters at which the chief officials have their offices. Here also the fire-prevention bureau is usually located when there is one. Then the city is divided into fire districts or precincts with a station in each. At every station there is a fire company consisting of an officer, five to fifteen men, and a unit of apparatus. Each station *Headquarters and stations.*

has at least one engine company and most of them have a ladder company as well. A company, in any event, is assigned to each important unit of fire fighting or rescue apparatus, because it is the smallest division in the department. A captain or a lieutenant is in command. It does not require a whole company of from five to fifteen men to man a pumping engine or a rescue ladder, but under the two-platoon system (as will be explained later) half the men are always off duty.

The distribution of men and apparatus. Companies at various stations within a district are sometimes organized into battalions, each under the command of a battalion chief. Occasionally a district will have several stations, but now that fire apparatus has become motorized the tendency is to reduce the number. In the downtown districts the present estimate is that the apparatus and men at a single fire station can adequately serve about one square mile of area. In the residential sections this range can be doubled, or even more than doubled without impairing the protection given. It is not the population of the district that determines the need. A heavily industrialized area or a retail business section requires close protection even though few people may live in it. Stations, apparatus, and men are distributed according to the principles of fire-fighting strategy. Hence the distribution should be changed whenever local conditions undergo any appreciable alteration, but this is not always done. A fire station cannot be moved at will, and the tendency is to keep on using it after the location has become obviously unsuitable. To acquire the logical sites for new fire stations, moreover, is not always easy. Often there are vehement protests from the immediate neighborhood in which structures are proposed to be located. This is because most property owners believe that the proximity of a fire station, with its roaring motors and shrieking sirens, is a detriment to real estate values.

The three purposes which a fire station serves. Fire stations serve three purposes. They house the apparatus, including the pumping engines, ladders, hose reels, and chemical extinguishers. They also provide a dormitory in which some of the firemen sleep during their night hours on duty. Finally, they provide outposts of the fire-alarm system in articulation with central headquarters. Precinct or district stations vary in equipment and personnel according to the extent and character of the area which they serve. Hence a fire station may have only a single piece of apparatus or it may have several; its complement of men may

FIRE PROTECTION

number only a half-dozen men or it may be four times that number. Everything depends upon the property values, the congestion, the fire hazards, the topographical features and the other characteristics of the district in which the station is located. Some cities have pursued the practice of combining police and fire stations in the same building. Such a combination often serves the interest of economy and is unobjectionable from any other point of view.

Fire departments are organized on a semi-military model. Men enter it at the bottom. In most of the larger cities they are appointed in accordance with civil service rules, which involve a competitive examination. These tests are both physical and mental, with a good deal of weight given to the former. But the practice of giving preference to veterans has virtually disbarred all but former service men from much chance of success in these competitions. In some states the preference is an absolute one, in other words any veteran who passes the tests must be put at the head of the eligible list. In others the preference is merely a qualified one, which means that a former service man gets a certain percentage added to his score on the tests, which does not always suffice to put him at the top. So far as fire departments are concerned this complication will come to an end, however, in the course of a few years because former service men will then be beyond the age limits which are usually set for new appointments. *The selection of firemen.*

The usual practice, until about twenty years ago, was to place a fireman on active duty immediately after his appointment without giving him any special training. New York City, however, inaugurated the experiment of a training school for probationary firemen and the example of the metropolis has been followed by virtually all the larger cities of the country. The course of training covers a period which ranges in different schools from fifteen to sixty days, during which time the recruits are instructed in fire-prevention regulations, the proper handling and care of fire-fighting apparatus, wall scaling and rescue work, the use of pulmotors for resuscitation, as well as in fire-fighting tactics. In the best organized fire departments, moreover, there are regular drills in which all the men take part, and the instruction of the firemen is sometimes continued after they have been through the training school, a few hours in each week being devoted to it. *Training schools.*

One of the difficult problems connected with fire-department administration is that of keeping the men from growing stale. Even *The use of free time.*

with drills and instruction they have a great deal of free time on their hands. A fireman who is on "active" duty for ten hours a day may spend half these hours in the station with no duties to do. Two parts heroism, three parts drudgery, and five parts idleness—that is about the usual distribution of a fire-fighter's time. The men polish up the apparatus till it glistens and do the routine chores, but for the rest of the hours they sit around, exchange gossip with one another, play cards, listen for an alarm, and watch the clock. The profitable use of this spare time is a problem for which no fire department has yet been able to find a satisfactory solution. The suggestion has been made that opportunities for vocational education should be given to the firemen, with classes held at each station, but this has not yet been found practicable.

Promotions and discipline. Promotions in the fire department are invariably made from the ranks, usually on a basis of seniority, but with deviations from this rule depending upon personal efficiency as judged by the higher officers. The maintenance of discipline is usually a responsibility of the fire chief or fire commissioner, but in some cities it is the practice to have all serious breaches of discipline tried by a board of three officers or by a disciplinary board on which both officers and men are given representation. Penalties are usually imposed in the form of extra duty, deprivation of pay, suspension for a designated time, or dismissal from the force in the case of serious offenses. When members of the fire department have been appointed under civil service rules they cannot usually be dismissed except on definite charges and after a formal hearing. In most large cities a fireman is entitled to retire on a pension when he reaches a certain age, usually sixty or sixty-five years, provided he has completed a designated term of service. Sometimes the city treasury provides all the money for these pensions, but more commonly the allowances are paid from a fund to which the firemen contribute a certain percentage of their pay.

The platoon system of duty. Until recent years it was the general practice to require members of the fire department to stay on duty continuously for a specified number of days at a time. They were then allowed one day off in seven, or in five, or in three, as the case might be. Such an arrangement was unsatisfactory in that it precluded anything akin to normal home life on the part of the men. Eventually it led to a demand for the establishment of a two-platoon system such as had been devised for the police department. This request, which was not unreasonable, has now been granted in all the larger cities. Under the two-platoon system the entire force is divided into two equal groups, each of which is on duty for a ten-hour day or a fourteen-hour night, the day and night shifts being changed from time to time. It is considered desirable to have the officers alternate in such a way that all of them will be frequently brought into contact with the men of each shift. In a few cities the firemen are now suggesting the desirability of a three-platoon plan with an eight-hour shift, but the granting of this request would necessitate a considerable increase in the size of the force with a large addition to the fire department budget.

The ideal equipment for an engine company consists of two units of apparatus, both motorized,—a pumping engine and a combined chemical engine and hose wagon, the latter commonly known as a combination wagon. To fight a large fire, however, more than one company is required, hence arrangements are always made for calling out several companies or even several battalions when this becomes necessary. The usual rule is that a second alarm calls out all the companies in a given district, while a general alarm calls out all the companies in several adjacent districts. When the chief's strategic plans are well worked out, every captain knows his place in the general line of battle and moves his apparatus accordingly. The objective is to mobilize the maximum fire-fighting strength in the shortest space of time at any large fire no matter where it may occur, while at the same time distributing the rest of the available force in such way as to leave no portion of the territory unprotected. *Mobilization for large fires.*

Where several cities and towns are situated close together, it is customary for their fire chiefs to get together and work out arrangements for systematic coöperation in the event of a serious fire at any point in the entire area. Then if a downtown conflagration gets under way, the companies from all the outlying residential stations are summoned to help fight it, whereupon detachments from surrounding cities and towns move in to take their places. All hydrant couplings are standardized to make this coöperation possible. *Inter-city mobilization.*

The equipment of a modern fire department comprises hydrants, gasoline pumping engines, chemical engines, hose wagons (with or without chemical tanks), ladder trucks, fuel wagons, water towers, appliances for handling powerful streams, automobile run- *The variety of equipment used.*

abouts for the higher officers, gas masks, pulmotors, and various subsidiary apparatus. In seaport cities there are fireboats for use in dealing with fires at the docks or along the water front. All varieties of fire-fighting equipment have undergone a notable improvement during the last twenty years—since the day of horse-drawn steam pumpers. Still fundamental in its importance, however, is the hydrant. It is the point of contact between the fire and water departments. Hydrants should be placed at close and convenient intervals along the street, and access to them should always be unobstructed. They should be easy to open and of such standard construction that connection with stream hose or engine may be made quickly. Hydrants should never be located in close proximity to lumber piles, oil tanks, or buildings of a very inflammable character. If the water pressure in the mains is sufficient, the hose is attached and a direct stream obtained, but in most cases the hydrant is merely used to supply the engine which steps-up the pressure and thus provides a stream of sufficient force and volume. A good hydrant will supply more than one engine. To ensure their always being ready for service, it is necessary to inspect hydrants frequently and in northern cities they must be protected carefully against freezing.

Engines and accessory apparatus. The steam pumping engine, which replaced the hand pump of an earlier generation, has now become obsolete and is being everywhere superseded by engines of the internal combustion type. A modern motor-pumper will deliver up to fifteen hundred gallons of water a minute. Horse-drawn apparatus has now disappeared from the streets. Incidentally the elimination of horses from the fire stations has made these buildings much less offensive to the neighborhoods in which they are located. Great progress has also been made in the development of chemical engines. The chemical engine is merely a truck carrying tanks of diluted bicarbonate of soda in which a bottle of sulphuric acid is suspended so that overturning the bottle or loosening the stopper will release the contents. The acid, mixing with the soda solution, generates carbonic acid gas which provides the pressure for forcing the contents of the tank through the attached hose. Various types of chemical engines are now on the market, some of them using no acid but carrying an extra tank of compressed air to furnish the pressure. Progress has also been made in the improvement of fire hose and in the development of such apparatus as water towers, ladder trucks,

FIRE PROTECTION

turret nozzles, pulmotors, gas masks, and smoke helmets. These accessories now make it possible for firemen to fight fires under conditions which would have been impossible even a few years ago. The water tower is a truck-mounted turret or standpipe which can be elevated to a height of fifty or sixty feet and a stream directed through it upon a fire which is too high for streams from the street to reach.

For small fires the large pumping engines are not needed. They weigh about ten tons and are costly to buy, maintain, and operate. Hence many cities have adopted the practice of putting small light-weight engines in their suburban districts. These engines pump about three hundred and fifty gallons of water per minute and can be more easily maneuvered to the proximity of burning houses. A popular type of apparatus is known as the triple combination. It consists of a small pumping engine, a chemical tank, and a hose reel, all mounted on the same chassis. Special rescue cars have also been coming into use during recent years. These cars carry a stock of life-saving appliances consisting of nets for catching persons who leap from windows, pulmotors, gas masks, smoke helmets, acetylene torches for cutting metals, tools for making forcible entry, hand pumps, axes, and other tools. In some cities the rescue car responds to all first-alarm fires in thickly populated areas. *Triple combinations.*

The fire-alarm system is a vital adjunct of the entire protective service. The call boxes should be so located and spaced as to be easily and quickly reached from any place in the city. They should be simple to operate and difficult to put out of order. When a box is pulled, its number and location are automatically recorded at headquarters, whereupon the information is relayed to the nearest station and then to all other stations so that they may be prepared for a second alarm if it becomes necessary. On arrival at a fire, if the captain finds the situation too serious for him to handle alone he rings in the second alarm. The central station should be in a building of fire-resisting construction isolated from other structures. The transmission of fire alarms by telephone is becoming increasingly common, so much so that the alarm box system is not often used in some cities for day calls. But the telephone switchboards are not always functioning at night or on Sundays in the business district where the prompt sending of an alarm is essential. There has been some discussion concerning the possible *The fire-alarm system.*

use of radio transmission from street boxes to the central station, but the experiment has not yet been carried to a satisfactory conclusion.

Fire protection and the water supply.

People have the impression that very large amounts of water are used in putting out fires, and one sometimes hears it argued that the water reservoirs must be made much larger to stand the heavy measure of extra strain. But the fact is that even a serious fire does not make large demands upon the reservoirs. A modern pumping engine will normally deliver about 1,000 gallons of water per minute when working at a pressure of one hundred pounds to the square inch. On this basis it would take a battery of seventeen big pumpers to use a million gallons in the course of an hour; but a city of 200,000 people will use that much water for other purposes every hour in the day. Taking the year around, it is very rarely that the fire department's consumption of water amounts to even one per cent of the total.

High pressure systems.

One of the notable developments of the past thirty years is the separate high pressure system. An engine working at maximum pressure can deliver an effective stream to about one hundred feet in height, whereas the upper stories of the modern skyscraper are far above that level. Some of the largest cities have therefore installed throughout their downtown districts a separate system of large mains and hydrants strong enough to carry water under heavy pressure—as high as 300 pounds to the square inch. Streams can be played from the ground by means of water towers, or the connection can be made to the interior standpipes with which most tall buildings are now equipped. With a high pressure system a large number of powerful streams can be played on a fire in a very short time with fewer men than are needed to serve the engines. This system, moreover, eliminates the confusion which often occurs when many engines are concentrated at a fire. The high pressure mains are served by a central pumping station equipped with power centrifugal pumps operated by electric motors. The high pressure is not kept up at all times but only when an alarm comes in from the district covered by the system. Raising the pressure takes less than a minute. Such stations, of course, should be located outside the conflagration zone.

Work of the police at fires.

Provision is usually made for notifying the police department whenever apparatus starts for a fire, so that one or more policemen can be sent to the spot. This is important because the work of the

FIRE PROTECTION

firemen may be greatly impeded by the horde of motor cars which usually rush to the vicinity when a fire of any considerable size breaks out, as well as by the crowding of people through the lines. The police, not the firemen, are responsible for keeping the area clear. They ought also to be at hand as a means of preventing the pillage of burning buildings by volunteer salvagers, of whom there is never a scarcity at any large fire.

The public fire-protection service is being supplemented, more and more, by private protection in the case of factories, theaters, office buildings, hotels, warehouses, and large stores. Many such buildings have watchmen on duty both day and night. These watchmen are usually checked up, being required to carry a clock which has to be wound half-hourly or oftener and the keys to which are fastened in various parts of the building. Standpipes, with hose attached and ready for service, are a feature in nearly all new buildings above a certain height. Chemical hand extinguishers are kept ready for use almost everywhere. Automatic sprinkler installations are being generally required in all buildings where the hazard is considerable. Such an installation consists of a network of pipes, laid just below the ceilings, through which water is carried to all parts of the building. At intervals of every few feet these pipes are fitted with sprinkler heads which are sealed with a fusible metal or solder which melts at a designated temperature. When a fire breaks out in any part of the building the heat quickly melts the solder and lets the water pour out against a circular disc which deflects a spray in all directions. Each sprinkler head, when supplied with water under adequate pressure, will throughly drench an area about one hundred feet square. The pipes and sprinkler heads should be installed in all parts of the building—in the basement, the attic, under the stairs, even in the closets and elevator wells; for the automatic sprinklers are intended to quench a fire before it gets well started, and fires often get started in out-of-the-way places. Sometimes, on a very hot night or by an accident, a sprinkler head gets into play and does a lot of damage before it is discovered. The most up-to-date systems are now equipped with an electric device which automatically sounds an alarm whenever a sprinkler head lets go.

Private fire protection.

Fire-protection services in American cities represent a very high standard of technical efficiency. One reason for this is the existence of an outside agency which has put continuous pressure upon the

The outside pressure for high standards.

municipal authorities to keep things that way. The National Board of Fire Underwriters, an organization representing all the important fire insurance companies, has for many years made a practice of rating cities on a basis of their ability to protect themselves against fires. This rating is figured on the adequacy of their water supply, the efficiency of their fire department, the strictness of their fire-prevention rules, and the success with which these rules are enforced. Every city is put into one of ten groups and the rates for fire insurance are adjusted accordingly. When a city is demoted from a higher group to a lower one because of a drop in the efficiency of its fire-protection service, all insurance rates on public and private property are raised, whereupon a barrage of protests is launched upon the city authorities by the chamber of commerce, the merchants' association, and by householders in general. If every other department had some such outside agency continually pressing for higher standards, the general efficiency of American municipal administration would be notably improved.

REFERENCES

In addition to the books listed at the close of Chapter XXX, it may be well to mention E. F. Croker, *Fire Prevention* (New York, 1912), a readable book on actual fire fighting by a one-time head of the New York fire department. John Kenlon, *Fires and Fire Fighters* (New York, 1913) and Luke Flanagan, *The Science of Fire Fighting* (New York, 1920) are volumes of much the same type. A book on the elements of fire-fighting strategy and tactics entitled *What Every Fire Fighter Should Know* (New York, 1928) is published by the editors of the weekly magazine *Fire Engineering*. W. B. Johnson, *Fire-Fighting by Land, Sea, and Air* (London, 1927) is a more systematic study.

Technical information concerning the proper use of fire streams and motor pumping equipment is published in Frederick Shepperd, *Simplified Fire Department Hydraulics* (New York, 1925), and much other data of a professional character is contained in the *Fire Chief's Handbook* by the same author (New York, 1932). The *Field Practice Handbook* of the National Fire Protection Association is also valuable (2nd edition, Boston, 1929). Material relating to the construction, care, and operation of motor apparatus is included in R. H. McNeish, *The Automobile Fire Apparatus Operator* (Los Angeles, 1926).

More than forty useful pamphlets on various phases of fire protection (*e.g.*, municipal fire-alarm systems, sprinkler equipments, fire pumps, etc.)

have been prepared by committees of the National Fire Protection Association during the past ten years. These pamphlets, which range in size from 5 to 250 pages, may be had from the National Board of Fire Underwriters (85 John St., New York). *Fire Protection,* a monthly magazine, is published in Indianapolis.

CHAPTER XXXII

SCHOOL ADMINISTRATION

> I shall detain you no longer in the demonstration of what we should not do, but straight conduct ye to a hillside, where I will point ye out the right path of a virtuous and noble education; laborious indeed at the first ascent, but else so smooth, so green, so full of goodly prospect and melodious sounds on every side that the harp of Orpheus was not more charming.—*John Milton.*

An introductory question.

If you ask anyone why he is going to school or college, he will probably tell you that he is doing it to get an education. But why should anyone want an education and why should the public authorities go to the expense of providing it? Even more, why should they put themselves to the trouble of compelling everyone to attend school, during several years of his life, whether he wants to do it or not? Individual citizens must feel that education has a high value, otherwise so many of them would not be seeking it. It must also be looked upon as having a high value to the social order, otherwise so much of the taxpayer's money would not be spent upon it. So what is the purpose of education and why is it the public function upon which the average American city spends about one-fourth of its entire annual income,—more than it expends on health work, police and fire protection, parks, street maintenance, and public libraries, all put together?

The threefold purpose of education:

1. Economic.

In general the purpose of education is threefold. First, it aims to give young men and women the sort of training which will enable them to become self-supporting. It makes them better able to earn their own living. This is a fundamental purpose because earning a living is one of the most insistent problems that most people have to solve, especially in times of business depression. Until men and women are able to handle that problem they cannot solve any others. This economic objective of education is steadily increasing its importance, moreover, because of the high specialization which is being developed in all fields of work. In our present-day economic organization there is no place whatever for illiterates, and almost no place outside the ranks of unskilled labor for the semi-illiterate whose education has not progressed beyond the most elementary stage. There was a time when mere ability to read and write served as a passport to steady jobs, but that day has now gone by. Earning power has become closely linked with education.[1]

But helping people to earn a living is not the sole purpose of education, and an educational system which confined itself to this alone would be seriously defective. A second objective in education is to develop the personality of the individual. It is the function of the school to search out the native abilities and inclinations of each pupil so that these qualities may be trained and developed. Personal aptitudes which are not directly connected with the work of earning a living may nevertheless be worth developing because the durable satisfactions of life are not entirely dependent on the amount of income that anyone earns. The balance sheet of a happy life cannot be cast in tables of assets and liabilities. To live a contented life it is necessary that an individual shall know what is going on in the world, appreciate its significance, understand its varied implications, and have a share in its cultural activities. Education likewise encourages the individual to develop a versatility of interests and thus enables him to make profitable use of his leisure time. 2. Cultural.

The third purpose of education, the social purpose, is nowadays regarded as the most important of the three. Above all things else, public education has come to be looked upon as a process of training in good citizenship. In democratic communities such training is of vital importance because democracy rests upon the good sense and tolerance of the people. It is the social purpose of education to train men to think before they speak or act, to remember that there are two sides to every question and hence to approach public issues with thoughtfulness and discrimination. As economic activities have become more intricate, so government has grown increasingly complex. This is particularly true of municipal government. The services which the city now renders to its citizens are more numerous, more technical, and more expensive than ever before. 3. Civic.

Popular government cannot function effectively unless the people know what they are getting from their rulers and what they are expected to give in return. Information on such matters The relation of the schools to citizenship.

[1] On the general topic of educational purposes there is a good discussion in Boyd H. Bode, *Fundamentals of Education* (New York, 1922).

will come to them from a wide variety of sources, some accurate and reliable; others biased, partisan, and misleading. It is only through education that people can be taught the art of discriminating between the true and the false, or between the half-true and the half-false, which is a much harder differentiation to make. It is only through education that they can be enabled to distinguish clearly between what is good sense and what is mere sophistry in the vast amount of information and misinformation which comes to them through the newspapers, over the radio, and in their daily conversations with other people. In large measure, accordingly, the cost of public education is an outlay for the upbuilding of an intelligent and discriminating citizenship. James Russell Lowell once wrote that "in making education not only common to all, but in some sense compulsory on all, the destiny of free republics in America was practically settled." And it is only by such means that the safeguarding of that destiny can be assured.

The spread of free public education in the United States.

Until about a hundred years ago free education was everywhere regarded as a form of high-grade charity. Those who could pay for the elementary schooling of their children were expected to do it in private seminaries, while those who could not afford this luxury sent their children to public or tax-supported schools. A century ago, when Andrew Jackson was President of the United States, at least one-fourth of the people were absolutely illiterate and about one-half of them were without any education beyond the most elementary stage. The proportion of illiteracy among women was especially large because so little provision had been made for the education of girls. But the movement for the establishment of free public schools spread steadily and by the middle of the nineteenth century the system of public elementary education had spread itself over the greater portion of the country. Since the close of the Civil War the policy of making elementary education not only free but compulsory has been adopted in all parts of the United States. The total enrollment in American public schools is now more than twenty-five millions, and the cost of educating this vast army of young citizens is about two billion dollars a year.

Education as a state function.

Since the national constitution gives the federal government no powers with respect to public education, the entire responsibility rests with the several states. It is true that the federal government maintains in the Department of the Interior a bureau known as the

SCHOOL ADMINISTRATION

Office of Education, but this office has no mandatory powers. Its functions are merely to collect statistics and facts showing the condition and progress of education in the several states, to help local school systems by furnishing them with information, and to render general services of an advisory nature.[1] Education in all its branches is wholly under state supervision and every state has assumed the duty of establishing a public school system. The detailed arrangements, however, vary from one state to another. In some of them the management of the public schools is largely centralized in the hands of the state authorities, while in others it is left almost entirely to the school boards of counties, cities, towns, or school districts. Everywhere there is a state department of education with a board or a superintendent in charge, some states having both. This department exercises a certain degree of control or supervision over the local school authorities, but the scope and strictness of this control depends upon the general organization and traditions of the state educational system.[2] In general there is more local autonomy or educational home rule in the older states of the East than in the newer states of the West.

This raises a question concerning the extent to which the state authorities should control the administration of the local schools.[3] On the one hand it is argued that every community has educational problems and requirements which are peculiar to itself and should be allowed to deal with these in its own way without having to comply with uniform state-wide regulations. It is pointed out, moreover, that in most states the chief burden of supporting the public schools is placed upon the local taxpayer. If he is paying more than half the cost, ought he not to have a dominant voice in deciding questions of school policy, organization, and management? On the other hand it stands to reason that if every city, town, and village is left free to manage its schools without any central control, there will be no uniformity in the subjects taught, the qualifications of teachers, the financing of the schools, or the scholastic standards. Such a system would not only be

State vs. local control of schools.

---

[1] For further information see Paul V. Betters, *Federal Services to Municipal Governments*, Municipal Administration Service, Publication No. 24 (New York, 1931), pp. 49–54.

[2] H. E. Schrammel, *The Organization of State Departments of Education* (Columbus, 1926), and W. G. Reeder, *The Chief State School Officer*, Bulletin of the United States Office of Education, No. 5 (Washington, 1924).

[3] See E. P. Cubberley, *State School Administration* (Boston, 1927), especially chap. xi.

wasteful but it would present serious difficulties in connection with the transfer of pupils from one school to another outside the same community. It would mean that some school systems would be kept at a high pitch of efficiency while others would fail to achieve the main purposes for which they are established.

<small>How far should state supervision extend?</small>

The public school system is maintained for the benefit of the whole people, not for portions of the people here and there. When the state laws make education compulsory, and when the state treasury grants money to local schools, as it does to some extent in virtually every state of the Union, it would seem to be within the province of the state authorities to make sure that the money is judiciously spent. A certain amount of central control seems therefore to be necessary, but it is not for the best interests of public education that every school throughout the state should be conducted in exactly the same way. Some discretion and independence should be given to the local school authorities to meet the varying needs of their own communities and to make experiments which they think would be of educational value. In other words the state should exercise so much control, and no more, as is necessary to secure reasonable uniformity in the whole educational system and to guarantee the maintenance of minimum standards; it should leave everything else to the local authorities.

<small>School districts and school boards.</small>

The unit of local school administration in the United States is the school district. In urban areas this district is usually, but not always, coterminous in its boundaries with the limits of a city or town. The governing organ of the district is a school board or board of education. This body varies considerably in size from city to city; and its members are sometimes appointed, although more commonly elected. Appointive boards exist in New York, Chicago, and San Francisco, the appointments being made by the mayor; whereas in Philadelphia, Detroit, Cleveland, and Los Angeles the members of the school board are elected by popular vote. Taking the remaining cities of the country, about four-fifths of them have elective boards. A few elect members by wards of the city, but the great majority have now adopted the plan of election at large.

<small>Appointive vs. elective boards.</small>

A generation ago it was frequently argued that by making school boards appointive, the work of school administration could be taken out of politics. Men and women who would not campaign for election, it was said, might be induced to accept appointive membership on the school board where their special capacities and interests would be utilized without their being forced continually to play politics in order to obtain reëlection. It has been found by experience, however, that appointive boards have not been of noticeably better quality than those elected by the people, nor have they kept the school administration any more free from the taint of partisan politics.

Students of municipal administration are now in fairly general agreement that the school board should be relatively small in size, containing not more than seven or nine members. These members ought to be elected for terms of from three to five years with one or two retiring annually. They should be chosen by the voters of the city at large, on a non-partisan ballot at a special school election. Service on school boards should be unpaid. There should be no salaries or allowances for meetings because even a small salary or allowance is apt to be an attraction to inferior candidates. It is frequently asserted that school boards in large communities have so much to do, and hence make such heavy demands on the time of their members, that it is impossible for men to serve on such boards without sacrificing their own personal interests. For this sacrifice, it is argued, there ought to be appropriate compensation. *The right kind of local board.*

But the trouble is that members of school boards have been taking too much upon themselves. They could save their own time, without detriment to the best interests of school administration, by giving more freedom of action to the superintendent and reserving fewer details for their own decision. When a school board finds it necessary to meet two or three times per week as well as to hold several committee meetings and conferences, one can be certain that the board is usurping functions which do not belong to it. With a proper organization in the offices of the superintendent and business manager, there is no reason why members of school boards should feel it necessary to devote any considerable part of their time to the work of school administration. The essential functions of a school board, as a board, can be performed in a very few hours per week. Directors of large business concerns customarily meet only once a month, but they could find excuse for meeting every day if they set out to deal with all the administrative details which school boards frequently try to settle. A school board has only one important duty, which is to reflect in a broad and catholic spirit the judgment and sense of the commu- *Its proper functions.*

nity in matters of school policy. To manage the schools is not its business.

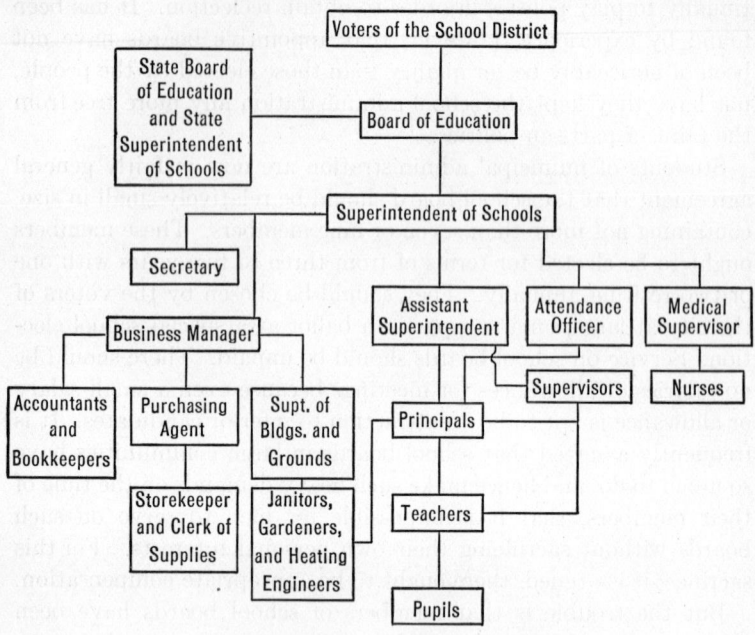

ORGANIZATION OF A SCHOOL DISTRICT

Why school boards should be kept small.

One reason for keeping school boards small in size is to avoid the waste of time in fruitless debates and discussions. A school board of fifteen or twenty members affords a forum for oratory, while a small group of five, seven, or nine does not. Moreover, when school boards are large, it becomes virtually essential to appoint committees and to have a good deal of the work done by these committees,—by committees on school buildings, on the appointment and promotion of teachers, on textbooks, on courses of study, and so on. This policy not only increases the amount of time which each member of the board must devote to his official duties, but it divides responsibility and puts a premium on secrecy in the conduct of school affairs. What is even worse, the committees often become centers for the distribution of patronage. The fact that service on a school board is unpaid does not deter the politician from striving to get himself elected to this body if by so doing he can get a share in the award of contracts, the appointment of janitors, and the making of dickers with publishing houses for the use of their textbooks. Politicians believe in committees, plenty of them, whether in city councils or in school boards, because the committee system enables them to help their friends at the public expense without such action becoming too widely known.

Most people are agreed on the proposition that party politics and political patronage should have no place in the management of the city schools, but it is easier to agree upon this principle than to make it an actuality of government. School elections in many American communities are still contested on party lines, or, if not avowedly so, upon lines of cleavage which closely coincide with party affiliations. In some parts of the country the school elections are considerably influenced by racial or religious divisions. In still other communities the school teachers and their friends have built themselves into what is virtually a political organization which tries to encompass the election of its own candidates. Very often the broader issues of educational policy are lost to view at school elections and the contest is largely a battle of special interests. *Keeping the schools out of politics.*

The best way to keep the schools out of politics, and out of factional campaigns, is to deprive school boards of their power to distribute lucrative patronage among political workers. This can be done by establishing strict rules relating to the acquisition of land for school sites, the award of contracts for buildings, the purchase of supplies and textbooks, the appointment and promotion of teachers, the hiring of janitors, and the fixing of pay-schedules. School administration cannot be kept clear of politics in any other way, for so long as there is valuable patronage to be distributed at the discretion of elective officials there will be a vigorous effort on the part of politicians to manipulate the elections at which these officials are chosen. *The abolition of patronage.*

The most important responsibility of a school board is the selection of a superintendent. This office is the pivotal point in school administration and determines its entire character. The superintendent should be a man or woman with special training for the post, a professional educator with administrative capacity and preferably with administrative experience. He should be well paid, chosen for a reasonably long term, and given adequate assurance of continued tenure in office so long as his work is satisfactory. The choice should be made with the greatest care because the *The superintendent of schools:*

1. His qualities.

superintendent's office is the center at which all the lines of authority and inspiration converge. No matter how competent an educator the superintendent may be, his work will fail of the best results if he is not also a good executive. For he is not only the eyes and ears of the board but its brain and conscience as well. Measured by its opportunities, therefore, the post of school superintendent is one of the most important in the entire municipal service. For it is in this office that the educational tone of the whole community is determined.

2. His functions. What are the superintendent's functions? It is often said that the school board should deal only with matters of general policy, leaving all administrative decisions to the superintendent; but the practical difficulty comes in drawing a line of demarcation between the two. Broadly speaking, however, the superintendent is the board's adviser on all technical or professional matters. He is presumed to take the initiative in the adoption of new methods, hence he must know his community, must forecast its needs, and prepare to meet them. He is expected to lay before the board his plans with respect to new school buildings, new courses of study, and all other matters affecting the school curriculum. As a rule it is also his duty to recommend the appointment, promotion, and retirement of teachers, together with their assignments of work. But the division of responsibility between the superintendent and the school board in all such matters cannot be made hard and fast. There must be some give-and-take on both sides because questions which seem to involve mere matters of administrative detail may create precedents which set the course of general policy. Everything depends upon the competence and tact of the superintendent, the good sense and forbearance of the board and, most of all, upon the measure of confidence which each reposes in the other.

The business manager. In large cities it is impossible for the superintendent of schools to bestow personal attention on all his duties, hence he is usually given the help of one or more assistant superintendents among whom he may apportion some of his responsibilities, more particularly those which involve contacts with the supervisors of teaching and with the school principals. In smaller cities the superintendent is usually expected to prepare the annual budget and to handle all sorts of business matters connected with the work of the schools; but in many of the larger communities it has now become the practice of school boards to engage a business manager or business agent for this work. When such an official is employed it becomes his duty to look after the preparation of the annual budget, the construction and maintenance of school buildings, the making of the monthly payroll, the purchase, storage, and distribution of supplies, the supervision of janitors, the approval of bills, and the keeping of the school accounts. Occasionally the business manager is directly responsible to the school board, but more often, and preferably, his immediate responsibility is to the superintendent.[1]

Finding a capable business manager for a large school system, or a well-qualified assistant superintendent to take charge of school business in a smaller one, is almost as difficult as finding a capable superintendent, for the position requires not only business capacity and judgment but integrity and resourcefulness. In other words it is not enough that the business manager shall be a good business man; he must also have a familiarity with educational purposes, methods, and problems. Otherwise he is apt to spend his energies in effecting economies at the expense of educational effectiveness.

Under the general jurisdiction of the superintendent come the supervisors, principals, and teachers. In early days the selection of teachers was made by the members of the school board directly. This practice is still maintained in some small cities where candidates for appointment are interviewed by the board, or by its committee on teachers, in order to determine which applicants seem to have the highest personal qualifications. But in the larger cities the appointments are now made on the recommendation of the superintendent. His selections must be made, however, from among applicants who possess the educational qualifications established by the state laws or by the rules of the local school board. The laws in many of the states now provide that no one may be appointed to a teaching position in any elementary or secondary school unless he or she is in possession of a teaching credential issued by the state department of education. To obtain such a credential one must have not only completed a certain amount of general academic training but must have pursued designated courses in a teacher-training institution. The requirements differ from state to state and in the various classes of schools, those established for high school teachers being considerably above those required of teachers in the elementary grades. Many of the

The school staff:

How selected.

---

[1] This issue is fully discussed in H. P. Smith, *Business Administration of the Public Schools* (Yonkers, N. Y., 1929), chap. iv.

largest cities now have normal schools for the training of elementary teachers, but appointments are not usually restricted to persons who have received their training in these schools. Applicants from outside the city are also eligible, but in the larger school systems all those seeking appointment, whether trained locally or elsewhere, are customarily required to take a competitive examination.

<small>The teacher-tenure problem.</small> Supervisors, principals, and teachers are as a rule appointed for one school year only. This makes it essential that their contracts be renewed annually by the board of education upon the recommendation of the school superintendent. In most cases the reappointments are made as a matter of course, but the plan of annual contracts is one which opens the door to personal and political favoritism. It has often provided the occasion for the most unseemly wire-pulling and flagrant injustice. Not only that, but the plan of annual election gives the teachers a feeling of insecurity which is detrimental to the morale of the entire teaching staff. Accordingly it has been provided by law in some of the states that annual appointments shall be made only during a probationary period with permanence of tenure thereafter. But in remedying one evil, these teacher-tenure laws have produced another. Too often they serve as an encouragement to laxity and indifference on the part of those teachers who have completed the probationary term and feel themselves comfortably settled for life. Feeling secure in the tenure of their positions, there are some teachers who become stale, self-satisfied, unprogressive, lacking in alertness, and uncoöperative. It is true that even under the protection of tenure laws a teacher may be removed on charges, after a proper hearing; but this procedure is so distasteful to all concerned that teachers on permanent tenure are removed from service on the rarest occasions only.

<small>The turnover in the rank of teachers.</small> Between the plan of annual elections and that of life-tenure some reasonable compromise ought to be worked out, avoiding the evils of both. Probably this can be found by a provision that after a certain probationary term the teachers will not be subject to annual reëlection but will hold their posts during the pleasure of the board. Not all the difficulties, however, are connected with the providing of equitable tenure, or even with the matter of releasing inferior teachers from the school staff. A more perplexing problem is that of keeping the best teachers from leaving the service. Large numbers of young women go into elementary school

teaching with no intention of making it a permanent career but merely as a way of passing the time until matrimony beckons. Many young men likewise enter the teaching profession for a few years as a means of earning money to continue their post-graduate studies or for setting themselves up in business. Hence the turnover in the ranks of school teachers is high in comparison with that of college teachers or even compared with the higher ranks of business enterprise. City schools find it hard to get good teachers, and harder to keep them, for both of which difficulties there is but one remedy—the maintenance of salaries at a point where the schools cannot only secure but retain a high measure of teaching skill.

In most cities there is a minimum rate of compensation based upon the rate paid to new teachers in the lowest elementary grades. Higher salaries are then given to teachers in the more advanced grades with a stated annual increase until a certain maximum is reached.[1] Under the laws of some states these annual increases are automatic and must be granted without reference to the teacher's proficiency or lack of it. In other states the annual increase is optional with the superintendent and school board. This is by all means the preferable plan. In many of the larger cities it has become the practice to stipulate that no promotions will be made except as the result of promotional examinations or unless the teacher satisfactorily pursues certain studies at a recognized institution of higher education during vacation periods.

The scale of salaries.

Finally, some school systems have worked out a scheme of salary increases based upon efficiency records or rating scales. This plan has not proved altogether satisfactory, for although everybody seems to agree that promotions and increases of salaries for teachers ought to be based on merit, there is no general agreement as to the best method of ascertaining where the merit lies. As yet there are no objective tests of teaching efficiency which teachers are willing to accept as valid. Rating scales, howsoever devised, are necessarily subjective, that is, they represent the opinions of those who are set to do the rating—whether they be superintendents, supervisors, principals, or fellow-teachers. And such opinions will not be in all cases divorced from the influence of personal bias or favoritism. The plan of basing promotions and increases of salary on formal rating scales may be right in principle, but expe-

Efficiency ratings.

---

[1] See the discussion of salary schedules in A. B. Moehlman, *Public School Finance* (Chicago, 1927), chap. ix.

rience shows that teachers usually resent its use, lack confidence in its fairness, and criticize its results in no uncertain terms.

Compulsory school attendance. Originally it was assumed that free education ought to be provided at the public expense through the elementary grades and no further. Then the proposal was made, and in time found acceptance, that it should also include the high schools. Accordingly the generally accepted school period now extends over eight years of elementary education and four years of high school work. The age of compulsory attendance is fixed by state law, usually at fourteen or sixteen years unless the pupil completes his eight years of elementary work at an earlier age. But most children of subnormal or relatively low intelligence do not manage to complete the work of the elementary grades before reaching the age at which the compulsory attendance ends. It is now provided in some of the states that those who leave school at fourteen or sixteen years of age must attend continuation classes for a designated number of hours per week for a certain period thereafter. Attendance at these continuation classes is counted as part of the number of hours during which the labor of these young people is permitted by law. Outside the cities, however, the laws relating to compulsory school attendance have not been rigidly enforced and even in large communities they are sometimes not rigorously applied because of a disinclination to spend money for attendance officers. A sufficient number of these officials should be attached to every public school system. They should investigate all cases of non-attendance reported to them by principals, teachers, policemen, or juvenile court officers. Their function should be not only to investigate such cases but to discover the causes of truancy so that these may be remedied.

To what point should public education extend? Public support of education is now passing to a point beyond the elementary and high school grades. Many cities have established junior colleges which provide two years of college work, and a few municipalities maintain complete colleges or universities. Such institutions are found, for example, in Toledo, Akron, Cincinnati, Detroit, and New York. So the American taxpayer is now confronted with the question: At what point in the educational process does the obligation of the taxpayer come to an end? There are state universities, publicly supported, in many of the American commonwealths, but these institutions are not always situated in close proximity to the largest cities. Hence the widespread demand that collegiate facilities shall be brought right into the home communities where eligible students live. The junior colleges, which embody a halfway response to this demand, will doubtless materialize into full-fledged four-year institutions. And if they do it is obvious that a greatly increased burden of taxation for educational purposes is in sight.

More attention is nowadays being given by the school authorities to the subject of adult education. This involves the use of the school buildings after the regular hours for classes in citizenship, English composition, American history, and a considerable range of general instruction including vocational training adapted to the use of grown persons. This instruction is customarily provided by members of the regular school staff, hence it has in some cases involved an overloading of these teachers. While the cost of adult education programs is in some cases partially financed by state grants-in-aid, the planning and supervision of the work is usually under the local school authorities. With a shortening of the customary hours of weekly work in industries and the increased amount of leisure which will come as a result of this shortening, the demand for adult education on a broader scale will undoubtedly undergo a considerable increase during the next few years. The question therefore arises whether the entire cost ought to be borne from the public treasury or whether those who receive the advantages of adult education should be required to pay a portion of it. There are both economic and psychological arguments in favor of the latter policy. While adult education can hardly be expected to pay its way, it certainly ought to pay its share. *Adult education.*

Graduation from an elementary school has traditionally been looked upon as the logical point at which the general run of pupils should terminate their education and begin to earn their living. Even yet the majority of pupils leave school at that stage. Our system of school divisions has therefore brought it about that there is no logical breaking-off point between the age of fourteen (elementary school graduation) on the one hand, and eighteen (high school graduation) on the other. To remedy this situation it is now being advocated that the whole school course be divided into three parts by interposing a junior high school between the elementary and high school grades. Many communities have adopted this plan which is said to have the additional advantage of providing a more efficient system of instruction for pupils in the two highest elementary classes. The junior high school takes the seventh and *The school graduations.*

eighth grades from the grammar school, adds the first year of a regular high school course, and thus provides a 6-3-3 program. Graduation from the junior high school, normally at the age of fifteen, thus provides a logical stopping point which did not exist under the older arrangement. In a few cities this plan has been further elaborated into a 6-4-4 program, comprising six elementary grades, four years of junior high school, and four years of regular high school and junior college combined, thus taking the pupil all the way from five or six to nineteen or twenty years of age.

The old and the new curricula. To maintain the interest of pupils during the long stretch of schooling, as well as to make the training more useful to them in later life, the entire curriculum of the public schools has been undergoing a radical change. The old-time high school was in large measure a literary and cultural institution. It catered mainly to those who were expecting to enter college. Its course of study did not bear any direct relation to the present or future interests of the great majority who were not headed in that direction. This cultural tradition had come down from past generations when education was mainly the privilege of the leisure class and was primarily designed to develop cultured gentlemen. But since almost ninety per cent of all the pupils in the public schools go directly into some form of industrial or mercantile employment rather than into the learned professions, it can readily be seen that no program of cultural studies can meet the educational needs of a modern community. Hence the school authorities have been responding to the strong demand for vocational education. Such education includes three things: (a) a broad and practical foundation in elementary education of the ordinary type; (b) a study of the social and civic forces which control the life of the people; and, (c) definite training in some particular vocation or trade.

Vocational education. Vocational studies have therefore spread themselves all over the school curriculum during the past twenty-five years. They include such things as shop work, millinery, sewing, cooking, stenography, mechanical drawing, even carpentry and machine work. Place has been made for them by crowding the older high school studies, particularly the foreign languages and mathematics, into the background. The demand for vocational education comes from a variety of sources—from parents who believe that education ought to be directly related to earning power; from teachers who are convinced that there is little or no educational value to be had by drilling pupils in lessons which do not interest them; from a portion of the general public which has been led to believe that the schools are chiefly concerned with fitting pupils to earn their own living; and, finally, from enterprising employers who have seen in this form of education a chance to get a plentiful supply of partly trained workers.

No sensible person will regret that the schools have moved in this new direction; the only question is how far they ought to go. If the sole purpose of education were to teach the art of getting and holding a job, there would be no occasion to limit the drift of the schools to pure materialism; but man does not live by bread alone and it is a serious question whether the great emphasis that is now being placed upon purely vocational studies will not impair the effectiveness of American schools with respect to the attainment of the other high purposes for which they are maintained. The value of an education, whether in school or in college, does not depend upon the accumulation of knowledge in one field rather than in another. It is measured by the amount of self-propelled intellectual activity that it has inspired in the student. And some of the vocational subjects are of relatively slight service in that direction. *How far should it be carried?*

The various changes in the scope and drift of public instruction have made new and enlarged demands upon the school plant. The location, planning, and equipment of schoolhouses have become matters of much greater moment than they used to be. A good school should be in a region of relative quiet, not in close proximity to a railroad or an interurban street railway with heavy cars. Its site should be spacious enough to afford room for playgrounds, an athletic field, and other appurtenances besides the school building. The old idea was that a good school site must be centrally located, within convenient walking distance of all pupils attending it; but as respects a high school, this is no longer a vital consideration, and even elementary pupils who live at a distance can now be brought to and from the school in motor-busses. Convenience of location is still a matter of some importance, however, because the adults who resort to the schools for evening instruction cannot well be transported in that way. *The school plant.*

As for the school buildings, if they are more than a single story in height, they should be of fire-resisting construction, and if the city is located in an earthquake zone special measures should be *School buildings.*

taken to ensure their structural safety. Particular attention should be given to the ventilation, lighting, and heating of school buildings.[1] It is also desirable that these structures be so constructed that they can be readily and economically made over, for the local needs as respects the interior arrangements of school buildings undergo considerable changes within a relatively short term of years. Too often, unfortunately, the architects and the school authorities unite in the creation of massive structures, built at heavy expense, which cannot be remodelled without large outlays when the interior layout becomes ill suited to new conditions. The result of this is to prolong antiquated methods of instruction because of the limitations imposed by the physical plant.

No one knows what sort of school buildings a city will need twenty or thirty years hence; but we can be fairly certain that it will be something different from what is needed today. Wise school boards follow the policy of building inexpensively with the expectation that when a school building becomes out of date it can be remodelled without spending too much money. This does not mean, however, that the schoolhouses need be small, with accommodation for only a few classes. Larger structures are desirable from both a financial and an educational point of view; but even large schoolhouses can be built with an eye to economy.

Wider use of the school plant. Under ordinary conditions the rooms of a public school building are in use during an astonishingly few hours in the course of a year. Five hours a day or thereabouts, five days a week, for about forty weeks is the usual program. This relatively small use has involved a high per hour cost to the community. It has been suggested that greater use might be made of school buildings by the introduction of a platoon system, such as would enable the pupils, especially in the elementary grades, to be doubled up by the plan of having two half-day sessions. But experiments along this line have not proved popular.

Recreational uses. The use of the school plant for other than educational purposes, particularly by groups of citizens after school hours, has also been deemed practicable and to some extent has been encouraged by the authorities. School buildings are now used in most cities for

---

[1] F. B. Dresslar, *American Schoolhouses*, Bulletin of the United States Bureau of Education, No. 5 (Washington, 1910), is an old but excellent treatise on this subject. It should be supplemented by reference to *Standards for Elementary School Buildings* (New York, 1923) and *Standards for High School Buildings* (New York, 1924) by George D. Strayer and N. L. Engelhardt.

all manner of civic and social welfare meetings, and to some extent for purely recreational purposes as well. Many large schools have elaborate recreational facilities consisting of a school playground, tennis courts, athletic fields, a gymnasium, a swimming pool, an auditorium, and so on. These are an integral part of the community's educational plant, yet it is only within relatively recent years that the public has come to appreciate this fact and to understand the educational value of supervised play.

Public playgrounds and athletic fields for children, whether connected with the schools or located elsewhere, should therefore be under the jurisdiction of the school authorities. For these areas are not parks in any sense and there is no sound reason for placing them under the control of the city's park department, as is done in some cities. As respects athletic fields, tennis courts, and other recreational facilities for adults, the problem of jurisdiction is not so simple and it is by no means clear that these should be placed within the purview of the school authorities. Many cities have established regular departments of recreation which conduct some of their activities on school property, in which case the problem becomes one of working in coöperation with the school authorities.[1]

Jurisdiction over playgrounds.

Public education in the United States has become enormously more expensive during the past twenty years. School buildings have cost more to construct and maintain; the pay of teachers has been increased; the supplies used in schools have been steadily improving in quality and likewise in price. Newer methods of school organization and instruction, the wider use of the schools, the incoming of vocational education, the providing of free textbooks, the progress of health work in the schools, the establishment of evening schools, continuation schools, and junior colleges—all these advances have resulted in an ascending budget year after year. It is estimated that public education in the United States now costs about two billion dollars per annum, which is twice what it cost fifteen years ago. If the expenses double again within a similar period, it will be a serious problem to find the money.

The rising cost of public education.

Educational enthusiasts are prone to forget that the schools are not our only instrumentalities of public service. They must share the public income with other municipal departments—streets, health, poor relief, police, fire protection, water supply, sanitation —all of which are equally vital to the public well-being. It may

And the limit to community resources.

[1] See also Chapter XL.

be replied, of course, that the way to get more money for all of them is to keep raising the tax rates. This betrays the existence of a widespread delusion—that a city tax rate has the sky for its limit. The truth is that when taxes on property rise above a certain point they operate to discourage the erection of new buildings and to check the industrial progress of a community. Within certain flexible limits a city has only so much money to spend. If the schools get more than their share, other departments will be inadequately provided for.

School-budgets: Who should control them?

Some of the money that is needed for the support of the public schools is supplied by the taxpayers of the city or school district, and some of it by the state. In many parts of the country the annual contributions of the state treasury toward defraying the cost of local schools is very large. In some states the school board has independent authority to determine its own tax rate up to a certain maximum, but in others the board submits its requirements to the city council and is allowed such sums from the general tax levy as the council may choose to give it. The chief argument for placing the appropriation of school funds in the hands of the city council or the city commission is that it unifies the local taxing power, making one representative body responsible for all municipal expenditures. But experience demonstrates that there are serious objections to the policy of requiring the school board to come as a suppliant before the group of politicians who compose the average city council. Nothing is more certain to draw the schools into politics and keep them there. Under such an arrangement the members of the school board must play the game as the councilmen understand it; they must be ready to do favors or increased appropriations will not be forthcoming. The best policy, and the one which is now being followed by many of the cities, is to set a maximum limit within which the school board has its own taxing authority.

The per capita cost of the public schools.

The steady increase in the percentage of local revenues now absorbed by the schools has been the subject of much adverse comment in business circles. School expenditures constitute the largest item in local budgets. They have increased more rapidly, during the past twenty years, than expenditures for police, fire protection, sanitation, or health. Stated in round figures the sum of two billion dollars per annum seems a large sum for the country to spend on public education; it figures out to about sixteen dollars per capita or something like fifty dollars per family. Still it is not as much as the American people spend each year upon beer, tobacco, chewing gum, ice cream, perfumery, and cosmetics. It is probably a fact, moreover, that the taxpayer comes nearer to getting one hundred cents on the dollar for his expenditures on public education than he manages to secure from any other branch of municipal administration. Money for the schools will be forthcoming so long as people appreciate that this is the case. If existing sources of revenue will not stand the strain, others will be found.

But not all school expenditures can be defrayed by the levying of taxes. For large outlays such as are needed in connection with the acquisition of school sites and the construction of school buildings it is necessary to borrow money from time to time.[1] As a rule, however, no bonds can be issued on the credit of the school district without prior authorization by a majority of the voters. The general principles which apply to the issue and amortization of municipal bonds, as elsewhere explained, are applicable to these school obligations. The bonded indebtedness of school districts underwent a rapid increase during the decade 1920–1930, largely because of the elaborate building programs which many communities were induced to sponsor in an era of general prosperity. In a few of the largest cities the attempt has been made to maintain a pay-as-you-go plan of school financing by raising enough money in each year's tax levy to pay for such new school buildings as are needed. When a city reaches the point at which one or more new school buildings are required each year, the pay-as-you-go plan has obvious merits. For if a city in this situation does not adopt some such arrangement it will presently find itself borrowing money each year to pay for new school buildings and raising annually by taxation an equal or greater amount to pay off maturing bonds.

School bonds.

REFERENCES

Bibliographical aids of prime value in all branches of public education are W. S. Monroe, T. T. Hamilton, and V. T. Smith, *Locating Educational Information in Published Sources* (Urbana, Illinois, 1930), and the *Bibliography of Current Research Studies in Education* issued by the United States Bureau of Education in 1928.

[1] A discussion of school borrowing may be found in H. P. Smith, *Business Administration of the Schools* (Yonkers, N. Y., 1929), chap. xv. See also John G. Fowlkes, *School Bonds* (Milwaukee, 1924).

The best book on the matters which have been discussed in the foregoing chapter is Ellwood P. Cubberley, *Public School Administration* (new edition, Boston, 1929). In its arrangement of material, clarity of presentation, and excellence of style this volume has no equal among books of its kind. Good bibliographies are appended to each chapter. The same author's *History of Education* (Boston, 1920) is a serviceable source of information on earlier developments.

Books of interest and value, particularly on the financing of the public schools, are G. D. Strayer and others, *Problems in Educational Administration* (New York, 1925), E. W. Knight, *Education in the United States* (Boston, 1929), Arthur E. Moehlman, *Public School Finance* (Chicago, 1927), F. H. Swift, *Federal and State Policy in Public School Finance* (Boston, 1931), H. F. Clark, *The Cost of Government and the Support of Education* (New York, 1924), H. C. Morrison, *The Management of School Money* (Chicago, 1932), E. E. Lewis, *Personnel Problems of the Teaching Staff* (New York, 1925), N. L. and F. Engelhardt, *Public School Business Administration* (New York, 1927) and *Public School Organization and Administration* (Boston, 1931), H. P. Rainey, *Public School Finance* (New York, 1921), W. S. Deffenbaugh, *School Administration and Finance* (Washington, 1931), Harry P. Smith, *Business Administration of the Public Schools* (Yonkers, N. Y., 1929), W. G. Reeder, *The Business Administration of a School System* (Boston, 1929), and William H. Kirkpatrick, *Education for a Changing Civilization* (New York, 1927).

Many useful publications are issued by the United States Office of Education and material of current interest may be found in the *Educational Yearbook*, published in New York, the *Research Bulletins* and the *Journal* of the National Education Association, as well as in the *School Board Journal*, the latter two being published monthly.

CHAPTER XXXIII

PUBLIC LIBRARIES

We are building, in our public libraries, temples of happiness and wisdom common to all. No other institution which society has brought forth is so wide in its scope; so universal in its appeal; so near to every one of us; so inviting to both young and old; so fit to teach without arrogance the ignorant, and, without faltering, the wisest.—*John Cotton Dana.*

The public library is an institution owned by the municipality and opened to the public without charge. It is a part of the community's educational equipment and also an important agency of public recreation. For the resources of the public library enable the citizenship to combine intellectual and vocational self-improvement with an agreeable use of leisure hours. More than any other institution it is an index to the cultural standards and tastes of the city or town that it serves. Tell anyone what the community reads and he can tell you what kind of community it is. {The place of the library in the community.}

Until about a generation ago, however, the public library was a somewhat passive agency of education and service. For the most part it merely served as a gloomy storehouse for books, a sort of literary museum, to which free public access was not encouraged but on the contrary was looked upon as a disturbing intrusion. The services of the old-time public library were strictly limited to those who came of their own accord, undeterred by the intricacies of library rules and routine. Today this situation has changed or is changing. The public library has come to realize that its business is to bring books and readers into contact with one another. The test of a modern public library's usefulness is not the number of volumes on its shelves but the amount of daily patronage which it is able to obtain from all classes in the community.

Despite its importance from the standpoint of cultural advancement, the administration of the public library has always been looked upon by the municipal authorities as a relatively insignificant part of their responsibilities. The amount of money spent on the library each year is a mere trifle in municipal budgets. The earliest public libraries were either administered by the local {Library boards.}

school board or turned over to the custody of unpaid library trustees appointed by the city authorities. The latter plan became in time the common one and it is still the most typical form of public library administration in all parts of the United States. Members of this library board are elected by popular vote in many of the smaller cities, but in most of the larger ones they are appointed by the chief municipal executive. In a few cities the library trustees are a self-perpetuating body. And in a few others the selection is made by the board of education.

Libraries under the manager plan.

Under the city manager plan of government the library is sometimes placed directly within the manager's jurisdiction, but more often the board system is continued, with its members appointed by the city council.[1] Occasionally the library board is given the status of a separate corporation, with independent powers somewhat akin to those of the school authorities, but more frequently its administration is an integral part of the general city government, although with a somewhat greater independence than is accorded to the other municipal departments. The argument for this independence is usually based on the proposition that the library is an agency of public education entitled to something like the same administrative autonomy which is accorded to the schools.

Should the public library be organized as a separate department?

Most students of municipal government are inclined to the opinion that public library administration should be a regular and not an independent municipal function. But it should be organized as a department by itself and not combined within some larger city department such as public welfare or public recreation as has been done in some cities under the commission form of government. The public library department should be headed by a board with its members appointed by the mayor, or, in city manager cities, by the city council. It has been suggested that in the larger cities unpaid library boards should be abolished and their functions transferred to a full-time, well-paid commissioner or director of libraries, but this idea has not gained much favor, nor does it deserve to do so. For among all branches of municipal administration the library department is the one that most appropriately lends itself to the board system of management. Its problems are

---

[1] For a full discussion see the article by Carleton B. Joeckel on "The Public Library under the City Manager Form of Government" in the *Library Quarterly*, Vol. I, pp. 121–151 (April, 1931), and Vol. I, pp. 301–329 (July, 1931).

of the sort that can best be handled by common counsel, by deliberation, and by the reconciliation of honest but divergent views. Few decisions in library administration have to be made in a hurry. A board of influential citizens can perform great service by interpreting the library to the community and the community to the library.

The library board should be composed of not fewer than five nor more than nine members, depending upon the size of the city. Preferably these members should be appointed for five-year terms with approximately one-fifth of the membership retiring annually. No salaries should be paid to members of the library board, nor should there by any per diem allowance for meetings. For here is one branch of the city service in which it should never be difficult to obtain the services of competent men and women without remuneration. Nevertheless the selection of members for the library board ought to be made with the greatest care in order to afford proper representation to all elements in the community. And no one should be appointed to the board unless he or she is genuinely interested in the work of the library. Appointments to unpaid boards of this kind have been too frequently motivated by a desire to bestow official recognition upon prominent citizens whom the mayor or the city council wish to link up with the administration. Such appointments are rarely productive of beneficial results. The same is true of ex-officio members who are given places on the library board because they hold some other municipal office such as chairman of the city council or director of public recreation. They rarely attend meetings with any regularity or evince much interest when they come.

How members of library boards should be chosen.

The selection of board members should be made from among those citizens who have demonstrated their genuine interest in the library by making consistent use of it, from among lovers of books who appreciate the true function of a library and are ready to serve its interests at a personal sacrifice. The selections should not be made with a view to giving representation to any race, creed, or social class, and care should be taken to avoid the appointment of zealots or faddists who have their own special hobbies to promote. Members of a library board who attend its meetings regularly and show an active interest in their work should be reappointed, while those who prove ineffective should be dropped without any compunction when their terms come to an end. Continuity of member-

The kind of member who is most helpful.

ship is desirable, but the introduction of some new blood from time to time is equally advantageous. For if the composition of a library board is permitted to remain unchanged year after year, the whole administration of the library will presently become quite impervious to any suggestion of new policies, functions, or methods. That is what has happened in many instances.

The avoidance of committees. The library board ought to meet at least once a month and preferably should do its work without the intervention of committees. But if the board has more than seven or nine members it is difficult to avoid the committee system. A large board cannot quickly reach decisions in plenary session. Hence it is likely to feel the need of a finance committee, a committee on buildings and grounds, a committee on books, and various other committees, including perhaps an executive committee to do its work between the regular monthly meetings. Even with a fairly small board the committee system is helpful when there is much work to be done, but the objection is that the various committees gradually draw both the work and the responsibility into their own hands until the meetings of the board deteriorate into perfunctory sessions which merely ratify actions that have already been taken.

The board's functions. The principal duties of a library board are to appoint the librarian, approve the annual budget of the library for transmission to the regular appropriating authorities, and decide on the main features of library policy. It should function as a board of trustees, not as a board of managers, which means that it should concern itself with policies and results rather than with methods. What has been said in a previous chapter with reference to the work of a school board in relation to the superintendent of schools applies with equal force in this case. The library board should not usurp the functions of the administrative staff. It should never interfere with the routine or in the details of management. Having chosen a competent librarian it should expect him to exercise the initiative, do the work, and assume the responsibility for it. Nothing is more destructive of library morale than the over-zealous activity of committees and board members who imagine that good intentions can atone for their lack of good judgment.

The librarian. In this matter of a clear division of functions everything depends upon the choice of a competent librarian. The selection of this official is the most important function that a library board has to perform. It was not always so. Under conditions of a generation

PUBLIC LIBRARIES

ago the librarian's job was a relatively simple one. He had merely to see that books were bought, catalogued, and placed on the shelves where they could wait in innocuous desuetude until readers came to look for them. Such functions made a relatively small demand on any librarian's initiative, resourcefulness, or organizing power. But now this situation has entirely changed. The primary function of a public library head today is not merely to organize a collection of books but to organize and satisfy a constituency of readers. To accomplish this he must seek to develop a taste for reading among people of his community by establishing branch libraries and by the placing of books in various centers such as factories and schools; likewise he is expected to make contact with adult education classes, university extension courses, study clubs, and other groups to which the facilities of the library may be made of special service.

Moreover a well-organized public library must nowadays be able to render informational service to public officials, business organizations, newspapers, authors, and students of all grades. In addition city libraries now maintain juvenile departments in which an expert carefully chooses books that are likely to interest the young. Reading lists of interesting and timely subjects are also prepared and kept posted in accordance with the psychology of suggestion; arrangements are made with school teachers whereby their pupils are encouraged to use the library in connection with their essays and projects; illustrated lectures are often provided in the late afternoon hours and on Saturdays; reference rooms are provided with attendants who can help patrons of the library to find anything they may be looking for; newspapers, magazines, and other current literature are kept easy of access and up to date; seekers of books are permitted to browse around among the stacks and shelves; special exhibitions of rare, interesting, or timely books are arranged periodically; arrangements are made whereby books can be reserved by telephone and sometimes delivered by messenger; the whole atmosphere of a well-managed library has now become surcharged with the spirit of active and cheerful service. To make and keep this spirit robust is the librarian's principal responsibility today. *His newer responsibilities.*

To perform all the services which have been enumerated in the foregoing paragraph, and many others, the library must have a considerable staff including heads of divisions, assistants, cat- *The need for a good organizer.*

aloguers, desk attendants, and other subordinates, all of whom must work in close coöperation. This means that the librarian must be above all things else a good organizer, conversant with every phase of library work. But being a good organizer is not enough. To be successful the head of a public library must also be something of a diplomat, for the development of cordial relations between the library and its constituency make heavy demands in the way of patience, tact, and good humor. It goes without saying, moreover, that the librarian should be a person of good academic education supplemented by professional training in library science. Preferably he should be someone who has come up from a less important post such as the headship of a branch library or of one of the divisions in the main institution.

<small>Libraries that are behind the procession.</small> It should not be imagined, however, that all public libraries are fortunate enough to have librarians of this character or that they are everywhere alive to their possibilities for community service. There are plenty of public libraries throughout the country which have not yet been aroused from their nineteenth century stupor. Library boards in many American communities are still composed of well-meaning, highly respectable, and throughly complacent men and women who are far more concerned with the prestige of their positions than with the measure of service that the library might render. This spirit permeates from the board down the library staff until the whole organization becomes a circle of sublime indifference, engulfed by red tape and routine. What passes for the public library in some of these communities is merely a grim-visaged building with a musty odor in its public lobbies and a badly balanced assortment of books (mostly fiction) on its shelves, wherein some slow-moving spinsters stand behind the counters and with frowns on their faces hand out books that are called for. Libraries are making progress but many of them have still a long way to go.

<small>The library staff.</small> Having selected a competent librarian, the library board should expect him to make recommendations concerning appointments, promotions, and dismissals in the library staff. It should then be guided by these recommendations. Members of the board ought not to intervene with the librarian for the appointment or promotion of their own personal friends,—a point which would not need mention but for the fact that the practice is so common.

In many cities it is provided by law that appointments to positions in the public library must be made under civil service rules as a result of competitive examinations, but library boards and librarians seem to be, in general, rather out of sympathy with this method. Many of them feel that positions in the library should be exempt from civil service rules even when employees in all other branches of the municipal service are brought under it. They argue that "civil service regulations, enforced by an outside board, while they may be necessary to curb political or personal favoritism in those likely to exercise it, do not conduce to good administration when applied to bodies that are not likely to be prejudiced in either of these directions." [1] *Methods of selection.*

This exemplifies, however, a somewhat naïve but by no means uncommon point of view among heads of municipal departments. Virtually all the higher officials in city administration feel that civil service regulations are excellent for the other fellow. They do not relish the idea that a merit system, like charity, should begin at home. Civil service rules, they assure us, are quite justifiable where there is danger of favoritism or partisanship; but not in such high-minded and high-purposed departments as the schools, the library, or the hospital. One would suppose, however, that positions in the public library are of precisely the kind that ought to be filled by civil service competition, for the work is of such nature that qualifications for doing it can be more easily determined by the application of formal tests in this department than in almost any other. *Are civil service regulations desirable?*

This is the more so since appointments to positions in public libraries are now made, for the most part, from among those who have had special training. Library work has become a profession. There are special schools connected with universities, while others are adjuncts of large libraries. These schools are turning out each year a considerable number of graduates from among whom library assistants can be chosen by competitive examinations or by a scrutiny of their records under civil service rules. Unfortunately, however, the city authorities often feel that local applicants for positions in the public library ought to be given a *The training of library employees.*

---

[1] Arthur E. Bostwick, *The American Public Library* (New York, 1923), p. 21. "It is usually considered a serious handicap for the librarian to be obliged to recommend appointments from a list of candidates who have been declared eligible as a result of civil service examinations in which personality cannot be tested." John Adams Lowe, *Public Library Administration* (Chicago, 1928), p. 125.

preference and this shuts out many well-qualified persons who would otherwise be eligible.

Staff duties:
1. Administrative.

The duties of a library staff may be classified as administrative, clerical, informational, and mechanical. Administrative work consists in directing or supervising the work of the staff. This duty is performed by the librarian and by the heads of the various divisions. In large libraries these divisions include such branches of library work as circulation, reference, cataloguing, the bindery, the children's department, as well as the care of grounds and buildings. The heads of the several divisions have a varying number of assistants assigned to them.

2. Clerical.

Most of these assistants perform functions of a clerical nature. They take in and give out books over the counter, see that the records are accurately kept, make out library cards, send out notices in the case of overdue books, collect fines, and care for the considerable amount of correspondence which is necessary in connection with the purchase of books and with library work in general. Such clerical work does not differ greatly from that of other city departments and there seems to be no good reason why those who perform it should be selected in any different way.

3. Informational.

The informational work of the library staff, however, is of a more specialized character. It is performed by those employees who serve at the information desk, in the reference rooms, and in the children's department. It is their business to help readers find what they have come for. Much useful public service can be performed by competent and tactful library assistants in this field because a great many readers are perfectly helpless when confronted with the mass of cards in a library catalogue. They know in a hazy way what they want but not how to find it. Members of the staff whose business it is to help such readers must not only be quick-witted, resourceful, and throughly conversant with the contents of the library; they need also a vast endowment of patience and good nature. They are employed in educational work of the highest value.

4. Mechanical.

Under the head of mechanical work comes the checking of incoming shipments, the putting of shelf-marks on books, the affixing of labels and book pockets, the arrangement of the books on the shelves, the mending and rebinding of worn volumes, the arranging of current magazine files in their proper places, and a whole host of chores which have to be done around a library. In this category may also be placed the gardeners and the doorkeepers whose business it is to safeguard the library against the surreptitious removal of books.

Taking these four groups together, the employees of a public library may constitute a large staff,—sometimes running into the hundreds. They should be classified into definite, correlated grades according to an established plan. The positions falling within each grade ought to be clearly outlined in this plan and the qualifications, duties, and salaries should be specified. Salaries in the public library should be adjusted to meet the competition of business, teaching, and other vocations but should also take into account, on the credit side of the ledger, the relative security of tenure, the generous number of holidays which library employees usually obtain, and the opportunities for self-education that go with the work. *The salary schedules.*

The procedure by which books are selected for a public library seems arbitrary and mysterious to the average citizen who does not realize that books are selected by readers, not by librarians. In other words books are not chosen and bought in accordance with the whims of someone in the ordering department, but because the librarian and his assistants have reason to believe that if certain volumes are purchased they will be read. A librarian may believe this to be the case because the author of the book is a popular writer, or because the volume deals with a timely subject, or, more often, because a number of readers have asked for it. In selecting books for purchase every competent librarian pays careful attention to the character of the community which his library serves. His task is not merely to buy whatever books his readers may desire, for their desires may in many instances reflect a low standard of literary discrimination which in time would lower the whole tone of the library. Nor, on the other hand, is it merely a matter of selecting the books which the librarian thinks the community ought to read, for this would soon impair the library's popularity and detract from its service. The problem is to follow a judicious middle course, setting as high a standard as is practicable without stocking the shelves with books which, however worthy to be read, will fail to attract a circle of readers. *The problem of book selection.*

There are those in every community who feel that the shelves of a public library should be a resting place for the assembled souls of all that men hold wise, and for no others. They would admit *The public attitude.*

to this hallowed ground nothing that is ephemeral, risqué, or even radical. But when citizens of exalted intellectual and moral tastes criticize the library for buying so many low-voltage books, they should remember that this public institution does not cater mainly to readers of supernormal intelligence or of advanced education. People whose reading habits have been cultivated to the point where they can enjoy the best books are usually in a position to buy such volumes for themselves. Or, if not, they often have access to either private libraries or to the bookshelves of educational institutions. In any event the responsibility for the selection of books should rest with the librarian and his staff rather than with any book-choosing committee of outsiders, although an advisory committee of citizens can usually be of service by making suggestions. The library officials will make mistakes, of course, but they will make fewer of them than would be made by anyone else.

Financing the library by a direct tax or by appropriations.

Some public libraries have income from endowments which have been given them by public-spirited citizens, but the main income of practically all public libraries is derived from the municipal treasury. These funds may be obtained from a direct tax which is levied for library purposes in accordance with the provisions of the state law, or they may be obtained in the form of an annual appropriation made by the city council. The usual procedure in the latter case is for the librarian to make an estimate of financial needs for the oncoming fiscal year. These estimates, after having been approved by the library board are then presented to the mayor, city manager, or city council, as the case may be, for incorporation in the annual municipal budget. Usually the librarian or the members of the library board are given an opportunity to appear before the appropriating authorities in support of their estimates. The mayor, city manager, or city council may, however, reduce the estimates and make the appropriation less than was asked for,—which is what frequently happens.

How the direct tax plan operates.

Accordingly, most librarians and library boards regard the direct tax system as the better plan of financing. Under this system the state law or city charter provides that a city shall impose a special tax for the maintenance of its public library, with a proviso that such tax shall not exceed so much per thousand dollars of assessed valuation. In some states the law also establishes the minimum levy that must be made for this purpose. Under such a plan the library receives whatever the proceeds of the special tax may be, and neither the mayor, city manager, nor city council has any power to reduce the amount. As the city grows, moreover, and the property valuations increase, the library's revenue automatically goes up.

From the standpoint of library enthusiasts there is much to be said for the special tax method of financing. It removes the library from dependence upon the caprice of the mayor or city council as well as from the pressure of those civic organizations which are sometimes over-zealous in their efforts to have public expenditures kept down. On the other hand, if the library has a right to be exempted from the control of the regular appropriating authorities, why may not this right be claimed by other departments of municipal administration as well? Why should not the work of the health department be financed by a special tax levy? Or the department of public welfare? There is no argument for a special direct tax in the case of the public library which cannot be applied with equal force to several other departments. And if one department after another succeeds in obtaining an independent basis for its own financing, the annual tax rate of the city will ultimately represent something over which the appropriating authorities, elected by the people, have no control whatever.

Its merits and defects.

Every department of municipal administration, for its own good, should be under the necessity of submitting a detailed statement of its needs each year to some central authority. These estimates should then be gone over and carefully scrutinized, not from the standpoint of what the library would like to have but with due regard to what the taxpayers can afford. The library board is in most cases an appointive body. It is not directly responsible to the people, hence its expenditures should be placed within the purview of some municipal authority which does have such responsibility. In other words, the public library should sell itself to the public confidence as every other public activity is expected to do. That is the only way to be sure of getting adequate funds. Some years ago a committee of the American Library Association announced that "one dollar per capita of the population is a reasonable minimum annual revenue for the library in any community which desires to maintain a good public library system with trained librarians." Many public libraries receive

The library budget.

much less than this, while some are given a good deal more. On the whole, however, public libraries have been undernourished by the municipal treasuries.

The library site and building. The best site for a public library is one that is centrally located but not on one of the congested business streets. It should not have its natural light cut off by tall buildings near by, and preferably should have vacant ground on all four sides. When a city builds a civic center, the library is often included in the group without much heed being paid to the fact that an excellent location for a city hall or county building may be a poor place for an educational building. The library needs a situation that is easy of access from the residential districts, since it is from these districts that most of the patrons of the library come. As for the building itself, there is almost everywhere a popular idea that it ought to be an impressive, dignified, and rather monumental structure. But this is merely a hangover from the days when libraries were places of storage for costly books, whereas the modern public library is a community clubhouse. It is a people's rendezvous, not a safe deposit vault.

Essential features. In the older public libraries there was little space for anything but books. The modern library gives most of its space to people. It is a series of reading rooms, reference rooms, newspaper and magazine rooms, exhibition rooms, lecture halls, and open shelves, as well as of book stacks. That is why the building should be roomy without being palatial, of simple design, artistic without being ornate, well ventilated, with plenty of windows, and the best possible scheme of artificial lighting. A high standard of lighting is particularly important in rooms where the card catalogues are kept. The maintenance of a proper degree of humidity is also essential to the preservation of books and bindings. Floors in the public rooms should be of rubber or cork tile so that noise may be reduced to a minimum. And many other features of a good library building will readily come to the mind of anyone who has been in the habit of using the facilities of such an institution.

The people who use the library. What percentage of the people, in any city, make use of the public library? The fraction in many cases is pitiably small. There are whole neighborhoods in which the reading of a book is among the rarest of all phenomena. The minds of these people run in narrow grooves, never veering out of routine concentration on their own small affairs, or concerned with anything in the throbbing world outside. They read nothing but the newspaper headlines with a furtive glance now and then at the sports page or the comic strips. But these people of the proletarian stratum are not the only non-readers. At the other extreme is that element in every urban citizenship which can find no more profitable use for its leisure hours than playing bridge, drinking cocktails, and entertaining one another with small-talk futilities. Into the ranks of both these groups, into ghetto and gold coast alike, the public library should energetically press its campaign of adult education. It can be a great agency of civic enlightenment.

REFERENCES

All phases of library administration are well presented in Arthur E. Bostwick, *The American Public Library* (4th edition, New York, 1929). A smaller book on *Public Library Administration* by John Adams Lowe (Chicago, 1928) is also excellent. Some years ago the American Library Association (520 North Michigan Ave., Chicago) conducted an elaborate investigation, the results of which were published as *A Survey of Libraries in the United States* (4 vols., Chicago, 1926–1927). In the first volume of this series is a full discussion of administrative work in public libraries.

Other books that deserve mention are Carl Vitz, editor, *Current Problems in Public Library Finance* (Chicago, 1933), Joseph L. Wheeler, *The Library and the Community* (Chicago, 1924), and Jennie M. Flexner, *Circulation Work in Public Libraries* (Chicago, 1927). Attention should likewise be called to the various volumes in the series entitled *Classics of American Librarianship* edited by Arthur E. Bostwick, and to the several reports of studies made by the American Library Association, *e.g.*, *Libraries and Adult Education* (Chicago, 1926) and *Library Extension* (Chicago, 1926). Current discussions may be found in the *Library Quarterly*, the *Library Journal*, and *Public Libraries*.

CHAPTER XXXIV

HEALTH ADMINISTRATION

The public health is the foundation on which rest the happiness of the people and the welfare of the nation. The care of the public health is the first duty of the statesman.—Benjamin Disraeli.

Importance of public health work. Nothing among the functions of a city government is more important than the care for the public health. The value of this work cannot be measured in dollars and cents, for health is the greatest of all factors in personal efficiency. It is also important as a promoter of the social welfare, for ill health is an underlying cause of much human misery. Disease and poverty, sickness and dependency—they are linked together in a vicious circle of social maladjustment. Hence the safeguarding of the community's health is something that cannot be left to the discretion of individuals. It must be a group enterprise. A man's religious and political beliefs may be his own concern, but his convictions as to the source and spread of communicable disease are not. With millions of people living close together in crowded centers and coming into daily contact with one another, the protection of the public health must be a matter of social control; otherwise the ignorance or negligence of individual citizens would cause the spread of epidemics everywhere.

The crude ideas of earlier days. Primitive man was a pantheist who believed that diseases were due to the wrath of the gods. Recall, for example, the passage in Homer's *Iliad* where the sun-god in anger raised his terrible bow and with every twang of the bow-string sent brave warriors to their death by pestilence. Then came Hippocrates who moved a step nearer to the truth with his belief that the bodily ills of men were due to baleful emanations carried through the air. Hence fire was assumed to purify the atmosphere and dispel the miasma or contagium from swamps and decomposing matter. For many succeeding centuries the world suspected a certain connection between filth and disease, and believed that sickness could in some mysterious way be communicated from one person to another, but the major routes of infection were wholly unknown.

Plagues and epidemics swept over both Europe and Asia with nothing to stop them. By mediaeval Christians they were looked upon as visitations of wrath on the part of Heaven for the sins of the people. Consequently when an epidemic broke out, the people gathered together in the homes of the sick and offered up their prayers. A more effective way of spreading the plague could hardly have been devised.

Yet even as early as Roman times there were those who could put two and two together in tracing disease to its source. They saw, or thought they saw, a connection between night air and malaria—the "pestilence that walketh in darkness"—but it did not occur to them that the prolific mosquitoes of the Roman marshes which swarmed into the city after sundown were serving as the links of infection. And for nearly fifteen centuries after the fall of Rome the world remained almost entirely oblivious to what is now a commonplace of popular knowledge, namely, that food, water, and insects are the principal carriers of the great epidemics such as bubonic, typhus, typhoid, yellow fever, cholera, and malaria. Even in seventeenth century London so highly sophisticated a gentleman as the portly Pepys, when the plague raged all around him, did not take the precaution to keep aloof from the pest-houses but merely bought himself "some roll tobacco to smell and chew, which took away the apprehension."

Scientific public health work is largely the product of the last hundred years. It owes the largest part of its progress to the work of Louis Pasteur who was the first to establish the germ theory of disease; in other words, he was the first to demonstrate the direct relation between bacteria and physical ailments. In 1877 Pasteur published convincing proof that the process of organic decay is caused by minute living organisms. This was soon followed by the discovery that some of these organisms are pathogenic in their nature and consequently can serve as the progenitors of disease when they enter the human frame.

Scientific health work is a modern development.

The acceptance of the germ theory revolutionized the whole enterprise of public health. During the earlier decade of the nineteenth century, as in all previous generations, the measures taken for public health protection were crude and ineffective. Sanitary officials went around condemning everything that seemed offensive to sight or smell—stagnant water, manure piles, dead animals, rubbish heaps,—but without the slightest idea as to how these nui-

Old and new methods of health protection.

sances might transmit infection. Typhoid was often attributed to bad ventilation and smallpox to sewer gas. When people became sick they were dosed with quinine, ipecac, and other old-time drugs, but relatively little attention was paid to such precautions as the isolation of patients, quarantine, and disinfection. With the acceptance of the germ theory, however, the emphasis was gradually shifted from remedial to preventive measures such as the inspection of food and milk, the safeguarding of water supplies, the disinfection of sewage, the quarantining of homes in which communicable diseases are reported, and the eradication of insect disease-carriers. Today these measures form the foundations of public health protection.

The germ theory explained. To understand the far-reaching transformation wrought in this field by Pasteur's notable discoveries it is desirable to add a further word concerning the germ theory of disease. In its main outlines this may be stated as follows: Countless minute organisms, of which there are perhaps fifteen hundred different kinds (commonly known as microbes, bacteria, bacilli, or germs), exist in the air as well as in or upon nearly all other substances. These organisms are so small that they do not become visible to the eye except with the aid of a powerful microscope. Thousands of them can assemble in a single drop of water. Not all bacteria, however, are harmful; on the contrary most of them render a useful service. Without their aid we could not make cheese or vinegar. Nor could we have any fermented beverages. On the other hand almost all decay in organic matter is caused by the action of these same bacteria. When butter turns rancid, or milk sours, or fruit becomes rotten, it is all due to bacterial action. Under suitable conditions of temperature and in an appropriate medium the process goes on swiftly because nearly all bacteria multiply with great rapidity. In most cases they increase by division, that is, one bacillus divides itself into two, these two into four, and so on by geometrical progression. Hence one of these little fellows may find himself a great-grandfather within a very few hours.

The major routes of infection. By using laboratory methods it is possible to identify different species of bacilli, for they assume varying shapes and characteristics. The human body is a favorable environment for the propagation of microörganisms, and most disease-bearing varieties cannot live for more than a short time outside of it. Access is gained in

HEALTH ADMINISTRATION

various ways, but principally through direct or indirect personal contact, as well as through food and drink or through the bites of germ-carrying insects. Thus the bacilli of typhoid fever are usually found in polluted water, but they sometimes make their way into milk through the use of contaminated water in washing cans or other utensils. Hence the prevention of typhoid is largely a problem of protecting water supplies from pollution by sewage from hospitals and homes, in other words it is largely a matter of using care and spending money to close the major routes of transmission.

Yellow fever, malaria, and typhus are good examples of insect-borne diseases. The first two are transmitted by mosquitoes. Yellow fever was a scourge in tropical countries until the incoming of the twentieth century, and malaria is still prevalent in many of them. The most effective remedy in both cases is the eradication of the mosquito by various methods, some of which are explained in the next chapter. Typhus is carried from person to person by the common body louse. It is still a common pestilence in backward countries where the elements of public sanitation and personal hygiene are ignored. Bubonic plague, known during the Middle Ages as the Black Death, is spread by rat fleas. All these insect-borne diseases, however, have now been largely eradicated from civilized lands. Various diseases in addition to yellow fever, malaria, typhus, and bubonic are known to be spread by insects and some others are believed to be carried in that way although definite proofs of it are lacking.

Personal contact is likewise responsible for the transmission of human ills. Discharges from the mouth and nose are the means whereby diphtheria, scarlet fever, whooping cough, and various other ailments are spread. There is reason to believe that influenza and common colds are disseminated in the same way. Human sputum is now regarded as one of the main agencies in the conveyance of tuberculosis, which is the most extensive of all the serious human infections. In some cases the authorities do not know the agencies through which communicable disease is spread and hence are at a great disadvantage in trying to control certain epidemics such as sleeping sickness and infantile paralysis. There are various theories as to how some of these infections are periodically carried from one end of the world to the other, but none of them afford a satisfactory explanation of the extraordinary phenom-

The spread of disease through personal contact.

enon. It is not improbable that human "carriers," in other words persons who transmit the germs of a disease without being themselves ill at the time of transmission, are responsible for some of the mystery.[1]

Methods of disease control:

1. Quarantine.

First among the measures taken by the public authorities to prevent the spread of communicable diseases are the quarantine regulations which the national government enforces at all seaports under its authority. Day and night throughout the year the health officers stand guard at these ports to see that no disease-bearing persons are permitted to land. Every vessel leaving a foreign harbor for the United States must secure a bill-of-health from the American consul before it sails; and the first person who goes on board an incoming vessel after the pilot is the quarantine officer. This official permits no passenger to be landed until he has made sure that there are no quarantinable ailments aboard. If there are any such cases, the passengers are held until the danger is past.

The various states and cities also maintain systems of health inspection and quarantine. Certain diseases (including tuberculosis, smallpox, typhoid, scarlet fever, pneumonia, whooping cough, diphtheria, measles, and mumps) must be promptly reported to the state or municipal authorities. The health regulations usually require in cases of the more readily communicable diseases that the house be placarded, and in extreme cases the patients may be removed to an isolation hospital. This isolation of cases and carriers is of very great importance.

2. Disinfection.

After the illness has terminated, the regulations usually provide that the premises shall be disinfected under the supervision of an official from the health department. Every city and town now maintains general regulations relating to quarantine and disinfection, these being enforced by the local health authorities under central supervision. For the most part the enforcement of these regulations is left to the health boards or health officers of the various communities, but in the case of epidemics involving several municipalities the state health authorities may assume direct control and the national public health service may send assistance. Epidemics, like conflagrations, pay no heed to political boundaries, hence it sometimes happens that when a city by stringent measures

---

[1] There is a full discussion of the routes of infection in Herbert H. Waite, *Disease Prevention* (New York, 1926), and in A. J. McLaughlin, *The Communicable Diseases: How They Spread and How They May Be Controlled* (New York, 1923).

is able to rid itself of an epidemic disease there is a reinfection as a result of inadequate control or official negligence in other cities near by. For this reason a complete degree of municipal home rule in public health matters is neither practicable nor desirable.

In order that measures for preventing the spread of disease may be effective, they must be based upon a well-organized and accurate system of vital statistics.[1] These statistics include figures relating to births, deaths, and illness. They are compiled in the offices of the health authorities from the reports sent in by physicians or by heads of households. To be of real value they must be filed promptly and the laws usually require that all notifiable diseases shall be reported to the health department immediately after the diagnosis has been made. The standard notification blank now used in the larger cities is so framed as to elicit all essential information. By means of these statistics the health authorities can sense the beginnings of an epidemic, determine its source or cause, and immediately set the machinery in motion to ensure its control. When one physician reports a case of typhoid this may be of little significance; but if a dozen cases are reported on the same day, the necessity for an immediate investigation into the water and milk supplies becomes apparent. Not only this but the individual physician finds it easier to make his diagnosis when he can call upon the public health authorities for accurate statistical information.

3. The compilation of accurate statistics.

Every health officer knows, however, that the disease-resisting power of the individual is an important factor in stemming the spread of communicable illness. Indeed it may truly be said that immunity or resisting power is the overshadowing factor in the promotion of personal hygiene. The ability of the individual to resist disease may be acquired in various ways—by the development of a general physical vigor, by successfully conquering an infection, or by the artificial introduction of a serum, virus, vaccine, or suitable toxin into the human body. In the case of some diseases a single attack leaves the individual with a specific immunity against a recurrence of that particular disease. This immunity varies, however, in degree and duration. Other diseases

4. Building up individual resistance and immunity.

---

[1] There is a good chapter on "Vital Statistics" in Carl E. McCombs, *City Health Administration* (New York, 1927), pp. 75–104. The best treatises on the subject are George C. Whipple, *Vital Statistics* (2nd edition, New York, 1923), Sir Arthur Newsholme, *Elements of Vital Statistics* (new edition, London, 1923), I. D. Falk, *Principles of Vital Statistics* (New York, 1923), and Raymond Pearl, *Introduction to Medical Biometry and Statistics* (2nd edition, Philadelphia, 1930).

seem to predispose individuals to recurrent attacks. Varying degrees of specific immunity may also be procured, in the case of some diseases, by artificial vaccination or inoculation. It is also believed that a degree of specific immunity to certain diseases develops in all persons as they grow older. The positive work of the public health authorities is now very much concerned with the development of both the general and specific disease-resisting powers of the people.

5. Vaccination and inoculation. The practice of vaccinating healthy persons as a safeguard against disease has been used for more than a century. Prophylactic inoculations are also used nowadays to prevent or to mitigate diphtheria, typhoid, and rabies. The technique of inoculation differs, of course, in each case. All members of the American Expeditionary Forces during the World War were given anti-typhoid inoculations which consisted of injecting subcutaneously a quantity of dead and greatly attenuated typhoid bacilli. These bacilli were not capable of producing the disease but they were enough to set the resisting powers of the blood in motion and thus to ensure a certain degree of immunity from typhoid infection by the ordinary process.[1] How long this immunity continues we do not yet know.

Vaccination against smallpox is the process of transferring virus from the skin eruption of an animal having vaccinia (cowpox) to an abrasion in the skin of a human being. The process was discovered by Edward Jenner in 1796, and was the first specific prophylactic measure devised by man. Its efficiency was soon accepted and during the past hundred years it has been widely used. Vaccination of school children is compulsory in several of the American states and in many communities, although there is a good deal of objection to it among certain sections of the people. If smallpox were completely wiped off the face of the earth, there would be no need for universal vaccination; but so long as numerous cases exist, as they still do in many countries, compulsory vaccination is a justifiable measure of public safety. The reputed dangers of vaccination have been greatly magnified by its opponents.

6. The war on tuberculosis. Tuberculosis, the great white plague, is the most serious chronic disease with which the health authorities of the city have to deal.

---

[1] During the Spanish-American War (1898) a division of 12,000 troops was encamped at Jacksonville, Florida. It had nearly 3,000 cases of typhoid and about 250 deaths from this disease. During the World War (1917–1918) a division of more than 25,000 troops was encamped at about the same spot but not a single case of typhoid developed. This illuminates the progress made in two decades.

It is one of the most important single causes of death in the United States. But tuberculosis is a curable, or at any rate an arrestable, disease if properly treated in its early stages. The hospital clinic, the dispensary, the school medical examination, and the public health nurse as well as the private physician are the agencies through which incipient cases of this ailment are brought to light. Early diagnosis is of supreme importance and the health authorities should put forth every effort to ensure that all cases of tuberculosis are promptly reported. The control of this disease is largely a matter of public education but facilities should also be provided by the municipal authorities for the treatment of tuberculosis in special hospitals, sanitariums, open-air schools, and out-of-door living quarters.

Because of the unhygienic conditions which have been found to exist in workshops and factories, particularly in the large cities, various states have passed laws and made regulations to protect the health of employees in such establishments. Industrial hygiene, as it is called, has become an extremely important branch of preventive medicine since it deals with the health of workers who form a large element in urban populations. In various forms of industry, moreover, there are "occupational" diseases, many of them due to the inhalation of gases, vapors, or dust. Some of these trades, by reason of their danger to the health of the workers, are now being subjected to periodic health inspection and strict regulation. The "sweat-shops" or tenement rooms in which women and children formerly worked long hours for a mere pittance, crowded together with almost no ventilation—these industrial dungeons have either been legislated out of existence or are prohibited by the new business codes. Workshops and factories are now required to be commodious, well lighted, clean, and properly ventilated. Adequate sanitary equipment must be provided. It is the duty of the state factory inspectors to see that all these regulations are complied with, but the local health departments are expected to coöperate in the work.[1] Industrial hygiene, however, is a field in which the medical, economic, and legal aspects are closely interwoven. The preservation of health among the workers

7. Industrial hygiene.

[1] See the chapter on "Industrial Hygiene" in Victor M. Ehlers and Ernest W. Steel, *Municipal and Rural Sanitation* (New York, 1917), pp. 320–330; also E. R. Hayhurst and G. M. Kober, *Industrial Health* (Philadelphia, 1924), R. Goldberg, *Occupational Diseases in Relation to Compensation and Health Insurance* (New York, 1931), and Thomas Oliver, *Diseases of Occupation* (3rd edition, New York, 1916).

is not merely a matter of improving industrial environment but of regulating the wages, hours, and conditions of labor.

8. Public education in health matters. The basis of successful public health work is the education of the people in hygiene and sanitation. If the masses can be brought to realize the vital importance of the work, their coöperation will be assured, but without this coöperation very little can be accomplished. Where the health regulations are disobeyed, it is largely because their value to the individual, as well as to the community, has not been made clear to the people concerned. An effective method of educating the public is by means of health exhibits which demonstrate, with the aid of pictures, especially motion pictures, the value of proper hygienic conditions in the workshop and the home. But the ultimate education of the whole people in this field, as in all others, must be primarily the work of the schools. It is easier to teach hygiene and sanitation to children than to grown-ups. Adults have acquired habits of life and attitudes of mind which are hard to alter. Hence the education of children in all that relates to clean living, wholesome food, modern sanitation, and the avoidance of disease should be part of the regular work of the public schools, and especially of the high schools. Upon such instruction will depend, in no small degree, the future physical well-being of the nation.[1]

9. Medical inspection in the schools. In this connection the frequent medical inspection of children in the schools is a public health activity of self-evident importance.[2] By such means communicable diseases are detected in their early stages, while non-transmissible ailments or defects, which ordinarily would pass unnoticed, are discovered before they have developed to serious proportions. Correctable defects are in part responsible for inattention in the classroom, lack of interest in work, truancy, and retarded intellectual development. The majority of those who have to "repeat a grade" in the public schools owe their trouble to adenoids, defective eyesight, and other physical defects. Some taxpayers object to the paternalism which medical care of school children involves, but it is more economical to provide medical inspection, and even to pay for the correction of remediable

[1] K. W. Wooten, *A Health Education Procedure for the Grades and Grade Teachers* (New York, 1926).

[2] L. H. Gulick and L. P. Ayres, *Medical Inspection of Schools* (new edition, New York, 1925), and E. W. Nemayer, *Medical and Sanitary Inspection of Schools* (2nd edition, Philadelphia, 1924); also S. J. Baker, *Child Hygiene* (New York, 1925), and the joint report of the National Education Association and the American Medical Association on *Health Service in City Schools* (New York, 1922).

ailments, than to defray the cost of an extra year's schooling for the pupil.

Most of the inspectional work is done by school nurses, but with all important questions referred to the school physician. The nurses and physicians who perform these duties should be appointed by the city health department and the supervision of the entire work should be under its jurisdiction, although it is frequently contended by educators that a matter so closely related to the schools ought to be in the hands of the school authorities. It is true, no doubt, that there is danger of friction when an outside department is given authority to carry on its operations during school hours within the public school buildings. On the other hand a strong argument for not giving the responsibility to the school board may be found in the fact that many schools (parochial and private schools) are not under the jurisdiction of this board, yet such schools should not be left out of account in any comprehensive plan for the safeguarding of the public health. There are some communities in which as many as one-fourth of the children attend institutions other than the public schools. A well-organized program of child hygiene should not neglect this considerable fraction of pupils, yet it is neither advisable nor practicable to give the public school authorities any control over them. The city health department, on the other hand, is an agency which can appropriately assume city-wide jurisdiction in all health matters.

The control of such inspections.

Among all the foods of humanity, milk is probably the most important. It is the chief nutrition of children until they reach school age, and sometimes even longer. It forms a large factor in the diet of invalids. Even in the daily fare of robust adults, it is an item of no small importance. Health authorities believe that milk is responsible for more illness than all other foods combined. It has been a prolific carrier of tuberculosis, typhoid, septic sore throat, scarlet fever, and diphtheria. This is because no article of everyday commerce is so easily contaminated, and in the case of no other article are the results of pollution likely to be so serious. For when the germs of disease get into milk, they multiply with great rapidity and go directly into the diet of those who have the least power to withstand infection, the children and invalids of the community.[1]

10. Supervision of the milk supply.

[1] C. E. North, "Milk in Its Relation to Public Health," in M. P. Ravenel, *A Half-Century of Public Health Administration* (New York, 1921), pp. 236–289.

484 MUNICIPAL ADMINISTRATION

Milk standards. Milk, moreover, is of all foods the most readily subject to decomposition, hence it is the most difficult to collect, transport, and deliver in a fresh and clean condition. But the mere presence of bacteria in milk, even though in large numbers, does not necessarily indicate contamination; it is the *kind* of bacteria that matters. Nevertheless, a high bacterial content is good ground for suspicion that the milk is old, dirty, or otherwise below proper standards. The number of bacteria in milk is, on the whole, the best indication of its general freshness and cleanliness. Some cities permit the sale of milk containing as many as 300,000 bacteria per cubic centimeter; but it is the opinion of most public health experts that a much smaller number ought to be fixed as the maximum. In the case of certified milk, so called, the limit should be fixed a great deal lower.

Milk inspections. From its source on the farm milk passes through several hands before reaching the customer, and at each of these points there is a possibility of contamination. Careless milking, the storing of milk in unsanitary places or in unclean containers, the rinsing of utensils in polluted water, the handling of milk by persons who are just coming down with disease, or who have just recovered and are still germ-carriers, the lack of adequate precautions in transporting and delivering the milk,—any of these things involves a danger of infection and some of them are almost certain to take place when a city's milk supply is brought from thousands of farms. Most of the larger cities and many small ones have travelling inspectors who scrutinize the cattle, the barns, the equipment, and the methods of milking at these dairy farms. Their reports are given in the form of a rating scale, each dairy being graded in accordance wth the final score.[1]

Why thorough inspection is difficult. One of the fundamental handicaps in coping with the problem of milk purity arises from the fact that the supply comes from such a large number of widely scattered sources. This makes the problem of frequent inspection an exceedingly complicated one and increases the difficulty of safeguarding the milk while it is being transported. Yet inspection at the source and protection during transit are essential, no matter how laborious the work or how great the cost. An efficient milk inspector can cover seven or eight farm-dairies each day, or about two hundred per month. Samples are also taken at random from the delivery wagons in the city and

---

[1] The United States Public Health Service has prepared a standard dairy inspection form.

tested at the city's health laboratory. It would be better to have all milk inspection made a state function, thus providing a service of uniform standards and efficiency for all cities.

In view of the difficulties involved in the protection of milk supplies by inspection, some health authorities believe that it would be wise to insist upon a general requirement of pasteurization. This consists in heating the milk to a temperature of from 142° to 145° F. for half an hour and then chilling it to below 50° F. There is no impairment of the nutritive qualities. Such treatment, however, is not practicable as a matter of economics unless large quantities of milk are handled. Pasteurizing milk, however, does not make it either clean or fresh if it is dirty or sour. Pasteurized milk should not be confused with certified milk which is merely a superior grade of raw milk produced and distributed under special sanitary conditions prescribed by the health authorities and certified to this effect by a medical commission.

The question of pasteurization.

The close relation between infant mortality and impure milk has long been recognized by the medical profession.[1] Before active steps were taken to reduce the rate of infant mortality by preventive measures it was not uncommon to find this rate exceeding fifty per cent of the children born in any year. Even as late as 1900 there were some cities in which the infant death rate was above thirty per cent. But by reason of various measures, chief among which is the rigorous inspection and safeguarding of the milk supply, this mortality rate has been so reduced that in none of the largest cities is it much above ten per cent and in some it is as low as four per cent. The establishment of milk distribution stations in large cities has been of great value in that it enables people of limited means in the crowded sections to obtain pure milk at reasonable prices.

The marketing of impure or adulterated food is everywhere forbidden by laws and health regulations, but until comparatively recent years these rules were not strictly enforced. One reason for this lay in the fact that most articles of food are produced in one state to be sold in another; hence they are subjects of interstate commerce and not easily made amenable to municipal control. In 1906, however, Congress passed the Food and Drug Act, by the terms of which the national government assumed the duty of eliminating impure food from being transported across state

11. The inspection of food and drugs.

[1] Robert M. Woodbury, *Infant Mortality and Its Causes* (Baltimore, 1926).

boundaries. This act prohibits all interstate commerce in adulterated food and drugs; in addition it provides for the inspection of meats at the packing plants. Likewise it requires that all packages of food and drugs shall be correctly branded, and that when artificial preservatives are used the label shall state the fact. All impure, adulterated, or wrongly branded articles are prohibited by the federal authorities from being manufactured in one state for sale in another.

Local products. The supervision of the national government does not extend, however, to articles of food which are produced, distributed, and sold within the territory of a single state. As regards such products, the task of protecting the public against impurity and adulteration rests with the state and local health officers who are expected to work in coöperation but sometimes do not. These officers are responsible for the frequent inspection of foodstuffs at places where they are produced or sold. As a rule, however, there are too few inspectors to do the work thoroughly and they are not always resourceful enough to cope with the ingenious methods of adulteration which are being devised from time to time. Most forms of food adulteration, fortunately, are not seriously inimical to health; they are mainly employed by the manufacturer as a way of cheapening his product or making it more attractive in appearance. In such cases the main objection is in the defrauding of the consumer rather than in any possible injury to his health.

Diet and health. The importance of diet in relation to health has not been adequately appreciated until very recent years. Diet, however, is fundamental, not only in the growth and nutrition of the individual, but in the building up of resistance to disease throughout the community. To this end it is in the public interest that the diet of all the people, and especially of the children, shall be adequate and well balanced. This is the justification of what the school authorities do in the way of supplementing at the schools the deficient and ill-balanced diet which many of the poorer children obtain at home. Such action is not paternalism, as some grumbling taxpayers protest, but is merely a reasonable measure of public health conservation. It is much more economical to use public funds in building up a general resistance to disease than to spend what otherwise becomes essential in the way of clinics, dispensaries, and hospitals for the care of those whose powers of warding off disease have become impaired.

HEALTH ADMINISTRATION 487

The indiscriminate and unchecked sale of narcotic drugs (chiefly morphine, cocaine, and opium) resulted in serious evils for many years. Persons who could buy these drugs easily were led into the habit of using them freely and in the end became confirmed addicts. As such they contributed largely to the city's quota of physical wrecks, criminals, vice promoters, crooks, and gangsters. The drug habit grew to such dimensions, some years ago, that the national government stepped in and took the sale of narcotics under its own supervision. By the provisions of the Harrison Act, narcotic drugs cannot now be bought or sold except under strict regulations which usually necessitate a prescription from a licensed physician. The enforcement of these regulations is primarily in the hands of federal officers, but their work is supplemented by the vigilance of the city health authorities and the municipal police. Whether the drug evil is being substantially diminished in the cities is a matter on which there is some difference of opinion. Everyone knows, at any rate, that a great deal of traffic in narcotic drugs is still carried on through illicit channels.

12. Controlling the drug traffic.

The relation of the liquor traffic to the public health is a question upon which there has been much divergence of opinion among medical men, although most of them would concur in the proposition that the immoderate use of intoxicating liquors is not conducive to the development or maintenance of good health or bodily vigor. All ethical considerations aside, the fact remains that alcohol is a drug, a habit-forming drug. When used to excess it lowers bodily resistance, impairs physical and mental efficiency, fosters crime, diminishes self-control, promotes immorality, discourages thrift, and engenders economic waste. It clouds judgment, depresses will power, and stupefies the normal clarity of the human mind. That is why its manufacture, sale, and transportation are placed under varying degrees of public control in all countries. The cities exercise this control by means of their licensing power but look upon such licensing as a means of raising revenue rather than as a measure of health conservation.

Relation of intoxicants to the public health.

In most of the smaller cities and in some of the larger ones the traditional plan of public health administration has been to place the work in the hands of a board (usually called the board of health) made up of from three to five members. Sometimes there has been a requirement that one of the members must be a physician. Students of municipal administration, as well as men in active

Boards of health.

public life, were for many years disposed to regard the board system as a suitable one for the management of this department because of a feeling that the work of a health department was for the most part legislative in its nature. It involved the making of rules and regulations with the force of law. Such work, of course, should not be entrusted to the discretion of a single individual lest the way be opened for oppression and partiality. Twenty-odd years ago, a distinguished student of American municipal affairs expressed the conviction that "more may be said in behalf of a board for public health administration than perhaps any other branch of municipal government."[1]

Their place in the new program. And it is true that in the days when public health activities consisted chiefly of rule-making, rather than of rule-enforcing, there was a good deal of weight to the arguments in favor of board administration. If an epidemic broke out, the chief duty of the health authorities was to call upon everyone to observe various precautionary regulations. Then they would order everybody's yard cleaned up, or they would close the schools and advise householders to boil water before drinking it. But the nineteenth-century board of health did very little in the way of long-range, preventive health programs or even in the enforcement of its own makeshift regulations. This is still the situation in many small communities, but in all the larger cities the work of public health departments has been altogether transformed during the past generation. General health regulations are now framed, for the most part, by the state authorities. They are embodied in a code of public health laws or in the general regulations of the state health department. The principal duty of the municipal health department is to see that these laws and regulations are applied and enforced, although some local rules are also made from time to time. Hence the work of the municipal health department has now become almost wholly administrative.

Why unified administration is now desirable. Moreover, with rapid advances in the science of public hygiene this work has become steadily more extensive, more varied, and more technical in its character. It includes the supervision of chemical and bacteriological laboratories, the tabulation of vital statistics, the inspection of food, drugs, and milk, the maintenance of quarantines, the disinfection of premises, child hygiene, health education, and the exercise of a vigilant watch on all major chan-

---

[1] Charles A. Beard, *American City Government* (New York, 1912), p. 264.

nels of infection. In large communities this work can no longer be efficiently performed by a board of laymen, even though a physician be one of its members.[1] The need today is for a highly trained health officer, a qualified public health specialist, at the head of the department. This official should have the right to make his own plans and to act on his own initiative without having to seek the approval of a health board at every stage. Accordingly, most of the larger cities, and many of the smaller ones as well, have already made the change from the board to the single commissioner plan, and the rest will undoubtedly follow in time. The day of the old-fashioned board of health is rapidly drawing to a close.

The head of the health department, no matter what the size of the city, ought to be a full-time, well-paid, member of the medical profession, who has had special training in public health work. His duties are too important to be entrusted to the spare time of some local practitioner who looks upon the post as a means of supplementing his private fees. Public health work has become a specialized profession. The practitioner who claims to be a physician, surgeon, obstetrician, and public health expert is not likely to be very proficient in any of these lines. Effective public health administration, moreover, requires organizing and executive capacity which is by no means guaranteed by the mere possession of a license to practice medicine. Finally, and perhaps most important of all, is the fact that the work of the municipal health department cannot be well performed unless the man at its head gives it a primary claim on his time and attention every hour in the day and every day in the week.[2] No physician with any considerable private practice can give to public health problems the vigilant care that they are entitled to have in view of their vital importance to the whole community. Emergencies are constantly arising in the public health service and if these are to be met adequately they must be met immediately.

The head of the health department.

The title of the health department head ought to be health commissioner or health director rather than city physician. The latter designation is apt to imply that his main function is to at-

His functions and jurisdiction.

---

[1] A full discussion of the merits and defects of the board system may be found in Carl E. McCombs, *City Health Administration* (New York, 1927), pp. 37–49.

[2] Some years ago a survey undertaken by the United States Public Health Service disclosed that many cities of over 100,000 population were still employing part-time health officers.

tend patients who cannot afford a regular practitioner. The health commissioner or director should have no obligations to individuals. His duties should be confined to matters which concern the health of the whole people. He should have no responsibility for the management of the general city hospital, but if the municipality maintains an isolation hospital for the care of patients with communicable diseases this institution may properly be placed within his jurisdiction. Sanitary functions, such as street cleaning and garbage removal, which have only an incidental relation to the public health, should not ordinarily be included within the jurisdiction of his department. They can better be turned over to the department of public works. The health commissioner should have security of tenure, an adequate salary, a sufficient corps of assistants and inspectors, proper laboratory facilities, and, above all, the cordial support of the public. To be successful in his work he must have the full coöperation of the local physicians. The requirement that the health commissioner must be chosen from among the residents of the municipality should be abolished, leaving the city free to choose the best available man wherever he may be found. If there be any feeling that all this will lead to a bureaucratic administration of the health department, such fear can be allayed by providing for a board of laymen to act with the health officer in an advisory capacity.

Extensive nature of the department's work. The average citizen has a very inadequate conception of the extensive and varied functions which the health department of a large city is expected to perform. These duties cover a wide range and affect all classes in the community. For example, there is the inspection of alleyways, yards, slaughterhouses, factories, tenement houses, stables, cemeteries, swimming pools, artificial ice plants, barber shops, beauty parlors, public comfort stations, lodging houses, and bath and massage establishments. It has been reckoned that about 4,000 inspections for every 100,000 population are required every year by food establishments alone. This includes milk inspection, ice-cream inspection, water analysis, together with the health certification of all persons engaged in the handling of food. Smoke abatement, mosquito eradication, and the general abatement of nuisances is also within the health department's jurisdiction. Permits from the department are required for all manner of things, from the sale of candled eggs to the location of an auto camp. To accomplish all this work requires the full-time service of health inspectors who are in most of the large cities selected by civil service competition.

Compared with the outlay in other departments of city administration such as police or fire protection, the annual expenditure for public health work is relatively small. New York City, for example, has built up an elaborate and highly efficient health department; yet the cost of maintaining it was only five and a half million dollars in 1930 or less than a dollar per capita. Police administration cost five times as much. In Philadelphia the outlay was considerably less than one million dollars or only about fifty cents per head of the city's population.[1] The entire amount expended by all the cities of the United States for the care of health is just about what it costs to build a single battleship of modern design. Nor does the entire cost of public health work come from the municipal treasury. Much of it is covered by the levying of inspectional fees on restaurants, barber shops, dairies, slaughterhouses, and so on. Taking this into consideration our cities have been none too generous in their appropriations for public health work. This is partly because the work is new, but partly, also, because the health service provides a minimum of "patronage jobs" and hence does not acquire many friends among local politicians.

The cost of public health protection.

The guardianship of the public health is no longer a local enterprise to be carried on in each community as its health authorities deem best. Even though municipalities may not like the idea, there must be some central supervision over all of them, provided by the state. This is axiomatic, for the incompetence or laxity of officials in one community may visit penalties upon its neighbors. In every state of the Union, accordingly, a state department of health has now been established. This department is usually under the supervision of a state board of health, but in a few states a single health commissioner has been placed in charge, sometimes with a council to assist him. The powers and duties of these state departments vary a good deal throughout the country, but in many states they do not have much actual authority. They make investigations into the causes of disease, give advice to municipalities on health and sanitary problems, and actively assist the municipal health departments whenever an epidemic threatens

State supervision of local health work.

[1] See the table of expenditures in Publication No. 27 of the Municipal Administration Service entitled *The Administration of Regulatory Inspectional Services in American Cities* (New York, 1932), p. 64.

to spread beyond local control. In a few instances, however, the state governments have boldly taken over the control of all public health work, and have vested the appointment of the local health officers in the hands of the state health department. It is not improbable that the drift toward centralization in this field will grow steadily stronger.

Health work of the national government. In the Constitution of the United States, the national government is granted no specific powers with reference to the preservation of the national health. But conditions have made it essential that the national authorities should supplement the health work of the states, the more so because they alone can control immigration as well as the movement of the people from one part of the country to another. Consequently the United States Public Health Service was established in 1912 and given charge of quarantine at all ports of entry. Its assistance may also be obtained by the states at any time in coping with epidemics, and it maintains one of the world's best research laboratories for the study of questions affecting the public health. It is believed by many health authorities that the work of this bureau is so important that it ought to be made a regular department of the national administration with a member of the cabinet at its head.

The International Health Office. No matter how watchful a country may be in guarding the health of its people, it can never feel at ease so long as epidemics are raging in other lands. Travel and trade may carry disease across the best-guarded borders. International coöperation in health protection is accordingly most desirable if it can be secured. With a view to promoting such coöperation the Covenant of the League of Nations pledged all member-countries to take steps for the international prevention and control of disease. It also contained provisions for the establishment of an International Health Office with the function of gathering data relating to public health matters, promoting the acceptance of the best health regulations by the different countries, and securing common action in the case of widespread epidemics. It is interesting to see, therefore, how public health work, beginning on a neighborhood scale less than a century ago, has widened to a municipal, state, national, and even an international function.

A final word. Perhaps it may not be amiss to add a final word by way of driving home one of the lessons which this development in public health work ought to teach. The advance which the world has made in sanitation, hygiene, and preventive medicine during the past half-century is worthy to be numbered among the most remarkable achievements of western civilization. The history of this progress is a consistent record of one notable triumph after another, each contributing to the comfort, happiness, and prosperity of mankind. But who are they that have done all this? Certainly not the toilers in the fields and factories, nor yet the captains of industry to whose efforts we are so often told that all our progress is due. First and last it has all been the work of sanitary scientists and health experts, using the methods of experimental research in their laboratories. And if the advance is to be continued it must be in no other way. Perhaps those who like to scoff at higher education, science, and research can tell us how they would set about prolonging the days of a man's years.

REFERENCES

A *Bibliography on Public Health and Allied Topics* (4th edition, New York, 1926) and a *Catalogue of Health Books* (New York, 1928) are published by the American Public Health Association (450 Seventh Ave., New York). The same organization has also sponsored a *Model Health Code for Cities* and an *Appraisal Form for City Health Work*.

Important books of a general character in the field of public health are Carl E. McCombs, *City Health Administration* (New York, 1927), H. H. Waite, *Disease Prevention* (New York, 1926), Milton J. Rosenau, *Preventive Medicine and Hygiene* (new edition, New York, 1927), William H. Hallock, *Public Health and Hygiene* (New York, 1927), Courtenay Dinwiddie, *Child Health and the Community* (New York, 1931), Harry K. Moore, *Public Health in the United States* (New York, 1923), A. J. McLaughlin, *The Communicable Diseases: How They Are Spread and How They May Be Controlled* (New York, 1923), Sir Arthur Newsholme, *Health Problems in Organized Society* (London, 1928) and *Medicine and the State* (Baltimore, 1932), M. P. Ravenel, editor, *A Half-Century of Public Health* (New York, 1921), G. S. Luckett and H. F. Gray, *Elements of Public Health Administration* (Philadelphia, 1923), William H. Welch, *Public Health in Theory and Practice* (New Haven, 1925), Curtis M. Hilliard, *The Prevention of Disease in the Community* (New York, 1931), Ira V. Hiscock, editor, *Community Health Organization* (new edition, New York, 1932), R. D. Leigh, *Federal Health Administration in the United States* (New York, 1927), E. L. Bishop, *Public Health Organizations* (New York, 1932), N. Sinai, *Organization and Administration of Public Health* (Detroit, 1933), M. M. Davis and M. C. Jarrett, *A Health Inventory of New York City* (New York, 1929), Robert F. Steadman, *Public Health Organization*

494   MUNICIPAL ADMINISTRATION

in the Chicago Region (Chicago, 1930), and the United States Public Health Bulletin on *Municipal Health Department Practice* (Washington, 1926). James A. Tobey, *Riders of the Plagues: the Story of the Conquest of Disease* (New York, 1930) is a readable survey.

For books on vital statistics, see p. 479, *footnote*.

The legal phases of the subject are presented in H. B. Hemenway, *Legal Principles of Public Health Administration* (Chicago, 1914), and in J. A. Tobey, *Public Health Law* (Baltimore, 1926).

Special attention should be called to the various publications of the United States Public Health Service and the American Health Association. *The American Journal of Public Health*, issued monthly, contains useful information of a current nature.

See also the references at the close of Chapters XXXV–XXXVI.

CHAPTER XXXV

THE ABATEMENT OF NUISANCES

Nuisance signifies anything that worketh hurt, inconvenience, or damage.—*Blackstone.*

The local health authorities also have to do with the abatement of nuisances. The term is a very comprehensive one, including whatever is a menace to the life, health, morals, or convenience of the people. So whether a thing is a nuisance has to be determined by the circumstances of each individual case rather than by general rule. It becomes a question of fact, to be determined by a jury if need be. Things which might be accounted malodorous nuisances in a thickly settled community, such as slaughterhouses or oil wells, do not necessarily constitute nuisances in the open country. {What constitutes a nuisance.}

Most of the complaints which reach the municipal health authorities from day to day are concerned with some form of nuisance, real or imaginary. Many things are thought by the complainants to be a menace to public health when they are merely offensive to the public taste—establishments which emit unsavory smells, cluttered alleyways, ash piles, heaps of rubbish in backyards, and vacant lots overgrown with weeds. But however uncongenial such departures from orderliness may be to fastidious people, they have very little direct relation to the public health, and the health authorities ought not to have any responsibility for getting rid of them. In many cities, however, they are still expected to assume this responsibility, an arrangement which harks back to the days when everything that looked offensive was deemed to be a cause of disease. The enforced cleaning of alleyways, backyards, and vacant lots should be a responsibility of the officials who have charge of rubbish and garbage removal. {Nuisances and the public health.}

On the other hand there are various conditions in large cities which produce nuisances more or less directly related to the public health. Among these one of the most prevalent is the smoke nuisance. In many large industrial centers the continuous emission of smoke is a more serious menace to community health than people {The smoke nuisance.}

realize. Pure air is essential to the maintenance of bodily vigor, and rural parts of the country encounter no difficulty in providing themselves with plenty of it. But in nearly every large city the daily assault upon the purity of the atmosphere has become so formidable that official action has become necessary to protect the air from intolerable pollution. For in the absence of regulation smoke will be poured out of factory smokestacks, heating plants, and locomotives in such vast quantities that the outdoor ceiling becomes completely blanketed by it.

Twofold effect of it:

1. A menace to health.

The detrimental effect of the smoke nuisance upon the public health is twofold. First there is a deterioration in the quality of the atmosphere which induces physical ailments. The inhalation of smoke-filled air, hour after hour and day after day, contributes to numerous nose and throat irritations which lower the normal resistance of the respiratory organs to communicable disease. Heavy smoke also forms a menace to the public health by decreasing the amount of sunlight which reaches the earth. It is the ultra-violet rays in sunlight which make one of the best among natural germicides, but the blanket of smoke which is overlaid upon a large industrial city has the effect of blocking these rays from the sun on their way to the earth. Hence what the people get is denatured sunshine, stripped for the most part of its hygienic qualities. Averages for the whole year indicate that smoke steals about one-fifth of New York City's total sunlight. A survey made in Cleveland some years ago demonstrated that the city obtained only two-thirds of what the sun would have provided if the smoke nuisance had been out of the way.

2. The economic loss.

Then there is the economic loss which this nuisance entails. The vast amount of soot which is poured into the air by smoke-belching industries is the cause of monetary losses through the blackening of walls and decorations, the corrosion and tarnishing of metal work, the depositing of grime on household furnishings and draperies, and the injury of goods which are exposed for sale in mercantile establishments. Investigations have shown that in a heavily industrialized city, such as Pittsburgh, as much as one thousand tons of soot per square mile may be deposited in the course of a year. In other cities the figures disclose an average deposit of more than half that amount as a regular occurrence. Such an output is large enough to warrant its being curtailed by strict regulation. About the only ones whom the smoke nuisance

THE ABATEMENT OF NUISANCES

benefits are the soap manufacturers. To all others it is a source of expense,—to the individual citizen for extra laundry and cleaning bills, to the household for additional repairing and refurnishing, to owners of buildings for the periodic repainting or sand-blasting of exterior walls, to retail stores for the damage done to their merchandise, and even to the smoke-makers themselves because the excessive smoke indicates imperfect combustion and hence a waste of fuel. Many an industrial smokestack is merely an inverted wastebasket.

Indirectly, perhaps, the electric lighting companies make some profit from the smoke nuisance because this darkening of the sunlight by smoke, especially in the late afternoon hours or on cloudy days, is responsible for an increased use of artificial illumination. In large communities where buildings are crowded close together there is usually no excess of natural light under the best conditions. Hence when the effectiveness of sunlight is reduced by ten, twenty, or thirty per cent, this deficiency has to be made up by artificial means, that is, by turning on the electric switches an hour or two ahead of time. Eventually, moreover, the smoky air beclouds the window panes and skylights, thus further reducing the access of natural light into shops and offices. This not only adds to the monthly light bills but puts the owner or tenant to the expense of having his windows cleaned more often than would otherwise be necessary. Between what is cut off by the pall of smoke and by the soot-laden windows, the exclusion of natural sunlight at midday is in some cases as high as fifty per cent. It is not always easy to estimate the amount of needless outlay caused by the compulsory substitution of artificial for natural light by reason of the smoke nuisance; but it is beyond question that the loss runs far into millions of dollars every year.   *Smoke and the need for artificial lighting.*

The detrimental effect of smoke upon vegetation should also be reckoned on the debit side of the account. Soot in large quantities has an injurious effect upon the growth of trees, shrubs, and plants. It affects them in various ways,—by blocking the pores, thus impeding the transpiratory process, by coating the leaves so that the intensity of the sunlight is reduced, and by the poisonous action of the acids which the soot contains. One American city after another has had, during the past fifty years, an impressive demonstration of the injury which can be wrought to fine avenues of shade trees by a failure to control the smoke nuisance in time.   *Effects on vegetation.*

498   MUNICIPAL ADMINISTRATION

The trees are gone. A city cannot have parks or esplanades of thrifty trees and shrubs if it permits them to be smothered by smoke and soot. Only a few hardy trees can stand a smoke-laden atmosphere. Nor can attractive private grounds be maintained under such conditions. Even good lawns are impossible where the smoke belt spreads.

The psychological effect. Incidentally, the psychological effect of this particular nuisance should not be overlooked. Sunshine has a stimulating effect upon mind and body. To shut so much of it from the face of the earth, as many cities have permitted their industries to do, is to deprive themselves of what ought to be a stimulant to the spirits of their people. Life in a great city is depressing enough without adding an artificial contribution to the natural cloudiness which many cities have to tolerate for half the days of every year.

Can a smoke nuisance be beautiful? "Look at Chicago," writes a magazine rhapsodist, "with her halo of smoke as a chaplet of claret and mauve, garnet and gray, exceedingly lovely against the sunset sky. Buildings seem to blur into other buildings, with soft skies drooping lovingly above them." All of which shows how a wallow of aërial sewage can be transformed by the touch of a poetic pen! There are not many, however, who would defend the smoke nuisance on aesthetic grounds. Or, if by any stretch of the imagination it be deemed beautiful in itself, it remains the enemy of all other things beautiful, whether the handiwork of nature or of man. For no matter how skillfully an architect may plan his buildings, grounds, or public monuments, they will not remain attractive if smoke-fogs with soot and grime are permitted to do their work without interference. Smoke may soften the visage of a city but it is a type of facial treatment that costs high.

Smoke-abatement ordinances: To deal with this nuisance most of the larger cities have adopted smoke-abatement ordinances. The main source of the trouble is the incomplete combustion of coal and oil in industrial plants, railroad locomotives, and heating plants, but a surprisingly large percentage of the smoke comes from domestic furnaces. Hence regulations have been established to prohibit the excessive emission of smoke and the validity of these regulations has been upheld by the courts. Of course the courts do not hold smoke to be a nuisance *per se*. A certain amount of it is inevitable, and while this may constitute an annoyance to the community it is part of the price which people pay for the privilege of living as neighbors.

1. Their legality.

But when the smoke is so excessive as to interfere materially with the ordinary comforts of human existence it is the right and the duty of the public authorities to intervene by the exercise of their police power.

Smoke ordinances usually provide that no dense smoke shall be emitted from any stack or chimney for more than a certain number of minutes in any hour. But what constitutes dense smoke? To determine the degree of density certain standards have been set up, based on the capacity of the smoke to shut off a certain percentage of light as measured by an instrument known as an umbrascope. On this basis smoke has been classified into five grades, with from twenty to one hundred per cent density.[1] Smoke inspectors determine whether density from time to time exceeds the allowable maximum and then report cases in which the ordinance is being violated. Such violations are usually declared to be misdemeanors, punishable by the imposition of heavy fines. Occasionally, however, such attempts at enforcement have become tied up in prolonged litigation. Industrial establishments have sometimes contested the reasonableness of the regulation but without much success.

2. Their usual provisions.

Municipal ordinances are not very effective as regards the smoke which comes from the chimneys of private residences. A few inspectors can keep watch on industries, hotels, railway terminals, and heating plants, but it would take a whole battalion of them to cover the residential areas. Education, rather than a campaign of prosecution, is the need as respects the average householder. He must be shown that the discharge of dense smoke from his furnace chimney can be prevented to a large extent by alternate firing, that is, by piling the fuel on one side of the fire only. This allows the heat on the other side to consume the volatile matter. As respects industrial plants the same result can be accomplished by installing automatic stokers and by the use of various smoke-consuming devices. Hence a smoke-abatement ordinance should not content itself with the mere prohibition of heavy smoke but should make provision for informing and educating the public in order to secure general coöperation. When a first violation is reported, the procedure should be to notify the offender in a courteous way, indicating what changes in equipment, fuel, or

Educating the average householder.

---

[1] The United States Geological Survey suggests the use of the Ringelmann Chart as a means of specifying the degree of density which is permitted.

methods of firing would obviate the trouble. Prosecution should not be used except as a last resort.

The control of future installations. Moreover the ordinance ought to contain provisions which give the buildings department authority to control the types of boilers, stacks, and other equipment which may be placed in all future buildings. To this end some such provision as the following is desirable: "No person or corporation shall construct, install, reconstruct, alter, or repair any furnace, boiler, chimney, or smokestack, or any apparatus connected therewith until plans and specifications for the same have been filed with the Department of Buildings and a permit obtained for such work." Permits should not be granted unless the inspectors are satisfied that the chimney or stack is of adequate dimensions and height. They should be withheld unless the equipment is of a type which will keep dense smoke to a minimum. It has been estimated that ninety per cent of the smoke from industrial plants can be eliminated by the use of proper equipment and firing methods. The expense of installing this equipment is usually offset by the increased economy in use of fuel.

The enforcing authorities. The responsibility for securing an abatement of the smoke nuisance has usually been devolved upon the health authorities. This is because of the general idea that smoke is mainly a nuisance in its relation to the public health. Smoke inspectors appointed by the health department check up violations of the ordinance and send various notices to the offenders before proceeding to the issue of a court summons. But the health authorities are not the logical ones to take the responsibility for this work. The only effective way to control the smoke nuisance is to make sure that no furnaces, grates, boilers, stacks, or chimneys are so constructed as to encourage the trouble. Along with this should go a persistent campaign of education. Householders require enlightenment concerning the economic losses involved. In this way an appeal can be made to the pocket nerve. Smoke abatement ought, therefore, to be a function of a separate bureau of the buildings department, with a chief smoke inspector in charge of it. He should keep in his office a list of approved types of apparatus which can be consulted in advance by architects and builders. No other installations should be allowed. The smokeless city is still a long way off, but it will inevitably come if the authorities adhere to the policy of permitting no nuisance-making equipment to be installed and if the work of

THE ABATEMENT OF NUISANCES 501

educating the public is vigilantly pursued. In this latter connection the Smoke Abatement Leagues and other private organizations which are interested in the problem can be of great assistance.

Too much smoke is by no means unique among the avoidable nuisances of urban civilization. Too much water (in the wrong place) may be a nuisance of almost equal irritation. Much trouble arises, in other words, from pools of stagnant water, big and little, which are located here or there in the low-lying sections of nearly all large communities. For such places serve as the breeding places of mosquitoes and other insects which are responsible for the spread of serious diseases, some of which have played a notable part in the history of mankind. It is doubtful if the public has any adequate conception of the illness, suffering, and monetary losses which are occasioned by these bothersome insects, or fully realizes the manifold advantages which result from a vigorous campaign of mosquito eradication. *The mosquito nuisance.*

The indictment against the mosquito contains three principal counts, first, the annoyance, illness, and the deaths which are caused by insect-borne infections; second, the resulting expenditures for medical services, as well as the loss of the patient's time which the illness entails; and, third, the depreciation in property values which always results from the proximity of mosquito-breeding grounds.

Despite a vigorous campaign of public education on this matter there is even yet, in the mind of the populace, a very blurred notion of the part which the mosquito plays in the transmission of disease. An adult female mosquito lays eggs on a water surface, preferably a surface that is quiet and unruffled. After about twenty-four hours the eggs hatch into larvae which are popularly known as wigglers. These begin feeding on small water organisms and on disintegrated organic matter. They rapidly increase in size until the length of about one-eighth of an inch is reached, at which point they enter the pupa stage. A couple of days later, the pupa splits and an adult, full-winged mosquito emerges on the water surface from which it presently flies off into the air to begin its career as a trouble-maker. Thus the interval between birth and the prime of life occupies only about a week if conditions are favorable and especially if the weather is warm. But a water surface is absolutely necessary to the development of the mosquito life, hence there is no foundation for the popular notion that these *The mosquito's life cycle.*

insects come to life in shady spots which are merely damp or on the leaves of shrubbery after a rain.[1]

Types and varieties.

In the mosquito kingdom the female of the species is deadlier than the male. For the female alone is able to inflict annoyance upon mankind. The drilling apparatus of the male mosquito is too weak to penetrate the human skin. He gets his livelihood by extracting juices from tender plants. Among many species of mosquitoes, moreover, even the female does not bother humanity at all; on the other hand there are a few varieties which search out the uncovered portions of the human anatomy with a persistence worthy of a better cause. Among the mosquito population the most widely known troublers are the *anopheles* which transmits malaria and the *stegomyia* or *aedes aegypti* which is the carrier of yellow fever, but there are at least a hundred other species more or less common in the United States. As a rule mosquitoes do not travel over considerable distances and are rarely encountered more than a mile or two from their place of birth. When they go further it is usually because they are involuntarily carried by the wind. The expectation of life among mosquitoes does not usually exceed a few weeks, although mosquitoes have been kept alive in laboratories for several months and individual specimens of certain species have been known to hibernate throughout the winter.

The route of infection.

Of herself the female mosquito does not inoculate anyone with disease. She is merely the transmitter of germs from an infected person to someone else. Moreover the process of infective transmission requires a varying amount of time. In the case of malaria and yellow fever it takes from twelve to fourteen days to complete this process. Both these diseases are caused by microscopic parasites which can be found in the blood streams of infected persons. The mosquito imbibes some of these small organisms which work their way into her salivary gland and in due course are injected under the skin of the next victim.

Methods of mosquito eradication:

Efforts toward the eradication of mosquitoes after they have taken flight are of little value. The best control measures are those directed against the insect in its earlier stages. Such measures consist mainly of draining stagnant pools or putting oil on water

---

[1] A comprehensive and readable discussion of the subject, to which the present author is considerably indebted, may be found in Victor M. Ehlers and Ernest W. Steel, *Municipal and Rural Sanitation* (New York, 1927), pp. 141–188.

which cannot be drained, but the stocking of ponds with larvae-eating fish has also proved a useful method of eradication.

Anti-mosquito drainage should be so planned that no water will be allowed to stand for any length of time in drainage ditches or elsewhere. Moreover, while it is a recognized fact that mosquitoes do not breed in running water, this does not eliminate rivers as mosquito producers because even in rivers there are obstructions which check the current to an extent that permits mosquito breeding. The remedy in such cases is to clear the stream of vegetation and other obstructions.

1. Drainage.

Reservoirs in which the city's water supply is stored are also a source of mosquitoes, but this difficulty can be circumvented by carefully clearing the edges of the reservoir from all vegetation and stocking the water with a plentiful supply of small minnows. Much of the difficulty, however, does not come from streams or ponds or reservoirs but from open drains into which the rainfall is allowed to run and remain for weeks at a time, or from carelessly constructed culverts, or even from roof gutters and downspouts which are allowed to become obstructed.

2. Clearing the edges of reservoirs.

Oil as a larvacide has been used to great advantage in places where drainage is not possible and where the water is not to be used for public supply. When applied to the surface of the water the oil forms a thin film which the mosquito larvae are not able to penetrate because it chokes their breathing tubes. Kerosene is excellent for this purpose because it spreads rapidly and easily over the water's surface. It acts more quickly than crude oil but is also more expensive to apply and evaporates more quickly in dry weather. Fairly good results can be had at small cost by diluting crude oil with kerosene. In either case the oil is best applied by spraying it on water surfaces where there is no current. In the case of streams in which the water keeps moving there are various other ways of providing a continuous application. One of them is to anchor sacks of sawdust soaked in oil a short distance below the surface. This permits a slow exudation of the oil which rises to the surface and floats with the stream.

3. Spraying breeding places with oil.

Like all other living things the mosquito has its natural enemies, including dragon-flies, birds, and small fish. Among the fish that have proved most useful in this respect there are the several species of minnows, particularly the species commonly known as top-water minnows which feed voraciously on mosquito larvae. Stocking

4. The value of fish in mosquito eradication.

ponds and pools with these minnows is the cheapest method of mosquito eradication, but it is not effective under all conditions and it proves wholly ineffective whenever the water contains any considerable amount of floating matter or of vegetation which affords places of refuge in which the larvae can be safely deposited. Clearing such vegetation from the shores of a pond or small stream is sometimes very difficult. But where the water level is under control, as in reservoirs, the growth of marginal vegetation can be discouraged by changing this level from time to time.

Campaigns of eradication. Mosquito eradication is largely a matter of coöperative effort under the leadership of the municipal health authorities. Before any campaign of eradication is inaugurated, a survey should be made to establish the amount of work that is necessary and to obtain some idea of its probable cost. With this data in hand, an appropriation should be obtained from the municipal treasury, and if possible this ought to be supplemented by private subscriptions or by contributions from chambers of commerce, real estate associations, and other civic organizations. Some cities have adopted ordinances which prohibit the maintenance of pools or other places on private property in which mosquitoes may breed. A model ordinance has been prepared for this purpose by the United States Public Health Service.

The need of public education in this field. In general, however, the mere passage of an ordinance accomplishes little. Real results are only obtained by aggressive action, —by drainage, oiling, clearing of vegetation, and most of all by the education of householders to the fact that any quantity of still water, however small, may become a birthplace of mosquitoes by the thousand if left for a week or two in warm weather. Householders have often been amazed to be told that the infestation of their homes by swarms of these insects has had its origin in a bucket left standing under a water tap, or in the vase where a few flower bulbs have been placed to take root. Publicity and education are therefore of prime importance to success in anti-mosquito work. The responsibility for dealing with the problem should not be left to the health department alone, although this department should have an active part in the work. The coöperation of several city departments is needed.

The house fly nuisance. Mosquitoes are not the only insects that deserve obliteration as nuisances. Flies of various species are also known to be carriers of infection. The common house fly is one of the worst offenders. Un-

THE ABATEMENT OF NUISANCES

like the mosquito it does not inoculate anyone directly, but its hairy legs gather all sorts of germ-laden material which is subsequently deposited on food or in milk. As a rule flies do not travel long distances from the place of their origin, hence this nuisance can be best abated by removing or screening all materials in which the eggs are laid. The prompt collection of stable manure and its storage in water-tight, fly-proof bins or pits constitute an effective measure of prevention. Provision should also be made for the screening of all places in which the contamination of food might take place. In many cities the health ordinances now require these measures of protection.

Another malefactor is the common rat. Particularly in seaport cities the rodent population may become carriers of bubonic plague. This communicable disease is transmitted from one rat to another through the bites of rat fleas. When one rodent succumbs to bubonic, the fleas take refuge elsewhere, and often find lodgment on the person of a human being to whom they transfer the infection. Bubonic plague is prevalent in various parts of Asia, and as the rat is a migratory animal he frequently makes his way in the holds of vessels from one country to another. The federal quarantine authorities at American ports of entry have to exercise unceasing vigilance to prevent these stowaway rodents from coming ashore. As a rule vessels are required to fend off a distance of eight or ten feet from the wharf, using a submerged fender. All lines, hawsers, and cables should be equipped with circular rat guards and these should be freshly tarred each evening. Gangplanks and other connections with the shore should be removed at night.
The rat nuisance.

Rats are not only bearers of infection but are public enemies because of the economic losses which they cause. They devour food products in elevators, warehouses, barns, stores, and homes. They damage woodwork, fabrics, and furnishings. There is no way of estimating the total amount of their depredations but it must be very large if one takes the country as a whole. On many farms, it is said, the grain eaten and wasted by rats and mice would suffice to pay the farmer's taxes if it could be saved and sold. The loss in the cities is not proportionately so large, but the amount paid annually in toll to the rodent population is far in excess of what it ought to be.

Too little attention has been given by municipal authorities to the problem of rodent extermination. In view of the high cost
Anti-rat campaigns.

which this nuisance involves it is surprising that it should have been tolerated so long. Within the past few years, however, many cities have embarked upon anti-rodent campaigns and have been successful in their attacks upon the problem. Poison is the chief reliance in these campaigns, with powdered barium carbonate as the most effective medium. This poison works rather slowly, thus giving the rodents time to leave their places of refuge in search of water before they succumb. Fumigation is commonly used as a method of rodent extermination on vessels.

The rat-proofing of buildings. In the long run the surest method of controlling this nuisance is through the rat-proofing of buildings.[1] When new buildings are being erected, or old ones remodelled, the cost of making adequate provision against invasion by rodents is relatively small. The protection consists mainly of a rat-proof floor sealed into the walls surrounding it, with all cellar openings, as well as all openings around water and drain pipes, protected by wire mesh. Special attention is required in the case of stables and sheds. The protection of garbage from access by rats is also important. The sanitary inspectors should be instructed to keep careful watch on this precaution. Rats multiply where they are generously fed. Hence their increase in numbers can be most effectively prevented by keeping every kind of food supply out of their reach.

Miscellaneous nuisances. Various other nuisances are reported to the municipal authorities from time to time—obstructions in the streets and on the sidewalks, establishments which make an undue amount of noise during the night hours, dark corners in which gangs of idlers congregate, disorderly houses, unlicensed beer parlors, vacant lots on which weeds are allowed to grow and scatter seeds throughout the neighborhood, hog pens in thickly populated sections, vociferous canines that noisily salute the moon while the city sleeps—there is almost no end to the list of things which the citizen looks upon as major or minor nuisances. The old idea was that a nuisance could not be abated except on the complaint of someone who was affected by it. Today the initiative is usually taken by the public authorities without awaiting complaints. In any event the action taken to abate a nuisance must not go beyond the needs of the situation. If the use to which a building is put constitutes a nuisance, for example, such use can be stopped; but the building itself cannot

---

[1] A model ordinance covering the rat-proofing of buildings has been issued by the United States Public Health Service.

be ordered demolished. If an industry gives out too much smoke, it can be compelled to desist from that practice, but it is not allowable to go further and close down the establishment for having violated the smoke ordinance. Abatement proceedings are designed to achieve results, not to impose penalties.

REFERENCES

L. H. Cannon, *Smoke Abatement* (St. Louis, 1924) is a comprehensive work on the subject. Mention should also be made of John B. C. Kershaw, *Fuel Economy and Smoke Prevention* (New York, 1925), Napier Shaw and John S. Owens, *The Smoke Problem of Great Cities* (New York, 1925), and the *Manual of Smoke and Boiler Ordinances* issued by the Smoke Prevention Association (City Hall Square Building, Chicago, 1924). The most recent and most readable book in this field is Henry Obermeyer, *Stop That Smoke* (New York, 1933), a volume which contains an elaborate bibliography. Legal problems connected with this nuisance are fully discussed in Lucius H. Cannon, *Smoke Abatement—a Study of the Police Power as Embodied in Laws, Ordinances, and Court Decisions* (St. Louis, 1923). A *Proposed Standard Smoke Ordinance* has been prepared by the United States Bureau of Mines. *The Smoke Act Abatement Handbook*, issued by the National Smoke Abatement Society (Manchester, England, 1931), contains serviceable data. Current information can be had from the Smoke Prevention Association (City Hall Square Building, Chicago).

A volume on *City Noise* by E. F. Brown, E. B. Dennis, Jr., J. Henry, and G. Edward Pendray, editors (New York, 1930), discusses a growing urban nuisance that little has been done to remedy.

On mosquito eradication, the extermination of flies, and the control of rodents, there are excellent chapters in Victor M. Ehlers and Ernest W. Steel, *Municipal and Rural Sanitation* (New York, 1927). Mention should also be made of W. E. Hardenburg, *Mosquito Eradication* (New York, 1922), L. O. Howard, *The House Fly, Disease Carrier* (Columbus, Ohio, 1923), A. Moore Hogarth, *The Rat: a World Menace* (London, 1929), Charles A. R. Campbell, *Rats, Mosquitoes, and Dollars* (New York, 1925), Robert A. Wardle and Philip Buckle, *The Principles of Insect Control* (New York, 1923), and T. M. Hovell, *Rats and How to Destroy Them* (London, 1924). In 1928 the United States Department of Agriculture issued a useful bulletin on *Rat Control*, and various publications on insect extermination have also been published by the Bureau of Entomology in that Department.

The legal aspects of nuisance abatement are discussed in John F. Dillon, *Commentaries on the Law of Municipal Corporations* (5th edition, 5 vols., Boston, 1911), Vol. II, pp. 1034–1055; E. H. Pearce and Dougall Meston, *The Law Relating to Nuisances* (London, 1926), and J. A. Tobey, *Public Health Law* (Baltimore, 1926).

CHAPTER XXXVI

HOSPITALS

And ye brought that which was torn, and the lame, and the sick; thus ye brought an offering.—Malachi i, 13.

Private and public hospitals. For many centuries the care of the sick was looked upon as a responsibility of the church. It is still so regarded to a considerable extent. Hospitals under the sponsorship of religious organizations are maintained in a large number of American cities. But many non-sectarian hospitals have also been established as philanthropic enterprises, and private hospitals on a commercial basis are frequently operated in cities for the profit of those who own them. Likewise, during the past half-century, numerous public hospitals have been established and are maintained by counties or cities from the public revenue. These public hospitals are not intended to supply the entire needs of the community in the way of hospitalization but merely to supplement the services rendered by hospitals of the other types mentioned, as well as to care for the cases which for one reason or another cannot well be handled by other institutions. The most recent figures show nearly seven thousand hospitals in the United States, with a total of about a million beds. Of these nearly two-thirds are in public institutions. In some of the states the chief responsibility for the provision of public hospitals rests with the county authorities. In others the maintenance of such institutions is a municipal function.

The contract plan of public hospitalization. Most of the smaller cities do not maintain public hospitals of their own but make contracts with religious, philanthropic, or private institutions for the care of the indigent sick, usually on a basis of so much per day for each patient who is sent there by the overseers of the poor, or the public welfare department, or whatever authority has the dispensation of public charity in hand. In the largest municipalities, however, it is generally found more satisfactory and less expensive to have a general hospital under municipal control unless the county maintains such an institution available to the people of the city. And in any event the larger cities find it necessary to operate certain specialized hospitals as well. The latter are essential because certain types of illness cannot be satisfactorily handled by a single institution.

Consider the various classes of patients requiring treatment in public hospitals. First, there are those suffering from acute diseases or from serious injuries which require routine medical and nursing care for a relatively short space of time, not exceeding a few weeks. For such patients, if they cannot afford to pay for care in some private institution, a general public hospital is needed as an appropriate place of treatment. But there are also those afflicted with chronic ailments or infirmities which require medical and nursing care over a prolonged period, sometimes for the remaining years of their lives. A general hospital is obviously not the right place for such patients, whether viewed from a medical or an economic standpoint. Likewise there are those who unfortunately combine some physical affliction with mental troubles and hence require a measure of vigilant supervision which only a special hospital can provide. Among patients afflicted with acute illness, moreover, there will be some cases of highly communicable disease, such as diphtheria, scarlet fever, or measles. These, of course, cannot be taken to the general hospital wards. They must either be placed in isolated quarters connected with the general hospital or in a separate institution provided for such cases.

The various types of patients requiring hospital facilities.

Many large cities also find it essential to have emergency hospital facilities, centrally located, to which persons who are injured on the streets, or who for other reasons need immediate first-aid treatment, can be brought. Again, there will always be numerous cases in which free medical or surgical treatment is required, but not necessarily in hospitals. Such cases include those who are taken ill at their own homes but cannot afford the medical and nursing care which even a mild illness may require. It is more economical and usually more satisfactory to provide such patients with the services of a city physician and a visiting nurse than to arrange for their transfer to a hospital. Finally, some provision needs to be made for ambulatory patients who are not confined to either the hospital or their homes but nevertheless require therapeutic attention without being able to pay the full cost of it. For them it is customary to provide an out-patient clinic as well as a dispensary from which medicines may be obtained at a nominal cost or at no cost at all.

Emergency cases, home visitations, and clinics.

Hence a complete program of public hospital service and medical care involves not one but several institutions. It requires, in the first place, a general hospital for the care of the sick and injured who need routine medical and nursing care under conditions most suitably provided by a hospital, whether they are able to pay for it or not. Second, it includes an institution for the care of chronic diseases, more especially tuberculosis, and likewise a place which is equipped to care for those who are both ill and mentally unbalanced. Such a sanitarium, however, is not usually required when suitable hospitals for the insane are provided by the county or the state. A complete municipal program also necessitates an isolation wing or a special hospital for the care of those whose ailments have been diagnosed as communicable; and if the general hospital is located at a distance from the downtown section of the city, there is also need for a relief or emergency hospital at which first aid can be rendered. The welfare of indigent home patients usually demands the maintenance of a public health center, one or more city physicians, a corps of visiting nurses, a clinic, and a dispensary. This is a comprehensive program and very few cities are able to cover it entirely. For the most part they attempt only a portion of it, leaving the rest to private philanthropies or to centralized institutions maintained by the other public authorities.

The function of a general hospital is fourfold. In the first place it is expected to serve as a public health agency by assisting in the control of disease and by providing sick or injured persons with a quality of treatment which they could not obtain in their own homes. Hence a good public hospital is often patronized by patients who can afford to pay what the service costs, or at least a large portion of it. In every city hospital there are some patients who pay their way, but there is a much larger number of those who do not. As respects this latter class the hospital is not exclusively a health institution but an agency of health and charity combined. For this reason it has sometimes been argued that a free general hospital ought to be under the supervision of the public welfare authorities and should not constitute a responsibility of the city's health department. In some cases the issue has been settled by placing the isolation and emergency hospitals under the health department while the management of the general hospital is entrusted to a separate board or director working in close coöperation with the city's poor-relief authorities. While such a division may be a logical one, it is hardly conducive to economy or to the concentration of responsibility for the success of a public health program.

The balance of advantage would seem to lie with the policy of combining all the city's facilities for the care of the sick under a single administrative authority. This range of control should include not only the general hospital but all specialized health institutions, as well as home visitation by doctors and nurses, together with clinics, dispensaries, and convalescent camps. The care of the sick ought to be looked upon as a single unified public enterprise and not as a bifurcated municipal function to be apportioned among two or more departments on the basis of health versus charity. Where such a unified hospital department exists, it is usually under the supervision of an appointive board which assumes final responsibility for the selection and control of personnel as well as for hospital policy. Members of this board are usually appointed by the chief municipal executive and are expected to give their services without remuneration. The board then appoints a superintendent or director who acts as its executive officer. *The desirability of unified control.*

In some cities, however, there is no board of hospital trustees, but the director or superintendent of hospitals is appointed by the head of the city government or by the administrative head of the health department. In any event it is essential that the superintendent or director be given direct control over all branches of hospital management whether relating to in-patients or out-patients, and subject only to such supervision of his work as may be exercised by the hospital board or by his superior officer in the city government. The hospital board, where there is one, should not interfere in the management of the institution. It should make the major appointments, outline policies, develop a sound plan of financial operation, and scrutinize the results. There its functions should end. The superintendent, for his part, should follow the lines of policy laid down for him (or in consultation with him) and should produce the results which the board expects. To accomplish this he must keep all branches of the hospital service working effectively and harmoniously together. *Hospital boards.*

The personnel of a public hospital includes a variety of professional and trained workers who constitute a considerable group. First of all there are the physicians and surgeons who form the *The medical staff.*

professional staff of the hospital. A few of these may be resident at the hospital (one of them being designated as head physician or surgeon), but the majority are doctors engaged in private practice who come in from day to day to undertake the professional care of their own patients or of patients to whom they are assigned. Members of the professional staff may be appointed by the superintendent of the hospital or by the hospital board, but such appointments should not ordinarily be made except on the recommendation of those doctors who are already members. In the case of indigent patients the members of this medical staff give their services free or for a nominal compensation. Supplementing their work, every large public hospital has a group of internes,—young physicians and surgeons who are using their hospital experience as a means of securing professional training. Appointed for terms of one or two years, they serve as aides to members of the staff and usually receive a small amount of remuneration in addition to their maintenance. The resident-house physician or surgeon or other resident medical officer is responsible for the supervision of these internes so far as their professional work is concerned. In other respects they are under the jurisdiction of the superintendent.

2. As an institution for the training of nurses. The second function of a general public hospital is educational. It serves as a center of training for nurses. The nurses in charge of the various wards or special service units are usually graduates appointed by the superintendent and are under the immediate control of a head nurse. As respects their work with patients, however, these graduate nurses are subject to the orders of the attending medical staff. Graduate nurses are assisted by student nurses from the hospital training school which is attached to every large public hospital. The training of nurses is not an indispensable branch of public hospital work, but it has everywhere been found to be a desirable activity from the standpoint of both service and economy. For student nurses are utilized in the work of routine nursing under the supervision of graduates as part of their training, and thus increasing the amount of service which can be rendered at low cost. They also do a good deal of work which otherwise would necessitate the employment of additional maids and other helpers. The training period for these student nurses usually extends over two or three years, during which time they are given their maintenance and often a small monthly allowance as well.

In addition to their practical work they spend certain hours each day in the classroom receiving instruction from the director of nurses or from members of the medical staff. A director of the nurses' training school, appointed by the superintendent or board, is responsible for standards and discipline.

The third activity of a public hospital is connected with outdoor work and social service. Most public hospitals maintain one or more out-patient clinics. An out-patient clinic may be defined as an institution which organizes the professional skill of physicians and which provides special equipment for the prevention, diagnosis, and treatment of diseases or injuries among ambulatory patients. Usually certain ground-floor rooms of the hospital are set apart for this purpose. Out-patient clinics at public hospitals are intended for those who cannot afford to obtain medical advice or care in the ordinary way, but they are sometimes imposed upon by others. For this reason some public hospitals have adopted the plan of charging a small fee for all treatments given in the out-patient department with a proviso that such fees may be waived in cases of real necessity.

3. As an enterprise in social service.

This suggests that the relation between the medical and the social service of an out-patient clinic is a very intimate one. The relationship has been recognized in most large public hospitals by the organizing of a social service bureau or division, thus attaching a number of social workers to the clinic. Some of them are trained professionals, while others are volunteer workers. Their function is to obtain such information about the home circumstances of patients as may be useful to physicians in making a correct diagnosis or in determining the most desirable methods of treatment and care. The social history of a patient often throws light on the origins of his physical troubles. This is especially true of patients who have ailments connected with the nervous system. Social workers attached to the clinic are also expected to do follow-up work with convalescents. To this end they keep in touch with the city's department of public welfare or with private charitable organizations in the endeavor to promote both the physical and economic rehabilitation of patients. Their work indicates a widened recognition of the fact that illness is a prolific cause of social dependency.

Out-patient clinics and social workers.

Finally, the general hospital is an institution of research. It is a center in which medical and surgical specialists have an oppor-

4. As an institution of scientific research and medical education.

tunity to keep careful records of numerous cases, study them, and try hopeful experiments in the treatment of patients under controlled conditions. Many large hospitals are either associated with medical schools or have some arrangement under which their clinical facilities are made available for the encouragement of research and the improvement of medical education. Much of the advance in clinical medicine and in operative surgery has been due to research work conducted in hospitals.

The special services.

Various special services and responsibilities are connected with every large public hospital. For example, there is the supervision and management of the various laboratories, including the chemical, bacteriological, and X-ray laboratories, the operating room, the ambulance service, and the emergency ward. Provision is also made for special treatments in the way of medicated baths, massage, corrective exercises, and occupational therapy. The steady advance in medical science and in surgical ingenuity has imposed upon the hospitals an ever-growing demand for specialization. Each of these specialized services is placed under the immediate charge of a resident medical officer, an officer of the attending staff, an interne, or one of the head nurses. But in order to secure a complete articulation of the entire work the superintendent should have jurisdiction over them all. This ought to be axiomatic but in practice it is not always so regarded. Not all public hospitals are conducted on the principle that every working unit is an integral part of the whole and that unified authority is the prime requisite of its successful functioning.

Hospital housekeeping.

The foregoing brief enumeration does not by any means exhaust the list of functions which the authorities of the public hospital are expected to perform. For one thing, good hospital management requires the upkeep and maintenance of buildings, grounds, and equipment. In certain respects a hospital is a hotel with the obligation of properly lodging and feeding its guests. Hence, its kitchen equipment is quite elaborate. Then, in addition to the preparation and service of food, there is the work of cleaning the wards and rooms, operating a laundry, and caring for many other household duties which have to be performed with scrupulous attention because of the dangers which would result from carelessness. Nor should one overlook the considerable amount of work which has to be performed in connection with the inspection, receipt, storage, and distribution of hospital and food supplies, the keeping of records and accounts, as well as the purchasing of medicines, equipment, materials, and so forth.

The selection of a suitable site for a general municipal hospital is a problem of great importance. In the case of private institutions, which serve mainly those able to pay, accessibility of location is not a factor of great importance; but a public hospital deals mainly with people whose facilities in the way of transportation are very limited. The general hospital's out-patient department, as well as its dispensary and social service bureau, should therefore be so located that they can easily be reached by the population which they are intended to serve. It has been found that the usefulness of these institutions is greatly diminished if patients have to travel long distances in order to reach them on foot, by street car, or in the ambulance. When the general hospital is placed in an outlying section of the city it usually becomes essential to provide downdown locations for both the out-patient and emergency departments. This involves a duplication of equipment and an increase in overhead expenses. *The hospital site.*

A central location for the general hospital is also desirable from the standpoint of its medical staff, the members of which are for the most part practitioners who give their services free. These doctors should not be asked to spend an hour or more each day in getting to the hospital and returning from it. They should be within range, moreover, when their patients send out a hurry call. Ease of access by automobile, through the possibility of avoiding congested streets, is therefore of importance to all concerned. On the other hand the hospital and its auxiliary institutions ought to be located outside the zone of heavy traffic and persistent noise. To secure an ideal site is sometimes very difficult, however, because most neighborhoods do not welcome a public hospital into their midst. Plenty of land in an easily accessible downtown location, together with an agreeable environment, are rarely to be found in combination. A generous amount of land is needed because hospital buildings should have light and air on all sides. Pleasant surroundings are important from the standpoint of patients, medical staff, and nurses. Freedom from disagreeable sights, sounds, and odors is obviously desirable. Nevertheless, it is not uncommon to find public hospitals placed in congested neighborhoods surrounded by unkempt streets and noisy or odorous industries. *Why a central location is desirable.*

The buildings.

As for the hospital building itself, it should be so planned as to keep the cost of operation and maintenance within economical limits. To achieve this result there must be the closest coöperation between architects and hospital authorities. It is also essential that the building be so constructed that additional facilities can be added without undue cost when they are required. Likewise the possibility of economical remodelling should be kept in mind. Hospital technique is steadily improving and changing. In keeping with these changes the interior arrangements of a hospital building need to be altered from time to time. As in the case of schools, however, the tendency has been to erect structures of an imposing and ornate character which do not lend themselves to interior alterations without excessive cost.

Hospital finance.

Hospitals are expensive to operate—more so than the average taxpayer realizes. The special dietary service is costly; the service has to be kept at a high standard; the amount of cleaning, laundering, and disinfecting that needs to be done is very large, while the amount expended for instruments, medicines, surgical supplies, and laboratory materials is steadily growing. This explains why the daily cost per patient is so large. Public hospitals occasionally have some income from endowment, but for the most part their maintenance is a charge upon the municipal budget. This item in public budgets has been steadily increasing in size because of the enlarged demands for service being made by the people. What once were merely places of care for the sick have now become health centers where education, research, and social service are carried on as well.

REFERENCES

Useful books in this field are Frank E. Chapman, *Hospital Organization and Operation* (New York, 1924), C. E. A. Winslow and Josephine Goldmark, *Nursing Education in the United States* (New York, 1923), Mary S. Gardner, *Public Health Nursing* (New York, 1924), Michael M. Davis, *Clinics, Hospitals and Health Centers* (New York, 1927), J. J. Weber, *First Steps in Organizing a Hospital* (New York, 1924), C. R. Rorem, *The Public's Investment in Hospitals* (Chicago, 1930), M. M. Davis and C. R. Rorem, *The Crisis in Hospital Finance and Other Studies in Hospital Economics* (Chicago, 1932), Niles Carpenter, *Hospital Service for Patients of Moderate Means* (Washington, 1930), E. F. Stevens, *The American Hospital of the Twentieth Century* (2nd edition, New York, 1928), and

HOSPITALS

Ira V. Hiscock, *Community Health Organization* (new edition, New York, 1932).

Mention should also be made of the useful information contained in the *Kansas City Health and Hospital Survey* by W. F. Walker and associates (Kansas City, 1931). An illuminating report on *The Cost of Medical Care* was issued in 1928 by the Committee on Cost of Medical Care (910 Seventeenth St., N. W., Washington). *The Modern Hospital Year Book*, published annually in Chicago, is a useful book, and bibliographical bulletins are published from time to time by the Hospital Library and Service Bureau (22 East Ontario St., Chicago).

Current discussions may be found in *The Modern Hospital*, published monthly.

See also the references appended to Chapter XXXIV.

CHAPTER XXXVII

PUBLIC WELFARE AND SOCIAL INSURANCE

> Poor naked wretches, whoso'er you are,
> That bide the pelting of this pitiless storm,
> How shall your houseless heads and unfed sides,
> Your looped and windowed raggedness, defend you
> From seasons such as these?
>
> —*King Lear.*

An age-old problem. Poverty is one of the oldest among human problems. Two thousand years ago, in Biblical times, the world was endeavoring to find a solution for it, and it has kept trying ever since. In every generation of men there have been those who, by their own fault or the fault of others, have proved unable to support themselves. Since the day when man was condemned to eat bread in the sweat of his brow he has been trying to get the most bread for the least sweat. He must work to live. Hence if he is out of work or unable to work or unwilling to work, he becomes dependent on the exertions of others. People are said to be in poverty when they find themselves unable through their own efforts to maintain that minimum standard of living which is essential to health and working efficiency. This means, of course, that poverty is a relative term. It depends upon what the minimum standard of living is considered to be. In some American communities an individual might reckon himself in abject poverty and yet be better fed and better clothed than millions of his fellow men who are maintaining the customary standard of living in India or China.

Poverty and city life. For the most part poverty is an urban problem. Except in case of famine or other catastrophe, it rarely becomes a serious problem in the rural areas. "He that tilleth his land shall have plenty of bread."[1] So long as a country remains in the agricultural stage its people may live in very modest circumstances, but the number of those who cannot support themselves will be small. In the United States the problem of poor relief did not become a serious one until after the frontier had vanished and free land had become no longer available. In other words, the problem of poor relief

[1] Proverbs xxviii, 19.

is one that seems to have accentuated in difficulty with the advance of civilization and the rise of great urban communities.

In the cities of the United States there is no way of measuring the exact dimensions of this problem. We do not know how many persons require relief or how much is spent upon them year by year because the official figures cover only those who are being maintained in institutions of charity or who receive assistance from the public treasury. No reliable figures are available with respect to those dependent persons who receive aid from church organizations, welfare societies, fraternal orders, community chests, social agencies, and private individuals. In any event the total would vary enormously from year to year. In an era of business depression it grows to several times its normal size. The first of our handicaps in dealing with the problem of poverty arises from the fact that we do not know just how serious the problem has become at any given time.

Its extent.

What are the causes of poverty? The sociologists usually divide them into two general groups which they designate as individual and social causes. Among the individual causes of poverty are illness, accidents, old age, bereavement, and personal incompetence. Illness is a double-edged misfortune because it increases the family expenses and decreases the income. Accidents, resulting in either temporary or permanent incapacity to do full work, have been an important cause of poverty in the past but are now becoming much less so by reason of the provisions which have been made by law for workmen's compensation. Old age comes to everyone in time and there are many who make no provision for its coming. Hence they have to be supported by their relatives or by the public authorities. The problem of public support for the aged has become so serious in European countries that virtually all of them have now established something in the way of an old age pension system. And several American states have in recent years made a beginning in the same direction. Dependency is also caused, in many instances, by the death of the bread winners, leaving wife and children with no means of support. Finally, there is the prolific cause of poverty which, for want of a better term, is set down as personal incompetence or maladjustment. This deficiency may be physical, mental, moral, or all three combined. Some unfortunates are born blind, deaf, feeble-minded, or crippled. Others meet with mishaps which burden them with par-

The causes of poverty:
1. Individual causes.

tial or total disability. Such persons obviously find it difficult to make their way in a world of keen competition and hence are forced to seek assistance from others. Shiftlessness, intemperance, laziness, and bad habits are all additional causes of varying importance; but contrary to the popular impression they are not responsible for the major part of the problem.

2. Social causes.

Nor do the individual causes of poverty account for nearly the whole of it. Social causes arising chiefly from the vicissitudes of industrial society are contributing factors of great importance, especially in times of economic depression. Unemployment is chief among the social causes of dependency and in a prolonged period of industrial recession it becomes more important than all other causes combined. The burden which it places upon the normal facilities for poor relief is sometimes much heavier than they can bear. These periodic eras of widespread and prolonged unemployment point to serious defects in the existing industrial order. They are the outcome of bad planning and overproduction, or unbalanced production, or of the failure of credit to keep itself adjusted to industrial needs. With a general rise in the standard of living, moreover, the danger of serious depression under a régime of economic *laissez-faire* becomes greater than ever. For when the standard of living is low, most of the agricultural and industrial production is related to the actual necessities of life. But as the standard rises there is a diversion of labor to the production of non-essentials, the demand for which may suffer an abrupt falling-off at any time. And when that occurs the problem of poor relief merges into the larger and more fundamental one of getting work for those who have been thrown out of it.

Some examples of social ineptitude.

National prosperity, however, does not by any means eliminate unemployment. There are seasonal variations in the demand for labor even during industrial booms. Moreover the inequalities in the distribution of income often lead to the underpayment of workers, especially those with large families. Large families and inability to educate them properly result in recruiting the supply of workers who can be had for low wages. Immigration had a similar effect until it was curtailed. Unsanitary conditions of living and overcrowding are also environmental causes of poverty because they lead to illness and throw people out of work. Corruption in public office, the waste of public funds, and misgovernment in all its forms should likewise be reckoned among the causes of poverty

PUBLIC WELFARE AND SOCIAL INSURANCE

because they place an undue burden upon industry, prevent the enactment of desirable legislation, and interfere with the enforcement of the laws. The failure to prevent the employment of child labor, for example, has thrown large numbers of physically weakened and poorly educated workers into a losing competition with those who are more fit. Earning power is low where the percentage of illiteracy is high. Hence, compulsory public education is one of the most effective measures for the prevention of poverty that a country can take.

For many centuries the world's attitude toward poverty was a fatalistic one. "The poor ye have with you always." Poverty had always existed and would continue to the end of time. People looked upon this problem as many of them now do upon the possibility of abolishing war. Then, in due course, came social reformers who argued that all poverty was due to a single cause. Malthus believed it due to the pressure of population upon subsistence. Karl Marx taught that it was the inevitable outcome of a capitalistic system. Henry George argued that poverty was attributable to the existence of landlords and could be abolished only by the adoption of a single tax system. It is only within relatively recent years that the complex nature of the causes has gained full recognition and with it a realization that poverty is in considerable measure a social disease for which there is no single panacea and which can be eradicated only by persistent effort along many lines. *The older attitude toward the problem of poverty.*

Even yet, however, the amelioration of poverty is not regarded in the United States as primarily a public problem. Most of the responsibility is still remitted by the public authorities to private charitable organizations. In every large city there are literally hundreds of organizations engaged in some form of relief and remedial work, such as child welfare, or the care of the aged, the sick, the blind, the crippled, or the unemployed. There are orphanages, homes for the aged, institutions for the deaf and blind, hospitals, preventoriums, clinics, district nursing associations, day nurseries, midnight missions, free lodging houses, soup kitchens, and other relief agencies bearing names almost without number. Virtually all these organizations and institutions are financed by income from endowments or by gifts from benevolent individuals. Sometimes each agency raises its own funds; in other cases they are financed from a community chest. This central fund is obtained by a great money-raising campaign once a year and the proceeds *Private and public contributions toward its solution.*

Community chests.

are then allocated to the different agencies. The public treasury, in the main, provides relief only for those who cannot obtain it from private sources. In times of industrial depression, however, this residual responsibility becomes very great because the private agencies are unable to bear the increased load.

Public welfare administration.

When the responsibility for the relief of distress is placed upon the municipality, the function of caring for dependent persons is usually entrusted to a department of public welfare or a department of charities. In the early stages of American municipal history this department was almost invariably placed under a board of overseers. These overseers of the poor were public-spirited citizens who gave a part of their time to the work without being paid for it. Such boards still exist in many communities. But the more common practice nowadays is to place a director of public welfare or a superintendent of public charities at the head of the department, although he is sometimes assisted by an advisory board of citizens. Everywhere the tendency is to discard such terms as poor relief or charity and to substitute public welfare as a less humiliating designation. The director of the public welfare department should be a person fully qualified by training and experience for the work, appointed by the chief municipal executive, and the members of his advisory board should be similarly appointed. He should have control over all branches of public welfare activity and should receive a remuneration commensurate with the importance of his work. For here is a post with respect to which a low salary prefigures false economy, because there is no other city department in which public money can be more readily wasted through incompetence or lack of vigilant supervision.

Boards of overseers and single directors.

Outdoor relief.

Public provision for the relief of distress usually (but not always) takes the form of outdoor relief. This involves the giving of food, clothing, fuel, or even money to individuals and families for use in maintaining themselves in their own homes. Outdoor relief is favored by the public authorities because it is believed to be more expedient and less expensive to hold a family together as a unit than to scatter its members around among public institutions. Applications for this kind of assistance, however, must be patiently and carefully investigated by competent social workers, otherwise there will be a waste of public money on a large scale. Most people realize this need, yet public opinion is strangely intolerant of any procedure which keeps an applicant waiting until his circumstances have been looked into. It prefers to give twice by giving quickly—which is what quick giving often amounts to. Unless there is a careful investigation of every case by trained officials of the public welfare department, the allowances given are likely to be so generous as to place a premium on idleness. And in any event outdoor relief should not be continued in individual cases any longer than is absolutely necessary, for it is nothing but a makeshift, a palliative that does not go to the sources of the trouble at all. It is sometimes said that the world owes every man a living, which is true with the reservation that it is up to him to go out and collect it. Any charitable endeavor which wholly loses sight of this ultimate obligation is bound in the long run to demoralize those concerned in it.

Indoor relief, on the other hand, is the term used to describe the method of caring for distress in public institutions. Many persons cannot be kept in their own homes because they have no homes or because they need special care which cannot be given them at their homes. Hence there is usually a public almshouse, or house of refuge, or county farm, or city home, or whatever it may be called. This institution is burdened with the handicap of bad ancestry. For generations it was known, both in England and America, as a place of coarse food and inhuman treatment where the aged poor dragged out the final years of their drab existence amid the cold charities of man to man. Even yet, in twentieth century America, the public almshouse is often inhumanly administered. Too frequently its superintendent is chosen under the inspiration of local politics and possesses neither the intelligence nor the ideals which his work requires. He, in turn, appoints subordinates of his own type. Food supplies of inferior quality are bought at high prices from personal or political friends; indolent employees let the place get into an unsanitary condition; uncouth attendants bully the inmates until the institution becomes a conspicuous illustration of the commonplace that political malfeasance invariably falls with redoubled weight upon the helpless portion of the community.

Indoor relief.

In addition to a general place of indoor relief the larger cities maintain various specialized institutions. These include a juvenile hall or temporary refuge for homeless children, a municipal lodging house for transients, and sometimes an institution for ine-

Specialized public welfare institutions.

briates. Another municipal activity which closely connects itself with the problem of helping those who are out of work is the free employment bureau. This is an office, maintained at the city hall or elsewhere, for the purpose of bringing vacant jobs and unemployed workers into contact with one another. Employers are asked to telephone their needs which are promptly supplied from names of those on file at the bureau. Here again, however, the efficiency of the service has often been impaired by the habit of placing some deserving politician rather than a trained employment manager in charge of the office.

Public works as relief agencies. During periods of industrial depression the cities endeavor to lessen the ranks of the unemployed by spending additional money on public works, these funds being usually obtained through the issue of bonds or by subsidies from the federal government. While the urgency of the relief problem may force cities into a program of this sort, there is not a great deal to be said for it in the last analysis. A large part of the expenditure goes for materials, not for labor, and the cost of the work usually proves to be far in excess of what it would be if the element of relief were excluded. Men are put on the work because they are needy, not because they are competent. Such a program, moreover, offers very little to the "white collar" workers, or to unemployed women, both of whom are quite as deserving and often even more in need than are the artisans and laborers who can be helped by a program of emergency public construction. On the other hand it is better to give people work, so far as it goes, than to be under the necessity of supporting them by direct relief from the public treasury.

Legal aid bureaus. Another public welfare service which some cities provide is represented by the legal aid bureau. Its purpose is to afford legal advice and assistance at nominal cost, or at no cost at all, for those who cannot afford to pay the customary legal fees. The staff of the bureau is made up of young lawyers who give their services for a certain number of hours per week without compensation. They listen to the grievances and complaints of those who believe that their wages have been wrongfully withheld, or who have been unfairly treated by landlords, or who have suffered from something else that rankles as an injustice. Most of these naturally turn to the city hall as a place where wrongs are set right and grievances adjusted. The legal aid clinic is of great service in protecting the otherwise helpless against the exactions of avaricious

PUBLIC WELFARE AND SOCIAL INSURANCE 525

employers, iron-fisted landlords, shyster lawyers, and other predatory amphibians. In many cities this service is performed as a private philanthropy, not as a regular function of the municipality.

The waste involved in public welfare work is inevitably large. This is because so many organizations, official and unofficial, are engaged in it. The number of such agencies, in any large city, will run into the hundreds. Naturally there is much duplication of effort and piling-up of overhead expenses. Until not many years ago each organization functioned without much regard to the others, with the result that malingerers and impostors often found it relatively easy to tap several sources of relief and make a good living thereby. But nowadays, in nearly all cities, a confidential exchange has been established as a clearing house of information concerning all individuals who come into contact with any of the agencies. When an applicant comes to any public welfare organization and tells his story, it can be checked up by calling the confidential exchange and finding out if he is being helped from some other source. Sometimes this exchange is maintained by the city, but more often it is operated by the various private organizations as a common enterprise. *Preventing duplication of relief.*

Among all branches of municipal administration there is probably none that has made more tardy progress toward a final solution of its problems than the department which has to do with the amelioration of distress. Most of its work has been of a makeshift character. Those in charge of municipal poor relief have only vaguely sensed the idea that their problem is not merely to distribute a weekly dole, but to devise measures for getting the recipients back upon their own feet again. Every case that comes to them ought to be a problem in social diagnosis; that is, it should be made the subject of a careful inquiry into causes and possible remedies. Too little of this has been done, largely because the public mind in times of emergency is concentrated on relief rather than on rehabilitation. *The slow progress of scientific public welfare work.*

Other city departments, however, have learned to reach beyond the immediate urgencies of the situation. The city health department has not concerned itself solely or even mainly with the care of those who have become sick; it has put forth even greater effort toward the prevention of disease by the eradication of its causes. To this end it has fully utilized the results of medical research. But public welfare departments in American cities have given *A comparison with other departments.*

little attention to the problem of prevention. They have not been pioneers or leaders in the movement for social insurance or for the inauguration of a better industrial economy. To a surprisingly small degree have they utilized the results of research in the field of dependency. Consequently the large expenditures made by cities through their public welfare departments have accomplished relatively little in bringing public action to the roots of the problem. It is probably true that poverty can never be wholly eliminated, but there is reason to believe that well-planned and well-administered measures of prevention would some day reduce it to a minimum. Some measures of this kind have already been taken on the initiative of the state governments, and others will follow in the course of time.

Social insurance as a remedy: What can be done in the way of prevention? In the first place it has already been pointed out that accidents, illness, old age, and unemployment are among the chief causes of individual dependency and distress. Of course these causes cannot themselves be altogether eliminated, but their sinister social effects can undoubtedly be mollified by rational prevision. As a matter of fact the first cause of dependency above mentioned, namely, industrial accidents, is now being almost wholly removed from the list through the operation of workmen's compensation laws.[1] These laws, which are now in effect throughout the greater portion of the United States, virtually compel employers to take out industrial accident insurance for the support of their workers in case of accident. The usual arrangement is that every workman, injured in the course of his employment, becomes entitled to compensation no matter how the accident may have been caused. The amount of compensation is generally based on the wages of the injured worker and the percentage varies with the seriousness of the injury. Most of the states have a maximum limit of compensation per week and many of them also set a limit on the number of weeks during which the payments may be made. Employers usually arrange with a regular insurance company or with the state insurance department to pay this compensation in return for an annual premium. Thus the cost of workmen's compensation becomes one of the regular expenses of conducting the business, like rent, taxes, or fire insurance. If an employer does not arrange for insurance he must pay the compensation from his own pocket. Any contro-

1. Industrial accident insurance.

[1] E. H. Downey, *Workmen's Compensation* (New York, 1924).

versies which arise with respect to the payments are adjusted by a state body commonly known as the industrial accident board. Agricultural workers and domestic employees are usually excluded from the scope of these compensation laws.

Protection against dependency as a result of illness is now being provided by compulsory health insurance in several European countries. The premiums on this insurance are paid partly by the workers and the employers, but a subsidy from the public treasury is usually added. In Great Britain the system is administered by a number of approved non-profit organizations under the supervision of the Ministry of Health.[1] Some attempts have been made to secure legislation establishing compulsory health insurance in several American states, but thus far none of them have been successful, although the plan has a great deal to commend it.[2] Meanwhile a good deal is being done in the way of sickness benefits by labor unions and fraternal organizations.

2. Health insurance.

Old age and the infirmities of age are everywhere a prolific cause of the heavy strain upon the public relief funds. Most wage-earners do not, and probably cannot, save enough to provide for themselves when they are no longer able to work. Hence they have to be supported by their children, or, failing this, they become dependent on assistance from private or public agencies. To cope with this problem virtually all the more important countries of Europe have now established systems of old age pensions or weekly allowances for those workers who have reached a stated age and are no longer self-supporting. The necessary funds are in some countries contributed by employers, workers, and the state jointly, while in others they are entirely provided from the public revenues. During the past few years a number of American states have made a beginning in the way of old age gratuities, and it will probably not be long before the idea receives general adoption throughout the country. Meanwhile the pension idea is spreading along other lines. Most of the states have made provision for allowances to needy mothers for the support of their children. These are paid from the public welfare funds. Pensions to war veterans, as well as to policemen, firemen, and various other civil employees, are being provided on a generous scale. Many private industries and educational institutions have established super-

3. Old age pensions.

---

[1] W. H. Aggs, *The National Insurance Act, 1924* (London, 1925).
[2] Gerald Morgan, *The Public Relief of Sickness* (New York, 1922).

annuation allowances for their employees after a designated term of service. Insurance companies through their endowment policies, and all manner of thrift organizations, are doing their best to encourage the habit of saving. In spite of these various efforts, however, it would seem that adequate provision for old age, as a means of eradicating dependency, will ultimately require compulsory insurance or a pension system on a nation-wide scale.

4. Unemployment insurance. Finally, there is the most difficult problem of all—that of providing social insurance to ameliorate the widespread distress which is caused from time to time by unemployment. This is perhaps the most urgent need of our day, for unemployment not only deprives the worker of his income but impairs his efficiency and undermines his sense of responsibility. It tends to weaken the existing order by promoting discontent, unrest, and defiance of law. Many industrial establishments in American cities have adopted the plan of setting aside each week a certain percentage of the total payroll as an unemployment reserve. Then, when the workers are laid off by reason of slackened business, and not through any fault of their own, a certain weekly allowance is paid to them. In a time of prolonged depression, however, the reserve is likely to prove inadequate.

European experience with it. Social insurance against unemployment has had a considerable trial in European countries, more particularly in Great Britain, but in Italy and Germany as well. The British system was inaugurated in 1911, but has been greatly extended in scope since that time. At the outset the plan contemplated that the employer, the employee, and the public treasury should all make stated contributions to the insurance fund. After the close of the World War, however, the amount of unemployment was so great that the fund could not take care of all the weekly allowances required. Hence arose the practice of having the national government subsidize the fund far beyond its anticipated contribution. Various defects in the administration of the system, moreover, have permitted it to be abused, but in recent years many of the more serious weaknesses have been corrected.[1]

The philosophy of unemployment insurance. The idea which lies at the basis of unemployment insurance is fundamentally sound. For so long as our industrial system is subject to vicissitudes which throw large numbers of men out of work, it is self-evident that the public authorities should devise

[1] J. L. Cohen, *Social Insurance Unified* (London, 1924).

some plan whereby the resultant hardships to large groups of citizens can be ameliorated without subjecting both private philanthropy and the public treasury to an emergency strain which neither of them is readily able to bear. The cost of individual dependency due to unemployment is bound to fall upon the community in any case. When distress arising from unemployment is relieved by the action of private charitable organizations, the cost is certainly not less than when it is defrayed from the public funds. It is merely that the expense in the former case is scattered around and disguised. Moreover, if employers have to contribute their share toward unemployment insurance, they will take greater pains to keep their industries going, just as they have been more interested in the prevention of industrial accidents since the burden of workmen's compensation has been placed upon them. On the other hand a scheme of unemployment insurance, however carefully it may be safeguarded against the ingenuity of work shirkers, is bound to be abused. The chief problem is to keep the insurance from becoming a dole.

Minimum wage laws have proved of service in preventing the gross underpayment of labor and to that extent have reduced the rank of the partially dependent. It should be impressed upon every student of social science that when labor is underpaid, overworked, or thrown out of work, the community as a whole has to pay for it. The issue, therefore, is not one that concerns the employer and his men alone. It is one of vital importance to every taxpayer. For the future it is proposed that all such matters as minimum wages, maximum hours of labor, collective bargaining, and conditions of work shall be covered in officially ratified codes which each industry is required by the National Industrial Recovery Act to set up for itself. The success of this great social experiment, if it does succeed, will go a considerable distance in the direction of solving the city's problems of public welfare.

5. Minimum wage laws.

Social progress comes by way of social experimentation. If all the available remedies for poverty and distress are given a fair trial, some of them will inevitably prove successful and to that extent they will reduce the immensity of the public welfare tasks that are now thrown upon the municipal authorities But the process of trial and error requires both time and patience. The danger is that governments will be stampeded by an impatient electorate into the adoption of crude, unpromising, poorly thought-

Public welfare and social experimentation.

out schemes which have little or no chance of yielding permanent advantage. Undertaking hastily planned programs of public work, for example, as a means of affording additional employment have been proved by European experience to be among the most expensive and least effective ways of attacking a serious problem. Placing oppressive super-taxes on the incomes of the rich in order to finance these large public enterprises for the benefit of the poor will never bring a land to normal prosperity. If the poor could be made richer by the simple expedient of making the rich poor, the world would have discovered it long ago, for it has tried the experiment a great many times.

REFERENCES

A. G. Warner, S. A. Queen, and E. B. Harper, *American Charities and Social Work* (4th edition, New York, 1930), and Frank D. Watson, *The Charity Movement in the United States* (New York, 1922) are good books on the subject of poor relief. Mention should also be made of H. W. Odum and D. W. Willard, *Systems of Public Welfare* (Chapel Hill, N. C., 1925), J. L. Gillin, *Poverty and Dependency* (revised edition, New York, 1926), Elwood Street, *Social Work Administration* (New York, 1931), S. P. Breckinridge, *Family Welfare Work in a Metropolitan Community* (Chicago, 1924) and *Public Welfare Administration in the United States* (Chicago, 1927), Robert W. Kelso, *The Science of Public Welfare* (New York, 1928), and Arlien Johnson, *Public Policy and Private Charities* (Chicago, 1931). Volume CV of the Annals of the American Academy of Political and Social Science, January, 1923, is devoted to articles on *Public Welfare in the United States*.

Discussions of workmen's compensation may be found in E. H. Downey, *Workmen's Compensation* (New York, 1924), G. F. Michelbacher and T. M. Nial, *Workmen's Compensation Insurance* (New York, 1925), and F. R. Buechner, *Municipal Self-Insurance of Workmen's Compensation* (Chicago, 1931).

The problem of unemployment is discussed in Sir William H. Beveridge, *Unemployment* (new edition, London, 1930), Paul H. Douglas and Aaron Director, *The Problem of Unemployment* (Chicago, 1931), Gordon S. Watkins, *Labor Problems* (new edition, New York, 1929), and Shelby M. Harrison, *Public Employment Offices* (New York, 1924).

On unemployment insurance there are many books, including Bryce M. Stewart, *Unemployment Benefits in the United States* (New York, 1930), A. Epstein, *Insecurity: a Challenge to America* (New York, 1933), M. B. Gilson, *Unemployment Insurance* (Chicago, 1933), E. C. Buehler, *Compulsory Unemployment Insurance* (New York, 1931), Paul H. Douglas,

PUBLIC WELFARE AND SOCIAL INSURANCE 531

Standards of Unemployment Insurance (Chicago, 1933), the report of the National Industrial Conference Board on *Unemployment Benefits and Insurance* (New York, 1931), and the report of the President's Research Committee on *Recent Social Trends* (2 vols., New York, 1933).

Material relating to health insurance may be found in J. L. Cohen, *Social Insurance Unified* (London, 1924), M. M. Davis, *Paying Your Sickness Bill* (Chicago, 1931), and the bulletin on *Health Insurance* issued in 1931 by the Metropolitan Life Insurance Company.

Old age pension systems are explained in I. M. Rubinow, *The Care of the Aged* (Chicago, 1931), A. Epstein, *Facing Old Age* (New York, 1922), and *The Challenge of the Aged* (New York, 1928), and the Bulletin of the United States Bureau of Labor Statistics on *Public Old-Age Insurance in the United States and Foreign Countries* (No. 561, Washington, 1932). Mention should also be made of the report issued in 1930 by the National Association of Manufacturers on *Public Old Age Pensions* and by the National Industrial Conference Board on *The Support of the Aged* (New York, 1931). A good bibliography covering this subject is contained in the *Encyclopaedia of the Social Sciences*, Vol. XI, pp. 461–462.

Current material relating to public welfare and social insurance is published in the annual *Proceedings* and the quarterly *Bulletin* of the National Conference of Social Work (227 East Long St., Columbus, Ohio), the *Journal of Social Forces*, the *American Labor Legislation Review* (quarterly), and the various economic journals listed at the close of Chapter XI.

CHAPTER XXXVIII

HOUSING

>Whereas there are such great multitudes of people brought to inhabit in small rooms, whereof a great part are very poor, and they heaped up together and smothered with many families of children and servants in one house or small tenement; For remedy thereof Her Majesty doth charge and straightly command all manner of persons to desist and forbear from any new buildings or any house or tenement within three miles of the gates of the City of London to serve for habitation or lodging where no former house hath been known to have been within the memory of men now living, and also to forbear from letting any more families than one only to inhabit from henceforth in any one house that heretofore hath been inhabited.—*From a Proclamation of Queen Elizabeth (1580).*

An ancient perplexity. The quotation which stands at the head of this page would seem to indicate that the problem of housing the people is not a new one. Ancient Rome had a housing problem, a very serious one. Her million inhabitants were crowded into one area only three miles square. Hence most of them had to live in tenements (*insulae*) which were often four or five stories high, the lower apartments occupied by the well-to-do while the poorer tenants huddled together under the roof-tiles. Mediaeval London was similarly congested and remained so into modern times. We are accustomed to think of the housing problem as a by-product of the factory system and the concentration of industry, but it was bothering the cities long before the factories came.

Overcrowding and the industrial revolution. The industrial revolution and the rise of the factory system merely made a bad situation worse. The worker had to live within walking distance of his work and this accentuated the congestion in the immediate neighborhood of the industries. Anyone who reads the narratives of life in an English factory town during the early years of the nineteenth century will be appalled by the wretchedness and squalor of the human habitations, with their thousands of men, women, and children packed into sweltering attics and unlighted cellars. It was not until England had reformed both her national and local governments (1832–1835) that the worst of the housing evils began to be remedied. This was partly because most Englishmen clung to the belief that a man's house was his castle and that he could put as many people into it as he chose. Not until it had been made plain that the crowded tenements were nurseries of disease did the authorities intervene in any effective way.

American cities also had their housing problems during the nineteenth century but not in such an acute form. Virtually nothing was done in the way of comprehensive remedy until the enactment of the New York tenement-house law of 1901. This pioneer statute was passed by the legislature because an investigation of housing conditions in New York City demonstrated that great numbers of people were living in rooms with no natural light, located in fire-trap buildings, with no sanitary equipment whatever and often under conditions of overcrowding which were a menace both to health and morality.[1] Almost as many more were inhabiting the so-termed dumb-bell tenements in which the kitchens and bedrooms received their meager percolation of sunlight by way of a narrow air-shaft. The occupants usually found this air-shaft to be a convenient receptacle for the easy disposition of rubbish and garbage, so that the small windows had to be kept closed to exclude the odors and the neighbors' profanity. (There are still over 10,000 of these dumb-bell tenements in New York City.)

The housing problem in America.

The law of 1901 was a comprehensive enactment of far-reaching implications. It inaugurated throughout the United States a new era in legislation with respect to housing. Its provisions, which were deemed very drastic at the time, established rules with respect to the construction, sanitation, and capacity of tenement houses, besides setting up administrative machinery for enforcement. More specifically the statute restricted the height of tenements and limited the percentage of the lot that might be built upon. It prohibited the future erection of air-shaft tenements and required that all rooms be given direct access to light and air. Rules with respect to fire prevention were included as well as provision for adequate sanitary equipment Finally, it was stipulated in the law that no room in any tenement should be occupied by more than one adult or two children for each 400 cubic feet of air space. Other large cities soon followed the example of New York and today there is hardly an urban community in the United States that does not have a series of regulations governing the conditions under

A pioneer housing statute: New York Tenement House Law of 1901.

---

[1] In 1901 there were over 350,000 dark interior rooms in New York tenements.

which the people may be housed. These regulations, however, are not always embodied in a separate housing ordinance, for it has become the common practice to include them among the provisions of the general building code.

Why cities have a housing problem.

The overcrowding of people in tenements is not due to any perversity of human nature. Everyone desires to have enough space for comfort if he can find it. On the other hand the worker naturally desires to live within convenient distance of the place where he is employed. He is led to this desire by motives of convenience and economy as well as by the preference of his family who prefer to be near the centers of recreation and amusement. The cost of food, moreover, is usually less in thickly populated districts than in the outer suburban areas, and this is especially true of the cheaper foods which the workman's household uses. Adequate and cheap transportation facilities do a good deal to relieve housing congestion in the immediate neighborhood of industry, but these facilities rarely keep pace with the growth of population. Moreover, it is generally to the interest of transportation companies to discourage the spreading of population over too great an area because short-haul traffic is more profitable to them than long-haul. Street railways carrying passengers at a flat-rate fare are likely to lose money if any large proportion of their patrons move to the outer suburbs.

High land values and congestion.

For these various reasons the pressure on the land available for economical housing becomes strong, and this in turn increases land values. As these values rise, the owners find it necessary to secure a return on this valuation by utilizing the land to the utmost. They try to make every inch of it yield a revenue by increasing the bulk and height of the buildings, reducing the size of the rooms, and leaving no more free space for light and air than the laws require. High land values in the tenement house district are looked upon as the primary cause of congestion but they are not wholly to blame for it. Land speculation, which keeps available ground unbuilt upon while waiting for a rise, is often a contributing factor. The unintelligent planning of multiple-family buildings is also responsible in part. And the ignorance or carelessness of tenants, who fail to make good use of the space that they have, is frequently instrumental in making a bad situation worse. Low wages similarly have their relation to the problem because so many families who live in crowded tenements feel that they must take in one or more lodgers as a means of supplementing the weekly income. Economic factors thus combine to promote bigger tenements with smaller apartments and more people in them.

Everywhere in urban centers, therefore, the single-family dwelling is losing ground. In downtown New York a new private residence is an object of curiosity; not more than a half-dozen of them are erected each year. In other large cities almost the same situation prevails. Even in smaller communities the multiple-dwelling is crowding houses out of the way.[1] It is true that many large industries are moving to the suburbs of cities but they do not always draw their workers after them. On the contrary there is often encountered the spectacle of great industries located in the outer areas while their workers live in the tenement house districts downtown. So it seems probable that the in-town housing areas will continue to be thickly populated no matter what the shops and factories may do. And serious overcrowding is bound to be the result unless it is curbed by the regulative and constructive action of the public authorities. *The future of urban housing.*

The evils of overcrowding require no detailed exposition. In the first place housing congestion results in an abnormally high death rate. Repeated investigations have shown that the children who live in crowded tenements are undersized, physically weakened, and become an easy prey to communicable diseases. The overcrowding of families in small apartments makes the isolation of the sick impracticable, hence when one child becomes ill with a communicable ailment the others come down with it also. Tuberculosis, as the spot-maps of city health departments prove, is to a large extent a disease of the tenements, a class disease. Public health experts are convinced that room overcrowding is one of the most important causative factors in the spread of this and other respiratory diseases.[2] *The effects of housing congestion: 1. On health.*

Associated with inadequate housing, likewise, are problems of crime and immorality. Studies in a number of cities have shown a *2. On conduct.*

---

[1] Figures compiled by the United States Bureau of Labor Statistics, covering more than 250 cities, for the year 1929 indicated that only about forty per cent of all the dwellings constructed during that year were for single-family use, while almost sixty per cent were for occupancy by more than one family. More than forty-eight per cent of all the dwellings constructed that year were for occupancy by more than two families. These figures disclose, moreover, that the larger the city, the higher is the percentage of families for whom provision is made in multifamily houses.

[2] See the article by Henry F. Vaughan on "Room Overcrowding and Its Effect upon Health," in *Proceedings of the National Housing Conference*, Vol. VIII, pp. 183–197 (1920).

definite correlation between overcrowded tenements and juvenile delinquency. Gangs and gangsters are usually recruited from the slums. Cramped, unsanitary living quarters make for discomfort of body and discontent of soul. They accentuate the bitterness of class antagonism. To what extent they foster industrial unrest and social discontent no one can venture to say because there is no way of measuring it. But where honest toil can purchase nothing but squalor there need be no wonder that unsocial tempers arise. Grown children, finding nothing in the way of elementary comfort at home, take to the streets. And when they go wrong, society pays the bills—by supporting reformatories, foundling hospitals, police courts, probation officers, and houses of refuge.

On political attitudes. The west side knows little about the east side, and the residential suburbs know little about the city of the tenements, except that it votes for the wrong candidates on election day. This city of the tenements is just a sprawling area into which thousands and tens of thousands of men, women, and children are herded together. Most of them pass their lives in small, ill-ventilated rooms, often half-dark and musty, where the sunlight never enters except in a furtive way and where fresh air ranks among the rarities. The windows, most of them, open into air-shafts or look out upon rubbish heaps in the neighbors' back yard. Here are whole streets of shabby house-fronts, unlighted hallways, dilapidated stairs, broken-down plumbing, and roofs that leak,—homes with neither peace nor privacy. Walk through some of these streets on a hot summer evening and inquire of your own conscience whether the city of the tenements is a place from which one can fairly expect high ideals of citizenship to emanate. Yet in the larger urban communities it is from these cheerless and drab rows of brick or wooden buildings that most of the votes are cast. New York City has over 100,000 tenements of all varieties, housing nearly four million persons. In one relatively small portion of the metropolis (the area lying south of Fourteenth Street and east of Broadway) there is a solid phalanx of such buildings inhabited by more than half a million people, a great city in itself, but not "a city into which there entereth nothing that defileth or worketh abomination."

Legal and popular definitions of a tenement house. What is a tenement house? How is it to be differentiated from any other kind of dwelling place? In a legal sense a tenement house is any building, or portion of a building, which is leased to be occupied, in whole or in part, as the home of three or more families

HOUSING

living independently of each other. This definition includes apartment houses but not hotels; because people in hotels do not live in families or independently. It often happens, however, that a legal definition does not synchronize with popular acceptation of the same term, and such is what happens in this instance. For a tenement, in ordinary parlance, is any apartment house in which the accommodations are poor and the rent low. As a rule, tenement houses are located in sections which were once favored by the well-to-do but from which they have moved away. When such an exodus commences, the vacated dwellings are often converted into two- or three-family houses, but ultimately these are pulled down and replaced by large tenements of the customary type. In every large city there is what may be called a zone of deterioration, with good housing going out and poor housing coming in. During the transition period this area often presents the worst of tenement conditions, although it may not show a high density of population per acre.

This raises a question as to what yardstick can be used to determine whether a section of the city is overcrowded? Density of population, in other words the number of persons per acre, will not serve. Tables of relative density may be quite misleading because they do not take into consideration the height or character of the buildings on a given area of land. Some districts of a city may have a very high density because they include big hotels and tall apartment houses, yet the housing conditions in such districts may be of the very best. Other districts, with only half the density, may be acutely overcrowded if they are covered with houses which were built for single families but have been roughly remodelled to accommodate three or four. On Manhattan Island in New York City the average density is about 150 persons per acre, but this figure really means nothing because an acre of ground will satisfactorily accommodate three or four times that number if properly built upon. *The test of overcrowding.*

There is no simple formula wherewith one can determine whether a given area of urban land is over-populated. The problem relates itself to housing space, not to land. The number of persons per room, or per house, is similarly an inaccurate yardstick. One cannot say that a room is overcrowded when more than two persons live in it, or that an apartment is overcrowded when a dozen people occupy it; everything depends upon the location, cubic area, layout, *Air space and density.*

and other characteristics of the room or apartment. Nor can congestion be detected by the mere ratio of human beings to cubic feet of space. Adults require more elbow-room than children. Persons of a single family can get along comfortably with less housing space than a group of equal size which includes two or three boarders. There is only one way of accurately determining whether a tenement house is overcrowded, which is by a careful inspection of all its facilities, including a count and classification of the persons occupying it.

<small>The interests concerned in the problem:</small>

<small>1. The public.</small>

In approaching the question of measures for the relief of housing congestion it is well to remember that three important interests are concerned. First, and most vital of all, is the interest of the community. Its standards of safety, health, and morals are adversely affected wherever serious overcrowding is permitted. No other interest is on a level with this one. The proprietary rights of the owner and the liberty of the tenant are subsidiary to it. Hence the starting point in housing reform ought to be the safeguarding of the general welfare, which is paramount to all other considerations.

<small>2. The tenants.</small>

Second comes the interest of the occupants, the people who as tenants or lodgers have to spend a large part of their lives in the tenements. They are the ones who bear the brunt when the public authorities fail to afford them adequate protection. Theoretically, these people have a right to live where and as they choose, but as a matter of grim reality they have little or no choice at all. They must take what is at hand and within their means. To the extent that this is the case they should be wards of the public authorities.

<small>3. The owner.</small>

Finally, there is the interest of the owner. Traditionally this interest has been regarded as the most important one. Yet overcrowding and the misery which goes with it affect him least of all. Indeed, the more people he packs into his building, and the less he spends in making things convenient for them, the more profitable his investment is likely to be. His interest, therefore, is often at variance with good public policy. Still, the owners of tenement houses are entitled to be fairly protected against economic injustice. They have both a legal and a moral right not to be deprived of their property without due process of law. The exercise of their proprietary rights should be restrained to the extent that the general welfare requires, but no further.

As a matter of actual experience, however, the simple philosophy

HOUSING

of housing control which has been outlined in the preceding paragraph has not found general acceptance. Projects of housing reform, ever since the days of the Gracchi, have almost invariably met with opposition from land owners, house owners, building contractors, house-renting agents, and from those who have building materials to sell. These interests are usually in league to convince public opinion that a stiffening of the regulations with respect to the design and equipment of tenement houses will depreciate the value of all property, place a serious check on building operations, keep workers from getting employment, and raise the level of rents. The influence of preachments along these lines would not carry far if the great body of tenants were in a mood to demand stricter regulations, but they are not. As a rule they are either indifferent to the issue or can be convinced by the landlords that stringent tenement house laws operate to the disadvantage of the poor. "Those who fight for the poor," as Jacob A. Riis once said, "must fight the poor to do it." [1] Hence when improvements have been secured in housing conditions, the credit has been largely due to the activities of social workers and public officials who are neither the owners nor occupants of tenement houses.

Why remedial measures are hard to apply.

For many years it was the inclination of social workers to believe that the housing problem could be solved by direct action on the part of the public authorities through the building of city-owned tenements. Both German and British cities were induced to try this plan on a considerable scale, with results that were said to be satisfactory so far as they went. But even when the policy of building municipal tenements is pursued in a comprehensive way, it does not make a sizable dent in the problem. London, for example, has built more workmen's dwellings than any other city in the world, yet fewer than one per cent of London's workers are housed in publicly owned tenements. To rehouse the half-million people who inhabit a single section of New York's most congested area would probably cost a billion dollars if the city were letting the contracts and paying the bills. Even so, the expenditure of so large a sum would afford no direct relief to the eighty per cent who live in remaining privately owned tenements save in so far as the competition of the municipal buildings would reduce rents elsewhere.

Public housing as a remedy.

[1] *How the Other Half Lives* (New York, 1890).

Municipal tenements do not pay.

Virtually all schemes of municipal housing, moreover, have resulted in a financial loss to the public treasury. This is not surprising because the business of buying land, building houses, renting them, collecting the rents, and keeping the houses in repair—all this constitutes a highly specialized vocation in which only the most assiduous realtors ever succeed. Certainly the work cannot be done successfully, and the enterprise made to yield a profit, by municipal employees of the usual type. European cities have not been able to make their municipal tenements pay, yet most of them are much better equipped to do it than are cities on this side of the Atlantic where the spoils system still continues in active operation. Those American cities which embark on rehousing schemes, even with aid from the federal government, are in all probability preparing a new burden for future taxpayers to carry.

Nor do they always benefit those for whom they are intended.

Another difficulty of a practical sort arises with respect to the occupancy of tenements erected and owned by the public authorities. Such buildings, it has been found, do not usually draw their tenants from the poorest of private tenements but merely enter into competition with the better ones. When a slum area is cleared and new buildings are erected upon it, the old residents do not come back to occupy the modern structures; on the contrary the new buildings quickly become populated by families which have been living in fairly good quarters but who now see an opportunity to get something just as satisfactory at a lower cost. Public housing, therefore, does not usually reach the people whom it is intended to help.

Poor tenements and shoestring financing.

So on the whole it seems improbable that the housing problem in American cities will be solved by public initiative alone. Even though the municipal authorities may undertake housing schemes on an extensive scale, the great majority of tenements are likely to be built by private capital, that is, by promoters and speculators. In all large cities the erection of tenements has been largely in the hands of such men and too often they operate on a shoestring. The usual procedure is this: The promoter provides a small amount of money, often a very small amount. Then he goes to a bank, or to a building and loan association and endeavors to borrow fifty, sixty, or even seventy per cent of the estimated cost of land and structure, giving a first mortgage and perhaps a second mortgage on the property to secure the loan. All that the promoter expects to own in the property, therefore, is the equity, in other words

HOUSING

the difference between the market value and the amount of his mortgages. If he succeeds in borrowing the money, he builds as cheaply as the laws will permit and then sells the property as speedily as he can in order to avoid paying interest, taxes, and other expenses. Moreover, he wants to get his money back quickly so that he can start another enterprise in the same way. If everything goes well, if he sells the building without delay and it stays sold, he nets a profit; but if anything goes wrong he stands to lose all that he has put into the venture when his mortgages are foreclosed on him. Under such conditions the building of tenements has become a highly speculative enterprise carried through under conditions which are rarely advantageous to the solid growth of a community.

What is needed, therefore, is a code of well-framed housing regulations which will make it impossible for flimsy, unsanitary, badly lighted, badly ventilated, or badly equipped houses to be erected in the first instance. These rules should determine what proportion of a building lot may be covered by the structure and how much must be left free for light and air. Usually the prescribed fraction of free space is set at one-quarter to one-third of the whole area. The regulations should also fix minimum standards with respect to the general design, materials, equipment, and occupancy of all buildings in which three or more families make their homes. The maximum height of buildings used for residential purposes should likewise be specified. A comprehensive housing ordinance should also prohibit windowless rooms (except small closets) and should fix a minimum size in the case of rooms used for living purposes. The usual minimum is one hundred feet of floor area. The square footage of window space should be at least one-seventh of this. Minimum standards should similarly be prescribed as respects water supply and sanitary fixtures. In all cases the underlying aim of the housing rules should be to ensure a reasonable degree of safety, cleanliness, and convenience without unduly increasing the expense. *The regulation of housing by law.*

But no matter how admirable the housing regulations may be with respect to structural layouts and sanitary equipment, they will fail of their purpose if too many occupants are permitted to crowd into the buildings. Hence there is need for some way of restricting occupancy in relation to space. Some cities, following the example of New York, have set up a uniform requirement of *Provisions as to occupancy.*

room space, amounting to 400 cubic feet for every adult and half that amount for every child under twelve years of age. The practice of imposing an arbitrary minimum of this kind is defended on the ground that no better method of safeguarding houses against overcrowding has yet been found practicable. It is well recognized, however, that a uniform minimum will not fit all conditions. Four hundred cubic feet of air space in a room that has large windows fronting a wide street is an altogether different thing from the same cubic area in a dark hall bedroom which looks out into a narrow air-shaft. The air-space standard is admittedly defective but it is used in lieu of a better alternative.

<small>The enforcement of these rules.</small>
Regulations to prevent overcrowding are in any event much easier to frame than to enforce. The city's building inspectors can apply strict rules relating to the structure and sanitary equipment of tenement houses if they are diligent and honest, but the restrictions upon maximum occupancy can be violated in ways which defy ascertainment except by the periodic raiding of tenements during the night hours, and public opinion does not tolerate such drastic procedure very long. A generation ago the tenement house authorities in New York City tried some raiding experiments in their endeavor to abate overcrowding in various east side areas occupied mainly by foreign-born families. A small squad of police officers would start out at a late hour each evening and make their rounds to one tenement after another, banging on the doors and arousing the occupants to be counted. They usually found themselves confronted by various sleepy members of a badly frightened family of all ages and sexes in various stages of undress, holding lighted candles or lamps, while the rest were making their exit into the open air by way of the fire escape. A squad of reporters followed to see the fun. But since it was usually impossible to make arrests or to secure convictions, the "get up and be counted" raids were soon abandoned. It has been suggested that the landlord rather than the tenant ought to be held responsible for any violation of the rules with respect to overcrowding houses, but he is sometimes the last one to know that the evil exists.

<small>The lodging and rooming house problem.</small>
Many cities have a lodging and a rooming problem as well as a housing problem. This arises in connection with the provision of rooms for those working men and women who live by themselves, apart from families. Without family ties they constitute a very mobile group. The line of demarcation between a tenement

house, a lodging house, and a rooming house is not always clear, but in general a tenement house is one occupied by families who rent their quarters by the month and live independently. A rooming house accepts families or individuals by the week or longer, and they do not live independently, while a lodging house is one that accommodates transients for a night or two at a time. The old-style boarding house, with its common dining room and parlor which gave facilities for inter-acquaintance, has largely disappeared in the cities. The cafés, cafeterias, and quick-lunch counters have taken its meal patronage away. But rooming and lodging houses have undergone an increase in number during the past generation, due to the partial breakdown of family ties and the increased fluidity of the population. In the larger cities there are thousands who flit from one place to another for a night or a week at a time. Homeless, they have no end of homes. The keepers of these rooming houses change almost as frequently as the roomers. Nobody knows who is in the room next to him, for both of them are in today and out tomorrow. Anonymity thus links itself with mobility.

Rooming houses run to a type, but lodging houses disclose wide variations in accommodations and quality. Some of them are maintained by charitable or religious organizations for the benefit of homeless men or women who cannot afford to pay even a small sum for shelter. Although the accommodations in these houses may be free, the patrons are often required or expected to attend a religious service. Other eleemosynary lodging houses make a small charge for a bed or a cubicle, and sometimes they conduct a wood yard in which the men are expected to do some work in return for bed and breakfast if they have no money. In some cities there are municipal lodging houses which have been established as a substitute for the free accommodation which was formerly given to transients at the police station. As a rule these municipal establishments make no charge, although they sometimes try to have their lodgers do whatever work is necessary around the place. Model municipal lodging houses have been erected in some European cities, but in the United States nearly all experiments along this line have been conducted under private auspices. Finally, and most common of all, are the commercial lodging houses, among which the poorest type are commonly known to the underworld as "flop joints" where men are permitted to sleep on the floor or in bare wooden bunks for a nickel or a thin dime. A notch above

Types of lodging houses.

this level is the place with small rooms or cubicles in which one can get a bed with a mattress and blankets for a quarter of a dollar, and above this, again, comes the fifty-cent hotel. All such places need the vigilant supervision of the health authorities, for the ventilation is usually bad, the sanitary equipment inadequate, and the rooms unclean, while the vermin are prolific, well-organized, and enterprising.[1]

Keeping the rules enforced. In most cities the responsibility for enforcing tenement house regulations, and for the supervision of rooming or lodging houses, has rarely been concentrated in the hands of any single officer or department. Rules relating to the structure of the building are commonly left for enforcement to the buildings department, and occasionally the fire department is expected to enforce the regulations with respect to fire prevention. Sometimes the responsibility for seeing that proper sanitary equipment is installed devolves upon the health department; while various matters requiring periodic inspection, such as the cleaning of cellars, the removal of rubbish, the prevention of overcrowding, and the behavior of occupants, are all assumed to be under the supervision of the police. This division of authority naturally encourages a lax enforcement of the laws. On the other hand, it is not easy to secure complete unity of official action in the administration of the housing rules. For the housing problem is a many-sided one, with ramifications which carry into many departments—city planning, buildings, health, fire prevention, police, and public recreation. New York City maintains a separate tenement house department with control over all matters relating to the structure, equipment, and occupancy of buildings which contain three or more families living independently of each other. The head of this department is appointed by the mayor and is assisted by a large staff of inspectors, clerks, and investigators, most of whom are chosen under civil service regulations. Very few cities have as yet followed New York's example, but the present tendency is in that direction.

REFERENCES

A full discussion of housing conditions a generation ago may be found in R. W. DeForest and Lawrence Veiller, *The Tenement House Problem* (2 vols., New York, 1903). Later books of notable value are Lawrence

[1] For a full description of the various types of lodging houses see Maurice R. Davie, *Problems of City Life* (New York, 1932), pp. 128–143; also Nels Anderson, *The Hobo* (New York, 1923).

Veiller, *Model Housing Law* (revised edition, New York, 1920), Edith E. Wood, *Housing of the Unskilled Wage Earner* (New York, 1919), and *Recent Trends in American Housing* (New York, 1931), Louis H. Pink, *The New Day in Housing* (New York, 1928), J. J. Clarke, *Housing in Relation to Public Health* (Liverpool, 1926), Morris Knowles, *Industrial Housing* (New York, 1920), B. J. Newman, *Housing in Philadelphia* (Philadelphia, 1924), B. S. Townroe, *The Slum Problem* (New York, 1928), E. D. Simon, *How to Abolish Slums* (New York, 1929), E. L. Allen, *American Housing as Affected by Social and Economic Conditions* (Peoria, Illinois, 1930), Carol Aronovici, *Housing and the Housing Problem* (Chicago, 1920), and the *First Report of the Joint Legislative Committee on Housing*, New York State Legislature (Albany, 1923).

Three publications edited by John M. Gries and James Ford entitled *Housing and the Community*, *Slums—Large Scale Housing*, and *Housing Objectives and Programs*, all of them published in Washington during 1932, are valuable contributions, the outgrowth of the President's Conference on Home Building and Home Ownership.

Attention should also be called to the study of "Housing Conditions in the New York Region" which is included in the publications of the Regional Plan of New York and Its Environs (New York, 1931), Vol. VI, chap. ii, and to the publication by Charles S. Ascher, entitled *Elements of a Low-Cost Housing Law and Its Administration* issued as a Supplement to the *National Municipal Review*, Vol. XXII, pp. 85–113 (February, 1933), as well as to the special report on "The Housing Situation in the United States" published by the International Labor Office in its *Studies and Reports* (Geneva, 1925).

The experience of European cities in dealing with the housing problem is set forth in the *Handwörterbuch des Wohnungswesens* edited by G. Albrecht and others (Jena, 1930).

CHAPTER XXXIX

PUBLIC MARKETS

Invendibili merce oportet ultro emptorem adducere; proba merx facile emptorem reperit, tametsi in abtruso sita sit.—Plautus.[1]

Food costs and incomes. The average worker who lives in the city and is the head of a family spends nearly half his wages for food. He spends more on food, as a rule, than on shelter, clothing, and fuel combined. His cost of living, therefore, depends primarily upon the expense involved in securing daily fare for himself and his family. It is not so with those who stand higher in the scale of earnings. With them the cost of food becomes a relatively smaller item in the family budget. It drops to one-fourth of the total, or even to a much smaller fraction in the case of the well-to-do. In general, therefore, even a moderate increase in the cost of foodstuffs may work a considerable amount of hardship in the ranks of those who are at or near the minimum in the established wage scale.

The step-up between producer and consumer. The cost of food, moreover, is not mainly the cost of producing it. The expense of bringing it to him from the place of production is in many instances an even larger item. The cost of getting meat, vegetables, fruit, and milk from the original producer to the ultimate consumer is frequently equal to, or even greater than, what was originally paid for these products. In other words the high cost of living in cities is largely due to an elongated, involved, and expensive mechanism of food distribution. Investigations have shown that the excess of the price paid by the consumer, over that received by the producer, ranges from fifty to one hundred and fifty per cent. This is mainly because the products pass through several hands on the way, each of them adding an increment to the price. It is also due to the fact that the foodstuffs are often brought from a distance at considerable expense for transportation. Likewise it arises, in some cases, from the inadequate facilities for storage and the high cost of transshipment from place to place within the city.

---

[1] Buyers must be coaxed to buy unsalable wares, but good merchandise readily finds a purchaser, even though it be hidden out of sight.

PUBLIC MARKETS

Most of the staple foodstuffs required by the average family in a city or large town are bought from retail stores, usually from neighborhood stores. This is especially true of meats, vegetables, bread, eggs, fruits, canned goods, and incidental groceries. The retailer's profit on such products must be substantial, particularly in the case of perishable products, because his volume of business is usually small and his expenses are relatively large. So it is not uncommon for the small market to have an average mark-up of from twenty-five to fifty per cent. But the retailer has made his purchases from a jobber, wholesaler, or commission merchant. He, likewise, has added a sizable fraction of profit to the cost. And in the case of certain products these middlemen have bought from a packing company, cannery, or manufacturer who in turn has obtained the raw materials from the cattle-raiser, fruit grower, vegetable farmer, dairyman, or whoever produces them. Between their source and their destination, accordingly, many staple food products pass through at least three hands and sometimes through four or five. Adding to their profits the cost of transport, storage, handling, and distribution, there need be no reason for surprise that the city household often pays for its meat, vegetables, butter, cheese, canned goods, milk, fish, and shelf-groceries at least twice, and sometimes more than twice, what the rancher, farmer, fisherman, or other original producer received. *Reasons for it.*

In most European cities the separation between producer and consumer is by no means so wide nor is it so costly as it is in the United States. Through the provision of public markets and the almost universal patronage which is given to them, a direct contact between farmers and householders is established. A large part of the foodstuffs needed each day by every European community is brought from surrounding farms during the early morning hours by the producers themselves. They are placed on the public market and sold directly to the people without the intervention of commission merchants, jobbers, or retailers. This direct method of feeding a city exists in Europe because it is traditional and also because economic pressure has compelled resort to it. The European housewife goes to the public market every morning because she knows that she can save money and because she does not mind the small inconvenience involved. Going to market with a basket on one's arm is part of the regular daily routine in European households. It has been so for generations. *European and American marketing.*

548   MUNICIPAL ADMINISTRATION

The desire for personal convenience.

In the cities of the United States there is a different tradition. Most American households prefer to patronize a retail store or private market with its telephone facilities, monthly bills, and prompt delivery of goods. The producers of foodstuffs, similarly, prefer to have their milk, vegetables, fruit, and other products collected at their doors by a jobber or commission merchant who saves them the inconvenience of bringing these things to town even though he pays lower prices than they would obtain by direct sale to the consumer. They complain that middlemen are making too much profit but have not, to any large extent, devised methods for eliminating him. This method saves time, trouble, inconvenience—in fact it saves everything but money. The relative prosperity of the United States over a long period of time has served to engender a feeling of indifference to minor economies such as one nowhere finds in European communities.

Lack of storage facilities in American homes.

Other factors have also had an influence in developing the present marketing habits of the American family. The almost universal use of furnace heat in city homes, for example, has made it virtually impossible to use the cellar for storing a winter's supply of apples, butter, eggs, potatoes, and various other vegetables as was the general custom a generation or two ago. On the other hand the ubiquity of household refrigeration has made it possible to keep small quantities of perishable products in good condition for a varying number of days. The ordinances in many cities still provide that any bona fide farmer may peddle his produce from door to door without a license, but relatively little is obtained by city households in this way. On the other hand the professional huckster of fruits and vegetables, who visits his customer each morning, is an important factor in serving those who prefer to save the time which is necessarily consumed in patronizing public or private markets.

The value of public farmers' markets.

Many retail markets in American cities do most of their business by telephones and on credit, although the vogue of cash-and-carry establishments has greatly increased in recent years. The consequence is that retail food stores and small private markets exist too numerously in cities while public markets are few and often poorly patronized. One of the most effective ways of reducing the cost of living in urban communities is by the construction, operation, and encouragement of public farmers' markets. To be successful, however, such markets must have support from two sources. It does not avail to have producers come with things to sell unless consumers are there in sufficient numbers with both money and inclination to buy. And the consumers will not patronize a public market in large numbers unless the prices, quality, and range of choice are substantially better than in retail stores and private markets.

Municipal markets of this type are not new in the United States. At one time they were to be found in almost every city and town, but their popularity has dwindled steadily during the past forty years. There are exceptions, of course, but taking the country as a whole the public farmers' market has been losing ground. Such markets are still maintained in a good many communities, but among the cities above 30,000 population which reported to the United States Bureau of Census for 1930, more than half indicated no expenditures for public markets of any kind, while many others reported an expenditure of negligible proportions. Not one city in five throughout the United States is now devoting any considerable attention to the provision of public markets as a means of keeping the cost of living within bounds. This contrasts strongly with developments in Europe where there seems to have been no appreciable decline in the popularity and patronage of these institutions. *Their decline in popularity.*

Municipal authorities in the United States, moreover, often seem to think that their responsibility for public marketing comes to an end when they have provided a suitable market-place and made arrangements for keeping it in order. In some American cities the public market is merely a tract of land or a building in which space is leased to retailers or private marketmen who do not produce anything but have merely bought their produce from others. Very little in the way of reducing costs is ever accomplished by a so-termed public market of this type. What is needed is the active encouragement of a producers' market so that the cost of double handling and the middleman's profit can be eliminated. It is something of a convenience, of course, to have a central location in which a large number of private markets and retail food stores can be concentrated; but this does not assure any lowering of the price level nor does such an institution constitute a public market in the true sense of the term. *One reason for it.*

A public market, for the advantage of consumers, should be a place where they are brought into direct contact with the original

Essentials of a good municipal market.

producer. Such a market should be located where it is easy of access to both parties. Like any other business establishment it cannot be popularized except by active effort. Some cities have found that the patronage of a public market can be increased by the daily publication of current market prices, thus demonstrating to householders that a substantial saving can be made by doing their buying there. The saving must be demonstrably substantial, for the average American housewife believes that time is money. Along with lower prices there should be such rigid municipal inspection and supervision of the public market as will ensure the cleanliness and purity of foodstuffs as well as the use of honest weights and measures. Most American cities have yet to learn that municipal markets do not become successful without energetic and consistent encouragement on the part of the public authorities.

Wholesale and jobbing markets.

Wholesale and jobbing markets ought also to be provided. In addition to the producers' market-place where farmers, market gardeners, dairymen, poultry raisers, and others can come with their merchandise for direct sale, a comprehensive marketing program requires the establishment of a wholesale or jobbers' market to which produce from a considerable distance can be brought by rail in carload lots or can be trucked to the city in large quantities. Having been brought to such a central point, the foodstuffs are then distributed in smaller lots to retailers. Markets of this type exist in all the more important European cities. The largest and best known among these wholesale terminal markets are the *Halles Centrales* in Paris, with a covered and uncovered area of nearly twenty-five acres. Into this world-renowned marketing place the food supplies of Paris are brought by railroad, by boats on the Seine, and by trucks from all over France, to a total amount of about a million tons per year. Much of this is sold directly to consumers in such portions of the market-place as are reserved for this purpose, while the rest is jobbed out to retailers of all kinds.

The procedure at terminal markets.

In most large American cities the major part of the general food supply (including meats, vegetables, poultry, eggs, and milk) likewise comes in by rail, boat, or truck but not always to a single terminal market. Often there are several private terminal markets, one for each railroad entering the city. Whatever comes to these points, day by day, is first handled by the big jobbers who buy in carload or truckload lots. They in turn may resell to wholesalers or commission merchants as a rule, but frequently to retailers as well. This practice varies from place to place. When retailers are permitted to do so they come with their cars each morning and load up the day's supply. More often, especially in the larger cities, retailers do not come to the terminal markets but are supplied at secondary wholesale markets which specialize in single classes of produce.

From every point of view it is a great advantage to have a conveniently located, adequately equipped, and well-administered terminal market at which this process of receiving produce in bulk and distributing it can take place without unnecessary loss of time or needless inconvenience to those engaged in it. Such a market should be situated at a point which is convenient of access by railroad, water, or highway. Where several railroads enter the city the primary or terminal market should be located on the belt line or other rail link which connects them. It should be roomy enough to accommodate a large number of vehicles. If used exclusively for wholesale marketing it is by no means certain that this terminal market should be owned by the city, but the municipal authorities should at least make certain that suitable facilities are provided by somebody. Otherwise the ultimate consumer will be forced to pay, in excessive food prices, for the lack of a well-planned center. *Essentials of a good terminal market.*

A well-planned terminal center for receiving and distributing perishable food products should include adequate yard space for holding railway cars until the produce is sold. It should be provided with switch tracks to which the cars can be shunted and then unloaded directly to the buyers' trucks. Provision should also be made for ample cold storage warehouses as well as for storage sheds of the ordinary type. Likewise some terminal markets have auction rooms in which the carloads of fruit or other highly perishable produce are put up for speedy sale as soon as they arrive. Inspection can also be conveniently made at the terminal market. By a congressional act of 1917 (modified in 1919 and in 1923) the Department of Agriculture is authorized to provide for the federal inspection of fruits, vegetables, and other perishable farm products "at such central markets as the Secretary of Agriculture may designate or at points which can conveniently be reached therefrom." This inspectional work is now carried on at a large number of terminal and producers' markets, the cost being defrayed by the imposition of fees. *Storage and inspection.*

Curbstone markets.

In addition to their producers' retail market and their terminal market, many European cities set aside certain streets for curbstone markets either all day or during certain hours of the day. Sometimes there are a dozen or more of these and they are of all varieties. No special facilities are provided—merely the right to do business on the designated streets when the weather is good enough. Markets of this sort exist in some American cities also but not on such an extensive scale as in Europe. At a curbstone market the vendor backs his vehicle to the curb and sells from it directly to his customers. It is a straight cash-and-carry, pay-as-you-go, take-your-chance transaction. Sometimes the city authorities charge a small daily fee from each vehicle for the use of the curbstone market. This rarely suffices to pay for the extensive clean-up that is necessary after the marketing is done for the day. Vigilant inspection by the city authorities is also essential to ensure that those who use the curbstone market are bona fide producers and not peddlers who resort to the place as a way of saving rent or avoiding the cost of a peddlers' license; but push-cart vendors are permitted to use such markets under certain conditions.

Why they have dwindled.

Twenty years or more ago these curbstone markets were more common in American cities than they are today. It is rather significant that they have so generally gone out of fashion because they served a useful purpose by placing a check on the level of prices for farm and garden products. During the war era, however, and in the years of general prosperity which followed the war, the scale of wages rose to a point where economies in the family budget did not seem to be imperative. People gave up the habit of going to market, preferring to make use of the telephone and delivery service. Or, in many cases, the housewife adopted the practice of driving around in her motor car to a private market downtown. Something may also be attributed to the development of non-domestic activities on the part of large numbers of American women during this period as evidenced by the extraordinary growth of women's clubs, parent-teachers' associations, lecture courses for women, and so on. At any rate, curbstone markets and marketing went out of vogue during this era in most of the cities.

Some objectionable features.

Markets of this type, moreover, are open to some serious objections. Having no protection from sun or rain, besides being constantly exposed to dust and flies, the foodstuffs exposed for sale at a curbstone market are not always up to the hygienic standards of the city's health department. Accordingly it has sometimes been deemed expedient to provide that no food products shall be sold at such markets except those which need to be washed, peeled, or cooked before being eaten, or unless they are sold in dustproof containers. Other regulations have had to be provided by health departments to ensure that market garbage shall not be thrown around to litter the streets but shall be kept in approved receptacles and gathered every day when the marketing hours are over. All things considered, there is not a great deal to be said for the curbstone type of public market except that it is an inexpensive institution, involving no investment on the city's part, while at the same time giving the people an opportunity to buy in small quantities at low prices if they are willing to take the time and trouble involved. A curbstone market can be moved from one location to another whenever the occasion arises, and in fact it is practicable to have several such markets serving different parts of the same city.

A word should be said with respect to the competition which public markets are now meeting at the hands of roadside stands in the rural areas surrounding the cities. These rather primitive rural establishments cater to large numbers of automobile owners who combine shopping with recreation. But roadside markets are seasonal markets, for the most part, and in many cases do most of their business on Saturdays or Sundays during the summer months. They have the advantage of fresh local-grown products and of low prices due to the absence of any expense for rentals or delivery service. Thus far, moreover, they have been left for the most part unregulated and have been subjected to no regular inspection. Whether this competition with the city-owned market (and with private markets as well) is merely a passing phase or destined to be a permanent feature of the marketing process it is not yet possible to predict. *Roadside stands.*

The desire to afford protection against the weather has led in many cities to the purchase of land and the erection of market buildings. Such buildings are usually provided with stalls which can be rented to farmers or to retail dealers for the sale of fruits and vegetables, meat, dairy products, poultry, fish, or even canned goods. But for the most part these covered markets, although sometimes erected at considerable cost, have not rendered a great deal of service to the community. Retail dealers usually get control of the best stalls and sell their products at the same price that is *Municipal market buildings.*

current elsewhere throughout the city. The farmers and market gardeners presently drop out of the picture. Moreover the chain-store markets which have sprung up in neighborhood centers all over the city are more convenient of access and their prices are usually as low or lower than those charged by the individual retailers who have stalls at the public market. These chain-store markets have the advantage which comes from buying in large quantities through their chain connections. Likewise they have a well-trained personnel and their accounting methods are usually much superior to those of the average individual retailer. Their merchandising is reduced to a science. They have plenty of capital behind them. It is not easy for the small individually owned private market to compete successfully with them.

A market program. At the present time the general opinion seems to be that the most effective field of municipal service, so far as public markets are concerned, lies in the establishment of the combination market in which both wholesale and retail trading can be carried on. Such a market need involve no heavy investment in the form of an expensive building. Preferably it should occupy a tract of land owned by the city in a convenient location and should be provided with overhead protection against rain. For greater convenience in the winter months, moreover, a portion of the land should be provided with enclosed accommodations sufficient to keep out the extreme cold. No charge, or at most a very nominal charge, should be made for the use of these accommodations.

Wholesale and retail marketing in combination. Farmers, dairymen, and market gardeners who bring their truckloads into the city should be given the opportunity of selling at this market either in wholesale or retail quantities as they think best. Jobbers who have bought at the terminal market can likewise do their distributing to retailers here. Under such circumstances it will usually happen that the wholesale selling takes place in the early morning hours, followed by retail sales to the public during the rest of the forenoon. In this way those who have time and inclination to patronize the public market get fresh produce at low prices, while others who prefer to buy from retail stores get exactly the same foodstuffs but pay a little more for them. The main thing is to keep the channel between producer and consumer as direct as possible, making sure that not more than one middleman intervenes. If the market is restricted to retail selling, it cannot serve the needs of jobbers or wholesalers. Moreover, many local producers who bring their goods in large quantities will not use it. Finally, a strictly retail market is likely to arouse the vigorous opposition of merchants' associations and similar bodies. They feel that those who rent shops and pay taxes ought not to have competition from vendors in city-owned locations who pay no taxes. Many advantages arise, on the other hand, from having a combination market in which sales of all kinds may take place—to jobbers, wholesalers, retailers, or individual consumers as the case may be. But it is difficult to find a location which is large enough, properly located, and equally convenient to all concerned.

In small cities the public market is frequently administered by the health department or the buildings department. In the larger municipalities it is usually supervised by a market director or a market board. Usually this branch of municipal activity is not regarded as sufficiently important to call for the creation of a separate department and consequently the supervision of markets is often combined with some other administrative function. To secure proper study and encouragement it is most desirable that the market service should at least be a separate bureau in one of the larger departments.

Market supervision.

REFERENCES

Sources of information in this field are Arthur E. Goodwin, *Markets, Public and Private—Their Establishment and Administration* (Seattle, 1929), F. E. Clark and L. D. H. Weld, *Marketing Agricultural Products in the United States* (New York, 1932), Henry E. Erdman, *American Produce Markets* (Boston, 1928), W. P. Hedden, *How Great Cities Are Fed* (Boston, 1929), Charles Thom and Albert C. Hunter, *Hygienic Fundamentals of Food Handling* (Baltimore, 1924), H. F. Holtzclaw, *Agricultural Marketing* (New York, 1931), J. C. Grinnalds, "Report on Public Markets" in *Proceedings of the American Society for Municipal Improvements* (1923), pp. 14–25, L. M. Barton, *A Study of All American Markets* (4th edition, New York, 1931), Benjamin H. Hibbard, *Marketing Agricultural Products* (New York, 1921), and Wells A. Sherman, *Merchandising Fruits and Vegetables* (New York, 1928).

CHAPTER XL

PARKS AND PUBLIC RECREATION

> Come forth into the light of things,
> Let Nature be your teacher.
> —*Wordsworth.*

The growth of leisure. Leisure has increased in cities during the past half-century. Once the heritage of the few, it has become the privilege of the many. This is due to a number of causes—the shorter working day, better rates of wages, higher standards of living, and more convenient transportation facilities. During the past fifty years the addition to the leisure of the average American worker has been about three hours per day. Not all of this spare time is spent out of doors, of course, although the extension of automobile ownership has greatly enhanced the recreational opportunities of the road and the rural areas. For the thousands and tens of thousands who do not have this facility, however, the city must provide open spaces nearer home. Private enterprise can supply, and should supply, a considerable part of what the people of any community may need in the way of outdoor recreation, but there remains an essential part which cannot be provided except at the public expense.

Urban recreational facilities of a half-century ago:

1. Vacant lots. The city of fifty years ago left its people to provide their own recreation facilities. In most urban communities there was plenty of undeveloped land within a reasonable distance to which people could go for their games and outings. Even closer at hand were numerous vacant lots which the children of the neighborhood could seize for use as playgrounds. The youthful years of every American city dweller during the nineteenth century were closely associated with play time spent on these sand lots and other unbuilt tracts which lay scattered along the residential streets. About

2. The formal park. all that the city did, by way of encouraging outdoor recreation, was to provide a number of formal parks, big and little, in which the people could walk or sit around when they had nothing else to do. But these parks rarely made any provision for games or play. Every city had at least one of them, planted with trees and dotted with flower beds. It was maintained as a show place, and to keep it immaculate the people were warned by ubiquitous notices to keep off the grass.

Likewise in most cities there were various small open spaces which usually took the form of squares or gardens, rarely more than an acre in extent and sometimes much smaller. These were designed to serve a triple purpose, namely, to afford light and air for the buildings adjacent to them, to provide places where the people of the neighborhood might cool themselves in hot weather, and more particularly to improve the general appearance of the street intersections. Sometimes they were so placed as to afford an agreeable foreground or approach to public buildings. In a day when cheap and rapid transportation in and out of the city was lacking, these small open spaces served a very useful purpose. Today they still exist but are largely deserted except by the unemployed who sit upon the benches. As places of active recreation they have little or no value. *3. Small squares and gardens.*

With the development of better transportation services there came a demand for public recreation facilities of a more active sort. During the latter years of the nineteenth century many cities began to provide themselves with considerable areas of ground beyond the outskirts of the city, chiefly land which was endowed with certain natural attractions such as would ensure its popularity as a place of public resort. Among these acquisitions were stretches of ocean frontage, or of land surrounding a lake, which could be used for bathing purposes. Frequently, moreover, the new reservations included woodlands, mountain areas, canyons, or other regions which could suitably be used by large bodies of people for picnics, all-day outings, or even as camping grounds. Land of a level character within convenient access was also acquired in many cases for use as an athletic field. More attention was likewise given to the building of parkways and scenic roads such as might be used for pleasure-driving by owners of automobiles. Meanwhile the old-fashioned park and small public garden obtained less attention from the public and from the municipal authorities. But such reservations still possess a large share of their original usefulness. They retain the function of civic embellishment. Changes in our habits of life and in the public attitude toward recreation have not impaired the aesthetic serviceability of these near-by havens of greensward and foliage. *The newer public recreation program.*

Outlying parks, beaches, and athletic fields.

558 MUNICIPAL ADMINISTRATION

Places of entertainment.

Losing sight of this aesthetic consideration, there is a great deal of pressure in many cities to transform the older parks into playgrounds, baseball fields, and locations for tennis courts, or even to utilize them as sites for public buildings, such as an aquarium, an aviary, a zoo, or an arboretum. Indeed it is frequently advocated that portions of these parks should be turned into picnic grounds and filled with concessions such as refreshment stands, merry-go-rounds, and outdoor dance pavilions. While fully appreciating the public need for amusement opportunities of this nature, it seems desirable that the transformation of city parks into centers of noisy entertainment should be strongly resisted, for a single tract of ground cannot serve two purposes and do both of them equally well. Playgrounds, for example, constitute a problem of their own as respects appropriate location and equipment. The same is true of athletic fields, picnic grounds, and amusement centers. For all such uses it is the best policy to acquire new recreation areas with an eye to their special suitability for the purpose in hand. Moreover, these recreation grounds should not be concentrated but should be distributed in various parts of the city.

Balance and variety in a city's park system.

The strength of a park and recreation system depends upon its balance, proportion, and variety, not on its acreage alone. Figures of area do not tell the whole story. A city may have more land than it needs for park purposes in the traditional sense, and yet be badly deficient in neighborhood playgrounds, athletic fields, bathing beaches, picnic grounds, swimming pools, parkways, or scenic driveways. What a city needs, at any given time, is dependent upon what it already has. A well-rounded and comprehensive system of parks and recreation grounds will include at least a half-dozen types of public property.

The acquisition of natural beauty spots.

Almost every large community has in its neighborhood some place which nature seems to have designed for public recreation, a fine stretch of seashore, the banks of a stream or lake, a mountain peak, canyon, arroyo, virgin forest, unspoiled woodland or waterfall—something that combines outstanding attractiveness with reasonable accessibility to the center of population. Such places should be acquired by the municipal authorities before they pass under private control and exploitation. For sooner or later, under private ownership, they become commercialized, in which case the people of the city may have to pay more for the privilege of using them than it would have cost to buy the land outright.

PARKS AND PUBLIC RECREATION

Beaches, shores, mountains, and forests are natural monopolies, being strictly limited in extent so far as any one community is concerned. They are things which cannot be duplicated by human effort. For purposes of public recreation, however, many of them have been already ruined by commercial exploiters.

Some of the larger cities have shown commendable foresight in acquiring such tracts of outlying territory for public use. Often they have been purchased at a relatively small cost, being made up of wild land, unused water frontage, or tracts that are not valuable for any other immediate use. But with the growth of the city and the crowding of its people in the downtown areas, such places soon become great adult playgrounds which provide a goal of exodus for many thousands during the warm weather. The street railway companies have usually coöperated in making these recreation grounds accessible through the provision of extra service on Saturday afternoons, Sundays, and legal holidays. By the building of paved highways, moreover, they have been brought within easy access by motor-bus and private automobile even when located several miles outside the boundaries of the city itself. Auto transportation has greatly extended the radius of those who desire to utilize their leisure time in short excursions out of the city. It has transformed what used to be a semi-occasional event for the masses into an almost daily habit.

Value of such reservations.

The maintenance of these reservations, and their proper administration, are matters which present some serious problems. Obviously they should be developed in such way as to make and keep them attractive to the largest number of visitors, but unhappily it is not easy to achieve this result without destroying to some extent the natural beauty and attractiveness of the regions concerned. Large numbers of people, for example, desire that the reservation shall be provided with cheap and rapid transportation, which means that it soon becomes defaced by car tracks, paved roadways, and auto parking places. Likewise the sweltering crowds who resort to these public beaches or mountain reservations during the summer months have their own ideas as to what the city ought to provide for them. Usually they want the place turned into an amusement park, with roller coasters, popcorn vendors, dime shows, dance halls, refreshment stands, and even gambling devices of a mild sort. The result is that the natural attractiveness is often sacrificed to this public demand. Then,

Some problems connected with them.

with the coming of large crowds, there arises the problem of regulating and policing the resorts in the interest of fire prevention, law observance, and public morals. Most of the people who come to these recreation places want to enjoy themselves in their own way and expect to be given full liberty in doing it, but there is a point at which the authorities feel bound to interpose with their rules and regulations. This problem of making rules which are reasonably liberal and yet adequately safeguard the public interest is often a troublesome one.

Parkways. The city park system includes not only parks but parkways. A parkway is an avenue of more than ordinary width which is given a park-like appearance by the reservation of ample space for shade trees and shrubbery. Such thoroughfares are for pleasure driving, hence heavy teaming is usually excluded from them. Parkways, as a rule, are the connecting thoroughfares between two or more parks or other public reservations, but some parkways lead from the outlying woodlands or beaches into the heart of the city. For the most part these avenues do not follow the shortest route between two points but are laid out as winding roads which follow the natural contour of the regions through which they pass. Being part of the city's general street plan, however, they are to some extent used by ordinary traffic, especially by private cars coming into the city from outlying communities. There is some difference of opinion as to whether parkways should be built and maintained by the street department or by the park authorities. They fall in the twilight zone between these two jurisdictions. Some cities have adjusted the matter by providing that the street department shall build and maintain the roadway, while the park department assumes responsibility for the shrubbery, trees, and grass plots.

Park administration. Traditionally the city parks have been administered by park boards, usually of three or five appointive members. In many cities, especially in the smaller ones, this is still the method of organizing the park department. These boards are made up of public-spirited citizens who serve without pay and in many instances their loyal interest has been of great value to the development of the municipal park system. The general drift, however, is nowadays in the direction of placing the city parks under the control of a single head, known as the park commissioner or superintendent. It is believed that better results can be obtained at less

PARKS AND PUBLIC RECREATION 561

cost in this way if a thoroughly competent official is placed at the head of the department. Nevertheless, there is much to be said for the old-fashioned park board if appointments to its membership can be kept clear of politics. Unhappily the doing of this is difficult. The temptation to make the selections on a political basis is usually strong, and when members of a park board are chosen in that way they look upon their posts as affording an opportunity to put their friends on the city payroll.

Money for the acquisition of park lands is usually obtained by the issue of bonds, but in some cases it is raised by levying special assessments on all private property in the neighborhood. This is done on the theory that the presence of a well-kept park enhances the value of surrounding land. It should be borne in mind, however, that it takes several years for a park to become developed. Trees and shrubbery require time to become full-grown. Hence it is advisable to pay for park land by issuing general bonds, or local improvement bonds, in such way that the burden of interest and repayment will fall less heavily in the early than in the later years of the bond period. This can be done by arranging the maturity of the serial obligations accordingly. As for the cost of maintaining the parks, the entire amount usually comes out of the city's current revenues. Parks produce no income, or almost none.

Park finance.

The smaller open spaces which the cities provided in earlier days at certain street intersections were not intended to be used as playgrounds. They were too small for that purpose, and in any event they were usually planted with trees in such formal fashion as to preclude games of any kind. Hence the youngsters resorted to the streets, alleyways, and vacant private land. Nowadays, when the streets are filled with rapidly moving automobile traffic, we do not easily realize that these highways were once upon a time the city's chief playgrounds, for in the era of horse-drawn vehicles they could be used for such recreational purposes with relatively little danger. But the advent of the automobile and the disappearance of vacant lots in the downtown residential sections—these developments created a new situation with respect to play space. The change necessitated the provision of new spaces for play off the streets.

Playgrounds.

Hence extensive programs of public playground development have been carried through in all large cities during the past thirty years. Such programs have involved the acquisition of land for playgrounds in the different sections of the city, usually small tracts which had not yet been built upon, but in some instances the providing of downtown playgrounds has necessitated the demolition of existing buildings. Moreover, the city authorities are now insisting that whenever new subdivisions of property are opened up, the plans shall provide a sufficient amount of public playground space, just as they are required to dedicate an adequate percentage of the land for street purposes. A neighborhood playground should include from half an acre to two acres of ground, depending on the age of the children who are likely to use it.

Neighborhood and district playgrounds. A distinction is sometimes made between neighborhood playgrounds and district playgrounds. The former are intended for the use of small children, while the latter are designed to meet the needs of those who have reached high school age. Neighborhood playgrounds should be located within a half-mile radius of those who are likely to use them. This means that a considerable number of such playgrounds are needed. Most educators are of the opinion that the best location for a neighborhood playground is in close proximity to an elementary school. When so located the playground does not require any considerable amount of special supervision or direction. With a proper arrangement of apparatus a large number of younger children can amuse themselves on a relatively small tract of land, but in the case of district playgrounds, especially those intended for football and baseball games, tennis, field hockey, and other outdoor sports, the facilities are of little value without expert supervision at all times.

Playground supervision. Unsupervised athletic grounds or playfields become the rendezvous of idlers and bullies who make such places disagreeable to the well-behaved. Such playgrounds should therefore be under adequate supervision and direction continuously, with provision for additional service on Saturdays and holidays. By supervision, moreover, one does not mean a mere custodian but one or more adult leaders who have been trained in the art of organizing games and keeping them going. The active organization and general direction of a sports program is the chief function of these playground supervisors or directors. The maintenance of proper conduct on the playground follows as a matter of course.

Swimming pools. The heaviest demands on public playgrounds are made during the school vacations. At such times, especially during the long summer vacation, the regular playground spaces are likely to be overcrowded unless relief is afforded by the provision of swimming pools, bathing beaches, and summer camps. Virtually every city of any considerable size now has a swimming pool, and the larger ones have several of them. Some are owned by clubs and associations; others are maintained by the public authorities. Those conducted by the city are usually open without charge, but a nominal charge is generally made for the use of bathing suits and towels. The close association of many persons in a public swimming pool, with the water as an effective agency of infection, is bound to present an element of danger unless the most rigid sanitary precautions are taken. These precautions involve the frequent recirculation of the water as well as the disinfection of the pool, usually by the application of liquid chlorine. Bacteriological tests of water samples should also be made at frequent intervals. In addition a strict limitation should be placed on the number of bathers using the pool at any one time. This limit is usually reckoned at twenty persons for every thousand gallons of clean water added to the pool. Economy in the use of water requires that a filtering plant be installed, preferably one of the pressure type, so that the same water may be used repeatedly.

The necessity of requiring swimmers to pass through shower baths before entering the pool is generally recognized but not always enforced. The quality of the water in a public swimming pool is largely dependent upon the degree with which this requirement of a preliminary cleansing is observed. To be effective the shower bath should be taken before bathing suits are put on, and warm water should be provided to encourage observance of the rule. In public swimming pools the patrons are usually allowed to bring their own bathing suits, but health authorities believe it better policy to require that all suits be furnished by the pool management in order that they may be washed and sterilized after each use. If dressing rooms, showers, and toilets are inadequate or badly arranged, the maintenance of sanitary conditions in the pool itself is made extremely difficult, no matter how excellent the system of recirculation and disinfection may be. No one should be permitted to use the municipal swimming pool at any time unless an attendant is on duty, and public pools should have at least one attendant for every hundred persons using them. There should be a pulmotor available to resuscitate persons in the event of an emergency.

Regulations and auxiliary equipment.

Bathing beaches. Public bathing beaches, or places set apart for bathing in the ocean or in fresh water streams or lakes, need no such elaborate regulations or equipment. But bathhouses and dressing rooms have to be supplied and kept under supervision. Endeavors have been made to make these establishments wholly self-supporting but not usually with much success. This is partly because the patronage is concentrated into a few months of the year. Even during these months, moreover, the facilities are overtaxed on Sundays, legal holidays, and on week days when the weather is very warm, but not on other days. The overhead expense, and many of the current expenses, go on whether the patronage is large or small.

Municipal golf courses. A few cities have established municipal golf courses. This has been done on the principle that adults as well as the younger generation have a claim upon facilities for outdoor recreation. Golf has become popular because it provides a vigorous (but not too strenuous) bodily exercise combined with mental relaxation, thus serving as an antidote to the strain of city life. An eighteen-hole golf course, however, requires a considerable tract of land, from 125 to 175 acres, which ought to be in reasonably close proximity to the business section of the city so that those using the course will not have to travel too far. In acquiring land for a municipal golf course it is desirable to provide additional areas so that practice fairways can be built for the use of beginners. Sometimes it is practicable to combine the preservation of a scenic area with golfing facilities of a superior type. Adjacent to the municipal golf course there should be a clubhouse properly equipped with shower baths, dressing rooms, and a lounging place. This need not be a large structure, but it should be dignified and attractive. Municipal golf courses in cities which have a mild climate during most of the year can usually be made to pay their way, but elsewhere they are almost always operated at a loss. This is because the municipal golf course caters chiefly to those who are not members of private golf clubs and who feel that they cannot pay more than a nominal green fee for the use of the course. The management should be under the immediate charge of a professional who may be employed by the city and paid a salary or may be granted certain privileges (selling golf balls, repairing clubs, or giving lessons) in return for his services. The former plan has proved to be the better one.

It has become the custom of cities to provide band concerts in the public parks and other open spaces during the summer months. Such occasions are popular and draw large crowds of people. Concerts of vocal music are also provided in some cities on Sunday afternoons, a stage with an appropriate background in one of the public parks being provided for this purpose. And concerts of this type are occasionally provided by the city during the winter months in its civic auditorium. Neighborhood dances, under the sponsorship of the city recreation department, are also conducted in some communities. As a rule these dances are held in the school buildings, particularly in the school gymnasium; but during the summer months they may be held out of doors, using the tennis courts as a dance floor. Likewise there has grown up in recent years the custom of having evening dances during the summer months on a paved street, especially in those parts of the city populated by the foreign born.

Public concerts and dances.

Indoor dances and motion picture shows, if sponsored by the city, ought to be self-supporting. The same is true of concerts in the civic auditorium or other public halls. Such entertainments are in their way competitive with commercial enterprises which pay a share of the municipal taxes, and there is no good reason why free entertainments of this nature should be furnished to the public as a charge on the municipal budget. People show a greater appreciation of such privileges, moreover, when they have to contribute something from their own pockets. The tendency has been to look upon community recreation, even in its specialized forms, as something which ought to be provided without cost to those who enjoy it. Frequently the cost has been loaded upon the school budget because school buildings are commonly used as community centers by musical clubs, dancing classes, and dramatic organizations. Such activities should be under the direction of the city's department of public recreation and so far as practicable they should be made to pay their way.

Financing public recreation.

No city undertakes to provide the larger part of the recreation which its people desire. Motion picture houses, commercial dance halls, dine-and-dance establishments, and evening resorts of many other kinds supply the greater portion of the recreation opportunities in every large center. These commercial enterprises have a legitimate place in the life of the modern city, but they require a considerable amount of censorship on the part of the municipal authorities in order that proper standards shall be enforced.

The control of commercialized recreation.

Theaters of all kinds, dance halls, vaudeville shows, pool and billiard parlors, and amusement concessions are usually required to be licensed. The licenses are issued by the city's recreation authorities or by some other department on their recommendation. In the case of motion picture houses, most cities have an official censor or board of censorship from which a permit must be had before any picture can be shown. Some cities entrust this function to the police, which is not a good plan if one may judge from their experience with it. In the case of all other forms of commercialized recreation it is necessary to provide for periodic inspection to ensure that standards of conduct are being maintained. This inspection may be undertaken by officials of the recreation department or it may be left to the police. One advantage of having women police in the department is that they can be used for this inspectional service in the case of commercial dance halls and amusement parks.

Municipal auto camps. The growth of travel by automobile has led to the establishment of auto camps in or adjacent to cities. An auto camp is a tract of land with numerous tents or small huts erected on it. These quarters are available for hire by transient tourists who desire more economical accommodations than are provided by the city hotels. Usually there is a small store adjacent to the auto camp from which food supplies can be obtained, and common cooking facilities are also provided as a rule. Most cities now require that privately operated camps shall be licensed as a means of keeping them under police surveillance and ensuring the provision of proper sanitary facilities. In many instances, however, an auto camp or tourist camp is provided by the city itself. This is done as a police measure to prevent indiscriminate camping on roadsides or other unsuitable places. A small fee per day is charged at these camps, the proceeds going to maintain the place and pay the caretaker.

Recreational administration. Under what form of administration should all these activities be placed? It might be thought at first glance that the maintenance of parkways and reservations on the one hand, and of playgrounds, swimming pools, athletic fields, community centers, and amusement grounds on the other are closely enough related to warrant their being combined under the jurisdiction of a single department. A little consideration, however, will show that such is not the case. The problems of maintaining parks, reservations, and parkways are chiefly of a physical character. They relate mainly to construction, upkeep, and care. But in the case of playgrounds the day-to-day problems are mainly of a personal character, being connected with supervision, instruction, and the effective organization of play. Athletic fields, swimming pools, golf courses, bathing beaches, auto camps, the sponsoring of band concerts and dances, together with the control of commercialized recreation—all these present a variety of problems which have no close relation to park administration in the ordinary sense of the term. On the other hand they are sufficiently alike among themselves and in their totality are important enough to warrant their being handled by a separate department of public recreation in any large community. In smaller cities it may be expedient for reasons of economy to include parks and recreation in the same department, but in larger municipalities this is not a wise combination to make. The strictly recreational activities of cities are expanding rapidly, both in scope and in cost, so that they are now sufficiently extensive to have a department of their own.

This department should be headed by a director or superintendent of public recreation, but it is advisable that he be given the assistance of an advisory board made up of interested citizens who are willing to serve without pay. Many cities have recreation boards (sometimes they are combined park and recreation boards) which assume direct control, but experience shows that better results are usually obtained when a single executive head is placed in charge. He should be someone fully qualified by training and experience for the work of organizing and conducting the city's recreational program. All phases of the work should be concentrated under his supervision. All positions other than that of the department head should be filled under civil service regulations. Otherwise the recreation department will become a refuge for those friends of politicians who cannot qualify for appointment elsewhere.

Organization of a public recreation department.

REFERENCES

L. H. Weir, editor, *Parks: a Manual of Municipal and County Parks* (2 vols., New York, 1928) is the great comprehensive work in this field. It was compiled as the result of a nation-wide survey covering parks, playgrounds, and open spaces of all varieties. George Burnap, *Parks: Their Design, Equipment, and Use* (Philadelphia, 1916) relates particularly to small city parks. W. T. Lyle, *Parks and Park Engineering* (New York,

1916) should also be mentioned. Much useful information may be found in the annual reports of the City Parks Association (701 Stephen Girard Building, Philadelphia) and in the publications of the American Institute of Park Executives and American Park Society.

Many books are available in the field of organized public recreation. Bibliographical references may be found in M. P. Williams, *Sources of Information on Play and Recreation* (New York, 1927). Among general works mention may be made of W. P. Bowen and E. D. Mitchell, *The Theory and Practice of Organized Play* (New York, 1927), Clarence E. Rainwater, *The Play Movement in the United States* (Chicago, 1922), Jay B. Nash, *The Organization and Administration of Playgrounds and Recreation* (New York, 1927), J. C. Elsom, *Community Recreation* (New York, 1929), Jessie F. Steiner, *Community Organization* (New York, 1930), A. G. Truxal, *Outdoor Recreation* (New York, 1929), and the volume on *The Normal Course in Play* issued by the Playgrounds and Recreation Association of America (New York, 1925). This organization has issued various other books and pamphlets in addition to its *Park and Recreation Manual* and its monthly periodical. *Standard of Play and Recreation Administration* by Jay B. Nash is published as a Supplement to the *National Municipal Review*, Vol. XX, pp. 485-506 (July, 1931).

Leisure and Its Use by Herbert L. May and Dorothy Petgen (New York, 1928) is an interesting volume. A good general discussion of public recreation is included in Maurice R. Davie, *Problems of City Life* (New York, 1932), pp. 565-714. Mention should also be made of Raymond Moley, *Commercial Recreation* (New York, 1920).

Attention should likewise be called to various recreational surveys, *e.g.*, L. H. Weir, *Recreation Survey of Buffalo* (Buffalo, 1925), the recreational survey of Indianapolis, published as *The Leisure of a People* under the editorship of Eugene T. Lies (Indianapolis, 1929), and the study of *Public Recreation* by Lee F. Hammer which is included in the publications of the Regional Plan of New York and Its Environs (New York, 1928).

References to books and articles on various phases of public recreation may be found from time to time in *The American City*.

See also the references appended to Chapter XVII.

CHAPTER XLI

WATER SUPPLY

And the rest of the acts of Hezekiah, . . . how he made a pool and a conduit, and brought water into the city, are they not written in the chronicles of the kings of Judah?—*II Kings xx, 20.*

Water is an essential of life. Even primitive peoples realized this and guided their habitats to oases and streams. Water supplies have determined, in the course of history, the routes of caravans, the location of towns, the development of industry, and even the prosperity of modern states. Hence the desirability and even the necessity of providing an adequate water supply are now recognized in all civilized communities. This is not only required for the promotion of sanitary progress and the safeguarding of health; it is essential to the progress of industry, to the protection of property against fire, and to the maintenance of civic comfort and beauty through the cleaning of streets and the watering of both public and private open spaces during dry weather. {An essential of civilized existence.}

The history of public water supply is almost as old as the history of man. We have definite evidence of such enterprises in Egypt twenty centuries before the beginning of the Christian era. Vast irrigation works were constructed in the valleys of the Tigris and the Euphrates by the early Assyrian kings. In early Athens the water was brought to the public wells and fountains in aqueducts from the brooks in the neighboring hills. Rome, however, was the primate of all ancient communities in this field. The scope and excellence of the water-supply system in the city of the Caesars is one of the marvels of ancient civilization, for the aqueducts which supplied Rome totalled nearly four hundred miles in length. They were built along the hydraulic grade lines because pressure conduits were not available, iron pipe being unknown at the time. Lead pipe was in use for smaller connections but of course could not be utilized to carry high pressures. The total capacity of the Roman aqueducts is estimated to have been about 75 million gallons per day. Much of this water was used for irrigating lands outside the city.[1] {Early history of public water supply.}

[1] We know a good deal about the water supply of ancient Rome because Fron-

Later developments.

The Romans also provided systems of water supply in their provincial cities, but after the collapse of the empire these were allowed to go into disuse and decay. During the long era of the Dark Ages the people drew their water supply from any source that lay near at hand, however polluted it might be. Consequently the whole of Western Europe was swept by frequent epidemics of cholera, dysentery, and fever. Some progress in the way of bringing clean water to the larger cities began to be made during the later Middle Ages and in the early modern era, but the great renaissance in water-supply construction did not come until the invention of cast-iron pipe and of steam-driven pumps at the close of the eighteenth century. Then the development proceeded everywhere at a rapid pace until nowadays virtually all urban communities are equipped with public water supplies.

Factors in the daily consumption of water by cities:

How much water does a modern city require? The answer is usually expressed in gallons per capita on a basis of all water pumped into the distributing system, without deduction for wastage. In American cities the amount runs from a hundred to two hundred gallons per person daily. Reduced to avoirdupois, this is from over 800 to over 1,600 pounds of water. Or, reckoning four persons to the average family, it implies a minimum of a ton and a half of water daily. Of course no ordinary household uses anything like so much water. The domestic use of water, that is, its use in kitchens, in bathrooms, and for drinking purposes, does not ordinarily amount to more than from thirty to forty gallons per person daily. It is not the largest factor in the total consumption. Yet most people think of the city's water supply in terms of domestic use and are apt to overlook four other factors which, taken together, make a much heavier daily draft on the system.

1. Domestic use.

2. Industrial use.

One of these is the use of water by industries. Factories and shops require water, sometimes a great deal of it, as in the case of laundries, dyeing establishments, and bottling plants. Railroad terminals and steamship docks likewise make heavy demands, as do all other establishments which use steam boilers, condensers, and similar water-consuming appliances. Hotels and restaurants, with dish-washing machines, are by no means frugal consumers. On the other hand there are many large industries which use

---

tinus, in his *De Aquis Urbi Romae*, gives a detailed account of it. This book has been translated into English by Clemens Herschel under the title *The Two Books of the Water Supply of Rome* (Boston, 1899).

relatively little water. Hence the volume of industrial and commercial demand is subject to much variation from city to city, depending not only on the number but on the nature of its industries. It ranges from twenty to fifty gallons per capita daily.

Again there is the use of water for irrigation and sprinkling, especially in cities which have little or no rainfall during the summer months. Gardens in the suburban districts and lawns all over the city are given a wetting-down at frequent intervals. In some cities the daily water consumption during July and August runs fifty per cent above the figures for March and April. The total amount of water used for irrigation and sprinkling is very large, and much of it represents a sheer wastage. For water sprinkled on gardens or lawns during the morning hours of a hot summer day gives little service because of the rapid evaporation. Most city lawns are oversoaked with water anyhow. If the owners would use more fertilizer and less water they would get better results.

3. Irrigation.

Then there is public consumption, in other words the use of water by the city authorities themselves—in fighting fires, flushing sewers, washing down the streets, watering parks and public golf courses, supplying bathhouses and fountains, and providing a water supply for all kinds of public buildings such as schools, hospitals, police stations, and the like. This factor in the total water consumption cannot be accurately estimated because it is seldom measured and no charge is usually made for it. Public officials often waste water because it is not charged against their appropriations. Some time ago in one eastern city it was found that the gallonage used at the municipal cemetery was higher per capita for the interments than for the living population outside. When John F. Hylan was mayor of New York, he endeared himself to the people of the tenements by roping off portions of certain streets during hot summer evenings and turning these spaces into community shower-baths with the aid of the fire hydrants. The use of water by the various public services may run as high as twenty or thirty gallons per capita, particularly in the summer months. People have an idea that the fire department must use up a great deal of water in its work because they see the streams being played at high pressure on a burning structure now and then. But the extinguishing of fires is an almost negligible factor in a city's annual water consumption, as has already been pointed out.

4. Public use.

5. The item of waste.

Finally, there is waste. It is a big item almost everywhere. Of the total amount of water pumped into the mains, it is figured that the wastage sometimes runs as high as twenty or even thirty per cent. Part of this is due to leaks in the water pipes under the streets or in connections to the houses. Wastage of this kind is to some extent unavoidable because leaks cannot always be immediately detected and a considerable loss of water may take place before repairs can be made. On a much larger scale the loss of water is due to defective plumbing fixtures in houses, shops, and industrial plants. Taps, toilets, and garden hydrants are left dripping, day and night, for months at a time. Even a small drip will account for several gallons of water in the course of twenty-four hours. Carelessness on the part of water consumers is especially noticeable when their services are not metered. A frequent house-to-house inspection of all fixtures, by officials of the water department, is the best way to keep this wastage within bounds. In northern portions of the country there is a considerable misuse of water on cold winter nights owing to the common household practice of leaving the taps partly open to keep the fixtures from freezing.

How it can be reduced.

Water wastage depends in part upon the pressure that is carried in the mains. High pressures mean more leaks. A change of a few pounds per square inch in pressure has been found to increase the total water consumption by a substantial fraction. Cities, therefore, should use the lowest pressures that are compatible with satisfactory service. Waste is also affected by the scale of charges for water. It naturally goes down as the water rates go up. The excessive use of water, again, is relatively much more common in the well-to-do residential sections of the city where servants are employed than in the small homes and tenements where those who use the water have to pay for it. If the avoidable waste of water could be entirely eliminated, it is certain that the figures of total consumption would be substantially cut down in most American communities. People do not increase their ice bills by negligently leaving their refrigerator doors open. They are also scrupulous about turning off the electric lights in their homes when light is not needed. But they seem to have no such scruples about turning their water taps off tightly. Many of them need education in this respect.

In recapitulation, then, it may be said that domestic use, industrial use, the use of water for irrigation, its use by the public authorities, and various forms of waste account for the total per capita consumption of half a ton or more per day. Only a very small portion of this—not more than five per cent, perhaps,—is used for purposes which require pure water, in other words, for drinking purposes or in preparing food. But the whole supply has to be safeguarded against pathogenic bacteria because there is no practicable way of separating this five per cent from the other ninety-five. It is for this reason that cities go to the great expense of protecting their entire watersheds or filtering the whole volume of supply. Of course there is a touch of absurdity in the practice of protecting and filtering these enormous quantities of water, billions of gallons, and then using it to flush sewers, extinguish fires, feed steam boilers, and sprinkle parkways—but there seems to be nothing else to do. Separate distributing mains for *eau potable* and for *eau non potable* are used in some European cities, notably in Paris, but the general results have not been altogether satisfactory nor is it certain that the plan conduces to any financial saving in the long run. The need for safeguarding the entire supply.

Water, as supplied to a city, is not a raw product but a manufactured commodity. It has to be procured in sufficient quantity, stored, protected, purified, and distributed. In many cases the available supply is limited. Providing a city with a satisfactory public water supply is not merely a matter of finding a lake or stream which can be diverted into mains and aqueducts. Usually it involves the building of dams and impounding reservoirs, the protection of these storage basins against pollution or the filtering of the water where protection is not practicable; likewise it necessitates the planning, erection, and maintenance of pumping plants together with an elaborate distribution system including the installation of meters and provisions for a system of water accounting. All this costs a great deal of money and the marvel is that cities can supply water in homes or shops, and make a profit out of it, at rates which average less than five cents a ton, as they do in many cases. What this involves.

What are the sources from which cities' public water supplies are obtained? There are only two sources, namely, ground waters or surface waters. The former is water that has pushed its way from the surface, through sand, gravel, or rock, to an underground basin,—frequently an old river formation which has become filled Sources of public water supply:
1. Ground water.

with porous matter. It is then reached by driving wells, sometimes several hundred feet below the surface. There is a popular impression that water pumped from deep wells is always suitable for use without any form of treatment; but such is not always the case. Subsurface water may be well filtered by its percolation through the sand or gravel, and thus denuded of bacteria; but it is usually affected by mineral matter in the process and thus becomes too hard or otherwise not well suited for industrial use. Many small cities, however, depend on ground waters and wells without any form of water-softening or other treatment.

2. Surface water.

Surface water may be drawn from natural lakes and rivers or from impounded watersheds. Many cities and towns on the Great Lakes obtain their supplies directly from these great bodies of water. Chicago, Detroit, Cleveland, and Buffalo are examples. Unfortunately much sewage is also poured into the Great Lakes, hence their usefulness as a source of supply has been endangered to a point where the diversion or treatment of the sewage has become essential. Small cities often find lakes or ponds which can be connected up to meet their needs. Large rivers, of course, provide an abundant supply for cities located on their banks, although the quality of the water may leave much to be desired. St. Louis draws from the Mississippi and the Missouri, New Orleans from the Mississippi, Washington from the Potomac, and Philadelphia from its two adjacent streams, the Delaware and the Schuylkill; but in all these cases the raw water is put through an elaborate treatment works before being used.

The impounding of surface supplies.

Geography, in other words, is kind to some cities and not to others. Many of the less favored communities have had to go far afield, gathering up their supplies at high cost from several small watersheds. Such waters are then impounded behind artificial dams or in storage reservoirs, to be drawn upon as needed. New York City has tapped the Croton and Catskill areas;[1] Boston draws from the watersheds of mid-Massachusetts, while Los Angeles brings her supply from an area near the Nevada frontier, a distance of two hundred and fifty miles. With the completion of the Boulder Dam the cities of Southern California will draw much of their water from the Colorado River, at a still greater distance. Baltimore, Seattle, and other cities also derive their supplies from catchment areas located some distance away. As

[1] Lazarus White, *The Catskill Water Supply of New York City* (New York, 1913).

these watersheds are usually inhabited, and sometimes thickly inhabited, the problem of protecting the impounded waters against pollution often becomes a very difficult one.

But whatever the source, it is essential that the water shall be "good water" when it goes into the mains. This expression, good water, may seem at first sight to be an easily understandable one, but it is by no means as simple as it sounds. What qualities is water required to have in order that it may be good water for public use? First, it should be substantially free from disease-bearing bacteria. That, obviously, is the most important of all considerations, but it is by no means the only one. Good water should also be colorless, otherwise it is unsuitable for use by laundries, dyeworks, ice-making plants, and other industrial establishments which require large amounts of it. Good water must likewise be free from suspended matter of any kind, and it should have neither taste nor odor. Furthermore it should be neither too hard nor too soft; and finally, it ought to be of reasonably agreeable temperature in hot weather, otherwise it is unpalatable to most people unless ice is used with it. *What is meant by "good water."*

Of course raw water rarely satisfies these requirements in their entirety. Almost invariably it has to be treated for impurity, color, taste, odor, or hardness. One supply requires sedimentation; another needs prolonged storage either with or without exposure to sunlight; another filtration or disinfection with chlorine preparations, while still others may have to be run through a water-softening plant. Good water is not, therefore, a simple combination of oxygen and hydrogen, drawn from some natural source and supplied to the consumer just as it happens to come. It should be classed as a finished product which the city procures in raw form and often puts through an elaborate process to make it marketable. *Raw water is rarely fit for public use.*

Surface water, especially from small lakes, ponds, and streams, is often slightly colored as the result of contact with algae and other growths. The presence of algae may likewise give a slight taste and odor. This may also result from contact with peat and certain soils. Surface water may also be cloudy or turbid by reason of the small particles of clay and sand which it picks up. And water from either surface or ground sources is sometimes affected by contact with certain chemical substances in the ground, such as mineral salts or sulphides. Water is also, at times, too hard for *Reasons why this is the case.*

domestic use, that is, when it contains too much lime. Likewise water becomes unpalatable for drinking purposes in the summer months when its temperature runs above 60° Fahrenheit at the tap.

The pollution of water supplies by sewage.

All such defects in a water supply can be remedied, in whole or in part, by appropriate methods of water treatment. Disease-bearing bacteria gain access to water sources through the flow of sewage into it, and in no other way. Natural water is harmless. It can only be polluted by the action of human or animal life. So the obvious way to preserve the natural purity of a water supply is by keeping pollution away from it, that is, by making sure that all sewage effluent is carefully diverted somewhere else. But this is often difficult, or even impossible, in the case of surface water supplies which come from areas that are heavily inhabited. The protection must be absolute, complete, and continuous; otherwise there is danger to the public health because a relatively slight pollution may start an epidemic. Typhoid is the most common and the most serious of the diseases caused by water-borne bacteria. It is spread by typhoid bacilli (*B. typhosi*) which belong to the colon bacillus group. The presence of *B. coli* in water is now generally regarded by public health authorities as a reasonably conclusive indication that it has been in contact with sewage.

Storage as a remedy.

Water which is subject to a mild pollution can usually be made safe for human consumption by storing it in protected reservoirs for a sufficient length of time. Harmful bacilli do not multiply in impounded water, at least not when exposed to air and sunlight. On the contrary they decrease rapidly. The length of time necessary to ensure this safety through storage depends on the extent of the pollution, the depth of the reservoir, the temperature, and various other factors; but a couple of months is ample under ordinary conditions. New York and Boston depend largely upon the storage-time factor in handling their water supplies.

Water disinfection.

If the pollution is considerable, however, or if storage for a sufficient length of time is not practicable, there is a relatively inexpensive method of water disinfection. This is by chlorination, in other words by sterilizing the water with chloride of lime or with liquid chlorine gas. Chloride of lime is commonly known as bleaching powder. It is an inexpensive chemical which, after being dissolved in water, can be injected into the reservoir at its intake. This method has now become obsolete because the use of liquid chlorine gas is less expensive and at the same time more effective in its results. Chlorination, however, is not satisfactory as a germicide when the water is heavily turbid. In such cases the chlorine treatment ought to be preceded by sedimentation. This involves keeping the water in large settling basins for a short time. To hasten the process of sedimentation as respects the smaller suspended particles, a coagulant such as alum or sulphate or iron is commonly used. The proper employment of chlorination is as a supplement to storage, sedimentation, or some similar method of preliminary water treatment. It is also useful in emergencies when a filtering plant breaks down or when surface water finds its way into a reservoir.

Filtration has the advantage of removing both the bacteria and the suspended matter in water. There are two types of filtration plants, namely, the English or slow sand filtering process, and the American rapid or mechanical filtration method. The slow sand filter is man's adaptation of nature's methods as used in river beds where water percolates through layers of sand and gravel until it reaches springs or wells in a clarified condition. The construction of a slow sand filter is a relatively simple problem. First a large water-tight basin, usually of concrete, is built with suitable underdrains or outlet pipes. The basin is then partly filled with broken stone and covered with sand. Raw water from the lake or river is allowed to flow in at the top of the basin and to work its way through the sand and stone to the outlets below. During this process the bacteria and the suspended particles of matter which happen to be in the water adhere to the grains of sand or to the film which forms on them.

Filtration:

1. The slow sand filter.

When this film has had time to become developed, the slow sand filter will remove ninety-nine per cent or more of the bacterial content, but it does not in all cases eliminate taste or discoloration. Hence it is sometimes necessary, when the raw water is badly discolored, to employ some supplementary treatment, such as aëration, or to run the water through the filters a second time.[1] Slow sand filtration, coupled with aëration, is said to eliminate tastes and odors better than any other method of water treatment. But without a preliminary sedimentation the slow sand filter is not well adapted for use with waters which, like

Its effectiveness.

---

[1] While aëration has been and still is effective for eliminating tastes and odors, the use of activated carbon has been adopted in many plants especially in connection with rapid filtration systems. It is sold under various trade names.

those of the Ohio or Mississippi, are turbid or muddy. Even with relatively clear waters, such as those of the New England rivers, the surface of the filters must be cleaned at intervals. Sand filters are usually built in pairs, therefore, so as to permit one of them to be in use while the other is having its periodical cleansing.[1]

2. The mechanical filter. The other type of filtration plant, the rapid or mechanical filter, has been coming into more general use during recent years. There are several types of mechanical filter, but all of them use a bed of sand enclosed in a covered tank or container made of concrete, bronze, or other durable material. The raw water, having first been treated with a chemical coagulant, is forced under high pressure into this container where it passes down through the sand at a rapid rate leaving the coagulated particles to accumulate on the top of the bed. Daily or oftener this top layer of sediment is cleared off by forcing water or air through the filter in the reverse direction. Many of the new installations are rapid filters placed in open concrete tanks with the circulation produced by gravity. These seem to be displacing the older type of mechanical filter.

Relative merits of the two processes. There is a popular impression, somewhat encouraged by filter-construction companies, that these two filtration plans are rival processes, either of which a city may choose at its discretion. Sanitary engineers are well aware, however, that this is not the case. Each method has its own appropriate field. The mechanical filter is preferable where the water is muddy but not badly polluted. It is effective in removing a large percentage of the bacteria; how large is still a matter of some disagreement among the experts. In any event the water can be chlorinated after it comes from the mechanical filter and thus rendered safe. With a sufficient use of coagulants the mechanical process removes all turbidity and discoloration.

By using this process a city is able to handle about one hundred and twenty-five million gallons per acre of filtering area daily,— the normal supply for a million people. This is about forty times the usual rate for slow sand filters. Mechanical filters are usually

[1] During recent years a filter-washing machine has been developed and is now coming into extensive use. It consists of a box-like arrangement carried upon a bridge which spans the width of the filter and moves from end to end. This box is lowered upon the filter bed, completely cutting off the enclosed surface from the rest of the filter surface. Clear water is then forced into the upper few inches of the enclosed filter bed while a wash pump withdraws the muddy water produced by the washing operation. With this machine a slow sand filter can be maintained in continuous operation and still be kept in good condition.

less expensive than slow sand filters to install, but more expensive to operate. The selection of one or the other method depends upon local conditions; it cannot be determined by any general rule. The nature of the raw water, whether clear or turbid, discolored or not, badly polluted or not, is the most important factor but not the only one. Consideration must also be given to what sites are available and what they cost, likewise to what the city can afford to spend.

Filtration does not of itself soften hard water. To accomplish this a water-softening plant is necessary. These plants add some chemical to the water, usually soda. When water contains more than 100 to 150 parts of calcium per million, it ought to be softened. Many cities, however, do not realize this. They pump hard water into their mains and let the large consumers (factories, hotels, laundries, etc.) do their own softening. That is an inconvenient and expensive way to do it. Likewise the supplying of unduly hard water to homes involves increased expenditures for soap and washing powders far in excess of what a centralized softening treatment would cost. *Softening water for public use.*

When a water supply has been made ready for use, it goes into the distribution system. This includes reservoirs, standpipes, pumps, and mains. Reservoirs are necessary in order to ensure a supply of water which can be used in emergencies such as conflagration, drought, or a breakdown in the pumping plant. Such reservoirs should be covered, for filtered water deteriorates when exposed to strong light in warm weather. Uncovered reservoirs also permit the growth of algae and are more difficult to safeguard against surreptitious bathers. The distribution system may be such that water is pumped from the source or treatment plant into the reservoirs at a high level and then flows by gravity into the mains; or it may flow to a reservoir on a lower level and be pumped out. The former plan is preferable when topography permits. Standpipes and water towers are used in some cities to equalize the operation of the pumps by providing a reserve during periods of high water consumption. *The water distribution system:* *1. Reservoirs and pumps.*

The correct and safe location of water mains, the determination of proper water pressures, and the designing of the pumping plants are engineering problems which must be carefully worked out if the public water system is to function satisfactorily. No matter how excellent the water itself may be, no system of public *2. Mains and house connections.*

supply will give full satisfaction unless the arrangements for distribution receive their appropriate share of attention. The mains are usually of cast iron or steel, although they are sometimes of reinforced concrete. In ordinary residential streets a six- or eight-inch water main is sufficient, but trunk mains should be several times larger. House connections are of pipe not exceeding two inches in diameter. All mains and house connections should have shut-off valves for use in emergencies. A pressure of from thirty to fifty pounds per square inch at the street level is sufficient for ordinary purposes; but many of the larger cities have installed additional high-pressure services in their downtown areas and these can be stepped up to a couple of hundred pounds. The installation of a high-pressure service, approved by the National Board of Fire Underwriters, results in lower fire insurance rates throughout the area which it serves and hence is regarded as a good investment. This service is usually operated by the fire department, not by the regular water authorities.

How distribution systems are constructed. The amount of money invested in the public water-supply systems of the United States at the present time is well in excess of a billion dollars. In most cities the work of maintenance and extension, which includes the laying of new mains and the installation of meters, is handled by the regular employees of the water department, but large projects of new construction (basins, reservoirs, pumping plants, and high-pressure services) are generally carried out by using the contract plan. The construction of municipal waterworks has suffered less from political jobbery and corruption, on the whole, than the paving of streets or the laying of sewers. One reason may be found in the fact that water department funds have usually been kept separate from the general funds of the city and more carefully safeguarded.

Water finance. Hence, water department finance deserves a word. The original installation of a public water supply is covered, in virtually all cases, by the issue of water bonds which are backed by the general credit of the city and run for a varying term of years. Then the cost of later extensions and of new equipment is sometimes paid out of surplus income from the water rates, but more generally it also is financed by borrowing money. The interest upon these loans, and the contributions necessary to amortize them, are fixed charges upon the water department's revenue. Thus they do not come as a burden upon the general tax rate. Hence the water-

WATER SUPPLY

supply system is commonly looked upon as a "reproductive" enterprise, able to pay its own way and perhaps contribute a little to the city's general expenses besides.

Water rates are fixed on this basis, that is, on a scale sufficient to pay all interest and sinking fund charges, together with all costs of operation including ordinary replacements, and yet provide a small surplus. The water department's contribution to the city's general revenue does not usually take the form of a cash payment. More often it merely provides free water for all the other departments, and some of them use a great deal of it,—for example, the parks and public buildings departments. This practice is not an economical one because departments which find themselves entitled to an unlimited amount of free water are very likely to be wasteful of it. *A self-supporting enterprise.*

The price of water to the consumer is supposed to be based upon the cost of service, but it is difficult to arrange a schedule of water rates which will provide just enough revenue and no more. For the cost of operating a water department, year by year, varies with the level of wages and prices, and these may undergo considerable changes within a very short time. But when a schedule of rates is once fixed, there are difficulties in the way of getting it revised upwards because the changes must have the approval of the city council. The members of this body, of course, dislike to approve anything that is going to be unpopular with the voters and an upward revision of the water rates never brings any applause at the polls. Rather strangely, people seem to resist increased charges for water even more strenuously than they oppose higher rates for gas or electricity. *The schedule of water rates.*

As to the methods of arranging the schedule of water rates, there has been considerable diversity of practice, and one might almost say that no two cities have followed exactly the same methods; but in a general way there are three ways of making consumers pay for water, namely, the flat-rate plan, the classified plan, and the measured-service plan. Selling water at a flat rate, irrespective of the amount used, was the common practice in American cities a generation ago, especially in the smaller municipalities. But this method came to be generally regarded as unbusinesslike, unfair to the small consumer, and an incentive to wastefulness. Thereupon cities adopted the plan of classifying their consumers according to the nature or value of the premises *Various ways of arranging it.*

served, or according to the size of the connection between premises and water main, or according to the number of faucets in the house, or on some other such basis. Every building was thus given a rating which was assumed to bear a rough approximation to the amount of water used. This arrangement marked a step in the direction of greater fairness, but it was not very effective in preventing waste and it aroused much discontent among consumers who sometimes discovered that their neighbors were paying less and using more water than they themselves.

Spread of the metered service. So the practice of metering each individual service came into vogue and during the past twenty years it has been rapidly extended. Metering began with the large industries and business establishments where the waste was thought to be greatest. Then it was extended to small shops, tenements, and individual homes. In some cities practically the entire service is now on a metered basis; in others this goal is being approached as rapidly as the meters can be purchased and installed by using the surplus earnings of the water department. Under the metered system it is the usual practice to fix a certain rate per hundred cubic feet for water used up to a designated amount, with a lower rate for all water above this figure. Some cities have an elaborate sliding scale of rates in which a differentiation is made not only on the basis of consumption but as between the various types of water users, agricultural, industrial, and domestic.

Advantages of this plan. The superior merits of the metered system are easy enough to point out. On the face of things there is no good reason why water, being a marketable commodity, should be sold on a different basis from any other merchandise. No one expects to buy gas or electric current on a flat-rate basis. From a purely economic standpoint the measured-service plan is the only one that deals fairly with all concerned, including the city which sells the water, and in addition it has the outstanding merit of providing a definite check upon wastage. But there are offsetting considerations which must not be overlooked. For one thing the general installation of meters involves large and continuing expenditures, since many thousands of meters have to be bought and installed; then they get out of order and register wrongly. Like all other mechanical devices, moreover, they deteriorate or grow obsolescent and in time have to be replaced. Despite all this it is good business policy to pay the cost and save the water.

WATER SUPPLY

The progress of metering has been somewhat retarded, moreover, by political opposition to the plan. Much popular opposition has been aroused against the idea of charging by the gallon or by the cubic foot for something which the city is assumed to get for nothing. A good deal of this opposition has been inspired by the large consumers (including the newspapers) who find that the installation of a measured service increases their water bills. Some of it has also been stirred up by social workers who believe that the plan tends to discourage the needful and legitimate use of water for sanitary purposes in the poorer sections of the city. Especially where the landlord pays the water rates it is asserted that the meter system encourages him to reduce the sanitary conveniences in tenement houses to the minimum quota permitted by law. Resentment is also created by the fact that the schedules which are worked out in connection with a metered service usually give lower rates per hundred cubic feet to large industrial consumers than to domestic users. This policy of giving lower rates to large consumers is deemed to be sound economics and in addition it is designed to encourage the location of new industries in the community. The average householder, on the other hand, is inclined to agree with the politician who tells him that "the city ought to treat everyone alike." In spite of all this opposition, however, the meter system continues to make headway. Water department authorities are everywhere a unit in favor of it. *Common objections to it.*

Meters are of two general types, known as displacement and inferential meters. In one case the flow is measured by the motion of a disk and in the other by the revolutions of a screw. Disk meters are the more generally used. The installation of meters should be at the water department's expense; it should not be charged to the consumers. This enables a standardization of the meters and simplifies the work of keeping them in good working order. Even at the best there will be a small margin of error in meter measurement, and this slip increases with the age of the meter unless it is frequently tested and kept in adjustment. *Types of meters.*

The reading of the meters, monthly or quarterly, is done by the water department's employees. The city, for this purpose, is mapped off into sections and one reader is assigned to each. The work is simple but requires care and honesty. The records are turned in each day and entered on the cards at water department headquarters. Bills are then prepared and sent out. If they are *Meter reading and water bills.*

not paid within a designated time the water service to the delinquent premises may be shut off.

Organization of the water department. The organization of the water department shows considerable variation in cities throughout the country. In most of them there is a water board of from three to five members. These are sometimes elected by popular vote but more often they are appointed by the mayor or city commission. This board selects the superintendent of the water service who has charge of the actual operations. In city manager municipalities it is the more common practice to have the manager appoint the water superintendent directly. Many of the larger cities have a water commissioner, appointed by the mayor. This branch of municipal administration lends itself better to unified than to board control. In cities of any considerable size it is likely that water boards will everywhere be replaced in time by a well-qualified individual head of the department.

Its several functions. In any event the internal organization of a water department presents a number of problems. Several functions of a widely differing character come within its jurisdiction. The most important work of the department is, of course, concerned with projects of an engineering character, such as planning, construction, maintenance, and repairs; but it also includes such matters as water analysis and water treatment, things which call for the help of sanitary experts; and it must likewise care for the financial end of the business, which includes the responsibility for preparing rate schedules, keeping accounts, and collecting bills.

Division of work with other departments. A well-organized water department must make provision for the proper handling of all these things. This does not mean, however, that all of them must be done by the department's own officials, for such an arrangement would involve much needless duplication in smaller cities. Except in the larger municipalities, where there is work enough to employ a separate engineering staff for the water department alone, the plans and specifications for work in the water department can be furnished by the city engineer's office. The collection of water bills, again, may be turned over to the office of the city treasurer or collector of taxes, unless the work is sufficiently extensive to demand the establishment of a special income bureau within the water department itself. In the smaller cities, accordingly, the problem is that of coöperating effectively with the other departments.

So far as its subordinate officials and employees are concerned, the water department lends itself very well to the policy of selection on a civil service basis. Its problems, as has been said, are largely technical. With the exception of the laborers employed in the work of construction, extension, and repair, the employees of a water department are entrusted with functions which require a high degree of intelligence. Miscalculations in the laying of mains, errors in water analysis, and mistakes in water accounting are all easy to make, and indeed they are almost certain to be made with costly repetition unless the city takes reasonable precautions to keep political patronage out of the department. *Civil service in water departments.*

In a day when the laws require that even the village pharmacist shall be rigidly examined and licensed because otherwise his lack of expertness may bring death or illness to some customer, is it not an anomaly that any city should tolerate the blunderings of political spoilsmen in such vital matters as the adequacy and safety of water supply, the engineering problems of reservoirs, pumps, mains, and pressures, and the highly technical questions of water analysis and water purification? Practically every regular position in the city's water department involves duties of a definable character, and whether or not a man is capable of performing them can be determined by means of a practical test. A typhoid epidemic is one of the penalties that a community is likely to pay for letting its water department drift under the sway of the politicians, and a severe penalty it is. The assertion has been made by health experts, and there is some force to it, that for every outbreak of typhoid due to water impurities somebody ought to be put in jail. In public administration, however, it is far better to prevent than to punish. *The exclusion of politics.*

The earliest public water-supply services in the United States were owned by water companies; but municipal ownership began to make headway during the nineteenth century and today virtually all the plants are owned by the cities. Private ownership of the municipal water system is now quite exceptional. This is not surprising because public ownership is demanded in this field by several considerations which do not apply to other public utilities such as lighting plants, street railways, and telephones. The water supply, in point of adequacy and purity, has a relation to the public health which the others have not. The city cannot leave the control of its illness-and-death-rates in the hands of any profit-seeking concern and should not be asked to do so. *Municipal ownership of public water supplies. The reasons for it.*

The arguments for public ownership are convincing.

Again, the city itself is the largest individual customer of the water plant. The park department, the street-cleaning service, the sewer-cleaning division, the fire department, and many other branches of municipal administration are all large users of water; along with the public buildings they sometimes take as much as one-fifth of the entire daily supply. Finally, there is a public interest that may be adversely affected by a private water company's rate-making policy. One method of charging for water may encourage the coming of new industries; another may drive them away. One schedule may discourage the owners of crowded tenements from putting in proper sanitary arrangements; another may provide an incentive for them to do so. Water should be supplied to the people at cost, or nearly at cost, and a private company cannot be expected to operate its plant on this basis. For these various reasons water supply is a public utility that stands in a class by itself. The issue of public or private ownership cannot here be settled on economic grounds alone. Social considerations bulk large. One may therefore be a strong advocate of public ownership in this field, and yet be strongly opposed to the municipalization of electric lighting plants or street railways.

The future.

And what of the future? It is within the bounds of conservatism to say that before another generation has passed the public water-supply systems will everywhere be publicly owned, that all water supplied for public use will be filtered or otherwise rendered absolutely safe, that the meter system will be universally adopted, that scientific progress will greatly simplify the problems of water treatment, and that a large percentage of the present-day waste will be eliminated by improvements in household plumbing. In spite of this waste elimination, however, the per capita consumption of water seems likely to keep increasing, and if it continues to increase as it has been doing the problem of obtaining an adequate supply is going to present a serious problem in some of our cities.

REFERENCES

Harold E. Babbitt and James J. Doland, *Water Supply Engineering* (2nd edition, New York, 1931) is one of the latest and best treatises in this field. It is a comprehensive work, covering thoroughly all phases of the subject. Of high value also is F. E. Turneaure and H. L. Russell, *Public Water Supplies* (3rd edition, New York, 1924).

Other useful sources of information are the volume on *Water Works Practice*, issued under the auspices of the American Water Works Association (Baltimore, 1925), Donald M. Baker and Harold Conkling, *Water Supply and Utilization* (New York, 1930), Frank Dixey, *Practical Handbook of Water Supply* (New York, 1931), George C. Whipple, *The Microscopy of Drinking Water* (4th edition by G. M. Fair and M. C. Whipple, New York, 1927), A. M. Buswell, *The Chemistry of Water and Sewage Treatment* (New York, 1928), Allen Hazen, *Meter Rates for Water Works* (New York, 1919), Joseph W. Ellms, *Water Purification* (2nd edition, New York, 1928), A. P. Folwell, *Water Supply Engineering* (3rd edition, New York, 1917), Milton F. Stein, *Water Purification Plants and Their Operation* (3rd edition, New York, 1926), and the 423-page bulletin of the United States Public Health Service, by H. W. Streeter, entitled *Studies of the Efficiency of Water Purification Processes* (Public Health Bulletin No. 172, Washington, 1928).

Another federal bulletin of interest and value is W. D. Collins, *The Relations between Quality of Water and Industrial Development in the United States* (Washington, 1926). Mention should also be made of the publication issued in 1925 by the American Public Health Association on *Standard Methods for the Examination of Water and Sewage*. The third edition of the *Waterworks Handbook*, published in 1927 by A. D. Flinn, R. S. Weston, and C. L. Bogert, contains much serviceable data. A popular survey of the subject is given in Hope Holway, *The Story of Water Supply* (New York, 1929).

Current discussions can be found in the annual *Proceedings* and in the monthly *Journal* of the American Water Works Association. The Water Works Research Bureau (50 East 42nd St., New York) has issued some useful pamphlets, *e.g.*, its discussion of *Water Meters and the Elimination of Waste* (1927). *The Municipal Index* (published annually) gives statistics and bibliographical references.

CHAPTER XLII

PUBLIC LIGHTING

These blessed candles of the night.—The Merchant of Venice.

The handmaid of civilization.
Among the triumphs of man the production and use of artificial light rank high. In the promotion of human efficiency no other achievement surpasses it. For without its aid the activities of mankind would be restricted to the daylight hours. As it is, we work and play, or we travel on land, at sea, and in the air, all piloted by light of our own making. Maeterlinck, in his *Blue Bird* makes Light, "in pale gold shot with silver," the faithful companion of man. For light goes with him everywhere except into the abode of evils, and always it is the symbol of goodness, truth, and knowledge. Darkness is no longer its equal. In the great cities of today there has been for all practical purposes a fulfillment of the prophecy that the sun shall no more go down.

Public lighting in earlier days.
We do not know when or where the practice of public lighting began. There were no street lights in ancient Rome and no one in the imperial city dared to go out of doors after nightfall unless accompanied by friends or slaves with blazing torches. Nor were there lights in the streets of mediaeval cities. The world in those days barred its doors and went to bed when darkness came, for there was nothing else to do. London appears to have made the pioneer attempt at street lighting in 1416–1417 when it was ordained that lanterns with candles should be hung in front of houses on winter evenings. But the ordinance does not appear to have been heeded, for two centuries later most of the London streets were still unlighted while "the sons of Belial, flown with insolence and wine," roamed the dark thoroughfares. Oil lanterns came into use during the era preceding the American Revolution. It took fifteen thousand of them to light the streets of London in 1750.

Shortly after the incoming of the nineteenth century, however, London replaced these lanterns by gas lamps. Other cities throughout the civilized world hastened to light their streets with this new illuminant, but not without a good deal of opposition from the more conservative elements. It was argued that the attempt to turn night into day by artificial illumination was an interference with the divine order of things which had decreed that nights should be dark. Medical men protested that the emanations from the illuminating gas would be injurious to the public health. Moreover, it was predicted that lighted streets would induce people to stay up late and remain out of doors, getting fatigued and making themselves unfitted for work the next day. And many taxpayers cried out against the policy of making the whole people pay for lighting the streets when only a portion of them ever went out after dark.

But in spite of all such objections the practice of public lighting made rapid headway and within the next fifty years the streets of all cities were lined with flickering gas lamps which threw a weird illumination over the sidewalks and a portion of the roadway. Gas held undisputed sway until about 1880 when electricity leaped into the field and gradually pushed the older illuminant aside. The open arc lamp came first, but it was an unsteady light source with a poor distribution. Presently it gave way to the enclosed arc and this in turn was supplanted by the magnetite arc. Meanwhile the incandescent lamp made its appearance and has been steadily improved by the introduction of the tungsten filament and bulbs filled with inert gases. Thus the art of public lighting has made more progress during the past fifty years than it was able to make in the preceding five thousand.[1]

The spread of public lighting during the past century.

Most people do not realize the enormity of the change which the progress of electric lighting during the past half-century has made in the routine of urban life. It has freed the cities from their bondage to the sun and the moon. Industries are enabled to operate in double shifts, and some great enterprises crowd most of their work into the night hours, the morning newspapers for example. Adequate lighting increases production, decreases waste, and is a very important factor in the prevention of industrial accidents. Much of our transportation by water, by rail, by road, and even by air is now made possible by artificial lighting. The planning of large buildings has been simplified by the fact that care need no longer be taken to provide all the rooms with natural light. A considerable part of every great city's trade and industry is nowadays carried on in places to which the sun's rays rarely or never penetrate. For

Its effect on human activities.

---

[1] The details may be found in Henry Schroeder, *The History of Electric Light*, Smithsonian Institution Publication No. 2717 (Washington, 1923).

proof of this one need only walk through any large retail establishment or office building and note the amount of artificial illumination that is used during the day hours.

Its influence upon public recreation.   Without high-powered artificial lighting, moreover, the city's recreation facilities, both public and private, could never have been elaborated to their present extent. To take only a single example, the most widely popular among all present-day forms of recreation, the motion picture shows, could not have been developed without it. Artificial light has some advantages over that which nature provides. It can be controlled in color and intensity. It is more dependable. On the other hand it is obviously more expensive, but not so much so as might be imagined, for even windows cost a good deal to install, to keep clean, and to repair when they get broken. In any event the universal use of artificial light has made mankind independent of the setting sun. For many centuries the world dreaded the coming of the night wherein no man could work, and it is small wonder that among primitive peoples the sun and the moon became objects of reverence and worship. The faithful, throughout the Dark Ages, lifted up their eyes unto the New Jerusalem and were comforted by the scriptural promise that "there shall be no night there."

The purpose of public lighting.   Public lighting, when it came, was looked upon as a matter of public safety, a means of helping people to avoid accidents and safeguarding them against the assaults of malefactors. Hence the street lamps in earlier days were sometimes known as silent policemen, and statistics were adduced to prove that crimes were least prevalent in the best-lighted sections of the community. Nowadays, however, public lighting is more a matter of public convenience than of public security. The congestion in the streets due to motor traffic has made a high degree of public illumination imperative. Part of this illumination, of course, represents an outlay for advertising. Brilliantly lighted streets are thought to be attractive; they draw the crowds and are supposed to stimulate business. Even small cities have come to this conclusion, as is shown by the frequent over-illumination of their principal thoroughfares. There are few of them, anywhere in the country, which have failed to provide themselves with at least a miniature of the original "great white way."

The lighting of the public streets is therefore designed to serve two purposes, first, to provide such illumination as will allow vehicles and pedestrians to move about during the night hours without danger of accident or risk of being molested; and, second, to do this in such a way that the general appearance of the city will not be marred by day and will be considerably improved by night. The phenomenal increase in motor traffic during the past quarter of a century has accentuated the difficulty of fulfilling the former purpose, while the development of aesthetic tastes on the part of the people has enhanced the cost of fulfilling the latter. The expense of providing public light now forms a substantial item in the annual budget of every progressive municipality. And this is not surprising when it is borne in mind that the streets usually comprise at least one-quarter of the entire acreage within the city limits. Except in the downtown business section the street areas usually exceed the entire floor space of the buildings on both sides. Even though a minimum of public illumination is supplied on certain streets, the amount of electricity required to cover this vast acreage with light must necessarily be very large. *Efficiency and aesthetics in lighting.*

Public lighting in American cities has been severely criticized by illuminating engineers. The main counts in the indictment, as given by one of them, but which seem somewhat too severe, are as follows: *General shortcomings of public lighting systems in America.*

1. City streets with certain exceptions are inadequately illuminated and cities as a whole are insufficiently lighted.
2. The street lighting of many cities is disorderly, due to haphazard growth without comprehensive plans.
3. There are inconsistent associations, also gaps, in passing from one section of a city to another.
4. There is a lack of standardization in energy distribution, equipments employed, and amount of light used.
5. Streets are seldom carefully classified as to traffic or property values and rarely is there unity in treatment of streets of like character.
6. There are too many unsightly streets because of insufficient attention to architecture in street lighting.
7. As is natural in pioneering sections, there has been too much temporary construction.
8. The large cities that can afford to do so have applied too little correlated intelligent effort, research, and talent to street lighting.
9. Many street-lighting installations are poorly maintained. Contracts often impose outage penalties but do not enforce regular cleaning. As a result, fixtures become so dirty that they are in effect semi-outages, causing, in many instances, the loss of more light than that due to total outages.

The lighting of public buildings. The problems of public lighting are mainly connected with (a) public buildings, (b) parks, and (c) streets and squares. In the case of public buildings the requirements do not differ materially from what is needed in private halls or offices. They should conform to the recognized standards of good interior lighting. Very often, however, they have not done so. The interior illumination of public buildings, all over the country, is usually poor. Post offices, city halls, police stations, and other public structures are often lighted with little regard for public convenience or governmental economy. The lights are sometimes badly placed, without proper globes or reflectors, hence there is a large consumption of current without satisfactory results. Even the reading rooms of public libraries have sometimes left a good deal to be desired in the way of efficient lighting, although the comfort of patrons depends heavily upon it. Nowadays, however, more attention is being paid to the lighting of public buildings and the advice of a competent illuminating engineer is frequently sought when such structures are being planned. Such assistance ought to be enlisted in all cases.

Park lighting. With respect to parks and public gardens the problem of illumination is merely one of providing enough light to assure the maintenance of public order and decency without impairing the beauty of the layout. From a police point of view the best results are obtained by placing the lights irregularly, wherever dark spots among the trees or shrubbery call for them, and especially in out-of-the-way places. But the park designer usually prefers to have the lights ranged along the curved walk and driveways in such way as to accentuate these features of his circulation plan. It is not easy to serve both purposes by using the same arrangement, hence the outcome is usually a compromise between the two points of view. Obviously, however, the use of high-powered lights in public parks (except on such parkways as are arteries of traffic) involves a waste of money. No greater degree of illumination is needed than that usually given to minor residential streets. Playgrounds, athletic fields, and such places of public amusement, on the other hand, require a much higher standard of illumination if they are to be made available for use after dark. Many cities, both in England and America, have made their playing fields usable at night by the installation of floodlights, and have found that this policy justifies what it costs for light and supervision.

PUBLIC LIGHTING

More than ninety per cent of the public illumination goes on the streets, squares, and alleyways. In the case of minor residential streets, on which there is little night traffic, a relatively small amount of illumination is needed. Major residential streets require somewhat more, while retail business streets, especially those in the theater and recreation district, demand a still higher level of illumination. Even in the same section of a city, however, the amount of light may need to be varied considerably from street to street. For it is not the importance of a thoroughfare during the day hours that determines its lighting requirements. Some streets which are densely thronged with traffic during the day may be almost deserted after six o'clock—the streets of the wholesale and financial districts, for example. Conversely it sometimes happens, although not so often, that theaters and other places of evening recreation are located on streets in which there is relatively little traffic during the daytime. *How street lighting needs are determined.*

Thus it comes to pass, somewhat paradoxically, that a street may be paved for dense traffic and lighted for almost no traffic at all. Every street, in a word, presents its own lighting problems. It is obvious, therefore, that the requirements for any thoroughfare, as respects illumination, cannot be determined by rule or formula, but are ascertainable only through a careful survey. Such a survey makes it possible to classify or zone streets in accordance with their respective lighting needs, thus assuring each a sufficient minimum of light on the one hand and avoiding wasteful expenditure on the other. Streets should be zoned for lighting as for other purposes. In most large cities this zoning will cause them to be grouped into several classifications, with one or more subdivisions in each. Some streets, moreover, will be found to fall on the border line between two classes or to change their classification at different stretches along their length. *Street-lighting surveys.*

First of all, there are certain streets or parts of streets into which great throngs of people, either in motor cars or afoot, are drawn as though by an irresistible urge, night after night. In small cities the main retail business streets are the ones that allure the crowds, but in larger communities this is not necessarily the case. Lower Broadway is more densely thronged at midnight than Fifth Avenue. State Street carries more pedestrians in the evening hours than Michigan Boulevard. The location of the motion picture houses, the theaters, the cafés, the hotels, and the other focal *Types of streets in relation to the lighting problem:*

1. Promenade streets.

points of night life determine the direction of the popular current; but when this drift once becomes fixed it often remains in obedience to tradition and habit. Indeed it will sometimes compel a transformation in the character of the street rather than alter its own fixed ways. It is difficult to find a good term for the general classification to which these night-life thoroughfares belong, but let us designate them as promenade streets for want of a better term.

Private contributions to the lighting of these highways.

It is obvious, at any rate, that these streets which attract great bodies of people in the evening hours require a high degree of lighting in the interest of public convenience.[1] But the proprietors of stores, restaurants, theaters, and other enterprises along these streets are alive to the psychological magnetism of bright lights, and they usually supplement the amount of illumination which is supplied by the city. This they do by huge lighted signs, illuminated store-fronts, and electric advertising devices of every sort. The result is that some portions of these areas are super-saturated with light, far beyond any reasonable requirement during the early evening hours. This does not mean, however, that the city can economize by leaving the illumination of such streets, or portions of them, to private initiative. For much of this private illumination has only an incidental relation to the street surface. Being designed for advertising purposes it is placed where it will catch the public eye, not where it will throw beams of light on the pavement. Much of it, as a matter of fact, is projected far above the zone of traffic. The Neon signs, which now line the street-fronts of buildings in such profusion and which have added greatly to the attractiveness of exterior private lighting, add relatively little to the illumination of the street surface between the curbs. Most of this private lighting, moreover, is cut off at midnight or thereabouts, leaving the city to provide the entire illumination from then until dawn.

2. Retail business streets.

Second, there are the streets of the retail business sections where a considerable amount of traffic and shopping goes on in the evening hours, although the congestion is not so great as in the category of promenade streets. These retail shopping streets require a moderately high degree of illumination with dignified lighting equip-

---

[1] State Street, in Chicago, has a public lighting installation of about 2,000 lumens per linear foot; on Washington Boulevard and Woodward Avenue in Detroit the figure is 1,900 lumens. Market Street in San Francisco gets along with 750 and Broadway in Los Angeles with about 500 lumens. For an explanation of the term "lumens," see p. 596, *note*.

ment in the way of posts and lamps. This can be supplied by the use of direct current luminous arc lamps which use copper as the upper electrode and a magnetite stick as the lower. This type of lamp has a high degree of efficiency and gives a steady light of white color. Or, as a preferable alternative, high-powered incandescent lamps of lower intensity can be used if spaced at closer intervals.[1] Too often, however, the illumination of these shopping streets is made unduly expensive by the insistence of local merchants upon fancy posts and fixtures which are costly to install and maintain but give no increased lighting efficiency.

Third come the arterial traffic streets, the cross-city thoroughfares which carry a considerable amount of rapidly moving vehicle traffic during the evening hours, but are not much used by pedestrians. Such through-streets, when the paving is good, draw large numbers of motor cars and ought to have a level of illumination to ensure safety. For there is a very close relation between poor lighting and motor accidents on streets of this type, as has been repeatedly disclosed by surveys in both American and foreign cities. In London, during the World War, the street lamps on the main thoroughfares were dimmed in order to diminish the danger from Zeppelin raids. At once the number of traffic accidents showed a marked increase. In American cities it has been estimated that about seventeen per cent of night traffic accidents are due to inadequate illumination.[2] Improved lighting has in some cases materially reduced this percentage of accidents, especially by diminishing the number which occur on arterial thoroughfares. The efficient lighting of such highways does not depend on the intensity of the illumination alone, but on its proper distribution over the whole street surface and its freedom from glare.

3. Arterial traffic streets.

In the fourth category one may place the streets of the wholesale, financial, and office districts, as well as those which serve the market and shipping sections of the city. Such streets bulk large in the day life of the community and contain vast amounts of valuable property. But they are very little used after the sun goes down, and by nine o'clock in the evening they are as quiet as a village

4. Streets in the wholesale and shopping districts.

---

[1] The gas-filled incandescent, especially the 1,000-watt lamp which produces about 20 lumens per watt, is rapidly displacing the magnetite arc. A new sodium vapor lamp, which is said to produce as high as 50 lumens per watt, may in turn displace the incandescent.

[2] Ward Harrison, O. F. Haas, and Kirk M. Reid, *Street Lighting Practice* (New York, 1930), p. 22.

roadway. Efficient public lighting here becomes a matter of police protection rather than of serving to facilitate the flow of traffic. Half as much light as is given to major retail shopping streets will usually meet the requirements. City authorities have not always recognized this fact, however, and their sense of the great importance of these streets by day seems to exert a subconscious influence upon their action in providing more light than is needed by night.

5. Residential streets: Their variety.

The four classes above named do not by any means include a majority of our urban highways. Most of the city streets come within the category of residential streets, a term which includes thoroughfares of great variety, broad and narrow, crooked and straight, with trees and without, with long rows of tenements set flush to the sidewalk or with the houses of the well-to-do standing a dignified distance back from the street line. If one were disposed to divide and subdivide the general category of residential streets, it would be possible to keep up the process almost without end. For there are major and minor residential streets, broad avenues and narrow slits between rows of tall apartment houses, long residential thoroughfares that romp along for miles, and little uptown cross-streets that start from nowhere and reach the same destination.

Their needs.

The type and the degree of illumination which are required by these residential streets must inevitably depend upon their width, their grade (whether level or hilly), the character of the abutting property, the presence or absence of shade trees, and the other factors involved. If the street is wide, level, and straight, without being heavily shaded, and not used as a through-traffic artery by night, it ordinarily has no need for a higher degree of illumination than the moonlight standard.[1] If, however, the street is narrow, crooked, heavily shaded, and considerably used after nightfall

---

[1] The amount of light given by the full moon on a clear night—which is about $1/25$th of a foot-candle. A foot-candle is the degree of illumination produced on a plane one foot distant from a single standard candle. A rough idea of a foot-candle of illumination may be obtained by trying to read a book held twelve inches away from an ordinary candle. It seems adequate at the outset but in a few minutes the reader will call for more light. A brilliantly lighted room will run to ten or more foot-candles. Lights are now usually rated in "lumens," rather than in "candle power." A lumen is the amount of light intercepted from one standard candle through an opening one foot square in a black sphere of one foot radius. In other words, one foot-candle represents one lumen falling on a square foot or ten lumens on ten square feet. Hence if foot-candles are multiplied by square feet, lumens result.

by motor traffic, the illumination requirements will run much higher.

Finally, there are alleyways and subsidiary passages in which lighting is simply a matter of police protection. There are no aesthetic considerations involved. Patrolmen, garbage collectors, and others have to wend their way through these byways after dark. Unlighted alleys become a hiding place for wrongdoers. Even less than the moonlight standard suffices in the case of these subsidiary passages.

6. Alleyways.

A serious obstacle to the efficient and economical lighting of residential streets is often found in the perverseness of the property owner. Sometimes the city pays for the installation of street lights in residential sections out of its public funds; but more often, especially in western cities, the cost of installation is levied as a local improvement tax upon the adjacent property. In either case the owners feel themselves entitled to a voice in determining what type of lighting shall be used. They have their own ideas as to what kind of lighting fixtures will look best and sometimes these ideas have been drummed into them by enterprising propagandists who have a particular type of fixture to sell. Accordingly, the actual needs of the street in the way of effective and economical illumination are often disregarded for something that is more ornate or more distinctive but which also proves more costly to maintain. Property owners (or their wives) frequently insist that the new lamps on their street shall be hung from the post like a pendant, or arranged in clusters, or placed at a designated height from the ground—merely because they think that the lamps look better that way, and altogether regardless of lighting efficiency.

The attitude of property owners.

In no department of municipal administration, as a matter of fact, has the percentage of actual waste been larger than in the field of public lighting. This is not because of corruption or intentional malfeasance on the part of the public authorities; but largely because the preference of the property owners is for equipment that sends a considerable fraction of the light elsewhere than on the street pavement where it is supposed to go. The only way to avoid such waste is to have a comprehensive public lighting program covering all the streets of the city, each of them zoned into its appropriate class, with a standardized installation prescribed for each classification. The burden of proof should then be upon those who ask for departures from the established policy.

How this often leads to waste.

598   MUNICIPAL ADMINISTRATION

Tabulations of lighting requirements.   Tabulations have been printed from time to time showing the appropriate amount of illumination required by different classes of city streets, but no two of these tables are alike. The matter is one on which the best authorities have not been able to agree. But in a general way there is a unity of opinion that promenade streets ought to have an illumination intensity of from one-half to a foot-candle, or from about five hundred to a thousand lumens per linear foot. The principal retail business streets should get along with half this intensity, while major residential streets do not usually need more than one-tenth of it. These generalizations ought not to be relied upon, however, for there are differences among streets of the same class as respects the amount of illumination that they require. The exact requirements cannot be determined by referring to tabulations or to some layman's rule-of-thumb. They ought to have careful study and exact photometer calculations on the ground.

Present-day lighting practice.   Virtually all street lighting in American cities today is now supplied by luminous arc lamps with an efficiency of from eight to twenty-five lumens per watt or by gas-filled (Mazda) incandescent lamps. The arc lamps are usually set singly, but sometimes in clusters, chiefly on the promenade and retail business streets as well as on the arterial thoroughfares. The incandescent lamp is used to a very large extent on residential streets. It has a great range, being available for street lighting in small or large units. Gas is still used for public lighting in some small cities and in the alleyways of a few larger ones, especially in those parts of the country where cheap natural gas is obtainable. But the day of gas as a public illuminant seems to have come to a close. The cost of lighting and extinguishing the gas lamps by hand has proved a serious obstacle in the competition with electricity. For many years it was hoped that someone would invent an automatic lighting and extinguishing device for gas lamps that would be safe, economical to install and to operate, dependable, and not unsightly. This hope was never realized.

Lighting equipment and efficiency.   Efficiency in street lighting depends not only upon the character of the light used, but also upon height, spacing, reflectors, and other provisions for uniformity of distribution. Not only must there be enough light, but it should be distributed so as to illuminate the entire street surface with reasonable uniformity, leaving no dark spots or shadows. Look at the full moon on a clear night. She does not give a high degree of intensity anywhere, but in point of uniform distribution, steadiness, mellowness, and the absence of glare, no system of lighting devised by the hand of man compares with lunar illumination. Street lighting should seek to approximate this ideal, which means that the lamps should not only be of the right intensity but properly located with reference to the other lights, correctly designed with reference to globes and reflectors, free from glare, and set at such an elevation that the illumination will not be intercepted by the foliage of trees. A street is no better lighted than its darkest spot.

There is no standard height or spacing for all lamps, no single type of fixture which can be profitably given city-wide adoption, and no arrangement of lamps, whether singly or in clusters, that can be set down as preferable to all others. The needs of streets in the matter of lighting are as diverse as in paving or cleaning; but unhappily most city councilmen have not come to a clear recognition of this fact. They do not venture to tell the head of the street-cleaning department what type of rotary sweeper he ought to use or what kind of pumping engine the water department should buy, but they are quite ready to pass judgment on anything connected with a public lighting installation. Many cities, even of considerable size, have no lighting plan and no lighting policy; some of them do not even have lamp maps showing where the existing lights are located. The city council merely directs that a pole be put up and a lamp placed on it whenever a few influential citizens petition for more light. The result is a haphazard allocation in which some streets get too much light, while others get too little. Most heads of families are scrupulous in avoiding any waste of artificial light in their own homes, for they know that such wastage will reflect itself on the monthly light bill. But even a flagrant and continuous waste of light on the public thoroughfares seems to make very little impression on the average mind. When a street light goes out, the neighbors will telephone their complaints, but who ever heard of their calling up to say that a street light should be turned off because the moon was adequately on the job? In ancient Athens it was calculated by Aristophanes that the light of the full moon was worth one drachma (eighteen cents) per month to every Athenian. It is worth even more than that to every city dweller in the United States, although he does not realize it.

Street lighting and the public psychology.

MUNICIPAL ADMINISTRATION

Regular and moonlight schedules. Street lights are placed on circuits and operated in accordance with a regular schedule. Most of them are turned on thirty minutes after sunset and shut off thirty minutes before sunrise. Under this all-night schedule a light burns about 4,000 hours per year. In many cases there is a variation from this all-night schedule which provides for shutting off every second or third light at midnight or even earlier. Some progressive cities have made provision whereby a considerable portion of all the lights are extinguished whenever the lunar illumination permits this to be done, but such an arrangement is by no means general. Contracts for street lighting are generally made on a basis of so much per lamp per year with a general understanding as to the number of hours involved. An adjustment is then made for reported outages or for lamps shut off at the city's request.

The cost of street lighting. The cost of public lighting in any city can be accurately calculated, but general tabulations of comparative costs for different cities are usually misleading. Such tabulations are usually figured per capita, or per lamp, or per mile of streets illuminated, or per unit of candle power, or per kilowatt hour, without reference to varying local conditions. Now and then one finds in the newspapers a set of tabloid figures which purport to show that the cost per capita, or per mile, or per something else, is a great deal higher in one city than in other communities near by. At once it is assumed that the high figure must represent waste or an overcharge. But such assumptions are usually unfair because innumerable factors enter into the actual cost of street lighting and in no two cities are these alike. The quality of the public lighting equipment (conduits, poles, reflectors, globes, etc.), the labor costs, the difference in the laws relating to maximum hours of labor and payment for overtime work by public utilities, the efficiency of the illumination on the street surface, the amount of taxes that have to be paid by the operating company, the cost of fuel, and many other matters must be taken into account when one sets out to determine what is a fair price for public lighting in any community. It makes a world of difference, for example, whether the wires are placed in conduits underground or are strung overhead in the city streets. In the latter case the city may pay a good deal less per mile for lighting, but it more than makes up the difference in the disfigurement of its highways. The cost per capita may be higher in one city than in another for the simple reason that the terms of its lighting contract require more expensive equipment and higher quality of service. The only sure way to determine whether a city is paying a private company too much for its public lighting is to have an analysis made by a qualified and impartial illuminating engineer, which is sometimes a long job and usually an expensive one.

The majority of American cities, both large and small, secure their public lighting by making contracts with electric light and power companies. A minority of them operate their own electric lighting plants. In the framing of a public lighting contract many difficult questions arise and unhappily they have not always been settled to the city's advantage. For how long a period should such a contract be made? Should the city provide the lighting equipment (mains, conduits, wires, poles, lamps, and fixtures), leaving the company to supply the current only? Or should the contract include the furnishing of this equipment? In the latter case how may the city authorities make sure that the equipment will be kept in good repair and not allowed to become obsolete? How should the intensity of the lamps be specified, and how may the full measure of intensity be maintained by adequate inspection to ensure the replacement and cleaning of lamps and fixtures? What is a fair price per annum for a street lamp of designated wattage, lumens, or candle power? What reduction should be allowed for shortened schedules, and what adjustment should be made for outages? Under what conditions should the city be permitted to terminate the contract and do its own public lighting? *Contracts for public lighting.*

These and many other difficult questions always come to the front when the representatives of a city and of the electric lighting company sit down at a table to settle the terms on which a new contract is to be made or an old one remade. On the one hand they must face the fact that a lighting contract is a document in black and white, with its terms fixed for a period of years. On the other hand there is the equally obvious consideration that the city's needs, in the matter of public illumination, are changing all the time and sometimes changing rapidly. The science of illumination is making steady progress, and the technique of public lighting is keeping pace with it. How, then, can a contract be made sufficiently rigid to protect the financial interests of both parties and yet be left sufficiently flexible to permit the standards of service to keep pace with the times? Engineers and lawyers have worked *Rigid contracts and changing technique.*

on this problem in many cities during the past fifty years and their experience is now available to cities that care to use it.

Ways of reconciling them. Appreciating the difficulty of covering every detail of service in a written contract, various cities have tried the plan of leaving all such questions to be adjusted by some impartial arbitrating body as they arise. This may be a group of arbiters, designated in part by the city and in part by the company. A common arrangement is to provide that each shall select one arbiter, leaving these two to choose the third. In practice, however, the settlement of lighting controversies by arbitration has been found to be slow, expensive, and often unsatisfactory to both sides. A better plan is to designate some governmental body, such as the state public service commission, to settle disputed points in the contract. These public service commissions are assumed to be impartial, and in most cases they prove to be so. Moreover they are provided with legal and engineering skill which enables them to get at the merits of a controversy with reasonable speed and without undue expense.

Contracts and franchises. The necessity of making any contract at all is avoided, of course, by having the city own and operate the electric lighting plant itself; but this raises the whole question of franchises and the municipal ownership of lighting plants, which are subjects to be discussed in later chapters of this book. At this point it should be explained, however, that a lighting contract and a lighting franchise are two different things. An electric lighting company cannot operate in any city without a franchise; but it may have a franchise for selling light and power to private individuals without holding a lighting contract with the city. As a rule, of course, the company has both, but its franchise runs for a longer term than its contract.

Public lighting contracts are ordinarily made for five or ten years, while franchises run for twenty years or more and sometimes for an indeterminate period. Thus, the contract may come to an end while the franchise runs on. If the contract for public lighting is not renewed, the company can still go on supplying light and power to its private customers so long as its franchise continues, and this constitutes by far the greater part of its business. In a large city the amount of current used for public lighting is not usually more than two or three per cent of the total current used for light and power. Hence it rarely pays a city to own and operate a plant for public lighting alone. To make the venture profita-

PUBLIC LIGHTING

ble it must take over the private lighting and power business also. In other words, municipal ownership must usually be prepared to go the whole way or not enter the field at all.

REFERENCES

A volume entitled *Street Lighting Practice* by Ward Harrison, O. F. Haas, and Kirk M. Reid (New York, 1930) contains a comprehensive and valuable survey of this subject. Mention should also be made of Charles J. Stahl, *Electric Street Lighting* (New York, 1929), a volume which covers all phases of the problem. Other useful books are M. Luckiesh, *Artificial Light* (New York, 1920), D. J. Bolton, *Electrical Engineering Economics* (London, 1928), William E. Mosher and others, *Electrical Utilities* (New York, 1929), Olin J. Ferguson, *Electric Lighting* (New York, 1920), C. F. Marsh, *Trade Unionism in the Electric Light and Power Industry* (Urbana, Illinois, 1928), Francis E. Cady and Henry B. Dates, *Illuminating Engineering* (New York, 1925), and the report on *Street Lighting Costs in the Larger Cities of the United States* issued by F. W. Ballard & Co. (Cleveland, 1925).

Attention should also be called to the booklet by F. L. Bird on *The Management of Small Municipal Light Plants* issued by the Municipal Administration Service (New York, 1932), and to the various *Bulletins* issued by the Edison Lamp Works of the General Electric Company at Schenectady, N. Y. Interesting discussions are included from time to time in the monthly *Transactions* of the Illuminating Engineering Society and in the monthly *Journal* of the American Institute of Electrical Engineers (33 West 39th St., New York). In 1930 the Electrical Illuminating Society (29 West 39th St., New York), through its Street Lighting Committee, prepared a "Code of Street Lighting" which has since served as a guide for street-lighting practice in the United States.

CHAPTER XLIII

MUNICIPAL AIRPORTS

Type of the wise who soar but never roam,
True to the kindred points of heaven and home.
—*Wordsworth.*

A rapid development.
The rapid expansion of airplane transportation has been one of the striking developments of the past ten years. In 1920 the airport facilities of the United States were almost entirely limited to the aërodromes of the army and navy. Today there are nearly six hundred municipal airports in the United States and an even larger number of commercial air stations.[1] Even this large number of airports, however, is by no means sufficient to meet the needs of a rapidly growing industry, and small cities are beginning to realize that they cannot remain any longer without adequate facilities in the way of air terminals. Airports are the harbors of aircraft. A community without an airport cannot use transportation by air, for air lines obviously cannot operate without landing fields any more than railroads can be run without passenger stations or steamship lines without docks.

And the penalties of haste.
The multiplication of municipal airports has been so rapid that many mistakes have undoubtedly been made in location, design, and management. Chambers of commerce and other civic organizations have frequently insisted that the municipal authorities act at once, and under pressure of urgency many airports have been constructed at sites which will ultimately prove unsatisfactory. Some of these will probably have to be abandoned at heavy loss. Political considerations, moreover, have frequently influenced the choice of airport locations, pressure being applied to the municipal authorities by influential interests with tracts of land to sell. It is inevitable that mistakes will be frequent and sometimes serious during the early stages in the development of any new utility. The science of airport planning is even yet in its infancy and it is not likely to become an exact science rapidly,

---

[1] These figures do not include intermediate landing fields, auxiliary fields, army aërodromes, navy air stations, or miscellaneous private airports.

for the experience of one community is not always a safe guide to action in another.

Every community, with its particular topography, meteorological and other local conditions, presents a different problem in the matter of selecting a satisfactory airport site. It is not possible to lay down hard and fast rules governing the selection. The problem is one which requires careful study on the ground by experts in airport engineering. Cities should not be deterred by the fact that such a study involves time and expense, for the construction of an airport involves a heavy financial investment and any errors due to deficient preliminary study are apt to be costly in the end.

The problem of a site.

Certain general requirements of an airport site are now well established. It should be a compact area of ample dimensions. Its length and breadth should be such that planes can take off or land in several directions, thus conforming to the prevailing winds. This means that a field which is located at about sea level should be spacious enough to provide landing strips of at least three thousand feet in length. In this connection it need hardly be explained that the take-off and landing areas have to be increased when the field is at a considerable elevation (say 1,000 feet or more) above sea level. This is because the lighter atmospheric densities at the higher altitudes afford less sustaining power with the result that higher speeds and longer runs are involved in landings and take-offs. In any event the site should have a firm, well-drained surface at all times and be reasonably free from surrounding obstructions. The surface should be such that it can be inexpensively graded to a slope of not more than two per cent in any direction. A perfectly level field is not desirable unless provided with catch basins and underdraining.

One of the important considerations in determining the suitability of a site for an airport is the matter of local atmospheric conditions. To a surprising degree these conditions differ within relatively short distances, even within a few miles. Fog, for example, is perhaps the most serious of all hazards to the safety of air transportation and it is well known that land located in close proximity to rivers or marshy areas is usually more susceptible to fog than is land on higher elevations. Blind flying to a landing through fog has not yet become a routine matter. Accordingly, if no suitable tract of high ground outside the fog area can be obtained within reasonable proximity to a city, it is advisable to

Meteorological factors:

1. Fog.

establish an auxiliary field which can be used in case the principal airport becomes fog-bound.

2. Smoke.   Smoke is also a detriment to safety in air transportation. Hence the location of an airport on the leeward side of a large industrial area is to be avoided because the prevailing winds are likely to carry large quantities of smoke over it, thus impairing the visibility. The direction and velocity of the wind are likewise to be taken into account. Pilots like to take off and land directly into the wind.

3. Wind constancy.   An airport which is so located in relation to the adjoining hills that it is subject to unpredictable air currents and eddies is likely to prove an undesirable field. Predictability and constancy of the prevailing wind are factors of considerable weight. Indeed it has generally been found wise to avoid selecting an airport site on the leeward side of high buildings or hills, because these obstructions, if located within a short distance of the airport, are likely to cause air conditions which militate against the safe and easy operation of the planes.

The airport approach.   A well-located airport should also permit landings and take-offs to be made in any direction without the risk of encountering either natural or artificial obstructions in close proximity to the field. Generally speaking, a plane will rise after it takes the air at a rate of one foot vertically for every seven feet travelled horizontally. In other words it will travel more than half a mile before it has achieved an elevation of five hundred feet. On its way to the landing it comes at the same ratio of descent to distance. This makes it essential that there shall be no artificial or natural obstructions extending upward into space within the zone of approach. This applies to high buildings, tall trees, smokestacks, power lines, radio masts, and more particularly to a range of hills or precipitous cliffs. No such obstructions should exist, to a height of 500 feet, within a radius of at least half a mile from the outer boundaries of the airport. This is necessary to leave a sufficient margin of safety. The close proximity of another airport likewise brings an element of hazard which it is desirable to avoid. Planes should have ample room to circle the airport at a low elevation before landing, and should be able to do this without the risk of encountering pilots who are circling for some other airport near by. Hence landing fields should be at least a mile apart, and this is not always easy to arrange when a city has several regular landing fields. In the region of New York City there are now more than thirty of them. Finally, there are obvious advantages in airport sites which can be seen from the air at considerable distances. Those situated in a pocket, obscured by surrounding high ground, are difficult to find.

Railways protect the approaches to their terminals by purchasing rights of way. Vessels have the approaches to their docks buoyed out and dredged for them. Ships of the air likewise need to have the approaches to their terminals protected for them, and the public authorities have endeavored by various means to afford such protection.[1] In some states the statutes permit the condemnation of surrounding obstructions by exercising the right of eminent domain. Zoning ordinances in some instances prohibit the future erection of any obstructions more than fifty feet in height within airport approaches on the basis of a seven to one gliding ratio. The fifty-foot exception is made because it would be obviously unjust to owners of immediately adjacent land if the right to build residential structures of normal height were denied them. When the airport is in close proximity to an already established industrial district, however, the problem of clearing the approach, and keeping it clear, is a more difficult one both at law and in fact. To compel the removal of smokestacks, electric signs, and so forth is harder than to prevent their erection. Airports should not be located in places where the problem of removal will arise.

How it can be protected.

Apart from these problems of visibility and a clear approach, there is the question of keeping the airport within convenient access for those whom it is intended to serve. This is not merely a matter of distance measured in miles, but of the time and expense in covering the ground between the airport and the downtown sections of the city. An airport site at a considerable distance from business or residential centers is not objectionable provided there are inexpensive and reasonably rapid transit facilities available. An airport served by taxicabs alone is not satisfactory, but an efficient motor-bus service will meet the requirements of economy and speed. A surface-car line does not ordinarily suffice, but a high-speed interurban railway, if one is close at hand, may be all that is needed. Moreover, since much of the airport's patronage comes by private motor car, the question of quick and easy access by

Convenience to other transportation terminals.

[1] Charles C. Rohlfling, *The Airport Approach* reprinted from the *Air Law Review*, April, 1933.

highway is important. The route between the airport and the center of the city should be direct, over well-paved and not-too-congested roads. It is not necessary, or perhaps even desirable, that the airport should be directly located on a main highway of this type, but it ought to be within convenient distance of such a route. In a word, the economy, convenience, speed, and frequency of the connecting service between the airport and the downtown urban area, including the hotels and railway terminals, are more important than the actual mileage.

Amphibian alternatives. In this connection it is desirable to keep in mind the advantage of having two airports, one on water and one on land. The past few years have witnessed some notable developments in amphibian planes and it is not improbable that the next decade will see all standard transport equipment provided with facilities for landing at both types of airport. Now it happens that practically all large American cities are located at tidewater or on lakes, rivers, or bays, hence a suitable seaplane airport can usually be provided within ready access of the central business section if the city so desires. With the development of amphibian transport planes the utilization of such centrally located water areas should go a long way toward solving the problem of accessibility for airport terminals. Passengers could then be picked up or dropped at the central water port under normal weather conditions, with the land port held in reserve as an auxiliary or emergency terminal.

The cost of land in relation to airport locations. Then there is the element of cost, which cannot be disregarded when the problem of locating an airport is under consideration. A great deal of land is needed for an airport,—from two hundred to a thousand acres. This is because the site must not only provide sufficient area for the take-off and landing strips, but also requires storage space for planes in hangars or otherwise, as well as sites for administrative offices and waiting rooms. It should also, if practicable, provide space for the parking of automobiles by those who come to the field as passengers or as friends of passengers. Some of the larger airports provide locations for a variety of other enterprises—a hotel, a restaurant, a swimming pool, a pilot's clubhouse, tennis courts, and a dance pavilion. The acquisition of so large a tract of reasonably level land, free from obstructions, natural or artificial, and provided with satisfactory channels of access to the city,—all this usually involves a large expenditure. Some of the largest air terminal locations have cost more than a million dollars. Hence city officials have occasionally been induced to eliminate the most desirable airport sites from consideration because of the high cost involved in purchasing the land. They have resorted to less satisfactory locations which happened to be available at a lower price per acre. But in the long run such action is not likely to prove economy at all. With the inevitable growth of air transportation it is almost certain that well-located airports will turn out to be profitable investments, even though the initial cost to the city may seem very large.

Various formulas have been suggested as a means of choosing between different available sites for airports. These formulas may serve a useful purpose by indicating the relative weight which ought to be given such factors as visibility, freedom from air disturbances, the absence of obstructions, convenience of access, cost of acquisition, good drainage of the ground, and so forth, but they are not of much value unless carefully applied by experts in airport engineering. For the weight to be assigned to these various considerations will depend upon the kind of patronage which the airport is likely to obtain. Some airports are used largely for long-distance travel, others for short-distance commuter service. Some are important air mail stations, while others are off the route of the regular air mail lines. Some, again, are considerably utilized by air-taxi services or by sightseeing or private planes. Still others are used for training pilots or testing planes, while some are expected to serve all these purposes, or most of them, in combination.

Relative importance of these various factors.

Convenience of access to the center of the city is obviously more vital to short-distance than to long-distance air traffic. If the airport is lacking in this convenience it cannot hope to get much commuter patronage. The absence of obstructions in the neighborhood of the field is a matter of importance under all conditions, but it becomes doubly so when the airport is used as a training base for those who are learning to fly. No hard-and-fast schedule of weighted requirements can therefore be used as a guide to the selection of an airport site, but in a general way the principal qualities of an ideal location may be recapitulated as follows: adequate area, possibility of future expansion, reasonable cost of acquisition, freedom from natural and artificial obstructions, good meteorological conditions, accessibility to the center of the city, suitable topography, reasonably level surface, satisfactory natural drainage and soil characteristics, ease of identification from

Airports and the railroads.

the air, and proximity to the already established lanes of air traffic.[1]

An airport site possessing all these advantages is, of course, not easy to find, yet it is not so difficult as might be supposed. For most cities have several stretches of waste land which can be acquired at small expense and either cut down or built up to afford a level surface. It is better to spend a good deal of money in making such land usable for airport purposes, provided it has all the other essentials, than to take a less satisfactorily located tract which needs no considerable putting in order. Adequate room for future expansion is a particularly important consideration, as the experience of the railroads with respect to their terminals has shown. In most of the large cities the original areas purchased for these terminals have long since proved wholly inadequate and surrounding property has had to be acquired for extensions at exorbitant cost. The suggestion has sometimes been made in this connection that the railroad yards which are now being used for the storage of idle cars might be roofed over and used as landing places for airplane services. It is pointed out that such locations would possess great advantages in the way of accessibility, but the problem of getting a clear approach would be, in many cases, a difficult one. Such an arrangement, moreover, would facilitate the transfer of passengers and mail from train to plane and vice versa. It would

---

[1] The following tabulation* of weighted factors was used by one important city as an aid to the selection of the best among several available sites:

Factors	Points
Freedom from fog (determined by observation)	15
Freedom from bad air currents (determined by actual flight tests)	10
Area of site (an area of 250 acres was decided upon as the required size, and sites smaller and larger were given reduced ratings in proportion)	10
Shape of site	5
Approaches and surroundings	8
Favorable prevailing winds	5
Proposed neighborhood development	4
Possibility of expansion of area	4
Accessibility to air travel (sites on the transcontinental airway were given full value, and others in proportion to distance from the airway)	10
Distance from the center of population	10
Distance from the railroad	4
Distance from the post office	10
Distance from aircraft factory sites	5
Total	100

* *Annals of the American Academy of Political and Social Science*, Volume CLI (September, 1930), p. 229.

also simplify the problem of economically supplying an airport with the large quantities of oil and gasoline which it needs to keep on hand. Finally, if air transportation ever develops to a point where considerable quantities of light freight are handled, it is self-evident that a close articulation with the railroads would be advantageous. Meanwhile the decentralization of transportation terminals is proceeding apace. Railroad, motor-bus, and air terminals are being located and maintained at varying distances apart. Whatever else may be said about such a development it is bound to increase the cost of travel.

Whenever it is proposed to locate an airport in the vicinity of a residential district, there is likely to be a chorus of protest from the entire neighborhood. And this is not surprising, for an airport is bound to be a somewhat noisy place, with dozens of planes coming and going at all hours of the day and night. Nor is there much hope that this noise can ever be eliminated. The sound made by a propeller in cutting its way through the air is likely to be heard so long as there are sensitive ears on the ground to hear it. But railway locomotives have also a high audibility, and in the early days there was a great deal of protest against the racket which they made. Now the people have become used to it and property values have adjusted themselves to the proximity of railway tracks or terminals. Some complaint has also been voiced against airports because of the dust which they are said to create, but where this nuisance exists it can be eradicated by proper surfacing of the landing areas. There are likewise those who believe that the night lighting of an airport is detrimental to the agreeableness of the neighborhood. In the case of residents whose property fronts directly on the airport grounds, this objection may be a valid one, but as respects non-contiguous property the objection can be overcome by the more careful design and shading of airport lights. *Airports as nuisances.*

Finally, there has been some discussion of the increased danger to life and property which the presence of an airport brings to the region in which it is located, and it is true that most airplane accidents occur in connection with the take-off or landing, but it should also be borne in mind that such accidents are steadily decreasing in frequency. Various other grievances of a minor sort are frequently voiced by those who live in the airport zone. It is alleged, for example, that the adjacent streets, like those surrounding a railroad terminal, become congested by the parking of *Minor objections to them.*

automobiles, which points to the desirability of providing adequate parking space within the confines of the airport itself. At any rate, whatever features of neighborhood disagreeableness it may have, an airport cannot, by its mere presence, be classed as a nuisance. However, it may become a nuisance by creating unnecessary noise or dust, and such annoyances may be abated by judicial process. Airports are public utilities and the courts have held them to be such. A city may therefore acquire by process of condemnation any land that it desires for an airport, irrespective of the wishes of owners or neighbors, provided the owners of the property are awarded just compensation.

Effects of airports on neighboring land values. What is the general effect of an airport on neighboring real estate values? The answer to this question is that we have not yet had sufficient experience to determine what the effects are likely to be. Thus far it has usually been found that the construction of an airport tends to raise neighboring values if it is located in a sparsely settled, low-priced district; but if it is placed on the borders of a high-class residential area the usual effect on land values seems to be in the other direction. Hence when the selection of an airport site is under discussion, the mercantile interests of the city insist that it be located where it will be the most readily accessible; the owners of undeveloped real estate subdivisions want it farther out where they can profit by the rise in values; while the better residential sections suggest that anywhere outside their own neighborhoods will be agreeable to them. Occasionally real estate promoters have offered a free site as an inducement to come their way. Thus the problem often becomes one of reconciling sectional preferences with considerations of suitability and cost. In such cases a compromise may be made, with results which are satisfactory to no one. A few cities have tried to solve the problem of acquiring an airport site by leasing rather than buying the land.

Aesthetic considerations in airport planning. Incidentally it may be suggested that some thought might well be given to the desirability of placing the landing field, other things being equal, at a point where the city will present a good appearance from the air. People get their initial impressions of a city from their route of approach to it. Hence many large American communities have acquired an undeserved reputation for ugliness because of the unattractiveness of the existing railroad and highway approaches. Passengers are ushered into the business district by motor-bus, or into the railway terminal through long stretches of rubbish dumps, backyards, rear balconies of tenement houses, flaming billboards, and sordid alleyways. With the growth of traffic by airplanes the importance of this aesthetic consideration will probably be recognized, but it ought to have attention before the approaches to the airport become defaced by a medley of huge painted signs on the roofs of factories and houses. Already some of the more aggressive advertisers are plastering their ballyhoo wherever it can be seen from the air in the neighborhood of the country's landing fields. Such measures as are practicable to preserve the reasonable sightliness of airport approaches deserve attention at the hands of the public authorities before it is too late.

By whom should airports be constructed and owned? Opponents of public ownership usually point to the fact that railroad and motor-bus terminals are owned and operated by private companies. Reasoning from analogy they argue that the creation and maintenance of airports should be left to private enterprise. On the other hand many steamship terminals are owned and operated by the public authorities. As a matter of fact the municipal authorities and the private companies have thus far divided the field of airport exploitation about equally between them. Public and commercial airports in the United States at the present time are not far apart in number, there being now about six hundred of each. Experience during the last ten years seems to indicate that while municipal ownership has its drawbacks in this as in other fields of business activity, it has served to some extent a useful purpose. In many instances, for example, the cities have stepped in and provided airport facilities when private enterprise has been unwilling to do it. Commercial investments are for the most part limited to communities from which a profit can be expected either at once or within a short time, and there are many small cities in which the traffic is not sufficient to maintain an airport on a profit-making basis. In such cases, if the municipality had not stepped in, there would be no air-transportation facilities at all. Many municipal airports, perhaps a majority of them, are operated at a loss and the deficit falls on the general taxpayer. In justification of this it is argued that by having an airport the city gets a place on the air map and gives the citizens an avenue of travel which they would not otherwise have. The air map, by the way, is much smaller than the rail map, as the accompanying scaled diagram discloses. The airplane has reduced the United

Public vs. private ownership of airports.

States to a fraction of its former area as respects potential rapidity of travel.

It is also contended that being on a line of air transportation, with airport facilities, is a good thing for business in any city,—a contention which does not appear to have much real basis under present conditions. Furthermore there is the argument that a municipal airport will accord equal treatment to everyone using it, whereas if the field is owned by an air-transport company, as frequently happens when it is built by private initiative, the planes

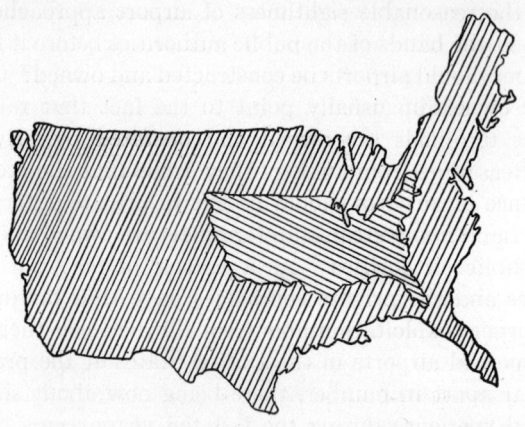

THE AREA OF THE UNITED STATES RECKONED IN TERMS OF RAIL-SPEED TRAVEL AND OF AIR-SPEED TRAVEL

of this company will get preference and all others may be given inferior service. Inter-municipal rivalry has doubtless been a more effective instigator of municipal airports than has logic or argument. When one city builds a fine field, its neighbors feel that they must be equally progressive. Out of this rivalry has developed a competition in locations and equipment. Whether for this reason or for some other, it seems to be true that municipally owned airports are for the most part larger and better equipped, although not usually better managed, than are those owned and operated by private companies. A majority of the most outstanding airports in the United States have been developed under public ownership.

Airport expenses and revenues. How much does it cost to operate an airport and how can enough revenue to cover the cost be obtained? The first part of the question does not lend itself to a confident answer because the accounts of airports have not been kept in such form that figures of comparative expenses can be readily obtained. To some extent, moreover, the cost of operating an airport depends on the overhead charges resulting from the cost of the site, and this may be anywhere from a few dollars to several thousand dollars per acre. The expense involved in making the land level is also a variable. Money for the purchase of municipal airport sites has usually been obtained by the issue of bonds, but such issues have not usually sufficed to cover the entire cost of improvements, hence a certain amount of capital outlay has been found necessary after most municipal airports are in operation. Revenue is obtained from landing fees and passenger tolls, from leased land and concessions as well as from charges for the storage of planes. Some profits are made from the sale of gasoline and oil. But relatively few municipal airports show a balance on the right side at the end of the fiscal year.

Air service, however, is a new enterprise. As such it needs encouragement. Accordingly there has been a feeling that landing facilities should be provided on a basis of ability to pay rather than on the general principle of fixing the schedule of fees at such figures as will provide a fair return on the investment. Municipal airports have served to a considerable extent as a medium through which air transportation can be subsidized from the public treasury. When the industry becomes full-grown, however, this policy will have to be abandoned. Airports, both public and commercial, will be expected to pay their way. In all probability the municipal airports will take longer to reach this point because their management is likely to be less efficient and less economical. There is no reason to expect that a municipality will manage its airports with any greater economy than its parks, public buildings, or water supply. *Maintaining public airports at a loss.*

If the various types of airport use could be kept separate, it would be appropriate to have certain fields owned by private concerns while others would more properly be kept under municipal control. In the case of airports used for training or testing purposes, there is obviously a strong presumption in favor of private ownership. Incidentally, the tendency now is to exclude this kind of flying from the regular fields because of the hazard that it creates. But those landing fields which are used in connection with the carrying of the mails, or of long-distance passengers, can put up an equally strong claim for public ownership. As it happens, how- *The case for public ownership.*

ever, most large airports perform a combination of several services. That being the case, the determination of airport ownership must be decided by local conditions. Where a private company has been prompt to come forward and build the airport, the city has usually kept out. But when no move has been forthcoming from private sources, the municipality has felt itself under obligation to step in and see that the facilities are provided even at the risk of an annual deficit.

Airport administration. When an airport is established by the municipal authorities, some arrangement must be made for administration. What department of the city government should be vested with the responsibility for its management? Should it be placed within the jurisdiction of the park department, for example, or the department of public works, or the public utilities department? Or should a separate department of aëronautics be created to take charge of it? Some cities have decided this issue in one way and some in another. It is argued that the city's park department is well equipped to take charge of the municipal airport because the problems of management are quite similar to those encountered in park administration. For the airport is a tract of land which has to be cleared, levelled, maintained, lighted, and made usable—in a word it presents problems of ground management. But equally plausible arguments can be advanced in favor of its administration by the public works department, for the airport includes not only land but buildings. It requires paved roadways, a water supply, sewerage connections, and the upkeep of its various structures,—in all of which things the public works department is assumed to be proficient. Likewise the public utilities department puts in its claim, for the air service is essentially a public utility, like a railroad or street railway, in that it serves as a common carrier and as such should be subject to regulation in the public interest. Airport management therefore includes the fixing of rates and tolls as well as the provision of facilities for carrying passengers from the airport to the center of the city.

A municipal department of aëronautics. All of these contentions, however, are more plausible than convincing. The fact is that airport administration is a new departure in municipal government. It is not exactly analogous to anything that municipalities have been doing in the past. Every consideration, save perhaps that of economy, suggests that its administration be placed in the hands of a separate department. In many cities, therefore, a department of aëronautics has been created with a director or an air board at its head. The director of the department of aëronautics is usually appointed by the mayor or by the city manager. Where an air board is created, its members are likewise appointed by the chief municipal executive. Very little can be said in favor of the board system as applied to this branch of municipal administration. On the contrary, everything points to the desirability of a unified command under a single director. A few cities, including Atlanta and San Francisco, have placed their airports under the supervision of council committees. Among all forms of airport administration this one is likely to prove the least satisfactory. When a separate department of aëronautics is created, it is usually given full charge of the construction, extension, maintenance, and operation of the city's facilities for air transportation. In case the city has a seaplane landing area, this also is placed under the department's jurisdiction. When the department has a director at its head, he usually serves as the airport manager with the assistance of a field superintendent and various other subordinates.

One of the functions of good management is the promotion of business at the airport. This promotion work takes a variety of forms but is mainly directed to impressing upon the public the relative safety and convenience of travel by air. A well-planned and well-regulated airport, at which planes arrive with clock-like regularity, is in itself an impressive advertisement for the new method of travel.

REFERENCES

The best book on this subject is Henry V. Hubbard, Miller McClintock, and Frank B. Williams, *Airports: Their Location, Administration, and Legal Basis* (Cambridge, Mass., 1930), a volume to which the foregoing chapter is considerably indebted. Mention should also be made of Archibald Black, *Civil Airports and Airways* (New York, 1929) and *Transport Aviation* (2nd edition, New York, 1929), Thomas G. Holt, *Aërial Transport* (London, 1920), I. A. E. Edwards and F. Tymms, *Commercial Air Transport* (London, 1926), R. R. Bennett, *Aviation: Its Commercial and Financial Aspects* (New York, 1929), Donald Duke, *Airports and Airways* (New York, 1927), T. H. Kennedy, *An Introduction to the Economics of Air Transportation* (New York, 1924), James G. Woolley and Earl W. Hill, *Airplane Transportation* (Hollywood, Calif., 1929), and Stedman S. Hanks, *International Airports* (New York, 1929).

An extensive discussion of "Airport Problems of American Cities" by Austin F. Macdonald is printed as a Supplement to the *Annals of the American Academy of Political and Social Science*, Vol. CLI, pp. 225–283 (September, 1930), and a discussion of *Airports as a Factor in City Planning* by Ernest P. Goodrich was issued as a Supplement to the *National Municipal Review*, Vol. XVII, pp. 181–194 (March, 1928). The Aëronautics Branch of the United States Department of Commerce has issued a number of bulletins dealing with airport problems, *e.g.*, Bulletin No. 5 on *Airports and Landing Fields* (revised edition, January, 1930), and Bulletin No. 17 on *Airport Management* (July, 1929). Good articles on municipal airports (with bibliographies) are usually included in the annual issues of *The Municipal Index*, and a periodical entitled *Airports* (published monthly) contains current discussions.

The legal aspects of air transport are covered in C. F. G. Zollman, *Law of the Air* (Milwaukee, 1927) and *Cases on Air Law* (St. Paul, 1932), R. W. Fixel, *Law of Aviation* (New York, 1927), and F. J. Davis, *Aëronautical Law* (Los Angeles, 1930).

CHAPTER XLIV

URBAN TRANSPORTATION

Man is created of hastiness.—The Koran.

During the past century urban transportation has passed through four stages. Prior to 1850 no city made any general provision for transporting its people from one section to another. There were stage coaches, of course, which went from city to city, and in some of the larger communities these conveyances carried passengers from the outlying sections into the central portions of the town. But this form of transit was relatively expensive, hence it became necessary for the great majority of people to live within walking distance of their work. Then, first of all, horse-car lines were laid, the earliest being established in New York City in 1852. They proved popular from the start, and within the next twenty-five years this method of passenger transportation found general adoption in the larger communities.

All these horse-car lines were built and operated by private companies under franchises which were given to them for long terms. New companies were formed as the demand for service increased, so that eventually it became common to find several companies operating in different parts of the same city. A single horse or a pair of horses formed the motive power; the cars were small and the rails were light; hence the companies did not have to be heavily capitalized and it was practicable for them to engage in transportation on a small scale, sometimes confining their operations to a single long street. Eventually, however, there took place a merging or consolidation of the various small companies until in most cities a single organization managed to obtain complete control. This merging of the old horse-power lines was frequently accompanied by a good deal of financial manipulation and an inflation of capital beyond the actual values.

Transportation by horse cars, however, was never entirely satisfactory.[1] It was slow and could not be operated readily on heavy grades. The cars were small and could not carry many passengers

History of urban transit:

1. Horse-car lines.

Duplications and mergers.

Drawbacks of horse-car transportation.

---

[1] G. F. Train, *Observations on Horse Railways* (London, 1860).

at once, and the service was usually infrequent. During the winter months in the colder sections of the country a snowstorm often put the whole system out of commission, and in any event there was no convenient way of keeping the cars heated. Accordingly inventors turned their attention to the development of some form of mechanical power which could be utilized to propel the cars. Steam propulsion was tried but quickly proved impractical in the city streets. Failure also attended various experiments with compressed air, coal gas, and carbonic acid as agencies for supplying motive power.

2. Cable car lines.

The first experiment with artificial motive power to achieve any considerable measure of success was embodied in the so-termed cable car, perfected about 1875. This was a car operated by a continuous cable which ran in a conduit beneath the street surface and was itself driven by steam power at a central plant. To this endless cable the car attached itself by means of a grip or clutch and was drawn along at a rate of six or eight miles per hour. It was brought to a stop by releasing this grip and applying the brakes. But there were technical difficulties involved. For one thing it required great skill on the part of the "gripman" to avoid disagreeable jolts in starting or stopping, inasmuch as the cable was kept running at a uniform speed. To install a cable car system, moreover, involved a heavy investment, for the expense included not only the cars and tracks but street excavations, conduits, cables, and a central power station. Moreover, in the winter months snow and ice often clogged the narrow slot through which the grip made its contact with the cable. Nevertheless the cable car would probably have enjoyed a longer career if the electric trolley had not so quickly made its appearance, but against the competition of the trolley it had no chance. The latter system cost less to install and less to operate. It provided cars of greater and more flexible rates of speed. These cars, moreover, could be started and stopped without jolting their passengers. So cables and conduits went to the scrap heap, but not before large amounts of capital had been invested and lost in cable enterprises.

3. Surface trolley car lines.

Experiments in the propulsion of street cars by electric motors were carried on during the late seventies, but it was not until after 1880 that the electric railway first demonstrated its commercial possibilities. Several American communities, including Richmond, Kansas City, Cleveland, and Baltimore claim to have had the earliest installation of street cars operated by electricity, but the fact seems to be that all four of them inaugurated this form of transportation on a small scale at about the same time. The new trolley cars at once achieved great popularity, for they showed themselves capable of travelling at a speed of fifteen or twenty miles an hour, which was an altogether unprecedented rapidity in urban transportation. During the next few years, accordingly, there was a widespread public demand for electric trolleys. The insistence was so strong in many instances that the horse-car companies, which held a strategic position through their ownership of unexpired franchises, were able to utilize this public clamor to their own advantage. Frequently they held out and would not agree to electrify their lines except on the condition that their franchises should be extended for long terms, or in some cases granted to them in perpetuity.

The change in motive power put a new face on the whole street railway problem. Stables gave place to electric power plants. Cars were doubled or even trebled in size, taking up more room in the streets. Moreover these heavy cars now moved at a rapid pace, increasing the danger to horse-drawn traffic and to pedestrians. Heavier rails had to be laid, and special foundations provided for them in the street pavements. Trolley poles, moreover, were now set in the sidewalks, with wires strung over the middle of the street, thus contributing to the defacement of the thoroughfares. Nevertheless a spirited competition took place among merchants on the main business streets, each group trying to swing the car lines to the highways in front of their own stores. Property on streets served by the new trolley lines increased in value, sometimes out of proportion to the benefit which the change brought with it. *A new era in urban transportation.*

All this gave opportunity for a good deal of financial juggling. The amount of money invested, and hence the capitalization of the street-car companies, underwent a vast increase. This expansion of capital structures often brought with it a good deal of stock-watering and other financial manipulation. Franchise values were capitalized along with rolling stock and other tangible assets. All this could be done without raising the five-cent fare which had been customary on the horse-car lines because the operating cost per passenger mile was lowered by using the new motive power. But the apparent prosperity of the traction companies soon drew the envious eyes of local politicians and in self-defense the corpora- *Street railway financing.*

tions frequently found themselves compelled to take a hand in municipal elections. In many places they became contributors to the campaign funds and maintained a powerful lobby at the city hall.

Rapid growth of the service. On the whole, however, the new service was exceedingly popular with its patrons, and the trolley lines kept spreading year after year until they had penetrated even small communities which could not supply enough patronage to make the business profitable. The companies discounted future growth too heavily. Some of them found financial salvation by linking themselves into a network of interurban lines, thus entering into competition with the steam railways. These interurban lines, situated mainly in New England, the Middle Atlantic states, and the Middle West, now include over forty per cent of the total electric railway mileage. In 1885 there were only about a hundred miles of electric railway trackage in the United States, but in 1930 this had expanded to nearly fifty thousand miles. During the year 1860 the horse-car lines of New York City carried about fifty million passengers; in 1930 the elevated, subway, and surface lines of this metropolis carried a total of more than two billion passengers. Taken together the electric street railways of the United States carry more than ten times as many passengers as the steam railroads.

The ratio of traffic to population. It is an axiom of transportation that the need for increased facilities develops more rapidly than the growth of population. The bigger the city, in other words, the more street railway traffic there is per thousand of population. In a city of a million people it has been estimated that under normal conditions there will be about a hundred paid fares per annum for every head of population; but in a city of five million there will be about four hundred paid fares per capita. These figures are sometimes reduced by the active operation of motor-busses which enter into direct competition with the street cars. But contrary to the popular impression the general use of private automobiles has not disastrously reduced the amount of street-car patronage. To be sure, the private automobile has made the well-to-do independent of the rails, but the great bulk of the population in most cities still continues to use the street cars. The automobile has cut into the Sunday and holiday patronage of the street railways, but on the other hand it has helped to develop the riding habit among the people on other days. It has tended to make walking unfashionable and to that extent has indirectly stimulated street railway business.[1]

There is a limit, however, to the number of cars which can be operated upon the city streets, and this means that when the population of a community reaches a certain point, surface transportation by street cars becomes more and more unsatisfactory. With the congestion of other traffic the average speed of the street car has been seriously cut down. In most large cities it does not now average more than ten to twelve miles per hour, and as respects transportation between the downtown and outlying sections this is too slow to be satisfactory. The suburbanite wants to be within a half-hour of his work. Hence it has become necessary to meet the competition of the street railways, so far as commuter traffic is concerned, by taking long stretches of street-car lines off the congested streets. To accomplish this there are only two practicable alternatives, namely, to put the tracks overhead or to put them underground. Some cities have tried one plan and some the other, while a few have experimented with both. Some have built elevated structures to carry the rails, while others have dug subways. New York and Boston have tried both plans on an extensive scale. *Street congestion and the need for rapid transit.*

Rapid transit presents some new and difficult problems. For example, should surface cars and rapid transit lines be operated by the same company as part of a single system? Or should they be operated separately? On the one hand it has been argued that unification saves overhead expense and facilitates the transfer of passengers from one branch of the transportation system to the other. Hence it benefits both the owners and the patrons. Under unified control it is also contended that the transportation system of the city can be better planned and coördinated as a whole. But on the other hand it is apparent that the two systems of transit are different in their problems and are subject to dissimilar demands. Surface transportation, to be satisfactory, must provide service of high frequency at a low rate of fare and preferably at a flat rate. The lines must also be rather ubiquitous and have stopping places at close intervals because people will not walk long distances in order to reach the surface cars. Service on rapid transit lines does *Some rapid transit problems.*

---

[1] The Boston Elevated Railway (which operates surface cars, elevated lines, and subways in the Boston metropolitan district) was carrying about a million passengers each week day in 1917. It was still carrying substantially that number in 1932, but patronage on Sundays and holidays fell off about twenty per cent during this fifteen-year interval.

not need to be so frequent, or so low-priced, or carried so close to the patron's place of abode; but it must be speedy.

This means, of course, that elevated and subway trains must run without frequent stops to take on or leave off passengers. One system transports passengers in relatively small groups at a moderate rate of speed over relatively short distances, while the other handles larger bodies of long-haul traffic at a much more rapid rate and at higher fares. In view of this difference in problems it is sometimes argued that elevated and subway lines should be operated independently of the surface traction system, but this arrangement has not generally commended itself either to the transportation companies or to the public authorities. When rapid transit became a necessity in the larger cities, the surface car companies were usually requested to provide it as an adjunct to their existing systems. In some instances, however, a separate company was formed to build and operate the elevated lines, while the city itself constructed the subways and leased them to either the surface company or to a new operating corporation.

Elevated *versus* subway transit.
The elevated system of rapid transit has only one advantage over the subway—it is cheaper to build. But as against this consideration of initial economy there is the serious obstruction to surface traffic which is caused by the supporting pillars, and there is the public objection to elevated lines as monstrosities of noise and unsightliness. Nor, indeed, is the economy so great as was anticipated, especially in parts of the city where property valuations are high. This is because owners of private property on both sides of an elevated railway feel that they are entitled to damages by reason of the fall in property values which results from the presence of the structure, and the courts have usually upheld their claims. The cost of liquidating these damages is sometimes very large. Regarded simply as an engineering enterprise it costs much less to elevate car tracks than to place them underground, but a subway does little or no damage to private property and this advantage tends to offset the difference in construction costs, especially in the zone of high values.

Effect on property values.
Moreover, one should take into account the damage to public property, that is, to the street and to the general appearance of the neighborhood. This does not have to be liquidated in monetary compensation to anyone, but it is a matter of consequence in days when large sums are being spent in city planning to improve the

sightliness of urban communities. Elevated structures have proved a detriment to the business districts of cities by congesting the streets, lowering property values, discouraging the erection of new buildings, and driving high-class establishments out of the immediate neighborhood. Subways, on the other hand, relieve traffic congestion and tend to increase property values. On the whole it seems probable that no more elevated lines will be built in the downtown districts of cities, and it is not unlikely that some of those now standing will ultimately be removed. Some such removals have already taken place. In the outer suburban areas, however, the elevated may well continue to hold its own because the cost of providing subway transit over long and thinly populated stretches of territory is virtually prohibitive.

Everywhere the people desire subways as a means of solving their rapid transit problems, but the question whether a subway can be profitably built and operated is obviously dependent upon the amount of traffic which is waiting to be carried. This, again, depends in a general way upon the population of the region traversed. The cost of carrying a subway passenger is made up of two items—overhead or fixed charges, and operating or current charges.[1] The first includes interest on the capital invested in the subway and rolling stock together with provision for the amortization of this investment. Such overhead expenses have to be borne irrespective of whether the amount of traffic is large or small. The second element in the cost of carrying a passenger is the operating expenses. This includes such items as the wages of the employees, the cost of supplying power to the cars, the wear-and-tear on rolling stock, and so on—all of which vary with the volume of traffic. In the case of surface cars the overhead cost per passenger-mile is relatively small, while the operating cost is relatively large. Subway cars are run in trains with a consequent saving of wages, and since they travel at high speed it is possible to carry a great many passengers per hour. This economy of operation is such that a subway can be profitably operated, despite high overhead charges, if there is enough traffic to employ its full capacity or nearly so. *Making a subway pay.*

But transit facilities are never used to their full capacity except at certain hours of the day, and not always even then. During at least eighteen hours out of every twenty-four the cars average *The uneven distribution of the passenger load.*

[1] For a detailed discussion of the subject see American Transit Association, *Economics of Rapid Transit* (New York, 1929).

much less than their potential capacity. In ordinary service a
large proportion of the traffic flows inward and outward during the
early morning and late afternoon hours. The peak load for the
entire year is almost always reached during the late afternoon
hours of the days just preceding Christmas. And in general it is by
no means uncommon for a street railway system to carry as much
as thirty-five or forty per cent of the entire day's traffic during
four or five hours out of the twenty-four. That is why people who
rarely use the cars except in going to or coming from their work
get the fixed notion that the cars are always crowded to capacity
and that the street railway system must be making a great deal of
money. But when the traffic is averaged over the whole working
day the figures tell an altogether different story. Reckoned on
that basis there are many more seats than passengers.

Absence of the diversity factor. In other words, the "diversity factor," which is of great assistance in the smooth operation of other public utilities, does not operate in the case of street railways at all. A passenger either rides or does not ride, hence there is no such thing as a quarter-load or a half-load so far as any one patron is concerned. A customer can reduce his use of gas or electricity by any desired percentage, but a patron of the street cars cannot easily do anything of that sort if he lives some miles away from his work. Hence the increases or decreases in street railway patronage are sometimes sharp and sudden. An electric lighting plant, moreover, can reduce its daily peaks by building up a demand for power during those hours when there is little demand for light; but a street railway has little or no opportunity of doing this. In handling peak loads, moreover, the street railway power stations and the electric lighting plant can be of relatively little assistance to one another because the maximum demand for current usually comes upon both at exactly the same time, that is, in the late afternoon hours of the pre-Christmas days. Were the two peaks at different times, each plant could help out the other.

Some problems arising from it. One of the serious practical difficulties connected with street railway operation arises from this uneven distribution of the load. The entire rolling stock and the maximum labor force is needed during the rush hours; then many cars have to be laid off for the rest of the day. But the overhead cost of this rolling stock goes on just the same,—interest on the investments, depreciation, and maintenance. This adjustment of service to traffic is one of the hardest problems in street railway operation. Utilizing the full time of employees likewise becomes a matter of difficulty; but schedules are worked out so that each conductor and motorman is provided with his assigned number of hours per day, which means that they must work in broken shifts. As a rule, moreover, a number of relief men, or extra men, are put on during rush hours. These are paid for the time they work, but usually with a guaranteed minimum per week. Arranging the work time-tables in such way that everyone will be kept within the maximum number of hours and yet be able to take care of the traffic satisfactorily is an enterprise that requires a high degree of expertness.

The street railway differs from every other public utility in that the rate of fare does not usually bear a direct relation to the amount of service which the passenger receives. Gas and electricity are sold by meter, hence the customer pays for what he uses. Water is now supplied on the same basis because cities have generally abandoned the old method of charging a lump sum for water service. The telephone companies for a long time provided their facilities to patrons at a flat rate within certain zones, but in most cities the measured-service plan is now being substituted. Steam railroads base their rates on mileage; so do motor-busses and taxicabs. In any of these utilities if you were to propose that every passenger be charged a fixed sum irrespective of the service which he receives, you would not only find your proposal promptly rejected but you would give people a poor opinion of your intelligence. Even parcel post rates are on a zone basis. Street-car fares continue to be the one outstanding exception to all this. In most street-car systems you pay a designated sum and ride as far as you wish by getting transfers when necessary. In a few cities, however, the zone system has recently made its appearance and an additional fare is charged to those passengers who ride beyond a certain limit.

The flat fare on street railways.

The use of the flat fare on American street railways is the outcome of an accident, fortified by habit. When horse-car lines were established, the maximum ride rarely exceeded a mile or two and the fare was placed at five cents. No attempt was made to grade the fares according to distance because of the inconvenience which would have been involved in making change. Then came the electrification of the lines and their extension over longer distances. The average ride per passenger lengthened, but the five-cent fare

American and European practice contrasted.

had become one of the traditions of urban life and the companies did not venture to alter it. "One city, one fare," became the slogan. That is not what happened in the cities of Great Britain. There the transportation companies have always adjusted their fares to the distance travelled. The farther you ride in London the more you pay. The English currency system facilitates doing this without inconvenience. The zone-fare plan is sound economics and, in the long run, good public policy. In the United States, however, the transit companies were able to maintain the five-cent fare for many years by increasing their business and introducing various economies; but with the steadily rising cost of transportation together with a reduction in traffic due to motor competition, the nickel ride has had to be abandoned in many cities. In some of them the flat rate has now been raised to six, seven, or even ten cents, but the adherence to uniformity is still fairly general.

The injustice of uniform fares.

A uniform fare is unjust to both the street railway company and its patrons, because the cost of carrying a passenger varies directly with the distance travelled.[1] The situation differs from city to city, but it has been estimated that under present conditions of cost and service a street railway company breaks even on the passenger who rides from two to three miles in a surface car for a five-cent fare. This means that the company makes money on every passenger who rides less than that distance and loses money on those who exceed it. In other words the downtown traffic gets less than it pays for, while the suburban passenger profits thereby. It likewise means that when a company operates under a flat fare it will naturally do everything it can to encourage short-haul traffic and nothing whatever to promote travel over long distances.

Flat fares and suburban development.

This points to the fundamental weakness which inheres in the flat-rate system. It is good public policy to get people out into the suburbs, thus relieving the congestion in the downtown areas. The street railway system ought to be a powerful factor in promoting this movement, yet it cannot serve as such except to its own financial detriment so long as it is required to carry everyone for a uniform five-, six-, or ten-cent fare. Moving the population to the outlying districts means that the amount of long-distance traffic will increase more rapidly than the amount of short-haul

[1] For a full discussion, see D. C. Jackson and D. F. McGrath, *Street Railway Fares: Their Relation to Length of Haul and Cost of Service* (New York, 1917), also Henry W. Blake and Walter Jackson, *Electric Railway Transportation* (2nd edition, New York, 1924), pp. 185–214.

traffic, and hence that the street railway company will find itself carrying an ever-increasing percentage of passengers at a loss. Economic justice and good public policy, therefore, demand that some arrangement be devised whereby these two objectives can be reconciled. Already the zone-fare system has been established on interurban street railways and in the course of time it will doubtless be applied to intra-urban systems as well. Only by some such device can the street railways be placed on a basis of sound financial operation.

Reference has been made to the fact that the cost of transportation has been greatly increased during the past generation by the rising rate of wages. The wages of labor form the largest element in the cost of street railway operation. For the degree of skill and the amount of experience involved in the operation of street cars, the level of wages has been pressed to a relatively high point. The work of a conductor or motorman necessitates a comparatively small amount of education or special training, far less than what is involved in most of the skilled vocations. But the general level of wages in the street railway service has been held up by two influences, first, the thorough organization of street railway employees and, second, the intervention of the public authorities whenever labor controversies arise. Street railways operate under the terms of a franchise and this is assumed to give the public authorities a right to insist upon concessions by the company whenever the danger of a strike for higher wages arises. A tie-up of the transportation system is likely to cause such a heavy loss to any community that street railway employees have had a marked advantage in bargaining for wages and terms of employment. Hence it is that they are among the best-paid workers in any community when one takes into account the moderate amount of skill required in the performance of their work. *Street railways and the wage problem.*

One of the serious problems confronting the street railway in recent years has been that of meeting motor competition. This includes competition from private cars, taxicabs, and more particularly from motor-busses. Motor-bus competition has been especially difficult to meet because the motor-bus has no tracks or trolley to keep in repair and no franchise taxes to pay. Motor-busses are usually under no obligation to maintain service when weather conditions are bad, or to pay their employees a designated rate of wages, or to assume bonded liability for accidents. They *Motor competition.*

change their rates whenever they feel like it, give no transfers to anyone, and no free rides to policemen, firemen, postmen, or other public officials, and when anyone rides on a motor-bus beyond a given distance he pays accordingly.

Moreover, they are not required by existing laws to pay their proper share of the public taxes.[1] The injustice of this has not been fully realized by the public. Some people are shortsighted enough to imagine that vigorous competition between street cars and motor-busses, each trying to undercut the other, must redound in the long run to the public advantage. Such unregulated competition, however, can have no other result than to impair the service rendered by both these utilities and eventually to increase the cost of transportation. In recognition of this fact, motor-busses are now being brought under regulation but as yet it is not particularly stringent. In some cities the street-car companies have countered by entering the motor-bus field and are using this form of transportation as a supplement to their own. American street railway companies have virtually stopped extending their lines into newly developed areas. Instead they are applying for bus franchises.

Taxicabs. In the larger cities an appreciable amount of the passenger traffic is carried by taxicabs.[2] These vehicles are patronized by people who desire more expeditious transportation than the surface cars provide, or who are carrying baggage with them, or who are going to places which the street-car lines do not serve. Patrons of hotels, theaters, and steam railways provide a good deal of the patronage which comes to these conveyances. Taxicabs, for the most part, are operated by companies and are subject to a certain amount of public regulation, chiefly as respects the rates of fare which they are permitted to charge. In most cases these rates are a combination of the flat-fare and mileage, with a minimum rate for the first half-mile and a graded charge thereafter. Public authorities are now fairly well agreed that taxicabs should be regulated by limiting their number, by compelling them to remain at stands rather than go cruising through congested streets, by requiring a high standard of equipment, and by prescribing the maximum fares to be charged. It is likely that cities will eventually adopt the policy of giving a single company the exclusive right to operate

[1] On this question see the National Conference Board's report on *The Taxation of Motor Vehicle Transportation* (New York, 1932).

[2] In 1930 there were nearly 20,000 taxicabs in New York City and they carried about 350,000,000 passengers during the year.

taxicabs in their streets, for it is much easier to enforce regulations under such an arrangement.

Street railways operate under public franchises. They are not permitted to use the streets, whether for surface cars, elevated structures, or subways, save in accordance with the terms of such franchises. In earlier days these franchises were granted by city councils and did not extend beyond the city limits. Accordingly a company which operated in several adjoining municipalities needed to have several franchises, and these frequently differed in their terms as well as in their dates of expiry. This inevitably led to complications and produced a situation which was unsatisfactory both to the company and to the public. Hence the state legislatures frequently intervened and assumed general supervision of the franchise-granting power. Along with this in many cases went the regulation of street railways as a state function. Public utility commissions were set up with state-wide jurisdiction over them. Today, in most cities, the municipal authorities have relatively little control over the fares or the quality of the service within their own boundaries. When the public authorities or the companies desire any change in the existing arrangements it is necessary to go before the state railway commission or some similar body which has statutory power to grant or deny the request.[1] *Street railway franchises.*

In return for their franchise privileges the street railway companies are subject to taxation, but the methods of levying these taxes vary in different parts of the country. Sometimes the tax is fixed at so much per annum for every mile of track or for every car used. This is not a satisfactory plan because it discourages the extension of service. More often the annual tax payment is based upon the value of the company's stock, or upon its gross earnings. An ad valorem tax on real estate owned by a street railway company is not usually a good arrangement where the company operates in more than one city, because it is impracticable for the assessors in each municipality to make a fair valuation of the street railway's property within its own bounds. To arrive at a proper valuation of a company's real estate one must take the road as a unit, as a going concern. On the whole it is usually found best to let the state do the taxing on a basis of gross earnings and then distribute the proceeds on some equitable basis among the cities in which the street railway operates. *Street railway taxation.*

[1] For a further discussion, see Chapter XLV.

The public attitude on this question.

As respects the taxing of street railways, however, there is a good deal of cloudiness in the public mind. Many people seem to think that the more the city can squeeze out of an operating company, the better it is for everyone except the stockholders. But it ought to be a self-evident proposition that whatever is levied on the street railways in the way of taxes must ultimately be borne by the car riders. It can come from no other source. All the revenue of the street railway is derived from its patrons, and it follows that all assessments levied upon it must be paid by them in the form of higher fares or more restricted service. It does not profit the city anything, in the long run, to make the street railway company pay for a share of the street paving on highways used by the cars, as has often been done in deference to popular sentiment. It merely means that the company collects the cost from its passengers. Heavy taxes and other public obligations upon a street railway are nothing more than devices whereby these burdens are shifted from the taxpayers to the car riders. Such taxes are particularly inequitable because the car riders are drawn for the most part from those elements of the community which can least afford the additional burden.

Service at cost.

A few large cities (including Boston, Cleveland, Cincinnati, Rochester, and Dallas) have tried the experiment of putting their street railways on a basis of service at cost. This is an arrangement whereby the rate of fare is automatically adjusted to the total cost of providing the service. In Boston the management of the street railway system is in the hands of the public authorities, although the property still belongs to the stockholders. In Cleveland the management remains in the hands of the street railway company subject to official control. Fundamentally it is a sound principle that a passenger should get what he pays for and pay for what he gets, but there are political difficulties in the way of carrying this principle into practice. The operation of a privately owned property by a board of public officials is an arrangement which seems to have the disadvantages of both company and municipal management with the advantages of neither. It usually means that the service will be given at less than cost and that the taxpayer will make good the deficit. There may be a halfway house between private and public ownership, but as a practical matter it is difficult to find.

American street railways have had a hard time of it during

recent years, with patronage declining more rapidly than expenses could be reduced. They have found their car loads and their income dwindling, while public utility commissions insist on high standards of service. The average citizen will gladly pay a hundred dollars for a more up-to-date automobile than his neighbor's, but he groans at the thought of an extra cent or two on the established street-car fare. Yet it ought to be obvious that when the street railway system cannot make both ends meet on a specified fare, there is nothing to be gained from the attempt to compel its operation at a loss. New York retains a five-cent fare, but it is nothing but a political slogan. The average ride in that city costs about eight cents and the taxpayer makes good the difference. Perhaps it is justifiable to have it that way, for the street railway is an essential public industry, hence some method for ensuring its continuous operation must be devised. If the public will not pay in one way, it must pay in another.

The future of our street railways.

This being the case, there are many who believe that the best solution of the urban transportation problem lies in the direct ownership and operation of the street railways by the municipal authorities. Three large American cities, San Francisco, Seattle, and Detroit, have undertaken experiments with municipal ownership of street railways. They have now acquired a considerable amount of experience in this field, but the municipally owned portion of the entire street railway mileage in the United States is less than two per cent. The general question of municipal *versus* private ownership of public utilities, however, is one of sufficient importance to have separate consideration in the next two chapters.

REFERENCES

Among important sources of information in this field are Stuart Daggett, *Principles of Inland Transportation* (New York, 1928), especially chap. v, H. W. Blake and W. Jackson, *Electrical Railway Transportation* (2nd edition, New York, 1924), E. S. Mason, *The Street Railway in Massachusetts* (Cambridge, 1932), H. C. Clark, *Service at Cost Plans* (New York, 1920), American Transit Association, *The Urban Transportation Problem* (New York, 1932), American Electric Railway Association, *Electric Railway Practices in 1925*, edited by H. H. Norris (New York, 1926), Delos F. Wilcox, *San Francisco's Street Railway Problem* (San Francisco, 1927), E. L. Lobdell, *Chicago's Transportation Problem* (Chicago, 1930), E. H. Spengler, *Land Values in New York in Relation to Transit*

Facilities (New York, 1930), G. L. Wilson, *Motor Traffic Management* (New York, 1928), Percival White, *Motor Transportation of Merchandise and Passengers* (New York, 1923), and the *Report of the Mayor's Commission on Taxicabs* (New York, 1930).

A great deal of valuable information is contained in the *Proceedings of the Federal Electric Railway Commission* (3 vols., Washington, 1921), and a summary of these *Proceedings* has been printed under the title *Analysis of the Electric Railway Problem* by Delos F. Wilcox (New York, 1921). In the publications issued by the Regional Plan of New York and Its Environs (Vol. IV) there is a discussion of *Transit and Transportation* by H. M. Lewis, W. J. Wilgus, and D. L. Turner (New York, 1928).

Statistics relating to this industry are published quinquennially by the United States Bureau of the Census, the latest compilation giving the figures for 1930 (Washington, 1933). *McGraw's Electric Railway Manual* and *Poor's Manual of Public Utilities*, both of which are revised annually, give current financial data on street railway systems.

The Electric Railway Journal is published monthly in New York. Interesting articles are published in *Aëra*, which is also a New York monthly publication devoted to transportation matters. An excellent article on "Municipal Transit," with further references, especially on street railway problems in European cities, may be found in the *Encyclopaedia of the Social Sciences*, Vol. XI, pp. 118–128 (New York, 1933).

CHAPTER XLV

THE CONTROL OF PUBLIC UTILITIES

> Forced into virtue thus, by self-defence,
> Even kings learned justice and benevolence;
> Self-love forsook the path it first pursued,
> And found the private in the public good.
> —*Alexander Pope.*

What is a public utility? Ordinarily it is a private enterprise which provides some essential or important service to the public. But not every service upon which the public depends for its existence or comfort is a public utility. Bread and meat are among the essentials of community life, but the bakery and the meat market are not public utilities. A public utility is a specialized type of business enterprise which, though under private ownership, makes use of public property and is a natural monopoly. What is a public utility?

The chief public utilities operating in cities are railroads, street railways, telegraph and telephone systems, water supply facilities, gas plants, and electric light and power plants. All of these find it necessary to use property which belongs to the people. A railroad must run its tracks across the public highways; a gas company finds it necessary to lay its pipes beneath the pavements; an electric lighting company must put some of its poles in the streets; and a street railway company, as its name implies, must make large use of the public thoroughfares. Moreover, they all desire the right to take by condemnation whatever private property they may need for their terminals, power houses, gas tanks, stations, and so on,—which is a right that only the governmental authorities can give. The right of eminent domain cannot be exercised except for a public purpose, hence any private enterprise which secures such a right is in a legal sense a public utility. The most characteristic legal earmark of a public utility, therefore, is its possession of special privileges in relation to public property. The lawyer's definition.

But public utilities are differentiated from ordinary business concerns in an economic as well as in a legal sense, for otherwise why should they be regulated in a different way from all other forms of business? The answer is that competition operates and The economist's definition.

affords protection in the one case but not in the other. In ordinary business, competition is a sufficient spur to low prices and good service. Sometimes it accomplishes too much in these directions. In any event, the customer who finds prices high or service poor at one drug store or haberdashery stops trading there and goes somewhere else. The merchant who is not satisfied with one jobber shifts his business to another. The wholesale dealer, if one factory does not send his goods promptly, or charges him too much, merely transfers his patronage to some other factory. All forms of ordinary business are in competition with other establishments of their own kind and, save to the extent that they are protected by industrial codes, must meet this competition in order to survive. Hence the rivalry of those who have goods or services to sell has usually been sufficient to afford the public a reasonable degree of protection against excessive prices and deficient quality. It has sometimes been possible, however, to stifle competition by some form of combination, and monopolies created in this way have been called artificial monopolies, for they are due to the cupidity of man.

Natural monopolies. But public utilities such as railroads, street railways, telegraph and telephone lines, water supply systems, as well as gas and electric plants, are natural monopolies. Freedom of trade, from the customer's point of view, does not exist in their case. Their rates and the quality of their service are not determined (or are determined to a very slight degree) by competition with other public utilities. The individual customer has rarely any choice but to take what is given him. If he desires to travel from one part of the city to another, he is not often so fortunate as to find two street railways competing for his patronage. If he thinks that the rates for gas are exorbitant, he cannot tell the company that he will buy gas from someone else, for he is dealing with the only concern which provides the service to houses on his street. The man who lives in Yonkers can send to New York City and buy his groceries there if he doesn't like the prices and quality which prevail in his own neighborhood, but he cannot get his telephone service or his electric light that way. For each form of public utility service he finds that there is only one concern with which he can deal.

They inevitably exclude competition. This limitation on his freedom of trade is not the result of human perversity. It cannot be altered by changing the laws or the ordinances. Public utilities are and must remain monopolies

CONTROL OF PUBLIC UTILITIES 637

because their business, from the way in which it is carried on, virtually excludes competition. No doubt it would be mechanically possible to have rival street railway companies competing on the same thoroughfare, or a couple of gas companies laying their mains under the same pavement, or several electric companies stringing their wires over it; but such a policy would soon transform public utilities into public nuisances. Moreover, it would so greatly increase the amount of fixed capital needed to provide the service, and thus so greatly increase the overhead cost, that higher prices to the public would be the only possible outcome of such competition. It would mean that each public utility must provide full-sized facilities for half-sized patronage. There would be no ultimate economy for anyone in that arrangement. Occasionally the city officials have been deluded into thinking that they could break down a natural monopoly by enfranchising two rival telephone or electric light companies and setting them to a lively competition in the same area. But the only result has been a merry rate-war for a little while with cheap but unsatisfactory service, followed by a merger of two rivals who then proceed to raise their schedules and get back all that they lost during the era of competition.

A moment's reflection ought to convince anyone that two telephone companies, operating in the same city, would avail the householder or business man nothing, even if their competition resulted in cutting the rates to half what they had been. To get full service everyone would have to install two telephones, consult two books, and get patiently accustomed to hearing two bells ringing at once. Rival lighting companies would not be so prolific in annoyances; but nowhere, for any length of time, have they brought a community better service at lower rates. The reason is that a natural monopoly cannot be successfully operated, over any considerable period of time, except by frankly recognizing it for what it is. Yet even today one can find plenty of men and women in almost every community who are convinced that the way to solve the problem of cheap and adequate service from public utilities is to promote competition between them. If a natural monopoly is a monopoly by predestination, there is nothing that laws or men can do to make it anything else. Public opinion ought to reconcile itself to the proposition that light, power, transportation, and communication can be more cheaply and more

The popular misapprehension on this point.

conveniently sold by one company which possesses a complete monopoly within a given area than by competing companies which do not have that advantage. It is many years since the English economist, John Stuart Mill, enunciated the doctrine that there can be no effective competition between public utilities operating in the same area, and it is a truism which has been repeatedly confirmed by public utility experience in all parts of the world.

Public utilities being natural monopolies must be regulated:

Now, if public utilities are monopolies by nature, and can never be anything else, it is essential that the public authorities shall exercise some control over them. For it is unthinkable that the people of any city will submit to being charged whatever rates the monopoly may see fit to impose and take whatever service it may choose to give. Especially is this the case in view of the propensity of all monopolies, when left unregulated, to enrich themselves at the expense of their customers or patrons. There have been some exceptions to this rule, it is true, but it is hardly in the nature of things that a public service company, immune from competition, will of its own accord choose a policy of lower rates to the public in preference to one of higher dividends to its own stockholders. For it must be remembered that utility companies are managed by directors and officials whom the stockholders elect and control. They are not chosen by the public, and their first duty is to those whose property interests they represent. Some public utility managements have pursued the enlightened policy of endeavoring to make larger profits by giving better and cheaper service, but it would hardly be safe to count upon all of them coming to this point of view. Hence it is necessary to exercise some degree of public regulation over rates and service to protect the consumer or patron.

1. To protect the consumer or patron.

2. To promote the general interests of the community.

There are other reasons why public utilities need regulation. The community which a public utility serves is more than the sum-total of its citizens. It has its own interests and ambitions. The expansion of a city, for example, depends in part upon the efficient planning and operation of its transportation facilities. Rapid transit at low fares will encourage the growth of outlying suburbs and relieve congestion downtown. But a street railway company plans and operates for profit, not for philanthropy. Under a flat-fare system it makes most of its profit out of short-haul traffic. Left to itself it will not be greatly interested in any other kind. The public authorities naturally feel that they ought to have a voice in determining what extensions shall be made, how adequate the service shall be, and within how wide a zone a passenger may ride for a minimum fare. These things are related to urban and suburban growth. They come within the purview of city planning. And so it is with public utilities which supply gas, power, and light. Rates and service in such cases have a relation to the growth of industry, the ensuring of public safety, and the promotion of the public convenience. Some degree of regulation is therefore essential in the interest of good city planning and the general promotion of community welfare.

From quite another point of view the regulation of public utilities, within reasonable bounds, is good for the companies themselves. For when their managements are allowed a free hand to do as they please, without any public supervision, they frequently do things which in the long run prove detrimental to the interest of their own stockholders. There is plenty of evidence to prove that many public utility managements, during the era which followed the World War, treated their own bondholders and stockholders even worse than they treated the public. They let themselves be drawn into the vortex of high finance; they advised their stockholders to trade securities which represented real property for the inflated shares of holding companies; they paid extra dividends which had not been earned, expanded their services unprofitably, gave excessive salaries to their principal officers, and abused their discretion in various other ways. Such things would not have happened if the stockholders had been afforded the measure of protection which the general public demanded and obtained.

3. To safeguard the interests of the utilities themselves.

So long as there are privately owned utilities there will be stockholders, and their proper protection is essential to the easy securing of capital for these enterprises. Capital will not be readily offered at reasonable rates of interest or dividend if the investor in public utility bonds or stock is open to be fleeced by any group of inside exploiters or outside manipulators who may happen to get control of the management. Only a few stockholders attend the company's meetings. They are not a homogeneous body; they have no convenient way of getting any information save such as the management gives them, and hence are often quite in the dark as to how the finances of their property are being conducted. Some degree of public regulation is therefore necessary in the interest of the utilities themselves and for the protection of those who own the property.

And to conserve their credit.

Public utility franchises. In brief, then, the individual citizen, the community, and the investors are entitled to the protection which a rational plan of public regulation affords. This protection is made practicable by the fact that public utilities, unlike ordinary industrial or mercantile concerns, must come to the state or city government for various special privileges which they find essential to the conduct of their business. Obviously they cannot put tracks on the street surface, or gas mains under it, or wires over it, until the public authorities have consented. Accordingly every public utility must needs obtain what is called a "franchise" before it can begin operations. And because it has to have a franchise it must bargain with the public authorities and agree to submit itself to such regulatory provisions as the latter may impose in granting it.

What a franchise is. To the mind of the average layman the term franchise connotes something complicated and unfathomable. But a franchise is nothing more than a general permit. Everyone knows that in order to place an obstruction in the streets an individual or corporation must first obtain permission from the public authorities. Thus a permit must be secured by the merchant who projects a sign beyond his property line, by the contractor who blocks the sidewalk with a bulkhead when he is erecting a building, and by the fruit vendor whose stand encroaches on public property. Each such permit is valid for a single privilege only; but public utilities find that they need a general permit covering privileges in a great many streets and holding good for a number of years. They require the right to scatter their tracks, poles, mains, conduits, or wires over a wide area. This general permission, which does not differ from an individual permit except in its broader scope and longer duration, is known as a franchise. Hence a franchise may be defined as a broad grant of permission to use public property (the streets, particularly) for a term of years or in perpetuity subject to certain conditions which have been agreed upon. To obtain a franchise the public utility company must negotiate with the authorities of the state, city, town, or township as the case may be. If such negotiations eventuate successfully the company obtains the rights and the public authorities impose the conditions.

Legal status of franchises. From the lawyer's standpoint a public utility franchise is a contract. Both the company and the city are under obligation to live up to its terms. The courts have held, however, that if, at the time the franchise is granted, there are general reservations in

CONTROL OF PUBLIC UTILITIES

the state constitution or laws with respect to the future revocation or modification of all franchises, these reservations are paramount to any stipulations which individual franchises may contain. No city, for example, can grant a valid franchise in perpetuity if the state constitution or general laws provide that all franchises should be limited to a maximum term of years. The provisions of a franchise, moreover, do not operate to prevent the reasonable exercise of the city's police power if the occasion arises. It may be provided in a lighting franchise, for example, that the company shall have the right to make openings in the street for the laying of conduits; but this does not entitle it to make such openings in a way that endangers the public safety.

Franchises of fifty years ago were usually one-sided affairs. Public utility companies obtained extensive rights for long terms of years, or sometimes even in perpetuity, but were subjected to very few obligations in return. Sometimes they were virtually permitted to charge what they pleased. The chief reason for this liberality was the impatience of the people to obtain immediate service. The public wanted electric light or street-car service without delay, and in their haste to comply with this demand the city officials often gave a great deal more than they got. The franchise-seeker, during the last quarter of the nineteenth century, was usually welcomed as a public benefactor who would give a much-needed service quickly and wait patiently for his reward. But he invariably got more than he gave, which is what he came for. A few technical phrases, innocent enough in appearance but judiciously distributed at strategic points in the franchise, were sometimes good for many millions. *Early municipal experience with franchises.*

In some cases such one-sided bargains were the outcome of corrupt deals and dickers between the companies and the local bosses. These were days when boards of aldermen and city councils seemed less sensitive to public criticism than they have since become. The first street railway franchises in New York City, for example, were granted by a bevy of aldermen who became known as "The Forty Thieves" and well deserved the name. Their successors in office likewise gave many franchises without limit of time, with no provision for extensions of service, or for public control over the gross earnings of the companies. The same story, with some slight variations, was repeated in almost every large city. Valuable privileges were bartered away for next to nothing by public officials who *Corruption in franchise granting.*

betrayed the interests of the city which they had sworn to serve. These franchises were the nucleus of many private fortunes,—gas fortunes, traction fortunes, telephone fortunes, and other fortunes that were piled high by audacious promoters of public utility enterprises.

The era of franchise restrictions. Public opinion, however, was gradually aroused to the belief that public utility franchises were worth far more than the cities were getting for them, especially when various investigations disclosed that political grafters and "boodle aldermen" were enriching themselves by their franchise votes. A wave of public indignation followed, and presently the state legislatures began to pass laws forbidding the grant of any franchise without a public hearing, or without some provision being made for open competition among those desiring to bid for it. In 1886 the New York legislature provided that thenceforth all new franchises in New York City should be sold at auction to the highest bidder. Perpetual franchises, without provision for revocation, were also banned by laws of many states, but city councils sometimes evaded this prohibition by granting franchises for the limited term of 999 years. The provisions for publicity were also reduced to nullity in many instances by various devices, such as that of giving inadequate public notice when franchise hearings were held. Consequently the restrictions were further stiffened until they sometimes provided that no franchise should be given without the approval of the people at the polls.

What a franchise now includes. So the public utility franchise of today is a different thing from the franchise of fifty or sixty years ago. The modern franchise runs for a fixed term of from ten to forty years, although sometimes it is given for an indeterminate period but subject to revocation at any time if cause can be shown to the satisfaction of some designated administrative body. It contains numerous detailed stipulations as to rates, quality of service, equipment, and so on. It provides for such extensions of service as may be required to meet the needs of a growing community. It determines what share the city shall receive from the profits of the public utility. Sometimes it contains a statement of the terms under which the city may itself take over the service and operate it directly. And it usually makes provision that all controversies between city and company shall be settled by arbitration or by referring them to the regulating body which the state has created for this purpose.

CONTROL OF PUBLIC UTILITIES 643

Hence a franchise is neither a short nor simple document. It is a voluminous agreement, the framing of which requires both legal and technical skill. The public utility companies have usually had command of the best legal and engineering talent that money could buy, while the city has too often been represented by its own law and engineering departments, neither of which is especially proficient in franchise drafting. Consequently these departments have often been out-matched by the high-grade and high-paid experts to whom the companies entrust their side of the negotiations. The city is at a further disadvantage in that it must make its terms public and have them openly discussed by city councilmen who befog the issues with futile suggestions, while the company can work out its strategy at private conferences among its legal, technical, and financial advisers. So regularly did the city get the short end of the bargain in earlier days that some reformers believed its only hope to be in giving no franchises at all. "The only good franchise," said Mayor Tom L. Johnson of Cleveland, "is a dead one." More recently, however, the situation has much improved. The cities have profited by their setbacks and are now taking more care to be skillfully, as well as honestly, represented in all franchise negotiations. Rarely does a city go into such things nowadays without retaining one or more outside experts to advise its own officials. Moreover, most of the artifices by which the cities were tricked in the older days have become well known and can no longer be used.

The city's disadvantage in negotiating a franchise.

In the course of the negotiations for a franchise a number of questions come forward to be settled. How many years should a franchise run? Ought it to be made for an indefinite term with provision for revocation whenever good cause for such action is shown? If the franchise is revoked or not renewed, what arrangement should be made for operating the plant? Street car lines, electric lighting plants, and telephone switchboards cannot be shut down whenever some franchise trouble arises. The people depend on them, hence provision must be made for keeping these services in operation whether the franchise runs or terminates. Should the city be empowered to take over and operate the plant when the franchise expires? In that event how should the compensation to be paid the company by the city be determined? Meanwhile, during the term of the franchise what share of the company's profits should go to the city in return for the use of its

Some franchise problems.

streets? Should it be based on the company's gross earnings, or net profits, or capital stock, or assessed franchise value? And in any event how may the full payment of the city's share be ensured? To this end should it have the right to investigate the company's financial operations? These and many similar questions arise whenever a franchise is being negotiated.

<small>Keeping the franchise provisions up to date.</small>
The most difficult of all franchise problems, however, is this: How can the public be guaranteed good service at reasonable rates? It is easy enough to specify a schedule of maximum rates for certain standards of service in the same document; but to do this is to disregard the fact that costs and conditions of service may undergo great changes within a few years. The cost of operating a public utility depends upon the general scale of wages and prices. For that reason a reasonable scale of rates, as fixed today, may be too high or too low a few years hence. Considerable changes, up or down, often take place within a short time in the price of coal, steel, copper, and oil (all of which are largely used by public utilities). Similar variations occur in the wages of labor. On the other hand some new invention may greatly simplify and thus reduce the cost of operating the utility. Progress is continually being made in the equipment of power plants, in the design of street cars, and in the technical aspects of the telephone service.

<small>The need for flexibility.</small>
Hence if regulation is to be effective it must be flexible enough to adapt the schedule of rates and the standard of service to new conditions of cost and technique. In other words, the franchise should not try to specify such things in rigid detail but should set up some arrangement whereby they can be determined at intervals as the need may appear. Regulation, in this way, should be made to march with changed conditions and not fall behind them. To embalm a host of detailed provisions in a franchise, with no simple arrangement for modifying them, or settling controversies that arise concerning them, is to supply endless opportunities for friction and evasion with a good deal of political maneuvering and some lawsuits thrown in. If the specific franchise provisions are so onerous that the company cannot give service except at a loss, they fail of their purpose. In such cases the state authorities or the courts usually step in and relieve the company of such obligations as are deemed to have become oppressive.

As a means of putting flexibility into franchises it has therefore become the practice of cities to provide that all controversies per-

CONTROL OF PUBLIC UTILITIES

taining to rates and standards of service shall be referred for decision to the public service commission at the state capitol or some such body. These commissions, which now function in virtually all the states, are an outgrowth of the earlier state boards for regulating the railroads. Their jurisdiction has generally been extended to cover motor-bus, light and power, gas, water, street railway, telephone, and even air transport companies. Delaware is the only state that does not have such a commission.

<small>Regulation by public service commissions.</small>

Some cities have tried the plan of maintaining their own municipal commissions to perform this regulatory service, but there are several reasons which make it desirable that the supervision of public utilities should be handed over to a state board with state-wide jurisdiction. A single street railway, electric lighting, or telephone company may operate in several neighboring communities. Municipal regulation in such instances would subject the company to a variety of rules, thus making it difficult to unify the service as a whole. Public regulation, moreover, is rarely effective unless a good deal of money is spent to make it so. It necessitates the employment of skilled investigators and experts of various kinds. For each city to maintain such a staff involves duplication and waste. It is better to have the state do it for them all. Finally there is a flavor of unfairness in having a city-appointed body decide controversies to which the city itself is a party. So it is becoming the general practice to make the state board serve as arbiter in all disputes arising between cities and public utility companies operating under municipal franchises. This arrangement has the advantage of encouraging the companies to keep out of local politics. When city councils or municipal regulating boards have the power, it is natural that the public utility companies should bestir themselves to keep their own friends in the membership of these bodies; but when the jurisdiction is transferred to a state commission the chief reason for such political activity disappears.

<small>They should be state-appointed bodies.</small>

Public service commissions ordinarily consist of three to five members. In most of the states they are appointed by the governor; but in a considerable number of them the commissioners are elected by popular vote. In a few of the latter states they are also subject to the recall. Appointment has generally proved to be the more satisfactory plan, but it does not always ensure that the commission shall be either a competent or an impartial body.

<small>How such commissions are organized.</small>

Partisan governors appoint partisan commissioners. When the public utilities help them to get elected they sometimes return the favor by putting pro-utility men on the commission. The terms of members vary from two to ten years, and in most cases substantial salaries are paid for the service. The commission is assisted by a staff organization which includes engineers, attorneys, statisticians, accountants, investigators, and secretaries. The material on which the commissioners base their decisions is prepared by these assistants. In a general way the data relates to standards of service, schedules of rates, the methods of public utility accounting, and the financial policy of the companies, including the issue of new securities.

The need for impartiality. The success or failure of public utility regulation depends primarily upon the competence and integrity of the men who constitute the state commission. But it also hinges in some measure upon the skill and impartiality with which the material on which they rely is prepared for them by members of their technical staff. A public service commission is a quasi-judicial body. Its function is to protect both the public and the companies, each against unreasonable actions on the part of the other. But governors sometimes appoint, and the people more often elect, men whose chief claim to preferment is their open hostility to what they term the vested interests. Such men cannot be expected to serve impartially. Nor, on the other hand, can impartiality be expected from those commissioners whom pliant governors sometimes appoint because of pressure exerted upon them by the companies. The same care should be exercised in the selection of public service commissioners that is bestowed upon the choice of judges for the higher courts.

The public attitude toward regulation. Even when the membership of a public service commission represents a high level of competence and impartiality it is difficult to hold a just and even balancing of the scales. For public opinion often assumes a very factious attitude toward those commissioners who are sincerely trying to deal in a judicial spirit with matters coming before them. When the commission orders a reduction in rates, for example, its action is sure to be loudly applauded; but when it permits a public utility to increase rates, or to change some service feature in the interests of more economical operation, there is an equally spirited chorus of protests, which is often fomented by local politicians for their own advantage. Thus the labor organizations are urged to protest when a public service commission sanctions the use of one-man cars on the street railways or permits the telephone company to replace its switchboard operators by an automatic calling-device. Householders are urged to show their resentment when the public service commission approves a sliding scale of lighting rates which bears more heavily upon the small consumer than on the large one. Many voters seem to feel that when a public service commission rules in favor of the company on any point it is playing false to a public trust and hence that its members ought to be promptly removed from office. They forget that these commissioners are sworn to deal justly with all concerned and that only by such rectitude can the public interest be served in the long run.

With what matters is a public service commission chiefly concerned? Broadly stated, the commission's principal function is to see that the companies live up to the terms of their franchises and obey the general laws relating to public utilities. The commission hears complaints concerning rates and service, obtains the company's side of the case, and after due investigation makes such rulings as the matter seems to require. Rates have no meaning except in relation to service, and the converse is also true. Whether a given schedule of rates is reasonable or unreasonable depends upon the standards of service that are being maintained. The determination of reasonable rates is therefore a highly technical problem and one that cannot be solved by the application of any simple formula. {What public service commissions do:} {1. Regulation of rates and service.}

Likewise the commission seeks to prevent discrimination in favor of one class of patrons or customers as against another, by insisting that service of approved quantity and quality be given to all. It likewise requires financial reports from the various companies and to this end may order that all public utility accounts be kept in a uniform manner. These accounts, in order to facilitate the work of the commission in making its decisions, must show the actual investment, the costs of operation, the revenues, the allowances for depreciation, and many other general items,—all set forth in the prescribed detail. The usual contention of a public utility, when requested to revise its rates downward, or to modify its standards of service upward, is that the company cannot afford to comply. Data drawn from a uniform system of accounts and reports enable the commission's staff of accountants to check this contention. The approval of new stock and bond issues by public {2. Regulation of finances.}

utilities also comes within the purview of the commission. So do such matters as the extension or abandonment of service, safety appliances, inter-company contracts, the substitution of one type of equipment for another, the imposition of special service charges, and various other details of operation.

Their procedure. The usual procedure, when complaints are made, or when a public utility company desires approval for some proposed action, is for the commission to order a hearing. In some cases the commission may take up matters on its own initiative without waiting for complaints or petitions to be filed. But if there are complainants they appear at the hearing and state their case, supporting it with such testimony as they care to present, then the company, through its representatives, submits its answer; similarly with an array of facts and figures. If the hearing does not arise out of complaints but is held on the petition of the company for increased rates or a change of service, the company is allowed to present its data and arguments first. The opposition (if there is any) then takes the floor. Hearings are going on all the time, in fact they have become so numerous in some states that they are not conducted by the commission as a whole but by individual members of it, thus enabling more than one controversy to be heard simultaneously. This also saves expense because the single commissioner can proceed to the city in which the controversy has arisen and examine into its merits on the ground.

Orders and rulings. When the hearing on any important issue is concluded, the commission does not usually make its decision at once. It sets its own engineers, attorneys, and accountants to examine the data that have been submitted by both sides and to make such independent investigations as may be deemed advisable. Not until all this has been finished, and the results carefully studied, can a vote of the commissioners be taken. In the event of a difference of judgment among the members of the commission, a majority decides. The decision is announced by the issue of an order or ruling. If either side is dissatisfied, an appeal can usually be taken to the courts.

Precedents and appeals. Public service commissions began their work, a generation ago, with a clean slate. They had no precedents to guide them, and for a time were forced to decide each case on its own merits. Gradually, however, they began to evolve some general rules covering cases of substantially the same sort and there has now been developed a considerable body of public utility jurisprudence. While a commission is not bound to follow its own precedents, much less those of commissions in other states, it has become the practice to give weight to both. The orders and rulings of a public service commission are usually accepted by both parties, but appeals are sometimes taken to the courts, particularly in cases where an order is regarded as denying the company a fair return on its investment and thus constituting "a deprivation of property without due process of law,"—something which the national and state constitutions forbid. No state can authorize its public service commission to take away the property of an individual or a corporation by compelling it to reduce rates below the point at which a reasonable and fair return on its investment can be obtained.

But what constitutes a fair return and what is the base upon which it should be calculated? If you ask the average layman, he will tell you that "five or six per cent" is a fair return; but five or six per cent upon what? On the outstanding capital of the company? On the amount that has been actually invested in the plant, less an allowance for depreciation? The amount that would have constituted a prudent investment? On the present market value? On the replacement value at current prices? *Reasonable rates and a fair return.*

That is a question which cannot be given a categorical answer. The subject is still in some degree of confusion. For many years it was the general tendency of the commissions to fix the valuation of public utilities on a basis of the amount of capital "honestly and prudently invested, and devoted to the public service." The actual investment was taken and scanned to see what proportion, if any, could be regarded as coming outside the category of prudent investment, and the balance was then taken as a fair and definite basis for determining reasonable rates. But during recent years the tendency has been swinging over to the "reproduction cost" theory, due to the dicta of the United States Supreme Court in several decisions. In one of these cases the court held in general that there must be a fair return on the reasonable value of the property at the time that it is being used for the public, and that if the property had increased in value since it was acquired the public utility company is entitled to the benefit of such increase. In other words the estimated cost of reproducing the property at the prevailing price levels was set up as the proper basis.[1] At the present *The basis of valuation.*

[1] For example, see the decision in McCardle *vs.* Indianapolis Water Co., 272 *U. S.* 400 (1926).

juncture it is not possible to predict whether the "cost of reproduction" principle will be permanently accepted, or the "prudent investment" theory recover its lost ground, or some other basis of valuation supplant both of them.

Judicial restraints on rate reductions.
Much of the public dissatisfaction that has been manifested toward regulatory commissions is related to this matter of valuation. The customers and patrons of a public utility want the minimum rates given to the maximum number of people and they do not think that a regulatory commission is performing its duty unless it can bring this about. They overlook the fact that constitutions and courts are still functioning with their guarantees of protection to private property. A citizen's lands and goods do not cease to be his property because they are used by him and his associates in the service of the public. Regulatory commissions have to remember that their orders will be set aside if the courts find them to be in contravention of the constitution or the laws. They cannot set up their own arbitrary valuation of a public utility and use this as a rate-making base. They must follow the principles which the courts, in interpreting the laws of the land, have laid down for them in such cases.

Why cities so often lose in contestations with public utility companies.
City officials frequently complain that too many adverse rulings are handed out to them by public service commissions. The city is so often overruled that they wonder what is the matter. One reason may be found in the fact that municipalities are inclined to ask too much. Every citizen who has a grievance expects the city to champion it for him. Civic organizations vote to protest this or that, or to petition for this or that, without going into either the legal or the practical aspects of the question. City councils, under the inspiration of these organizations, often do the same. Moreover, when a controversy comes up for hearing, the company is likely to have its case better prepared and better presented. This is particularly true when small municipalities are concerned. The large city can keep on its legal, engineering, and accounting staff a group of men who are specialists in public utility matters, and thus meet the company on even terms; but the smaller communities cannot do this. They must make use of such local talent as they have, and it usually proves unequal to the task of getting the facts and arguments before the commission in a way that will prove convincing.

There is a considerable body of municipal opinion which believes

CONTROL OF PUBLIC UTILITIES

that public regulation of the utilities has been a failure and that it can never provide a permanent solution of the problem with which it has been trying to deal. Where it has been effective, some say, it has throttled the initiative of the companies; and where regulation has been ineffective it has failed to protect the interest of the public. In neither case does it satisfy. One should bear in mind, however, that administrative regulation is a relatively new development in the United States. It should be given time to work out a satisfactory technique. Nor should one forget that public regulation of the utilities has had many obstacles to surmount. Political appointments to public service commissions, inadequate appropriations with which to finance thorough investigations, the impatience and frequent unreasonableness of the public, the lack of a well-established basis for the making of valuations, the rapidity with which the utilities have expanded, and the great mass of technical details that have had to be studied,—all these considerations explain why regulation has not yet had a fair chance to show what it can accomplish. The alternative to public regulation is public ownership. Whether this alternative would be preferable is a question to be discussed, but not answered, in the next chapter.

Has public regulation failed?

REFERENCES

There is a vast amount of material in this field, but most of it is embedded in the official reports and decisions of the public utilities boards in the several states, as well as in the annual reports of the public utility companies themselves. In the endeavor to keep track of developments, however, the publications issued by Public Utility Reports, Inc. (20 Exchange St., Rochester, N. Y.), will be found valuable.

Among the more useful treatises and monographs of a general character are Eliot Jones and T. C. Bigham, *Principles of Public Utilities* (New York, 1931), Martin G. Glaeser, *Outlines of Public Utility Economics* (New York, 1927), L. R. Nash, *The Economics of Public Utilities* (New York, 1925), Herbert B. Dorau, *Materials for the Study of Public Utility Economics* (New York, 1930), and William G. Raymond, *The Public and Its Utilities* (New York, 1925).

On franchises and public utility regulation some well-known books are John Bauer, *The Effective Regulation of Public Utilities* (New York, 1925) and the same author's *Standards for Modern Public Utility Franchises* (Municipal Administration Service Publication No. 17, New York, 1930), W. E. Mosher and Finla G. Crawford, *Public Utility Regulation* (New York, 1933), C. M. Clay, *The Regulation of Public Utilities* (New York,

1932), N. L. Smith, *The Fair Rate of Return in Public Utility Regulation* (Boston, 1932), Morris L. Cooke, *Public Utility Regulation* (New York, 1924), Ellsworth Nichols, *Public Utility Service and Discrimination* (Rochester, 1928), Henry C. Spurr, *Guiding Principles of Public Utility Regulation* (2 vols., Rochester, 1924–1926), C. M. Kneier, *State Regulation of Public Utilities in Illinois* (Chicago, 1927), and I. R. Barnes, *Public Utility Control in Massachusetts* (New Haven, 1930).

Questions of public utility valuation and depreciation are fully discussed in W. H. Maltbie, *The Theory and Practice of Public Utility Valuation* (New York, 1924), Robert H. Whitten, *The Valuation of Public Service Corporations* (2nd edition, 2 vols., New York, 1928), Henry E. Riggs, *Depreciation of Public Utility Properties* (New York, 1922), and Delos F. Wilcox, *Depreciation in Public Utilities* (New York, 1926).

Discussions of rate-making and various other public utility problems may be found in Lamar Lyndon, *Rate Making for Public Utilities* (New York, 1923), J. C. Bonbright and G. C. Means, *The Holding Company* (New York, 1932), Walter E. Lagerquist, *Public Utility Finance* (New York, 1927), W. G. Bailey and D. E. Knowles, *Accounting Procedure for Public Utilities* (New York, 1926), Philip Cabot and Deane W. Malott, *Problems in Public Utility Management* (2nd edition, New York, 1930), and William Z. Ripley, *Main Street and Wall Street* (Boston, 1927).

Useful books on the legal aspects of public utility regulation are Oscar L. Pond, *Treatise on the Law of Public Utilities* (3rd edition, Indianapolis, 1925), William M. Wherry, *Public Utilities and the Law* (New York, 1925), and Gustavus H. Robinson, *Cases and Authorities on Public Utilities* (Chicago, 1926).

Current material may be found in the *Journal of Land and Public Utility Economics*, the *Proceedings* of the National Association of Railroad and Utilities Commissioners (270 Madison Ave., New York), the *Journal* of the American Institute of Electrical Engineers (33 West 39th St., New York), the monthly periodical known as *Aëra* issued by the American Electric Railway Association (292 Madison Ave., New York), and *Public Ownership*, the organ of the Public Ownership League of America (127 North Dearborn St., Chicago), as well as in the *Annals of the American Academy of Political and Social Science* and the various economic journals listed at the close of Chapter XI.

See also the references appended to Chapters XLII, XLIV, and XLVI.

CHAPTER XLVI

MUNICIPAL OWNERSHIP

Communis utilitas societatis maximum vinculum est.[1]—*Livy.*

Public regulation of privately owned utilities has been a success in some places and a failure in others. Whether the balance is a plus or a minus quantity, taking the country as a whole, would be hard to say. The answer to that question would depend, in most cases, upon individual temperament and point of view. In any event there is a good deal of dissatisfaction with it, chiefly on the part of those who do not appreciate the serious difficulties which stand in the way of making public regulation effective. And this dissatisfaction has manifested itself in the demand that it be abolished in favor of the direct ownership and operation of the utilities by the city government. Those who look upon public regulation as a failure point out that a community has only two alternatives with respect to its public utilities, and that if it is not satisfied with the one, it must necessarily take the other. The only issue is between public regulation and municipal ownership. *The only alternative to regulation.*

But let us first be sure of our terminology, for much confusion results from the use of terms which do not mean what they say. The words "municipal ownership" do not convey an adequate idea of the policy which they are intended to connote. For it is not ownership but management that the advocates of municipalization desire to lay their principal stress upon. Philadelphia, for example, owns a gas plant, Cincinnati a railroad, and New York a network of subways, but because these properties are leased to private corporations, and are operated under private management, no one speaks of these utilities as examples of municipal ownership. In Boston, on the other hand, the street railway system belongs to a private company, but because it is operated by the public authorities there are frequent references to this Boston experiment as a venture into the field of public ownership. *What "municipal ownership" means.*

Strictly speaking, the term municipal ownership implies both ownership and operation, with the emphasis on the latter. It is

[1] The common good is the greatest cohesive force in society.

from actual public operation, not from mere public ownership, that virtually all the advantages and disadvantages arise. In England the customary term is municipal trading, and on the Continent the policy is called municipal socialism, which includes something more than Americans have in mind by municipal ownership. For municipal socialism includes the public ownership and operation not only of public utilities such as lighting plants and street railways but in addition such enterprises as municipal tenements, savings banks, theaters, bakeries, abattoirs, and even pawnshops. Municipal ownership, as Americans use the phrase, has reference to the major public utilities only—water, gas, electricity, and transportation. And since the water supply has now been taken over by most of the cities, the controversy over municipal ownership in the United States has narrowed itself down to the two fields of lighting and transportation.

The public attitude toward municipal ownership in Europe.

Municipal ownership, using the term as above defined, has made far greater progress in Europe than in the United States. This applies to gas, electricity, and transportation alike. The municipalization of these utilities has spread widely in all European countries, but more especially in Great Britain and in Germany. In Europe municipal ownership is taken, not as a matter of course, but at least as the rule rather than the exception. The contrast between the Old and the New Continent in this respect is quite striking and various reasons account for it. One is the greater administrative efficiency of the European city. The business affairs of cities in Europe are managed by men who have been chosen for their special qualifications and who are kept in office long enough to show what they can do. The European municipality, whether it be in Great Britain, France, Germany, or Italy, has its permanent officials who are free to manage the business enterprises of the city in their own way, without constantly truckling to the exigencies of local politics.

And in America.

In the United States, on the other hand, with the spoils system holding sway (as is still the case in many cities), it has been apparent to every thoughtful citizen that municipal ownership of the public utilities would simply mean a large increase in the patronage available to politicians for distribution among their friends. When politics mix into business, whether public or private, it is always to the detriment of business. Before the people of an American city can safely own and operate their public utilities they must first learn how to own and operate their streets, police stations, parks, and public works. Municipal ownership, as a policy, would make more rapid progress in the United States if the people had greater confidence in the efficiency and honesty with which the roadways are paved, the public buildings constructed, the ordinances enforced, and the taxes collected. So long as there are padded payrolls and crooked contracts in those departments which the city already operates, there will be voters who oppose the expansion of public activity into more difficult fields of administration.

There is another reason for the relatively slow development of municipal ownership in American cities, namely, the venturesome spirit which private capital has displayed in the public utility field. Long ago it acquired the habit of taking chances. It proved ready to build railroads, irrigation works, telegraph and telephone lines, street railways, and lighting plants when the public authorities were afraid to take the risks of financial loss which were involved. During the second half of the nineteenth century, there were many medium-sized and small cities which, but for the initiative of private capital, would not have had adequate public utilities at all. Private enterprise jumped at the opportunity when public enterprise was slow. With villages growing into towns, and towns into cities, the race went to the swift. The people of these expanding communities were not willing to wait until mayors and aldermen could supply them with water, gas, electricity, telephones, and street railways. So they summoned private capital to their aid, and private capital responded. But in their impatience the people often gave away franchise privileges of great value and it has not been easy to get them back into the city's hands. *Why privately owned utilities have made such headway in the United States.*

The American concept of government, as well as the system of legal and constitutional limitations, has also had something to do with the slow progress of municipal ownership in this country. European cities have been expected to pioneer in the field of public utilities, and to this end they have been given broad grants of powers. Subject to the approval of certain higher administrative authorities they may engage in almost any field of public service. But in the United States the traditional presumption has been against the government's doing what could be done by private enterprise. Hence the American city has usually been given a relatively narrow range of authority and discretion. Its carefully enumerated powers, granted by the state constitution or laws, do *Legal and other obstacles to municipalization.*

not customarily include the right to engage in profit-making enterprises. Special legislation has ordinarily been needed before an American city could take over a public utility, or at least before it could raise the necessary funds by the issue of bonds. In most instances an affirmative vote of the people is also required before the policy of municipal ownership can be undertaken or extended. Supplementing these various difficulties is the fact that the unexpired franchises of privately owned utilities are property. If the city wants to take them over it must pay for them, even though the franchises may have been originally given without exacting any money payment. The process of municipalizing an existing utility is often a tedious and expensive one, with a likelihood of prolonged litigation. Cities have sometimes voted to embark on a policy of municipal ownership and have then found the financial difficulties too great.

The present situation in American cities. Nevertheless some progress in the direction of municipalization has been made by American cities, especially during the past thirty-five years. There are now about 6,000 electric light and power generating plants in the United States, of which one-third are publicly owned and operated. But they are for the most part in small communities. Taken as a whole these municipal plants have only about three per cent of the country's total generating capacity and supply less than six per cent of all the customers. Of gas plants there are approximately 900 in the United States, of which about fifty are publicly owned, and of these there are thirty-five plants serving communities of fewer than ten thousand population. Less than two per cent of the gas sold in the United States for heating and lighting purposes is supplied from municipal plants. The largest American cities operating their own gas plants are Duluth, Holyoke (Mass.), Omaha, and Richmond (Va.). There has been virtually no municipalization of telephones, chiefly because the service which this industry renders is that of communication and the system must therefore extend over an area much wider than a single city.[1] There are over eight hundred street railways operating in the United States, of which about a dozen are owned and operated by the public authorities. These comprise about 800 miles of trackage, which is less than two per cent of the total for the country as a whole. The most important are those of

[1] A few small communities have local systems which are owned and operated by the municipality.

Detroit, Seattle, and San Francisco, but a number of other cities operate rail transportation facilities in a limited way. The street railway system of the Boston metropolitan area is privately owned but operated by a state-appointed commission on a service-at-cost basis, the annual deficit being pro-rated among the cities and towns which the system serves.

Taken as a whole, this is not an extensive showing. But the policy of municipal ownership is likely to be extended as time goes on, particularly if municipal government in the United States becomes more efficient, as everyone hopes will be the case. The issue between public and private ownership is not one of principle but of expediency. There is no good reason why any city should engage in it unless the municipality is in a position to give better service at lower rates than a company can provide. On the other hand the general presumption is against the city's being able to achieve any such result unless the conditions affecting municipal ownership are of an uncommonly favorable character. The successful management of a municipally owned utility demands, first of all, the complete exclusion of local politics from all share in such management. There are relatively few American cities that can exclude politics from any branch of their local administration, whether police, fire protection, public works, or even the schools, hospitals, and public library. It demands, in the second place, security of tenure for those officials who are operating the municipal utility. Few cities in the United States can guarantee such continuity of service, even when the officials who render it are competent and faithful. Finally, the successful operation of a publicly owned utility necessitates honest accounting and the rendering of a financial statement to the people at regular intervals. Not all cities comply with this requirement as concerns their governmental departments, although to do so is by no means a difficult task.

An issue of expediency, not of principle.

There has been a vast outpouring of printer's ink on the question of municipal ownership, one group of authors and pamphleteers extolling it as a panacea for municipal ills of every kind, while another group declares that it will never bring anything but deficits and demoralization. They have been "pelting each other for the public good," as Cowper says. Figures in abundance have been produced on both sides, but they prove little except that the chief service of statistics in this field has been to befog the real issue.

Success is relative to local conditions.

For the merits and shortcomings of municipal ownership, as a general policy, cannot be determined by appealing to the outcome of this or that adventure in it. The policy of municipal ownership succeeds in one city and fails in another. It succeeds when applied to one utility and fails when applied to another, even in the same city. It has done better in Europe than in America, and better in some American cities than in others. Its success or failure depends upon the city, its traditions and its personnel, as well as upon the local problems of the utility concerned.

Profit is not the only test. Too often, again, the issue has been discussed as though it were one of profit and loss alone. Does municipal ownership pay? Can the city make a reduction in its tax rate through the profits earned from its operation of the public utilities? But the issue is not one of finances alone. It is not merely one of surplus or deficit. There are social gains and losses connected with the form of public utility operation which are too intangible to be set down on balance sheets but are of great importance none the less. If municipal ownership and the abolition of public utility franchises would eradicate a corrupting influence from political life, ensure the fair treatment of labor, and promote the well-being of the community in other ways, it might be a justifiable policy in spite of deficits. On the other hand if it results in making the political bosses more powerful by increasing the number of employees on the city payroll, and enlarging the amount of patronage, it is doubtful whether municipal ownership is a wise policy even though it yields a profit. So the issue cannot be settled by merely matching dollars and dimes. A public utility sells service to the people, and the amount of satisfaction which this service gives to them cannot be reckoned in terms of so many cents per kilowatt-hour or per passenger-mile. Municipal ownership is not altogether a question of economics, but of politics and social ethics as well.

The political implications. It is a question of politics because the private operation of public utilities has had far-reaching and frequently quite sinister effects upon the course of municipal politics. Differences of opinion on this point relate only to the extent and nature of such influence, for its existence is not denied. Some critics have gone so far as to brand the public service corporations as the greatest of all corrupting influences in American municipal life.[1] That is an exag-

---

[1] "If you will trace corruption in politics during the last half-century in American cities, Pittsburgh, San Francisco, New York, Boston, Minneapolis, and scores of

geration, of course, yet it will hardly be denied that the public service corporations in many American cities have contributed their full share to the debauching of municipal and state politics. It would be worth something to get rid of politically minded gas and traction companies provided something else, more sinister, did not presently appear in their place. That is the turn which things have sometimes taken. Municipal ownership increases the size of the city's working force. A general policy of municipalization would add to the public payroll all the employees of the gas plant, electric lighting company, and street railway. It would greatly strengthen a group which has been, of all groups in the electorate, the most active politically and sometimes the least concerned with anything except their own rates of pay, hours of work, leniency of discipline, and frequency of public holidays. It is by no means certain that there would be any profit for good government in an exchange of that sort.

The issue is also one of social ethics. All forms of business enterprise, whether publicly or privately owned, have their reactions upon the social life of the community. The safety and continuity of public utility operation, the hours and wages of labor, the degree of care taken for the health and recreation of the workers, the absence of discrimination in rates and fares, the courtesy with which service is rendered, the coöperation given by the utilities in city planning, and the avoidance of congestion,—these are things in which the entire community has a direct interest no matter who the owners of the enterprise may be. The public utilities serve millions of people; they are much in the public eye; and the influence of their example is far-reaching into all other forms of industry. They can contribute much, little, or nothing at all to the city's program of better homes, better health, better recreation, better people. They can keep their patrons, customers, and employees satisfied so that no serious controversies arise, or they can be engaged in a continual round of animosity with all three.

Social reactions.

This aspect of the matter is not to be lightly regarded, for a city is bound to protect its social interests just as it must conserve, if it

others, you will find without a single exception that the fountain head of the corruption was the privately owned public service corporation. In order to gain their ends they have joined hands with the saloon, the gambling house, and the red light district, but the head and front of the sinister combination is always the public service corporation." Amos Pinchot, quoted in C. C. Maxey, *Readings in Municipal Government* (New York, 1924), pp. 158–159.

can, the decency of its political life. The main thing is that whatever outlay the city makes for promoting the common good shall be effective to the end desired, even if this take the form of operating the public utilities at a financial loss. In short, the policy of municipal ownership is not necessarily to be condemned because it does not pay in the usual sense of the term. It may be recording a monetary loss while yielding a high social dividend.

The arguments in favor of municipal ownership:

What are the principal arguments usually advanced in favor of municipal ownership? The advocates of this policy commonly start with the flat assertion that regulation of privately owned utilities has been a failure and that the remedy for the failure of regulation is more of it, that is, complete regulation through public ownership. Regulation, it is quite true, has failed—sometimes,

1. It is the only alternative since regulation has failed.

and in some places, under some conditions. But it has not failed generally, and failure is not inherent in public regulation. Usually it has been due to the interference of politicians and the readiness of public opinion to tolerate this interference with the work of regulatory commissions. But would a public opinion which condones poor appointments to the membership of public service commissions be any more rigorous as regards the choice of managers for the municipally owned utilities? What reason is there to believe that the bosses who have dominated appointments in the one case would be unable to do so in the other? It is from the people that the boss derives his power. Hence a community which cannot, with the aid of the state authorities, satisfactorily regulate the rates and conditions of service on its street railways would surely not find the task of actually managing the lines any easier. Operating a public utility is more difficult than regulating it. It is hardly logical to argue that having proved unable to succeed with a smaller responsibility, the cities should be given a larger one.

2. It would reduce overhead expenses.

Then there is the claim that municipal ownership would lessen the overhead expenses of operating the public utilities. The chief items in the list of such expenses are the interest on bonds and the dividends on stock which a privately owned utility must pay. These amount to five or six per cent on the bonds and sometimes even more on the stock, under normal conditions. But the cities can borrow money at lower rates than this,—partly because they offer the investor a greater degree of security for his investment, and partly because municipal bonds enjoy certain exemptions from taxation. The differential in favor of the city may be as much as two per cent, or even more. This does not sound like a large saving, but when a public utility company is bonded and capitalized to the amount of many millions the economy in overhead is very considerable.

All this is usually joined with the further contention that under municipal ownership no dividends would be paid on inflated capitalization, as has frequently happened in the case of privately owned utilities. The city would borrow and pay interest on the exact amount of money needed for actual investment in the enterprise. It would finance the business by the issue of bonds on the general credit of the city and bearing a low rate of interest. There would be no capital stock and hence no dividends to be paid. Out of the utility's net earnings the city would then pay off a portion of the bonds each year and eventually there would be no fixed overhead charges at all. This argument, based upon the alleged general over-capitalization of public utilities, has been freely used in all discussions of the subject, but it has not been supported in most cases by anything in the way of definite evidence. Of course there is little doubt that public utilities have paid dividends on inflated capital in many cases, but there are also numerous instances in which the properties are worth a great deal more than the total outstanding bonds and stock. At any rate it has been found that when a city obtains a current valuation of any public utility, with the idea of purchasing it, the figure is rarely less than the book value of the plant. *And prevent overcapitalization.*

A third argument commonly advanced in favor of municipal ownership is that costs of operation would be reduced by the elimination of unduly large executive and managerial salaries. Under private operation each public utility maintains its own executive organization which usually includes a president, one or more vice-presidents, an executive committee, a board of directors, and a general manager or superintendent. Some of these officials receive a higher salary than is paid to the mayor of the city in which the utility operates. Under municipal ownership, it is contended, there would be no need for presidents, vice-presidents, directors, and the rest. One general manager for all the utilities, with a deputy in charge of each service (water, gas, electricity, and transportation), would be sufficient. It is also contended that this consolidation of all the utilities under a single head would permit economies in the buying of equipment, materials, and sup- *3. Managerial costs would be decreased.*

plies. The city's purchasing office could buy for the utilities as it does for the other municipal departments.

To all this it is usually replied that while privately owned utilities pay large salaries, they get what they pay for. It is easy to cut the salaries of presidents or managers and lose them, putting less competent men in their places. But such action does not usually conduce to economy in the end. One may doubt that public utilities get full value for the high salaries they sometimes pay; but there is even greater doubt that the average city gets full value for the more modest remuneration which it gives to its public officials. Under municipal ownership the city would probably pay less for managerial service, but whether this would be a real saving is another question. So it is with equipment, materials, and supplies. Perhaps a city could buy at lower prices than a utility company, but the way in which most cities have done their buying and contracting in the past does not endow such a hope with the color of probability.

4. It would benefit the public utility employees. Municipal ownership, it is said, would result in a more humane and more generous treatment of those who are employed in the various public utilities. Wages, as a rule, are higher in public than in private employment; the hours of labor are generally shorter; more holidays are allowed, and the discipline is rarely so strict. Labor organizations are usually in favor of public ownership, and frankly because they feel that workers stand to profit by the change. In this they are undoubtedly correct. Under municipal ownership the employee becomes his own employer, that is, in his capacity as a voter he has a substantial share in determining the conditions of his employment. And to the extent that he has this influence it will be directed to his own advantage. To expect him to exert it in any other direction would be asking too much of human nature.

5. It would remove a sinister influence from politics. The political advantages of municipal ownership are often given a great deal of emphasis. Public utility companies are under a natural temptation to take a hand in local politics in order to secure the election or reëlection of public officials who are friendly to them. As a rule they avoid doing this openly, but they can become quite a factor in under-cover politics. Through their lobbyists, moreover, they frequently influence the action of mayors and city councils, or even the action of state legislatures, in ways which are not always of advantage to the public well-being. Anyone who has followed the course of municipal politics from the inside will not deny that public utility companies have a good deal to answer for. But it is equally true that the companies do not mix into politics of their own volition. Frequently they have been driven to it by the instinct of self-preservation, because every municipal demagogue looks upon them as a good target. Political racketeers attack them, and hostile legislators put all manner of obstacles in their way. Most public utility companies would keep out of politics, and do it gladly if the politicians would let them alone.

Finally, the advocates of municipal ownership declare that where their policy has been given a full and fair trial it has proved successful. Sometimes they produce American examples of their success but more often they turn to the experiences of Glasgow, Manchester, London, or Berlin. The claim is made that both British and German cities are making substantial profits from their municipal utilities as well as giving good service at low rates. Such general assertions are easy to make, but quite impossible either to prove or disprove. No one knows, in many instances, whether a city is operating its public utilities at a profit or at a loss. No one can find out—with the accounts kept as they are. "Financial legerdemain, or at least incomplete and inaccurate reporting, characterizes practically every municipally owned utility in the country."[1] Capital accounts are sometimes inadequately debited with outlays; insufficient allowances for depreciation are made; and almost never is any sum charged to the utilities in lieu of taxes. Sometimes the profit statement is padded by overcharging the other city departments for service, or by undercharging the utility for services which these other departments render to it. Thus the utility may be given the services of the city's law department at a nominal cost, or may have its offices in the city hall without paying for them, or may be allowed to borrow expensive equipment from the street or park departments without paying a rental charge. Under such conditions it is not difficult to show a surplus on paper.

6. European cities have made it a success. Why can we not do the same?

In European cities the accounts are kept free from such financial jugglery and they indicate that municipal operation of the utilities has usually been successful over there; but this by no means creates any strong presumption that similar results would be

Is this point well taken?

[1] Lent D. Upson, *Practice of Municipal Administration* (New York, 1926), p. 557.

obtained in the United States. The European city has no spoils system, no payroll padding, no ward bosses, no constant interference on the part of state legislatures, no dismissing of competent public officials on partisan grounds, no awarding of contracts to political favorites, and no sacrificing of civic efficiency in order to build up political machines. On the other hand the cities of Europe have much wider powers than American cities possess; their mayors are not elected by popular vote; their officials hold office for long terms (often for life), and their financial affairs are vigilantly scrutinized by the higher administrative authorities. European cities have had no serious difficulty in regulating privately owned utilities. Where they have embarked on municipal ownership it is not because regulation had failed. Their success in municipal ownership is a tribute to the efficiency of their governmental machinery and traditions. It offers no lesson to American cities except the lesson that a well-governed city can administer its public utilities on the same plane as all its other departments and that a poorly governed municipality is likely to do the same.

7. It is essential to good social planning.

These are the high spots in the case for municipal ownership. The foregoing paragraphs outline a series of arguments based fundamentally on considerations of public convenience and social welfare. Municipal ownership aims at giving the city an opportunity to render the best possible service in public utility operation from the community standpoint without having to think primarily of profit and loss as private concerns must necessarily do. Hence municipal ownership is believed by many of its advocates to be essential to the proper fulfillment of a city plan, in its larger sense, for there can be no comprehensive directing of a community's growth unless the utilities coöperate. The relation of suburban development to the transportation system, for example, is so obvious as to require no explanation. Under ideal conditions of municipal administration the case for public ownership would be almost incontestable; but most American communities are still a long way from excellence in their governmental performances.

The arguments against municipal ownership:

Let us turn to the opponents of municipalization. As a rule they fire their first volley at the item of operating expenses. Theoretically there is no reason why a gas plant or a street railway should not be as economically operated by the city as by a private company. Materials, supplies, and labor have a rock-bottom price in the open market; there is no inherent reason why the city should have to pay higher figures. But there is a practical reason. Buying at the cheapest rates, hiring at the lowest figures, neither favoring your friends nor discriminating against your enemies—these things do not fit with the traditions of American municipal democracy. No city in the United States is run on strictly business principles, and no city administration that tried to run things in that way would be likely to survive the next election. Giving the people "a strictly business government" is merely a promise which candidates make before the election and then find quite impossible to fulfill. Hence the idea that a municipality can make a profit where private enterprise has failed is not shared by anyone who has ever warmed a swivel-chair in a city hall office. The plain fact is that any private business, managed in the way that the average city paves its streets, or builds its sewers, or buys its fire apparatus, would be in financial difficulties before the year was out. If evidence of this is desired, there are literally mountains of it in the records and reports of investigating commissions and committees, reform leagues, municipal research bureaus, grand juries, and other bodies which have probed into municipal affairs all over the country. *1. It would greatly increase the expenses of operation.*

The opponents of municipal ownership make much of the fact that the new policy would involve a large increase in the number of city employees. These workers, it is contended, would not be chosen on a merit basis. The local politicians would insist on jobs for their friends. Motormen on the municipal street railway would be appointed and promoted just as employees of the street department are now selected and advanced in most cities,—through the favor and influence of big and little politicians. And having the support of such friends they could not be disciplined or dismissed without a ruction. The same would be true of all other street railway employees and of workers in the municipal lighting plant. If there were not enough jobs to go around, more jobs would be created, as has been done in the other city departments. In this way the opponents of municipal ownership conjure up a dismal picture of increased political manipulation and wastefulness. *2. It would debauch local politics.*

If the policy of municipal ownership could guarantee increased labor efficiency, continuity of service, and the elimination of strikes in public utilities, these advantages might offset the higher wages and shorter hours which seem to be inevitable under public operation. But no such guarantee is in prospect. The transfer of a public utility from private to municipal operation has nowhere brought any increase in labor efficiency. More workers, higher wages, fewer hours, more time off, and less work accomplished per man—these have been the more common results of the change. Workers connected with the public utilities do not make any distinction between municipal and private ownership as respects their right to bargain collectively and to call a strike if need be.

3. It would interpose a barrier to technical progress.

Virtually all progress in the public utility field has been due to individuals rather than to governments. The men who discovered the art of public lighting by gas and electricity, of transmitting the human voice over a wire, and of propelling cars by electric current—none of them were government officials. A government seldom invents; it waits for private enterprise to make the experiments and expects private capital to take the risks of loss. It is only when a public utility becomes profitable that the public authorities have any desire to take it over. Sometimes one hears the claim that under municipal ownership it is possible to make public utility extensions without keeping an eye on the profit factor, but where municipalities have taken over private plants it does not appear that there has been any increased rapidity of expansion. Municipal utilities, on the whole, do not serve their communities more adequately than private companies, and they display, on the whole, less progressiveness in modernizing their equipment.

The reasons for this.

There are various reasons why publicly owned utilities tend to retain equipment and methods which are behind the times. The officials who direct these utilities are generally in office for short terms and hence cannot plan developments over any considerable period. The temptation is to get along with things as they are. Moreover, these officials cannot introduce new methods and mechanism on their own responsibility but must usually have the approval of the mayor or the city manager, as well as an appropriation from the city council. If there is opposition from any quarter, the inclination is to compromise or let well enough alone.

And there is likely to be opposition when changes in equipment or in methods are proposed. New appliances displace labor, as for example, when automatic switchboards are installed in the telephone exchange, or when one-man cars are put into service on the street railways. New methods change the employee's duties or compel a readjustment in his work. The manager of a municipalized utility, if he resorts to frequent changes in the interest of progress and economy, may easily incur the hostility of labor organizations and endanger his own position.

Municipal ownership would greatly increase the public debt. It would place the figures of total indebtedness far above the debt limits which have been established in cities as the safe maximum.[1] It will be replied, of course, that when a city pledges its credit by the issue of bonds in order to take over the utilities from their private owners it obtains valuable properties as an offset. If it assumes liabilities, it also acquires assets. And this would be an effective reply if we could be sure that the utilities, under municipal operation, would yield a net return sufficient to cover the interest on the indebtedness. Unhappily there can be no such assurance. Under some conditions it is virtually impossible for utilities to earn their fixed charges, no matter how skillfully and economically they are managed. When that situation exists, the bondholders take the loss in the case of a privately owned utility but under municipal ownership the deficit would have to be made good by the taxpayer. His tax burden would be increased. Having permitted the city to be drawn into an unprofitable investment, he would have to shoulder his share of the consequences.

4. It would increase municipal debts and taxes.

American cities have had a considerable range of experience in the field of municipal ownership during the past generation. The testimony relating to this experience is extensive and anyone who sets out to make a study of it will not lack materials, for there are books, pamphlets, dissertations, census bulletins, and reports of public service commissions, as well as great masses of data in the annual reports of the cities themselves. From this welter of statistics it is relatively easy to prove anything that one wishes to prove. Of only one thing can anybody be certain, namely, that his conclusions (whatever they are) will be controverted from the same data by somebody else. It is probably not far wide of the truth to say, however, that municipal ownership in the United States has been neither an unqualified success nor an unalloyed failure as the extreme partisans on either side would have us believe. Some cities have done well with it, while others have done badly. The

5. Conclusion.

---

[1] For a discussion of this topic see the article by L. L. Durisch on "Municipal Debt Limits and the Financing of Publicly Owned Utilities" in *National Municipal Review*, Vol. XX, pp. 460–465 (August, 1931).

majority do not appear to have accomplished anything more than private companies would have done if they had been left alone. American cities, on the whole, have managed their public utilities about as efficiently as their police, fire protection, public works, and health departments. That, in many instances, is not high praise.

Municipal ownership and municipal democracy. Municipal democracy seems to mean government by amateurs. It can be argued that this does not necessitate a spoils system, rotation in office, ward bosses, partisan dismissals, or any one of a dozen other brands of political racketeering. But as a matter of fact we have not succeeded, thus far, in sweeping it clear of these barnacles. And so long as this is the case it cannot be convincingly argued that city governments are in a position to manage their public utilities with any high degree of administrative efficiency. That is why this discussion returns to the proposition with which it began, namely, that the arguments for and against municipal ownership are all of them relative to the time, the place, and the circumstances. No one ought to declare himself a believer in municipal ownership on principle, or an opponent of it on principle. No principle is at issue. Considerations of expediency should control. A man may favor municipal ownership in one city and oppose it in another, without being either illogical or inconsistent. For it is a policy which is likely to succeed when conditions are favorable and to fail when they are not.

REFERENCES

A complete list of the earlier publications on this subject may be found in Don L. Stevens, *Bibliography of Municipal Utility Regulation and Municipal Ownership* (Cambridge, Mass., 1918). Important books published since the appearance of this volume are E. E. Lincoln, *The Results of Municipal Electric Lighting in Massachusetts* (Cambridge, 1918), Harry W. Laidler, *Public Ownership Here and Abroad, before, during and after the War* (New York, 1923), W. S. Murray, *Government Owned and Controlled, Compared with Privately Owned and Regulated, Electric Utilities* (New York, 1922), National Electric Light Association, *Political Ownership and the Electric Light and Power Industry* (New York, 1925), Carl D. Thompson, *Public Ownership* (New York, 1925) with an extensive bibliography, James Mavor, *Niagara in Politics* (New York, 1925), Frederick L. Bird and Frances M. Ryan, *Public Ownership on Trial* (New York, 1930), and Herbert B. Dorau, *The Changing Character and Extent of Municipal Ownership in the Electric Light and Power Industry*, issued by the Institute

MUNICIPAL OWNERSHIP 669

of Land and Public Utility Economics (Chicago, 1929). The Institute of Economic Research has also published a study of *Forces Affecting Municipally Owned Electric Plants in Wisconsin* by E. Orth Malott (Chicago, 1930).

An eighty-page booklet on *The Administration of Municipally Owned Utilities*, by Delos F. Wilcox, was issued by the Municipal Administration Service in 1931, which also published in 1932 a larger bulletin by Frederick L. Bird on *The Management of Small Municipal Lighting Plants*, and in 1934 a study of *Municipal Electric Plant Managers* by Edna C. Macmahon.

Mention should also be made of the pamphlet containing the address by Hon. Herbert C. Hoover on *Government Ownership* (Washington, 1924), and of several pamphlets issued by the National Electric Light Association (420 Lexington Ave., New York), as well as the various bulletins published from time to time by the Public Ownership League of America (127 North Dearborn St., Chicago). Articles on the subject appear in the *Journal of Land and Public Utility Economics* (e.g., "Municipal Ownership and the Changing Technology of the Electric Industry," Vol. VI, 1930, pp. 241–257, 386–398), as well as in the various economic periodicals which are listed at the close of Chapter XI.

A volume of *Selected Articles on Municipal Ownership* (3rd edition, Minneapolis, 1918) is included in the Debaters' Handbook Series.

See also the references appended to Chapters XLIV and XLV.

INDEX

Abbott, H. S., *Treatise on the Law of Municipal Corporations*, 88.
Absent voting, 72.
Accounting, municipal, general administration of, 188–193.
Activated sludge process, in sewage disposal, 307–308, 310.
Adam, J. Collyer, *Criminal Investigation*, 334.
Adams, S. H., *Modern Sewage Disposal and Hygienics*, 311.
Adams, T., Lewis, H. M., and Orton, L. M., *The Building of the City*, 236.
Adams, Thomas, and others, *Recent Advances in Town Planning*, 235.
Adeney, W. E., *Principles and Practice of the Dilution Method of Sewage Disposal*, 311.
Administration, municipal, and practical politics, 1–14; ordinance power as basis of, 1–2; separation of functions in, 2–3; political interference in, 4; non-partisanship in, 5; conduct of, compared with private business, 6–8; general framework of, 9–14; principles and problems of, 15–33; scope and variety of its work, 15; men and methods in, 17–18; law of increasing costs in, 156.
Adshead, S. D., *Town Planning and Town Development*, 235.
Adult education, 453.
Aëra, 634, 652.
Agg, Thomas R., *The Construction of Roads and Pavements*, 271, 284; and Brindley, John E., *Highway Administration and Finance*, 154, 284.
Aggs, W. H., *The National Insurance Act, 1924*, 527 n.
Agriculture, relation of, to city growth, 213.
Airports, municipal, 604–617; rapid development of, 604; problems in selecting sites for, 605–608; ownership of, 613–614, 615–616; expenses and revenues, 614–615; administration of, 616–617.
Akers, Kenneth F., *Fire Protection Engineering as Applied to Municipalities*, 426.

Akron, city manager plan of government in, 12; importance of rubber industry in, 214; municipal university in, 452.
Albrecht, G., and others (editors), *Handwörterbuch des Wohnungswesens*, 545.
Alexander, F., and Staub, H., *The Criminal, the Judge, and the Public*, 383.
Alice in Wonderland (American Version), quoted, 155.
Allen, E. L., *American Housing as Affected by Social and Economic Conditions*, 545.
Allotment budget, in cities, 165.
Amendments, to the city charter, functions of law department in connection with, 82.
American Automobile Association, publications of, 284.
American City, The, 284, 568.
American Economic Review, 140.
American Electric Railway Association, *Aëra*, 634, 652.
American Federation of Labor, affiliation of municipal employees with, 47; in relation to police, 332.
American Institute of Electrical Engineers, *Journal*, 603, 652.
American Institute of Park Executives, publications of, 568.
American Institute of Weights and Measures, *Our American System of Weights and Measures*, 409–410.
American Journal of Public Health, The, 494.
American Labor Legislation Review, 531.
American Library Association, on library financing, 471; *A Survey of Libraries in the United States*, 473; *Libraries and Adult Education*, 473; *Library Extension*, 473.
American Park Society, publications of, 568.
American Prison Association, *Proceedings*, 384.
American Public Health Association, *Standard Methods for the Examination of Water and Sewage*, 311, 587; *A Bibliography on Public Health*

671

672 INDEX

and Allied Topics, 493; *Catalogue of Health Books*, 493; *Model Health Code for Cities*, 493; *Appraisal Form for City Health Work*, 493; publications of, 494.
American Road Builders' Association, *Proceedings*, 284.
American Society for Testing Materials, *Book of Standards*, 399.
American Society of Civil Engineers, *Proceedings*, 247, 312; "Excess Condemnation in City Planning," 258; publications of, 284.
American Society of Municipal Engineers, *Proceedings*, 284.
American Transit Association, *Economics of Rapid Transit*, 625 n.; *The Urban Transportation Problem*, 633.
American Water Works Association, *Water Works Practice*, 587; *Proceedings*, 587; *Journal*, 587.
Amphibian airports, 608.
Anderson, Nels, *The Hobo*, 544 n.; and Lindeman, E. C., *Urban Sociology*, 218.
Anderson, William, *American City Government*, 34, 50.
Annals of the American Academy of Political and Social Science, "Zoning in the United States," 247; *Modern Crime: Its Prevention and Punishment*, 334, 384; *The Police and Crime Problem*, 334; *Planning for Street Traffic*, 352; *Public Welfare in the United States*, 530; tabulation of factors in selecting an airport site, 610 n., 652.
Ann Arbor, institutional forces in growth of, 214.
Appeal, the right of, from municipal assessments, 124–125; from municipal courts, 363; from buildings inspectors, 396–397; from rulings of public service commissions, 648–649.
Appointments, municipal, by mayor, 28–29; by city manager, 29; in relation to politics, 30; of subordinate employees, 37–44. *See also* Merit System, Employees.
Appropriations, municipal, how made, 158–159; transfers of, 164–165. *See also* Budgets.
Arkansas, voting requirements in, 52.
Armitage-Smith, G., *Principles and Methods of Taxation*, 140.
Aronovici, Carol, *Housing and the Housing Problem*, 545.
Ascher, Charles S., *Elements of a Low-Cost Housing Law and Its Administration*, 545.
Ashes, the removal of, 290.
Asphalt, use of, for street pavements, 277.
Asphalt Institute, publications of, 284.
Assessment of property for taxation, 116–125; defined, 116; procedure, 117–122; favoritism in, 123; of personal property, 123–124.
Athens, ancient, defensive location of, 201; historic associations of, 204; city planning in, 220; value of lunar illumination to, 599.
Athletic fields, municipal, 562. *See also* Playgrounds.
Atlanta, supervision of airports in, 617.
Atlantic City, climatic factor in location of, 204.
Auditor, city, functions of, 187–188.
Audits, municipal, 185–188.
Austin, political factor in growth of, 214.
Australian ballot, the, 68.
Auto camps, municipal, 566.
Automatic signals, in traffic regulation, 348–349.
Ayres, L. P. *See* Gulick, L. H.

Babbitt, Harold E., *Sewerage and Sewage Treatment*, 311; and Doland, James J., *Water Supply Engineering*, 586.
Babcock, Frederick M., *The Appraisal of Real Estate*, 123; *The Valuation of Urban Real Estate*, 123.
Babylon, early policing of, 313.
Bailey, W. G., and Knowles, D. E., *Accounting Procedure for Public Utilities*, 652.
Baker, Donald M., and Conkling, Harold, *Water Supply and Utilization*, 587.
Baker, Newman F., *Legal Aspects of Zoning*, 247–248.
Baker, S. J., *Child Hygiene*, 482 n.
Ballard & Co., F. W., *Street Lighting Costs in the Larger Cities of the United States*, 603.
Ballots, form of, in municipal elections, 67–68; rotation of names on, 69. *See also* Elections, Short Ballot.
Baltimore, sale of municipal bonds in, 177; breadth of economic base, 214; state control of municipal police in, 314; special traffic courts

INDEX

in, 351; source of water supply for, 574; early street cars in, 620.
Band concerts, municipal, 565.
Barnes, I. R., *Public Utility Control in Massachusetts*, 652.
Bartholomew, Harland, *Urban Land Uses*, 218.
Barton, L. M., *A Study of All American Markets*, 555.
Barton, W. H., and Doane, Louis H., *The Sampling and Testing of Highway Materials*, 284.
Bateman, J. H., *Highway Engineering*, 271.
Bates, F. G., and Field, O. P., *State Government*, 75.
Baths, public, location of, 233.
Batson, Harold E., *A Select Bibliography of Modern Economic Theory*, 139.
Battle Creek, importance of health restoration industry in, 214.
Bauer, John, *The Effective Regulation of Public Utilities*, 651; *Standards for Modern Public Utility Franchises*, 651.
Beaches, municipal ownership of, 564.
Beale, J. H., *Selection of Cases on Municipal Corporations*, 88.
Beard, Charles A., on financial administration of cities, 185; *American City Government*, 488 n.
Beccari method, in Italy, garbage disposal by, 293 n.–294 n.
Bedford, Scott E. W., *Readings in Urban Sociology*, 218, 247.
Belt-line thoroughfares, 344.
Bennett, R. R., *Aviation: Its Commercial and Financial Aspects*, 617.
Benoist, L., *Manuel de la prévention de l'incendie*, 426.
Bentham, Jeremy, quoted, 168; his attitude towards the criminal, 377.
Berkeley, educational forces as a means of growth, 204.
Berlin, early expansion of, 202; municipal federation in, 217; famous thoroughfares of, 263; sewage farms of, 309; annual fire losses in, 412; large proportion of fire-resisting buildings in, 413; municipal ownership in, 663.
Bernhard, H. A., *Das parliamentarische Wahlrecht*, 75.
Bertillon, Alphonse, his anthropometric method of criminal identification, 323.
Bessemer, a satellite city, 216.
Besson, F. S., *City Pavements*, 271, 271 n., 284.

Betters, Paul V., *Federal Services to Municipal Governments*, 443 n.
Beveridge, Sir William H., *Unemployment*, 530.
Beyle, H. C., *Governmental Reporting in Chicago*, 200.
Bids, competitive, in centralized purchasing, 109–110; sealed, 112–113.
Bigham, T. C. *See* Jones, Eliot.
Billboards, regulation of, 246–247.
Bingham, Robert F. *See* McMichael, Stanley.
Bird, Frederick L., *The Management of Small Municipal Lighting Plants*, 603, 669; and Ryan, Frances M., *Public Ownership on Trial*, 668.
Bishop, E. L., *Public Health Organizations*, 493.
Bishop, Ward L., *An Economic Analysis of the Constitutional Restrictions upon Municipal Indebtedness in Illinois*, 184.
Black, Archibald, *Civil Airports and Airways*, 617; *Transport Aviation*, 617.
Black, Russell Van Nest, *Planning for the Small American City*, 235.
Blackstone, Sir William, his attitude towards the criminal, 376–377; towards nuisances, 495.
Blake, Henry W., and Jackson, Walter, *Electric Railway Transportation*, 628 n., 633.
Blanchard, A. H., *The American Highway Engineer's Handbook*, 284; and Morrison, R. L., *Elements of Highway Engineering*, 284.
Board system, in municipal administration, disadvantages of, 26; merits of, 27; in registrations, 58–59; in elections, 63; in city planning, 226–227; in zoning, 239–240; in police administration, 316–317; in paroles, 379; of appeals, in regulation of buildings, 396; in fire department administration, 427; in school administration, 444–447; in the public library, 461–464; in health administration, 487–488; in hospitals, 511; in public welfare administration, 522; in park administration, 560; in water supply administration, 584.
Bode, Boyd H., *Fundamentals of Education*, 441 n.
Bogert, C. L. *See* Flinn, A. D.
Bolton, D. J., *Electrical Engineering Economics*, 603.
Bonbright, J. C., and Means, G. C., *The Holding Company*, 652.

INDEX

Bond, H. L. *See* McClintock, Miller.
Bonds, municipal, 83, 174–180; for school financing, 459.
Bonney, E. A. *See* Harger, W. G.
Borrowing, municipal, philosophy of, 168–169; anticipatory, 170.
Boston, strong-mayor plan of government in, 10; municipal departments in, 19; municipal printing plant in, 24; election board in, 53 *n.*; registration of voters, 55; location of, as a factor in growth, 203; topography in relation to development, 204; invasion of business in residential districts of, 211; breadth of economic base in, 214; a metropolitan city, 216–217; street layout in, 230; importance of streets in, 264; street excavations in, 281; state control of municipal police in, 314; police strike in, 332; source of water supply for, 574; rapid transit in, 623, 623 *n.*; management of street railway system in, 632, 653, 657.
Bostwick, Arthur E., *The American Public Library*, 467 *n.*, 473; (editor), *Classics of American Librarianship*, 473.
Bowen, W. P., and Mitchell, E. D., *The Theory and Practice of Organized Play*, 568.
Breckinridge, S. P., *Family Welfare Work in a Metropolitan Community*, 530; *Public Welfare Administration in the United States*, 530.
Brick pavements, 277.
Bridgeport, importance of machine tool industry in, 214.
Brindley, John E. *See* Agg, Thomas R.
Broad irrigation, sewage disposal by, 309.
Bronner, Augusta F. *See* Healy, William.
Brooks, R. C., *Political Parties and Electoral Problems*, 61, 75.
Brown, E. F., Dennis, E. B., Jr., Henry, J., and Pendray, G. Edward (editors), *City Noise*, 507.
Brown, Fraser, *Municipal Bonds*, 184.
Brown, H. G., *The Economics of Taxation*, 140.
Brown, V. J., and Conner, C. N., *Low-Cost Roads and Bridges*, 284.
Browning, Robert, quoted, 89.
Bruce, A. A., *The American Judge*, 367; and others, *Parole and the Indeterminate Sentence*, 384.

Bryan, W. B., *History of the National Capital*, 224 *n.*
Bryce, James (Viscount), quoted, 1; *Modern Democracies*, 14.
Buck, A. E., *Municipal Finance*, 115, 154, 167, 184, 196 *n.*, 199; *Public Budgeting*, 167; *Municipal Budgets and Budget Making*, 167; *Budgeting for Small Cities*, 167; and Cleveland, F. A., *The Budget and Responsible Government*, 167.
Buckle, Philip. *See* Wardle, Robert A.
Budgets and budget making, municipal, methods of compiling and adopting, 159–163; powers of mayor in relation to, 161, 162; under city manager plan, 162; types of, 163–167; for schools, 458; for libraries, 471.
Buechner, F. R., *Municipal Self-Insurance of Workmen's Compensation*, 530.
Buehler, E. C., *Compulsory Unemployment Insurance*, 530.
Buffalo, annual registration of voters in, 55; breadth of economic base of, 214; sewage disposal system of, 305; sources of water supply for, 574.
Building Officials' Conference of America, *Proceedings*, 399.
Buildings, public, planning the location of, 232–233; private, zoning regulations in relation to, 241; restricting height of as a remedy for traffic congestion, 342; regulation of, 385–398; in the interest of structural safety, 386; of fire prevention, 386, 421–423; of sanitation, 386; department of, 388–390; classification of, 393; code for, 393–394; permits for and inspections of, 395–398; rat-proofing of, as a sanitary measure, 506.
Bullock, C. J., *Selected Readings in Public Finance*, 139.
Bureau of Entomology. *See* United States Department of Agriculture.
Burgess, Ernest W., *The Urban Community*, 218.
Burnap, George, *Parks: Their Design, Equipment, and Use*, 567.
Burnstan, Arthur R., *Special Assessment Procedure*, 154.
Burton, Frank, "A Concise History of Building Codes from the Earliest Days," 385 *n.*
Burton, J. E. *See* Simpson, H. D.
Business, private, compared with city administration, 6–8; taxes on, 134.

INDEX

Buswell, Arthur M., *The Chemistry of Water and Sewage Treatment*, 311, 587.
Butte, importance of mining in, 214.
By-pass highways, in state road system, 343.

Cable Act (1923), 56.
Cabot, Philip, and Malott, Deane W., *Problems in Public Utility Management*, 652.
Cady, Francis E., and Dates, Henry B., *Illuminating Engineering*, 603.
Cahalane, Inspector Cornelius F., *The Policeman*, 333.
California, cities of, sewage farms in, 309.
Callender, C. N., *American Courts: Their Organization and Procedure*, 367.
Cambridge, England, educational forces in growth of, 204.
Campbell, Charles A. R., *Rats, Mosquitoes, and Dollars*, 507.
Cannon, Lucius H., *Smoke Abatement*, 507; *Smoke Abatement—a Study of the Police Power as Embodied in Laws, Ordinances, and Court Decisions*, 507.
Cantor, N. F., *Crime, Criminals, and Criminal Justice*, 383.
Carlyle, Thomas, quoted, 260.
Carpenter, Niles, *The Sociology of City Life*, 218; *Hospital Service for Patients of Moderate Means*, 516.
Catskill water supply system, 574.
Chamberlain, Lawrence, and Edwards, G. W., *The Principles of Bond Investment*, 184.
Chapel Hill, institutional forces in growth of, 214.
Chapman, Frank E., *Hospital Organization and Operation*, 516.
Chapman, George, quoted, 76.
Charter, city, separation of functions under, 2–3; legal restrictions in, 6; importance of provisions in, 13–14; departmental set-up under, 16–17.
Checks and balances, principle of, as to mayor, 3–4.
Chemical precipitation, in sewerage treatment, 306.
Chicago, strong-council plan of government in, 9; election board in, 53 *n.;* registration of voters in, 55; residence evasions in, 57; assessment manipulation in, 121; municipal obligations of, 169; importance of meat packing industry in location of, 203; invasion of business in residential districts of, 211; breadth of economic base in, 214; a metropolitan city, 216; planning in, 225–226; zoning survey in, 244; importance of streets in, 264; relief of traffic congestion in, 269; volume of urban wastes in, 286; drainage canal of, 298; the Sanitary District of, 303; jay-walking in, 341; double-decker streets in, to relieve traffic congestion, 342; special traffic courts in, 351; specialization in municipal courts of, 359; annual fire losses in, 412; appointment of board of education in, 444; rhapsody on smoke nuisance in, 498; sources of water supply for, 574; street lighting of, 594 *n.*
Chicago Bureau of Public Efficiency, *Proposed System of Registering and Canvassing the Registration Lists in Chicago*, 61.
Chicago Metropolitan Street Traffic Survey, 338 *n.*, 352.
Chlorination, of sewage, 310; of water supply, 576–577.
Cincinnati, city manager plan of government in, 12; municipal university in, 24, 452; topography in relation to growth of, 204; basis of street railway service in, 632.
Cities, principles of growth, 201–217; beginnings of, 201–203; relation of topography to, 204–205; expansion of, 205–207; centralization of business in, 208–211; localization in, 211–212; grouping of, 213–217.
Citizenship, and the suffrage, 56; relation of schools to, 441–442.
Citizens' Police Committee, *Chicago Police Problems*, 333.
City clerk, the, work of, 21; importance of, 89; manner of selection, 89–90; qualifications, 90–91; duties, 91–95.
City council, policy-determining functions of, 2–3; its relation to mayor, 3–4; to administrative officers, 4–5; diversity of interests in, 6; functions of, in strong-council plan of government, 9–10; in strong-mayor plan, 10; in city manager plan, 11–12; importance of, 12–13; selection of departmental heads by, 28; appointment of civil service commission by, 41; relation of city clerk to, 91–92; functions of, in relation to budget, 161–162.

City courts, 354–366. *See also* Courts, Municipal.
City manager plan of government, non-partisanship of, 5–6; administrative methods of, 11–12; departmental appointments under, 29–30; budget making under, 162; jurisdiction of libraries under, 462.
City Parks Association, annual reports of, 568.
City planning, 23, 219–235; scope and development of, 219–227; procedure in, 227–229; various factors of, 229–233; social phases of, 233–234; financial aspects of, 234; in relation to private property, 234–235; as a means of relieving future street congestion, 341–342.
City Planning (a periodical), 236.
City treasurer, the, functions of, 157; how chosen, 158.
Civil service. *See* Merit System.
Civil War, spread of crime as a result of, 372.
Claims, adjustment of, by legal department, 86.
Clark, F. E., and Weld, L. D. H., *Marketing Agricultural Products in the United States*, 555.
Clark, H. C., *Service at Cost Plans*, 633.
Clark, H. F., *The Cost of Government and the Support of Education*, 460.
Clarke, J. J., *Housing in Relation to Public Health*, 545.
Classified property tax, 130.
Clay, C. M., *The Regulation of Public Utilities*, 651.
Cleveland, election board in, 53 *n.*; registration in, 55; election workers in, 66; oil wells as a factor in location of, 203, 215; invasion of business in residential district of, 211; planning in, 225; civic center in, 232; importance of streets in, 264; sewage disposal system of, 305; sludge treatment plants in, 305 *n.*; special traffic courts in, 351; popular election of board of education in, 444; smoke nuisance in, 496; sources of water supply for, 574; early street cars in, 620; basis of street railway service in, 632.
Cleveland, F. A., and Buck, A. E., *The Budget and Responsible Government*, 167.
Cleveland, Grover, quoted, 36; veto message of, as mayor of Buffalo, 272.

Codes, traffic, 345–346; building, objectives of, 386; limitations on, 387; provisions of, 388; enforcement of, 388–391; flexible provisions in, 391–392; need for frequent revision in, 391; classification of buildings under, 393–394; machinery for enforcement of, 395–396; regulations of, in the interest of fire prevention, 414.
Cohen, J. L., *Social Insurance Unified*, 528 *n.*, 531.
Collins, W. D., *The Relations between Quality of Water and Industrial Development in the United States*, 587.
Collusive bidding, 102.
Colorado River, as a source of water supply, 574.
Colorado Springs, tourist trade in relation to growth of, 214.
Commerce, relation of, to city growth, 215–216.
Commerce Clearing House of Chicago, *Tax Magazine*, 140.
Commission plan of government, 11; departments in, 19.
Committee on Cost of Medical Care, *The Cost of Medical Care*, 517.
Community chests, 521–522.
Compensation, for land takings, how determined, 251–253.
Comptroller, functions of, 189.
Compulsory voting, 72–73.
Comstock, A. P., *Taxation in the Modern State*, 140.
Concrete pavements, 277.
Condemnation of land for public purposes, 251–254. *See also* Excess Condemnation.
Congestion, of traffic and its relief, 335–346; on main thoroughfares, 348–350; housing, in modern cities, 533–535; effects of, 535–538; remedies for, 539–542.
Conkling, Harold. *See* Baker, Donald M.
Conner, C. N. *See* Brown, V. J.
Consumption, of water in American cities, 570.
Contact beds, use of, in sewage treatment, 308–309.
Contracts, municipal, preparation and awarding of, 99–104; importance of inspection, 102–103; bonded, 103; for supplies, 113; for public lighting, 601–602.
Cooke, Morris L., *Public Utility Regulation*, 652.
Cooley, E. J., *Probation and Delinquency*, 384.

INDEX

Cooley, R. W., *Handbook of the Law of Municipal Corporations*, 88; *Illustrative Cases on Municipal Corporations*, 88.
Cooley, T. M., *Treatise on Constitutional Limitations*, 88.
Corporation cuts, 280–281.
Correction, institutions of, 22; theories in relation to, 376–377; methods of, 377–383. *See also* Crime.
Corrupt practices, in municipal elections, 73–74.
Courts, municipal, 22, 354–366; importance of, 354–356; development of, 356–357; present-day organization of, 357–359; functioning of, 360–366; need for reforms in procedure of, 366.
Courts of domestic relations, 359.
Cowper, William, quoted, 657.
Crawford, Finla G., *The Administration of the Gasoline Tax in the United States*, 134 n. *See also* Mosher, W. E.
Crime, definition of, 368; classification of, 368–369; causes of, 369–371; ratio of, in city and country, 371–373; localized centers of, 373–374; a typical biography of, 374–376; methods of dealing with, 376–377; modern methods of correction in relation to, 377–383.
Criminal investigation, organization of, 321–324.
Crohurst, H. R., *Municipal Wastes: Their Character, Collection, and Disposal*, 292 n.
Croker, E. F., *Fire Prevention*, 438.
Crosby, Everett U., Fiske, Henry A., and Forster, H. Walter, *Handbook of Fire Protection*, 426.
Crosby, W. W., and Crosby, George E., *Highway Location and Surveying*, 271.
Croton water supply system, 574.
Cubberley, E. P., *State School Administration*, 443 n.; *Public School Administration*, 460; *History of Education*, 460.
Curbs, construction of, 282.
Curbstone markets, 552–553.
Cushman, R. E., *Excess Condemnation*, 258.

Dactyloscopy, use of, in police departments, 323.
Daggett, Stuart, *Principles of Inland Transportation*, 633.
Dallas, basis of street railway service in, 632.

Dalton, H., *Principles of Public Finance*, 139.
Dana, Gorham, and Milne, William D., *Industrial Fire Hazards and an Encyclopedia of Hazardous Materials*, 426.
Dana, John Cotton, on libraries, 461.
Darby, Walter R., *Outline of Uniform System of Accounts for Municipalities*, 199.
Dates, Henry B. *See* Cady, Francis E.
Davie, Maurice R., *Problems of City Life*, 218, 544 n., 568.
Davis, F. J., *Aëronautical Law*, 618.
Davis, M. M., *Paying Your Sickness Bill*, 531; and Jarrett, M. C., *A Health Inventory of New York City*, 493; and Rorem, C. R., *The Crisis in Hospital Finance and Other Studies in Hospital Economics*, 516.
Davis, Michael M., *Clinics, Hospitals and Health Centers*, 516.
Dawson, R. M., *The Principle of Official Independence*, 14.
Day, Edmund E., *Statistical Analysis*, 199.
Dayton, importance of cash register industry in, 214.
Debaters' Handbook Series, *Selected Articles on Municipal Ownership*, 669.
Debt limits, municipal, 172–174.
Debts, municipal, 168–183; varieties of, 169–171; limitations on, 172–174; liquidation of, 177–180; causes of growth of, 180–183.
Deffenbaugh, W. S., *School Administration and Finance*, 460.
DeForest, R. W., and Veiller, Lawrence, *The Tenement House Problem*, 544.
Delaware River, as a source of water supply, 574.
Dennis, E. B., Jr. *See* Brown, E. F.
Denver, merit system in, 40; gold and silver as factors in location of, 203.
Departments, municipal, organization of, 16–18; number of, 18–20; general functions of, 20–26; heads of, 26; manner of selection, 28–30; qualities of, 30–31; internal organization of, 31–33. *See also* Civil Service.
Detectives. *See* Criminal Investigation.
Detroit, strong-mayor plan of government in, 10; municipal departments in, 19; registration of voters in, 55; importance of automobile industry in, 203, 214, 215; planning

678　INDEX

of, 231; sewage disposal system of, 305; special traffic courts in, 351; popular election of board of education in, 444; municipal university in, 452; sources of water supply for, 574; street lighting of, 594 n.; municipal ownership of street railways in, 633, 657.
Dickens, Charles, novels of, 371.
Diet, its importance in relation to health, 486.
Dillon, J. F., *Commentaries on the Law of Municipal Corporations*, 88, 507.
Dilution, sewage disposal by, 304–305.
Dinsmore, John C., *Purchasing Principles and Practices*, 115.
Dinwiddie, Courtenay, *Child Health and the Community*, 493.
Director, Aaron.　*See* Douglas, Paul H.
Direct tax plan, in library financing, 470–471.
Disease, germ theory of, 476–477; spread of, through personal contact, 477; methods of control, 478–487.
Disinfection, of premises as a health measure, 478–479.
Dismissals, of municipal employees, 45–46. *See also* Spoils System.
Disraeli, Benjamin, quoted, 116; on care of the public health, 474.
Dixey, Frank, *Practical Handbook of Water Supply*, 587.
Doane, Louis H.　*See* Barton, W. H.
Dodd, W. F., *State Government*, 75.
Doland, James J.　*See* Babbitt, Harold E.
D'Olier, W. L., *The Sanitation of Cities*, 297.
Dominge, Charles C., and Lincoln, Walter O., *Fire Insurance Inspection and Underwriting*, 426.
Dorau, Herbert B., *Materials for the Study of Public Utility Economics*, 651; *The Changing Character and Extent of Municipal Ownership in the Electric Light and Power Industry*, 668; and Hinman, Albert G., *Urban Land Economics*, 204 n., 217, 247.
Dougherty, T. F., and Kearney, P. W., *Fire*, 426.
Douglas, importance of mining in, 214.
Douglas, Paul H., *Standards of Unemployment Insurance*, 530–531; and Director, Aaron, *The Problem of Unemployment*, 530.

Douglass, H. Paul, *The Suburban Trend*, 218, 235.
Downey, E. H., *Workmen's Compensation*, 526 n., 530.
Doyle, Conan, his interest in the criminal, 371.
Dresslar, F. B., *American Schoolhouses*, 456 n.
Drugs, municipal inspection of, 485–486; narcotic, controlling the sale of, 487.
Drummond, Henry, quoted, 96.
Duffus, R. L., *Mastering a Metropolis*, 235.
Duke, Donald, *Airports and Airways*, 617.
Duluth, municipal gas plant in, 656.
Durisch, L. L., "Municipal Debt Limits and the Financing of Publicly Owned Utilities," 667 n.

Economic base, relation of the, to city growth, 213–217.
Eddy, Harrison P.　*See* Metcalf, Leonard.
Edinburgh, city planning in, 225.
Edison Lamp Works, General Electric Company, *Bulletins*, 603.
Education.　*See* School Administration.
Educational Yearbook, 460.
Edwards, G. W.　*See* Chamberlain, Lawrence.
Edwards, I. A. E., and Tymms, F., *Commercial Air Transport*, 617.
Eggert, E. G.　*See* Ehlers, Victor M.
Eggleston, DeWitt C., *Municipal Accounting*, 199.
Egypt, early water supply in, 569.
Ehlers, Victor M., and Steel, Ernest W., *Municipal and Rural Sanitation*, 293 n., 297, 301 n., 481 n., 502 n., 507; Eggert, E. G., and White, E. G., *Applied Municipal Sanitation*, 297.
Elections, municipal, 21; early procedure in, 62; state control of, 62–63; present methods of holding, 63–74; management of, by city clerk, 93.
Electric Railway Journal, The, 634.
Electrolysis, treatment of sewage by, 307.
Elevated railways, 623–625.
Elizabeth, Queen of England, proclamation on housing (1580), 532.
Elliott, C. B., *Principles of the Law of Municipal Corporations*, 88.
Ellms, Joseph W., *Water Purification*, 587.

INDEX 679

Elsom, J. C., *Community Recreation*, 568.
Emergency hospitals, 510.
Eminent domain, right of, 251.
Employees, municipal, compared with private employees, 36–37; appointment of, 37–45; removal of, 45–46; standardizing the position and pay of, 46–47; organizations of, 47; pensions for, 47–49; the education of, 49–50; relation of municipal ownership to, 662. *See also* Merit System.
Employment bureaus, in relation to public welfare administration, 524.
Emporia, Kansas, an agricultural service community, 213.
Encyclopaedia of the Social Sciences, 531; "Municipal Transit," 634.
Enforcement, of traffic code, 350; of building code, 388–391; machinery of, 395; of weights and measures' ordinances, 407–408; of fire prevention rules, 423–424; of housing regulations, 541–542, 544.
Engelhardt, N. L., and Engelhardt, F., *Public School Business Administration*, 460; *Public School Organization and Administration*, 460. *See also* Strayer, George D.
Engineering, department of, in cities, work of, 96–106.
Engineering News-Record, 284, 312.
English cities, registration procedure in, 54; elections in, 62; legal procedure in, 76 *n.;* clerk's office in, 89; betterment tax in, 143; municipal borrowing in, 174; large proportion of fire-resisting buildings in, 413; health insurance in, 527; system of unemployment insurance in, 528; public housing in, 539; municipal ownership in, 654.
Eno, William P., *Fundamentals of Highway Traffic Regulation*, 352.
Epstein, A., *Insecurity: a Challenge to America*, 530; *Facing Old Age*, 531; *The Challenge of the Aged*, 531.
Erdman, Henry E., *American Produce Markets*, 555.
Euclid, Ohio, zoning ordinance in, 244–245.
Euclid *vs.* Ambler Realty Company, 245 *n.*
Eugene, educational activities as a means of growth of, 214.
Excavations, in paved streets, 280–281.
Excess condemnation, 254–258.
Exemption, of property from taxation, 138.

Exodus, quoted from, 2.
Expenditures, municipal, expansion of, 155–157; of police departments in various cities, 331; for schools, 458–459.

Factories, fire protection in, 422.
Fair, G. N. *See* Imhoff, Karl.
Fairtrace, George D., "Overinsurance as a Factor in Fire Losses," 415 *n.*
Falk, I. D., *Principles of Vital Statistics*, 479 *n.*
Fares, on street railways, 627–629.
Fees, municipal revenue from, 135; for building permits, 397–398; for inspection of weights and measures, 406–407.
Ferguson, Olin J., *Electric Lighting*, 603.
Field, O. P. *See* Bates, F. G.
Filtration, of public water supplies, 577–578.
Finance, municipal, 21; of planning, 234; of street pavements, 278; of sanitation, 296; of police administration, 331; of school administration, 457–459; of libraries, 470–471; of health department, 491; of hospitals, 516; in acquisition of park lands, 561; in water department, 580–581; of street lighting, 600; of airports, 614–615; of street railways, 621–622. *See also* Expenditures, Indebtedness, Revenues, Taxation.
Fines, municipal revenue from, 135.
Finger prints, identification by. *See* Dactyloscopy.
Fire Engineering (editors), *What Every Fire Fighter Should Know*, 438.
Fire hazards, in cities, 419–420.
Fire losses, in European and American cities, 412–414.
Fire prevention, 411–426; lack of efficiency in, 411; annual fire waste in America and Europe, 412–416; causes of fires, 416–420; reduction of losses, 420–421; regulation of buildings in the interest of, 386, 421–423; enforcement of, 423–424; state control over, 424–425; public education in, 425–426.
Fire protection, 427–438; organization of fire department, 427–432; work of, 433–436; fire-fighting appliances, 433–435; fire alarm systems, 435–436; in relation to water supply, 436; private fire protection, 437; high standard of efficiency in, 437–438.

680　INDEX

Fire Protection, 439.
Fire zones, in cities, 420.
Fish, C. R., *The Civil Service and the Patronage*, 50.
Fisher, Ernest M., *Advanced Principles of Real Estate Practice*, 125; and Smith, R. F., *Land Subdividing and the Rate of Utilization*, 218.
Fiske, Henry A. *See* Crosby, Everett U.
Fitzpatrick, E. A., *Budget Making in a Democracy*, 167.
Fixel, R. W., *Law of Aviation*, 618.
Flanagan, Luke, *The Science of Fire Fighting*, 438.
Flexner, Jennie M., *Circulation Work in Public Libraries*, 473.
Flinn, A. D., Weston, R. S., and Bogert, C. L., *Waterworks Handbook*, 587.
Flint, a satellite city, 216.
Flouton, Allen B., *Outline of the Law of Municipal Corporations*, 88.
Fog, hazard in air transportation, 605–606.
Folwell, A. P., *Municipal Engineering Practice*, 106; *Sewerage*, 311; *Water Supply Engineering*, 587.
Food, municipal inspection of, 485–486.
Food and Drugs Act (1906), 485.
Forbes, Russell, *Governmental Purchasing*, 109 n., 115; *The Organization and Administration of a Governmental Purchasing Office*, 115; *Purchasing Laws for State, County and City Governments*, 115; *Purchasing for Small Cities*, 115.
Force account plan, in public construction, 103–104.
Ford, George B., *Building Height, Bulk and Form*, 235.
Ford, James. *See* Gries, J. M.
Forster, H. Walter. *See* Crosby, Everett U.
Fosdick, Raymond B., *European Police Systems*, 333; *American Police Systems*, 333.
Foulke, W. D., *Fighting the Spoilsmen*, 50.
Fowlkes, J. G., *School Bonds*, 184, 459 n.
Franchises, work of law department in relation to, 85–86; taxes on, 135–136; for electric lighting, 602; for street railways, 631; general discussion of, 640–644.
Francis, T. P., *Modern Sewage Treatment*, 311.

Frankfort-on-the-Main, zoning in, 237.
Freitag, Joseph K., *Fire Prevention and Fire Protection as Applied to Building Construction*, 426.
French cities, registration procedure in, 54; large proportion of fire-resisting buildings in, 413.
Fresno, California, an agricultural service community, 213.
Frontinus, *De Aquis Urbi Romae*, 570 n.
Fuld, L. F., *Civil Service Administration*, 50.
Fuller, G. W., and McClintock, J. R., *Sewage Problems*, 311.
Functions, of city governments, 20–24.

Gallagher, H. R., *Crime Prevention as a Municipal Function*, 333, 367.
Gallagher, Raymond M., *Public Personnel Problems and the Depression*, 50–51.
Garbage, collection of, 25.
Garbage, definition of, 291–292; disposal of, 292–294; methods of collecting, 294–296.
Gardner, Mary S., *Public Health Nursing*, 516.
Gary, Indiana, importance of steel in growth of, 214; a satellite city, 216.
Gas, public lighting by, 588–589.
General Filtration Co., *The Activated Sludge Process of Sewage Treatment*, 311.
General property tax, 129–130.
German cities, large proportion of fire-resisting buildings in, 413; unemployment insurance in, 528; public housing in, 539; municipal ownership in, 654.
Germ theory of disease, 476–477.
Gibbon, Edward, quoted, 107.
Gillin, John L., *Criminology and Penology*, 383; *Poverty and Dependency*, 530.
Gilson, M. B., *Unemployment Insurance*, 530.
Glaeser, Martin G., *Outlines of Public Utility Economics*, 651.
Glasgow, municipal ownership in, 663.
Gloucester, importance of fisheries in, 214.
Goldberg, R., *Occupational Diseases in Relation to Compensation and Health Insurance*, 481 n.
Goldman, M. C., *The Public Defender*, 367.

INDEX

Goldmark, Josephine. *See* Winslow, C. E. A.
Golf courses, municipal ownership of, 564.
Goodnow, Frank J., *Politics and Administration*, 14.
Goodrich, Ernest P., *Airports as a Factor in City Planning*, 618. *See also* Lewis, Harold M.
Good Roads, 284.
Goodwin, Arthur E., *Markets, Public and Private—Their Establishment and Administration*, 555.
Gordon, R. A., *Handbook on Compulsory Acquisition of Land and Compensation*, 258.
Gordon, W. D., and Lockwood, J., *Modern Accounting Systems*, 199.
Gosnell, H. F., *Why Europe Votes*, 75. *See also* Merriam, Charles E.
Göttingen, importance of educational forces in growth of, 204.
Governmental Research Conference, *The Character and Functioning of Municipal Civil Service Commissions in the United States*, 50.
Governor and Judges Plan for Detroit, 231.
Graham, G. A., *Special Assessments in Detroit*, 154.
Grais, Hue de, *Handbuch der Verfassung und Verwaltung in Preussen und im deutschen Reich*, 259.
Grand Rapids, Michigan, importance of lumber in location of, 203; dependence of, on a single industry, 214.
Granite blocks, use of, for street pavements, 277.
Graper, E. D., *American Police Administration*, 333.
Gray, H. F. *See* Luckett, G. S.
Greece, municipal voting in, 62.
Greeley, S. A. *See* Hering, Rudolph.
Greenman, E. D., "The Codification of Municipal Ordinances," 83 *n*.
Greer, Sarah, *A Bibliography of Public Administration* (1st edition), 75; (2nd edition), 14.
Greville, Fulke, quoted, 411.
Gridiron plan, of street layout, 230.
Gries, J. M., and Ford, James, *Planning for Residential Districts*, 218; (editors), *Housing and the Community*, 545; *Slums—Large Scale Housing*, 545; *Housing Objectives and Programs*, 545.
Griffeth, E. S., *Current Municipal Problems*, 34; *Modern Development of City Government in the United Kingdom and the United States*, 34.
Grinnalds, J. C., "Report on Public Markets," 555.
Grit chambers, 306.
Ground floor awards, 101.
Growth of cities in the United States, 202–217.
Gulick, L. H., and Ayres, L. P., *Medical Inspection of Schools*, 482 *n*.
Gutters, construction of, 282.

Haas, O. F. *See* Harrison, Ward.
Haines, C. G., and Haines, B. M., *Principles and Problems of Government*, 75.
Hallett, G. H. *See* Hoag, C. G.
Hallock, William H., *Public Health and Hygiene*, 493.
Hamilton, Mary E., *The Policewoman: Her Service and Ideals*, 334.
Hamilton, T. T. *See* Monroe, W. S.
Hammer, Lee F., *Public Recreation*, 568.
Hammond, a satellite city, 216.
Hanks, Stedman S., *International Airports*, 617.
Hardenburg, W. E., *Mosquito Eradication*, 507.
Harger, W. G., *Rural Highway Pavements—Maintenance and Reconstruction*, 284; and Bonney, E. A., *Handbook for Highway Engineers*, 284.
Harper, E. B. *See* Warner, A. G.
Harriman, N. F., *Principles of Scientific Purchasing*, 115.
Harris, Joseph P., *Registration of Voters in the United States*, 58 *n*., 60 *n*., 61; *Election Administration in the United States*, 75.
Harrisburg, location a factor in growth of, 203; political factor in development of, 214.
Harrison, Shelby M., *Public Employment Offices*, 530.
Harrison, Ward, Haas, O. F., and Reid, Kirk M., *Street Lighting Practice*, 595 *n*., 603.
Harrison Act, 487.
Hatfield, H. R., *Accounting: Its Principles and Problems*, 199.
Haussmann, Baron Georges-Eugène, replanning of Paris by, 231; land taking by, in Paris, 257; planning and reconstruction of Paris sewers by, 302.
Haverfield, F., *Ancient Town Planning*, 220 *n*.

682 INDEX

Hayhurst, E. R., and Kober, G. M., *Industrial Health*, 481 n.
Hazen, Allen, *Meter Rates for Water Works*, 587.
Heads of departments. See Departments.
Health administration, 22, 474–493; importance of, 474; old and new methods of protection, 474–477; methods of disease control, 478–487; boards of health, 487–488; head of health department, 488–490; work of, 490; financing, 490; state control over local work, 491–492; national and international health work, 492; hospitals in relation to, 510.
Health centers, 510.
Health exhibits, importance of, as a means of public education, 482.
Health insurance, 527.
Healy, William, and Bronner, Augusta F., *Delinquents and Criminals: Their Making and Unmaking*, 383.
Hedden, W. P., *How Great Cities Are Fed*, 555.
Heidelberg, educational forces in growth of, 204.
Hemenway, H. B., *Legal Principles of Public Health Administration*, 494.
Henry, J. See Brown, E. F.
Hering, Rudolph, and Greeley, S. A., *The Collection and Disposal of Municipal Refuse*, 297.
Herring, F. W., and others, *Municipal Costs and Finance*, 167.
Herschel, Clemens, *The Two Books of the Water Supply of Rome*, 570 n.
Hibbard, Benjamin H., *Marketing Agricultural Products*, 555.
High pressure systems, for fire protection, 436, 580.
Highway Education Board, publications of, 284.
Highway Research Board, of National Research Council, publications of, 284; "Traffic Survey Methods and Forms," 353.
Hill, Earl W. See Woolley, James G.
Hilliard, Curtis M., *The Prevention of Disease in the Community*, 493.
Hinman, Albert G. See Dorau, Herbert B.
Hippocrates, his idea of need for health protection, 474.
Hiscock, Ira V. (editor), *Community Health Organization*, 493, 517.
Hoag, C. G., and Hallett, G. H., *Proportional Representation*, 71 n.

Hogarth, A. Moore, *The Rat: a World Menace*, 507.
Holcombe, A. N., *State Government in the United States*, 75.
Holland Tunnel, in New York City, 343.
Hollywood, importance of motion picture industry in, 214.
Holmes, Oliver Wendell, quoted, 52.
Holt, Thomas G., *Aërial Transport*, 617.
Holtzclaw, H. F., *Agricultural Marketing*, 555.
Holway, Hope, *The Story of Water Supply*, 587.
Holyoke, Mass., municipal gas plant in, 656.
Homer, his interest in the criminal, 371; *Iliad*, 474.
Homestead, a satellite city, 216.
Hoover, Herbert C., *Government Ownership*, 669.
Hospital Library and Service Bureau, bibliographical bulletins published by, 517.
Hospitals, public, 508–516; program of general hospital, 508–510; functions of, 510–514; boards, 511; medical staff, 511–512; nurses, 512; location of, 515–516; financing, 516.
House fly nuisance, 504–505.
Housing, 532–544; in ancient cities, 532; in modern cities, 533–535; effects of congestion in, 535–538; interests concerned in problem of, 538–539; the improvement of, 539–544.
Hovell, T. M., *Rats and How to Destroy Them*, 507.
Howard, L. O., *The House Fly, Disease Carrier*, 507.
Hubbard, Henry V., McClintock, Miller, and Williams, Frank B., *Airports: Their Location, Administration, and Legal Basis*, 617. See also Hubbard, Theodora Kimball.
Hubbard, Theodora Kimball, and McNamara, Katherine, *Planning Information Up to Date*, 235; *Manual of Planning Information and Supplement*, 235; and Hubbard, Henry V., *Our Cities—Today and Tomorrow*, 235, 242 n.
Hughes, Charles Evans, quoted, on justice in the courts, 354.
Hughes, T. H., and Lamborn, E. A. G., *Towns and Town Planning: Ancient and Modern*, 221 n., 235.
Hugo, Victor, quoted, 368; interest of, in the criminal, 371.

INDEX

Hunter, Albert C. *See* Thom, Charles.
Hunter, M. H., *Outlines of Public Finance*, 139.
Hurd, R. M., *Principles of City Land Values*, 125, 217.
Hutchinson, R. G., *State-administered Locally-shared Taxes*, 140.
Hylan, John F., attitude of, toward public use of water, 571.

Illegal practices, in city elections, 74.
Illinois Constitutional Convention Bulletin, *Eminent Domain and Excess Condemnation*, 258.
Illinois Crime Survey, 362 n.
Illuminating Engineering Society, *Transactions*, 603; Street Lighting Committee, "Code of Street Lighting," 603.
Imhoff, Karl, and Fair, G. N., *The Arithmetic of Sewage Treatment Works*, 311.
Imhoff tanks, 307.
Improvements, public, plans of financing, 141, 145–146.
Incendiarism, 418.
Incineration, of rubbish, 291; of garbage, 294.
Income taxes, in cities, 130.
Indebtedness, municipal, general discussion of, 168–183.
Indeterminate sentences, 377.
Indiana, state control of municipal taxation in, 133; of municipal indebtedness in, 174; of local audits, 186.
Indoor relief, 523.
Industrial accidents, as a cause of poverty, 526–527.
Industrial hygiene, 481.
Industrial revolution, its relation to housing, 532.
Industry, the relation of, to city growth, 214–215.
Infant mortality, in cities, 485.
Initiative and referendum, 93.
Inoculation, as a public health measure, 480.
Inspection, in municipal contracts, importance of, 102–103; in centralized purchasing, 113–114; of buildings, 395–398; of weights and measures, 400–409; medical, in the schools, as a means of health protection, 482–483; of milk supply, 484–485; of public markets, 551.
Insurance, in relation to fire losses, 414–415. *See also* Social Insurance.
Intangibles, taxation of, 124.

Intermittent filtration systems, in sewage treatment, 308–309.
International Association of Police Chiefs, *Uniform Crime Reporting: a Complete Manual for Police*, 334.
International Association of Street Sanitation Officials, *The Measurement and Control of Municipal Sanitation*, 296 n., 297.
International Health Office, 492.
International Labor Office, "The Housing Situation in the United States," 545.
Iowa, state control of municipal indebtedness in, 174; of local audits, 186.
Isolation hospitals, 510.
Italy, Beccari method of garbage disposal in, 293 n.; unemployment insurance in, 528.
Ithaca, institutional forces in growth of, 214.
Ivorydale, a satellite city, 216.

Jackson, Andrew, and the evolution of municipal courts, 357; spread of free education, 442.
Jackson, D. C., and McGrath, D. F., *Street Railway Fares: Their Relation to Length of Haul and Cost of Service*, 628 n.
Jackson, Walter. *See* Blake, Henry W.
James (Revised Version) quoted, 427.
James, E. W., *Highway Construction, Administration and Finance*, 284.
James, Harlean, *Land Planning in the United States for the City, State and Nation*, 235.
Jarrett, M. C. *See* Davis, M. M.
Jay-walking, as a cause of traffic congestion, 340–341.
Jenner, Edward, his discovery of vaccination process, 480.
Jensen, J. P., *Problems of Public Finance*, 139; *Property Taxation in the United States*, 140.
Jerome, Harry, *Statistical Method*, 199.
Jerusalem, historical associations of, as a factor in growth, 204.
Jèze, Gaston, *Principes généraux du droit administratif*, 259.
Joeckel, Carleton B., "The Public Library under the City Manager Form of Government," 462 n.
Johnson, Arlien, *Public Policy and Private Charities*, 530.
Johnson, F. R., *Probation for Juveniles and Adults*, 384.
Johnson, Tom L., Mayor of Cleveland, on franchises, 643.

Johnson, W. B., *Fire-Fighting by Land, Sea, and Air*, 438.
Jones, Eliot, and Bigham, T. C., *Principles of Public Utilities*, 651.
Journal of Land and Public Utility Economics, 652; "Municipal Ownership and the Changing Technology of the Electric Industry," 669.
Journal of Political Economy, 140.
Journal of Social Forces, 531.
Journal of the American Institute of Criminal Law and Criminology, 384.
Journal of the American Judicature Society, 367.
Judd, D. L., *Budget Making and Administration with Special Reference to Cities*, 167.
Judges, of municipal courts, methods of selection, 360–361. See also Courts.
Jury, preparation of lists for the, 94; awards by, in land-taking cases, 253.
Juvenile courts, 359.

Kansas City, city manager plan of government in, 12; importance of meat packing industry in, 203; topography in relation to growth, 204; state control of municipal police in, 314; early street cars in, 620.
Kearney, P. W. See Dougherty, T. F.
Keay, G. E., *Fire Waste*, 426.
Kelso, Robert W., *The Science of Public Welfare*, 530.
Kenlon, John, *Fires and Fire Fighters*, 438.
Kennedy, John P., *The Basis of Real Estate Values*, 125.
Kennedy, T. H., *An Introduction to the Economics of Air Transportation*, 617.
Kent, Frank R., on the boss and the election, 62.
Kershaw, G. Bertram de B., *Sewage Purification and Disposal*, 311.
Kershaw, John B. C., *Fuel Economy and Smoke Prevention*, 507.
Kibbey, C. H., *The Principles of Sanitation*, 297.
Kimball, Theodora. *Manual of Information on City Planning and Zoning*, 235. See also Hubbard, Theodore Kimball.
Kings II, quoted, 569.
Kinnicutt, L. P., Winslow, C. E. A., and Pratt, R. W., *Sewage Disposal*, 311.

Kirby, James P., *Selected Articles on Criminal Justice*, 367.
Kirkpatrick, Wiiliam H., *Education for a Changing Civilization*, 460.
Kirkpatrick, Wylie, *Reporting Municipal Government*, 200.
Kneier, C. M., *State Regulation of Public Utilities in Illinois*, 652.
Knight, E. W., *Education in the United States*, 460.
Knowles, D. E. See Bailey, W. G.
Knowles, Morris, *Industrial Housing*, 545.
Knox, Charles, *Principles of Real Estate Appraising*, 125.
Kober, G. M. See Hayhurst, E. R.
Koran, The, quoted, 619.
Kuhlman, A. F., *A Guide to Material on Crime and Criminal Justice*, 383.
Kumm, Harold F., *The Law of Special Assessments*, 154.

Lagerquist, Walter E., *Public Utility Finance*, 652.
Laidler, Harry W., *Public Ownership Here and Abroad, before, during and after the War*, 668.
Lamborn, E. A. G. See Hughes, T. H.
Lancaster, Lane, *State Supervision of Municipal Indebtedness*, 184.
Lanchester, H. V., *The Art of Town Planning*, 235.
Land takings, for public improvements, 249–251; in relation to politics, 253–254. See also Excess Condemnation.
Larson, J. A., *The Single Fingerprint System*, 334.
Latin proverb, 249.
Law department, in municipal government, 20; head of, 76; manner of his selection, 76–78; functions of, 79–88.
Lawrence, institutional forces in growth of, 214.
Lawrence, W. B., *Cost Accounting*, 199.
League of Kansas Municipalities, *How to Conduct City Elections*, 75.
Legal aid bureaus, 524.
Legal residence, as a qualification for voting, 56–57.
Leigh, R. D., *Federal Health Administration in the United States*, 493.
Leighton, M. O. (editor), *Water Supply and Irrigation Paper No. 190*, 303 n.
Leisure, growth of, in cities, 556.
Leland, S. E., *The Classified Property Tax in the United States*, 140.

INDEX

L'Enfant, Major Pierre-Charles, planner of Washington, D. C., 223–224; street planning of Washington, 270.
Lepawsky, A., *The Judicial System of Metropolitan Chicago*, 367. *See also* Merriam, Charles E.
Lewis, E. E., *Personnel Problems of the Teaching Staff*, 460.
Lewis, Harold M., and Goodrich, Ernest P., *Highway Traffic in New York and Its Environs*, 352.
Lewis, H. M., Wilgus, W. J., and Turner, D. L., *Transit and Transportation*, 634. *See also* Adams, T.
Lewis, John, *A Treatise on the Law of Eminent Domain in the United States*, 258.
Lewis, Nelson P., *The Planning of the Modern City*, 235.
Libraries. *See* Public Libraries.
Library Journal, 473.
Library Quarterly, 473.
Licenses, municipal, revenue from, 135; proposed extension of, 138–139; for commercial amusements, 565–566.
Lies, Eugene T. (editor), *The Leisure of a People*, 568.
Lighting, public, 588–603; early development of, 588; modern development of, 589–591; purposes of, 590–591; short-comings of, 591; of buildings, 592; of parks and streets, 592–597; methods of, 598–600; cost of, 600–601; contracts for, 601–602; and franchises, 602–603.
Lincoln, Abraham, presidential ballot of, 67
Lincoln, E. E., *The Results of Municipal Electric Lighting in Massachusetts*, 668.
Lincoln, Walter O. *See* Dominge, Charles C.
Lindeman, E. C. *See* Anderson, Nels.
Liquor traffic, in relation to public health, 487.
Literacy, as a qualification for voting, 58.
Livy, quoted, 653.
Lobdell, E. L., *Chicago's Transportation Problem*, 633.
Local improvement bonds, issue of, in special assessments, 152–153.
Lockwood, J. *See* Gordon, W. D.
Lodging house problems, 542.
Logan, Edward B., *The Supervision of the Conduct of Elections and Returns with Special Reference to Pennsylvania*, 75.

Lohmann, Karl B., *Principles of City Planning*, 220 n., 235.
London, mediaeval, defensive facilities of, 201; municipal federation in, 217; Wren's plan for, 222–223; street layout in, 230; use of excess condemnation in, 257–258; famous thoroughfares of, 263; treatment of sewage in, 306; early police arrangements in, 313; congestion of traffic in, 335; annual fire losses in, 412; municipal housing in, 532, 539; early street lighting in, 588, 595; zone-fare system on street railways in, 628; municipal ownership in, 663.
Long Beach, climate as a factor in growth of, 204.
Los Angeles, strong-council plan of government in, 9; registration of voters in, 55; importance of citrus industry in, 203; breadth of economic base of, 214; a metropolitan city, 216; relief of street congestion in, 339; vehicular tunnels in, 343; popular election of board of education in, 444; sources of water supply for, 574; street lighting in, 594 n.
Lowe, John Adams, *Public Library Administration*, 467 n., 473.
Lowell, water power as an influence in location of, 203.
Lowell, James Russell, quoted on education, 442.
Luckett, G. S., and Gray, H. F., *Elements of Public Health Administration*, 493.
Luckiesh, M., *Artificial Light*, 603.
Lump sum budget, in cities, 163.
Lutz, H. L., *Public Finance*, 139, 184.
Lyle, W. T., *Parks and Park Engineering*, 567.
Lyndon, Lamar, *Rate Making for Public Utilities*, 652.
Lynn, importance of electrical products in, 203.

Macdonald, Austin F., *American City Government and Administration*, 34, 50, 247; *Planning for City Traffic*, 352; "Airport Problems of American Cities," 618.
MacKenzie, R. D., *The Metropolitan Community*, 218.
Macy, John E., *Selection of Cases on Municipal or Public Corporations*, 88.
Madrid, early expansion of, 202.
Maeterlinck, *Blue Bird*, 588.
Magistrates' courts, 359.

686 INDEX

Magna Carta, quoted, 400.
Malaria, the suppression of, 477.
Malott, Deane W. *See* Cabot, Philip.
Malott, E. Orth, *Forces Affecting Municipally Owned Electric Plants in Wisconsin*, 669.
Maltbie, W. H., *The Theory and Practice of Public Utility Valuation*, 652.
Manchester, England, municipal ownership in, 663.
Manchester, N. H., importance of textile industry in, 214.
Mann, D. M. *See* Queen, S. A.
Marsh, C. F., *Trade Unionism in the Electric Light and Power Industry*, 603.
Marsh, Edward C., *Civil Service: A Sketch of the Merit System*, 50.
Martin, A. J., *The Activated Sludge Process*, 311.
Mason, E. S., *The Street Railway in Massachusetts*, 633.
Massachusetts, civil service system of, 39–40; legislative bills in, 80; state control of local audits, 186; development of textile industry in cities of, 203.
Massachusetts Constitutional Convention Bulletin, *Excess Condemnation*, 258.
Massachusetts Institute of Technology, Division of Municipal and Industrial Research, *Principles of Sewage Disposal*, 312.
Mavor, James, *Niagara in Politics*, 668.
Maxey, C. C., *Readings in Municipal Government*, 659 n.
Maxey, Chester C., *Urban Democracy*, 34, 50.
May, Herbert L., and Petgen, Dorothy, *Leisure and Its Use*, 568.
Mayor, in relation to city council, 3–4; functions of, in strong-council plan of government, 9–10; in strong-mayor plan, 10; appointments made by, 28–29; appointment of city attorney by, 78; his relation to the budget, 161; veto power of, 162.
McBain, H. L., *American City Progress and the Law*, 88.
McCaffrey, G. A. *See* Post, A. J.
McCall, J. H., *Municipal Audits and Finance*, 199.
McCardle *vs.* Indianapolis Water Co., 649 n.
McClintock, J. R. *See* Fuller, G. W.
McClintock, Miller, *Street Traffic Control*, 336 n., 352; and Williams, Sidney J., *Municipal Organization for Street Traffic Control*, 352; and Bond, H. L., *The Problem of Fire Waste and Insurance Rates in the City of Boston*, 426. *See also* Hubbard, Henry V.
McCombs, Carl E., *City Health Administration*, 479 n., 489 n., 493.
McCracken, Dwight, "Methods for Studying Traffic Control Problems," 338 n.
McDonald, E. F., *Municipal Accounting*, 199.
McGrath, D. F. *See* Jackson, D. C.
McGraw's Electric Railway Manual, 634.
McLaughlin, A. J., *The Communicable Diseases: How They Spread and How They May Be Controlled*, 478 n., 493.
McLaughlin, Glenn E., "Industrial Diversification in American Cities," 215 n.
McMichael, Stanley, *McMichael's Appraising Manual*, 125; and Bingham, Robert F., *City Growth and Values*, 125; *City Growth Essentials*, 218, 247.
McNamara, Katherine, bibliography on zoning, 247. *See also* Hubbard, Theodora Kimball.
McNeish, R. H., *The Automobile Fire Apparatus Operator*, 438.
McQuillin, Eugene, *The Law of Municipal Corporations*, and *Supplement*, 88.
Means, G. C. *See* Bonbright, J. C.
Measures, inspection of. *See* Weights and Measures.
Mechanical filters, 578–579.
Medical inspection, in the schools, 482–483.
Memphis, location of, as a factor in growth, 203.
Merchants' Association of New York, *Proposed Building Code for New York City*, 399.
Meriam, Lewis, *Principles Governing the Retirement of Public Employees*, 51.
Merit system, selection of department heads under, 29; and municipal employees, 35–50; beginnings of the, 36; its purposes, 36–37; its essential features, 37–43; advantages and defects of, 43–46; standardization of positions and pay under, 46–47; pension problem under, 47–49; in police departments, 327–328; selection of build-

INDEX

ing inspectors by, 397; in the fire department, 431; in selection of library employees, 467; in water departments, 586.
Merriam, Charles E., *New Aspects of Politics*, 14; and Gosnell, H. F., *The American Party System*, 75; Parratt, S. D., and Lepawsky, A., *The Government of the Metropolitan Region of Chicago*, 217 n.
Meston, Dougall. *See* Pearce, E. H.
Metcalf, Leonard, and Eddy, Harrison P., *Sewerage and Sewage Disposal*, 307 n., 311; *American Sewerage Practice*, 311.
Meter system. *See* Water Rates.
Metropolitan cities, 216–217.
Metropolitan Life Insurance Company, *Health Insurance*, 531.
Metzenbaum, James, *The Law of Zoning*, 247.
Miami, tourist trade in development of, 214.
Michelbacher, G. F., and Nial, T. M., *Workmen's Compensation Insurance*, 530.
Milk supply, relation of the, to public health in cities, 483–485.
Mill, John Stuart, quoted, 15; doctrine of monopoly of public utilities, 638.
Mills, Earl O., "Zoning Survey and Procedure," 240 n.
Mills, M. C., and Starr, G. W., *Readings in Public Finance and Taxation*, 139.
Milne, William D. *See* Dana, Gorham.
Milton, John, quoted, on schools, 440.
Milwaukee, cost of registering voters in, 60 n.; sewage disposal system of, 305.
Minimum wage laws, 529.
Minneapolis, City of, *Report on Classification of Positions and Schedules of Compensation*, 51; importance of wheat in location of, 203; of water power, 203; flour industry in, 214; a metropolitan city, 216.
Mississippi River, as a source of water supply, 574.
Missouri *vs.* Illinois, 303 n.
Missouri River, as a source of water supply, 574.
Mitchell, E. D. *See* Bowen, W. P.
Modern Hospital, The, 517.
Modern Hospital Year Book, The, 517.
Modus operandi files, in criminal identification, 323–324.
Moehlman, A. B., *Public School Finance*, 451 n., 460.

Moley, Raymond (editor), *Cleveland Crime Survey*, 333; *Missouri Crime Survey*, 333; *Politics and Criminal Prosecution*, 367; *The Long Day in Court*, 367; *Our Criminal Courts*, 367; *Tribunes of the People*, 367; *Commercial Recreation*, 568.
Monroe, W. S., Hamilton, T. T., and Smith, V. T., *Locating Educational Information*, 459.
Montgomery, R. H., *Auditing Theory and Practice*, 199.
Montpazier, town plan of, 221–222.
Moonlight standard, 596 n., 600.
Moore, Harry K., *Public Health in the United States*, 493.
Morey, Lloyd, *Introduction to Governmental Accounting*, 199; *Manual of Municipal Accounting*, 199.
Morgan, Gerald, *The Public Relief of Sickness*, 527 n.
Morgan, Morris H., translation of Vitruvius' *Ten Books of Architecture*, 220 n.
Morrison, H. C., *The Management of School Money*, 460.
Morrison, R. L. *See* Blanchard, A. H.
Mosher, W. E., and Crawford, Finla G., *Public Utility Regulation*, 651.
Mosher, William E., and others, *Electrical Utilities*, 603.
Mosquito nuisance, 501–502; eradication of, 502–504.
Motion pictures, the censorship of, 566.
Motor-busses, competition of, with street railways, 629–630.
Municipal Administration Service, *The Administration of Regulatory Inspectional Services in American Cities*, 491 n.
Municipal Finance Officers' Association, publications of, 140.
Municipal Index, The, 248, 284, 297, 334; bibliography on "Traffic Control and Facilitation," 353; bibliography on "Fire Fighting and Fire Prevention," 426, 587; articles on municipal airports, 618.
Municipal ownership, of water supply in the United States, 585–586, 653–668; definition of, 653; extent of, in Europe and America, 654–657; the issues in, 657–660; arguments for, 660–664; arguments against, 664–668.
Munro, William B., *The Government of American Cities*, 9 n., 34, 86 n.; *The Government of European Cities*, 34; "A Danger Spot in the Zoning Movement," 242 n.

688   INDEX

Murphy, H. D., *The Fundamental Principle of Purchasing*, 115.
Murray, W. S., *Government Owned and Controlled, Compared with Privately Owned and Regulated, Electric Utilities*, 668.

Napoleon III, sewerage construction plan of Paris carried out by, 302.
Nash, Jay B., *The Organization and Administration of Playgrounds and Recreation*, 568; *Standard of Play and Recreation Administration*, 568.
Nash, L. R., *The Economics of Public Utilities*, 651.
National Assembly of Civil Service Commissions, *The Personnel Problem in the Public Service*, 50; *Proceedings*, 51.
National Association of Manufacturers, *Public Old Age Pensions*, 531.
National Association of Railroad and Utilities Commissioners, *Proceedings*, 652.
National Automobile Chamber of Commerce, statistics relating to automobiles published by, 336 n.
National Board of Fire Underwriters, *Fire Underwriters' Code*, 399; *Code of Suggested Ordinances for Small Municipalities*, 399; *Safeguarding the Nation against Fire: a Fire Prevention Manual for High Schools*, 417 n.; *Suggested Fire Prevention Ordinances*, 423 n.; publications of, 426; approval of high pressure water service, 580.
National Building Code Committee, recommendations of, in regard to building codes, 388.
National Civil Service Reform League, *Good Government*, 51.
National Commission on Law Observance and Law Enforcement (Wickersham Commission), 333; *Report on Criminal Procedure*, 355 n., 366; *Report on Prosecution*, 360 n., 366; *Report on Criminal Statistics*, 384.
National Committee on Municipal Reporting, *Public Reporting*, 200.
National Committee on Prisons and Prison Labor, publications of, 384.
National Conference Board, *The Taxation of Motor Vehicle Transportation*, 630 n.
National Conference of Social Work, *Proceedings*, 531; *Bulletin*, 531.
National Conference on Street and Highway Safety, statutes and ordinances drafted by, for traffic regulation, 345.
National Conference on Street and Highway Safety and Traffic Control and Facilitation, *A Model Municipal Traffic Ordinance*, 353.
National Conference on Weights and Measures, *Proceedings*, 409; work of, 409.
National Crime Commission, *Criminal Statistics and Identification of Criminals: on Pardons, Parole, Probation, Penal Laws, and Institutional Correction*, 384.
National Education Association, *Research Bulletins*, 460; *Journal*, 460; and the American Medical Association, *Health Service in City Schools*, 482 n.
National Electric Light Association, *Political Ownership and the Electric Light and Power Industry*, 668; pamphlets issued by, 669.
National Fire Protection Association, publications of, 426, 438–439; *Field Practice Handbook*, 438.
National Fire Waste Council, publications of, 426.
National Industrial Conference Board, tax studies by, 140; *Unemployment Benefits and Insurance*, 531; *The Support of the Aged*, 531.
National Municipal League, *Report of the Civil Service Committee*, 50; *Pensions in Public Employment*, 51; *A Model Registration System: Report of the Committee on Election Administration*, 53 n., 57 n., 59 n., 60 n., 61; *A Model Election Administration System: Report of the Committee on Election Administration*, 75; the Model City Charter of, 93; *Special Assessments*, 154; *Special Assessments for Local Improvements*, 154; *A Model Budget Law*, 167; *A Model Municipal Bond Law*, 184.
National Municipal Review, 61, 140, 184, 342 n., 385 n.
National Recovery Act, industrial codes under, 529.
National Smoke Abatement Society, *The Smoke Act Abatement Handbook*, 507.
National Society of Penal Information, *The Handbook of American Prisons*, 383.
National Tax Association, *Proceedings*, 140; *Bulletin*, 140.

INDEX 689

Neighborhood dances, 565.
Nemayer, E. W., *Medical and Sanitary Inspection of Schools*, 482 n.
New Haven, importance of higher education in growth of, 204.
New Jersey, civil service system of, 39–40.
Newman, B. J., *Housing in Philadelphia*, 545.
New Orleans, location of, as a factor in growth, 203; source of water supply for, 574.
Newport, climate as a factor in growth of, 204.
Newsholme, Sir Arthur, *Elements of Vital Statistics*, 479 n.; *Health Problems in Organized Society*, 493; *Medicine and the State*, 493.
Newspapers, influence of, in city government, 198.
New York City, strong-mayor plan of government in, 10; registration procedure in, 53, 53 n., 55; its election officials, 65–66; profusion of municipal ordinances in, 83; special assessments in, 146; law of increasing costs in, 157; municipal obligations of, 169; report of police department in, 196; location of, as a factor in growth, 203; invasion of business in residential districts of, 211; breadth of economic base in, 214; a metropolis, 216–217; planning of, 224–225; regional planning of, 226; street layout in, 230; zoning in, 239; regulation of building heights in, 244; important streets in, 263–264; work of street cleaning in, 287–288; garbage collection in, 295; beginnings of police system in, 313; size of police force, 320; hazards of motor traffic in, 335; street congestion in, 339; two-level streets in, for relief of traffic congestion, 342; vehicular tunnel in, 343; automatic signal system in, 349; traffic courts in, 351; early judicial authority in, 356; specialization in municipal courts of, 359; regulation of buildings in, 388–389; specialization in building inspection, 390; annual fire losses in, 412; training schools for firemen in, 431; appointment of board of education in, 444; municipal university in, 452; cost of maintaining health department in, 491; smoke nuisance in, 496; Tenement House Law, 533; housing conditions in, 533, 535, 536, 537, 539, 542; tenement house department in, 544; source of water supply for, 574; airports in, 606–607; horse-car lines in, 619; growth of urban transportation in, 622; rapid transit in, 623; taxicabs in, 630 n.; basis of street car fares in, 633; franchises in, 641, 642.
New York State, control of merit system in, 41; control of local audits, 186.
New York State Legislature, *First Report of the Joint Legislative Committee on Housing*, 545.
Nial, T. M. *See* Michelbacher, G. F.
Nice, climate as a factor in growth of, 204.
Nichols, Ellsworth, *Public Utility Service and Discrimination*, 652.
Nichols, J. C., "The Planning and Control of Outlying Shopping Centers," 213 n.
Nichols, Philip, *The Law of Eminent Domain*, 258.
Night courts, in cities, 359.
Nineveh, early policing of, 313.
Nolen, John, *New Towns for Old*, 235; *Twenty Years of City Planning Progress*, 235; *City Planning*, 235, 247.
Nolting, O. F. *See* Ridley, C. E.
Nominations, in cities. *See* Elections.
Non-voting, the causes of, 55, 72–73.
Norris, H. H. (editor), *Electric Railway Practices in 1925*, 633.
North, C. E., "Milk in Its Relation to Public Health," 483 n.
Nuisances, the abatement of, by local health authorities, 495–506.
Nurse, C. J., *Purification and Disposal of Sewage*, 311.
Nurses, training of, in public hospitals, 512–513.

Oakey, Francis, *Principles of Governmental Accounting and Reporting*, 199.
Oakland, city manager plan of government in, 12.
Obermeyer, Henry, *Stop That Smoke*, 507.
Odegarde, Peter, *Pressure Politics*, 14.
Odum, H. W., and Willard, D. W., *Systems of Public Welfare*, 530.
O'Hare, K. R., *In Prison*, 383.
Ohio, state control of merit system in, 41; of local audits, 186.
Old age pensions, in Europe and America, 527–528.

Oliver, Thomas, *Diseases of Occupation*, 481 n.
Olmsted, F. L. *See* Shurtleff, Flavel.
Omaha, meat packing industry as a factor in location of, 203; municipal gas plant in, 656.
Ordinances, city, as basis of administration, 1; policy-determining, 1–2; framing of, by law department, 82–83; zoning, drafting of, 240–241; enforcement of, 241–242; for control of smoke nuisance, 498–500.
Orton, L. M. *See* Adams, T.
Osborne, T. M., *Prisons and Common Sense*, 383.
Ostend, climate as a factor in growth of, 204.
Outdoor relief, 522–523.
Out-patient clinics, 513.
Owens, John S. *See* Shaw, Napier.
Owings, Chloe, *Women Police*, 334.
Oxford, educational forces in growth of, 204.

Palo Alto, educational activities as a means of growth of, 214.
Pardons, granting of, 379.
Paris, mediaeval, defensive location of, 201; planning in, 225; street layout in, 230–231; land takings for public improvements in, 257; famous thoroughfares of, 263; relief of traffic congestion in, 269; use of sewers for subsurface utilities in, 281; early sewers in, 302; sewage farms of, 309; criminal identification in, 323; wholesale terminal markets in, 550; dual system of water distribution in, 573.
Parking and Garage Problem of the Central Business District of Washington, D. C., 352.
Parking space, for automobiles, in city streets, 346–348.
Parks, municipal, 22; different types of, 556–560; administration of, 560–561; financing, 561; lighting of, 592.
Parkways, 25; planning and control of, 560.
Parole, releases on, 379.
Parratt, S. D. *See* Merriam, Charles E.
Parsons, Philip A., *Crime and the Criminal*, 383.
Pasteur, Louis, 285; discoverer of germ theory of disease, 476.
Pauperism. *See* Poverty.
Pavements, for city streets, relation of, to local needs, 272–273; selection of, 273–275; structure of, 276–278; repairing of, 279–281; relation of, to street cleaning, 287–288. *See also* Streets.
Pay-as-you-go plan, in financing of public improvements, 182–183; in school financing, 459.
Pearce, E. H., and Meston, Dougall, *The Law Relating to Nuisances*, 507.
Pearl, Raymond, *Introduction to Medical Biometry and Statistics*, 479 n.
Peck, H. W., *Taxation and Welfare*, 140.
Peel, Sir Robert, police reforms of, 313.
Pendray, G. Edward. *See* Brown, E. F.
Penn, William, original plan of Philadelphia by, 223.
Pensions, municipal, types of, 48–49; for police officers, 331.
Pepys, Samuel, his attitude towards health protection, 475.
Permits, for erection of buildings, 395.
Personal property, the assessment of, 123–124.
Personnel work, in city employment, 21, 41–42.
Philadelphia, strong-council plan of government in, 9; municipal departments in, 19; merit system in, 40; appointment of election board in, 53 n.; annual registration in, 55; municipal ordinances in, 83; sale of municipal bonds in, 177; location of, 203; breadth of economic base of, 214; original planning of, 223; sewage disposal system of, 305; special traffic courts in, 351; early judicial authority in, 356; election of board of education in, 444; cost of maintaining health department in, 491; source of water supply for, 574.
Phillipson, C., *Three Criminal Law Reformers: Beccaria, Bentham, Romilly*, 383.
Pigou, A. C., *A Study in Public Finance*, 139.
Pinchot, Amos, quoted, 658 n.–659 n.
Pink, Louis H., *The New Day in Housing*, 545.
Pirenne, Henri, *Mediaeval Cities*, 201 n.
Pittsburgh, iron and coal as factors in location of, 203; topography in relation to growth of, 204; importance of steel in, 214, 215; special

INDEX

traffic courts in, 351; smoke nuisance in, 496.
Plague (bubonic), the suppression of, 477.
Planning boards, in cities, 226–227. *See also* City Planning.
Platoon system, in police administration, 326; in fire protection service, 432; in education, 456.
Plautus, quoted, 546.
Playgrounds, 24; jurisdiction of school authorities over, 457; location and administration of, 561–563.
Playgrounds and Recreation Association of America, *The Normal Course in Play*, 568; *Park and Recreation Manual*, 568.
Plehn, C. C., *Introduction to Public Finance*, 139.
Plunkitt, George Washington, quoted, 35; political philosophy of, 35–36, 41.
Police administration, 313–333; history of police, 313; in America, 313–314; state police control, 314–316; organization of police, 316–317; police commissioners, 317–320; rank and file of police, 320–321; detective service in, 321–324; functions of, 324–326; platoon system, 326; methods of recruiting force, 327–328; training schools for, 328–329; promotions and discipline in, 329–330; women officers, 330–331; expenditures for, 331; European and American police compared, 331; pensions, 331; associations of, 332; enforcement of traffic regulations by, 350–351; traffic courts, relation of, to, 351; work of police at fires, 436–437.
Police Journal, The, 334.
Police power, of cities, in regulation of buildings, 387; in reducing fire hazards, 421.
Politics, practical, in municipal administration, 4–5; in the law department, 86; in the engineering department, 96–97; of budget-making, 161; in relation to land acquisitions, 253–254; in the police department, 319–320, 327; interference of, in judicial work, 361–362; in the fire department, 429; in school administration, 447.
Poll taxes, as a qualification for voting, 52 *n.*
Pollard, W. L. (editor), "Zoning in the United States," 247.

Pollock, W. W., and Scholz, K. W. H., *The Science and Practice of Urban Land Valuation*, 125.
Pond, Oscar L., *Treatise on the Law of Public Utilities*, 652.
Poor relief. *See* Public Welfare.
Poor's Manual of Public Utilities, 634.
Pope, Alexander, quoted, 141, 635.
Popular sovereignty, doctrine of, in French Revolution, 61.
Population, density of, in relation to crime, 372–373.
Portland, Oregon, cost of registering voters in, 60 *n.;* importance of salmon industry in, 203.
Post, A. J., and McCaffrey, G. A., *Street Name Signs*, 283 *n.*
Potomac River, as a source of water supply, 574.
Pound, Roscoe, *Criminal Justice in America*, 367; "The Administration of Justice in the Modern City," 367.
Poverty, extent and causes of, 518–521; methods of dealing with, 521–530.
Pratt, R. W. *See* Kinnicutt, L. P.
President's Research Committee, *Recent Social Trends*, 531.
Primary election, 63 *n.*
Princeton, importance of higher education in growth of, 204.
Prison reform, 380–383.
Private property, public debts as a lien on, 169; relation of city planning to, 234–235; fire protection of, 437.
Probation system, 378–379.
Proceedings of the Federal Electric Railway Commission, 634.
Proceedings of the National Conference on City Planning, 236.
Procter, A. W., *Principles of Public Personnel Administration*, 50, 51.
Promotions, in police department, 329; of firemen, 432; of teachers, 451.
Proportional representation, explained, 71.
Prosecuting attorney, functions of, 361–362.
Proverbs, quoted, 518.
Providence, topography in relation to growth of, 205; breadth of economic base of, 215.
Public Administration Service, *Municipal Debt Defaults: Their Prevention and Adjustment*, 184.
Public amusements, licensing of, 25.
Public defender, 364.

Public health. *See* Health Administration.
Public libraries, 25, 461–473; administration of, by boards, 461–464; the librarian, 464–467; selection and duties of employees, 467–468; salaries, 469; problem of book selection, 469–470; financing of, 470–471; location of, 472; adult education in, 472–473.
Public Libraries, 473.
Public lighting. *See* Lighting.
Public markets, 546–555; marketing in Europe and America, 547–548; value of, 548–550; procedure at, 550–553; buildings, 553–554; program of, 554–555.
Public Ownership League of America, *Public Ownership*, 652; bulletins of, 669.
Public Personnel Studies, 51.
Public recreation, use of school plant for, 456–457; 561–567.
Public safety, administration of, 21–22.
Public service commissions, organization of, 645–647; functions of, 647–650.
Public utilities, relations of city with, 23–24; negotiations of legal department with, 85–86; imposition of taxes on, 135–136; control of, 635–651; definitions of, 635–636; characteristics of, 636–638; need for regulation of, 638–639; franchises of, 640–644; administrative supervision over, 645–646; public attitude towards, 646–647; fixing rates for, 647–650. *See also* Municipal Ownership.
Public Utility Reports, Inc., publications of, 651.
Public welfare, 22–23; municipal problem of, 518–521; administration of, 522–526; and social insurance, 526–530.
Public works, 23; as a public welfare agency, 524.
Purchasing, centralized, older methods of, 107–108; department of, its head, 108–109; procedure in, 109–111; advantages of, 111–115.
Purdom, C. B., *The Building of Satellite Towns*, 216 *n*.
Purdy, Lawson, "The Assessment of Real Estate," 125.

Qualifications for voting, 55–60.
Quarantine, as a public health measure, 478.

Quarterly Journal of Economics, 140.
Queen, S. A., and Mann, D. M., *Social Pathology*, 383. *See also* Warner, A. G.

Radial plan, of street layout, 230–231.
Rainey, H. P., *Public School Finance*, 460.
Rainwater, Clarence E., *The Play Movement in the United States*, 568.
Rat nuisance, 505–506.
Rapid transit, the problem of, 623–624.
Ravenel, M. P. (editor), *A Half-Century of Public Health Administration*, 483 *n.*, 493.
Ray, P. O., *Introduction to Political Parties and Practical Politics*, 60, 74.
Raymond, W. L., *State and Municipal Bonds*, 184.
Raymond, William G., *The Public and Its Utilities*, 651.
Recreation, commercialized, 565. *See also* Public Recreation.
Reduction, of garbage, 293–294.
Reed, Thomas H., *Municipal Government in the United States*, 34.
Reeder, W. G., *The Chief State School Officer*, 443 *n.; The Business Administration of a School System*, 460.
Reeves, Cuthbert E., *The Appraisal of Urban Land and Buildings*, 125.
Refuse, collection and disposal of, 290–291.
Regional Plan of New York and Its Environs, *Major Economic Factors in Metropolitan Growth and Arrangement* (Vol. I), 218; *The Building of the City* (Vol. X), 235–236; *Highway Traffic* (Vol. III), 271; *Highway Traffic in New York and Its Environs*, 352; "Housing Conditions in the New York Region," 545; *Public Recreation*, 568; *Transit and Transportation* (Vol. IV), 634.
Registration of voters, 21, 52–61; procedure in, 52–55; qualifications for, 55–59; cost of, 59–60.
Reid, Kirk M. *See* Harrison, Ward.
Report of the Mayor's Commission on Taxicabs, 634.
Report on the Street Traffic Control Problem of San Francisco, 338 *n.*, 352.
Reports, municipal, 92–93, 196–199; the improvement of, 197–198.
Research, scientific, in public hospitals, 513–514.

INDEX

Resolutions, policy-determining by, 2.
Revenues, municipal, 126–139; need for expansion of, 126–127; chief sources of, 128–130; limitations on, 131–133; need for additional sources of, 134–139; work of city treasurer in connection with, 157–158.
Rhode Island, development of textile industry in cities of, 203.
Richmond, early street cars in, 620; municipal gas plant in, 656.
Ridley, C. E., and Nolting, O. F., *How Cities Can Cut Costs*, 167.
Riggs, Henry E., *Depreciation of Public Utility Properties*, 652.
Riis, Jacob A., *How the Other Half Lives*, 539.
Riordon, William L., *Plunkitt of Tammany Hall*, 36 n.
Ripley, William Z., *Main Street and Wall Street*, 652.
Roadside stands, 553.
Robinson, C. M., *Modern Civic Art*, 235; *City Planning with Special Reference to the Planning of Streets and Lots*, 271.
Robinson, Gustavus H., *Cases and Authorities on Public Utilities*, 652.
Robinson, L. N., *Penology in the United States*, 383.
Rocca, Helen M., *Registration Laws*, 61.
Rochester, city manager plan of government in, 12; kodak industry in, 214; basis of street railway service in, 632.
Rohlfing, Charles C., *The Airport Approach*, 607 n.
Rome, elections in, 62; special assessments in, 142–143; original defensive facilities of, 201; historic associations of, 204; city planning in, 220–221; sewerage system of, 298; early police system of, 313; early theory of disease in, 475; housing problems in, 532; water supply in, 569–570; lighting and public safety in, 588.
Rorem, C. R., *The Public's Investment in Hospitals*, 516. See also Davis, M. M.
Rosenau, Milton J., *Preventive Medicine and Hygiene*, 493.
Rosewater, Victor, *Special Assessments*, 154.
Rubbish, collection and disposal of, 290–291.
Rubinow, I. M., *The Care of the Aged*, 531.

Russell, H. L. *See* Turneaure, F. E.
Ryan, Frances M. *See* Bird, Frederick L.

Sacramento, political factor in growth of, 214.
Safety zones, use of, in congested streets, 340.
Saginaw, importance of lumber in location of, 203.
Sait, E. M., *American Parties and Elections*, 61, 75.
Salaries, of teachers, 451; of library employees, 469.
Sales taxes, 134.
Sand filters, 577.
San Diego, tourist trade in development of, 214.
San Francisco, election board in, 53 n.; registration of voters in, 55; checking of registrations in, 57; election workers in, 66; sale of municipal bonds in, 177; topography in relation to growth of, 204–205; planning in, 225; civic center in, 232; vehicular tunnels in, 343; appointment of board of education in, 444; street lighting of, 594 n.; supervision of airports in, 617; municipal ownership of street railways in, 633, 657.
Sanitation, modern development of, 285–286; scope and methods, 286–287. See also Sewerage, Waste Disposal.
Saratoga, climatic factor in location of, 204.
Satellite cities, 216.
Scavenger's Oath, the (twelfth century), 285.
Schenectady, importance of electric products in, 203, 214.
Scholz, K. W. H. *See* Pollock, W. W.
School administration, 440–459; purposes of, 440–442; state control of schools, 442–444; organization of school boards, 444–445; functions of school boards, 445–447; superintendent of schools, 447–448; school management, 448–452; new demands on city schools, 452–455, 456–457; school plant and equipment, 455–456; school finance, 457–459.
School Board Journal, 460.
School boards, 444–447.
Schrammel, H. E., *The Organization of State Departments of Education*, 443 n.

Schroeder, Henry, *The History of Electric Light,* 589.
Schuylkill River, as a source of water supply, 574.
Scranton, importance of coal production in, 214.
Screening, sewage treatment by, 305–306.
Seasongood, Murray, *Local Government in the United States,* 34.
Seattle, registration of voters in, 55; importance of lumber in location of, 203; topography in relation to growth of, 205; source of water supply for, 574; municipal ownership of street railways in, 633, 657.
Secrist, Horace, *Introduction to Statistical Methods,* 199.
Sedimentation, sewage treatment by, 306.
Segregated budget, in cities, 164.
Seligman, E. R. A., *Essays in Taxation,* 139, 154; *The Shifting and Incidence of Taxation,* 140.
Septic tanks, use of, in sewage disposal, 307.
Serial bonds, 177–180.
Sewage, definition of, 298; early methods of disposal, 298–299; volume, 299; varieties of, 299–300; disposal of, 303–305; modern methods of treating, 305–310.
Sewage Works Journal, 312.
Sewerage, 298–311; planning, 299–300; materials used in construction of sewers, 300–301; maintenance of, 301–302.
Shakespeare, William, quoted, 79; his interest in the criminal, 371; quoted from *King Henry IV,* 385; *King Lear,* 518; *The Merchant of Venice,* 588.
Shaw, Napier, and Owens, John S., *The Smoke Problem of Great Cities,* 507.
Shepperd, Frederick, *Simplified Fire Department Hydraulics,* 438; *Fire Chief's Handbook,* 438.
Sherman, Wells A., *Merchandising Fruits and Vegetables,* 555.
Shirras, G. Findlay, *The Science of Public Finance,* 139.
Short ballot, 69.
Shultz, W. J., *American Public Finance and Taxation,* 139.
Shurtleff, Flavel, and Olmsted, F. L., *Carrying Out the City Plan,* 258.
Sidewalks, width of, 268, 282; construction of, 282–283.

Silverman, H. A., *Taxation: Its Incidence and Effects,* 140.
Simon, E. D., *How to Abolish Slums,* 545.
Simpson, Herbert D., *Tax Racket and Tax Reform in Chicago,* 140.
Simpson, H. D., and Burton, J. E., *The Valuation of Vacant Land in Suburban Areas,* 125.
Sinai, N., *Organization and Administration of Public Health,* 493.
Sinking funds, 177–180.
Sioux City, Iowa, an agricultural service community, 213.
Smith, Bruce, *The State Police,* 316 n., 334.
Smith, H. P., *Business Administration of the Public Schools,* 449 n., 459 n., 460.
Smith, N. L., *The Fair Rate of Return in Public Utility Regulation,* 652.
Smith, R. F. See Fisher, Ernest M.
Smith, R. H., *Justice and the Poor,* 356 n., 367.
Smith, Ralph W., *Weights and Measures Administration,* 404 n., 409.
Smith, V. T. See Monroe, W. S.
Smoke nuisance, effects of, 495–497; control of, 498–501; in relation to air transportation, 606
Smoke Prevention Association, *Manual of Smoke and Boiler Ordinances,* 507.
Social amelioration, 521–530.
Social insurance, in Europe and America, 526–530.
Spanish-American War, spread of typhoid during, 480 n.
Special assessments, defined, 141–142; origin of, 143; merits and disadvantages of, 143–144; kinds of, 145–146; methods of apportioning, 147–148; procedure in financing, 149–153; in connection with land acquisitions, 250–251; in paving of streets, 279.
Specifications, for municipal public works, 99; evasion of, by contractors, 102; standardization of, in centralized purchasing, 111–112.
Speed limits, 346.
Spencer, Herbert, quoted, 313.
Spengler, E. H., *Land Values in New York in Relation to Transit Facilities,* 633–634.
Split contracts, 100–101.
Spoils system, in American cities, 35–36; danger of, in municipal ownership, 654–655.

INDEX   695

Spokane, water power as an influence in location of, 203.
Spot zoning, 242–243.
Sprinkling filters, for sewage treatment, 309.
Spurr, Henry C., *Guiding Principles of Public Utility Regulation*, 652.
Stahl, Charles J., *Electric Street Lighting*, 603.
Standardization, of positions and salaries in the municipal service, 46–47; of specifications in centralized purchasing, 111–112.
Standards, for inspecting weights and measures, 404–405.
Starr, G. W. *See* Mills, M. C.
State control, of cities, in elections, 62–63; over tax limits, 133–134; over local audits, 186; of municipal police, 314–316; of weights and measures' inspection, 400–401; of fire prevention, 424–425; of local education, 442–444; of local health work, 491–492.
Statistics, in cities, 193–196.
Staub, H. *See* Alexander, F.
Steadman, Robert F., *Public Health Organization in the Chicago Region*, 493–494.
Stecher, Gilbert E. *See* Stone, Harold A.
Steel, Ernest W. *See* Ehlers, Victor M.
Stein, Milton F., *Water Purification Plants and Their Operation*, 587.
Steiner, Jessie F., *Community Organization*, 568.
Stevens, Don L., *Bibliography of Municipal Utility Regulation and Municipal Ownership*, 668.
Stevens, E. F., *The American Hospital of the Twentieth Century*, 516.
Stewart, Bryce M., *Unemployment Benefits in the United States*, 530.
St. Louis, election board in, 53 n.; sale of municipal bonds in, 177; location a factor in growth of, 203; topography in relation to development of, 204; planning in, 225; pollution of water supply of, 303; state control of municipal police in, 314; sources of water supply for, 574.
Stone, Harold A., and Stecher, Gilbert E., *Organization and Operation of a Municipal Bureau of Fire Prevention*, 426.
Stoner, J. B., *Systems of Equalizing, Assessing and Collecting Taxes*, 125.
Stratford, historical associations of, 204.

Strayer, George D., and Engelhardt, N. L., *Standards for Elementary School Buildings*, 456 n.; *Standards for High School Buildings*, 456 n.; and others, *Problems in Educational Administration*, 460.
Street, Elwood, *Social Work Administration*, 530.
Street name signs, 283.
Street railways, in relation to city plan, 229; to traffic zones, 268–269; effect of, on pavements, 280. *See also* Transportation.
Streeter, H. W., *Studies of the Efficiency of Water Purification Processes*, 587.
Streets, city, planning of, 230–232; acquisition of land for, 249–250, 260–271; services of, 260–261; organization of department in charge of, 261–263; classification of, 264–266; width of, 266–270; area of, in various cities, 270–271; methods of constructing, 275–277; paving for, 278–280; car tracks in, 280; cleaning of, 287–290; traffic congestion of, 338–339; remedies, 341–346; the lighting of, 593–600.
Street Traffic Control Problem of the City of Boston, The, 338 n., 352.
Street Traffic Control Problem of the City of New Orleans, The, 352.
Strikes, in the police department, 332; on street railways, 629.
Studensky, Paul, *The Government of Metropolitan Areas*, 34, 217 n.; *Public Borrowing*, 184.
Stutzman, J. O., *Curing the Criminal*, 383.
Subways, the development and cost of, 624–625.
Sugar Creek, a satellite city, 216.
Superintendent, of schools, position and powers of, 447–451; of public charities, 522.
Survey, for a city plan, 227–228; of traffic, 337–338; for street lighting, 593.
Sutherland, E. H., *Criminology*, 383.
Swan, H. S., *The Law of Zoning*, 248.
Swift, F. H., *Federal and State Policy in Public School Finance*, 460.
Swift, Jonathan, quoted, 335.
Swimming pools, municipal, 562–563.
Syracuse, importance of salt wells in location of, 203.

Tannenbaum, Frank, *Wall Shadows: a Study in American Prisons*, 383.
Taussig, F. W., on taxation, 125.

Taxation, municipal, assessment of property for, 116–125; limitations on power of, 127–128; general sources of, 128–129; forms of, 129–131; fixing of rates for, 131–133; new sources of, 134–139; of street railways, 631–632.

Taxicabs, as a means of transportation, 630.

Taylor, Clarence P., *Traffic Officer's Training Manual*, 352.

Taylor, Graham R., *Satellite Cities*, 218.

Taylor, Robert E., *Municipal Budget Making*, 167.

Teachers, selection of, in cities, 449–451; salaries of, 451; promotions of, 451.

Tenement houses, fire prevention regulation of, 422–423. *See also* Housing.

Tenements, fire prevention regulations of, 422–423.

Tennyson, Alfred, quoted, 237.

Terminal markets, 550–551.

Texas, voting requirement in, 52.

Theaters, fire prevention in, 422.

Themistocles, quoted, on city growth, 201.

Thom, Charles, and Hunter, Albert C., *Hygienic Fundamentals of Food Handling*, 555.

Thomas, A. G., *Principles of Government Purchasing*, 115.

Thompson, Carl D., *Public Ownership*, 668.

Thompson, F. Longstreth, *Site Planning in Practice*, 218.

Thompson, G. N., *The Preparation and Revision of Local Building Codes*, 399.

Thompson, J. G., *Urbanization*, 218.

Tobey, James A., *Riders of the Plagues: the Story of the Conquest of Disease*, 494; *Public Health Law*, 494, 507.

Toledo, municipal university in, 452.

Tolerances, scale of, in inspection of weights and measures, 408–409.

Tooke, C. H., *Selection of Cases on the Law of Municipal Corporations*, 88.

Topeka, political factor in development of, 214.

Townroe, B. S., *The Slum Problem*, 545.

Traffic, in relation to city plan, 228–230; as dictating the plan of city streets, 264–266; zones, determination of, for, 267–270; in streets, relation of, to paving materials, 275–278; relation of police to, 331; regulation of, 335–352; problem of, 335–336; surveys of, 337–338; causes of congestion in, 338–340; remedies for, 341–346; police department regulation of, 348–350; courts, 351, 359; public attitude toward, 351–352.

Traffic Control Plan for Kansas City, 338 n., 352.

Traffic Survey, City of Providence, 352.

Train, G. F., *Observations on Horse Railways*, 619 n.

Training schools, for police, 328–329; for firemen, 431; for teachers, 449–450; for librarians, 467; for nurses, 512–513.

Transportation, urban, 619–633; history of, 619; evolution of, 619–621; financing, 621–622; problems of, 622–630; franchises for, 631; taxation, 631–632; future of, 633; public ownership of, 633.

Trickling filters. *See* Sprinkling Filters.

Troy, importance of collar-and-shirt industries in, 203, 214.

Trull, Edna, *The Administration of Regulatory Inspectional Services in American Cities*, 399, 406 n., 410.

Truxal, A. G., *Outdoor Recreation*, 568.

Tuberculosis, as a major health problem, 480–481.

Tucker, J. I., *Special Assessments in California*, 154.

Tulsa, importance of oil production in, 214.

Turneaure, F. E., and Russell, H. L., *Public Water Supplies*, 586.

Turner, D. L. *See* Lewis, H. M.

Tymms, F. *See* Edwards, I. A. E.

Typhoid, a preventable disease, 477.

Typhus, the suppression of, 477.

Unbalanced bidding, 101.

Underwriters' Laboratories, publications of, 426.

Unemployment insurance, 528–529.

Unit-costs, in municipal construction, 105–106; statistics of, 194.

United States Bureau of the Census, *Financial Statistics of Cities Having a Population of over 30,000*, 167, 184, 549; statistics relating to urban transportation, 634.

United States Bureau of Labor Statistics, *Public Old-Age Insurance in the United States and Foreign*

INDEX

Countries, 531; figures compiled by, in relation to housing, 535 *n.*
United States Bureau of Mines, *Proposed Standard Smoke Ordinance*, 507.
United States Bureau of Standards, *National Directory of Commodities Specifications*, 112 *n.*; "Recommended Minimum Requirements for Plumbing in Dwellings and Similar Buildings," 301 *n.*; survey of, in regard to building codes, 388; custodian of national standards of weights and measures, 400.
United States Department of Agriculture, Bureau of Public Roads, bulletins of, 284; *Rat Control*, 507; Bureau of Entomology, publications of, on insect extermination, 507; federal inspection of farm products at central markets by, 551.
United States Department of Commerce, Advisory Committee on Zoning, *Standard State Zoning Enabling Act*, 248; National Code Committee, *Recommended Practice for the Arrangement of Building Codes*, 399; *Tabulation of Building and Plumbing Codes*, 399; Aëronautics Branch, *Airports and Landing Fields*, 618; *Airport Management*, 618.
United States Geological Survey, 499 *n.*
United States Office of Education, Department of the Interior, *A Fire Prevention Manual for the School Children of America*, 425 *n.*, 442–443; *Bibliography of Current Research Studies in Education*, 459; publications of, 460.
United States Public Health Service, *Municipal Wastes: Their Character, Collection, and Disposal*, 297; *Sewage Treatment in the United States*, 311; standard dairy inspection form prepared by, 484 *n.*; survey of health administration, 489 *n.*; quarantine work of, 492; *Municipal Health Department Practice*, 494; publications of, 494; anti-mosquito campaign by, 504; model ordinance on rat-proofing of buildings issued by, 506 *n.*
Unwin, Raymond, *Town Planning in Practice*, 221 *n.*
Upson, Lent D., *Practice of Municipal Administration*, 34, 50, 167, 184, 199, 352 *n.*, 663 *n.*; *The Growth of a City Government*, 157 *n.*

Urbana, educational forces in growth of, 204.
Urban transportation, in relation to city planning, 229. *See also* Transportation.
Utilization, waste disposal by, 290–291; of garbage, 292–293.

Vaccination, as a public health measure, 480.
Vaughan, Henry F., "Room Overcrowding and Its Effect upon Health," 535 *n.*
Veal, T. H. P., *The Disposal of Sewage*, 311.
Vehicular tunnels, as a remedy for traffic congestion, 343.
Veiller, Lawrence, *Model Housing Law*, 544–545. *See also* DeForest, R. W.
Veterans, preference of, under merit system, 38–39; in fire departments, 431.
Veto power, of the mayor, 162.
Vienna, city planning in, 225; famous thoroughfares in, 263.
Vital statistics, in cities, 94–95; nature and importance of, 479.
Vitruvius, *Ten Books of Architecture*, 220.
Vitz, Carl, *Current Problems in Public Library Finance*, 473.
Vocational education, 454–459.
Voters' lists, how compiled, 52–55.
Votes, policy-determining by, 2.
Voting machines, 71–72.

Waite, Herbert H., *Disease Prevention*, 478 *n.*, 493.
Walker, Harvey, *Federal Limitations upon Ordinance Making Power*, 2 *n.*, 82 *n.*, 88.
Walker, M. L., *Municipal Expenditures*, 167.
Walker, W. F., and associates, *Kansas City Health and Hospital Survey*, 517.
Wallace, S. C., *State Administrative Supervision over Cities in the United States*, 34, 174 *n.*, 184.
Ward, Mrs. Humphry, quoted, 298.
Wardle, Robert A., and Buckle, Philip, *The Principles of Insect Control*, 507.
Warner, A. G., Queen, S. A., and Harper, E. B., *American Charities and Social Work*, 530.
Washburn, Roger D., *Principles of Real Estate Practice*, 125.
Washington, D. C., political factor in

698 INDEX

growth of, 214; the original planning of, 223–224; large area of streets in, 270; disposal of sewage in, 305; source of water supply for, 574.
Waste disposal, 285–297.
Watch committee, control of police by, in English cities, 313.
Water rates, various schedules of, 581–583.
Water supply, 569–586; history of, 569–570; daily consumption of, 570–573; elements of waste in, 572; improving the quality of, 573; sources of, 573–574; analysis of, 575; relation of, to disease, 576; methods of purifying, 576–579; distribution of, 579–580; financing, 580–581; charges for, 581–583; organization of, 584–585; municipal ownership of, 585–586.
Water Works Research Bureau, The, *Water Meters and the Elimination of Waste,* 587.
Watkins, Gordon S., *Labor Problems,* 530.
Watson, Frank D., *The Charity Movement in the United States,* 530.
Weber, G. A., *Organized Efforts for the Improvement of Methods of Administration in the United States,* 14.
Weber, J. J., *First Steps in Organizing a Hospital,* 516.
Weights and measures, inspection of, 400–409; plans of enforcement, 400–402; inspectors, functions of, 402–405; organization of, 405; training of, 405–406; number and nature of, 406–407; limits of variation, 408–409.
Weimar, historical associations of, 204.
Weir, L. H. (editor), *Parks: a Manual of Municipal and County Parks,* 567; *Recreation Survey of Buffalo,* 568.
Welch, William H., *Public Health in Theory and Practice,* 493.
Weld, L. D. H. *See* Clark, F. E.
Werner, Helen M., *The Constitutionality of Zoning Regulations,* 248.
Weston, R. S. *See* Flinn, A. D.
Whalen, Grover, police report of, 196.
Wheeler, Joseph L., *The Library and the Community,* 473.
Wherry, William M., *Public Utilities and the Law,* 652.
Whipple, George C., *Vital Statistics,* 479 n.; *The Microscopy of Drinking Water,* 587.

White, Edward F., *The Negligence of Municipal Corporations,* 88.
White, E. G. *See* Ehlers, Victor M.
White, Lazarus, *The Catskill Water Supply of New York City,* 574 n.
White, Leonard D., *Introduction to the Study of Public Administration,* 14, 50, 51; *Trends in Public Administration,* 14; *Civil Service in the Modern State,* 50, 51.
White, Percival, *Motor Transportation of Merchandise and Passengers,* 634.
Whitehead, S., *Municipal Accounting Systems,* 199.
Whitten, Robert H., *The Valuation of Public Service Corporations,* 652.
Wickersham Commission. *See* National Commission on Law Observance and Law Enforcement.
Wider use of the school plant, 456–457.
Wilcox, Delos F., *San Francisco's Street Railway Problem,* 633; *Analysis of the Electric Railway Problem,* 634; *Depreciation in Public Utilities,* 652; *The Administration of Municipally Owned Utilities,* 669.
Wilgus, W. J. *See* Lewis, H. M.
Willard, D. W. *See* Odum, H. W.
Williams, Frank B., *The Law of City Planning and Zoning,* 235, 258; summaries of recent legal decisions relating to zoning, 248. *See also* Hubbard, Henry V.
Williams, M. P., *Sources of Information on Play and Recreation,* 568.
Williams, Sidney J. *See* McClintock, Miller.
Willoughby, W. F., *Principles of Public Administration,* 14, 50, 51, 167; *The National Budget System with Suggestions for Its Improvement,* 167; *Principles of Judicial Administration,* 366.
Wilson, G. L., *Motor Traffic Management,* 634.
Wilson, Woodrow, legal residence of, 56.
Wines, F. H., *Punishment and Reformation,* 383.
Winslow, C. E. A., and Goldmark, Josephine, *Nursing Education in the United States,* 516. *See also* Kinnicutt, L. P.
Women's courts, in cities, 359.
Wood, A. E., *Community Problems,* 235.
Wood, Edith E., *Housing of the Unskilled Wage Earner,* 545; *Recent Trends in American Housing,* 545.

INDEX

Wood, H. B., *Sanitation Practically Applied*, 297.
Wood blocks, use of, for street pavements, 277.
Woodbury, Robert M., *Infant Mortality and Its Causes*, 485 n.
Woods, Arthur, *The Policeman and the Public*, 333; *Crime Prevention*, 333.
Woolley, James G., and Hill, Earl W., *Airplane Transportation*, 617.
Wooten, K. W., *A Health Education Procedure for the Grades and Grade Teachers*, 482 n.
Wordsworth, William, quoted, 556, 604.
Workmen's compensation, 526–527.
World War, spread of crime as a result of, 372; safeguarding the health of troops during, 480.
Wren, Sir Christopher, quoted, 219; plan of London prepared by, 222–223.

Wright, Joseph, *Selected Readings in Municipal Problems*, 50.

Yellow fever, its suppression, 477.
Youngstown, importance of steel in growth of, 214.

Zangerle, John A., *Principles of Real Estate Appraising and Unit Value Land Maps*, 119 n., 125.
Zola, Émile, books by, in relation to criminals, 371.
Zollman, C. F. G., *Law of the Air*, 618; *Cases on Air Law*, 618.
Zoning, in cities, 237–247; value of, 237–238; history of, 239; scope of, 239–244; constitutionality of, 244–245; regional, 246; in relation to billboards, 246–247; as a means of relieving future street congestion, 341–342.
Zukerman, T. D., *The Voting Machine*, 75.